Lecture Notes in Computer Science 10941

Commenced Publication in 1973
Founding and Former Series Editors:
Gerhard Goos, Juris Hartmanis, and Jan van Leeuwen

More information about this series at http://www.springer.com/series/7407

Ying Tan · Yuhui Shi
Qirong Tang (Eds.)

Advances
in Swarm Intelligence

9th International Conference, ICSI 2018
Shanghai, China, June 17–22, 2018
Proceedings, Part I

 Springer

Editors
Ying Tan
Peking University
Beijing
China

Qirong Tang
Tongji University
Shanghai
China

Yuhui Shi
Southern University of Science
  and Technology
Shenzhen
China

ISSN 0302-9743   ISSN 1611-3349   (electronic)
Lecture Notes in Computer Science
ISBN 978-3-319-93814-1   ISBN 978-3-319-93815-8   (eBook)
https://doi.org/10.1007/978-3-319-93815-8

Library of Congress Control Number: 2018947347

LNCS Sublibrary: SL1 – Theoretical Computer Science and General Issues

Printed on acid-free paper

This Springer imprint is published by the registered company Springer International Publishing AG
part of Springer Nature
The registered company address is: Gewerbestrasse 11, 6330 Cham, Switzerland

Preface

This book and its companion volumes, LNCS vols. 10941 and 10942, constitute the proceedings of the 9th International Conference on Swarm Intelligence (ICSI 2018) held during June 17–22, 2018, in Shanghai, China.

The theme of ICSI 2018 was "Serving Life with Intelligence Science." ICSI 2018 provided an excellent opportunity and/or an academic forum for academics and practitioners to present and discuss the latest scientific results and methods, innovative ideas, and advantages in theories, technologies, and applications in swarm intelligence. The technical program covered most aspects of swarm intelligence and its related areas.

ICSI 2018 was the ninth international gathering in the world for researchers working on swarm intelligence, following successful events in Fukuoka (ICSI 2017), Bali (ICSI 2016), Beijing (ICSI-CCI 2015), Hefei (ICSI 2014), Harbin (ICSI 2013), Shenzhen (ICSI 2012), Chongqing (ICSI 2011), and Beijing (ICSI 2010). The conference provided a high-level academic forum for participants to disseminate their new research findings and discuss emerging areas of research. It also created a stimulating environment for participants to interact and exchange information on future challenges and opportunities in the field of swarm intelligence research. ICSI 2018 was held in conjunction with the Third International Conference on Data Mining and Big Data (DMBD 2018) at Shanghai, China, with the aim of sharing common mutual ideas, promoting transverse fusion, and stimulating innovation.

ICSI 2018 took place at the Anting Crowne Plaza Holiday Hotel in Shanghai, which is the first five-star international hotel in the Jiading District of Grand Shanghai. Shanghai, Hu for short, also known as Shen, is the largest and the most developed metropolis with both modern and traditional Chinese features in China. It is also a global financial center and transport hub. Shanghai offers many spectacular views and different perspectives. It is a popular travel destination for visitors to sense the pulsating development of China. The participants of ICSI 2018 had the opportunity to enjoy traditional Hu operas, beautiful landscapes, and the hospitality of the Chinese people, Chinese cuisine, and modern Shanghai.

We received 197 submissions and invited submissions from about 488 authors in 38 countries and regions (Algeria, Argentina, Aruba, Australia, Austria, Bangladesh, Brazil, China, Colombia, Cuba, Czech Republic, Ecuador, Fiji, Finland, Germany, Hong Kong, India, Iran, Iraq, Italy, Japan, Malaysia, Mexico, New Zealand, Norway, Portugal, Romania, Russia, Serbia, Singapore, South Africa, Spain, Sweden, Chinese Taiwan, Thailand, UK, USA, Venezuela) across six continents (Asia, Europe, North America, South America, Africa, and Oceania). Each submission was reviewed by at least two reviewers, and on average 2.7 reviewers. Based on rigorous reviews by the Program Committee members and reviewers, 113 high-quality papers were selected for publication in this proceedings volume, with an acceptance rate of 57.36%. The papers are organized in 24 cohesive sections covering major topics of swarm intelligence, computational intelligence, and data science research and development.

On behalf of the Organizing Committee of ICSI 2018, we would like to express our sincere thanks to Tongji University, Peking University, and Southern University of Science and Technology for their sponsorship, and to the Robotics and Multi-body System Laboratory at the School of Mechanical Engineering of Tongji University, the Computational Intelligence Laboratory of Peking University, and the IEEE Beijing Chapter for its technical cosponsorship, as well as to our supporters: International Neural Network Society, World Federation on Soft Computing, Beijing Xinghui Hi-Tech Co., Bulinge, and Springer.

We would also like to thank the members of the Advisory Committee for their guidance, the members of the international Program Committee and additional reviewers for reviewing the papers, and the members of the Publications Committee for checking the accepted papers in a short period of time. We are particularly grateful to Springer for publishing the proceedings in the prestigious series of *Lecture Notes in Computer Science*. Moreover, we wish to express our heartfelt appreciation to the plenary speakers, session chairs, and student helpers. In addition, there are still many more colleagues, associates, friends, and supporters who helped us in immeasurable ways; we express our sincere gratitude to them all. Last but not the least, we would like to thank all the speakers, authors, and participants for their great contributions that made ICSI 2018 successful and all the hard work worthwhile.

May 2018   Ying Tan
                                                                                                          Yuhui Shi
                                                                                                        Qirong Tang

Organization

General Co-chairs

Ying Tan — Peking University, China
Russell C. Eberhart — IUPUI, USA

Program Committee Chair

Yuhui Shi — Southern University of Science and Technology, China

Organizing Committee Chair

Qirong Tang — Tongji University, China

Advisory Committee Chairs

Gary G. Yen — Oklahoma State University, USA
Qidi Wu — Ministry of Education, China

Technical Committee Co-chairs

Haibo He — University of Rhode Island Kingston, USA
Kay Chen Tan — City University of Hong Kong, SAR China
Nikola Kasabov — Aukland University of Technology, New Zealand
Ponnuthurai N. Suganthan — Nanyang Technological University, Singapore
Xiaodong Li — RMIT University, Australia
Hideyuki Takagi — Kyushu University, Japan
M.Middendorf — University of Leipzig, Germany
Mengjie Zhang — Victoria University of Wellington, New Zealand
Lei Wang — Tongji University, China

Plenary Session Co-chairs

Andreas Engelbrecht — University of Pretoria, South Africa
Chaoming Luo — University of Detroit Mercy, USA

Invited Session Co-chairs

Maoguo Gong — Northwest Polytechnic University, China
Weian Guo — Tongji University, China

Special Sessions Chairs

Ben Niu	Shenzhen University, China
Yinan Guo	China University of Mining and Technology, China

Tutorial Co-chairs

Milan Tuba	John Naisbitt University, Serbia
Hongtao Lu	Shanghai Jiaotong University, China

Publications Co-chairs

Swagatam Das	Indian Statistical Institute, India
Radu-Emil Precup	Politehnica University of Timisoara, Romania

Publicity Co-chairs

Yew-Soon Ong	Nanyang Technological University, Singapore
Carlos Coello	CINVESTAV-IPN, Mexico
Yaochu Jin	University of Surrey, UK

Finance and Registration Chairs

Andreas Janecek	University of Vienna, Austria
Suicheng Gu	Google Corporation, USA

Local Arrangements Co-chairs

Changhong Fu	Tongji University, China
Lulu Gong	Tongji University, China

Conference Secretariat

Jie Lee	Peking University, China

Program Committee

Kouzou Abdellah	University of Djelfa, Algeria
Peter Andras	Keele University, UK
Esther Andrés	INTA, Spain
Sz Apotecas	UAM-Cuajimalpa, Mexico
Carmelo J. A. Bastos Filho	University of Pernambuco, Brazil
Salim Bouzerdoum	University of Wollongong, Australia
Xinye Cai	Nanjing University of Aeronautics and Astronautics, China
David Camacho	Universidad Autonoma de Madrid, Spain

Bin Cao	Tsinghua University, China
Josu Ceberio	University of the Basque Country, Spain
Kit Yan Chan	DEBII, Australia
Junfeng Chen	Hohai University, China
Mu-Song Chen	Da-Yeh University, Taiwan, China
Walter Chen	National Taipei University of Technology, Taiwan, China
Xu Chen	Jiangsu University, China
Yiqiang Chen	Institute of Computing Technology, Chinese Academy of Sciences, China
Hui Cheng	Liverpool John Moores University, UK
Ran Cheng	University of Surrey, UK
Shi Cheng	Shaanxi Normal University, China
Prithviraj Dasgupta	University of Nebraska, USA
Kusum Deep	Indian Institute of Technology Roorkee, India
Mingcong Deng	Tokyo University of Agriculture and Technology, Japan
Bei Dong	Shaanxi Nomal University, China
Wei Du	East China University of Science and Technology, China
Mark Embrechts	RPI, USA
Andries Engelbrecht	University of Pretoria, South Africa
Zhun Fan	Technical University of Denmark, Denmark
Jianwu Fang	Xi'an Institute of Optics and Precision Mechanics of CAS, China
Wei Fang	Jiangnan University, China
Liang Feng	Chongqing University, China
A. H. Gandomi	Stevens Institute of Technology, USA
Kaizhou Gao	Liaocheng University, China
Liang Gao	Huazhong University of Science and Technology, China
Shangce Gao	University of Toyama, Japan
Ying Gao	Guangzhou University, China
Shenshen Gu	Shanghai University, China
Ping Guo	Beijing Normal University, China
Weian Guo	Tongji University, China
Ahmed Hafaifa	University of Djelfa, Algeria
Ran He	National Laboratory of Pattern Recognition, China
Jun Hu	Chinese Academy of Sciences, China
Xiaohui Hu	GE Digital, Inc., USA
Andreas Janecek	University of Vienna, Austria
Changan Jiang	Ritsumeikan University, Japan
Mingyan Jiang	Shandong University, China
Qiaoyong Jiang	Xi'an University of Technology, China
Colin Johnson	University of Kent, UK
Arun Khosla	National Institute of Technology Jalandhar, India

Pavel Kromer	VSB Technical University, Ostrava, Czech Republic
Germano Lambert-Torres	PS Solutions, USA
Xiujuan Lei	Shaanxi Normal University, China
Bin Li	University of Science and Technology of China, China
Xiaodong Li	RMIT University, Australia
Xuelong Li	Chinese Academy of Sciences, China
Yangyang Li	Xidian University, China
Jing Liang	Zhengzhou University, China
Andrei Lihu	Politehnica University of Timisoara, Romania
Jialin Liu	Queen Mary University of London, UK
Ju Liu	Shandong University, China
Qunfeng Liu	Dongguan University of Technology, China
Hui Lu	Beihang University, China
Wenlian Lu	Fudan University, China
Wenjian Luo	University of Science and Technology of China, China
Jinwen Ma	Peking University, China
Lianbo Ma	Northeastern University, USA
Katherine Malan	University of South Africa, South Africa
Chengying Mao	Jiangxi University of Finance and Economics, China
Michalis Mavrovouniotis	Nottingham Trent University, UK
Yi Mei	Victoria University of Wellington, New Zealand
Bernd Meyer	Monash University, Australia
Efrén Mezura-Montes	University of Veracruz, Mexico
Martin Middendorf	University of Leipzig, Germany
Renan Moioli	Santos Dumont Institute, Edmond and Lily Safra International Institute of Neuroscience, Brazil
Daniel Molina Cabrera	Universidad de Cádiz, Spain
Sanaz Mostaghim	Institute IWS, Germany
Carsten Mueller	University of Economics, Czech Republic
Ben Niu	Shenzhen University, China
Linqiang Pan	Huazhong University of Science and Technology, China
Quan-Ke Pan	Huazhong University of Science and Technology, China
Bijaya Ketan Panigrahi	IIT Delhi, India
Mario Pavone	University of Catania, Italy
Yan Pei	University of Aizu, Japan
Thomas Potok	ORNL, USA
Mukesh Prasad	University of Technology, Sydney, Australia
Radu-Emil Precup	Politehnica University of Timisoara, Romania
Kai Qin	Swinburne University of Technology, Australia
Quande Qin	Shenzhen University, China
Boyang Qu	Zhongyuan University of Technology, China
Robert Reynolds	Wayne State University, USA
Guangchen Ruan	Indiana University Bloomington, USA
Helem Sabina Sanchez	Universitat Politècnica de Catalunya, Spain

Yuji Sato	Hosei University, Japan
Carlos Segura	Centro de Investigación en Matemáticas, A.C. (CIMAT), Mexico
Zhongzhi Shi	Institute of Computing Technology Chinese Academy of Sciences, China
Joao Soares	GECAD, Germany
Ponnuthurai Suganthan	Nanyang Technological University, Singapore
Jianyong Sun	University of Nottingham, UK
Yifei Sun	Shaanxi Normal University, China
Hideyuki Takagi	Kyushu University, Japan
Ying Tan	Peking University, China
Qirong Tang	Tongji University, China
Qu Tianshu	Peking University, China
Mario Ventresca	Purdue University, USA
Cong Wang	Northeastern University, USA
Gai-Ge Wang	Chinese Ocean University, China
Handing Wang	University of Surrey, UK
Hong Wang	Shenzhen University, China
Lei Wang	Tongji University, China
Lipo Wang	Nanyang Technological University, Singapore
Qi Wang	Northwestern Polytechnical University, China
Rui Wang	National University of Defense Technology, China
Yuping Wang	Xidian University, China
Zhenzhen Wang	Jinling Institute of Technology, China
Ka-Chun Wong	City University of Hong Kong, SAR China
Man Leung Wong	Lingnan University, Hong Kong, SAR China
Guohua Wu	National University of Defense Technology, China
Zhou Wu	Chonqing University, China
Shunren Xia	Zhejiang University, China
Ning Xiong	Mälardalen University, Sweden
Benlian Xu	Changshu Institute of Technology, China
Rui Xu	Hohai University, China
Xuesong Yan	China University of Geosciences, China
Shengxiang Yang	De Montfort University, UK
Yingjie Yang	De Montfort University, UK
Zl Yang	Shenzhen Institute of Advanced Technology, Chinese Academy of Sciences, China
Wei-Chang Yeh	National Tsinghua University, Taiwan, China
Guo Yi-Nan	China University of Mining and Technology, China
Peng-Yeng Yin	National Chi Nan University, Taiwan, China
Jie Zhang	Newcastle University, UK
Junqi Zhang	Tongji University, China
Lifeng Zhang	Renmin University, China
Qieshi Zhang	Shenzhen Institutes of Advanced Technology, Chinese Academy of Sciences, China
Tao Zhang	Tianjin University, China

Xingyi Zhang	Anhui University, China
Zhenya Zhang	Anhui Jianzhu University, China
Zili Zhang	Deakin University, Australia
Jianjun Zhao	Kyushu University, Japan
Xinchao Zhao	Beijing University of Posts and Telecommunications, China
Wenming Zheng	Southeast University, China
Yujun Zheng	Zhejiang University, China
Zexuan Zhu	Shenzhen University, China
Xingquan Zuo	Beijing University of Posts and Telecommunications, China

Additional Reviewers

Cheng, Tingli
Ding, Jingyi
Dominguez, Saul
Gao, Chao
Jin, Xin
Lezama, Fernando
Li, Xiangtao
Lu, Cheng
Pan, Zhiwen
Song, Tengfei
Srivastava, Ankur
Su, Housheng

Tang, Chuangao
Tian, Yanling
Wang, Shusen
Xie, Yong
Xu, Gang
Yu, Jun
Zhang, Mengxuan
Zhang, Peng
Zhang, Shixiong
Zhang, Yuxin
Zuo, Lulu

Contents – Part I

Theories and Models of Swarm Intelligence

Semi-Markov Model of a Swarm Functioning. 3
  E. V. Larkin and M. A. Antonov

Modelling and Verification Analysis of the Predator-Prey System
via a Modal Logic Approach 14
  Zvi Retchkiman Konigsberg

The Access Model to Resources in Swarm System Based
on Competitive Processes. 22
  Eugene Larkin, Alexey Ivutin, Alexander Novikov, Anna Troshina,
  and Yulia Frantsuzova

Self-organization of Small-Scale Plankton Patchiness Described by Means
of the Object-Based Model. 32
  Elena Vasechkina

On the Cooperation Between Evolutionary Algorithms and Constraint
Handling Techniques. 42
  Chengyong Si, Jianqiang Shen, Weian Guo, and Lei Wang

An Ontological Framework for Cooperative Games. 51
  Manuel-Ignacio Balaguera, Jenny-Paola Lis-Gutierrez,
  Mercedes Gaitán-Angulo, Amelec Viloria, and Rafael Portillo-Medina

An Adaptive Game Model for Broadcasting in VANETs 58
  Xi Hu and Tao Wu

Soft Island Model for Population-Based Optimization Algorithms 68
  Shakhnaz Akhmedova, Vladimir Stanovov, and Eugene Semenkin

A Smart Initialization on the Swarm Intelligence Based Method
for Efficient Search of Optimal Minimum Energy Design 78
  Tun-Chieh Hsu and Frederick Kin Hing Phoa

Ant Colony Optimization

On the Application of a Modified Ant Algorithm to Optimize the Structure
of a Multiversion Software Package 91
M. V. Saramud, I. V. Kovalev, V. V. Losev, M. V. Karaseva,
and D. I. Kovalev

ACO Based Core-Attachment Method to Detect Protein Complexes
in Dynamic PPI Networks 101
Jing Liang, Xiujuan Lei, Ling Guo, and Ying Tan

Information-Centric Networking Routing Challenges
and Bio/ACO-Inspired Solution: A Review 113
Qingyi Zhang, Xingwei Wang, Min Huang, and Jianhui Lv

Particle Swarm Optimization

Particle Swarm Optimization Based on Pairwise Comparisons 125
JunQi Zhang, JianQing Chen, XiXun Zhu, and ChunHui Wang

Chemical Reaction Intermediate State Kinetic Optimization by Particle
Swarm Optimization 132
Fei Tan and Bin Xia

Artificial Bee Colony Algorithms

A Hyper-Heuristic of Artificial Bee Colony and Simulated Annealing
for Optimal Wind Turbine Placement 145
Peng-Yeng Yin and Geng-Shi Li

New Binary Artificial Bee Colony for the 0-1 Knapsack Problem 153
Mourad Nouioua, Zhiyong Li, and Shilong Jiang

Teaching-Learning-Based Artificial Bee Colony 166
Xu Chen and Bin Xu

An Improved Artificial Bee Colony Algorithm for the Task Assignment
in Heterogeneous Multicore Architectures 179
Tao Zhang, Xuan Li, and Ganjun Liu

Genetic Algorithms

Solving Vehicle Routing Problem Through a Tabu Bee Colony-Based
Genetic Algorithm................................... 191
Lingyan Lv, Yuxin Liu, Chao Gao, Jianjun Chen, and Zili Zhang

Generation of Walking Motions for the Biped Ascending Slopes Based
on Genetic Algorithm   201
  *Lulu Gong, Ruowei Zhao, Jinye Liang, Lei Li, Ming Zhu, Ying Xu,
  Xiaolu Tai, Xinchen Qiu, Haiyan He, Fangfei Guo, Jindong Yao,
  Zhihong Chen, and Chao Zhang*

On Island Model Performance for Cooperative Real-Valued Multi-objective
Genetic Algorithms   210
  *Christina Brester, Ivan Ryzhikov, Eugene Semenkin,
  and Mikko Kolehmainen*

Differential Evolution

Feature Subset Selection Using a Self-adaptive Strategy Based Differential
Evolution Method   223
  *Ben Niu, Xuesen Yang, Hong Wang, Kaishan Huang,
  and Sung-Shun Weng*

Improved Differential Evolution Based on Mutation Strategies   233
  John Saveca, Zenghui Wang, and Yanxia Sun

Applying a Multi-Objective Differential Evolution Algorithm in Translation
Control of an Immersed Tunnel Element   243
  Qing Liao and Qinqin Fan

Path Planning on Hierarchical Bundles with Differential Evolution   251
  Victor Parque and Tomoyuki Miyashita

Fireworks Algorithm

Accelerating the Fireworks Algorithm with an Estimated
Convergence Point   263
  Jun Yu, Hideyuki Takagi, and Ying Tan

Discrete Fireworks Algorithm for Clustering in Wireless Sensor Networks . . .   273
  Feng-Zeng Liu, Bing Xiao, Hao Li, and Li Cai

Bare Bones Fireworks Algorithm for Capacitated p-Median Problem   283
  Eva Tuba, Ivana Strumberger, Nebojsa Bacanin, and Milan Tuba

Bacterial Foraging Optimization

Differential Structure-Redesigned-Based Bacterial Foraging Optimization   295
  Lu Xiao, Jinsong Chen, Lulu Zuo, Huan Wang, and Lijing Tan

An Algorithm Based on the Bacterial Swarm and Its Application
in Autonomous Navigation Problems. 304
    Fredy Martínez, Angelica Rendón, and Mario Arbulú

Artificial Immune System

Comparison of Event-B and B Method: Application in Immune System. 317
    Sheng-rong Zou, Chen Wang, Si-ping Jiang, and Li Chen

A Large-Scale Data Clustering Algorithm Based on BIRCH and Artificial
Immune Network 327
    Yangyang Li, Guangyuan Liu, Peidao Li, and Licheng Jiao

Hydrologic Cycle Optimization

Hydrologic Cycle Optimization Part I: Background and Theory 341
    Xiaohui Yan and Ben Niu

Hydrologic Cycle Optimization Part II: Experiments
and Real-World Application. 350
    Ben Niu, Huan Liu, and Xiaohui Yan

Other Swarm-based Optimization Algorithms

Multiple Swarm Relay-Races with Alternative Routes 361
    *Eugene Larkin, Vladislav Kotov, Aleksandr Privalov,
    and Alexey Bogomolov*

Brain Storm Optimization with Multi-population Based Ensemble
of Creating Operations. 374
    Yuehong Sun, Ye Jin, and Dan Wang

A Novel Memetic Whale Optimization Algorithm for Optimization. 384
    Zhe Xu, Yang Yu, Hanaki Yachi, Junkai Ji, Yuki Todo, and Shangce Gao

Galactic Gravitational Search Algorithm for Numerical Optimization. 397
    *Sheng Li, Fenggang Yuan, Yang Yu, Junkai Ji, Yuki Todo,
    and Shangce Gao*

Research Optimization on Logistic Distribution Center Location Based
on Improved Harmony Search Algorithm. 410
    *Xiaobing Gan, Entao Jiang, Yingying Peng, Shuang Geng,
    and Mijat Kustudic*

Parameters Optimization of PID Controller Based on Improved Fruit Fly
Optimization Algorithm. 421
    Xiangyin Zhang, Guang Chen, and Songmin Jia

An Enhanced Monarch Butterfly Optimization with Self-adaptive Butterfly
Adjusting and Crossover Operators   432
    Gai-Ge Wang, Guo-Sheng Hao, and Zhihua Cui

Collaborative Firefly Algorithm for Solving Dynamic Control Model
of Chemical Reaction Process System   445
    Yuanbin Mo, Yanyue Lu, and Yanzhui Ma

Predator-Prey Behavior Firefly Algorithm for Solving 2-Chlorophenol
Reaction Kinetics Equation.   453
    Yuanbin Mo, Yanyue Lu, and Fuyong Liu

Hybrid Optimization Algorithms

A Hybrid Evolutionary Algorithm for Combined Road-Rail Emergency
Transportation Planning   465
    Zhong-Yu Rong, Min-Xia Zhang, Yi-Chen Du, and Yu-Jun Zheng

A Fast Hybrid Meta-Heuristic Algorithm for Economic/Environment Unit
Commitment with Renewables and Plug-In Electric Vehicles   477
    Zhile Yang, Qun Niu, Yuanjun Guo, Haiping Ma, and Boyang Qu

A Hybrid Differential Evolution Algorithm and Particle Swarm
Optimization with Alternative Replication Strategy   487
    Lulu Zuo, Lei Liu, Hong Wang, and Lijing Tan

A Hybrid GA-PSO Adaptive Neuro-Fuzzy Inference System
for Short-Term Wind Power Prediction   498
    Rendani Mbuvha, Ilyes Boulkaibet, Tshilidzi Marwala,
    and Fernando Buarque de Lima Neto

Multi-Objective Optimization

A Decomposition-Based Multiobjective Evolutionary Algorithm
for Sparse Reconstruction.   509
    Jiang Zhu, Muyao Cai, Shujuan Tian, Yanbing Xu, and Tingrui Pei

A Novel Many-Objective Bacterial Foraging Optimizer Based
on Multi-engine Cooperation Framework   520
    Shengminjie Chen, Rui Wang, Lianbo Ma, Zhao Gu, Xiaofan Du,
    and Yichuan Shao

Multi-indicator Bacterial Foraging Algorithm with Kriging Model
for Many-Objective Optimization   530
    Rui Wang, Shengminjie Chen, Lianbo Ma, Shi Cheng, and Yuhui Shi

An Improved Bacteria Foraging Optimization Algorithm for High
Dimensional Multi-objective Optimization Problems   540
   Yueliang Lu and Qingjian Ni

A Self-organizing Multi-objective Particle Swarm Optimization Algorithm
for Multimodal Multi-objective Problems   550
   Jing Liang, Qianqian Guo, Caitong Yue, Boyang Qu, and Kunjie Yu

A Decomposition Based Evolutionary Algorithm with Angle Penalty
Selection Strategy for Many-Objective Optimization   561
   Zhiyong Li, Ke Lin, Mourad Nouioua, and Shilong Jiang

A Personalized Recommendation Algorithm Based on MOEA-ProbS   572
   Xiaoyan Shi, Wei Fang, and Guizhu Zhang

Large-Scale Global Optimization

Adaptive Variable-Size Random Grouping for Evolutionary Large-Scale
Global Optimization   583
   Evgenii Sopov

A Dynamic Global Differential Grouping for Large-Scale
Black-Box Optimization.   593
   Shuai Wu, Zhitao Zou, and Wei Fang

A Method to Accelerate Convergence and Avoid Repeated Search
for Dynamic Optimization Problem   604
   Weiwei Zhang, Guoqing Li, Weizheng Zhang, and Menghua Zhang

Optimization of Steering Linkage Including the Effect of McPherson Strut
Front Suspension   612
   Suwin Sleesongsom and Sujin Bureerat

Multi-scale Quantum Harmonic Oscillator Algorithm with Individual
Stabilization Strategy.   624
   Peng Wang, Bo Li, Jin Jin, Lei Mu, Gang Xin, Yan Huang,
   and XingGui Ye

Author Index   635

Contents – Part II

Multi-agent Systems

Path Following of Autonomous Agents Under the Effect of Noise   3
Krishna Raghuwaiya, Bibhya Sharma, Jito Vanualailai,
and Parma Nand

Development of Adaptive Force-Following Impedance Control
for Interactive Robot   15
Huang Jianbin, Li Zhi, and Liu Hong

A Space Tendon-Driven Continuum Robot.   25
Shineng Geng, Youyu Wang, Cong Wang, and Rongjie Kang

A Real-Time Multiagent Strategy Learning Environment
and Experimental Framework   36
Hongda Zhang, Decai Li, Liying Yang, Feng Gu, and Yuqing He

Transaction Flows in Multi-agent Swarm Systems.   43
Eugene Larkin, Alexey Ivutin, Alexander Novikov, and Anna Troshina

Event-Triggered Communication Mechanism for Distributed Flocking
Control of Nonholonomic Multi-agent System   53
Weiwei Xun, Wei Yi, Xi Liu, Xiaodong Yi, and Yanzhen Wang

Deep Regression Models for Local Interaction in Multi-agent Robot Tasks. . . .   66
Fredy Martínez, Cristian Penagos, and Luis Pacheco

Multi-drone Framework for Cooperative Deployment of Dynamic Wireless
Sensor Networks.   74
Jon-Vegard Sørli and Olaf Hallan Graven

Swarm Robotics

Distributed Decision Making and Control for Cooperative Transportation
Using Mobile Robots.   89
Henrik Ebel and Peter Eberhard

Deep-Sarsa Based Multi-UAV Path Planning and Obstacle Avoidance
in a Dynamic Environment.   102
Wei Luo, Qirong Tang, Changhong Fu, and Peter Eberhard

Cooperative Search Strategies of Multiple UAVs Based on Clustering
Using Minimum Spanning Tree   112
    Tao Zhu, Weixiong He, Haifeng Ling, and Zhanliang Zhang

Learning Based Target Following Control for Underwater Vehicles........   122
    Zhou Hao, Huang Hai, and Zhou Zexing

Optimal Shape Design of an Autonomous Underwater Vehicle Based
on Gene Expression Programming.............................   132
    Qirong Tang, Yinghao Li, Zhenqiang Deng, Di Chen, Ruiqin Guo,
    and Hai Huang

GLANS: GIS Based Large-Scale Autonomous Navigation System   142
    Manhui Sun, Shaowu Yang, and Henzhu Liu

Fuzzy Logic Approaches

Extraction of Knowledge with Population-Based Metaheuristics Fuzzy
Rules Applied to Credit Risk   153
    Patricia Jimbo Santana, Laura Lanzarini, and Aurelio F. Bariviera

Fuzzy Logic Applied to the Performance Evaluation. Honduran Coffee
Sector Case   164
    Noel Varela Izquierdo, Omar Bonerge Pineda Lezama,
    Rafael Gómez Dorta, Amelec Viloria, Ivan Deras,
    and Lissette Hernández-Fernández

Fault Diagnosis on Electrical Distribution Systems Based on Fuzzy Logic ...   174
    Ramón Perez, Esteban Inga, Alexander Aguila, Carmen Vásquez,
    Liliana Lima, Amelec Viloria, and Maury-Ardila Henry

Planning and Routing Problems

Using FAHP-VIKOR for Operation Selection in the Flexible Job-Shop
Scheduling Problem: A Case Study in Textile Industry   189
    Miguel Ortíz-Barrios, Dionicio Neira-Rodado, Genett Jiménez-Delgado,
    and Hugo Hernández-Palma

A Solution Framework Based on Packet Scheduling and Dispatching Rule
for Job-Based Scheduling Problems............................   202
    Rongrong Zhou, Hui Lu, and Jinhua Shi

A Two-Stage Heuristic Approach for a Type of Rotation
Assignment Problem   212
    Ziran Zheng and Xiaoju Gong

An Improved Blind Optimization Algorithm for Hardware/Software
Partitioning and Scheduling   225
    Xin Zhao, Tao Zhang, Xinqi An, and Long Fan

Interactive Multi-model Target Maneuver Tracking Method Based
on the Adaptive Probability Correction   235
    Jiadong Ren, Xiaotong Zhang, Jiandang Sun, and Qingshuang Zeng

Recommendation in Social Media

Investigating Deciding Factors of Product Recommendation
in Social Media   249
    *Jou Yu Chen, Ping Yu Hsu, Ming Shien Cheng, Hong Tsuen Lei,
    Shih Hsiang Huang, Yen-Huei Ko, and Chen Wan Huang*

Using the Encoder Embedded Framework of Dimensionality Reduction
Based on Multiple Drugs Properties for Drug Recommendation   258
    Jun Ma, Ruisheng Zhang, Rongjing Hu, and Yong Mu

A Personalized Friend Recommendation Method Combining Network
Structure Features and Interaction Information   267
    Chen Yang, Tingting Liu, Lei Liu, Xiaohong Chen, and Zhiyong Hao

A Hybrid Movie Recommendation Method Based on Social Similarity
and Item Attributes   275
    Chen Yang, Xiaohong Chen, Lei Liu, Tingting Liu, and Shuang Geng

Multi-feature Collaborative Filtering Recommendation for Sparse Dataset . . .   286
    Zengda Guan

A Collaborative Filtering Algorithm Based on Attribution Theory   295
    Mao DeLei, Tang Yan, and Liu Bing

Investigating the Effectiveness of Helpful Reviews and Reviewers
in Hotel Industry   305
    *Yen Tzu Chao, Ping Yu Hsu, Ming Shien Cheng, Hong Tsuen Lei,
    Shih Hsiang Huang, Yen-Huei Ko, Grandys Frieska Prassida,
    and Chen Wan Huang*

Mapping the Landscapes, Hotspots and Trends of the Social Network
Analysis Research from 1975 to 2017   314
    Li Zeng, Zili Li, Zhao Zhao, and Meixin Mao

Predication

A Deep Prediction Architecture for Traffic Flow
with Precipitation Information.   329
　　Jingyuan Wang, Xiaofei Xu, Feishuang Wang, Chao Chen, and Ke Ren

Tag Prediction in Social Annotation Systems Based on CNN
and BiLSTM   339
　　Baiwei Li, Qingchuan Wang, Xiaoru Wang, and Wei Li

Classification

A Classification Method for Micro-Blog Popularity Prediction: Considering
the Semantic Information   351
　　Lei Liu, Chen Yang, Tingting Liu, Xiaohong Chen, and Sung-Shun Weng

VPSO-Based CCR-ELM for Imbalanced Classification   361
　　Yi-nan Guo, Pei Zhang, Ning Cui, JingJing Chen, and Jian Cheng

An Ensemble Classifier Based on Three-Way Decisions for Social Touch
Gesture Recognition   370
　　Gangqiang Zhang, Qun Liu, Yubin Shi, and Hongying Meng

Engineering Character Recognition Algorithm and Application Based
on BP Neural Network   380
　　Chen Rong and Yu Luqian

Hand Gesture Recognition Based on Multi Feature Fusion   389
　　Hongling Yang, Shibin Xuan, and Yuanbin Mo

Application of SVDD Single Categorical Data Description in Motor Fault
Identification Based on Health Redundant Data.   399
　　Jianjian Yang, Xiaolin Wang, Zhiwei Tang, Zirui Wang, Song Han,
　　Yinan Guo, and Miao Wu

Finding Patterns

Impact of Purchasing Power on User Rating Behavior
and Purchasing Decision   413
　　Yong Wang, Xiaofei Xu, Jun He, Chao Chen, and Ke Ren

Investigating the Relationship Between the Emotion of Blogs and the Price
of Index Futures   423
　　Yen Hao Kao, Ping Yu Hsu, Ming Shien Cheng, Hong Tsuen Lei,
　　Shih Hsiang Huang, Yen-Huei Ko, and Chen Wan Huang

A Novel Model for Finding Critical Products with Transaction Logs   432
Ping Yu Hsu, Chen Wan Huang, Shih Hsiang Huang, Pei Chi Chen,
and Ming Shien Cheng

Using Discrete-Event-Simulation for Improving Operational Efficiency
in Laboratories: A Case Study in Pharmaceutical Industry   440
Alexander Troncoso-Palacio, Dionicio Neira-Rodado,
Miguel Ortíz-Barrios, Genett Jiménez-Delgado,
and Hugo Hernández-Palma

Architecture of an Object-Oriented Modeling Framework
for Human Occupation.   452
Manuel-Ignacio Balaguera, María-Cristina Vargas,
Jenny-Paola Lis-Gutierrez, Amelec Viloria, and Luz Elena Malagón

A Building Energy Saving Software System Based on Configuration.   461
Jinlong Chen, Qinghao Zeng, Hang Pan, Xianjun Chen, and Rui Zhang

Measures of Concentration and Stability: Two Pedagogical Tools
for Industrial Organization Courses   471
Jenny-Paola Lis-Gutiérrez, Mercedes Gaitán-Angulo,
Linda Carolina Henao, Amelec Viloria, Doris Aguilera-Hernández,
and Rafael Portillo-Medina

Image Enhancement

The Analysis of Image Enhancement for Target Detection   483
Rui Zhang, Yongjun Jia, Lihui Shi, Hang Pan, Jinlong Chen,
and Xianjun Chen

Image Filtering Enhancement   493
Zhen Guo, Hang Pan, Jinlong Chen, and Xianjun Chen

Random Forest Based Gesture Segmentation from Depth Image   500
Renjun Tang, Hang Pan, Xianjun Chen, and Jinlong Chen

Deep Learning

DL-GSA: A Deep Learning Metaheuristic Approach to Missing
Data Imputation   513
Ayush Garg, Deepika Naryani, Garvit Aggarwal, and Swati Aggarwal

Research on Question-Answering System Based on Deep Learning   522
Bo Song, Yue Zhuo, and Xiaomei Li

A Deep Learning Model for Predicting Movie Box Office Based on Deep
Belief Network   530
    Wei Wang, Jiapeng Xiu, Zhengqiu Yang, and Chen Liu

A Deep-Layer Feature Selection Method Based on Deep Neural Networks. . .   542
    Chen Qiao, Ke-Feng Sun, and Bin Li

Video Vehicle Detection and Recognition Based on MapReduce
and Convolutional Neural Network   552
    Mingsong Chen, Weiguang Wang, Shi Dong, and Xinling Zhou

A Uniform Approach for the Comparison of Opposition-Based Learning   563
    Qingzheng Xu, Heng Yang, Na Wang, Rong Fei, and Guohua Wu

Author Index   575

Theories and Models of Swarm Intelligence

Semi-Markov Model of a Swarm Functioning

E. V. Larkin and M. A. Antonov[(✉)]

Tula State University, Tula 300012, Russia
elarkin@mail.ru, max0594@yandex.ru

Abstract. The method of a physical swarm modeling, based on application of semi-Markov process theory to description of swarm unit cyclograms is worked out. It is shown, that ordinary semi-Markov processes with structural states are abstract analogue of units cyclograms. The method of gathering of ordinary semi-Markov processes into M-parallel process and further transformation of it into complex semi-Markov process with functional states is proposed. It is shown that functional states may be obtained as Cartesian product of sets of ordinary semi-Markov processes states. Operation of semi-Markov matrices Cartesian product is introduced. Method of evaluation of elements of complex semi-Markov matrix is worked out.

Keywords: Swarm · Unit · Cyclogram · Structural state · Functional state
Parallel semi-Markov process · Complex semi-Markov process
Cartesian product

1 Introduction

At the present time physical swarms are widely used in various branches of human activity, such as industry, defense, ecology etc. [1–3]. Below a physical swarm is considered as a set of physical units, operated to realize a corporative aim [3]. Every unit within overall intention executes its own function, so it operates in accordance with its own co-algorithm. Every co-algorithm forms so called cyclogram of swarm unit operation. Other level of swarming is an operation of swarm unit onboard equipment. It also includes a set of physical blocks, every block operates due to its own cyclogram, and operation of equipment as a whole leads to realization a corporative aim of swarm [4].

Cyclograms have next features [5, 6]:

they are divided onto states and every state of a cyclogram fits the physical state of the proper swarm unit;
the time of residence of the unit in the state of cyclogram is a random one, and is known with exactness to density;
switches into neighboring states from the current state have a stochastic character;
all states of cyclogram are actual, i.e. from every state of cyclogram there is at least one possible way to all other states.

Swarm control predetermines necessity of knowledge of all unites current states. At now this problem may be solved by means of determining of current states of separate units. After determining the states other problem, namely time coordination of units operation emerges. In this aspect task solution, which permits to determine complex swarm state at any time, is preferable.

Features of cyclograms, mentioned above, permit to use for their modeling the semi-Markov process theory [7–11], but semi-Markov models of parallel process are not of widely used, and their creation is rather complicated scientific problem. This fact explains importance and relevance of investigations in this domain.

2 M-Parallel Semi-Markov Process

Let us consider the pair [7]

$$B = (\Omega, P), \tag{1}$$

where Ω - is the set of elementary events; P - probabilistic measure.

Set Ω may be performed as the next union of subsets:

$$\Omega = \Omega^t \cup \left(\bigcup_{m=1}^{M} \Omega_m^a \right);$$

$$\Omega^t \cap \left(\bigcup_{m=1}^{M} \Omega_m^a \right) = \varnothing; \tag{2}$$

$$\Omega_m^a \cap \Omega_n^a = \begin{cases} \varnothing, & \text{when } m \neq n; \\ \Omega_m^a, & \text{when } m = n, \end{cases}$$

where $\Omega_m^a = \left\{ \omega_{1(a,m)}^a, \ldots, \omega_{j(a,m)}^a, \ldots, \omega_{J(a,m)}^a \right\}$ are discrete countable subsets of elementary events, $1 \leq m \leq M$; $\Omega^t = \left[\omega_{1(t)}^t, \ldots, \omega_{j(t)}^t, \ldots \right]$ is the infinite ordered subset of elementary events constituting a continuum; $\varnothing$ is the empty set.

The function

$$\alpha \left(\bigcup_{m=1}^{M} \Omega_m^a \right) = \bigcup_{m=1}^{M} \alpha \left(\Omega_m^a \right), \tag{3}$$

where

$$\alpha \left(\Omega_{1m}^a \right) = \left\{ \alpha \left[\omega_{1(a,m)}^a \right], \ldots, \alpha \left[\omega_{j(a,m)}^a \right], \ldots, \alpha \left[\omega_{J(a,m)}^a \right] \right\}; \tag{4}$$

$$\alpha \left(\omega_{j(a)}^a \right) = a_{j(m)}, \tag{5}$$

forms the set of states

$$A = \{A_1, \ldots, A_m, \ldots, A_M\};\tag{6}$$

$$A_m = \{a_{1(m)}, \ldots, a_{j(m)}, \ldots, a_{J(m)}\},\tag{7}$$

where $a_{j(m)}$ is the abstract analogue of the $j(m)$-th physical state of m-th swarm unit cyclogram.

In the state $a_{j(m)}$ m-th unit resides from begin of $j(m)$-th operations, predetermined by m-th cyclogram, till its end. Function $\alpha\left(\omega_{j(a)}^a\right)$ of elementary event is discrete, single-placed and one-to-one function, and is such, that to the event $\omega_{j(a,m)}^a$ fits the state $a_{j(m)}$, and vice versa, to the state $a_{j(m)}$ fits the event $\omega_{j(a,m)}^a$.

Function

$$t_{j(t)} = \tau\left[\omega_{j(t)}^t\right]\tag{8}$$

describes real physical time aspects of swarm operation. In particular, $t_{j(t)}$ - is the time, which corresponds to the elementary event $\omega_{j(t)}^t$. Function (8) is continual, single-placed and one-to-one function, and is such, that to the event $\omega_{j(t)}^t$ fits the state $t_{j(t)}$, and vice versa, to the state $t_{j(t)}$ fits the event $\omega_{j(t)}^t$,

Application of (8) to Ω^t gives

$$\tau(\Omega^t) = t,\tag{9}$$

where t is the real physical time.

Notions «global time» and «time intervals» should be distinguished (Fig. 1). Global time t_G is the same for all units of the swarm, and starts from beginning of swarm existence.

On the Fig. 1 $t \geq 0$ - is the time of residence in $j(a,m)$-th physical state of m-th swarm unit cyclogram; t_G is the global time. Time interval counts out from the previous switch till the next switch.

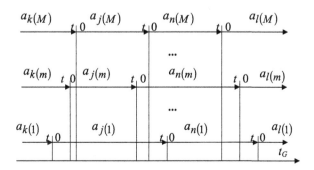

Fig. 1. Time intervals

Let us return to pair (1). Probabilistic measure

$$p_{j(m)} = P\lfloor a : a_{j(m)} \in A_m \rfloor \qquad (10)$$

may be aligned to subset Ω_m^a.

Measure (10) characterizes a residence of the m-th unit in one of states of subset A_m for external in relation, to mentioned unit, observer. The fact that the m-th unit may reside in one, and only one state, imposes next restriction on probabilities:

$$\sum_{j(m)=1(m)}^{J(m)} p_{j(m)} = 1. \qquad (11)$$

Nominate switch from $a_{j(m)}$ till $a_{n(m)}$ as

$$s_{j(m),n(m)} = \lfloor a_{j(m)}, a_{n(m)} \rfloor \in S_m, \qquad (12)$$

where S_m is the set of possible switches, which may be obtained by means of exponentiation into second Cartesian degree the set A_m:

$$S_m = (A_m)^2 = \{ s_{1(m),1(m)}, \ldots, s_{1(m),n(m)}, \ldots, s_{1(m),J(m)}, \ldots, s_{j(m),1(m)}, \ldots, \\ s_{j(m),n(m)}, \ldots, s_{j(m),J(m)}, \ldots, s_{J(m),1(m)}, \ldots, s_{J(m),n(m)}, \ldots, s_{J(m),J(m)}, \ldots, \}. \qquad (13)$$

To every pair of (13) may be aligned probabilistic measure

$$p_{j(m),n(m)} = P\lfloor s : s = (a^-, a^+) \in S_m, a^- = a_{j(m)}, a^+ = a_{n(m)} \rfloor, \qquad (14)$$

where a^- is the state of unit before switch, a^+ is the state of unit after switch.

The time interval of m-th cyclogram starts at the moment of switch from the state $a_{j(m)}$ till the state $a_{n(m)}$, $1 \leq j(m), n(m) \leq J(m))$. In such a way, on the global time axis t_G a flow of switches is generated which unites switch flows of units. Time interval between switches is random value, so for $j(m)$-th state, if it is known that next switch will be $s_{j(m),n(m)}$, probabilistic measure may be determined as follows:

$$f_{j(m),n(m)}\left(t_{j(t)}\right)dt = P\lfloor t : t\left(s_{k(m),j(m)}\right) = 0, t\left(s_{j(m),n(m)}\right) = t_{j(t)} \rfloor, \qquad (15)$$

where $t\left(s_{k(m),j(m)}\right)$ is the time of switch into the state $a_{j(m)}$; $t\left(s_{j(m),n(m)}\right)$ is the time of switch from the state $a_{j(m)}$, if there was decision, that next state will be $a_{n(m)}$.

If in (15) to omit the index $j(t)$, then time density $f_{j(m),n(m)}(t)$ is the probabilistic measure, which does not depend of pre-history of switches, but depends only of what state of cyclogram m-th unit switches next time.

So, conception (1) permits to formulate the notion of M-parallel semi-Markov process as follows;

$$\mu = \bigcup_{m=1}^{M} \mu_m, \tag{16}$$

$$\mu_m = \{A_m, \boldsymbol{h}_m(t)\}, \tag{17}$$

where μ_m is the ordinary semi-Markov process; A_m is the set of states, described as (7); $\boldsymbol{h}_m(t)$ is the semi-Markov matrix of size $J(m) \times J(m)$;

$$\boldsymbol{h}_m(t) = \left[h_{j(m),n(m)}(t)\right] = \boldsymbol{p}_m \quad \boldsymbol{f}_m(t); \tag{18}$$

$$\boldsymbol{p}_m = \int_0^{\infty} \boldsymbol{h}_m(t)dt = \left[p_{j(m),n(m)}\right]; \tag{19}$$

$$\boldsymbol{f}_m(t) = \left[\frac{h_{j(m),n(m)}(t)}{p_{j(m),n(m)}(t)}\right] = \left[f_{j(m),n(m)}(t)\right]. \tag{20}$$

Processes $\mu_m \ 1 \leq m \leq M$ belong to the category of ergodic semi-Markov processes. They operate simultaneously in all units, and for proper control the swarm as a whole it is necessary to build up the model of complex semi-Markov process.

3   Complex Semi-Markov Process

Events in complex semi-Markov process are shown on the bottom row of Fig. 1. This process may be defined as follows [12–14]:

$$^M\mu = \{^MA, {}^M\boldsymbol{h}(t)\}, \tag{21}$$

where ^MA is the set of states; $^M\boldsymbol{h}(t)$ - is the semi-Markov matrix.

Below notions «structural state» and «functional state» will be used (Fig. 2). Structural states are states of physical unit, follows from cyclogram of its functioning, so m-th unit have $J(m)$ states. Common number of structural states is equal to the sum

$$N_s = \sum_{m=1}^{M} |A_m| = \sum_{m=1}^{M} J(m). \tag{22}$$

The cartesian product of states A_m gives set of functional states

$$M_A = \prod_{m=1}^{M} {}^C A_m, \tag{23}$$

where $\prod^C$ is the nomination of group Cartesian product.

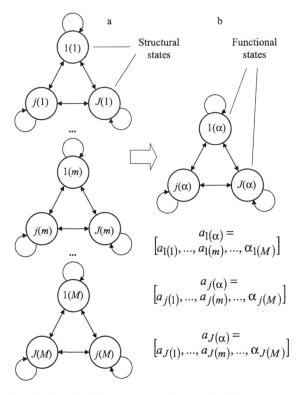

Fig. 2. Parallel (a) and complex (b) semi-Markov process

The set of functional states is as follows:

$$^{M}A = \{\alpha_{1(\alpha)}, \ldots, \alpha_{j(\alpha)}, \ldots, \alpha_{J(\alpha)}\} = \{[a_{1(1)}, \ldots a_{1(m)}, \ldots, \alpha_{1(M)}], \ldots,$$
$$[a_{j(1)}, \ldots, a_{j(m)}, \ldots, \alpha_{j(M)}], \ldots, [a_{j(1)}, \ldots, a_{j(m)}, \ldots, \alpha_{J(M)}]\}, \quad (24)$$

where $\alpha_{j(\alpha)} = [a_{j(1)}, \ldots, a_{j(m)}, \ldots, \alpha_{j(M)}]$ is the functional state;

$$J(\alpha) = \prod_{m=1}^{M} |A_m| = \prod_{m=1}^{M} J(m). \quad (25)$$

To define the semi-Markov matrix one should to consider the competition in M simplest semi-Markov processes

$$\tilde{\mu}_m = \left\{ \{b_{1(m)}, b_{2(m)}\}, \begin{bmatrix} 0 & f_m(t) \\ 0 & 0 \end{bmatrix} \right\}, 1 \le m \le M. \quad (26)$$

Process (26) is not ergodic, and it has starting state $b_{1(m)}$ and absorbing state $b_{2(m)}$. If all M processes start simultaneously, then weighted density of time of reaching the absorbing state $b_{2(m)}$ by m-th semi-Markov process $\tilde{\mu}_m$ is as follows;

$$\sum_{m=1}^{M} h_{wm}(t) = f_m(t) \prod_{\substack{k=1, \\ k \neq m}}^{M} [1 - F_k(t)], \tag{27}$$

where $F_k(t) = \int_0^t f_k(\tau)d\tau$.

From (27) probability and pure time density of reaching the absorbing state $b_{2(m)}$ by m-th semi-Markov process $\tilde{\mu}_m$ may be obtained as follows [15, 16]:

$$p_{wm} = \int_0^\infty f_m(t) \cdot \prod_{\substack{k=1 \\ k \neq m}}^{M} [1 - F_k(t)]dt; \tag{28}$$

$$f_{wm}(t) = \frac{h_{wm}(t)}{p_{wm}}. \tag{29}$$

Expectation and dispersion of $f_{wm}(t)$ are defined as usually:

$$T_{wm} = \int_0^\infty t f_{wm}(t)dt; \tag{30}$$

$$D_{wm} = \int_0^\infty (t - T_{wm})^2 f_{wm}(t)dt, \ 1 \leq m \leq M. \tag{31}$$

To define the semi-Markov matrix $^M\boldsymbol{h}(t)$ one should to define Cartesian product of matrices $\boldsymbol{h}_m(t)$ as follows:

$$^M\boldsymbol{h}(t) = \prod_{m=1}^{M} {}^C\boldsymbol{h}_m(t). \tag{32}$$

Rows and columns of $^M\boldsymbol{h}(t)$ should be numerated as follows:

$$\prod_{m=1}^{M} {}^C\{1(m),\ldots,j(m),\ldots,J(m)\}$$
$$= \{[1(1),\ldots,1(m),\ldots,1(M)],\ldots,[j(1),\ldots,j(m),\ldots,j(M)],\ldots, \tag{33}$$
$$[n(1),\ldots,n(m),\ldots,n(M),\ldots,[J(1),\ldots,J(m),\ldots,J(M)]]\}$$
$$= \{1(\alpha),\ldots,j(\alpha),\ldots,n(\alpha),\ldots,J(\alpha)\}.$$

Cartesian product of two semi-Markov may be defined as follows:

$$^2\boldsymbol{h}(t) = \boldsymbol{h}_k(t) \times \boldsymbol{h}_m(t) = \left[h_{j(k),n(k)}\right] \times \left[h_{j(k),n(k)}\right] = \left[h_{j(\alpha),n(\alpha)}(t)\right]. \qquad (34)$$

where $j(\alpha) = [j(k), j(m)], n(\alpha) = [n(k), n(m)]$ are indices in two-dimensional space.

Let us consider the functional state $a_{[j(k),j(m)]}$ of complex semi-Markov process, which represented with product (34). The functional state $a_{[j(k),j(m)]}$ describes the competition between processes in structural states $a_{j(k)}$ and $a_{j(m)}$. Let after a switch the functional state become $a_{[n(k),n(m)]}$. In the competition must be only one winner (probability of draw is vanishingly small), so the Hamming distance between the indices $j(\alpha)$ and $n(\alpha)$ must be as follows:

$$H = \begin{cases} 0, when\, j(k) = n(k),\, j(m) = n(m); \\ 2,\, when\, j(k) \neq n(k),\, j(m) \neq n(m); . \\ 1\, in\, all\, other\, cases. \end{cases} \qquad (35)$$

Time densities of residence the processes $\boldsymbol{h}_k(t)$, $\boldsymbol{h}_m(t)$ in structural states $a_{j(k)}$ are as follows:

$$f_{j(k)}(t) = \sum_{n=1}^{J(k)} h_{j(k),n(k)}(t),\ f_{j(m)}(t) = \sum_{n=1}^{J(m)} h_{j(m),n(m)}(t). \qquad (36)$$

Element of the semi-Markov matrix $^2\boldsymbol{h}(t)$, situated on the intersection of the $[j(k),j(m)]$-th row and $[n(k),n(m)]$-th column determines weighed time density of switch from the functional state $a_{[j(k),j(m)]}$ into the functional state $a_{[n(k),n(m)]}$. This element with use (27) may be obtained as follows:

if H = 0, then

$$\begin{aligned} h_{j(\alpha),n(\alpha)}(t) = f_{j(k),j(k)}(t) \left[1 - \sum_{n(m)=1}^{J(m)} H_{j(m,n(m))}(t) \right] \\ + f_{j(m),j(m)}(t) \left[1 - \sum_{n(k)=1}^{J(k)} H_{j(k,n(k))}(t) \right], \end{aligned} \qquad (37)$$

where $f_{j(k),j(k)}$ and $f_{j(m),j(m)}$ are determined as (18), (19), (20);

$$H_{j(k,n(k))}(t) = \int_0^t H_{j(k,n(k))}(\tau)dt;\ H_{j(m,n(m))}(t) = \int_0^t H_{j(m,n(m))}(\tau)d\tau;$$

if $H = 1, j(k) = n(k), j(m) \neq n(m)$, then

$$h_{j(\alpha),n(\alpha)}(t) = f_{j(m),n(m)}(t) \left[1 - \sum_{n(k)=1}^{J(k)} H_{j(k,n(k))}(t) \right], \tag{38}$$

If $H = 1$, $j(k) \neq n(k)$, $j(m) = n(m)$, then

$$h_{j(\alpha),n(\alpha)}(t) = f_{j(k),n(k)}(t) \left[1 - \sum_{n(m)=1}^{J(m)} H_{j(m,n(m))}(t) \right], \tag{39}$$

if $H = 2$, then

$$h_{j(\alpha),n(\alpha)}(t) = 0. \tag{40}$$

Semi-Markov matrix of complex process may be found with use the recursive procedure:

$$^{M}\boldsymbol{h}(t) = \prod_{m=1}^{M} {}^{C}\boldsymbol{h}_{m}(t) = {}^{M-1}\boldsymbol{h}(t) \times \boldsymbol{h}_{l}(t), \tag{41}$$

where $^{M-1}\boldsymbol{h}(t)$ is a Cartesian product of $M - 1$ ordinary semi Markov matrices; $\boldsymbol{h}_{l}(t)$ is the M-th semi-Markov matrix of ordinary process.

Permutation of factors in (34), (41) leads only to permutation in rows and in columns, and not change matrix as a whole. Also it is necessary to admit, that if all ordinary processes μ_{m}, $1 \leq m \leq M$, are the ergodic ones, then complex semi-Markov process $^{M}\mu$ is the ergodic too. Complex semi-Markov process obtained is just alike ordinary semi-Markov process with set of states and semi-Markov matrix (21). To solve the problem of evaluation time intervals of wandering through the process states, and probabilities of residence in states one can use known methods [5, 6, 8, 11] applied directly to (21).

4   Computer Experiment

To verify the proposed approach to parallel process modeling a direct computer experiment was carried out with use the Monte Carlo method. Structures of swarm cyclograms are shown on the Fig. 3a. Cyclograms structural states are On_k and off_k, $k = 1, 2, 3$. Time of residence in the structural states are defined as $^{on}f_k(t)$, $^{off}f_k(t)$. Expectations of time are as follows: $^{on}T_1 = 1$, $^{off}T_1 = 3$, $^{on}T_2 = 2$, $^{off}T_2 = 2$, $^{on}T_3 = 3$, $^{off}T_3 = 1$. Functional states of the swarm are $\{(On, On, On), \ldots, (Off, On, Off), \ldots, (Off, Off, Off)\}$. Calculated probabilities of residence in structural states in steady-state regime are as follows: $^{on}p_1 = 0,25$, $^{off}p_1 = 0,75$, $^{on}p_2 = 0,5$, $^{off}p_2 = 0,5$, $^{on}p_3 = 0,75$, $^{off}p_3 = 0,25$. Calculated probabilities of residence in functional states in steady-state regime are as follows:, $^{fs}p_{000} = 0,094$, $^{fs}p_{001} = 0,281$, $^{fs}p_{010} = 0,094$, $^{fs}p_{011} = 0,281$, $^{fs}p_{100} = 0,031$, $^{fs}p_{101} = 0,094$, $^{fs}p_{110} = 0,031$, $^{fs}p_{111} = 0,094$.

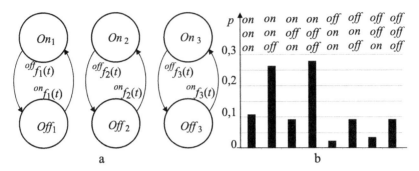

a   b

Fig. 3. The parallel semi-Markov process (a) and distribution of probabilities of residence in functional states (b)

Distribution of probabilities of residence in functional states, obtained with use Monte-Carlo method is shown on the Fig. 3b. The mean error, which gives proposed method is 0,7%.

5 Conclusion

In such a way common approach to analytical description of parallel semi-Markov processes is proposed. Approach permits to control the swarm states as a whole. After transformation M-parallel semi-Markov process into complex semi-Markov process time and probabilistic characteristics of the swarm states can be calculated with use rather simple known methods.

Further research in this area may be directed to building up the model of swarm, with description of unit behavior with use of strong Markov process abstraction. Further direction of development is linked with numerical methods of complex semi-Markov matrix parameters calculation with use numerical parameters of ordinary processes only.

The research was carried out within the state assignment of the Ministry of Education and Science of Russian Federation (No. 2.3121.2017/PCH).

References

1. Brambilla, M., Ferrante, E., Birattari, M., Dorigo, M.: Swarm robotics: A review from the swarm engineering perspective. Swarm Intell. **7**(1), 1–41 (2013)
2. Morin, P., Samson, C.: Motion control of wheeled mobile robots. In: Siciliano, B., Khatib, O. (eds.) Springer Handbook of Robotics. Springer, Heidelberg (2008). https://doi.org/10.1007/978-3-540-30301-5_35

3. Ivutin, A., Larkin, E., Kotov, V.: Established routine of swarm monitoring systems functioning. In: Tan, Y., Shi, Y., Buarque, F., Gelbukh, A., Das, S., Engelbrecht, A. (eds.) ICSI 2015. LNCS, vol. 9141, pp. 415–422. Springer, Cham (2015). https://doi.org/10.1007/978-3-319-20472-7_45

4. Kahar, S., Sulaiman, R., Prabuwono, A.S., Akma, N., Ahmad, S.A., Abu Hassan, M.A.: A review of wireless technology usage for mobile robot controller. In: 2012 International Conference on System Engineering and Modeling (ICSEM 2012), vol. 34, pp. 7–12. IACSIT Press, Singapore (2012)

5. Larkin, E.V., Ivutin, A.N.: Estimation of latency in embedded real-time systems. In: 3-rd Meditteranean Conference on Embedded Computing (MECO-2014), Budva, Montenegro, pp. 236–239 (2014)

6. Larkin, E., Ivutin, A., Kotov, V., Privalov, A.: Semi-markov modelling of commands execution by mobile robot. In: Ronzhin, A., Rigoll, G., Meshcheryakov, R. (eds.) ICR 2016. LNCS (LNAI), vol. 9812, pp. 189–198. Springer, Cham (2016). https://doi.org/10.1007/978-3-319-43955-6_23

7. Korolyuk, V., Swishchuk, A.: Semi-Markov Random Evolutions. Springer, Dordrecht (1995). https://doi.org/10.1007/978-94-011-1010-5

8. Limnios, N., Swishchuk, A.: Discrete-time semi-markov random evolutions and their applications. Adv. Appl. Probab. **45**(1), 214–240 (2013)

9. Markov, A.A.: Extension of the law of large numbers to dependent quantities. Izvestiia Fiz.-Matem. Obsch. Kazan Univ. (2-nd Ser.), pp. 135–156 (1906)

10. Bielecki, T.R., Jakubowski, J., Niewęgłowski, M.: Conditional Markov chains: properties, construction and structured dependence. Stoch. Processes Appl. **127**(4), 1125–1170 (2017)

11. Janssen, J., Manca, R.: Applied Semi-Markov Processes. Springer, Heidelberg (2005). https://doi.org/10.1007/0-387-29548-8

12. Larkin, E.V., Lutskov, Y., Ivutin, A.N., Novikov, A.S.: Simulation of concurrent process with petri-markov nets. Life Sci. J. **11**(11), 506–511 (2014)

13. Ivutin, A.N., Larkin, E.V.: Simulation of concurrent games. Bulletin of the South Ural State University. Mathematical Modeling, Programming and Computer Software, vol. 8 (2), pp. 43–54 (2015)

14. Larkin, E.V., Ivutin, A.N., Kotov, V.V., Privalov, A.N.: Simulation of relay-races. Bulletin of the South Ural State University. Mathematical Modelling, Programming and Computer Software, vol. 9 (4), pp. 117–128 (2016)

15. Bauer, H.: Probability Theory. Walter de Gruyter, Berlin (1996)

16. Shiryaev, A.N.: Probability. Springer, New York (1996). https://doi.org/10.1007/978-1-4757-2539-1

Modelling and Verification Analysis of the Predator-Prey System via a Modal Logic Approach

Zvi Retchkiman Konigsberg$^{(\boxtimes)}$

Centro de Investigacion en Computacion,
Instituto Politecnico Nacional, Mexico City, Mexico
mzvi@cic.ipn.mx

Abstract. Consider the interaction of populations, in which there are exactly two species, one of which the *predators* eat the *preys* thereby affecting each other. In the study of this interaction Lotka-Volterra models have been used. Other non-classical methodologies as Petri nets and first order logic have been employed too. This paper proposes a formal modeling and verification analysis methodology, which consists in representing the interaction behavior by means of a modal logic formula. Then, using the concept of logic implication, and transforming this logical implication relation into a set of clauses, a modal resolution qualitative method for verification (satisfiability) as well as performance issues, for some queries is applied.

Keywords: Predator-prey system · Modal logic · Model
Verification · Unsatisfiability · Modal resolution method

1 Introduction

Consider the interaction of populations, in which there are exactly two species, one of which the *predators* eat the *preys* thereby affecting each other. Such pairs exist throughout nature: fish and sharks, lions and gazelles, birds and insects, to mention some. In the study of this interaction Lotka-Volterra models have been used [1]. Other non-classical methodologies as Petri nets and first order logic have been employed too [2,3]. This paper proposes a well defined syntax modeling and verification analysis methodology which consists in representing the predator-prey interaction system as a modal logic formula. The modal logic approach introduces two new operators that enable abstract relations like necessarily true and possibly true to be expressed directly, called alethic modalities, what is not possible using first order logic. For example, the statement: 7 is a prime number, is necessarily true always and everywhere, in contrast, the statement the head of state of this country is a king is possibly true, because its truth changes from place to place and from time to time. Other modalities that have been formalized in modal logic include temporal modalities, or modalities

© Springer International Publishing AG, part of Springer Nature 2018
Y. Tan et al. (Eds.): ICSI 2018, LNCS 10941, pp. 14–21, 2018.
https://doi.org/10.1007/978-3-319-93815-8_2

of time, deontic modalities, epistemic modalities, and doxastic modalities. The main idea consists in modeling the predator-prey system by means of a modal logic formula. Then, using the concept of logic implication, and transforming this logical implication relation into a set of clauses, a modal resolution qualitative method for verification (satisfiability) as well as performance issues, for some queries is applied. The paper is organized as follows. In Sect. 2, a modal logic background summary is given. In Sect. 3, the modal resolution principle for unsatisfiability is recalled. In Sect. 4, the predator-prey problem is addressed. Finally, the paper ends with some conclusions.

2   Modal Logic Background

This section presents a summary of modal logic theory. The reader interested in more details is encouraged to see [4,5].

Definition 1. *A modal language $\mathcal{L}$ is an infinite collection of distinct symbols, no one of which is properly contained in another, separated into the following categories: parentheses, connectives, possibility modality, necessity modality, proposition variables $\Phi_0 = \{p_1, p_2, \cdots\}$ (called atoms), contradiction (falsity), true (tautology).*

Definition 2. *Well-formed formulas, or formulas for short, in modal logic are defined recursively as follows: (i). An atom is a formula, $\perp$ (false is a formula), T (true is a formula) (ii). If F and G are formulas then, $\sim (F)$, $(F \vee G)$, $(F \wedge G)$, $(F \leftrightarrow G)$, $\Box F$, $\Diamond F$, are formulas. $\Diamond A \equiv \sim \Box \sim A$. Formulas are generated only by a finite number of applications of (i) and (ii), therefore the set of welled formed formulas is enumerable infinite.*

Remark 1. It is important to underline the unique readability of the formulas which is secured by the assumption that the operators are one to one.

Definition 3. *A Kripke frame (frame) $\mathcal{F}$ is a pair $(W, \mathcal{R})$ in which W is a set of worlds (time, states, etc.), and $\mathcal{R} \subseteq W \times W$ is a binary relation over W.*

Definition 4. *A Kripke model (model) $\mathcal{M}$ over frame $\mathcal{F}$ is a triple $(\mathcal{F}, \pi) = (W, \mathcal{R}, \pi)$ where $\pi : \Phi_0 \to 2^W$ the set of worlds where each element of Φ_0 is true is an assignment or interpretation.*

Definition 5. *Given any model $\mathcal{M}$, a world $w \, \varepsilon \, W$, the notion of true at w is defined as follows:*

- $\mathcal{M}, w \models p_n \Leftrightarrow w \, \varepsilon \, \pi(p_n), n = 1, 2, \cdots$
- $\mathcal{M}, w \models \sim F \Leftrightarrow w \nvDash F$
- $\mathcal{M}, w \models F \wedge G \Leftrightarrow w \models F$ *and* $w \models G$
- $\mathcal{M}, w \models F \vee G \Leftrightarrow w \models F$ *or* $w \models G$
- $\mathcal{M}, w \models F \to G \Leftrightarrow$ *if* $w \models F$ *then* $w \models G$
- $\mathcal{M}, w \models F \equiv G \Leftrightarrow w \models F$ *iff* $w \models G$

  - $\mathcal{M}, w \models \diamond F \Leftrightarrow$ *there exists* $u \varepsilon W$ *such that* $(w, u) \varepsilon \mathcal{R}, \mathcal{M}, u \models F$
  - $\mathcal{M}, w \models \Box F \Leftrightarrow$ *for all* $u \varepsilon W$ *such that* $(w, u) \varepsilon \mathcal{R}, \mathcal{M}, u \models F$

Definition 6. *A formula F is consistent (satisfiable, true at w) in a model $\mathcal{M}$ in a world $w \varepsilon W$ iff $\mathcal{M}, w \models F$, then we say that $\mathcal{M}$ is a. model for F. If this happens for all worlds $w \varepsilon W$ then we say it is true.*

Definition 7. *A formula F is inconsistent (unsatisfiable) in a model $\mathcal{M}$ iff $\mathcal{M}, w \not\models F$ for every world $w \varepsilon W$, then we say that $\mathcal{M}$ is a countermodel for F.*

Definition 8. *A formula F is valid in a class of models $\mathcal{CM}$ if and only if it is true for all models in the class. This will be denoted by $\models_{\mathcal{CM}} F$.*

Definition 9. *A formula F is valid iff it is valid for every class of models $\mathcal{CM}$. This will be denoted by $\models F$.*

Definition 10. *A formula G is a logical implication of formulas $F_1, F_2, \ldots, F_n$ if and only if for every model $\mathcal{M}$, that makes $F_1, F_2, \ldots, F_n$ true, G is also true in $\mathcal{M}$.*

The following characterization of logical implication plays a very important role as will be shown in the rest of the paper.

Theorem 1. *Given formulas $F_1, F_2, \ldots, F_n, G$, G is a logical implication of $F_1, F_2, \ldots, F_n$ if and only if the formula $((F_1 \wedge F_2 \wedge \ldots, \wedge F_n) \to G)$ is valid in a class of models if and only if the formula $(F_1 \wedge F_2 \wedge \ldots \wedge F_n \wedge \sim (G))$ is unsatisfiable.*

Proof. Setting the class of models equal to all the models that make $F_1 \wedge F_2 \wedge \ldots, \wedge F_n$ true. The first iff follows directly by the definition of validity in a class of models, and logical implication. For the second one, since $F_1 \wedge F_2 \wedge \ldots, \wedge F_n \to G$ is valid in a class of models, every model that makes $F_1 \wedge F_2 \wedge \ldots, \wedge F_n$ true does not satisfy $\sim (G)$, therefore $(F_1 \wedge F_2 \wedge \ldots \wedge F_n \wedge \sim (G))$ can not be satisfied. Reversing this last argument we obtain the last implication.

Next, given a class of models $\mathcal{CM}$, we define the syntactic mechanisms capable of generating the formulas valid on $\mathcal{CM}$.

  Axioms: (1) All instances of propositional logic tautologies.
  (2) $\Box(F \to G) \to \Box F \to \Box G$.
  Rules of inference: (1) Modus ponens

$$\frac{F, F \to G}{G}$$

(2) Necessitation

$$\frac{F}{\Box G}$$

We write $\vdash F$ if F can be deduced from the axioms and the inference rules.

Theorem 2 *(Completeness* [4]*). A formula F is valid iff it is provable i.e.,
$\models F \Leftrightarrow \vdash F$.*

Definition 11. *A formula F in modal logic is said to be in disjunctive normal
form normal (DNF) if and only if is a disjunction (perhaps with zero disjunct)
of the form $F == L_1 \vee L_2 \vee \cdots L_n \vee \Box D_1 \vee \Box D_2 \vee \cdots \Box D_m \vee \Diamond H_1 \vee \Diamond H_2 \vee \cdots \Diamond H_j$,
where each L_i is an atom or its negation, each D_i is a DNF, and each H_i is
a CNF (next defined). A formula G is said to be in conjunctive normal form
(CNF) if it is a conjunction of F_i DNF i.e., $G = F_1 \wedge F_2 \wedge \cdots \wedge F_n$ which will
be denoted by the set $G = \{F_1, F_2, \ldots, F_n\}$.*

Definition 12. *A formula in DNF is called a clause. A clause with only one
element is called a unit clause. A clause with zero disjunct is empty and it will
be denoted by the $\bot$ symbol. Since the empty clause has no literal that can be
satisfied by a model, the empty clause is always false.*

Definition 13. *The modal degree of a formula F denoted by $d(F)$ is recursively
defined as follows:*

– *if F is a literal then its degree is zero*
– $d(F \bigtriangleup G) = max(d(F), d(G))$, *where $\bigtriangleup$ is $\wedge$ or $\vee$*
– $d(\sim F) = d(F)$
– $d(\nabla F) = d(F) + 1$, *where ∇ stands for $\Box$ or $\Diamond$*

Given a formula F, the following inductive procedure transforms F into a CNF
in such a way that the original formula is equal to its CNF form therefore
satisfying validity. (1) Using axioms 1 and 2, the definition $\sim \Box F \equiv \Diamond \sim F$
and the inference rules, eliminate all propositional other than $\wedge, \vee, \sim$ and move
negations inside so that they are immediately before propositional variables, (2)
If $d(F) = 0$ then apply the propositional procedure [6], (3) If $F = \Box F_1$ with F_1
in CNF, apply the theorem $\Box(F \wedge G) \equiv \Box F \wedge \Box G$ to distribute the $\Box$ operator
(this is proved with the aid of axiom 2). (4) If $F = \Diamond F_1$ with F_1 in CNF, then
do not do anything. (5) Otherwise, we have a combination of different formulas
which can be handled using the preceding rules.
Therefore, we have proved the following result.

Theorem 3. *Let S be a set of clauses that represents a formula F in its CNF.
Then F is unsatisfiable if and only if S is unsatisfiable.*

3   The Modal Logic Resolution Principle

We shall next present the resolution principle inspired by the propositional
logic resolution principle introduced by Robinson (see [6], the references quoted
therein, and [7]). It can be applied directly to any set S of clauses to test the
unsatisfiability of S. Resolution is a decidable, sound and complete proof system i.e., a formula in clausal form is unsatisfiable if and only if there exists

an algorithm reporting that it is unsatisfiable. Therefore it provides a consistent methodology free of contradictions. It is composed of rules for computing resolvents, simplification rules and rules of inference. The first ones compute resolvents, simplified by the simplification rules, and then inferred by the rules of inference.

Definition 14 [7]. *Let $\Sigma(A, B) \rightarrow C$, and $\Gamma(A) \rightarrow C$ be two relations on clauses defined by the following formal system:*

Axioms:
(1). $\Sigma(p, \sim p) \rightarrow \bot$.
(2). $\Sigma(\bot, A) \rightarrow \bot$.
Σ rules:

$$\vee - \text{rule} : \frac{\Sigma(A, B) \rightarrow C}{\Sigma(A \vee D_1, B \vee D_2) \rightarrow C \vee D_1 \vee D_2}$$

$$\Box \diamond - \text{rule} : \frac{\Sigma(A, B) \rightarrow C}{\Sigma(\Box A, \diamond(B, E)) \rightarrow \diamond(B, C, E)}$$

$$\Box\Box - \text{rule} : \frac{\Sigma(A, B) \rightarrow C}{\Sigma(\Box A, \Box B) \rightarrow \Box C}$$

Γ rules:

$$\diamond - \text{rule} \quad 1 : \frac{\Sigma(A, B) \rightarrow C}{\Gamma(\diamond(A, B, F)) \rightarrow \diamond(A, B, C, F)}$$

$$\diamond - \text{rule} \quad 2 : \frac{\Gamma(A) \rightarrow B}{\Gamma(\diamond(A, F)) \rightarrow \diamond(B, A, F)}$$

$$\vee - \text{rule} : \frac{\Gamma(A) \rightarrow B}{\Gamma(A \vee C) \rightarrow B \vee C}$$

$$\Box - \text{rule} : \frac{\Gamma(A) \rightarrow B}{\Gamma(\Box A) \rightarrow \Box B}$$

where A, B, C, D, D_1, D_2, denote general clauses, E, F denote sets (conjunctions) of clauses, and $(A < E)$ denotes the result of appending the clauses A to the set E.

Simplification Rules: The relation 'A can be simplified in B' denoted $A \simeq B$ is the least congruence relation containing: (S1) $\diamond \bot \simeq \bot$, (S2) $\bot \vee D \simeq D$, (S3) $\bot, E \simeq \bot$, (S4) $A \vee A \vee D \simeq A \vee D$. The simplified formula obtained is called the normal form of the original formula and is the one to be considered when computing resolvents.

Inference rules:
(R1)

$$\frac{C}{D} \quad if \quad \Gamma(C) \rightarrow D$$

(R2)

$$\frac{C_1 \quad C_2}{D} \quad \text{if} \quad \Sigma(C_1, C_2) \to D,$$

where C, C_1, C_2, D are general clauses.

A deduction of a clause D from a set S of clauses can be seen as a tree whose root is D, whose leaves are clauses of S, and every internal node C has sons A and B (respectively A) iff the rule R2 (respectively Rl) can be applied with premises A and B (respectively A) and conclusion C. The size of a deduction is the number of nodes of this tree. We say that D is a-consequence of S iff there is a deduction of D from S denoted by $S \vdash D$. These definitions and notations are extended to sets of consequences: if S' is a set of clauses, $S \vdash S'$ iff $S \vdash D$ for every $D \varepsilon S'$. A deduction of $\perp$ from S is a refutation of S.

Theorem 4 [7]. *The resolution proof system is decidable.*

The main two results of this subsection: the completeness theorem for the resolution proof system, and that proofs in the resolution proof system are actually proofs in our modal logic axiomatic system are next presented.

Theorem 5 [7]. *A set S of clauses is unsatisfiable if and only if there is a deduction of the empty clause $\perp$ from S.*

Theorem 6. *If there exists a deduction D from S in the resolution proof system then there is a deduction D from S in our modal logic axiomatic system.*

Proof. Let us proceed by induction on the size of the deduction. Base case: the deduction is an axiom i.e., it is either $\Sigma(p, \sim p) \to \perp$ or $\Sigma(\perp, A) \to \perp$ which in our modal logic system correspond to $p \wedge \sim p \to \perp$ and $\perp \wedge A \to \perp$ which are propositional logic tautologies. Next, let us assume that the conclusion holds for every deduction of size less than or equal to $k - 1$. Then, we have a deduction of S_{k-1} from S in our modal logic system and a one length deduction in the resolution proof system of S_k from S_{k-1} which turns out to be also a deduction in our modal logic system (due to the induction hypothesis). Therefore concatenating both we get a deduction of S_k from S.

4   Predator-Prey System

Consider the interaction of populations, in which there are exactly two species, one of which the *predators* eats the other the *preys* thereby affecting each other's growth rates. Such pairs exist throughout nature: fish and sharks, lions and gazelles, birds and insects, to mention some. It is assumed that, the predator species is totally dependent on a single prey species as its only food supply, the prey has unlimited food supply, and that there is no threat to the pray other than the specific predator. The predator-prey system behavior is described as follows: (1) Propositional variables: S: preys are safe, D: the preys are in danger, B: the preys are being eaten, I: the predators are idle, L: the predators are in search for a prey, CL: the predators continue searching for a prey, A: the predators attack the preys, F: the predator has finished eating the prey, P: the predator dies; (2) Rules of Inference: (a) if S and L then CL, (b) if S and CL then $\diamond P$, (c) if D and (L or CL) then A, (d) if A then B, (e) if D then $\diamond A$, (F) if L or CL and $\diamond A$ then $\Box A$, (G) if $\Box A$ then A, (i) if B then F (j) if F then I, (k) if I then L.

Remark 2. The main idea consists of: the predator-prey behavior is expressed by a modal logic formula, some query is expressed as an additional formula. The query is assumed to be a logical implication of the predator-prey formula (see Theorem 1). Then, transforming this logical implication relation into a set of clauses by using the techniques given in Sect. 2, its validity can be checked. It is important to point out that other type of behaviors can be incorporated in to the model by the modeler, making it as close to reality as needed.

The formula that models the predator-prey behavior turns out to be:

$$[S \wedge L \to CL] \wedge [S \wedge CL \to \diamond P] \wedge [D \wedge (L \vee CL) \to A] \wedge [A \to B] \wedge [D \to \diamond A] \wedge \quad (1)$$
$$[(L \vee CL) \wedge \diamond A \to \Box A] \wedge [\Box A \to A] \wedge [B \to F] \wedge [F \to I] \wedge [I \to L]$$

We are interested in verifying, the following statements:

(S1) Claim: We want to know that if the predators are in search or are continuing searching for a prey and there is a possibility of attack then the prey will be eaten. Specifically, we want to know if the following formula If (L or CL) and $\diamond A$ then B is a consequence of formula 1.
The set of clauses for this case is given by:

$$S = \{(\sim S \vee \sim L \vee CL), (\sim S \vee \sim CL \vee \diamond P), (\sim D \vee \sim L \vee A), (\sim D \vee \sim CL \vee A),$$
$$(\sim A \vee B), (\sim D \vee \diamond A), (\Box \sim A \vee \sim L \vee \Box A), (\Box \sim AV \sim CL \vee \Box A), (\diamond \sim A \vee A),$$
$$(\sim B \vee F), (\sim F \vee I), (\sim I \vee L), (L \vee CL), (\diamond A), (\sim B)\}$$

Then a resolution refutation proof for S, is as follows:

(a) $(\Box \sim A \vee \sim L \vee \Box A)(\diamond A) \to (\Box A \vee \sim L)(\diamond \sim A \vee A) \to (\sim L \vee A)$
(b) $(\Box \sim A \vee \sim CL \vee \Box A)(\diamond A) \to (\Box A \vee \sim CL)(\diamond \sim A \vee A) \to (\sim CL \vee A)$
(c) $(\sim A \vee B)(\sim B) \to (\sim A)$
(d) From (a) and (c) we get $(\sim L)$
(e) From (b) and (c) we get $(\sim CL)$
(f) From (d) we get $(\sim L)(L \vee CL) \to (CL)$
(g) Finally, from (e) and (f) we get a deduction of the empty clause $\bot$.

Therefore we have proved that the claim is true, this result is consistent with reality.

(S2) Claim: We want to know that if the predators are in search or are continuing searching for a prey and there is a possibility of attack then the predator will be idle. Specifically, we want to know if the following formula If (L or CL) and $\diamond A$ then I is a consequence of formula 1.

The set of clauses for this case is given by:

$$S = \{(\sim S \vee \sim L \vee CL), (\sim S \vee \sim CL \vee \diamond P), (\sim D \vee \sim L \vee A), (\sim D \vee \sim CL \vee A),$$
$$(\sim A \vee B), (\sim D \vee \diamond A), (\Box \sim A \vee \sim L \vee \Box A), (\Box \sim A \vee \sim CL \vee \Box A), (\diamond \sim A \vee A),$$
$$(\sim B \vee F), (\sim F \vee I), (\sim I \vee L), (L \vee CL), (\diamond A), (\sim I)\}$$

Then a resolution refutation for S is as follows:

(a) $(\Box \sim A \vee \sim L \vee \Box A)(\diamond A) \rightarrow (\Box A \vee \sim L)(\diamond \sim A \vee A) \rightarrow (\sim L \vee A)$
(b) $(\Box \sim A \vee \sim CL \vee \Box A)(\diamond A) \rightarrow (\Box A \vee \sim CL)(\diamond \sim A \vee A) \rightarrow (\sim CL \vee A)$
(c) $(\sim F \vee I)(\sim I) \rightarrow (\sim F)(\sim B \vee F) \rightarrow (\sim B)(\sim A \vee B) \rightarrow (\sim A)$
(d) From (a) and (c) we get $(\sim L)$
(e) From (b) and (c) we get $(\sim CL)$
(f) From (d) we get $(\sim L)(L \vee CL) \rightarrow (CL)$
(g) Finally, from (e) and (f) we get a deduction of the empty clause $\bot$.

Therefore, the claim holds, and the same conclusion given in (S1) extrapolates for this case.

5   Conclusions

The main contribution of the paper consists in the study of the predator-pray system by means of a formal reasoning deductive methodology based on modal logic theory. The modal logic approach introduces new operators that enable abstract relations like necessarily true and possibly true to be expressed directly. The results obtained are consistent with how the predator-prey system behaves in real life.

Acknowledgement. This work was supported by a grant provided by Honeywell Centro de Investigacion y Desarrollo SRL de CV through Comision de Operacion y Fomento de Actividades Academicas del IPN.

References

1. Haberman, R.: Mathematical Models in Mechanical Vibrations, Population Dynamics, and Traffic Flow. Prentice Hall, Englewood Cliffs (1977)
2. Retchkiman Konigsberg, Z.: Stability problem for a predator-prey system. In: Tan, Y., Shi, Y., Tan, K.C. (eds.) ICSI 2010. LNCS, vol. 6145, pp. 1–10. Springer, Heidelberg (2010). https://doi.org/10.1007/978-3-642-13495-1_1
3. Retchkiman, Z.: Modelling and verification analysis of a two species ecosystem via a first order logic approach. IJPAM **104**(3), 583–592 (2017)
4. Chellas, B.F.: Modal Logic: An Introduction. Cambridge University Press, Cambridge (1980)
5. Blackburn, P., Benthem, J., Wolter, F.: Handbook of Modal Logic. Elsevier, Amsterdam (2007)
6. Davis, M., et al.: Computability, Complexity and Languages. Academic Press, New York (1983)
7. Enjalbert, P., del Cerro, L.F.: Modal resolution in clausal form. Theoret. Comput. Sci. **65**(1), 1–33 (1989)

The Access Model to Resources in Swarm System Based on Competitive Processes

Eugene Larkin$^{(\boxtimes)}$, Alexey Ivutin, Alexander Novikov,
Anna Troshina, and Yulia Frantsuzova

Tula State University, Tula, Russia
elarkin@mail.ru, atroshina@mail.ru,
julianna_1204@mail.ru,
alexey.ivutin@gmail.com, alsnovikov@yandex.ru

Abstract. The article describes the approach to evaluation of the results of "competitions" arising from the access of intellectual agents to resources in distributed swarm systems. A mathematical model of "competitions" based on Petri-Markov nets was developed. Expressions for calculation of time and probabilistic characteristics of "competitions" are defined. Methods of simulation modelling of the process of "competition" and experimental determination of time parameters are proposed. The obtained results can be used for planning information processes of swarm distributed system.

Keywords: Intellectual agents · Access to resources · Competition process
Group concurrent games · Petri-Markov nets · Effectiveness
The penalty of a participant

1 Introduction

In recent years, game theory has been increasingly used in industry, economy, military spheres and cybernetics as a powerful mechanism for system modelling. Traditional game theory has been developed for static games with their value matrices and player strategies that can lead to the winning or loss of any resources. In computer science, game theory is used to model interactions within networks, between processors, computing modules, peripherals, and so on [1].

So far, the focus has been on pure antagonistic games (for example, zero-sum games), useful for modelling systems developing in a "hostile" environment. The temporal aspects of the evolution of games have been paid attention quite insufficiently. In particular, mathematical formalism has not been worked out to determine the price of "victory" ("loss"), if the price is reduced to a temporary factor, with group "competitions" of agents [2, 3].

In this paper we discuss the use of the apparatus of Petri-Markov nets [4] for the mathematical description of competitive processes that arise when the separate intellectual units of swarm system are trying to gain access to shared resources and can be considered as parallel random processes with a time factor. The introduction of the Petri-Markov formalism [5–7] allows us to take into account the time parameter and determine the payments of the participants in the game and, thus, its full price.

© Springer International Publishing AG, part of Springer Nature 2018
Y. Tan et al. (Eds.): ICSI 2018, LNCS 10941, pp. 22–31, 2018.
https://doi.org/10.1007/978-3-319-93815-8_3

2 The "Competition" Model, Based on Petri-Markov Nets

"Competition" is an important factor that determines the ability and speed of access to the resources (including information) of swarm system by individual intellectual agents. Any "competition" is one of the aspects of the interaction investigated in [4]. When accessing to an object, there are restrictions on the response time. If the response of an object to the process impact is too great, it can lead to a violation of the interaction of separate units, the breaking of information links, and ultimately reduces the effectiveness of swarm system as whole.

Thus, the study of the competition is connected with the determination of the waiting time for the elementary processes that have already ended, and processes that have not yet been completed. Any competition can be reduced to a competition of two processes, which is modeled by the Petri-Markov net (PMN) shown in Fig. 1.

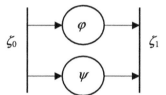

Fig. 1. "Competition" of two half-steps

Petri-Markov net has a structure:

$$\Pi = \left\{ \{\varphi, \ \psi\}, \ \{\zeta_0, \ \zeta_1\}, \ \begin{pmatrix} 0 & 1 \\ 0 & 1 \end{pmatrix}, \ \begin{pmatrix} 1 & 1 \\ 0 & 0 \end{pmatrix} \right\};$$
$$M = \left\{ (1, \ 0), \ \begin{bmatrix} 0 & f_1(t) \\ 0 & f_2(t) \end{bmatrix}, \ \begin{bmatrix} 1 & 1 \\ 0 & 0 \end{bmatrix} \right\}, \tag{1}$$

where φ, ψ - places simulating the functioning of the hardware of the simulator and the action of the trained operator, respectively; ζ_0 - the starting transition modeling the beginning of the "competition", ζ_1- the final transition modeling the fixing of the outcome of the "competition". $f_1(t), f_2(t)$ is the distribution density of the completion time of the "competition" by the first and second participant, respectively.

The distribution of the time spent by the tokens in places φ and ψ PMN is determined by densities, respectively, $\varphi(t)$ and $\psi(t)$.

At the beginning of the "competition" the half-steps $\sigma_{0\varphi}$ and $\sigma_{0\psi}$ are happening simultaneously. The density of distribution of the difference in the time intervals for achieving a transition ζ_1 when these half steps are made is determined in the form of a correlation $\int\limits_{0}^{\infty} \varphi(\tau)\psi(t+\tau)d\tau$.

The probability that the difference of random time intervals will be positive and negative are, respectively, $\int\limits_{t=0}^{\infty} \Phi(t)d\Psi(t)$ and $\int\limits_{t=0}^{\infty} \Psi(t)d\Phi(t)$. Hence, the waiting time by the half-step $\sigma_{0\varphi}$ for the event of half-step $\sigma_{0\psi}$ completion is determined by the expression:

$$f_{\varphi \to \psi}(t) = \frac{1(t) \int\limits_0^\infty \varphi(\tau)\psi(t+\tau)d\tau}{\int\limits_{t=0}^\infty \Phi(t)d\Psi(t)} \qquad (2)$$

where τ is an auxiliary variable having a physical sense of time; $\Phi(t), \Psi(t)$ - the corresponding distribution functions; 1(t) - is the Heaviside unit function.

It should be noted that operation (2) is not commutative. Accordingly, the waiting time by the half-step $\sigma_{0\varphi}$ for the event of half-step $\sigma_{0\psi}$ completion is equal to:

$$f_{\psi \to \varphi}(t) = \frac{1(t) \int\limits_0^\infty \psi(\tau)\varphi(t+\tau)d\tau}{\int\limits_{t=0}^\infty \Psi(t)d\Phi(t)}, \qquad (3)$$

and in the general case $f_{\varphi \to \psi}(t) \neq f_{\psi \to \varphi}(t)$.

In a frequently occurring practical case, K processes are divided into two groups. Without violating the degree of generality, we will assume that the first group has numbers from 1 to N, and the second group from the $(N + 1)$ to K. Distribution density of the execution time of the corresponding groups of processes are determined by the dependencies:

$$f_{1 \leftrightarrow N}(t) = \sum_{m=1}^N \tilde{f}_{j(mz)j(zn)}(t) \prod_{\substack{k=1 \\ k \neq m}}^N \tilde{F}_{j(kz)j(zn)}(t), \qquad (4)$$

$$f_{N+1 \leftrightarrow K}(t) = \sum_{m=N+1}^K \tilde{f}_{j(mz)j(zn)}(t) \prod_{\substack{k=N+1 \\ k \neq m}}^K \tilde{F}_{j(kz)j(zn)}(t). \qquad (5)$$

The distribution densities of the waiting time by the first group of the moment when the processes of the second group are completed are determined by the dependence:

$$f_{(1 \leftrightarrow N) \to (N+1 \leftrightarrow K)}(t) = \frac{1(t) \int\limits_0^\infty f_{1 \leftrightarrow N}(\tau)f_{N+1 \leftrightarrow K}(t+\tau)d\tau}{\int\limits_{t=0}^\infty F_{1 \leftrightarrow N}(t)dF_{N+1 \leftrightarrow K}(t)}. \qquad (6)$$

The distribution density of the waiting time by the second group of the moment, when the processes of the first group are completed, is determined by the dependence:

$$f_{(N+1\leftrightarrow K)\rightarrow(1\leftrightarrow N)}(t) = \frac{1(t)\int\limits_0^\infty f_{N+1\leftrightarrow K}(\tau)f_{1\leftrightarrow N}(t+\tau)d\tau}{\int\limits_{t=0}^\infty F_{N+1\leftrightarrow K}(t)dF_{1\leftrightarrow N}(t)}. \tag{7}$$

As an example of determining the distribution density of the waiting time, a number of important practical cases should be considered.

Case 1. Density $\varphi(t) = \delta(t - T_\varphi)$ is δ-function, $\psi(t)$ is an arbitrary function with a domain of non-zero values $T_{\psi min} \leq t \leq T_{\psi max}$ and a mathematical expectation T_ψ. Expression (2) for this case takes the form:

$$f_{\varphi\rightarrow\psi}(t) = \frac{1(t)\int\limits_0^\infty \delta(\tau - T_\varphi)\psi(t+\tau)d\tau}{\int\limits_{t=0}^\infty 1(t - T_\varphi)d\Psi(t)} = \frac{1(t)\psi(t+T_\varphi)}{\int\limits_{t=0}^\infty 1(t - T_\varphi)d\Psi(t)}, \tag{8}$$

where $1(t - T_\varphi)$ is the Heaviside unit function.

Depending on the location $\varphi(t)$ and $\psi(t)$ on the time axis, the following situations are possible (see Fig. 2).

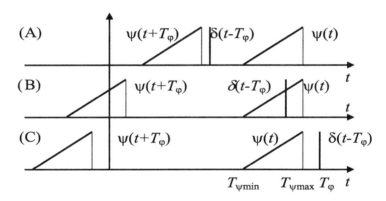

Fig. 2. Different cases of waiting at $\varphi(t) = \delta(t - T_\varphi)$

(A) $T_\varphi < T_{\psi min}$. In this situation, the denominator of the fraction (2) is defined as follows: $\int\limits_{t=T_\varphi}^\infty d\Psi(t) = 1 - \Psi(T_\varphi)$.

Expression (2) takes the form: $f_{\varphi\rightarrow\psi}(t) = \frac{1(t)\psi(t+T_\varphi)}{1-\Psi(T_\varphi)}$.

The range of non-zero values is defined as: $0 \leq t \leq T_{\psi max} - T_\varphi$.

(B) $T_\varphi > T_{\psi max}$. In this situation, expression (2) does not make sense, because the distribution density of the difference of the two random variables is completely shifted to the negative time range that is not possible (the process that ends in principle later can't wait for the process ending earlier).

Case 2. The density $\psi(t) = \delta(t - T_\psi)$ is a δ-function, and $\varphi(t)$ is an arbitrary function with a domain of non-zero values $T_{\varphi min} \leq t \leq T_{\varphi max}$ and a mathematical expectation T_φ. Expression (2) for this case takes the form:

$$f_{\varphi \to \psi}(t) = \frac{1(t)\int\limits_0^\infty \delta(t+\tau - T_\psi)\varphi(\tau)d\tau}{\int\limits_{t=0}^\infty \Phi(t)d1(t - T_\psi)}. \tag{9}$$

Depending on the location $\varphi(t)$ and $\psi(t)$ the time axis, the following situations are possible (Fig. 3).

(A) $T_\psi < T_{\varphi min}$. In this situation, expression (2) does not make sense.
(B) $T_{\varphi min} \leq T_\psi \leq T_{\varphi max}$. In this situation, the denominator of the fraction (2) is defined as: $\int\limits_{t=T_\psi}^\infty \Phi(t)d1(t - T_\psi) = 1 - \int\limits_{t=T_\psi}^\infty 1(t - T_\psi)d\Phi(T_\psi) = \Phi(T_\psi)$.

Expression (2) takes the form: $f_{\varphi \to \psi}(t) = \frac{1(t)\varphi(T_\psi - t)}{\Phi(T_\psi)}$.
The range of non-zero values $f_{\varphi \to \psi}(t)$ is defined as: $0 \leq t \leq T_\psi - T_{\varphi min}$.

(C) $T_\psi > T_{\varphi max}$. In this situation, the denominator of fraction (2) becomes equal to one, expression (2) and expression for the range of non-zero values (2) takes the form, respectively: $f_{\varphi \to \psi}(t) = \varphi(T_\psi - t)$, $T_\psi - T_{\varphi max} \leq t \leq T_\psi - T_{\varphi min}$.

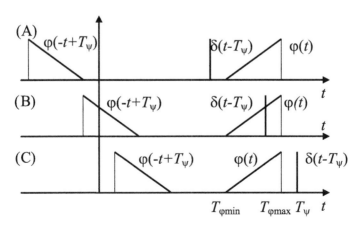

Fig. 3. Different waiting times for $\psi(t) = \delta(t - T_\psi)$

Case 3. Density $\psi(t) = \lambda \exp(-\lambda t)$ is an exponential distribution $\varphi(t)$, and is an arbitrary distribution density (the exponential distribution law is often used in the classical reliability theory for mathematical flow simulation without failure/failure recovery of complex systems).

Expression (2) for the case under consideration takes the form:

$$f_{\varphi \to \psi}(t) = \frac{1(t) \int\limits_0^\infty \varphi(\tau)\lambda \exp[-\lambda(t+\tau)]d\tau}{1 - \int\limits_{t=0}^\infty [1 - \exp(-\lambda t)]d\Phi(t)} = \frac{1(t) \int\limits_0^\infty \varphi(\tau)\lambda \exp(-\lambda t)\exp(-\lambda \tau)d\tau}{1 - \int\limits_{t=0}^\infty d\Phi(t) + \int\limits_0^\infty \exp(-\lambda t)\varphi(t)dt}$$

$$= \frac{1(t)\lambda \exp(-\lambda t) \int\limits_0^\infty \varphi(\tau)\exp(-\lambda \tau)d\tau}{\int\limits_0^\infty \varphi(t)\exp(-\lambda t)dt} = \lambda \exp(-\lambda t).$$

$$(10)$$

Obviously, the case considered reflects the property of the absence of aftereffect in strictly Markov processes with continuous time, which can be formulated as follows. If the time distribution between any two events in the system is distributed according to an exponential law, the time remaining until the next event from the point of view of the external observer will be distributed according to an exponential law, regardless of the time of the beginning of the system observation. In this case, the distribution density $\varphi(t)$ simulates an external observer, who enters into competition with the Markov process. If in the process the next event occurs before the observation, from the moment of the beginning of observation for the competition a new countdown begins.

For the distribution densities (2) and (3), the main numerical characteristics, namely, mathematical expectation and dispersion, can be found:

$$T_{\varphi \to \psi} = \int\limits_0^\infty \frac{\int\limits_0^\infty \varphi(\tau)\psi(t+\tau)d\tau}{\int\limits_{t=0}^\infty \Phi(t)d\Psi(t)}\, t\, dt, \qquad (11)$$

$$T_{\psi \to \varphi}(t) = \int\limits_0^\infty \frac{\int\limits_0^\infty \psi(\tau)\varphi(t+\tau)d\tau}{\int\limits_{t=0}^\infty \Psi(t)d\Phi(t)}\, t\, dt, \qquad (12)$$

$$D_{\varphi \to \psi} = \int\limits_0^\infty \frac{\int\limits_0^\infty \varphi(\tau)\psi(t+\tau)d\tau}{\int\limits_{t=0}^\infty \Phi(t)d\Psi(t)}\,\left(t - T_{\varphi \to \psi}\right)^2 dt, \qquad (13)$$

$$D_{\psi \to \varphi}(t) = \int_0^\infty \frac{\int_0^\infty \psi(\tau)\varphi(t+\tau)d\tau}{\int_{t=0}^\infty \Psi(t)d\Phi(t)} \left(t - T_{\psi \to \varphi}\right)^2 dt. \tag{14}$$

3 The Procedure of Simulation Modelling of "Competitive" Processes

The basic numerical characteristics and the density of the distribution of the waiting time by the process φ completion of the process ψ can be found by simulation if the densities are known $\varphi(t)$ and $\psi(t)$. Determination of numerical characteristics is carried out according to the following procedure.

Method 1. Determination of the distribution density of the waiting time by the process $\varphi(t)$ for the completion process $\psi(t)$ using the simulation model.

1. Start the random number generator and determine the value of some auxiliary random variable $0 < \tau < 1$ distributed equally.
2. From equation:

$$\Phi(t_\varphi) = \tau \tag{15}$$

   determine the value t_φ.
3. Start the random number generator and determine the value of the random variable $0 < \tau < 1$.
4. From equation:

$$\Psi(t_\psi) = \tau \tag{16}$$

   determine the value t_ψ
5. Compare the values t_φ and t_ψ. If $t_\varphi > t_\psi$, then counter $N_{\varphi \to \psi}$ is increased by one, and the array $M_{\varphi \to \psi}$ is updated with the value $t_{\varphi \to \psi} = t_\psi - t_\varphi$. If $t_\varphi < t_\psi$, then counter $N_{\psi \to \varphi}$ is increased by one, and the array $M_{\psi \to \varphi}$ is updated with the value $t_{\psi \to \varphi} = t_\varphi - t_\psi$.
6. Steps 1–5 is repeated N times.
7. Following the results of the simulation experiment, determine the following values:

   – the probability of waiting time by the process $\varphi(t)$ for the completion of the process $\psi(t)$:

$$p_{\varphi \to \psi}(t) = \frac{N_{\varphi \to \psi}}{N}; \tag{17}$$

– the probability of waiting time by the process $\psi(t)$ for the completion of the process $\varphi(t)$:

$$p_{\psi \to \varphi}(t) = \frac{N_{\psi \to \varphi}}{N} ; \tag{18}$$

– the statistical average of waiting time by the process $\varphi(t)$ for the completion of the process $\psi(t)$:

$$M^* \left[T_{\varphi \to \psi} \right] = \frac{\sum\limits_{n(\varphi \to \psi)=1}^{N_{\varphi \to \psi}} (t_{\varphi \to \psi})_{n(\varphi \to \psi)}}{N_{\varphi \to \psi}} ; \tag{19}$$

– the statistical average of waiting time by the process $\psi(t)$ for the completion of the process $\varphi(t)$:

$$M^* \left[T_{\psi \to \varphi} \right] = \frac{\sum\limits_{n(\psi \to \varphi)=1}^{N_{\psi \to \varphi}} (t_{\psi \to \varphi})_{n(\psi \to \varphi)}}{N_{\psi \to \varphi}} ; \tag{20}$$

– statistical dispersion of the waiting time by the process $\varphi(t)$ for the completion of the process $\psi(t)$:

$$D^* \left[T_{\varphi \to \psi} \right] = \frac{\sum\limits_{n(\varphi \to \psi)=1}^{N_{\varphi \to \psi}} \left\{ (t_{\varphi \to \psi})_{n(\varphi \to \psi)} - M^* \left[T_{\varphi \to \psi} \right] \right\}^2}{N_{\varphi \to \psi}} ; \tag{21}$$

– statistical dispersion of the waiting time by the process $\psi(t)$ for the completion of the process $\varphi(t)$:

$$D^* \left[T_{\psi \to \varphi} \right] = \frac{\sum\limits_{n(\psi \to \varphi)=1}^{N_{\psi \to \varphi}} \left\{ (t_{\psi \to \varphi})_{n(\psi \to \varphi)} - M^* \left[T_{\psi \to \varphi} \right] \right\}^2}{N_{\psi \to \varphi}} . \tag{22}$$

8. Align of the statistical time series of the waiting time by the process $\varphi(t)$ for the completion of the process $\psi(t)$ and the statistical time series of the waiting time by the process $\psi(t)$ for the completion of the process $\varphi(t)$.

4 Technique of Experimental Determination of Time Characteristics of "Competition"

The basic numerical characteristics and the density of the distribution of the waiting time by the process φ for the completion of the process ψ can be found by means of simulation, if the distribution density $\varphi(t)$ of the access time of an intellectual agent to resource is known, and the distribution density of the response time $\psi(t)$ of the information resource is measured.

Method 2. Determination of the density of the distribution of the waiting time by the process $\varphi(t)$ for the completion of the process $\psi(t)$ using the simulation model.

1. Start the random number generator and determine the value of some auxiliary random variable $0 < \tau < 1$ distributed equally.
2. From equation:

$$\Phi(t_\varphi) = \tau \tag{23}$$

   determine the value t_φ.
3. Using the software developed by the authors of PMTimeTester, the values $t_\psi - t_\varphi$ or $t_\varphi - t_\psi$ are determined.
4. Steps 1–3 repeat N times.
5. Based on the results of the simulation experiment, the values listed in point 7 of methodology 1 are determined.
6. Align of the statistical time series of the waiting time by the process $\varphi(t)$ for the completion of the process $\psi(t)$ and the statistical time series of the waiting time by the process $\psi(t)$ for the completion of the process $\varphi(t)$.

5 Conclusion

The paper presents a mathematical model of "competitions" that occur during the accessing intellectual agents of swarm system to shared resources, based on the mathematical formalism of Petri-Markov networks, which has shown its effectiveness for modelling the considered class of processes. The temporal and probabilistic characteristics of the competition were obtained in a general form, methods were proposed for practical determination of the results of competitions on the basis of simulation modelling.

The obtained results can be used both for planning the processes of information exchange between separate units of swarm system in various scenarios of its functioning, and for implementing the optimal mechanism for accessing to resources. The proposed methods can become a base for creating mathematical models for solving problems in the classical theory of games: optimization of game strategy, generation of target functions, etc.

Acknowledgements. The research was carried out within the state assignment of the Ministry of Education and Science of Russian Federation (No 2.3121.2017/PCH).

References

1. von Neumann, J., Morgenstern, O.: Theory of Games and Economic Behavior. Princeton University Press, Princeton (2007)
2. Ivutin, A.N., Larkin, E.V.: Simulation of concurrent games. Bull. S. Ural State Univ. **8**(2), 43–54 (2015). Series: Mathematical Modelling, Programming and Computer Software
3. Ivutin, A.N., Larkin, E.V., Novikov, A.S.: Mathematical modeling of group concurrency in game theory. J. Comput. Eng. Math. **2**(2), 3–12 (2015)
4. Ivutin, A.N., Larkin, E.V., Lutskov, Y.I., Novikov, A.S.: Simulation of concurrent process with Petri-Markov nets. Life Sci. J. **11**(11), 506–511 (2014)
5. Petri, C.A.: Nets, time and space. Theor. Comput. Sci. **153**(1–2), 3–48 (1996)
6. Jensen, K.: Coloured Petri Nets: Basic Concepts, Analysis Methods And Practical Use. Volume 1. Springer, London (1996). https://doi.org/10.1007/978-3-662-03241-1
7. Ramaswamy, S.: Hierarchical time-extended petri nets (H- EPN) based error identification and recovery for hierarchical system. IEEE Trans. Syst. Man Cybern. Part B Cybern. **26**(1), 164–175 (1996)

Self-organization of Small-Scale Plankton Patchiness Described by Means of the Object-Based Model

Elena Vasechkina$^{(\boxtimes)}$ (iD)

Marine Hydrophysical Institute of RAS, Sevastopol, Russia
vasechkina.elena@gmail.com

Abstract. The article presents a multi-species object-based model of a marine plankton community. The model was constructed using the synthesis of Lagrangian and Eulerian descriptions: we described the living components of an ecosystem by the individual-based approach and the non-living components (hydrochemical fields) – in a traditional way as concentrations in the nodes of a regular computational grid. A set of interacting objects simulated a plankton community. Each object modeled behavior of a group of identical plankters characterized by species, age, stage of development, biomass, abundance, and rates of physiological processes. Bioenergetic interaction between the objects and the environment was a source of population dynamics. We studied self-organization of plankton spatial distribution with no significant hydrophysical influences. Lloyd's index of mean crowding, spectral and wavelet analyses were used to investigate patterns of simulated spatial variability. We compared spectra of simulated plankton patchiness with those estimated according to observation data collected by the Video Plankton Recorder (VPR).

Keywords: Emergence · Plankton patchiness
Individual-based coupled physical biological model
Spatial heterogeneity of plankton distribution

1 Introduction

Spatial variability is an important attribute of marine ecosystems. Heterogeneity of plankton distribution has a great influence on population dynamics, reproductive processes, trophic relationships and structure of a plankton community, as reported earlier, e.g. [5, 12]. A number of published papers describe this phenomenon at different scales using observation data, but the spectral structure of plankton patchiness is not studied well enough. Large-scale and small-scale zooplankton patchiness is caused by different mechanisms. Large patches, heterogeneous inside, can correlate with spots of higher phytoplankton concentration or peculiarities of a temperature field. It suggests that their origin is connected with ocean eddies or other hydrodynamic phenomena. Small-scale heterogeneity (less than 10 km) does not generally correlate with hydrological and hydrochemical variables, and can occur under almost uniform distribution of these characteristics. We can assume that the reasons for such zooplankton variability are trophic interactions between the components of a plankton community and

© Springer International Publishing AG, part of Springer Nature 2018
Y. Tan et al. (Eds.): ICSI 2018, LNCS 10941, pp. 32–41, 2018.
https://doi.org/10.1007/978-3-319-93815-8_4

active movement of organisms and groups. At the moment, field data on small-scale spatial plankton variability are very limited. Therefore, simulation seems to be a convenient way to study the formation of marine plankton spatio-temporal patterns.

In recent decades, the method of complex natural systems simulation based on an evolutionary approach has been actively developing. According to this approach, the sustainable state of an ecosystem grows from the bottom up, from its smallest parts to the level of a population or community. There are several types of modeling techniques, which differ in the choice of basic objects as the smallest particles of the system. We considered the individual-based approach the most appropriate for simulation of a plankton community. As a methodological basis of modeling, individual-based approach has several advantages and problems. It has a great potential benefit for understanding the processes in a marine ecosystem, since it inherently involves individual variability induced by local interactions between the individuals and their resources [6]. Miller [11] published a review of studies using this approach for modeling plankton fish stages. He considered individual-based coupled physical biological models (ICPBM) combining low-level individual-based models with hydrophysical ocean models. He concluded that such models can gain a better understanding of the processes in an ecosystem, but reliability of findings from these models depends on the accuracy of the hydrographic model and adequacy of tracking algorithms [11].

The underlying model of ocean physics forcing by weather conditions plays a crucial role in marine ecosystem modeling. For example, representation of turbulent mixing in the upper ocean is of vital importance for coupled models, since it directly affects distribution of nutrient chemicals [9]. Recent experience in using individual-based models for marine plankton simulation was discussed during the workshop held in the framework of the Fifth International Zooplankton Production Symposium in Pucón, Chile [4]. In his thesis, Lange [9] presented a new ICPBM. He coupled an individual-based plankton ecosystem model with a general-purpose ocean model using an adaptive unstructured finite element mesh. The author proved that such coupled model could be used to combine individual and population-based methods in a single virtual ecosystem model.

All cited articles considered hydrodynamic impact on biological components of the ecosystem. The aim of this article is to study small-scale patchiness emergence caused by trophic interrelations within a plankton community in absense of significant hydrodynamic influences. For this purpose, we used the original object-based model of plankton ecosystem dynamics [16, 17]. Simulated spatio-temporal plankton fields were compared with observational data collected by VPR. We used the Lloyd's index of mean crowding, spectral and wavelet analyses, cross-correlation of wavelet amplitudes.

2   Methods

The object-oriented model of plankton ecosystem [17] was based on a combination of Eulerian and Lagrangian approaches. The living components of a marine ecosystem were described using individual-based approach (they are considered to be Lagrangian particles), while the non-living ones – as spatial field variables. In comparison with other ICPBMs it has some peculiarities.

- We considered a set of identical plankters together with their nearest environment as a basic structure element of the model [17]. The reasons for the choice were based on the research by Piontkovsky and Williams [13]. They discovered that the process of fragmentation of inhomogeneous biological fields had a certain finite spatial scale, which corresponded to the scale of elementary non-divided aggregations. The size of these elementary clusters depended on the species. The basic model objects can penetrate into each other and move. Food intake was calculated in proportion to the area of intersection of the objects (or an object and a grid cell in case of non-living resources). Since an arbitrarily large number of model objects can exist at the same point in space and time penetrating into each other, it seems that such description could be used to simulate the existing plankton diversity adequately.
- Metabolic costs, consumption, assimilation, excretion, and growth rate of an object were determined by its individual characteristics as well as external conditions, which depend on the movement of objects, growth of populations, abundance of resources, etc. Bioenergetic interaction between the objects and the objects and the environment was a source of the system dynamics.
- Mortality consisted of two parts. The first part was general mortality; it was calculated in proportion to biomass. The second part, due to predation, was calculated explicitly as a part of a group in a "prey object" that was eliminated during consumption of a "predator object". We named this part "consumption".
- Existing ICPBMs usually determine the hydrophysical forcing as the most significant factor for patchiness emergency. Contrary to this view, we studied the self-organization of plankton patchiness in absence of advection or noticeable hydrophysical influences. It is known that hydrophysical forcing can largely change plankton patterns. For example, James et al. [7] compared dominant scales of phytoplankton patches in lakes in summer and winter when ice covered the surface. The lack of wind mixing led to a reduction in patches' size by more than 20 times. The temperature field was flat and constant during the simulation, since influence of temperature variability on the growth of plankton population was excluded too.

In the framework of this model approach, a set of interacting objects described a zooplankton community. Each object simulated behavior of a group of identical plankters. The number of the objects in a system was usually tens of thousands. Population dynamics arose because of these objects' activities, which depend on the environment and change it too. Phytoplankton, dissolved oxygen, organic, and inorganic resources were embedded as arrays of concentrations in the nodes of a horizontal grid covering the vertically integrated simulation domain. Living objects could interchange with these resources by means of a special procedure.

The model described the dynamics of a plankton community in a coastal pelagic ecosystem that included seven compartments: phytoplankton p, bacteria b, ciliates a, nanophages f (with length <1 mm), small mesoplanktonic euryphages v (1–3 mm), small predators s (1–3 mm), large euryphages g_1 (3–30 mm), and large predators g_2 (3–30 mm). These groups were interconnected by trophic relations described by the matrix of food preferences, which was constructed using the estimates of Shushkina et al. [14] (Appendix [18]).

According to the definition, a basic model object had the properties inherent to simulated plankters and some other properties that determined behavior of a plankton cluster. Therefore, a sub-model of object dynamics included the functions that parameterize vitalities of the specimen and their behavioral rules. An object was specified by its position within a computational domain, size, plankton group, weight of an organism, biomass, and abundance. We supposed that the objects were homogenous ignoring the vertical biomass distribution. The object's biomass was calculated by multiplying the weight of an organism by the number of individuals in a unit volume.

Biomass dynamics of the objects were simulated using the energy balance approach based on the studies [8, 19]. Detailed description of the model is in the Appendix [18]. Plankton objects can estimate the gradient of the main resource (phytoplankton) within the limits of their area and move to improve their living conditions. Growing objects can divide and form new entities simulating plankton reproduction. The reproduction procedure included three stages, and conditions for their implementation were checked at each time step. These conditions and stages were:

1. If the mass of an organism inside any object exceeded the maximum value, reproduction was imitated. Individual mass became equal to the minimal accepted mass of an organism, and a new value of plankton abundance was calculated. Biomass of an object remained the same.
2. If an object's density exceeded the maximum value, its volume doubled by increasing the object's radius;
3. If an object's radius exceeded the maximum value, the object was bisected. A random number defined the position of a new object; the distance between the centers of two objects was determined equal to the diameter of the initial object.

The objects can be eliminated when their density decreased below the threshold level. If this happened, an object's mass entered a pool of suspended organic matter increasing its concentration in the corresponding grid cells.

Initial distributions of hydrochemical elements were defined as random fields with mean concentrations typical of the coastal zone. Computational grid contained 60×128 nodes with a spatial step of 100 m. The water temperature was 20 °C. Random number generator determined initial coordinates of the objects and their radiuses. At the initial time, they had minimal mass.

The model reproduced evolution of plankton objects as they interacted with each other and the environment. Self-organization of this system during simulation resulted in quasi-stable heterogeneous spatial distribution of zooplankton groups. We performed a series of simulations changing the spatial step (from 50 m to 100 m), the size of the calculation grid (30×128, 60×128, 90×128), the temperature and the initial distribution of objects and their number at the initial time. The results presented below are typical and refer to the end of the simulation. We pre-processed them to obtain discrete two-dimensional fields of plankton biomass in the following way. Plankton objects were "projected" onto the computational grid. Contribution of an object to the total biomass within a grid cell was calculated in proportion to the intersection area of an object and a grid cell. After processing all objects of one type, we obtained a discrete approximation of two-dimensional biomass field of this plankton group. Then we studied these fields using spectral analysis and wavelet transformation. Lloyd's index analysis was applied to number of objects within grid cells.

3   Results and Discussion

We analyzed the degree of inhomogeneity of the spatial plankton distribution by calculating Lloyd's index of patchiness according to [10]. We found a relation between individual properties (averaged specific metabolic costs) of a planktonic specimen and the spatial structure of biomass distribution at the population level – growth of specific metabolic costs led to more aggregate spatial distribution of this planktonic group. Figure 1 shows an example of the revealed dependence of this indicator on average specific metabolic costs estimated according to simulation data. In simulations without predators other groups of the plankton community demonstrated less aggregated distribution; their Lloyd's indices were lower. Predators formed denser patches compared to euryphages having approximately the same specific metabolic costs – the line connecting points for s and g_2 in Fig. 1 is above the approximate curve for all other groups.

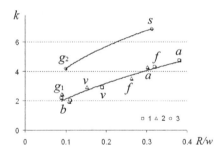

Fig. 1. The relationship between mean specific metabolic costs (organism level) of simulated plankton groups and the degree of crowding (population level) estimated by Lloyd's index: 1 – bacteria and euryphages; 2 – the same in the absence of predators; 3 – predators

Small plankton organisms (with higher specific metabolism) formed more aggregate spatial distribution characterized by patches of smaller scale and greater relative density inside:

$$D_{rel} = \left(D^{max} - D^{min}\right)/\overline{D}$$

Here D is a discretized biomass field $D(x, y)$ of a plankton group. D_{rel} decreased as the population grew and became relatively stable by the 40th day of simulation. For example, D_{rel} was 10.6 for small nanophages (f) and 3.6 for large euryphages (g_1). We also observed dependence of this indicator on the character of feeding – in the group of predators it was higher: 7.8 for predators (g_2) in comparison with 5.7 for euryphages of the same size (g_1).

Spatial spectra were calculated along the longer axis of the computational domain with averaging over 30 periodograms. Figure 2a shows spectra of nutrient, phytoplankton and large euryphages (g_1) biomass. In the shortwave range, phytoplankton and zooplankton spectra are close to each other; their slopes are much smaller than the slope of the resource spectrum. These features were also marked by other authors, for example [1, 15], who analyzed the spectra based upon data of numeric simulations with their plankton models. According to our estimates, mean slopes of spatial spectra in the shortwave range were –2.7 for resource, –1.5 for phytoplankton, and –1.2 for large zooplankton. These estimates well agreed with the data of the other authors and experimental evaluation.

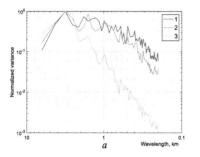 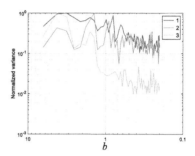

Fig. 2. Spatial spectra evaluated by the results of simulation – *a*: large zooplankton – 1; phytoplankton – 2; nutrient – 3. Spatial spectra estimated on data of the truncated transect (shallow region above the Georges Bank) – *b*: *Calanus* sp. abundance – 1; fluorescence – 2; light transmission – 3.

Consider the shortwave range of spatial spectra using pre-filtering of longwave components by subtracting a moving average. Figure 3 shows the dynamics of spatial spectra of all plankton groups and inorganic resource.

Firstly, one can observe low level of inorganic resource dispersion in the wavelength range less than 3 km during the simulation (Fig. 3, *a*). Therefore, we can conclude that plankton patchiness in this range was not connected with the resource field; it was caused by trophic relationships in the simulated plankton community. Formation of plankton patches of all trophic groups, except for predators, begins at small scales at a shortwave spectrum. These patches gradually merge, and the dominant scale of spatial heterogeneity increases. However, mesoplanktonic and large euryphages demonstrate small-scale patchiness throughout the simulation. This may be due to their character of feeding, because ciliates and nanophages forming small clusters are prey for these animals. Under sharp competition for phytoplankton, animal food becomes more important for these groups. We can observe multiscale variability of plankton spatial distribution with two most common ranges of scales: 1.5–1.8 km and 3–4 km. The second is the dominant scale of phytoplankton spatial variability (Fig. 3, *b*) that is probably determined by aggregations of zooplankton, which has a significant fraction of phytoplankton in its ration.

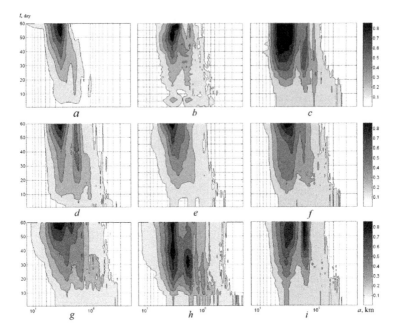

Fig. 3. Temporal dynamics of the spatial spectra of: a – nutrient; b – phytoplankton (p); c – bacteria (b); d – ciliates (a); e – nanophages (f); f – mesoplanktonic euryphages (v); g – small predators (s); h – large euryphages (g_1); and i – large predators (g_2).

We performed wavelet transformation of the simulated fields and calculated cross covariance between wavelet coefficients of the interacting plankton groups. We found that wavelet components correlated at several scales (Fig. 4). The X-axis in Fig. 4 is the spatial shift and the Y-axis is the spatial scale. Sinusoid shape of the correlation function and its maximum modulus point to the previously identified dominant spatial scales.

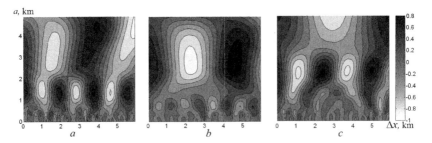

Fig. 4. Cross-correlation functions of spatial wavelet components of simulated fields of zooplankton and ciliates – a; phytoplankton and mesoplanktonic euryphages – b; phytoplankton and small predators – c.

3.1   Comparison with Observation Data

Consider the available observation data on spatial distribution of zooplankton and phytoplankton collected by the VPR. During U.S. GLOBEC Georges Bank Project, several experiments were performed to study small-scale plankton patchiness by means of VPR observations [2, 3]. The VPR was towed at 2 m/s collecting data from surface to bottom. It was equipped with video cameras, temperature and conductivity probes, fluorometer and transmissometer. Transects across Georges Bank were conducted in three different months in 1994 and 1995. *Calanus finmarchicus* was the dominant zooplankton taxon present in the observations of all three transects, but abundances of this group differed significantly in these experiments. Maximum abundances of *Calanus* sp. and *Phaeocystis* spp. protocolonies were observed in March 1995. We chose this deployment (EN262) to compare with our model results. It was carried out from 41° N, 66.3° W to 42.3° N, 67.5 W during 6–8 March 1995 [2]. We assumed that *Calanus* sp. could be compared with the model 'large euryphages', and observed fluorescence – with model phytoplankton.

The data were collected along a zigzagged path, from surface to bottom, so vertical and horizontal variability were mixed. Each data point contained horizontal coordinates, pressure (depth), and measured characteristics: temperature, salinity, fluorescence, light transmission, taxon abundance, etc. The step of the zigzagged path was larger in deep-water regions and approximately 2.4 km above the Georges Bank. To exclude this period from our analyses we took fluorescence measurements in the layer from 20 to 30 m and interpolated these data to obtain regular measurements with a distance of 0.1 km as it was in our simulations. As a matter of fact, during this procedure, we lost some portion of small-scale variability, but it was the only way to exclude vertical variability from the fluorescence measurements. Vertical distribution of *Calanus* sp. was quasi homogeneous, therefore we could take all data to obtain the average value in a 100 m bit of a transect. We prepared the observed data so that they could be compared with our simulated data. Figure 2*b* demonstrates spectra estimated by the VPR data that we compared with spectra shown in Fig. 2*a*. Dominant spatial scales of 3–4 km, 1.5 km, and 1–0.9 km are present in both diagrams. The spectra of fluorescence and light transmission had high peaks at 1.5 km scale. Similar peaks were observed on the spectra of *Calanus* sp. and *Phaeocystis* spp. Another local maximum is present on spectra of all components except for light transmission at the scale of 1.0–0.8 km.

Figure 5 shows the cross-correlation function between wavelet components of fluorescence, light transmission, zooplankton and phytoplankton. Sinusoidal sharp of the cross-correlation function on spatial scales 1–2 km and 3–4 km proved that the most intense interaction of phyto- and zooplankton took place at these scales. This could be associated with aggregations of aquatic organisms. Naturally, smaller patches are present in multiscale variability of plankton fields. Quasi-horizontal shape of the spectrum in the shortwave range indicates that there is no cascade fall of energy, which is typical of a turbulence spectrum. Therefore, we can suppose that aggregations of the analyzed scales include tightly packed small patches divided by distances that could be neglected in comparison with the scale of patches. According to our estimates, phytoplankton and zooplankton fields did not correlate at the scales less than 0.5 km.

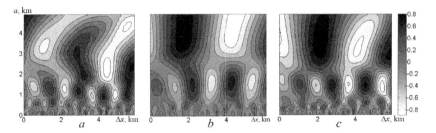

Fig. 5. The cross-correlation functions of spatial wavelet components of: *Calanus* sp. and *Phaeocystis* spp. abundances – *a*; light transmission and fluorescence – *b*; fluorescence and *Phaeocystis* spp. abundance – *c*.

4   Conclusion

We can conclude that the proposed object-based model of multi-species plankton community gives reasonable results comparable to the observations data, and gives an insight to the possible mechanisms of small-scale patchiness formation. There were no external driving forces that could be considered as reasons for patchiness emergence in our simulations. Multiscale patchiness appeared because of plankton growth and reproduction, objects movement, their interaction with each other and with the environment. We found similar scales in observed variability. This allows us to assume that the revealed mechanism of patchiness formation really exists. Thus, we can assume that such self-organizing patchiness is immanent to a plankton community and could be observed in cases where it is not overshadowed by external effects, which may be more intense, such as in lakes or semi-enclosed bays in calm weather. The model does not claim to describe the whole spectrum of plankton patchiness. It has several limitations, which define its applicability. However, according to the simulation results we can assume that some frequently observed peaks in spatial variability spectrum can be explained by trophic taxis and trophic interrelations within a plankton community.

The typical scales of self-organized patchiness are associated with the size and physiological parameters of planktonic animals. We have found a dependence of Lloyd's index of mean crowding on average specific metabolic costs of a plankton specimen. It is known that body size is an important parameter influencing ecological processes in a pelagic plankton ecosystem. Many studies, both empirical and theoretical, reflect its role in ecosystem dynamics. In our research, we have also found the connection between individual and population based properties of marine plankton. Body size defines the rates of the main physiological processes in an organism, and these rates regulate dynamics of a plankton community. There were no direct links between physiological rate parameters and simulated plankton fields in our model, but we have obtained these connections during the analysis of simulated fields. This conclusion can be considered as a confirmation of adequacy of the proposed object-based approximation of a plankton community.

References

1. Abraham, E.A.: The generation of plankton patchiness by turbulent stirring. Nature **391**, 577–580 (1998)
2. Ashjian, C.J., Davis, C.S., Gallager, S.M., Alatalo, P.: Distribution of plankton, particles, and hydrographic features across Georges Bank described using the Video Plankton Recorder. Deep-Sea Res. II. **48**, 245–282 (2001)
3. Ashjian, C.J.: VPR_ashjian_nonzero. Biological and Chemical Oceanography Data System. BCO DMO, WHOI. iPub: 26 July 2012. http://www.bco-dmo.org/dataset-deployment/455332/data. Accessed 10 Feb 2015
4. Batchelder, H.P., Speirs, D.C., Gentleman, W.C.: Workshop on "Individual-based models of Zooplankton". PICES Press **19**, 18–21 (2011)
5. Folt, C.L., Burns, C.W.: Biological drivers of Zooplankton patchiness. Trends Ecol. Evol. **14**, 300–305 (1999)
6. Grimm, V., Railsback, S.F.: Agent-based models in ecology: patterns and alternative theories of adaptive behaviour. In: Billari, F., Fent, T., Prskawetz, A., Scheffran, J. (eds.) Agent-Based Computational Modelling – Applications in Demography, Social, Economic and Environmental Sciences. Contributions to Economics, pp. 139–152. Physica, Heidelberg (2006)
7. James, E.C., Andrea, E.A., Brian, E.C., Heller, T.: Seasonal changes in the spatial distribution of phytoplankton in small, temperate-zone lakes. J. Plank. Res. **14**, 1017–1024 (1992)
8. Khailov, K.M., Popov, A.E.: Concentration of live mass as a regulator of aquatic organism functioning. Ekol. Morya **15**, 3–15 (1983)
9. Lange, M.: Embedding individual-based plankton ecosystem models in a finite element ocean model. Imperial College London, Department of Computing. Thesis, 188 p. (2014). https://spiral.imperial.ac.uk/handle/10044/1/18051
10. Lloyd, M.: Mean crowding. J. Anim. Ecol. **36**, 1–30 (1967)
11. Miller, T.J.: Contribution of individual-based coupled physical biological models to understanding recruitment in marine fish populations. Mar. Ecol. Prog. Ser. **347**, 127–138 (2007)
12. Pinel-Alloul, B.: Spatial heterogeneity as a multiscale characteristic of Zooplankton community. Hydrobiologia **300**(301), 17–42 (1995)
13. Piontkovski, S.A., Williams, R.: Multiscale variability of tropical ocean Zooplankton biomass. ICES J. Mar. Sci. **52**, 643–656 (1995)
14. Shushkina, E.A., Vinogradov, M.E., Lebedeva, L.P.: Processes of detritus production and fluxes of organic matter from epipelagic zones in different ocean regions. Oceanology **40**, 183–191 (2000)
15. Tzella, A., Haynes, P.H.: Small-scale spatial structure in plankton distributions. Biogeosciences **4**, 173–179 (2007)
16. Vasechkina, E.F., Yarin, V.D.: Modeling of the dynamics of age structure of the populations of free-floating copepods in the Black Sea. Phys. Oceanogr. **20**, 58–75 (2009)
17. Vasechkina, E.F., Yarin, V.D.: Object-oriented model of functioning of the plankton community of the shelf. Phys. Oceanogr. **14**, 360–376 (2004)
18. Vasechkina, E.: Appendix. Energy balance model of a plankton object. https://www.researchgate.net/publication/324521863_Energy_balance_model_of_a_plankton_object
19. Vinogradov, M.E., Shushkina, E.A., Kukina, I.N.: Functional characteristic of the plankton community of equatorial upwelling. Oceanology **16**(1), 122–137 (1976)

On the Cooperation Between Evolutionary Algorithms and Constraint Handling Techniques

Chengyong Si[1](✉), Jianqiang Shen[1], Weian Guo[2], and Lei Wang[3]

[1] Shanghai-Hamburg College,
University of Shanghai for Science and Technology, Shanghai 200093, China
sichengyong_sh@163.com
[2] Sino-German College of Applied Science,
Tongji University, Shanghai 201804, China
[3] College of Electronics and Information Engineering,
Tongji University, Shanghai 201804, China
wanglei@tongji.edu.cn

Abstract. During the past few decades, many Evolutionary Algorithms (EAs) together with the Constraint Handling Techniques (CHTs) have been developed to solve the constrained optimization problems (COPs). To obtain competitive performance, an effective CHT needs to be in conjunction with an efficient EA. In the previous paper, how the Differential Evolution influence the relationship between problems and penalty parameters was studied. In this paper, further study on how much can be improved through good evolutionary algorithms, or whether a good enough EA can make up the shortcoming of a simple CHT, and which factors are related will be the focus. Four different EAs are taken as an example, and Deb's feasibility-based rule is taken as the CHT for its simplicity. Experimental results show that better performance in EAs is not necessarily the reason for the improved performance of constrained optimization evolutionary algorithms (COEAs), and the key point is to find the shortcoming of the CHT and improve the shortcoming in the corresponding revision of EA.

Keywords: Constrained optimization · Constraint handling techniques
Evolutionary algorithms · Cooperation

1 Introduction

Constrained Optimization Problems (COPs) are very common and important in the real-world applications. The COPs can be generally expressed by the following formulations:

Minimize $f(\vec{x})$

Subject to: $g_j(\vec{x}) \leq 0, \quad j = 1, \cdots, l$

$$h_j(\vec{x}) = 0, \quad j = l+1, \cdots, m .\tag{1}$$

© Springer International Publishing AG, part of Springer Nature 2018
Y. Tan et al. (Eds.): ICSI 2018, LNCS 10941, pp. 42–50, 2018.
https://doi.org/10.1007/978-3-319-93815-8_5

where $\vec{x} = (x_1, \cdots, x_n)$ is the decision variable. The decision variable is bounded by the decision space S which is defined by the constraints:

$$L_i \leq x_i \leq U_i, \quad 1 \leq i \leq n. \tag{2}$$

where l is the number of inequality constraints and m-l is the number of equality constraints.

The Evolutionary Algorithms (EAs) are essentially unconstraint search techniques and play an important role in generating solutions. After solution generating, how to choose the better solutions especially for the COPs is another equivalently important issue, which leads to the development of various constrained optimization evolutionary algorithms (COEAs) [1]. The three most frequently used constraint handling techniques (CHTs) in COEAs are penalty functions, biasing feasible over infeasible solutions and multi-objective optimization.

Besides these basic CHTs, some other concepts like cooperative coevolution [2] and ensemble [3] have also been proposed, which can be seen as a dynamic adjustment process. Also, some other dynamic approaches based on the three different situations in solving COPs [4] have been developed.

Some researchers tried to solve the problem from the aspect of problem characteristics [5, 6].

As Li *et al.* [7] mentioned, the experimental comparisons on different constraint-handling techniques remain scarce. They compared different constraint-handling techniques in evolutionary constrained multiobjective optimization. Three representative constraint-handling techniques (i.e., Constrained-domination Principle, Self-adaptive Penalty, and Adaptive Tradeoff Model) are combined with nondominated sorting genetic algorithm II to study the performance difference on various conditions. The three properties of the problems are also summarized: the shape of Pareto front, the dimension of decision vector, and the size of feasible region. This research also gives some conclusion on these three different CHTs.

Kukkonen *et al.* [8] compared two existing constraint handling approaches with Differential Evolution (DE) as the searching algorithm. The two constraint handling approaches both prefer feasible solution candidates over infeasible, but when choosing between two infeasible solutions, one calculates the sum of constraint violations while the other approach uses Pareto dominance of constraint violations. This paper got the conclusion that neither of the constraint handling approaches can be judged to be better than the other.

We should also notice that when solving COPs, researchers mainly focus on the design of the search algorithms, i.e., trying to improve the performance of the EAs so as to make up the shortcoming of CHTs without carefully studied the characteristics of CHTs. But whether this works, or how much the search algorithm can make up for the CHTs, e.g., supposing the CHT is a very inefficient method, is few studied. A simple idea is the EAs should be in conjunction with an effective CHT so as to get a competitive performance. And that is what we try to study in this paper.

In the previous paper [9], how the Differential Evolution influence the relationship between problems and penalty parameters was studied. In this paper, we will give further study on how much can be improved through good EAs.

In the final revision period of this paper, a constrained composite differential evolution (called C^2oDE) [15] was proposed, which makes use of the idea of CoDE [10] to solve COPs. The method carefully selects three different trial vectors of DE to strike a balance between diversity and convergence. Besides, two CHTs, i.e., the feasibility rule and the ε constrained method, are combined for selection. Moreover, a restart scheme is also added. It should be pointed out the main purpose of the paper (C^2oDE) is to get a better performance, while this paper tries to verify whether the good EAs can make up for the CHTs through the comparison among different EAs. The paper of C^2oDE can also help to explain that good EAs need to be in cooperation with CHTs to get better performance (as two CHTs are carefully adopted).

The rest of this paper is organized as follows. Section 2 illustrates the basic idea and the CHT used in this paper. The experimental results and analysis are presented in Sect. 3. Finally, Sect. 4 concludes this paper and provides some possible paths for future research.

2   On the Cooperation Between EAs and CHTs

2.1   Basic Idea

The flowchart of COEAs is illustrated as in Fig. 1. After initialization, the EAs are mainly for generating solutions while the CHTs are mainly for solution ranking, then the chosen solution will be the parents in the EAs for the next generation.

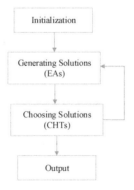

Fig. 1. Flowchart of COEAs

In the previous paper [9], to compare whether the evolutionary algorithm will influence the relationship between constrained optimization problems and penalty parameters, Ori-DE and CoDE [10] were adopted.

In this paper, to deeply understand the effect and to check the cooperation between EAs and CHTs, besides the two DE algorithms adopted in the previous paper, two PSO algorithms (Ori-PSO [11], CLPSO [12]) are also introduced, and the CHT adopted is the simple Deb's feasibility-based rule [13], as shown in Fig. 2.

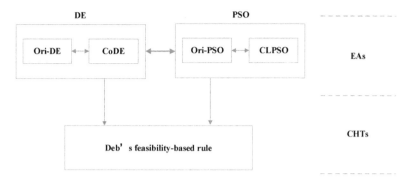

Fig. 2. Illustration of the basic idea

For page limited, the basic operators of DE and PSO are not introduced.

2.2 Deb's Feasibility-Based Rule

In this section, the CHT adopted (i.e., Deb's feasibility-based rule) is given.

Unlike the penalty function method which uses the penalty parameter to decide the balance between objective function and constraint violation, Deb's feasibility-based rule is one of the methods which compare separately the objective functions and constraint violations. It pair-wise compare individuals based on the rules below:

(1) Any feasible solution is preferred to any infeasible solution.
(2) Among two feasible solutions, the one having better objective function value is preferred.
(3) Among two infeasible solutions, the one having smaller constraint violation is preferred.

Deb's feasibility-based rule is very simple, and easy to understand, though it has some drawbacks, e.g., missing the information of some useful infeasible solutions, on the other hand, it is also the characteristics we want to use to compare with the EAs.

3 Experimental Study

3.1 Experimental Settings

24 benchmark functions from IEEE CEC2006 [14] were used in our experiment. The details of these benchmark functions are reported in Table 1, where n is the number of decision variables, $\rho = |F|/|S|$ is the estimated ratio between the feasible region and the search space, *LI, NI, LE, NE* is the number of linear inequality constraints, nonlinear inequality constraints, linear equality constraints and nonlinear equality constraints respectively, a is the number of active constraints at the optimal solution and $f(\overrightarrow{x^*})$ is the objective function value of the best known solution.

Table 1. Details of the benchmark functions from IEEE CEC2006

Prob.	N	Type of obj. fun.	ρ	LI	NI	LE	NE	a	$f(\vec{x}^*)$
g01	13	quadratic	0.0111%	9	0	0	0	6	−15.0000000000
g02	20	nonlinear	99.9971%	0	2	0	0	1	−0.8036191042
g03	10	polynomial	0.0000%	0	0	0	1	1	−1.0005001000
g04	5	quadratic	52.1230%	0	6	0	0	2	−30665.5386717834
g05	4	cubic	0.0000%	2	0	0	3	3	5126.4967140071
g06	2	cubic	0.0066%	0	2	0	0	2	−6961.8138755802
g07	10	quadratic	0.0003%	3	5	0	0	6	24.3062090681
g08	2	nonlinear	0.8560%	0	2	0	0	0	−0.0958250415
g09	7	polynomial	0.5121%	0	4	0	0	2	680.6300573745
g10	8	linear	0.0010%	3	3	0	0	6	7049.2480205286
g11	2	quadratic	0.0000%	0	0	0	1	1	−0.7499000000
g12	3	quadratic	4.7713%	0	1	0	0	0	−1.0000000000
g13	5	nonlinear	0.0000%	0	0	0	3	3	0.0539415140
g14	10	nonlinear	0.0000%	0	0	3	0	3	−47.7648884595
g15	3	quadratic	0.0000%	0	0	1	1	2	961.7150222899
g16	5	nonlinear	0.0204%	4	34	0	0	4	−1.9051552586
g17	6	nonlinear	0.0000%	0	0	0	4	4	8853.5396748065
g18	9	quadratic	0.0000%	0	13	0	0	6	−0.8660254038
g19	15	nonlinear	33.4761%	0	5	0	0	0	32.6555929502
g20	24	linear	0.0000%	0	6	2	12	16	0.2049794002
g21	7	linear	0.0000%	0	1	0	5	6	193.7245100700
g22	22	linear	0.0000%	0	1	8	11	19	236.4309755040
g23	9	linear	0.0000%	0	2	3	1	6	−400.0551000000
g24	2	linear	79.6556%	0	2	0	0	2	−5.5080132716

In the previous paper, *DE/rand/1/bin* and CoDE [10] was adopted as the search algorithm. To better compare the influence of different evolutionary algorithms, two variants of PSO (Ori-PSO [11], CLPSO [12]) are also introduced.

CLPSO uses a novel learning strategy whereby all other particles' historical best information can be used to update a particle's velocity. This strategy enables the diversity of the swarm to be preserved to discourage premature convergence.

In CoDE, several trial vector generation strategies with a number of control parameter settings are randomly combined at each generation to create new trial vectors. The three selected trial vector generation strategies are *DE/rand/1/bin*, *DE/rand/2/bin*, and *DE/current-to-rand/1*. The three control parameter settings are $[F = 1.0, Cr = 0.1]$, $[F = 1.0, Cr = 0.9]$, and $[F = 0.8, Cr = 0.2]$. It should be pointed out that some minor changes have been made to the selection operation of CoDE, i.e., the offspring are selected from the pool which is composed by all the trial vectors and target vectors.

The parameters in the Ori-DE are set as follows: the population size (NP) is set to 100; the scaling factor (F) is randomly chosen between 0.5 and 0.6, and the crossover control parameter (Cr) is randomly chosen between 0.9 and 0.95.

The parameters in the Ori-PSO are set as follows: the population size (NP) is set to 100; acceleration constants (c1, c2) are set to 1.49445, inertia weight (ω) is linearly decreasing between 0.9 and 0.4.

Besides the same setting as Ori-PSO, CLPSO adopts some other parameters: refreshing gap (m) is set to 5, Learning Probability (Pc) is set as

$$Pc_i = 0.00 + 0.50 * \frac{\left(\exp\left(\frac{5(i-1)}{NP-1}\right) - 1\right)}{(\exp(5) - 1)} \tag{3}$$

3.2 Experimental Results

25 independent runs were performed for each test function using 5×10^5 FES at maximum, as suggested by Liang et al. [14]. Additionally, the tolerance value δ for the equality constraints was set to 0.0001, and the constraints were not normalization.

Tables 2 and 3 shows the feasible rate (the percentage of runs where at least one feasible solution is found in MAX_FES, denoted as FR), the success rate (the percentage of runs where the algorithm finds a solution that satisfies the success condition, denoted as SR) on different problems with different EAs respectively.

Table 2. Feasible Rate for Ori-DE, CoDE, Ori-PSO, and CLPSO

Algo.	Prob.							
	g01	g02	g03	g04	g05	g06	g07	g08
Ori-DE	**1**	1	1	1	**1**	1	1	1
CoDE	0.32	1	1	1	0.36	1	1	1
Ori-PSO	1	1	**1**	1	**0.8**	0.32	1	1
CLPSO	1	1	0.28	1	0	1	1	1

Algo.	Prob.							
	g09	g10	g11	g12	g13	g14	g15	g16
Ori-DE	1	1	1	1	1	**1**	1	1
CoDE	1	1	1	1	1	0	1	1
Ori-PSO	1	0.96	**1**	1	**1**	0.8	0.92	1
CLPSO	1	1	0.16	1	0	0	0	1

Algo.	Prob.							
	g17	g18	g19	g20	g21	g22	g23	g24
Ori-DE	1	1	1	0	**1**	0	1	1
CoDE	1	1	1	0	0	0	1	1
Ori-PSO	**0.68**	1	1	**0.08**	0	0	**0.84**	1
CLPSO	0	1	1	0	0	0	0	1

Table 3. Success Rate for Ori-DE, CoDE, Ori-PSO, and CLPSO

Algo.	Prob.							
	g01	g02	g03	g04	g05	g06	g07	g08
Ori-DE	**1**	**0.88**	0	1	0	0	1	1
CoDE	0.32	0.44	0	1	**0.36**	**1**	1	1
Ori-PSO	0	0	0	1	0	**0.32**	0	1
CLPSO	**1**	0	0	0	0	0	0	1

Algo.	Prob.							
	g09	g10	g11	g12	g13	g14	g15	g16
Ori-DE	1	0	0.64	1	0	**0.24**	0.12	1
CoDE	1	0	**1**	1	**0.16**	0	**1**	1
Ori-PSO	0	0	0	1	0	0	0	0.2
CLPSO	0	0	0.04	1	0	0	0	**1**

Algo.	Prob.							
	g17	g18	19	g20	g21	g22	g23	g24
Ori-DE	0	**1**	**1**	0	0	0	0	1
CoDE	**0.8**	0.04	0.84	0	0	0	0	1
Ori-PSO	0	0.04	0	0.04	0	0	0	1
CLPSO	0	0	0	0	0	0	0	1

3.3 Comparison

From Tables 2 and 3, we can find some useful information:

(1) As to FR (Table 2), Ori-DE is better than or equal to CoDE in all problems. The similar situation can be observed between Ori-PSO and CLPSO where CLPSO only shows better performance at g06.

(2) As to SR (Table 3), Ori-DE gets a better performance at g01, g02, g14, g18 and g19 while CoDE obtains a better performance at g05, g06, g11, g13, g 15 and g17; there is not so much difference between Ori-PSO and CLPSO, where Ori-PSO shows a better performance at g04, g06 and CLPSO performs better at g01and g16.

(3) When compared between Ori-DE and Ori-PSO, Ori-DE performs slightly better as to FR. As to SR, the better performance of Ori-DE is more obvious. Ori-PSO shows a better performance only at g06.

Through these comparisons, some interesting conclusions can be obtained:

(1) Better performance in EAs is not necessarily resulting in the improved performance of COEAs. If the EAs are not in conjunction with the CHT, the performance may get even worse.

(2) As to different kinds of EAs, PSO is well-known for its fast convergence while DE is good at keeping the diversity. And Deb's feasibility-based rule also shows a fast speed without considering the information of many infeasible solutions. So if the fast convergence of PSO meets the fast speed of Deb's feasibility-based rule and if they find the right direction at the beginning, then the result will be very good; otherwise, the result will be much worse, as shown above.

4 Conclusion

In this paper, the relationship between EAs and CHTs when solving COPs are further studied. Four different evolutionary algorithms are taken as the search engines, while Deb's feasibility-based rule is taken as the CHT for its simplicity. Experimental results show that better performance in EAs is not necessarily the reason for the improved performance of COEAs and the key point is the cooperation between EAs and CHTs. To get a deeper understanding, more EAs together with CHTs, and test functions are needed for experiments. Besides, the inner mechanisms study, e.g., which factors or what characteristics affect the performance will be the focus for further research.

Acknowledgments. This work was supported by Shanghai Sailing Program (18YF1417400), the National Natural Science Foundation of China under Grants 61503287, Shanghai Young Teachers' Training Program under Grants ZZslg15087.

References

1. Mezura-Montes, E., Coello Coello, C.A.: Constraint-handling in nature-inspired numerical optimization: past, present and future. Swarm Evol. Comput. **1**(4), 173–194 (2011)
2. Li, X., Yao, X.: Cooperatively coevolving particle swarm for large scale optimization. IEEE Trans. Evol. Comput. **16**(2), 210–224 (2012)
3. Mallipeddi, R., Suganthan, P.N.: Ensemble of constraint handling techniques. IEEE Trans. Evol. Comput. **14**(4), 561–579 (2010)
4. Wang, Y., Cai, Z., Zhou, Y., Zeng, W.: An adaptive tradeoff model for constrained evolutionary optimization. IEEE Trans. Evol. Comput. **12**(1), 80–92 (2008)
5. Tsang, E., Kwan, A.: Mapping constraint satisfaction problems to algorithms and heuristics. Technical Report, CSM-198 (1993)
6. Si, C., Hu, J., Lan, T., Wang, L., Wu, Q.: A combined constraint handling framework: an empirical study. Memetic Comput. **9**(1), 69–88 (2017)
7. Li, J., Wang, Y., Yang, S., Cai, Z.: A comparative study of constraint-handling techniques in evolutionary constrained multiobjective optimization. In: Proceedings of CEC, pp. 4175–4182 (2016)
8. Kukkonen, S., Mezura-Montes, E.: An experimental comparison of two constraint handling approaches used with differential evolution. In: Proceedings of CEC, pp. 2691–2697 (2017)
9. Si, C., Shen, J., Zou, X., Wang, L., Wu, Q.: Comparison of differential evolution algorithms on the mapping between problems and penalty parameters. In: Proceedings of ICSI, pp. 420–428 (2017)
10. Wang, Y., Cai, Z., Zhang, Q.: Differential evolution with composite trial vector generation strategies and control parameters. IEEE Trans. Evol. Comput. **15**(1), 55–66 (2011)
11. Shi, Y., Eberhart, R.C.: A modified particle swarm optimizer. In: Proceedings of CEC, pp. 69–73 (1998)
12. Liang, J., Qin, K., Suganthan, P.N., Baskar, S.: Comprehensive learning particle swarm optimizer for global optimization of multimodal functions. IEEE Trans. Evol. Comput. **10**(3), 281–295 (2006)
13. Deb, K.: An efficient constraint handling method for genetic algorithms. Comput. Methods Appl. Mech. Eng. **186**(2–4), 311–338 (2000)

14. Liang, J.J., Runarsson, T.P., Mezura-Montes, E., Clerc, M., Suganthan, P.N., Coello Coello, C.A., Deb, K.: Problem definitions and evaluation criteria for the CEC 2006. Technical Report, Special Session on Constrained Real-Parameter Optimization (2006)
15. Wang, B., Li, H., Li, J., Wang, Y.: Composite differential evolution for constrained evolutionary optimization. IEEE Trans. Syst. Man, Cybern. Syst. **8**(3), 406 (2018). https://doi.org/10.1109/TSMC.2018.2807785

An Ontological Framework for Cooperative Games

Manuel-Ignacio Balaguera[1]([✉]), Jenny-Paola Lis-Gutierrez[1],
Mercedes Gaitán-Angulo[1], Amelec Viloria[2],
and Rafael Portillo-Medina[2]

[1] Fundación Universitaria Konrad Lorenz, Bogotá D.C., Colombia
{manueli.balagueraj,jenny.lis,
mercedes.gaitana}@konradlorenz.edu.co
[2] Universidad de la Costa, Barranquilla, Colombia
{aviloria7,rportill3}@cuc.edu.co

Abstract. Social intelligence is an emerging property of a system composed of agents that consists of the ability of this system to conceive, design, implement and execute strategies to solve problems and thus achieve a collective state of the system that is concurrently satisfactory for all and each one of the agents that compose it. In order to make decisions when dealing with complex problems related to social systems and take advantage of social intelligence, cooperative games theory constitutes the standard theoretical framework. In the present work, an ontological framework for cooperative games modeling and simulation is presented.

Keywords: Cooperative · Games theory · Ontology · Ontological framework
Simulation model · Clusters · Cooperation

1 Introduction

Social (collective) intelligence [1–3] is an emerging property of a system composed of agents that consists of the ability of this system to conceive, design, implement and execute strategies to solve problems and thus achieve a collective state of the system that is concurrently satisfactory for all and each one of the agents that compose it.

Any collective purpose competes with the selfish tendency of each agent consisting of believing, usually mistakenly, that his individual intelligence, as opposed to collective intelligence, can lead him to obtain a better result operating from his dimension and individual perspective than that which I would get if I worked from a strategy focused on trust and agreements designed to give the greatest value to the collective interest and the search for a state of equilibrium or a long-term metastable state. A perfect example of the above reflection is the system "humanity" in its various hierarchical levels of organization: global, regional, national, business, even family, in which throughout history have been very rare periods of social stability obtained from agreements and mutual trust.

When considering business organizations, companies all over the world strive to gain bigger market shares and optimize their operations in the existing globalized and

© Springer International Publishing AG, part of Springer Nature 2018
Y. Tan et al. (Eds.): ICSI 2018, LNCS 10941, pp. 51–57, 2018.
https://doi.org/10.1007/978-3-319-93815-8_6

competitive markets. In order to deal with this scenario, the collective intelligence of companies and organizations has produced the emergent system called "cluster" [2, 4, 5]. A cluster is known as a group of interconnected companies that share geographical boundaries or perform common practices, as they are related to the same supply chain. According to [6], clusters dominate today's economic world map, and this is a relevant feature of virtually every national, regional, state, and even metropolitan economy, especially in more developed nations.

Clusters are based on cooperation activities. Nevertheless Patti, [3, 7–9] states that, clusters benefit from both competition and cooperation. Specifically, in the case of cooperation, much of this has been evidenced at a vertical level of the supply chain and at a horizontal level if there is no direct competition or any external threat to the cluster existence. Yet, as this author highlights, trust among companies and the face-to-face interactions are key factors for cluster success.

In order to design robust clusters, which are not very vulnerable to the actions of their individual components and the changing environmental conditions, in addition to maximizing the benefits for component companies, it is very important to have tools that make it easier to predict the effect each agreement will have. and each game rule present in the framework of the creation of the cluster.

Cooperative game theory [4, 10, 11] provides a theoretical framework which may be used in order to develop software tool to assist the decision making process in the choice and design of agreements and game rules present in the coalition framework of a cluster. However, the process that allows developing a software system to support decision making based on the theoretical framework of cooperative game theory [5, 12, 13] is not a straightforward process, it requires: first, a very flexible and intuitive modeling environment (called a "modeling framework" in the software engineering literature) that allows to a user who is not a software engineering expert to identify and represent the components of the cooperative game as well as identify and represent the attributes and behaviors of each static component and, in addition, the decision rules of the autonomous components ("agents") present in the game. Second, the proposed decision support system requires a "simulation framework" to facilitate the creation of diverse simulation scenarios and its integration to a "simulation engine" in order to reproduce a particular game dynamics. In order to facilitate the appropriate processing and interpretation of the simulation results, the decision support system also should include a scientific visualization engine.

A crucial step in the development of a software framework intended to support the decision making phase of a cluster design, based in the cooperative game theory, is the abstraction process. Abstraction is the most powerful resource to reduce and manage the complexity of a system in the treatment of its associated problems.

2 Ontological Frameworks

In reference to the importance of the abstraction process and its relation to complexity, Grady Booch writes: "an individual can comprehend only about seven, plus or minus two, chunks of information at one time. This number appears to be independent of information content. […], "The span of absolute judgment and the span of immediate memory impose severe limitations on the amount of information that we are able to receive, process and remember. By organizing the stimulus input simultaneously into several dimensions and successively into a sequence of chunks, we manage to break… this informational bottleneck" [6]. In contemporary terms, we call this process chunking or abstraction.

As Wulf describes it, "We (humans) have developed an exceptionally powerful technique for dealing with complexity. We abstract from it. Unable to master the entirety of a complex object, we choose to ignore its inessential details, dealing instead with the generalized, idealized model of the object" [7]. For example, when studying how photosynthesis works in a plant, we can focus on the chemical reactions in certain cells in a leaf and ignore all other parts, such as the roots and stems. We are still constrained by the number of things that we can comprehend at one time, but through abstraction, we use chunks of information with increasingly greater semantic content. This is especially true if we take an object-oriented view of the world because objects, as abstractions of entities in the real world, represent a particularly dense and cohesive clustering of information".

In the last thirty years, software engineering has evolved from the "structured programming paradigm" to contemporary methods of artificial intelligence, of which game theory and agent-based modeling are essential components.

Under the paradigm of structured programming the words "program", "model" and "simulation" represented the same concept: an algorithm for the treatment and solution of a problem and not the computational implementation of a model that captures by abstraction the system's identity which is relevant in the context of a problem, and in this way, to allow its controlled manipulation according to a given scenario, what in modern times is called "a simulation" [8].

At the present, in the beginning of the 21 century, societies confront complex problems which require the development and use of software frameworks to support the forecasting of the behavior and evolution of a social system for a given set of possible scenarios and with it, to support the decision making process necessary for the problem solution under controlled risk.

The search for solutions in the treatment of complex problems has produced and consolidated the paradigm of "operations research" in which, knowing a multiplicity of possible solutions, it is necessary to choose the solution that maximizes or minimizes (optimizes) simultaneously a given set of "objective functions", see Fig. 1.

In the application of the operations research paradigm, the most critical issue is the model development. In order to simultaneously attain model controllability and realism it is relevant the process of abstraction: the selection of the system's components that should be ignored and those that should be considered. In addition, when modeling each system's component it is also relevant the same selection regarding the component's attributes and components to be considered. To facilitate this process, this paper proposes the use of "ontological frameworks".

"An ontology is a formal description of concepts and relationships that can exist for a community of human and/or machine agents. The notion of ontologies is crucial for the purpose of enabling knowledge sharing and reuse" [9, 13–15]. From this definition of ontology, an "ontological framework" is considered as a "semantic network"

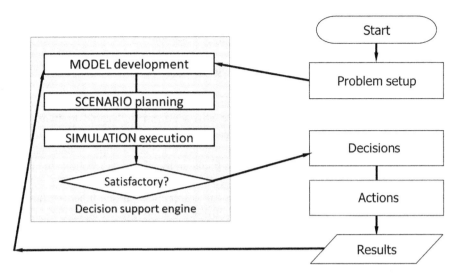

Fig. 1. Operations research life cycle for dealing with a problem

[10, 16–18] containing the minimally satisfactory set of concepts necessary to represent an object or a system in the process of a model development.

3   Ontological Framework for Cooperative Games

"There are applications of game theory for which the assumption of maximizing individual interests, with max-min as the resulting criterion for choice and with the use of randomization as the means for creating mixed strategies, may be changed. The means for doing so is called "bargaining" and the resulting games are called "cooperative games."

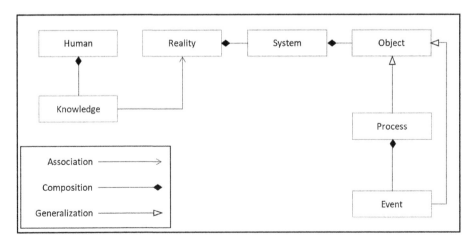

Fig. 2. Human knowledge ontology diagram

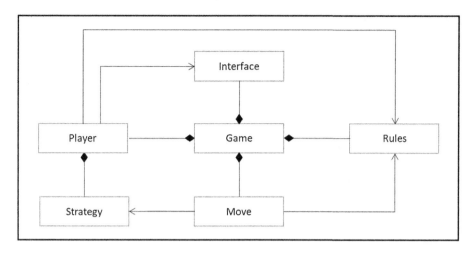

Fig. 3. Generic game ontology diagram

Basically bargaining is a process of making offers and demands with the objective of achieving total, joint results that are better than can be obtained from simply the competitive game. In such bargaining, of course, the competitive game sits in the background as the fall-back position in the event that bargaining fails and there is no cooperation in arriving at the solution" [11, 19–23] (Fig. 4).

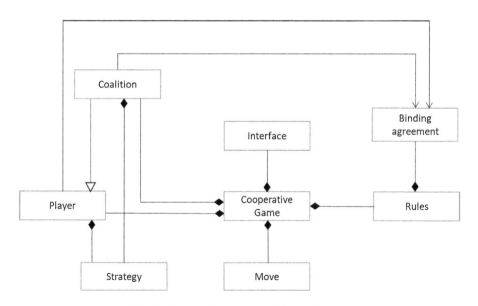

Fig. 4. Cooperative game ontology diagram

4 Discussion and Conclusions

Figure 1 shows the general context where game theory has its ontological roots. In this level of the ontological framework, in addition to the primitive concepts from which game theory concept components are derived, three kind of relations are defined: association, composition and generalization.

An association relation represents a dependency between two classes (object categories) where the origin node uses the end node. As an example in Fig. 1 one instance of the "Human" class requires one instance of the "Knowledge" class in order to enter in relation with a given reality. A composition relation indicates that the origin node is a component of the end node, for example, any instance of the class "Knowledge" is a component of the "Human" class. Finally, a generalization relation (also called "inheritance relation") indicates that the origin node is a subclass or "specialized" class of the ending node, which is equivalent to say that the ending node is a "generalization" of the beginning node [24–29].

Figure 2 presents the second level in the hierarchical structure of the proposed ontological framework for cooperative games, where it is stated that a game is composed by instances of the classes: player, interface, moves and rules. In addition, this ontology diagram specifies the relations between players and strategies (composition) and between players and interface, players and rules, and between moves and rules and between moves and strategies [30, 31].

Finally, the ontology diagram in Fig. 3 specifies cooperative games as an extension of general games where the additional elements are the coalition class, a specialization of the player class and the binding agreements class as a specialization of the rules class. In cooperative games players can make binding agreements, i.e. agreements they must keep. In cooperative games the interest is on the formation of coalitions and on the sharing of the benefits of cooperation rather than the means to achieve these.

References

1. Suárez, E., Bucheli, V., Zarama, R., Garcia, Á.: Collective intelligence: analysis and modelling. Kybernetes **44**(6/7), 1122–1133 (2015)
2. Gedai, E., Kóczy, L.Á., Zombori, Z.: Cluster Games a Novel, Game Theory-Based Approach to Better Understand Incentives and Stability in Clusters. Danish Ministry for Science, Technology and Innovation, DASTI (Copenhagen), Copenhagen (2012)
3. Patti, A.L.: Economic clusters and the supply chain: a case study. Supply Chain Manage. Int. J. **11**(3), 266–270 (2006)
4. Sedano, C.I., Carvalho, M.B., Secco, N., Longstreet, C.S.: Collaborative and cooperative games: facts and assumptions. In: 2013 International Conference on Collaboration Technologies and Systems (CTS), San Diego, CA. USA (2013)
5. Cano-Berlanga, S., Giménez-Gómez, J., Vilella, C.: Enjoying cooperative games: the R package GameTheory. Appl. Math. Comput. **305**, 381–393 (2017)
6. Miller, G.A.: The magical number seven, plus or minus two some limits on our capacity for processing information. Psychol. Rev. **101**(2), 343–352 (2001)
7. Shaw, M.: ALPHARD: Form and Content. Springer, New York (1981). https://doi.org/10.1007/978-1-4612-5979-4

8. Booch, G., Maksimchuk, R., Engle, M., Young, B., Conallen, J., Houston, K.: Object-Oriented Analysis and Design with Applications. Addison Wesley, Boston (2007)
9. Guarino, N., Oberle, D., Staab, S.: What is an ontology? In: Staab, S., Studer, R. (eds.) Handbook on Ontologies, pp. 1–3. Springer, Heidelberg (2009). https://doi.org/10.1007/978-3-540-92673-3
10. Sowa, J.: Semantic networks. In: Encyclopedia of Artificial Intelligence, pp. 1011–1024. Wiley, New York (1987)
11. Hayes, R.: Cooperative game theoretic models for decision-making in contexts of library cooperation. Libr. Trends **51**(3), 441–461 (2003)
12. Javid, A.A., Hoseinpour, P.: A game-theoretic analysis for coordinating cooperative advertising in a supply chain. J. Optim. Theory Appl. **149**(1), 138–150 (2011)
13. Alaei, S., Alaei, R., Salimi, P.: A game theoretical study of cooperative advertising in a single-manufacturer-two-retailers supply chain. Int. J. Adv. Manuf. Technol. **74**, 101–111 (2014)
14. Anderson, P.: Complexity theory and organization science. Organ. Sci. **10**(3), 216–232 (1999)
15. Aust, G., Buscher, U.: Vertical cooperative advertising in a retailer duopoly. Comput. Ind. Eng. **72**, 247–254 (2014)
16. Bahinipati, B., Kanda, A., Deshmukh, S.: Revenue sharing in semiconductor industry supply chain: cooperative game theoretic approach. Sadhana **34**(3), 501–527 (2009)
17. Carsetti, A.: Epistemic Complexity and Knowledge Construction. Springer, Roma (2013). https://doi.org/10.1007/978-94-007-6013-4
18. Castellani, B., Hafferty, F.W.: Sociology and Complexity Science. Springer, Heidelberg (2009). https://doi.org/10.1007/978-3-540-88462-0
19. Forrester, J.W.: Counterintuitive behavior of social systems. Reason **2**(2), 4–13 (1971)
20. Fritzson, P.: Principles of Object-Oriented Modeling and Simulation with Modelica 3.3: A Cyber-Physical Approach. Wiley-IEEE Press, Linköping (2014)
21. Johansen, O.: Introducción a la Teoría General de Sistemas. Limusa, Mexico D.F. (2007)
22. Law, L., Wilson, A., Wilson, D.: Las Estructuras Jerárquicas. Alianza Universidad, Madrid (1973)
23. Lewin, R.: Complexity, Life at the Edge of Chaos. University of Chicago Press, Chicago (2000)
24. Lin, C.-C., Hsieh, C.-C.: A cooperative coalitional game in duopolistic supply-chain competition. Netw. Spat. Econ. **12**, 129–146 (2012)
25. López-Paredes, A.: Ingeniería de Sistemas Sociales. Universidad de Valladolid, Valladolid (2004)
26. Mitchell, M.: Complexity: A Guided Tour. Oxford University Press, Santa Fe (2011)
27. Nakai, Y., Koyama, Y., Terano, T.: Agent-Based Approaches in Economic and Social Complex Systems VIII. Springer, New York (2013). https://doi.org/10.1007/978-4-431-55236-9
28. y Gasset, J.O.: History as a System and Other Essays Toward a Philosophy of History, W.W. Norton & Company (1962)
29. Parunak, H., Odell, J.: Representing social structures in UML. In: AOSE 2001, Montreal Canada (2002)
30. Rumbaugh, J., Jacobson, I., Booch, G.: The Unified Modeling language Reference Manual. Addison Wesley Longman Inc., Cambridge (1999)
31. Viloria, A., Robayo, P.V.: Virtual network level of application composed IP networks connected with systems - (NETS Peer-to- Peer). Indian J. Sci. Technol. (2016). ISSN 0974-5645

An Adaptive Game Model for Broadcasting in VANETs

Xi Hu[✉] and Tao Wu

Northeastern University at Qinhuangdao, Qinhuangdao 066004, Hebei, China
neuqhx@126.com

Abstract. Broadcasting is a popular and important way to information dissemination in vehicular ad-hoc networks (VANETs). But the weakness of broadcasting which is called broadcasting storm also reduces the performance of VANETs. In this paper, an adaptive game model for broadcasting in VANETs is proposed firstly. Then we optimize the proposed model adapting to the distance between two neighbor vehicles and use this optimizing game model to realize the probabilistic broadcasting. The simulation results show that the proposed adaptive game model can release the broadcasting storm, and make the performance better.

Keywords: Broadcasting · VANET · Game model · Probabilistic broadcast
Simulation

1 Introduction

Vehicular Ad-hoc Networks (VANETs), which is a kind of Mobile Ad-hoc Networks (MANETs), have been considered as an essential part of Intelligent Transportation System (ITS) [1]. In VANETs, there are many kinds of information disseminated between vehicle-to-infrastructure (V2I) and vehicle-to-vehicle (V2V) [2].

Due to the high mobility and restricted mobility patterns of vehicles, it is challenging work to design message dissemination scheme with low delay and high reliability. Broadcasting is a widely used dissemination technique in VANETs, but it also can cause some problems as shown in works [3, 4].

Blind Flooding (BF) [5] is a simple broadcasting scheme. In BF, vehicles always rebroadcast the messages received for the first or more times. However obviously, as the increasing of the density, it will cause a large amount of redundant messages in VANET, and also leads to the collision and congestion which degrade the availability of broadcasting.

X-persistence Broadcasting [6] contains three broadcasting schemes: weighted p-persistence, slotted 1-persistence, and slotted p-persistence schemes. In these schemes, when a node receives a message, it calculates a rebroadcast probability according to the distance from the sender. Generally, a node with a larger distance from the sender obtains a higher rebroadcast probability.

BBBR [7] is a multi-hop broadcasting protocol based on network coding aiming to minimize message retransmissions. Simulation results show that BBBR can decrease

© Springer International Publishing AG, part of Springer Nature 2018
Y. Tan et al. (Eds.): ICSI 2018, LNCS 10941, pp. 58–67, 2018.
https://doi.org/10.1007/978-3-319-93815-8_7

data packet rebroadcasting and reduce delay. However, using single forwarder node to transmit bidirectional emergency messages may induce additional delays.

PREDAT [8] provides a broadcast storm mitigation solution without periodic beacons. A circle-shaped communication area is divided into four quadrants. Four subareas chose in each quadrant respectively are defined as the sweet spot. PREDAT gets not only a high delivery ratio but a high overhead which is for the geographic distribution of sweet spots.

TURBO [9] broadcasts messages to a group of vehicles. It employs two mechanisms: a store-carry forwarding and a broadcast suppression. In store-carry forwarding, each vehicle carries the message for a determined time and retransmits it when intermittently connected network problems occur. In broadcast suppression, some specific vehicles are selected to rebroadcast the messages. Despite being a beacon-oriented approach, it does not implement any beacon congestion control.

DPS [10] selects a relay node to rebroadcast the message at each hop. To reduce delay and collisions, DPS uses both the local density and the inter-vehicle distance in the selection for selecting the vehicle farthest from the sender as the relay. DPS suffers from excessive overhead caused by broadcast storm.

Fast-OB-VAN [11] aims to reduce the delay and to increase the delivery ratio. Distances are represented by a 10-bit sequence. Vehicles having the most significant bit in this sequence set to one may contend to transmit the packet. This method allows the packet transmission by the farthest candidate relay. Fast-OB-VAN also suffers from a high overhead as DPS.

In this paper, we propose an adaptive game mode for broadcasting in VANETs. Using the proposed model, each in-between neighbor vehicle can calculate its broadcasting probability according to the local network situations independently, such as the distance to neighbors in our work.

2   Game Model for Broadcasting

2.1   Game Model

Considering a realistic broadcasting scene in VANET, there are r vehicles covered by the communication range of vehicle a, i.e. vehicle a has r neighbors. So when vehicle a generates and broadcasts a packet, all neighbors can hear the broadcasting. Then these neighbors have two choices to handle the received broadcasting packets: rebroadcast or discard. When some of neighbors choose rebroadcast, they will pay out a price themselves, and bring gains to the others.

Based on the above descriptions, we firstly define the neighbor set Γ of vehicle a as shown in Eq. (1)

$$\Gamma = \{n_1, \ n_2, \ n_3, \ \ldots, \ n_r\} \qquad (1)$$

Then, we model this broadcasting scene as a game named G among all the neighbors in Γ:

Players: r neighbors in Γ $(r \geq 2)$;

Strategy set: we define strategy set H = {B, D}, then each neighbor independently chooses its strategy within H. Here, B and D signify reBroadcast and Discard respectively.

Preferences: The preference to some strategy is determined by the expected value of the utility function, i.e. the payoff gained by every neighbors. Equation (2) shows the payoff of neighbor n_j with three different cases. Here, $u_j(h)$ is the utility function of n_j, v is the gain gained for other neighbors' rebroadcasting and c $(0 < c < v)$ is the cost paid for its rebroadcasting. Furthermore, $h \in H$, $n_i \in \Gamma$, $n_j \in \Gamma$.

$$u_j(h) = \begin{cases} v & \text{if } h_j = D \text{ and } h_i = B \text{ for } \exists i \neq j \\ v - c & \text{if } h_j = B \text{ for } \exists n_j \in \Gamma \\ 0 & \text{if } h_j = D \text{ for } \forall n_j \in \Gamma \end{cases} \tag{2}$$

2.2   Payoff Matrix of Game G

We define two proper subsets of the neighbor set Γ,

$$\Gamma_j = \{n_j \mid n_j \in \Gamma\}$$

$$\Gamma_{-j} = \eth_U \Gamma_j$$

which subject to $\Gamma_j \cup \Gamma_{-j} = \Gamma$ and $\Gamma_j \cap \Gamma_{-j} = \varnothing$.

Then, the combination (Γ_j, Γ_{-j}) can have four choices in H: (B, D), (B, B), (D, B) and (D, D). Here, (•, B) represents at least one vehicle in Γ_{-j} chooses B, and (•, D) represents all vehicles in Γ_{-j} choose D. Therefore, the payoff matrix of game G can be illustrated in Fig. 1. Here, $1 \leq k \leq r - 1$ and k $\in \mathbb{Z}$.

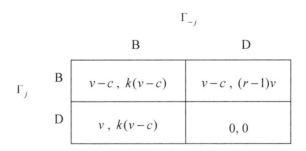

Fig. 1. Payoff matrix of game G

2.3 Symmetric Mixed Strategy Nash Equilibrium of Game G

In game G, all players share the same strategy set H. Furthermore, there are only two strategies B and D in H, so according to the existence of mixed strategy Nash equilibrium in finite game, G has a symmetric mixed strategy Nash equilibrium.

Firstly, we define a joint probability distribution (p_j, p_{-j}) as the mixed strategy of G over H, and the details of p_j and p_{-j} are shown in Eq. (3),

$$
\begin{aligned}
p_j &= (p_{jB}, \ p_{jD}) \\
p_{-j} &= (p_{-jB}, \ p_{-jD})
\end{aligned}
\tag{3}
$$

Here, $0 < p_{jB}, \ p_{jD}, p_{-jB}, \ p_{-jD} < 1$ and $p_{jB} + p_{jD} = 1$, $p_{-jB} + p_{-jD} = 1$. Therefore, the expected payoff of Γ_j is shown in Eq. (4),

$$
\begin{aligned}
u_j(p_j, \ p_{-j}) &= [p_{jB} \ \ p_{jD}] \begin{bmatrix} u_j(B, \ p_{-j}) \\ u_j(D, \ p_{-j}) \end{bmatrix} \\
&= p_{jB} \ \cdot \ u_j(B, \ p_{-j}) + p_{jD} \ \cdot \ u_j(D, \ p_{-j})
\end{aligned}
\tag{4}
$$

Let p $(0 < p < 1)$ be the probability of choosing B, then Eq. (5) can be easily drawn,

$$
\begin{aligned}
p_{jB} &= p \\
p_{jD} &= 1 - p
\end{aligned}
\tag{5}
$$

Substituting Eq. (5) into (4), we get

$$
u_j(p_j, \ p_{-j}) = p \ \cdot \ u_j(B, \ p_{-j}) + (1 - p) \ \cdot \ u_j(D, \ p_{-j})
\tag{6}
$$

Secondly, in Nash equilibrium, the mix strategy of any player is the optimal reaction to that of the others, so it should satisfy the condition shown in Eq. (7).

$$
\frac{\partial u_j(p_j, \ p_{-j})}{\partial p} = 0
\tag{7}
$$

Calculating Eq. (7), we get the result shown in Eq. (8),

$$
u_j(B, \ p_{-j}) - u_j(D, \ p_{-j}) = 0
\tag{8}
$$

Here,

$$
\begin{aligned}
u_j(B, \ p_{-j}) &= [u_j(B, \ B) \ \ u_j(B, \ D)] \begin{bmatrix} p_{-jB} \\ p_{-jD} \end{bmatrix} \\
&= p_{-jB} \ \cdot \ u_j(B, \ B) + p_{-jD} \ \cdot \ u_j(B, D)
\end{aligned}
\tag{9}
$$

$$u_j(D, \ p_{-j}) = [\, u_j(D, \ B) \quad u_j(D, \ D)\,] \begin{bmatrix} p_{-jB} \\ p_{-jD} \end{bmatrix} \tag{10}$$

$$= p_{-jB} \ \cdot \ u_j(D, \ B) + p_{-jD} \ \cdot \ u_j(D, \ D)$$

$$p_{-jB} = 1 - \prod_{i \neq j}^{r} (1 - p) \tag{11}$$

$$p_{-jD} = \prod_{i \neq j}^{r} (1 - p)$$

Substituting Eqs. (9), (10) and (11) into Eq. (8), we get

$$(1 - \prod_{i \neq j}^{r} (1 - p)) \cdot (v - c) + (\prod_{i \neq j}^{r} (1 - p)) \cdot (v - c) - [(1 - \prod_{i \neq j}^{r} (1 - p)) \cdot v + (\prod_{i \neq j}^{r} (1 - p)) \cdot 0] = 0 \tag{12}$$

Calculating Eq. (12), the optimal value of p is calculated as Eq. (13),

$$p^* = 1 - (\frac{c}{v})^{\frac{1}{r-1}} \tag{13}$$

Therefore, in the Nash equilibrium of G, the optimal mix strategy for each player is $(p^*, \ 1 - p^*)$, which means that the expected payoff from choosing B equals that from choosing D for any players.

2.4 Optimizing the Game Model

In an ideal broadcasting, only the neighbors which locate on the edge of communication range are needed to rebroadcast, and all of the others are redundant. So, we take v and c as two functions about the distance of two neighbors which are represented by $V(d)$ and $C(d)$ respectively. Then, Eq. (13) can be optimized to Eq. (14),

$$P(r, \ d) = 1 - (\frac{C(d)}{V(d)})^{\frac{1}{r-1}} \tag{14}$$

Here, $C(d)$ is a monotonic decreasing function about d which means that the lower the distance is, the more costs paid, and $V(d)$ is a monotonic increasing function about d which means that the lower the distance is, the more gains obtained.

Therefore, we can see that the broadcasting probability decreases with the increasing of the number of neighbors, and increases with the increasing of the distance from Eq. (14). These properties have two advantages: first, it can increase the probability for selecting the farthest neighbors to rebroadcast sequentially; second, it can reduce the broadcasting redundancy effectively in dense VANET environment.

We define $f(d) = \frac{C(d)}{V(d)}$, thus $f(d)$ should satisfy the following conditions: (1) $f(d)$ is a monotonic decreasing function about d; (2) $f(d) \in (0, \ 1)$; (3) $f(d) = 1$ when $d = 0$, and $f(d) = 0$ when $d = R$. Here, R represents the communication range. Based on these conditions, we choose a simplest form of $f(d)$ as shown in Eq. (15),

$$f(d) = (1 - \frac{d}{R})^{\alpha} \tag{15}$$

Here, α ($\alpha \in \mathbb{N}$) is an adjustment factor which can change the degree of the monotonic decreasing of $f(d)$. Thus, we can get the resulting calculation of p based on Eqs. (14) and (15),

$$P(r, d) = 1 - (1 - \frac{d}{R})^{\frac{\alpha}{r-1}} \tag{16}$$

3   Game Based Broadcasting Algorithm

In our Game based Broadcasting algorithm named GB for short, vehicles use periodic Hello packets to collect neighbor information, such as ID, location, velocity and so on.

When a source vehicle generates and broadcasts a broadcasting packet, which is a tuple like this <source, destination, pre-hop, pre-hop location, sequence number>. Every neighbor heard this broadcasting packet starts GB algorithm. The details of GB algorithm is shown in Fig. 2.

Algorithm 1. Game based Broadcasting (GB) Algorithm

---

one neighbor vehicle receives the broadcasting packet
IF this packet is a duplicated one which comes from the same source s
THEN
    discards the packet
ELSE
    updates the record items with the information carried by this packet
    calculates rebroadcasting probability p for this packet using Eqn. (16)
    generates an uniform random number Y between 0 and 1
    IF $Y <= p$ **THEN**
        updates this packet with the information itself
        broadcasts the updated packet sequentially
    ELSE
        discards this packet
    ENDIF
ENDIF

Fig. 2. Game based Broadcasting (GB) algorithm

4 Performance Evaluation

We evaluate the performance with NS2.35 and VanetMobiSim. VanetMobiSim is used to generate simulating traffic scenes. The basic parameter settings are shown in Table 1.

Table 1. The parameter settings

Parameter	Value
Scene	1000 m × 1000 m
Number of vehicles	10, 30, 50, 70, 90
Communication range	250 m
Velocity	Min: 5 m/s, Max: 10, 15, 20, 25, 30 m/s
Pause time	0 s
Data	CBR, 512 Bytes/packet
Packet generating rate	1 packet/s, 4 sources
Simulation time	600 s
Parameter α	10

4.1 Performance Metrics

(1) Saved-ReBroadcast (SRB). It is the ratio between the numbers of vehicles receiving a packet and the number of vehicles actually rebroadcasting the packet.
(2) Average Delay (AD). It is defined as the dissemination delay of the packet from the source vehicle to the last receiver. The faster the packet propagates, the more efficient the corresponding protocol.

The results shown in the following section are the average value from five simulations.

4.2 Performance Evaluation

We evaluate the performance of GB by comparing it to other two broadcasting algorithms BF [5] and Weighted-p [6] in two different simulations. One simulation uses different number of vehicles but fixed maximum velocity 20 m/s, and the other uses different maximum velocity but fixed number of vehicles 50.

As shown in Fig. 3, the SRB of GB is better than that of Weighted-p and BF. Furthermore, the SRB of GB and Weighted-p increases clearly as the number of vehicles increases, but that of BF algorithm is nearly zero. It is because that BF uses pure flooding scheme to broadcast, and then the other two algorithms realize the probability broadcasting. As shown in Fig. 4, our GB algorithm has the least average delay compared to the other algorithms. Furthermore, the average delay of BF decreases as the number of vehicles increases, but that of the other algorithms increases.

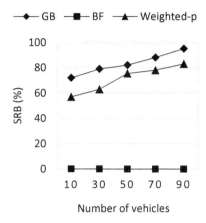

Fig. 3. SRB vs. Num. of vehicles

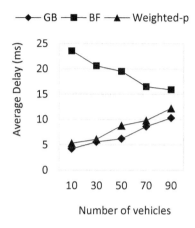

Fig. 4. AD vs. Num. of vehicles

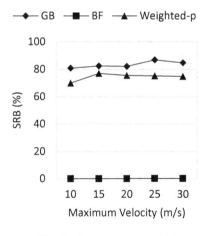

Fig. 5. SRB vs. Max. velocity

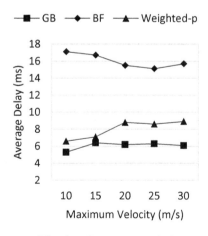

Fig. 6. AD vs. Max. velocity

As shown in Fig. 5, the SRB of GB and Weighted-p are fluctuating with the increasing of velocity, and that of BF algorithm is nearly zero again. As shown in Fig. 6, the average delay of GB is less than that of Weighted-p, and BF has the maximum delay. Furthermore, we also can see that the impact of velocity on average delay is smaller than that of the density.

5   Conclusion

In VANETs, broadcast storm may happen if vehicles rebroadcast the identical packet received more than once. Based on the analyses using game theory, the proposed game based broadcasting algorithm GB can promote the performance of VANETs. Simulation results show that GB has higher efficiency and reliability.

Acknowledgement. The research is sponsored by the National Natural Science Foundation of China (Grant No. 61501102).

References

1. Campolo, C., Molinaro, A., Scopigno, R.: From today's VANETs to tomorrow's planning and the bets for the day after. Veh. Commun. **2**, 158–171 (2015)
2. Dey, K.C., Rayamajhi, A., et al.: Vehicle-to-vehicle (V2V) and vehicle-to-infrastructure (V2I) communication in a heterogeneous wireless network – Performance evaluation. Transp. Res. Part C **68**, 168–184 (2016)
3. Basheer, H.S., Bassil, C.: A review of broadcasting safety data in V2V: weaknesses and requirements. Ad Hoc Netw. **65**, 13–25 (2017)
4. Cunha, F., Villas, L., et al.: Data communication in VANETs: Protocols, applications and challenges. Ad Hoc Netw. **44**, 90–103 (2016)
5. Aravindhan, K., Kavitha, G., Dhas, C.S.G.: Plummeting data loss for multihop wireless broadcast using position based routing in VANET. In: International Conference on IEEE Science Engineering and Management Research (ICSEMR), pp. 1–5 (2014)
6. Wisitpongphan, N., Tonguz, O.K., et al.: Broadcast storm mitigation techniques in vehicular ad hoc networks. IEEE Wirel. Commun. **6**(14), 84–94 (2008)
7. Wu, C., Ohzahata, S., Ji, Y., Kato, T.: Multi-hop broadcasting in VANETs integrating intra-flow and inter-flow network coding. In: Proceedings of the Eightieth IEEE Vehicular Technology Conference (VTC2014-Fall), pp. 1–6 (2014)
8. Meneguette, R.I., Boukerche, A., et al.: A self-adaptive data dissemination solution for intelligent transportation systems. In: Proceedings of the Eleventh ACM Symposium on Performance Evaluation of Wireless Ad Hoc, Sensor, & Ubiquitous Networks, PE-WASUN 2014, pp. 69–76 (2014)
9. Akabane, A.T., Villas, L.A., Madeira, E.R.M.: An adaptive solution for data dissemination under diverse road traffic conditions in urban scenarios. In: Proceedings of the 2015 IEEE Wireless Communications and Networking Conference (WCNC), pp. 1654–1659 (2015)

10. Rayeni, M.S., Hafid, A., Sahu, P.K.: Dynamic spatial partition density-based emergency message dissemination in VANETs. Veh. Commun. **2**(4), 208–222 (2015)
11. Gonzalez, S., Ramos, V.: Fast-OB-VAN: a fast opportunistic broadcast protocol for VANETs. In: Proceedings of the Ninth International Conference on Next Generation Mobile Applications, Services and Technologies, pp. 114–119 (2015)

Soft Island Model for Population-Based Optimization Algorithms

Shakhnaz Akhmedova, Vladimir Stanovov[✉], and Eugene Semenkin

Reshetnev Siberian State University of Science and Technology,
"Krasnoyarskiy Rabochiy" av. 31, 660037 Krasnoyarsk, Russia
shahnaz@inbox.ru,
{vladimirstanovov, eugenesemenkin}@yandex.ru

Abstract. Population-based optimization algorithms adopt a regular network as topologies with one set of potential solutions, which may encounter the problem of premature convergence. In order to improve the performance of optimization techniques, this paper proposes a soft island model topology. The initial population is virtually separated into several subpopulations, and the connection between individuals from subpopulations is probabilistic. The workability of the proposed model was demonstrated through its implementation to the Particle Swarm Optimization and Differential Evolution algorithms and their modifications. Experiments were conducted on benchmark functions taken from the CEC'2017 competition. The best parameters for the new topology adaptation mechanism were found. Results verify the effectiveness of the population-based algorithms with the proposed model when compared with the same algorithms without the model. It was established that by applying this topology adaptation mechanism, the population-based algorithms are able to balance their exploitation and exploration abilities during the search process.

Keywords: Island model · Population-based algorithms · Optimization
Particle swarm optimization · Differential evolution

1 Introduction

Many real-world problems in engineering and related areas can be reduced to optimization problems, which usually have many local optima, so it is difficult to find their global optima. For solving such problems, researchers have presented many methods in recent years and population-based algorithms are among them [1]. Such algorithms do not require any properties of the objective function (for instance, gradient information). Therefore, more attention has been paid to population-based algorithms, and many effective algorithms have been presented, including Differential Evolution (DE) [2] and Particle Swarm Optimization (PSO) [3].

Although population-based algorithms have been applied successfully in solving many difficult optimization problems, for example [4], they also have difficulties in keeping the balance between exploration and exploitation when solving complex multimodal problems. In order to achieve better performance for population-based algorithms, various modifications of the existing algorithms and also new techniques have been developed.

In this paper, the problem of premature convergence and search diversification was solved by dividing the initial population into several subgroups. All subgroups communicate with each other with some probability, while each subpopulation has its own current best found solution and other necessary features, depending on the population-based algorithm. The developed technique was called the 'Soft Island Model' or SIM. The SIM approach was applied to the mentioned PSO and DE algorithms and their variants. The efficiency of the mentioned algorithms with or without the soft island model implementation was examined on test problems from the CEC'2017 competition [5]. Experimental results demonstrated an improvement of their work with the soft island model compared to the original versions.

Therefore, in this paper firstly the soft island model is described, and the population-based algorithms used in this study to prove its usefulness are listed. Then brief descriptions of the mentioned population-based algorithms, namely of the PSO and the DE algorithms and their modifications, are presented. In the next section, the experimental results obtained by both the used population-based algorithms with the soft island model and the same algorithms without the model are discussed. After that, the best parameters for the proposed soft island model were found. Finally, some conclusions are given in the last section.

2 Soft Island Model

In this study, the soft island model (SIM) for improving the search diversity is introduced. The key concept of the proposed technique SIM is that the initial population is virtually separated into several subpopulations, and the connection between individuals from the different subpopulations or islands is probabilistic. More specifically, each island (subpopulation), when performing various operations on individuals, has a higher probability of choosing individuals for these operations from the current island than from other islands. The operations to be performed depend on the optimization technique nature, as well as the features of each subpopulation that should exist for each particular algorithm to work, for example, the best found solution.

The soft island model can be described with the following pseudo-code:

```
Let the number of islands be M
The islands are I = {I_k}, where k = 1, ... , M
The probability to choose a solution from current
island: P - equal for all islands
For individual i in the population:
          Let i belong to I_k
          Generate a random number R from the range
          [0,1]
          Individuals required for operation: Ind =
          {Ind_j}, where j = 1, ..., H; H depends on the
          algorithm
          For the every Ind_j:
            If R < P then:
              Choose Ind_j from I_k
            Else:
              Choose Ind_j from I\I_k
          End For
          Perform algorithm-specific operations with
          chosen Ind
End For.
```

The individuals can be assigned to islands in any convenient manner, depending on the algorithm. In case of an operation requiring several individuals, each of them can be chosen from either the current island with a probability P or any island with a probability $1 - P$.

The soft island model implements migration implicitly in a probabilistic manner, specifically, the islands exchange information, and the information rate exchange depends on the locality of each island. The migration strategy depends on the operators used by the population-based algorithm. If the probability P is set to 1.0, then the exchange between islands is eliminated, resulting in the optimization problem being simply solved several times.

Let us consider several examples of SIM realization for the Differential Evolution (DE) [2] and Particle Swarm Optimization (PSO) [3] algorithms. In the case of DE, the main operator is mutation, which may use several randomly chosen individuals from the population. The typical DE strategies are rand/1, rand/2, best/1, best/2 and target-to-best/1 [6]. Also in this study, the soft island model was applied to the following variants of the PSO algorithm in addition to the original version: Gaussian PSO [7], Cauchy and Gaussian-Based PSO [8], PSOs with linear- and exponent-decreasing inertia coefficient [9, 10] and PSO with the simulated annealing inertia coefficient [11].

3   Population-Based Optimization Algorithms

As was mentioned before, the Particle Swarm Optimization (PSO) [2] and the Differential Evolution (DE) [3] algorithms (and their various modifications) were used for the experiments. These algorithms were chosen due their high performance on various optimization problems. Besides, both of them lay the foundations for different biology-inspired algorithms (in the case of PSO) and evolutionary algorithms (in the case of DE). Thus, in this section brief descriptions of the considered population-based algorithms for solving the optimization problems to which the soft island model was applied are presented.

Particle Swarm Optimization or PSO is an optimization technique inspired by the social behaviour of bird flocking and fish schooling in search of food and was originally developed by Eberhart and Kennedy in 1995. The PSO algorithm is well-known for its easy implementation, robustness to control parameters and computation efficiency compared with other existing heuristic algorithms such as a genetic algorithm in a continuous problem.

In the original version of the PSO approach, each individual (or particle) modifies its movement according to its own experience and the experience of its neighbouring particle. Each particle is described by its coordinates in the search space (position) and velocity. Therefore, two equations are used in the PSO algorithm: the position update equation and the velocity update equation [2]. The position and velocity of the particle change in each iteration of the PSO algorithm to converge the optimum solution.

The most commonly used PSO variants consist in the modification of the inertia weight or the position update equation, for example [9, 10] or [11]. However, there are studies, for example [7], which suggested that a Gaussian distribution could be used in the PSO position update rule. In addition, a PSO model that employs both Cauchy and Gaussian distributions for sampling was later proposed [8].

Differential evolution (DE) is the continuous optimization technique first introduced by Price and Storn in 1997 [3]. Over the last 20 years, it has become one of the most popular and often prize-winning optimization techniques due to its simplicity in implementation and several important features. As with other biology-inspired methods, DE is a population-based algorithm, and the population contains a number of solutions. One of the main features of DE is the mutation scheme, which was shown to automatically adapt to the scale of the optimized function, improving the performance. The algorithm also contains crossover and selection schemes, which will be briefly described.

The key idea of differential evolution is in constructing a mutant vector using the difference between two other vectors from the current population. There are several popular mutations schemes, each having different behaviour, namely DE/rand/1, DE/rand/2, DE/best/1, DE/best/2, DE/target-to-best/1 (DE/current-to-best/1) [6] and many others.

There are various modifications of the DE algorithm, including jDE [12], JADE [13], SHADE [14], L-SHADE [15] and many others, which mainly focus on the control parameter and population size adaptation. However, here we will only consider basic algorithms and their performance when using the soft island model concept. The listed modifications could also be used with SIM.

4 Experimental Results

Applying SIM to population-based algorithms requires some modifications of these algorithms. First of all, if the algorithm uses the best solution in the population, this best solution has to be different for each island. So, in the PSO algorithm with SIM, each island has its own local best solution, and during the particle velocity calculation, the choice of the best solution to follow is probabilistic: with the locality probability of P, the best solution from the current island is chosen, otherwise it is chosen from any other island.

In the case of DE, for DE/rand/1 and DE/rand/2, the random indexes $r1 - r5$ could be chosen from either the current island or another island with the probability P. For DE/best/1, DE/best/2 and DE/current-to-best/1, the best solutions could also be chosen from other islands.

The two main parameters of the SIM are the number of islands and the locality probability P. To discover the influence of these two parameters on the algorithm efficiency, a number of experiments have been performed using CEC'2017 optimization problems [5] introduced in the competitions for bound-constrained continuous optimization. In these experiments, only problems with a dimension of 10 were used.

For all variants of PSO and DE, firstly the classical algorithms, i.e. 1 island, were tested; and then the algorithms with 2, 3, 4, and 5 islands. The locality probability for 2 islands was tested from 0.5 to 1.0 with a 0.05 step. For 3 and more islands, the probability changed from 0.35 to 1.0 with a 0.05 step. Note that the probability of 1.0 means that there is no exchange between islands, i.e. this corresponds to solving the optimization problem several times with a smaller population size.

The population size for DE was set to 150, and the individuals belonging to islands did not change during the optimization process. The total number of fitness calculations available for all algorithms was equal to 100,000.

To measure the efficiency of the possible variants of the soft island model, 51 tests for all 30 test functions have been performed. The difference between the function value at the optimum and the achieved function value in the best found position is used as the efficiency measure. The median value over 51 tests on each function and mean value over all functions were calculated. Figure 1 shows the resulting efficiency for three DE mutation strategies, namely best/1, best/2 and target-to-best/1 for 2, 3, 4 and 5 islands; Fig. 2 shows the results for rand/1 and rand/2 strategies for the same number of islands.

Increasing the locality of each island improves the efficiency of the three first variants of DE, which will be observed by the overall trend for these algorithms. The probability value of around 0.90–0.95 appears to be the best choice for all mutation strategies, while the probability of 1.0 (independent islands) results in a significant loss of efficiency.

For two other variants of DE which do not have a separate best solution saved for each island, it can be observed that the probability of 1.0 is better than any other probability value. This is due to the nature of these mutation strategies, which are focused on exploration, rather than exploitation. Allowing the islands to be independent and having a smaller island size improves the exploitation abilities simply due to the fact that this is the same as restarting the algorithm several times.

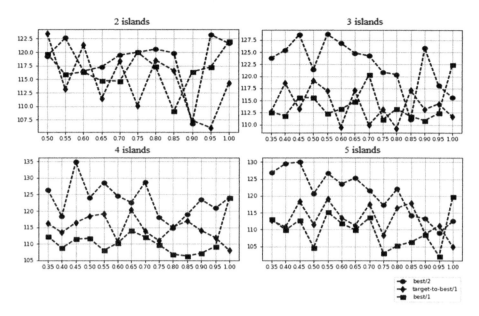

Fig. 1. DE efficiency for different numbers of islands and different probabilities, strategies DE/best/1, DE/best/2 and DE/target-to-best/1.

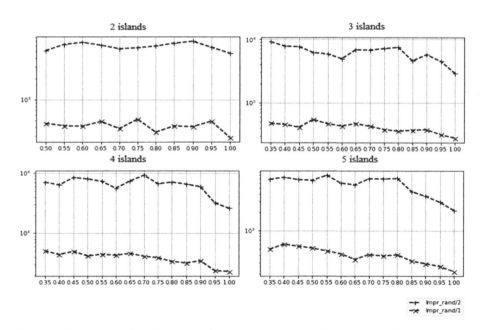

Fig. 2. DE efficiency for different numbers of islands and different probabilities, strategies DE/rand/1 and DE/rand/2.

In addition to considering averaged values, also the Mann-Whitney statistical tests ($p = 0.01$) have been performed to estimate if there was really a significant improvement in the efficiency of each algorithm. For this purpose, statistical tests comparing the basic algorithm with one island with all the other SIM variants separately for all 30 functions have been performed. After this, the number of functions with significant improvement according to the statistical test was calculated. The improvement was determined as the number of cases where the efficiency significantly increased minus the number of cases where the efficiency significantly dropped. Figure 3 shows the graphs for the differential evolution.

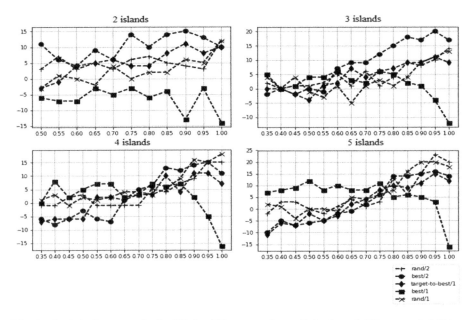

Fig. 3. Statistical tests results for DE for different numbers of islands and different probabilities, all mutation strategies.

The figures show that the overall trend is that increasing the locality of islands for most mutation strategies significantly improves the performance of most algorithms. However, the DE/best/1 strategy seems to suffer from a lack of exploration possibilities, because increasing the probability over 0.8 results in a loss in efficiency. This can be explained by the behaviour of the mutation strategy: it tends to search around the best solution and, as a result, often stagnates next to the local optima. It may also be observed that, for example, in the case of 4 or 5 islands, DE/best/1 is better than a single island algorithm for small probabilities because the SIM provides several best solutions to follow with an almost identical probability.

As for other mutation schemes, including DE/best/2, which appears to be more robust, the probabilities of 0.9-0.95 are the best available choice. Increasing the probability to the maximum value of 1.0 usually leads to a drop in efficiency for all algorithms and numbers of islands. This happens due to the need of islands to exchange information in order to balance exploration and exploitation.

The next series of experiments was performed for the PSO algorithms. The experimental setup was the same, and as long as all the used PSO variants have star topology in their base, for the SIM operation each island had its own best solution. During the particle position change, there is a chance to select the best solution from either the current island with a locality probability, or from any other island.

The averaged median values over all runs and all functions are presented in Fig. 4. For all PSO variants the trend is similar to the one that had been observed for DE: a larger locality of islands results in better solutions being received by the algorithms. The probability of 0.9−0.95 seems like an optimal solution for all PSO variants. At the same time, increasing the probability to 1.0 and making islands independent results in a lower overall performance.

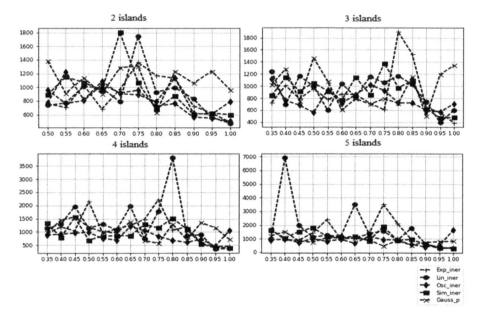

Fig. 4. PSO efficiency for different numbers of islands and different probabilities.

The performed statistical tests for PSO present a different picture (Fig. 5): increasing the number of islands usually gives better performance even with a small number of islands. This can be observed even for small probability values, though not for all the PSO variants.

With large numbers of islands, for example 5 islands, which corresponds to a topology, when every island has weak connections to other islands and has the possibility to use their information about the best solution, a larger number of significant improvements when increasing the probability value was received.

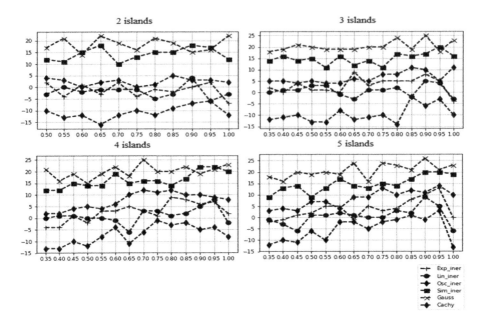

Fig. 5. Statistical tests results for PSO for different numbers of islands and different probabilities.

For Gauss PSO, improvements were achieved on 25 functions out of 30 for probability $P = 0.9$. As before, setting $P = 1.0$ significantly decreases the algorithm performance, which proves the importance of the modification.

5   Conclusions

In this paper, a novel island model, in which the interconnection between islands is probabilistic, i.e. there is no explicit migration operator, was presented. The locality of each island and, consequently, its connectivity level to other islands is controlled by a single parameter, the probability to choose a solution for the operation from another island. The SIM is relatively easy to implement, and it can be applied to any evolutionary, biology-inspired or other population-based optimization techniques, which require in their operators the use of several solutions at once. The experiments described in this study have shown that SIM allows higher performance rates to be achieved compared to the original algorithm, which was also proved by the Mann-Whitney statistical tests. The probability of 1.0 or close to 0.35−0.5 is worse than the probability of 0.9 or 0.95. It confirms that the observed improvement happens due to the fact that the larger probabilities allow information exchange to be limited, but without disabling it completely, which improves both the exploration and exploitation abilities of different algorithm schemes.

Further work for improving the SIM may include the automatic adjustment of the locality of each island, depending on their performance and similarity, dynamic island reallocation, applying islands of different types, the dynamic change of the type of islands and so on.

Acknowledgments. Research is performed with the support of the Ministry of Education and Science of the Russian Federation within State Assignment project № 2.1680.2017/ПЧ.

References

1. Eberhart, R., Shi, Y.: Computational Intelligence: Concepts to Implementations. Morgan Kaufmann, San Francisco (2007)
2. Kennedy, J., Eberhart, R.: Particle swarm optimization. In: IEEE International Conference on Neural networks, IV, pp. 1942–1948 (1995)
3. Storn, R., Price, K.: Differential evolution – a simple and efficient heuristic for global optimization over continuous spaces. J. Global Optim. **11**(4), 341–359 (1997)
4. Ryzhikov, I., Brester, Ch., Semenkin, E.: A multi-objective approach with a restart meta-heuristic for the linear dynamical systems inverse mathematical problem. Int. J. Inf. Technol. Secur. **10**(1), 93–102 (2018)
5. Awad, N.H., Ali, M.Z., Liang, J.J., Qu, B.Y., Suganthan, P.N.: Problem Definitions and Evaluation Criteria for the CEC 2017 Special Session and Competition on Single Objective Bound Constrained Real-Parameter Numerical Optimization. Technical Report, Nanyang Technological University, Singapore (2016)
6. Das, S., Mullick, S.S., Suganthan, P.N.: Recent advances in differential evolution - an updated survey. Swarm Evol. Comput. **27**, 1–30 (2016)
7. Kennedy, J.: Bare bones particle swarms. In: IEEE Swarm Intelligence Symposium, pp. 80–87 (2003)
8. Li, X., Yao, X.: Cooperatively coevolving particle swarms for large scale optimization. IEEE Trans. Evol. Comput. **16**(2), 210–224 (2012)
9. Xin, J., Chen, G., Hai, Y.: A particle swarm optimizer with multistage linearly-decreasing inertia weight. In: International Joint Conference on Computational Sciences and Optimization, vol. 1, pp. 505–508 (2009)
10. Li, H.R., Gao, Y.L.: Particle swarm optimization algorithm with exponent decreasing inertia weight and stochastic mutation. In: Second International Conference on Information and Computing Science, pp. 66–69 (2009)
11. Al-Hassan, W., Fayek, M.B., Shaheen, S.I.: PSOSA: an optimized particle swarm technique for solving the urban planning problem. In: International Conference on Computer Engineering and Systems, pp. 401–405 (2007)
12. Brest, J., Greiner, S., Bošković, B., Mernik, M., Žumer, V.: Self-adapting control parameters in differential evolution: a comparative study on numerical benchmark problems. IEEE Trans. Evol. Comput. **10**(6), 646–657 (2006)
13. Zhang, J., Sanderson, A.C.: JADE: adaptive differential evolution with optional external archive. IEEE Trans. Evol. Comput. **13**(5), 945–958 (2009)
14. Tanabe R., Fukunaga, A.: Success-history based parameter adaptation for differential evolution. In: IEEE Congress on Evolutionary Computation, pp. 71–78 (2013)
15. Tanabe, R., Fukunaga, A.: Improving the search performance of shade using linear population size reduction. In: IEEE Congress on Evolutionary Computation, pp. 1658–1665 (2014)

A Smart Initialization on the Swarm Intelligence Based Method for Efficient Search of Optimal Minimum Energy Design

Tun-Chieh Hsu[1] and Frederick Kin Hing Phoa[2(✉)]

[1] Department of Statistical Science, Duke University, Durham, USA
[2] Institute of Statistical Science, Academia Sinica, Taipei, Taiwan
fredphoa@stat.sinica.edu.tw

Abstract. Swarm intelligence is well-known to enjoy fast convergence towards optimum. Recently, the Swarm Intelligence Based (SIB) method was proposed to deal with discrete optimization problems in mathematics and statistics. Whether it was the traditional framework or the augmented version, the initialization of the particles were always done randomly. In this work, we introduced a smart initialization procedure to improve the computational efficiency of the SIB method. We demonstrated the use of the SIB method, initialized by both the uniform pool (standard procedure) and the MCMC pool (smart initialization), on the search of optimal minimum energy designs, which were a new class of designs for computer experiments that considered uneven or functional gradients on the search domain. We compared two initialization approaches and showed that the SIB method with smart initialization could save much experimental resources and obtain better optimal solutions within equivalent number of iterations or time.

Keywords: Swarm Intelligence Based (SIB) method
Smart initialization · Minimum energy designs (MEDs)
Computer experiments · Nature-inspired metaheuristic algorithm

1 Introduction

In the past few years, there was a debate between spending long computing time to obtain the best results and spending short computing time to obtain adequately good results. For most practical problems in our real world, most leaned on the latter position for cost efficiency. Nature-inspired metaheuristic algorithms attempted to solve complicated optimization problems from natural inspirations via simulating the composition, evolution, thinking, foraging and many other behaviors of human, nature or animals [1]. Swarm intelligence, a major class of metaheuristics, referred to the concept intrigued by the natural collective behavior of decentralized, self-organized system. Particle Swarm

© Springer International Publishing AG, part of Springer Nature 2018
Y. Tan et al. (Eds.): ICSI 2018, LNCS 10941, pp. 78–87, 2018.
https://doi.org/10.1007/978-3-319-93815-8_9

Optimization [2], Shuffled Frog Leaping [3], Artificial Bee Colony [4] and many others belonged to this class. Although these state-of-the-art algorithms were widely used in many engineering problems for decades, they were not popular in traditional optimization problems in mathematics and statistics mainly because of the discrete domain.

[5] proposed a new nature-inspired metaheuristic optimization method called the Swarm Intelligence Based (SIB) method. It apparently worked well in discrete optimization problems in mathematics and statistics, such as the search of circulant partial Hadamard matrices with maximum number of columns [6], the optimal $E(s^2)$ supersaturated designs [7] and the optimal Latin hypercube design under multiple objectives [8]. It also worked well in engineering problems with continuous domain, like an efficient construction of confidence regions for target localization [9]. Recently, an augmented version of the SIB method, namely the SIB 2.0, was proposed with the ability to change the particle sizes during the optimization procedure, it was applied to some timely problems like irregular-shaped community detection and change point analysis [10].

The SIB method inherited an excellent divide-and-conquer property from most swarm intelligence approaches, and this property allowed the algorithm to compute efficiently via parallel computing [11]. However, due to the curse of dimensionality, the algorithm could not be efficient when the search domain or the number of possible solutions was too large to handle. This work aims at providing a remedy to effectively improve the efficiency of the SIB method via a smart initialization. We demonstrate this remedy by searching a new class of computer experimental design called the minimum energy design.

The rest of this paper was organized as follows. We introduced the minimum energy design in Sect. 2. Then we recalled some basic concepts of the SIB method and proposed the smart initialization in Sect. 3. We applied the new SIB method to search for the best designs in Sect. 4. We provided some concluding remarks in the last section.

2   Minimum Energy Design (MED): An Introduction

Modern experiments were capable of investigating large-scale systems with complex response surface, but the cost reduction in terms of time, labor and other monetary resources became the key issues for the design of experiments to achieve cost-efficiency. Researches in experimental designs recently focused on computer experiments, but it was nontrivial to assure if the deterministic computer codes and the corresponding surrogate models accurately capture most variability of the responses and represent actual systems respectively. As a result, the initialization to assign representative and meaningful samples became a recent focus to the statisticians. Space filling designs attempted to assign samples to cover the available domain as apart as possible, aiming at gaining maximum insights from the domain using the fewest number of samples. Such designs became useful in complex meta-modeling [12] such as Krigin [13]. Extended studies of such designs were referred to [14].

An underlying assumption behind the formulation of traditional space filling designs was that the domain is always flat or follows a constant function. However, some non-constant functions might be imposed in the domain in reality. Traditional space filling designs lacked the ability to incorporate this information, and thus failed to achieve optimal uniformity accordingly. This led to the birth of Minimum Energy Design (MED), which was a new kind of space filling design proposed in [15]. Unlike traditional space filling designs, MED was able to adapt different types of design region and objective. It used a physical system analogy of electrical particles inside a box to motivate the design. The particles with the same charge repelled each other and occupied the positions where the total potential energy among the system could be minimized. This repulsive characteristics connected the MED to the famous maximin distance design proposed in [16].

Following [15], a MED D with its design points $\{x_1, \ldots, x_n\}$ was optimal if it satisfied the criterion

$$\max_{D} \min_{i,j} \frac{d(x_i, x_j)}{q(x_i)q(x_j)}. \tag{1}$$

and the charge function was defined as

$$q(x) = \frac{1}{\{f(x)\}^{1/(2p)}}. \tag{2}$$

where $f(x)$ was a desired density of the representative samples or the underlying domain function. This formulation was inspired from the potential energy between two particles. The detailed description of the formulation was referred to [15]. The optimization procedure of MED was computationally difficult or sometimes infeasible within reasonable time frame, so we proposed to tackle via the SIB method.

3   Swarm Intelligence Based Method and the Smart Initialization

We briefly review each step of the SIB method proposed in [5] below.

0: Randomly generate a set of initial particles.
   Evaluate objective function value of each particle.
   Initialize the local best (LB) for all particles and the global best (GB).
1: For each particle, perform the MIX operation.
2: For each particle, perform the MOVE operation
3: Evaluate the objective function value of each particle
4: Update the LB for all particles and the GB.
5: If the updated value is not converge or the algorithm does not reach the setting iterations, repeat Step 1 to Step 4.

Prior to the initialization step, several parameters and information were required, including the stopping criteria, the swarm size N, and the numbers of exchanges with the local best (LB) particle q_{LB} and the global best (GB) particle q_{GB}. Then N initial particles were generated from a random pool of particle units and objective function values were calculated, then the LB and GB particles were defined accordingly.

The MIX operation was a unit exchange procedure. To exchange with the LB (or GB) particle, the units in the current particle was first ranked and the worst q_{LB} (or q_{GB}) units with the least contribution to the objective function values were deleted. Then the best q_{LB} (or q_{GB}) units from the LB (or GB) particle were added to the reduced particle. Therefore, the MIX operation creates two hybrid particles for the MOVE operation to compare with the current particle in terms of the objective function values. If either best particle was the best among three, it was updated as the current particle in the next iteration. If the current particle was still the best, some random components were added to the reduced particle to form a new hybrid particle. The latter step ensures the particle to escape from the local attractor. The search continued until the objective function value reached its optimum or the number of iteration hit its limit.

As discussed in [5], there were several settings that governed the computational efficiency of the SIB method. It included the initial number of seeds, the domain size and the number of unit exchanges with the best particles. It was obvious that the larger initial number of seeds the faster the convergence to the optimum, and the smaller the domain size the faster the convergence to the optimum. It was an art to pick the adequate unit number of exchanges with the best particles, and it required domain knowledge from the field experts. If one chose the number to be too small, the convergence rate would be too slow to the optimum. However, the particles would easily trap in local attractors if one chose the number to be too large.

[5] did not mention that there was another key setting of governing computational efficiency. It was the method of selecting the initial units and the formation of the sample pool. Whether it was the traditional SIB method or the SIB 2.0, the sample pool was always the complete possible set and the selection of initial units to form a particle was always done randomly. It was similar to imposing a uniform sampling on a group of numbers that was known in prior to follow a specific distribution.

We propose in this work a smart initialization step that overwrites the random selection of units for creating initial particles. It is not a defined step but a concept. One can perform a screening-like procedure to pick the potentially useful units in prior, or one can impose different weights or probabilities on all units. The key idea is to select units not equally by utilizing some prior knowledge or information. This new step may spend slightly additional computational time before the traditional first step is performed, but it is usually worth to do as the time of convergence towards optimum can be shortened significantly, or better results can be obtained under the same amount of computational time. We demonstrate this idea via the search of optimal MED in the next section.

4 A Search of Optimal Minimum Energy Designs via Swarm Intelligence

In this section, we take the two-dimensional probability distribution with banana-shaped contour discussed in [17] as a demonstration. The density function was given by

$$f_B = f_d \circ \phi_B \tag{3}$$

where f_d is the density of a d-dimensional multivariate normal distribution, $N(0, diag(100, 1, 1, ..., 1))$, and $\phi_B(x_1, \ldots, x_d) = (x_1, x_2 + Bx_1^2 - 100B, x_3, \ldots, x_d)$ with constant $B > 0$. Thus,

$$f_B(x_1, \ldots, x_d) \propto \exp(\frac{-x_1^2}{200} - \frac{1}{2}(x_2 + Bx_1{}^2 - 100B)^2 - \frac{1}{2}(x_3^2 + x_4^2 + ... + x_d^2). \tag{4}$$

The dimension and constant was chosen as $d = 2$ and $B = 0.03$ for demonstration purposes.

We first proposed the SIB algorithm to search for optimal MED:

0: (Random or Smart) Generate a set of initial MEDs.
   Evaluate (1) of each MED.
   Initialize the local best (LB) for all MEDs and the global best (GB).
1: For each MED, perform the MIX operation.
2: For each MED, perform the MOVE operation.
3: Evaluate (1) of each updated MED.
4: Update the LB for all MEDs and the GB.
5: If the algorithm does not reach the setting iterations, repeat Step 1 to Step 4.

In Step 0, the initial MEDs were generated by two different approaches and we compared the performance of these two approaches. The first approach was the "random" initialization that commonly used in the standard SIB method. We first defined the objective function as Eq. 1, where Eq. 4 was considered as the $f(x)$ shown in Eq. 2. Then we set up the candidate pool by generating 10000 banana-shaped random samples uniformly scattered in the experimental region $[-20, -20] \times [-10, 5]$. We called it the "Uniform Pool" in the rest of the paper. After the optimization was performed via the SIB method, these scattered points eventually converged to the ideal banana-shaped distribution. Figure 1 illustrated the sample points that were well-spread over all region of the banana-shaped contour plot. This result successfully demonstrated that the SIB method could capture the characteristic of the density with only a few points, that greatly reduced the experimental and prediction costs in many industrial practices, especially each data point was expensive.

In the second approach, we cooperated prior knowledge of the density and "pre-selected" data points into the candidate pool via a Markov Chain Monte Carlo (MCMC) sampling method. On top of the standard MCMC framework, there were many extensions from MCMC algorithms that were widely used in statistical inference. We chose the adaptive MCMC algorithm to approximate the

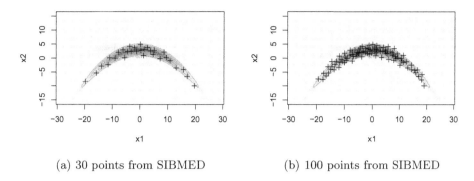

(a) 30 points from SIBMED   (b) 100 points from SIBMED

Fig. 1. Different amount of banana-shaped random samples generated from SIBMED method with 50 iterations.

data distribution by automatically earning better parameter values of MCMC algorithms while they ran. Readers could refer to [17,18] for detailed introduction and method comparison. The smart initialization via unit "pre-selection" sharpened the focus of the search domain that followed the target distribution, and ensured that the random jump would not deviate too much for the target distribution. We set up the candidate pool by pre-selecting 10000 data points via adaptive MCMC sampling that were distributed in a banana shape shown in Fig. 2.

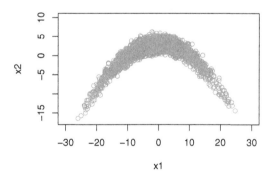

Fig. 2. The initiated MCMC pool

We call it the "MCMC Pool" in the rest of the paper. After the optimization was performed via the SIB method, these pre-selected points also converged to the ideal banana-shaped distribution illustrated in Fig. 3.

It was not trivial to observe the difference of data point distributions between Figs. 1 and 3. In fact, both the uniform pool and the MCMC pool were capable of generating representative sampling points, but samples from the MCMC pool had certain advantages in terms of extreme-point representations, energy value

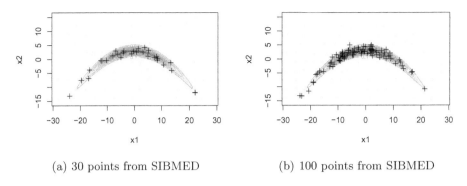

(a) 30 points from SIBMED   (b) 100 points from SIBMED

Fig. 3. Different amount of banana-shaped random samples generated from SIBMED using MCMC pool with 50 iterations.

and computational efficiency. First, under the same number of iterations, the SIBMED initialized via the MCMC pool successfully generates samples from two corners of the banana shapes when the MCMC pool is used in the initialization, but the SIBMED initialized via the uniform pool fails to do so. This difference is shown in the existence of samples in Fig. 3 but not in Fig. 1. In order to craft the complete shape of the function, it is actually important to include a few samples from the extreme regions, which are the regions that have very small but nonzero probability for samples to exist. Failure to do so may alter the true shape of the function.

Figure 4 recorded the performance of two initialization approaches. The left figure showed the decrease of energy values when the number of iteration increased. It was clear that the energy decreased more quickly when the MCMC pool was used than that when the uniform pool was used. In particular, the SIB initialized by the uniform pool required 30 iterations to obtain a MED with energy value -1.13, but the SIB initialized by the MCMC pool required only 10 iterations to obtain a MED with energy value -1.11, and it decreased to -1.17 with 20 iterations. This showed that given a fixed number of iteration, the SIB initialized by the MCMC pool could obtain a MED with lower energy value. One might argue that the time for one iteration in two approaches might not be the same. The right figure compared the time and iteration of two approaches. It was natural to see an increasing trend on time when the number of iteration increased. Although the time spent in the first 20 iterations were close for two approaches, the SIB initialized by the MCMC pool clearly spent less time than that initialized by the uniform pool to finish a single process.

In practice, one may likely be interested in how two pools are performed on minimizing the energy of the MEDs in terms of computing time (in minutes), which is shown in Table 1. Notice that the lower the energy, the better the space-filling property of the MED. It is obvious that the computing time is much lower when MCMC pool is used. The last row of the table shows the efficiency ratio when comparing the computing time spent when MCMC pool is used instead of the uniform pool. We define it as the ratio of computing time between the MCMC

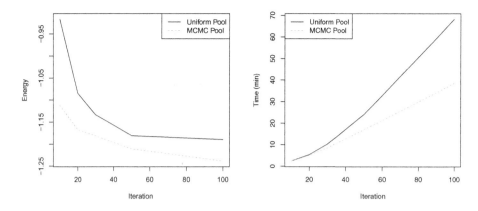

Fig. 4. The potential energy and converging time when generating 30 samples.

Table 1. Energy of designs and computing time using different pools

Pool	Energy			
	-1.10	-1.14	-1.18	-1.20
Uniform pool	7.3	11.2	24.1	68.1
MCMC pool	2.4	4.0	8.6	16.1
Efficiency ratio	32.88%	35.71%	35/68%	23.64%

pool (numerator) and the uniform pool (denominator). To obtain a MED that achieves a certain level of energy, the computing times being used in MCMC pool are only 20–35% of those used in uniform pool. This shows the efficiency of using MCMC pool in conjunction to the SIB method in the problem of optimization.

5   Discussion and Conclusion

The main contribution of this work was to introduce a smart initialization procedure to improve the computational efficiency of the SIB method. This new procedure could be applied universally in all forms of the SIB method, or perhaps some other nature-inspired metaheuristics algorithms. We demonstrated the use of the SIB method, initialized by both the uniform pool (standard procedure) and the MCMC pool (smart initialization), on the search of optimal minimum energy designs (MEDs). This class of designs was useful and more realistic when a computer experiment with uneven or functional gradient was imposed on the solution domain. A comparison between two initialization approaches showed that the SIB method initialized by the MCMC pool could save much experimental resources and obtain better MEDs.

There were still several potential improvements from this work. For example, although we demonstrated the adaptability of the SIB method on the search of optimal MEDs to improve the computational efficiency by cooperating with prior knowledge as the smart initialization, the modification or selection of the prior knowledge could potentially be an important issue for investigation. A consideration of inappropriate pool might neglect the uncertainties and led to missing searches on important regions of the response surface. The topic of the candidate pool selection to improve efficiency without overlooking useful information was still under investigation.

There were several approaches for sampling from arbitrary distributions in the literature. The most simplest approach was the inverse probability transformation method. The sampling procedure started from taking a uniform sample u where $u \in [0, 1]$ and then returns the largest number x from the domain of the distribution $P(X)$ such that $P(-\infty < X < x) \leq u$. However, it required a close form expression and thus was of limited use when the inverse function did not exist or was difficult to obtain. An alternative approach was the Markov Chain Monte Carlo (MCMC) method, which approximated the target posterior distribution by drawing values of θ from the approximate distribution, then sequentially updating those draws according to the most recent value. However, the sampling results might not be as representative as what the SIB method obtained. Therefore, this work introduced the SIB method to search for optimal MED, which could be applied to obtain a representative sample from a complex density. In specific, MED was able to reconstruct underlying distribution by appropriately selecting the charge function, so that the sample points would stay as far apart as possible but still retained the feature of the distribution.

Acknowledgement. This work is supported by Career Development Award of Academia Sinica (Taiwan) grant number 103-CDA-M04 and the Ministry of Science and Technology (Taiwan) grant numbers 105-2118-M-001-007-MY2.

References

1. Gogna, A., Tayal, A.: Metaheuristics: review and application. J. Exp. Theor. Artif. Intell. **25**(4), 503–526 (2013)
2. Kennedy, J.: Particle swarm optimization. In: Gass, S.I., Fu, M.C. (eds.) Encyclopedia of Machine Learning, pp. 760–766. Springer, Boston (2011). https://doi.org/10.1007/978-1-4419-1153-7_200581
3. Eusuff, M., Lansey, K., Pasha, F.: Shuffled frog-leaping algorithm: a memetic metaheuristic for discrete optimization. Eng. Optim. **38**(2), 129–154 (2006)
4. Karaboga, D., Basturk, B.: A powerful and efficient algorithm for numerical function optimization: artificial bee colony (ABC) algorithm. J. Glob. Optim. **39**(3), 459–471 (2007)
5. Phoa, F.K.H.: A Swarm Intelligence Based (SIB) method for optimization in designs of experiments. Nat. Comput. **16**, 597–605 (2017)
6. Phoa, F.K.H., Lin, Y.-L., Wang, T.-C.: Using swarm intelligence to search for circulant partial hadamard matrices. In: Tan, Y., Shi, Y., Coello, C.A.C. (eds.) ICSI 2014. LNCS, vol. 8794, pp. 158–164. Springer, Cham (2014). https://doi.org/10.1007/978-3-319-11857-4_18
7. Phoa, F.K.H., Chen, R.B., Wang, W.C., Wong, W.K.: Optimizing two-level supersaturated designs via swarm intelligence techniques. Technometrics **58**, 43–49 (2016)

8. Phoa, F.K.H., Chang, L.L.N.: A multi-objective implementation in swarm intelligence with application in design of computer experiments. In: Proceedings of ICNC-FSKD 2016, pp. 253–258 (2016)
9. Lin, F.P.C., Phoa, F.K.H.: An efficient construction of confidence regions via swarm intelligence and its application in target localization. IEEE Access **6**, 8610–8618 (2017)
10. Phoa, F.K.H., Wang, T.C., Chang, L.L.N.: An augmented version of the swarm intelligence based method (SIB 2.0). Swarm and Evolutionary Computation, in revision (2018)
11. Lin, F.P.C., Phoa, F.K.H.: A performance study on SSD analysis with parallel programming between general purpose GPU and CPU. In: Proceedings of ISMSI 2017, pp. 1–5 (2017)
12. Wang, G.G., Shan, S.: Review of metamodeling techniques in support of engineering design optimization. J. Mech. Des. **129**(4), 370–380 (2007)
13. Pronzato, L., Müller, W.G.: Design of computer experiments: space filling and beyond. Stat. Comput. **22**(3), 681–701 (2012)
14. Myers, R.H., Montgomery, D.C., Anderson-Cook, C.M.: Response Surface Methodology: Process and Product Optimization using Designed Experiments. Wiley, Hoboken (2016)
15. Joseph, V.R., Dasgupta, T., Tuo, R., Wu, C.F.J.: Sequential exploration of complex surfaces using minimum energy designs. Technometrics **57**(1), 64–74 (2015)
16. Johnson, M.E., Moore, L.M., Ylvisaker, D.: Minimax and maximin distance designs. J. Stat. Plann. Inference **26**(2), 131–148 (1990)
17. Haario, H., Saksman, E., Tamminen, J.: An adaptive metropolis algorithm. Bernoulli **7**, 223–242 (2001)
18. Roberts, G.O., Rosenthal, J.S.: Examples of adaptive MCMC. J. Comput. Graph. Stat. **18**(2), 349–367 (2009)

Ant Colony Optimization

On the Application of a Modified Ant Algorithm to Optimize the Structure of a Multiversion Software Package

M. V. Saramud$^{(\boxtimes)}$, I. V. Kovalev, V. V. Losev, M. V. Karaseva,
and D. I. Kovalev

Reshetnev Siberian State University of Science and Technology,
31 Krasnoyarsky Rabochy Av., Krasnoyarsk 660014, Russian Federation
msaramud@gmail.com

Abstract. The article considers the possibility of applying an optimization algorithm based on the behavior of an ant colony to the problem of forming a multiversion fault-tolerant software package. The necessary modifications of the basic algorithm and a model of graph construction for the implementation of the ant algorithm for the chosen problem are proposed. The optimization takes into account such features as cost, reliability and evaluation of the successful implementation of each version with the specified characteristics. A certain combination of versions in each module affects the characteristics of the module, and each characteristic of the module affects the characteristics of the system, so it is important to choose the optimal structure for each module to ensure the required characteristics of the system as a whole. The program system that implements the proposed algorithm is considered. The simulation results obtained with the help of the proposed software tool are considered. The results confirm the applicability of the ant algorithms to the problem of forming a multiversion software package, and they show their effectiveness.

Keywords: Ant algorithm · Multiversion programming · Software redundancy
Reliability · Optimization

1 Introduction

In recent years, industries that require reliable, fault-tolerant control systems i.e. high-technology industries [1], using composite and dangerous materials, autonomous unmanned objects, from multi-rotor systems delivering goods to vehicles with autopilot function are developing. Increasingly, the problem of developing fault-tolerant control systems becomes urgent. Nowadays the most relevant approach is N-version programming. N-version programming [2] offers parallel execution of N independently developed functionally equivalent versions with the selection of the correct output by the decision block, usually based on voting. Each N versions transmits the results to the decision block. The voting block accepts all N outputs as input data and uses them to determine the correct or the best output. As a rule, there is no need to interrupt the operation of the whole system while voting. To increase the fault tolerance of software systems, the software redundancy is introduced into them in the most important

© Springer International Publishing AG, part of Springer Nature 2018
Y. Tan et al. (Eds.): ICSI 2018, LNCS 10941, pp. 91–100, 2018.
https://doi.org/10.1007/978-3-319-93815-8_10

modules. There exist several such modules as a rule. In our example we will consider the software with 10 modules (m1–m10). Each module is a solution to a specific problem in the program that can be solved in various ways using different algorithms. We will assume that there exist 10 implementation types, i.e. 10 versions for each module. Each version has its own characteristics: cost of implementation, reliability and probability of successful implementation, i.e., the probability that it will be possible to implement a version with the chosen algorithms and functionality for the declared cost and it will have the predicted reliability. The last parameter is important for the risk evaluation to develop fault-tolerant systems. The characteristics are evaluated and determined on the basis of experience in this field, and, if it is necessary, a prototype method [3] could be used to obtain more reliable evaluation of the characteristics. A certain combination of versions in each module gives us the characteristics of the module, and each characteristic of the module affects the characteristics of the whole system, so it is important to choose the optimal structure of each module to provide the required characteristics to the system as a whole. The structure development of the multiversion software package is an important optimization problem that can be solved in various ways, from simple enumeration to the genetic algorithms getting the popularity recently. Thus, we proposed a method and tool for the software control by configuration of the components of the fault-tolerant software and the control system as a whole.

2 Ant Algorithm

Nowadays "natural algorithms" which are the optimization algorithms based on the natural ways of decision making are actively investigated by a lot of scientists [4]. One of those algorithms is the ant colony optimization algorithm (ACO) [5]. That algorithm is a result of the combined work of scientists who study the behavior of social insects and the IT specialists. The base of that algorithm is the ant behavior and their ability to find the shortest route to a food source.

An ant colony is a multiagent system. Despite the simplicity of its separate parts, that system can solve very sophisticated problems. Every single member of the colony tries to find the shortest route to a source of food. While doing that, it does not have an access to the knowledge of other members; therefore, there should be a way that can help them to combine their knowledge. The ant ability to mark a route with pheromones is a way to combine their knowledge. If an ant finds a source of food, it marks its route using pheromones on the way back to the colony. The other ants will use that signal while searching for food. The more pheromones are used to mark the route the higher probability that an ant will choose that route in his search for food is.

That mechanism of self-organization became a base for the ant colony algorithm. The main idea of the algorithm is that the agents having the behavior that models the behavior of ants are united into a set to solve the optimization problem. The agents coordinate their work with the help of stigmergy which is a mechanism of the indirect collaboration using the alterations in the common environment. In case of ACO that mechanism is pheromones. The agents mark the traversed path with the help of pheromones increasing the probability of choosing that route among other versions.

There is a mechanism which is known as the evaporation of the pheromones and it is used to prevent a situation when the algorithm goes irreversibly to the area of the local extremum. That mechanism is used to make the paths which were chosen as a solution by a mistake, less attractive by evaporating the pheromones on them. At the same time, the routes which were selected by agents during the decision making process will increase their attractiveness and that should lead to a situation where all the agents will select a general solution [6].

3 Modification of the Ant Algorithm

We have a problem concerning the graph according to which ants will move. Our case will differ from the traveling salesman problem that is often provided as an example of the ant algorithms operation [7, 8]. In our case, it will be a directed graph where an ant will receive M solutions according to the number of modules in the system; in this example this number is 10. Each time the arcs will represent all possible implementations of this module. The required number of versions for the multiversion voting is N > 2; we have only 10 types of versions. So we will consider all possible combinations of these versions in the module at N from 3 to 10. Each version can be included into the module only once, as the use of duplication in software systems does not make any sense unlike the duplication in hardware systems because we copy all the errors contained in it while copying the version [9]. Therefore, we cannot build a module from more than 10 non-repeating versions. We will take into account all theoretically possible combinations with the given constrains for a number of versions. The possible number of these combinations will be 968 for each module, i.e., an ant will choose from 968 arcs at each step at N from 3 to 10: {1;2;3}... {1;4;8;9;10}... {2;3;5;7;8;9}... {1;2;3;4;5;6;7;8;9;10}. The total number of the implementation versions of the system will be 968 m, where m is a number of modules in the system. To simplify the calculations checking, we take a structure of the software where all the modules from 1 to m are performed sequentially with the probability P = 1. It should be noted that the software implementation of our approach helps to specify any software structure due to a minor correction of the program code since the calculation of the system's characteristics is implemented as a separate function.

The weight of each arc will be calculated according to the formula

$$W_{ij} = \frac{(R * V)^{\beta}}{C}, \tag{1}$$

and the probability of the transition along this arc is

$$P_{ij} = \frac{\tau_{ij}^{\alpha} * W_{ij}}{\sum \left(\tau_{ij}^{\alpha} * W_{ij} \right)}, \tag{2}$$

where τ_{ij} is a value of the pheromone on this arc, $\alpha и \beta$ are coefficients that affect the operation of the algorithm: the larger α, the more the ant's solution depends on the pheromone level; the larger β, the larger the ant's solution depends on the weight of the arc [10]. It is important to note that in our case, the arc has no length as in the classical algorithm, and the weight is more of an inverse characteristic, i.e. the more weight, the more "attractive" the arc is.

In the classical model, when an ant traversed a route successfully it leaves a trace on all the passed edges inversely proportional to the length of the traversed route. In our implementation the pheromone value will increase by the set values in two cases: if an ant selects a structure that satisfies the constraints (for example, when optimizing according to the cost one should set constraints on minimum reliability and evaluation of successful implementation of the system) and in the case when a structure replaces the optimal solution. Further the given evaluation will be called as a successful ratio. This change was done due to the same number of edges traversed by all ants (according to the number of modules when each arc is a specific combination of versions in the module) and the absence of a length indicator replaced by a weight indicator. Moreover, the traces of the pheromone evaporate, i.e., the intensity of pheromone decreases on all the edges of each iteration of the algorithm. Thus, it is necessary to update the intensity values.

4   Software Implementation

Let's consider the software implementation of the proposed modified algorithm. Figure 1 shows the program interface and the optimization results of work at minimum cost and minimum system reliability of 0.95 and the minimum successful ratio of 0.95. It is possible to load version values from a file or generate values randomly with the help of this program. In case of random generation, all versions get a cost value from 15 to 200, the reliability from 0.60 to 0.99, the probability of successful implementation from 0.65 to 0.99. Randomly generated values can also be written to a file and used later. The form specifies the minimum and maximum version values, by default from 3 to 10; the program generates all possible combinations of 3, 4, 5, 6, 7, 8, 9, 10 non-repeating versions in the module. When the "Getweight" button is pressed, the cost, reliability and probability of successful implementation of all possible combinations of each module are calculated. For example, it is possible to take the first module, made up of the following versions $\{1; 2; 3\}$. The cost is calculated as $Cm1 = C11 + C12 + C13$, reliability is calculated as $Rm1 = R11 + (1–R11)*R12 + (1–(R11 + (1–R11)* R12))* R13$, the probability of successful implementation is calculated as $Vm1 = V11* V12* V13$.

Further all the necessary parameters are given on the form in order: the coefficients α and β affecting the calculation of the probability of the ant moving to the certain arc, pheromone evaporation rate after each iteration, a number of ants in each iteration, constraints according to the cost, reliability, successful ratio for optimization, the coefficients of increasing pheromones for routes that satisfy the constraints and route that replaced the global best solution, and the selection of the optimization regimes: maximum reliability, maximum successful ratio of the system, the maximum of their product, the minimum cost of the system implementation. It should be noted that to optimize according to the selected parameter, constraints by the remaining parameters

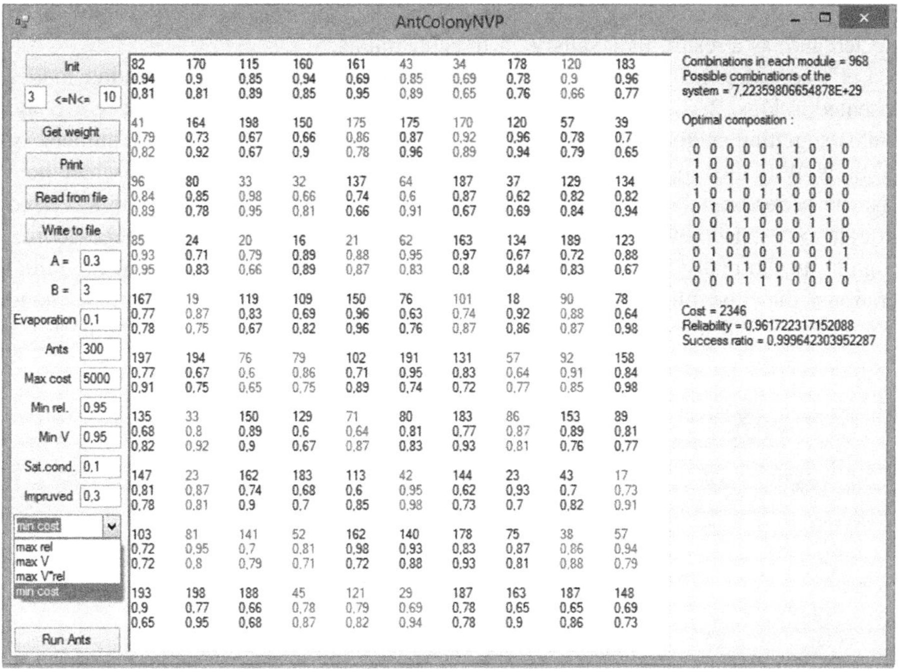

AntColonyNVP

Init	82	170	115	160	161	43	34	178	120	183
	0.94	0.9	0.85	0.94	0.69	0.85	0.69	0.78	0.9	0.96
3 <=N<= 10	0.81	0.81	0.89	0.85	0.95	0.89	0.65	0.76	0.66	0.77
Get weight	41	164	198	150	175	175	170	120	57	39
	0.79	0.73	0.67	0.66	0.86	0.87	0.92	0.96	0.78	0.7
Print	0.82	0.92	0.67	0.9	0.78	0.96	0.89	0.94	0.79	0.65
Read from file	96	80	33	32	137	64	187	37	129	134
	0.84	0.85	0.98	0.66	0.74	0.6	0.87	0.62	0.82	0.82
Write to file	0.89	0.78	0.95	0.81	0.66	0.91	0.67	0.69	0.84	0.94
	85	24	20	16	21	62	163	134	189	123
A = 0.3	0.93	0.71	0.79	0.89	0.88	0.95	0.97	0.67	0.72	0.88
	0.95	0.83	0.66	0.89	0.87	0.83	0.8	0.84	0.83	0.67
B = 3	167	19	119	109	150	76	101	18	90	78
Evaporation 0.1	0.87	0.87	0.83	0.69	0.96	0.63	0.74	0.92	0.88	0.64
	0.78	0.75	0.67	0.82	0.96	0.76	0.87	0.86	0.87	0.98
Ants 300	197	194	76	79	102	191	131	57	92	158
	0.77	0.67	0.6	0.86	0.71	0.95	0.83	0.64	0.91	0.84
Max cost 5000	0.91	0.75	0.65	0.75	0.89	0.74	0.72	0.77	0.85	0.98
	135	33	150	129	71	80	183	86	153	89
Min rel. 0.95	0.68	0.8	0.89	0.6	0.64	0.81	0.77	0.87	0.89	0.81
Min V 0.95	0.82	0.92	0.9	0.67	0.87	0.83	0.93	0.81	0.76	0.77
Sat.cond. 0.1	147	23	162	183	113	42	144	23	43	17
	0.81	0.87	0.74	0.68	0.6	0.95	0.62	0.93	0.7	0.73
Impruved 0.3	0.78	0.81	0.9	0.7	0.85	0.98	0.73	0.7	0.82	0.91
min cost	103	81	141	52	162	140	178	75	38	57
max rel	0.72	0.95	0.7	0.81	0.98	0.93	0.83	0.87	0.86	0.94
max V	0.72	0.8	0.79	0.71	0.72	0.88	0.93	0.81	0.88	0.79
min cost	193	198	188	45	121	29	187	163	187	148
	0.9	0.77	0.66	0.78	0.79	0.69	0.78	0.65	0.65	0.69
Run Ants	0.65	0.95	0.68	0.87	0.82	0.94	0.78	0.9	0.86	0.73

Combinations in each module = 968
Possible combinations of the
system = 7,22359805654878E+29

Optimal composition :

```
0 0 0 0 0 1 1 0 1 0
1 0 0 0 1 0 1 0 0 0
1 0 1 1 0 1 0 0 0 0
1 0 1 0 1 1 0 0 0 0
0 1 0 0 0 0 1 0 1 0
0 0 1 1 0 0 0 1 1 0
0 1 0 0 1 0 0 1 0 0
0 1 0 0 0 1 0 0 0 1
0 1 1 1 0 0 0 0 1 1
0 0 0 1 1 1 0 0 0 0
```

Cost = 2346
Reliability = 0,961722317152088
Success ratio = 0,999642303952287

Fig. 1. Result of work at optimizing by cost

are used; the constraint by the selected parameter is not checked, the program tries only to maximize (minimize) the parameter with the remaining constraints.

In the middle part of the form the characteristics of all versions for all modules are displayed, lines correspond to the modules, columns correspond to the versions, cost, reliability and probability of successful implementation are given for each version. On the right there is the output area of the calculation results. They are a number of possible combinations of versions for each module, a number of possible combinations of the system from the given number of modules, the selected optimal structure in the form of a matrix, characteristics of the system for the selected optimal structure. The cost of the whole system, its reliability and successful ratio are present. Also the parameters of the selected versions for each module are highlighted in red in the characteristics area of all available versions. Let's consider the result of cost the optimization presented in Fig. 1. It can be evident that the minimum number of versions required is 3 for the majority of modules. The optimal structure satisfies the constrains and gives the price of the system in 2346. It is possible to notice that not always the most successful versions are used if one studies the characteristics of all versions carefully. For example, version 8 for module 5 has a reliability of 0.92 at the cost of 18 and the probability of successful implementation is 0.86, but it is not selected. This leads to the conclusion that the resulting solution is not absolutely optimal and ants for the given number of iterations did not pass a more optimal route, but the resulting solution as a whole is acceptable and successful, since the majority of the cheapest and the most reliable versions have been selected and, as a result, they satisfy all the constraints.

Let's consider the results of the system operation in various optimization modes presented in Figs. 2, 3, 4. It is clear from the results that the algorithm works correctly; it allows getting a good structure of the system for a relatively small number of iterations. With the repeated starts of ants, the solution continues to improve when there exist the better branches in the neighborhood of the most successful of the traversed through routes. However, if any ants haven't traversed through the branches corresponding to the really optimal solution, or close to the optimal solutions at the initial iterations, then the pheromones evaporate on them and the probability of passing through them, and therefore improving the global best solution, is greatly reduced.

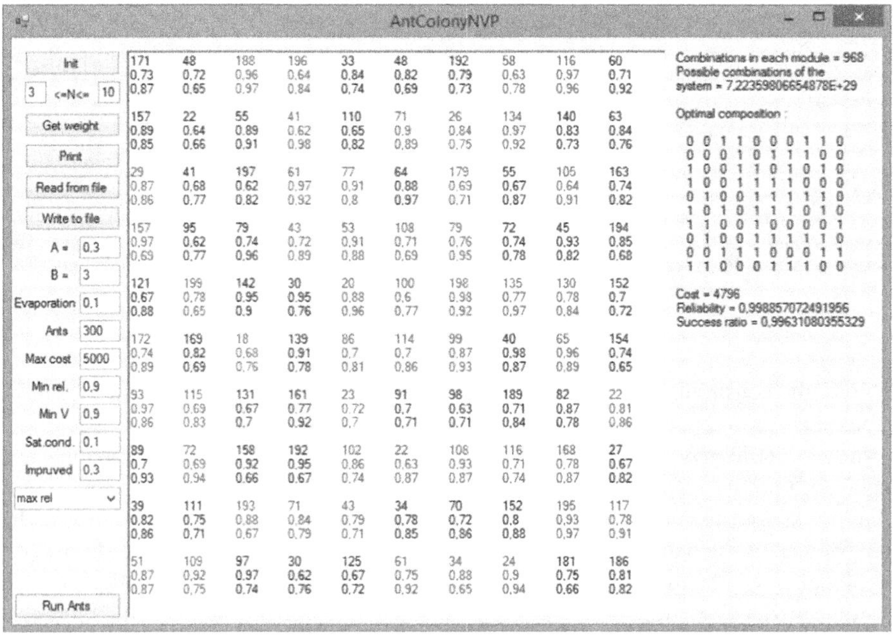

Fig. 2. Result of work in the optimization by reliability

It also depends on the chosen coefficients α and β. However, the selection of β values that are much higher than α, although it will allow to avoid such situations, firstly will turn the algorithm into greedy reducing the influence of pheromones, and in our case even less intelligent since with little effect pheromone on the probability of branching, they will remain close, and hence the choice is more random.

Table 1 presents the results of the program with different coefficients alpha and beta.

The cost optimization is performed with constraints by the reliability and the successful ratio when the reliability and successful ratio are more than 0.9. Every implementation contains 10 iterations of 300 ants. According to the results one can that an increase in the coefficient α with respect to β leads to a deterioration of the solution

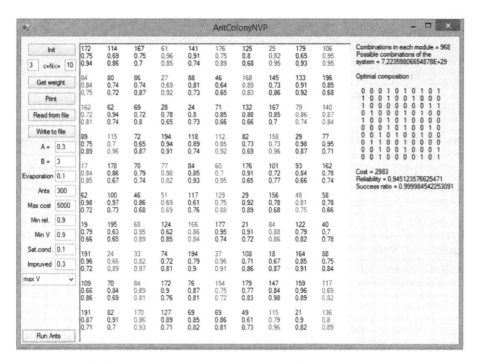

Fig. 3. Result of work in the optimization of the successful ratio

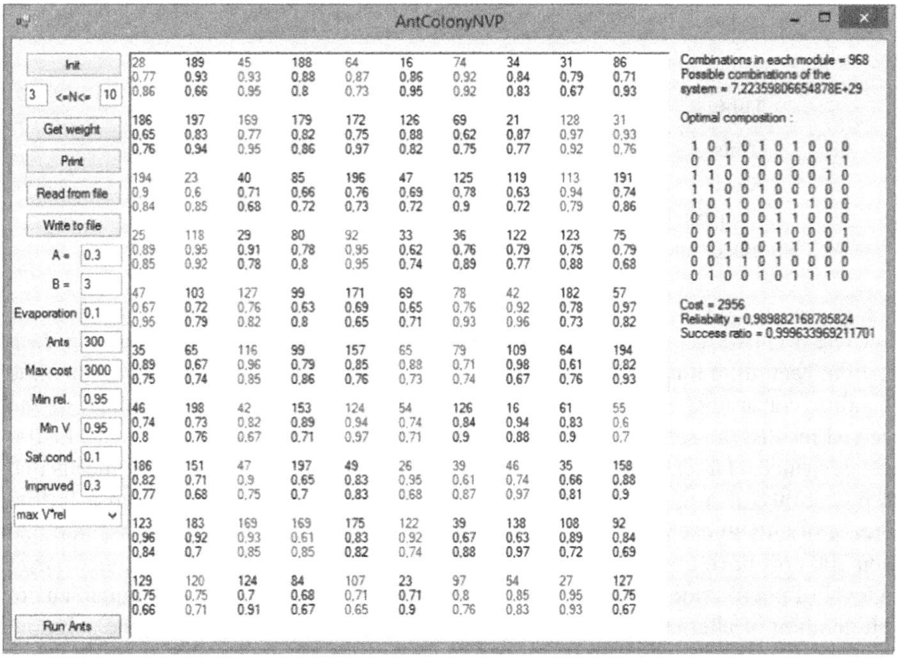

Fig. 4. Result of work in the optimization by R*V

Table 1. Results of changes in the coefficients α and β

$\alpha; \beta$	0.3;3	0.6; 2	1;1.5	2;1	3;0.5
Cost	2589	2828	3078	3103	3226
Reliability	0.9245	0.9207	0.9378	0.9761	0.9312
Succ. ratio	0.9997	0.9999	0.9994	0.9994	0.9975

since when selecting a route the arc weight is not so important for the ant. Therefore the ant is unlikely to choose a more optimal route.

Table 2 shows the results of the program with different cost constraints. Then the optimization by the reliability is performed. According to the results, as the cost constraint increases the system collects much more reliable system structure. However, after the cost of 4000, the reliability practically stops to increase, if with the constraints of 2500–4000 the optimal structure has almost reached the constraint, then with the constraint of 5000, the optimal structure costs 4227. That is far enough from the constraint which means that with the specified version characteristics, further increase in cost does not make sense in the case when a goal is to maximize the reliability.

Table 2. Results of changes in the maximum cost

Max cost	2500	3000	4000	5000
Cost	2490	2976	3990	4227
Reliability	0.9478	0.9701	0.9970	0.9985
Succ. ratio	0.9999	0.9992	0.9981	0.9955

Table 3. Results of changes in the ants number in the iteration

Ants	10	50	100	200	300	600
Cost	3200	2869	2655	2309	2512	2440
Reliability	0.9557	0.9283	0.9212	0.9551	09699	0.9163
Succ. ratio	0.9987	0.9998	0.9999	0.9999	0.9999	0.9999

Table 3 shows the results of the program with various numbers of ants in each iteration; each time it takes 10 iterations. The cost optimization is performed when the reliability constraints and a successful ratio are more than 0.9. According to the received results, the solution is more successful when a number of ants from 10 to 200 increases since a larger number of ants capture more variants of routes. That means that the probability of a more optimal path increases. An interesting result with a further increase of ants in each iteration. The solution stops to improve. One can assume that when 200 ants have traversed, the most successful paths receive a sufficient increase in the level of pheromone. It greatly reduces the probability of finding subsequent ants in each iteration of alternative route s that could lead to the improvement in the solution. There exists another regularity that with an increase in the number of ants, the "randomness" of the solution is reduced slightly. Table 3 shows the most successful solutions from a set of experiments. If a number of ants is 10, the spread in the resulting solutions is substantial (more than a thousand by value), then a number of ants is 300 and more, the close values are always obtained (the spread by value does not exceed 200).

5 Conclusion

The results of modeling in the proposed software environment show the applicability of ant algorithms to the problems of forming the optimal structure of a multiversion software package. The proposed algorithm has good performance as it allows obtaining an acceptable solution for 100–3000 iterations. It is much faster than the comparison of 968 m combinations for the classic search for the optimal solution by going through all the versions. The sensitivity of the algorithm to changes in the parameters of the operation is investigated; regularities and optimal values of the parameters are revealed. However, the result of the ant algorithm work is highly dependent on the passing of the first group of ants that is almost random, since at the beginning the pheromone values are the same, and the weights of the arcs are relatively close. The arcs will get an increase in the value of pheromone when the first ants are selecting the routes that are far from optimal, but improving the solution. However, the pheromone will evaporate from really optimal but not used arcs. That will reduce the chance to find a really optimal solution. To improve the operation of the algorithm further, one can suggest the following variant: to run the first few groups of ants, compare the results obtained by them at the first iteration, choose the best one and continue further modeling with only the best group. It does not complicate the calculations significantly, but it will eliminate the cases when the arcs far from the optimal solution received a high value of pheromone at the beginning of the simulation and even a large number of further iterations does not allow improving the solution.

Acknowledgments. This work was supported by Ministry of Education and Science of Russian Federation within limits of state contract № 2.2867.2017/4.6.

References

1. Kovalev, I., Voroshilova, A., Losev, V., Saramud, V., Chuvashova, M., Medvedev, A.: Comparative tests of decision making algorithms for a multiversion execution environment of the fault tolerance software. In: Proceedings of 2017 European Conference on Electrical Engineering and Computer Science (EECS 2017) (2017)
2. Kovalev, I., Losev, V., Saramud, M., Petrosyan, M.: Model implementation of the simulation environment of voting algorithms, as a dynamic system for increasing the reliability of the control complex of autonomous unmanned objects. In: MATEC Web of Conferences, vol. 132, 31 October 2017, No. 04011 (2017)
3. Kovalev, I.: The assessment methodology and improve the reliability of software and information technologies and structures [Monograph]. Kovalev, I., Semenko, T., Tsarev, R. Feder. Education Agency, Krasnoyarsk state technical University, 160 p. (2005)
4. Dorigo, M., Birattari, M.: Swarm intelligence. Scholarpedia 2(9), 1462 (2007)

5. Dorigo, M., Di Caro, G., Gambardella, L.M.: Ant algorithm for discrete optimization. Artif. Life **5**(2), 137–172 (1999)
6. Kovalev, I., Zelenkov, P., Karaseva, M., Kovalev, D.: Ant Algorithm Modification for Multi-Version Software Building. In: Tan, Y., Shi, Y., Buarque, F., Gelbukh, A., Das, S., Engelbrecht, A. (eds.) ICSI 2015. LNCS, vol. 9140, pp. 222–228. Springer, Cham (2015). https://doi.org/10.1007/978-3-319-20466-6_24
7. Dorigo, M., Gambardella, L.M.: Ant colonies for the travelling salesman problem. BioSystems **43**(2), 73–81 (1997)
8. Boats, L., Rodriguez, V., Alvarez, M.J., Robusté, F.: Algorithm Based on Ant Colony Optimization by Solving the Problem of Freight From Multiple Sources to Multiple Desti-nos. Santander, Spain (2002)
9. Laprie, J.-C., Arlat, J., Beounes, C., Kanoun, K.: Definition and Analysis of hardware- and software-fault-tolerant architectures. IEEE Computer, **23**(7), 39–51 (1990). Reprinted in Pham, H. (ed.) Fault-Tolerant Software Systems: Techniques and Applications, pp. 5–17. IEEE Computer Society Press (1992)
10. Dorigo, M., Blum, C.: Ant colony optimization theory: a survey (2007)

ACO Based Core-Attachment Method to Detect Protein Complexes in Dynamic PPI Networks

Jing Liang[1], Xiujuan Lei[1(✉)], Ling Guo[2], and Ying Tan[3]

[1] School of Computer Science, Shaanxi Normal University,
Xi'an 710119, China
xjlei@snnu.edu.cn
[2] College of Life Science, Shaanxi Normal University, Xi'an 710119, China
[3] School of Electronics Engineering and Computer Science,
Peking University, Beijing 100871, China

Abstract. Proteins complexes accomplish biological functions such as transcription of DNA and translation of mRNA. Detecting protein complexes correctly and efficiently is becoming a challenging task. This paper presents a novel algorithm, core-attachment based on ant colony optimization (CA-ACO), which detects complexes in three stages. Firstly, initialize the similarity matrix. Secondly, complexes are predicted by clustering in the dynamic PPI networks. In the step, the clustering coefficient of every node is also computed. A node whose clustering coefficient is greater than the threshold is added to the core protein set. Then we mark every neighbor node of core proteins with unique core label during picking and dropping. Thirdly, filtering processes are carried out to obtain the final complex set. Experimental results show that CA-ACO algorithm had great superiority in *precision*, *recall* and *f-measure* compared with the state-of-the-art methods such as ClusterONE, DPClus, MCODE and so on.

Keywords: PPI networks · Protein complexes · Core-attachment
Ant colony optimization

1 Introduction

Protein complex is a basic structural unit that can cooperate with each other to complete the specific biological function [1, 2]. The protein-protein interaction (PPI) network [3] is composed of a number of complexes which are related to each other to perform certain functions.

In recent years, many methods have been proposed to predict protein complexes. These methods greatly promote the progress in the field of complexes prediction. According to the category of complex recognition algorithms, these algorithms can be divided into the following categories: recognition algorithm based on dense sub-graph, recognition algorithm based on hierarchical clustering, recognition algorithm based on core-attachment structure.

Based on the theory of dense sub-graph in PPI networks, lots of algorithms are proposed. In 2003, Spirin *et al.* [2] proposed the algorithm using the results of

© Springer International Publishing AG, part of Springer Nature 2018
Y. Tan et al. (Eds.): ICSI 2018, LNCS 10941, pp. 101–112, 2018.
https://doi.org/10.1007/978-3-319-93815-8_11

traversing the fully connected graphs to identify complexes. Bader *et al.* [4] proposed a method, called molecular complex detection (MCODE). Palla *et al.* [5] proposed clique percolation method (CPM) based on the close connection of sub-graph filtering algorithm. And the algorithm's application software is developed, called CFinder [6]. In 2006, Altaf-UI-Amin *et al.* [7] proposed the DPClus which can get the overlapping complexes. In 2008, Li *et al.* [8] proposed IPCA algorithm, which is based on dense sub-graph to identify overlapping complexes. In 2009, Liu *et al.* [9] proposed clustering based on maximal cliques (CMC) algorithm, which can dig out the dense sub-graph in PPI networks.

Hierarchical clustering theory is also used to predict protein complexes. In 2002, Aivan and Newman proposed GN algorithm [10], which is used to partition the modules in complex networks. In 2004, Hartuv *et al.* [11] proposed highly connected sub-graph (HCS) algorithm. In 2009, Li *et al.* [12] proposed a fast hierarchical clustering algorithm based on the local variable and edge clustering coefficient, and redefined the protein complex. In 2012, Wang *et al.* [13] proposed OMIM algorithm to predict duplicate complexes in hierarchical clustering system.

The core-attachment structure of complex is a significant view to detect protein complexes. Leung *et al.* [14] designed CORE algorithm which calculates the *p-value* for all pairs of proteins to detect cores. Wu *et al.* [15] proposed COACH algorithm.

Recently, swarm intelligence algorithms have been successfully applied to the detection of complexes in PPI networks [20]. In addition, there are many other algorithms, such as Markov Clustering (MCL) [16, 17] algorithm, ClusterONE [18] algorithm, SPICi [19] algorithm and so on.

In this paper, we proposed a protein complex prediction algorithm based on core-attachment structure and ant colony optimization method, CA-ACO. First, we adopt the weighted matrix of the dynamic PPI network as the similarity matrix of the undirected graph. Second, we use the clustering coefficient value of every node to obtain the core proteins. We mark every neighbor node of core protein with unique label through picking and dropping principle of ACO. Third, filtering processes are carried out to obtain the clustering result.

2   Methods

2.1   The ACO Based Core-Attachment Design

Since the protein is not always active in the cell cycle, in order to construct a dynamic model, we integrate the static PPI data and gene expression data because gene expression level and protein expression level are consistent. If the gene expression data at a certain timestamp is better than a threshold, then it can be considered that the protein is active at this timestamp. By using three-sigma [29] principle, active threshold is set. At a certain timestamp, if two proteins are active and interactional, it can be considered that there is an edge between the two proteins at this time. As gene expression data has 12 timestamps, the static network is divided into 12 sub-graphs which correspond to 12 timestamps. Eventually, the dynamic PPI network is constructed. Figure 1 shows a process of dynamic PPI networks construction.

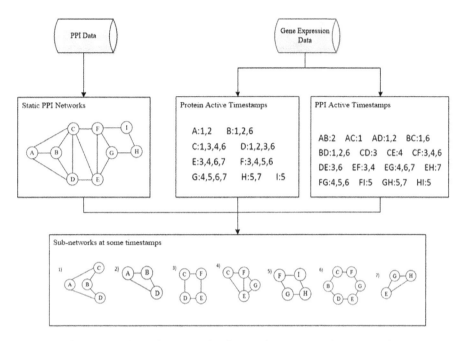

Fig. 1. An illustration example of dynamic PPI networks construction

Considering the organization of complexes, we combine the structure of core-attachment [14] with the principle of picking and dropping to predict complexes, and propose a novel algorithm, named CA-ACO. Figure 2 shows a part of the core-attachment formation design. There are two clusters which are in dotted circles of green and blue. Protein p and protein q are seed proteins. The connection between a protein and others is represented by a solid line or dotted line. The full line represents that two proteins belong to a cluster. Otherwise, they don't belong to a cluster. Taking p's neighbor protein a as an example, protein a does not belong to the cluster whose seed protein is protein p. Then, we should pick up a, and decide if protein a belongs to other cluster. Protein b is the neighbor protein of protein p and q. As the Fig. 2 shows, the protein b belongs to two clusters whose seed proteins are protein p and protein q. For protein c which is connected with protein p and protein q. Firstly, node c did not belong to cluster p and was picked up. Then, we have to decide its relationship with other seed nodes. There is a full line between c and q. Then, node c needs to be dropped out and put in the cluster whose seed node is protein q.

2.2   Description of CA-ACO Algorithm

The process of CA-ACO algorithm can be divided into 3 steps: similarity matrix initialization, clustering and purification.

In the first step, the similarity matrix of the dynamic PPI network is composed of 12 sub networks' weighted matrix. The greater the weight value is, the greater the

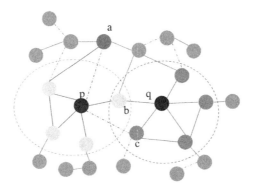

Fig. 2. A part of the core-attachment formation design (Color figure online)

similarity between the nodes is. The similarity matrix of PPI network initialization is shown in Eq. (1).

$$S(v_i, v_j) = \begin{cases} s(v_i, v_j) & if (v_i, v_j) \in E \\ 0 & else \end{cases} \quad (1)$$

Where $s(v_i, v_j)$ is weight value of edge (v_i, v_j). It represents the strength of the interaction of proteins v_i and protein v_j in weighted PPI network.

In the second step, we can obtain protein complex set from dynamic PPI network. There are two main processes: seed protein selection and attachment formation. In seed protein selection process, we need to compute the clustering coefficient value [30] of every protein by Eq. (2).

$$ccv(v_i) = \frac{2 \times n_i}{|neigh(v_i)| \times (|neigh(v_i)| - 1)} \quad (2)$$

where $neigh(v_i)$ is neighbor nodes set of a node v_i. A protein whose clustering coefficient value is greater than the threshold will be added to the core protein set. In attachment formation step, we need to access to neighbor protein set of every core protein. By carrying out the picking and dropping operation [21] of ACO, seed proteins' neighbor proteins can be clustered. The probability of picking is calculated by Eq. (3).

$$pp(v_j) = (\frac{k_p}{k_p + s(v_i, v_j)})^2 \quad (3)$$

where k_p is a picking constant whose range of values is from 0 to 1, $s(v_i, v_j)$ is the similarity between the protein v_j and the current core protein v_i. In the operation of picking, the probability of picking is compared with a random probability. When the probability of picking is more than the random probability, the operation of picking is executed. Otherwise, the protein v_j is labeled the complex whose seed protein is the protein v_i. The probability of dropping is calculated by Eq. (4).

$$pd(v_j) = \begin{cases} 2 \times s(v_i, v_j) & if \quad s(v_i, v_j) < k_d \\ 1 & else \end{cases} \tag{4}$$

where k_d is a dropping constant whose range of values is 0 to 1, $s(v_i, v_j)$ is the similarity between the protein v_j and the current core protein v_i. The probability of dropping is compared with random probability in the operation of dropping. When $pd(v_j)$ is more than a random probability, the operation of dropping is executed. Therefore, the protein v_j is labeled the complex whose seed protein is the protein v_i. Through the clustering process, we can get the initial clustering results where complexes have core-attachment structure.

In the third step, purification process is carried out. In the complex set, the complex with just one protein is deleted, and protein complex which has same proteins as others is removed. The protein complex set is obtained.

The pseudo-code of CA-ACO method is described as follows.

Algorithm: CA-ACO algorithm
Input: a dynamic PPI network G
Output: protein complexes set PC
Step 1: Initialization similarity matrix: the similarity matrix is shown in Eq.(1).
Step 2: Clustering:
        Initialization: Set various parameters.
        Seed selection: Compute the clustering coefficient of protein to obtain seed proteins by Eq.(2) .
        Attachment clustering:
          flag =0;
          For protein v_i in the core protein set
            For node v_j in the neigh(i)
              Compute the probability of picking up the protein v_j, pp, by Eq.(3)
              If pp < random value & *flag*=0
                Then label node v_j as v_i cluster, continue
                Else pick up node v_j , *flag* = 1
                For other core protein v_k except protein v_i
                  Compute the probability of dropping out the protein v_j, pd, by Eq.(4)
                  If pd > random value
                    Then drop down protein v_j, label v_j as v_k , *flag*=0, continue
                  End If
                End For
              End If
            End For
            If *flag*=1
              Drop down protein v_j, don't label and *flag*=0
            End If
          End For
        Put proteins with same labels into a cluster, get clustering results
        Return the protein complexes set dd from the PPI network
Step 3: Refinement: filtering the protein complexes of Step 2. Return the protein complex set PC

---

3   Experiments and Results

3.1   Experimental Dataset

In this paper, we adopt the PPI data of *S.cerevisiae* from DIP [24], MIPS [31] and Krogan database [32]. Dynamic PPI networks [3] at 12 timestamps correspond to 12 static PPI subnets. Different subnets have different size, as shown in Table 1.

Table 1. The number of proteins and interactions in each subnet of different PPI networks

Data	Timestamp	1	2	3	4	5	6	7	8	9	10	11	12
DIP	Proteins	797	941	796	623	601	530	493	944	1090	592	661	461
	Interactions	981	1444	1188	745	750	646	573	1705	2185	856	974	526
MIPS	Proteins	737	897	781	583	570	531	470	839	1014	523	616	402
	Interactions	1097	1443	1183	754	684	642	504	1238	1637	878	1207	700
Krogan	Proteins	336	379	320	256	206	189	202	580	626	304	330	250
	Interactions	334	464	331	234	210	184	213	1025	1081	314	373	258

In this paper, we use the standard known protein complex set, CYC2008 [25], which contains 408 complexes and 1,628 proteins. The biggest cluster has 81 proteins while the smallest cluster has 2 proteins in protein complexes of CYC2008.

3.2   Evaluation Criteria

The *precision* [24] indicates the proportion of the predicted protein complexes successfully matched by the standard protein complexes in the prediction of the complex. It can be defined as:

$$precision = \frac{N_{cp}}{|P|} \tag{5}$$

where $|P|$ represents the number of predicted protein complexes, and N_{cp} indicates that the number of the predicted complexes successfully matched by the known protein complexes.

The *recall* [24] indicates the proportion of the known protein complexes successfully matched by the predicted complexes in the standard of the complex. It can be defined as:

$$recall = \frac{N_{cb}}{|B|} \tag{6}$$

where $|B|$ represents the number of known protein complexes, and N_{cb} indicates that the number of the standard protein complexes successfully matched by the predicted protein complexes.

The *f-measure* [24] denotes the harmonic mean of *precision* and *recall*. It can be defined as:

$$f - measure = \frac{2 \times precision \times recall}{precision + recall} \tag{7}$$

In order to further validate the biological significance of the predicted protein complexes, we need to carry out the functional enrichment analysis by using *p-value* [36] formulated as follows:

$$p - value = \sum_{i=m}^{n} \frac{\binom{M}{i}\binom{N-M}{n-i}}{\binom{N}{n}} \tag{8}$$

where N is the number of protein in the PPI network, M is the number of proteins in a GO term, n is the number of proteins which are annotated with the same GO term. Generally, the smaller the *p-value* of a protein complex is, the stronger biological significance the complex processes will be.

3.3 Comparison with Other Methods

To evaluate the performance of CA-ACO algorithm, we compare CA-ACO with CMC [9], MCODE [4], CFinder [6], ClusterONE [18], CORE [14], COACH [15], RNSC [25], DPClus [7], MCL [16, 17], ACO-MCL [26], HC-PIN [27], MOEPGA [28] and FOCA [20] in terms of *precision*, *recall* and *f-measure* in the DIP dataset. It is obvious that the *precision* value of our method is greater than other methods *precision* value. The *recall* values of CMC, MOEPGA and FOCA algorithms are superior to our method, which are 0.5900, 0.6000 and 0.6360 respectively. However, the *f-measure* value of our method is much higher than other typical algorithms' *f-measure* value. Our method's *f-measure* value is 0.6653. It indicates that the performance of CA-ACO algorithm is optimal. The above analysis can be shown in Fig. 3.

Moreover, we also compare our method with the following prediction methods: CSO [33], ClusterONE [18], COACH [15], CMC [9], HUNTER [34] and MCODE [4] in terms of *precision*, *recall* and *f-measure* in the MIPS and Krogran dataset. As shown in Fig. 4, our method achieves the highest *f-measure* of 0.6025, *recall* of 0.5524 and *precision* of 0.6665 in MIPS dataset. On the Fig. 5, our method achieves the highest *f-measure* of 0.5844, *recall* of 0.4347 and *precision* of 0.8920 in the Krogan dataset.

We use functional enrichment analysis to validate the biological significance of methods. We calculate the *p-value* of detected complexes whose size are greater than or equal to 3. A complex is considered significant when its *p-value* is less than 0.01.

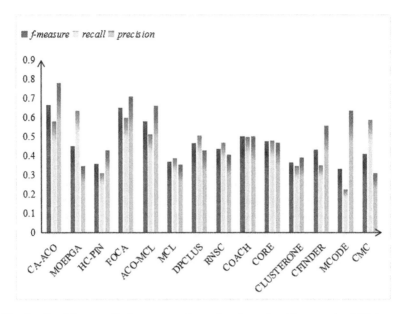

Fig. 3. *Precision, recall, f-measure* values of various algorithms on the DIP dataset

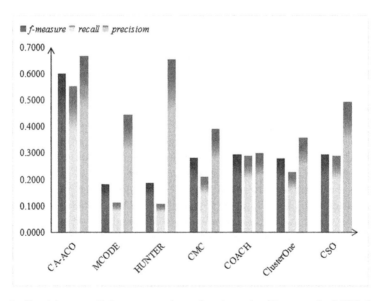

Fig. 4. *Precision, recall, f-measure* values of various algorithms on the MIPS dataset

Table 2 lists the number and percentage of the identified complexes whose *p-value* is in the range of <E−10, [E−10, E−5), [E−5, 0.01), >=0.01. Table 2 shows the comparison of the functional enrichment of complexes detected by CA-ACO, MCL, CORE and ClusterONE on DIP, MIPS and Krogan datasets. As shown in Table 2, we

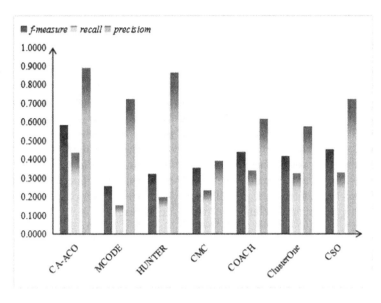

Fig. 5. *Precision, recall, f-measure* values of various algorithms on the Krogan dataset

Table 2. Functional enrichment analysis of complexes detected on DIP, MIPS and Krogan dataset

Dataset	Algorithm	PC	<E−10	[E−10,E−5)	[E−5, 0.01)	>=0.01
DIP	CA-ACO	481	15(3.12%)	107(22.25%)	254(52.81%)	105(21.83%)
	MCL	1053	66(6.26%)	183(17.38%)	362(34.38%)	442(41.98%)
	CORE	344	4(1.16%)	78(22.67%)	114(33.14%)	148(43.02%)
	ClusterONE	574	73(12.72%)	177(30.84%)	184(32.06%)	140(24.39%)
MIPS	CA-ACO	223	2(0.90%)	42(18.83%)	135(60.54%)	44(19.73%)
	MCL	606	18(2.98%)	94(15.51%)	220(36.30%)	274(45.21%)
	CORE	340	4(1.18%)	65(19.12%)	107(31.47%)	164(48.24%)
	ClusterONE	372	23(6.18%)	117(31.45%)	126(33.87%)	106(28.49%)
Krogan	CA-ACO	162	7(4.32%)	49(30.25%)	93(57.41%)	13(8.02%)
	MCL	403	59(14.64%)	103(25.56%)	119(29.53%)	122(30.27%)
	CORE	255	13(5.10%)	60(23.53%)	102(40.00%)	80(31.37%)
	ClusterONE	399	56(14.04%)	98(24.56%)	120(30.08%)	125(31.33%)

can obtain the number of predicted protein complexes by various methods on different datasets. The percentage and the amount of the predicted protein complexes with *p-value* fall into corresponding intervals. The percentage of complexes whose *p-value* is greater than 0.01 in predicted complexes by CA-ACO algorithm is the smallest. So, most of the predicted protein complexes by CA-ACO are meaningful. These illustrate that our proposed algorithm is competent to identified significant protein complexes in dynamic PPI networks.

4 Conclusions

Many of the current methods predicting protein complexes are running in a static PPI network, which ignoring the dynamic properties of the PPI network and the inherent organization of the protein complex. In this paper, we proposed a novel method for detecting protein complexes in dynamic protein interaction networks, CA-ACO, which is based on the core-attachment structure of protein complexes. We compare the performance of the CA-ACO algorithm with other state-of-the-art methods in DIP, MIPS and Krogan dataset. Experimental results show that CA-ACO algorithm is obviously superior to other methods. In addition, the shift from static PPI networks to dynamic PPI networks is important to analyze the biological significance of complexes identified from PPI networks. In the future, we will further optimize our algorithm to improve the efficiency of algorithm and the effect of biological research.

References

1. Gavin, A.C., Bösche, M., Krause, R., Grandi, P., Marzioch, M., Bauer, A., et al.: Functional organization of the yeast proteome by systematic analysis of protein complexes. Nature **415**, 141–147 (2002)
2. Spirin, V., Mirny, L.A.: Protein complexes and functional modules in molecular networks. Proc. Nat. Acad. Sci. U.S.A. **100**, 12123–12128 (2003)
3. Wang, J., Peng, X., Peng, W., Wu, F.X.: Dynamic protein interaction network construction and applications. Proteomics **14**, 338–352 (2014)
4. Bader, G.D., Hogue, C.W.V.: An automated method for finding molecular complexes in large protein interaction networks. BMC Bioinform. **4**, 2–28 (2003)
5. Palla, G., Derényi, I., Farkas, I., Vicsek, T.: Uncovering the overlapping community structure of complex networks in nature and society. Nature **435**, 814–818 (2005)
6. Adamcsek, B., Palla, G., Farkas, I.J., Vicsek, T.: CFinder: locating cliques and overlapping modules in biological networks. Bioinformatics **22**, 1021–1023 (2006)
7. Altaf-Ul-Amin, M., Shinbo, Y., Mihara, K., Kurokawa, K., Kanaya, S.: Development and implementation of an algorithm for detection of protein complexes in large interaction networks. BMC Bioinform. **7**, 207–219 (2006)
8. Li, M., Chen, J., Wang, J., Chen, G.: Modifying the DPClus algorithm for identifying protein complexes based on new topological structures. BMC Bioinform. **9**, 398–413 (2008)
9. Liu, G., Wong, L., Chua, H.N.: Complex discovery from weighted PPI networks. Bioinformatics **25**, 1891–1897 (2009)
10. Girvan, M., Newman, M.E.J.: Community structure in social and biological networks. Proc. Nat. Acad. Sci. **99**, 7821–7826 (2002)
11. Hartuv, E., Shamir, R.: A clustering algorithm based on graph connectivity. Inf. Process. Lett. **76**, 175–181 (2000)
12. Li, M., Wang, J., Chen, J., Pan, Y.: Hierarchical organization of functional modules in weighted protein interaction networks using clustering coefficient. Bioinform. Res. Appl. **5542**, 75–86 (2009)
13. Wang, X., Li, L., Cheng, Y.: An overlapping module identification method in protein-protein interaction networks. BMC Bioinform. **13**, S4 (2012)
14. Leung, H.C., Xiang, Q., Yiu, S.M., Chin, F.Y.: Predicting protein complexes from PPI data: a core-attachment approach. J. Comput. Biol. **16**, 133–144 (2009)

15. Wu, M., Li, X., Kwoh, C.K.: A core-attachment based method to detect protein complexes in PPI networks. BMC Bioinform. **10**, 169–184 (2009)
16. Leal, J.P., Enright, A., Ouzounis, C.A.: Detection of functional modules from protein interaction networks. Proteins Struct. Funct. Bioinform. **54**, 49–57 (2003)
17. Van Dongen, S.M.: Graph clustering by flow simulation (2001)
18. Nepusz, T., Yu, H., Paccanaro, A.: Detecting overlapping protein complexes in protein-protein interaction networks. Nat. Meth. **9**, 471–472 (2012)
19. Jiang, P., Singh, M.: SPICi: a fast clustering algorithm for large biological networks. Bioinform. **26**, 1105–1111 (2010)
20. Lei, X., Ding, Y., Hamido, F., Zhang, A.: Identification of dynamic protein complexes based on fruit fly optimization algorithm. Knowl. Based Syst. **105**, 270–277 (2016)
21. Leumer, E., Faieta, B.: Diversity and adaption in populations of clustering ants. In: Proceedings of the 3rd International Conference on Simulation of Adaptive Behavior: From Animal to Animals, pp. 499–508. MIT Press, Cambridge (1994)
22. Xenarios, I., Salwínski, L., Duan, X.J., Higney, P., Kim, S., Eisenberg, D.: DIP: the database of interaction proteins: a research tool for studying cellular networks of protein interactions. Nucleic Acids Res. **30**, 303–305 (2002)
23. Pu, S., Wong, J., Turner, B., Cho, E., Wodak, S.J.: Up-to-date catalogues of yeast protein complexes. Nucleic Acids Res. **37**, 825–831 (2009)
24. Keretsu, S., Sarmah, R.: Weighted edge based clustering to identify protein complexes in protein–protein interaction networks incorporating gene expression profile. Comput. Biol. Chem. **65**, 69–79 (2016)
25. King, A.D., Pržulj, N., Jurisica, I.: Protein complex prediction via cost-based clustering. Bioinformatics **20**, 3013–3020 (2004)
26. Seçkiner, S.U., Eroglu, Y., Emrullah, M., Dereli, T.: Ant colony optimization for continuous functions by using novel pheromone updating. Appl. Math. Comput. **219**, 4163–4175 (2013)
27. Wang, J., Li, M., Chen, J., Pan, Y.: A fast hierarchical clustering algorithm for functional modules discovery in protein interaction networks. Comput. Biol. Bioinform. **8**, 607–620 (2011)
28. Cao, B., Luo, J., Liang, C., Wang, S., Song, D.: MOEPGA: a novel method to detect protein complexes in yeast protein–protein interaction networks based on MultiObjective Evolutionary Programming Genetic Algorithm. Comput. Biol. Chem. **58**, 173–181 (2015)
29. Vlasblom, J., Wodak, S.J.: Markov clustering versus affinity propagation for the partitioning of protein interaction graphs. BMC Bioinform. **10**, 99 (2009)
30. Dimitrakopoulosa, C., Theofilatosa, K., Pegkasb, A., Likothanassis, S., Mavroudi, S.: Predicting overlapping protein complexes from weighted protein interaction graphs by gradually expanding dense neighborhoods. Artif. Intell. Med. **71**, 62–69 (2016)
31. Güldener, U., Münsterkötter, M., Oesterheld, M., Pagel, P., Ruepp, A., Mewes, H., et al.: MPact: the MIPS protein interaction resource on Yeast. Nucleic Acids Res. **34**, 436–441 (2006)
32. Krogan, N., Cagney, G., Yu, H., Zhong, G., Guo, X., Ignatchenko, A., et al.: Global landscape of protein complexes in the yeast Saccharomyces cerevisiae. Nature **440**(7084), 637–643 (2006)
33. Zhang, Y., Lin, H., Yang, Z., Wang, J., Li, Y., Xu, B.: Protein complex prediction in large ontology attributed protein-protein interaction networks. IEEE/ACM Trans. Comput. Biol. Bioinform. **10**, 729–741 (2013)
34. Chin, C., Chen, S., Ho, C., Ko, M., Lin, C.: A hub-attachment based method to detect functional modules from confidence-scored protein interactions and expression profiles. BMC Bioinform. **11**, S25 (2010)

35. Wang, J., Peng, X., Li, M., Pan, Y.: Construction and application of dynamic protein interaction network based on time course gene expression data. Proteomics **13**(2), 301–312 (2013)
36. Shen, X., Yi, L., Jiang, X., Zhao, Y., Hu, X., He, T., Yang, J.: Neighbor affinity based algorithm for discovering temporal protein complex from dynamic PPI network. Methods **110**, 90–96 (2016)

Information-Centric Networking Routing Challenges and Bio/ACO-Inspired Solution: A Review

Qingyi Zhang[1], Xingwei Wang[2(✉)], Min Huang[3], and Jianhui Lv[4]

[1] School of Computer Science and Engineering,
Northeastern University, Shenyang, China
zhangqingyi7@163.com
[2] College of Software, Northeastern University, Shenyang, China
wangxw@mail.neu.edu.cn
[3] State Key Laboratory of Synthetical Automation for Process Industries,
School of Information Science and Engineering, Northeastern University,
Shenyang, China
mhuang@mail.neu.edu.cn
[4] Central Research Institute, Network Technology Laboratory,
Huawei Technologies Co., Ltd., Shenzhen, China
lvjianhui@huawei.com

Abstract. Information-Centric Networking (ICN) aims to distribute and retrieve the content by name. In this paper, we review and approve the feasible Ant Colony Optimization (ACO)-inspired ICN routing solutions, i.e., applying ACO to solve ICN routing problem. At first, some significant challenges with respect to ICN routing are analyzed, such as explosive increasing of Forwarding Information Base (FIB), retrieval of closest content copy, uniform distribution of content and mobility support. Then, the solutions inspired by biology feature and behavior is reviewed. In addition, a general design thought of ACO-inspired solution is presented. Finally, the feasibility of ACO-inspired ICN routing solution is evaluated.

Keywords: ICN · Bio-inspired routing · ACO · Content retrieval

1 Introduction

Information-Centric Networking (ICN) [1] is a clean-slate design for accommodating the ever increasing growth of Internet traffic by regarding named content as network primitive. Some related projects have been developed, such as Data Oriented Network Architecture (DONA) [2], Network of Information (NetInf) [3], Publish/Subscribe Internet Technology (PURSUIT) [4] and Named Data Networking (NDN) [5].

The typical features of ICN are summarized as follows: (i) directly accessing content by a unique name, (ii) supporting in-network caching, (iii) consumer-driven communication model, i.e., contents are pulled by consumers' interests,

© Springer International Publishing AG, part of Springer Nature 2018
Y. Tan et al. (Eds.): ICSI 2018, LNCS 10941, pp. 113–122, 2018.
https://doi.org/10.1007/978-3-319-93815-8_12

and (iv) stateful forwarding, i.e., ICN forwarding plane will record the consumers' interests before they are satisfied. Although these features can effectively achieve content distribution and support mobility, there are some challenges to achieve efficient routing in ICN (See Sect. 2). Many kinds of ICN routing schemes have been proposed to solve the ICN routing problems, for example, translate the name of the interest into its locator and route the request by the locator. However, it is failed to exploit content copy in in-network caches in this routing scheme. Given this consideration, inspired by the natural behaviors when searching for the shortest path between nest and food source, the Bio-inspired solution has been investigated to solve the routing problems by many researchers. Without loss of generality, this paper aims at surveying the Bio/Ant Colony Optimization (ACO)-inspired ICN routing solution based on NDN architecture. The contributions of this paper are triple, i.e., (i) reviewing ICN routing challenges, (ii) discussing bio-inspired ICN routing development, and (iii) analyzing the feasibility of ACO-inspired ICN routing.

The rest of this paper is structured as follows. Section 2 analyzes some challenges of ICN routing. The potential of bio-inspired ICN routing is presented in Sect. 3. Finally, Sect. 4 proposes a general ACO-inspired ICN routing solution. Section 5 concludes the paper.

2   ICN Routing Challenges

2.1   Overview

In ICN, each Content Router (CR) has three tables, i.e., Content Store (CS), Pending Interest Table (PIT) and Forwarding Information Base (FIB). Besides, it can send two kinds of messages, i.e., interest packet which is sent by interest requester to request the desired content, and data packet which is sent by content provider to carry the corresponding content back to interest requester [6]. ICN forwarding depends on FIB and PIT to select the appropriate interface, thus ICN forwarding is stateful. ICN routing relies on the named-data link state protocol, which is an extension of OSPF [7]. ICN routing depends on lookup, record and forwarding with respect to CS, PIT and FIB, and it can be divided into three categories from three different perspectives, as follows.

• From the perspective of the number of forwarding interfaces, ICN routing consists of single-path and multi-path. The former is generated by selecting only one outgoing interface in FIB to forward interest request, which has considerably high demand on algorithm design, thus it is very difficult to retrieve the closest content copy. In fact, due to the capacity of in-network caching and multicast, ICN network usually has more than one content provider. In order to find all contents and further retrieve the closest content copy, some CRs select two or more outgoing interfaces to forward interest request [8].

• From the perspective of domain, ICN routing consists of intra-domain routing and inter-domain routing [9]. The former collects the link state information, such as delay, bandwidth, error rate and throughput, and accomplishes routing by coordinating lookup and forwarding among CS, PIT and FIB, which further demonstrates that the forwarding in ICN is stateful. The latter does the match between two domains according to the longest name prefix, which is similar to Border Gateway Protocol (BGP).

- From the perspective of efficiency improvement, ICN routing consists of adaptive forwarding and cache-aware routing. The first one focuses on selecting how many outgoing interfaces to forward interest request; the second one exploits the in-network caching during the data routing process in order to help the subsequent interest forwarding.

2.2   Challenges

However, ICN routing has some significant challenges, such as explosive increasing of FIB, retrieval of closest content copy, uniform distribution of content, mobility support and deployment at large-scale network, which cannot be effectively addressed by the current proposals and are introduced as follows.

Explosive Increasing of FIB. FIB is used to guide interest forwarding. CRs announce the provided content name prefix proactively by generating a certain amount of data packets, and then these announced data packets are transmitted within the network. When other CRs receive these data packets, basis on this, they construct their FIBs [10]. It is obvious that this results in the explosive increasing of FIB, because (i) the name length is variable and (ii) the number of content is huge.

Retrieval of Closest Content Copy. ICN enables users to retrieve the closest content copy from the CRs. However, how to obtain the cache information is a nontrivial task, because cache information cannot be broadcast throughout the network. What's worse, contents might have been removed by the time a request is routed to a specific node.

Uniform Distribution of Content. During the routing process, when the requested content is distributed at several CRs, consumers send interest packets to multiple outgoing interfaces. However, the network will face serious load and even congestion without considering congestion control because ICN does not inherently support the parallel transmission.

Mobility Support. The mobility in ICN usually consists of interest requester movement and content provider movement. However, the inherent mobility support refers to interest requester movement rather than content provider movement [11]. In general, interest requester movement can be addressed easily because ICN is an interest-driven mode. Under such condition, the mobile interest requester only needs to send new interest packet. On the contrary, content provider movement is very difficult to be addressed.

In fact, the mobility results from that most users have widely used mobile devices which join or leave the network at any time. When mobile devices which provide the content leave the network, interest requester cannot retrieve the content from the original mobile devices, which increases the difficulty and complexity of routing. Many methods have been proposed, such as topology-awareness [12], proxy point [13] and rendezvous point [14]. However, they all suffer from handoff latency.

Deployment at Large-Scale Network. An enormous number of contents will cause the explosive increasing of FIB. In addition, ICN adopts the named-data link state protocol. When the network scale becomes large, the information convergence speed becomes slow greatly [15], and thus decreases routing efficiency.

3   Bio-inspired ICN Routing Development

3.1   Bio-inspired Development

The bionics, as a classical discipline, was proposed in 1960. Regarding computer science in bionics, the research is usually divided into three fields, i.e., system, networking and computing [16], as shown in Fig. 1. Among them, the bio-inspired system is capable of adapting and learning how to react to unforeseen scenarios with emergent properties; the bio-inspired networking is capable of providing new services and applications by considering intrinsic networking features; the bio-inspired computing is capable of doing some operations according to the inherent computing rules and behaviors of biology.

Even though the bio-inspired system and computing (e.g., neural network) have already become widely useful, the application of bio-inspired networking has not been developed sufficiently [17]. In particular, the current bio-inspired researches do not fully incorporate system, networking and computing to solve the routing optimization problem in spite of bio-inspired solutions are regarded as a fruitful direction in networking and communication areas. Instead, an overwhelming majority of researches only pay attention to bio-inspired computing, even though some special issues from top journal were published [18–20].

3.2   Bio-inspired ICN Routing Solution

The typical features of biology are summarized as follows: self-evolution, self-organization, collaboration, survivability and adaptation [17]. Bio-inspired ICN routing solution is promising because it is capable of addressing the challenges mentioned in Sect. 2.2. At first, biologies can adapt to the dynamically varying environment, e.g., the explosive growth of FIB, such challenge is addressed by biological self-evolution. Secondly, biologies can intelligently retrieve the most suitable content copy by self-organization. Thirdly, biologies can easily accomplish uniform distribution of content by their frequent collaboration behaviors, which decreases network load and thus improves ICN routing efficiency. Fourthly,

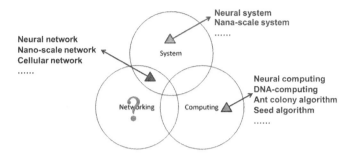

Fig. 1. Main research areas of bionics in computer science.

biologies have survivability to recover from failures caused by devices or links malfunction; the mobile phenomenon of either interest requester or content provider belongs to a subset of failures, such challenge regarding mobility is addressed by biological survivability. At last, biologies is adaptive to fully distributed environment, and further adapt to the large-scale network.

Bio-inspired ICN routing solution enables interest/data forwarding, traffic control and even other key operations to display self-organization and adaptation in order to improve routing efficiency, such as success rate, load balance and throughput. It is worth pointing out that when these features are exploited to address ICN routing challenges, they are not mutually independent. In general, collaboration and organization among a group of biologies are used to conduct interest/data forwarding, based on this, biologies adapt to external as well as internal environment by adaptation and self-evolution, which embodies biological survivability.

The design of bio-inspired ICN routing solution usually needs three main steps, as follows. (i) Analyze ICN routing problem to be solved, and designate an exactly bionic strategy because not all bionic strategies can fit a specific ICN routing scenario. (ii) Map the major modules from biological system into ICN networking layer by considering some special network features, and build the corresponding mathematical models. (iii) Solve ICN routing problem according to biological behaviors and rules. In fact, these three steps correspond to bio-inspired system, bio-inspired networking and bio-inspired computing respectively, which is a systematic design thought regarding all bio-inspired solutions. However, the current bio-inspired proposals usually focus on bio-inspired computing irrespective of its system and networking, and the corresponding design thought is summarized as two main steps, as follows. (i) Declare a network problem as NP-hard, and (ii) use bio-inspired computing to solve it. It is obvious that the design thought is not really bionic.

4   ACO-Inspired ICN Routing Proposal

4.1   Feasibility Analysis

To the best of our knowledge, ants always release the pheromone over their working trail. During the foraging process, ants can find food sources and determine the closest food source by indirectly communicating with others based on pheromone, including some notable features, such as self-organization, positive feedback, diversity, parallel computing, etc. Afterwards, the foraging behavior of ant is modeled as ACO, which was proposed and developed by Dorigo in 1992 [21] and 1996 [22] respectively. In particular, a classical application of ACO is to solve the Travelling Salesman Problem (TSP). To our minds, among many biological species, only ACO-inspired ICN routing solution is feasible, and some comprehensive illustrations are presented as follows.

• Concentrate on "what" instead of "where". ICN pays attention to the content rather than IP address. In other words, content provider is transparent relative to interest requester. Similarly, ants focus on what food is, and they do not know where food is because it is impossible to know food source before foraging. Thus, food source is transparent relative to ant.

• Consumer-driven. In ICN, requester pull the content by sending interests, that is, content provider has no corresponding operations until it is triggered by successive interest requests; when the content is found, it is returned to interest requester no matter which content provider it comes from; it is obvious that ICN is the interest-driven mode. Similarly, food is not likely to be provided for ant before food request is sent, which means that ACO is just as the ant-driven mode.

• Mobility support. ICN inherently supports movement of interest requester [23], that is, the content can be carried back to interest requester no matter where interest request moves. Similarly, ants can find food by their collaboration and self-organization no matter where food moves, which means that ACO supports mobility of food. In addition, ICN does not inherently support movement of content provider while ACO supports all mobile cases. Therefore, the mobile phenomenon of content provider can be addressed by ACO-inspired solution.

• Multiple resources. In ICN, a specific content may exist at multiple different content providers in the form of copy due to the inherent in-network caching. Similarly, there are many same food sources in nature. In addition, both content and food are diversified.

• Closest object retrieval. ICN inherently supports multicast and multi-path transmission, and its goal is to retrieve the closest content copy from multiple content providers. Similarly, ants can find all food sources by a distributed and parallel manner; especially when the number of iterations reaches a certain level, the closest food along the shortest path can be found.

• Naming style. ICN carries out the name-based routing, in which content name is persistent, available and authentic. The food name, similarly, is also unique in nature, that is, ants find food relying on the unique feature, i.e., food name. In addition, different contents have different names, which depends on naming rule in ICN. Also, different foods have different names, which depends on food odours

• Major system components. Each physical location in ACO is composed of Food Warehouse (FW) to store foods, Pheromone Matrix (PM) to percept and record pheromone, and Tabu Search Table (TST) to conduct forwarding of ant. Similarly, each CR in ICN consists of CS, PIT and FIB which can correspond to FW, PM and TST respectively.

According to the above seven interpretations, we believe that ACO-inspired ICN routing has potential in theory.

4.2   Routing Mapping

Figure 2 shows two scenarios, i.e., one is ant foraging in ACO, and the other one is content retrieval in ACO-inspired ICN routing. Specially, for an ant, the foraging process can be simply described as follows. Each ant starts its travel to find food from nest. When arriving at a location, it searches FW to see whether the requested food can be found. If yes, it accomplishes foraging and goes back to nest; otherwise, it percepts the surrounding pheromone by PM and begins the following travel by TST. Similarly, we map ant behaviors into ICN, and each interest ant retrieves the content starting from interest requester. When arriving at one CR, it checks CS to see whether the content exists. If yes, data ant goes back to interest requester and content retrieval is finished; otherwise, it percepts the surrounding pheromone by PIT and begins the following interest forwarding by FIB. Thus, we believe that using ACO to address ICN routing is feasible.

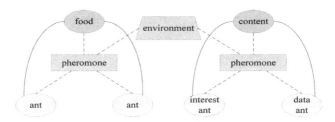

Fig. 2. ACO and ACO-inspired ICN.

In particular, during the process of designing ACO-inspired ICN routing solution, the updating strategy of pheromone is very significant, and the previous design model [24–28] on pheromone is presented as follows.

$$T_{i,j}(t, I) = (1 - \rho) \cdot T_{i,j}(t, I - 1) + cc_{i,j}(t, I). \tag{1}$$

Among them, $T_{i,j}(t, I)$ is the total pheromone over the edge between CR_i and CR_j (denoted by $e_{i,j}$) at time t after $I(\in \mathbb{N})$ iterations; ρ is a volatilization coefficient of pheromone, $1 - \rho$ is a residual factor of pheromone, and $0 < \rho < 1$

prevents the infinite accumulation of pheromone; $cc_{i,j}(t, I)$ is the pheromone over $e_{i,j}$ by some of m ($\in \mathbb{N}$) interest ants after the $I - th$ iteration.

However, Eq. (1) shows a discrete model, which neglects the actually continuous foraging behaviors. In order to make the modeling process fit the actual ant behaviors better, we propose a continuous model [23], as follows.

$$
\begin{aligned}
T_{i,j}(t, I) = {} & cc_{i,j}(t - \Delta t_{I-1} - \Delta t_{I-2} - \cdots - \Delta t_1, I) \\
& + cc_{i,j}(t - \Delta t_{I-2} - \cdots - \Delta t_1, I - 1) \\
& + \cdots + cc_{i,j}(t - \Delta t_1, 2) + cc_{i,j}(t, 1).
\end{aligned}
\tag{2}
$$

Regarding the proposed continuous model, Eq. (2), there are some related studies, such as [23, 29, 30], and the experimental results have demonstrated its feasibility.

4.3   Evaluation of Routing Hops

Based on the NSFNET and Deltacom topologies, the routing performance of above ACO-inspired ICN routing (ACOIR) is evaluated. Each CR stores 10,000 content items by adopting LRU replacement strategy. For comparison of the ACOIR, the AIRCS [29], the SoCCeR [31], the QAPSR [24] and the MuTR [25] are used as the benchmark method. In the simulations, the interest requests are set to 50, 100, 150, 200, 250, 300, 350 and 400 respectively by 100 times simulations. The performance of average routing hops is dispicted in Fig. 3.

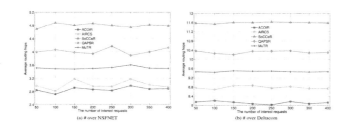

Fig. 3. Average routing hops of ACOIR, AIRCS, SoCCeR, QAPSR and MuTR.

Obviously, ACOIR has the smallest average routing hops. ACOIR can always retrieve the closest content copy, because of the diversity feature and positive feedback feature of inp-ant.

5   Conclusions

In this paper, we present a short review on ACO-inspired ICN routing solution. Firstly, three categories of ICN routing are reviewed, and some related challenges are analyzed. Secondly, bio-inspired ICN routing solution is presented, which includes bionic development, features and design thought. Finally, the feasibility of ACO-inspired ICN routing is summerized from seven different aspects. Furthermore, a continuous updating strategy regarding pheromone is proposed.

In future, we will do further research on the combination of bio-inspired system, bio-inspired networking and bio-inspired computing. In addition, ICN also has some potential to facilite advanced technologies, e.g., cloud computing, big data and 5G.

Acknowlegdment. This work is supported by the Major International (Regional) Joint Research Project of NSFC under Grant no. 71620107003, the National Natural Science Foundation of China under Grant no. 61572123, the Program for Liaoning Innovative Research Term in University under Grant No. LT2016007, and the MoE and China Mobile Joint Research Fund under no. MCM20160201.

References

1. Xylomenos, G., Ververidis, C.N., Siris, V.A., Fotiou, N., Tsilopoulos, C., Vasilakos, X., Katsaros, K.V., Polyzos, G.C.: A survey of information-centric networking research. IEEE Commun. Surv. Tutor. **16**(2), 1024–1049 (2014)
2. Koponen, T., Chawla, M., Chun, B., Ermolinskiy, A., Kim, K.H., Shenker, C., Stoica, I.: A data-oriented (and beyond) network architecture. In: ACM SIGCOMM, pp. 181–192. ACM Press, New York (2007)
3. Dannewitz, C., Golic, J., Ohlman, B., Ahlgren, B.: Secure naming for a network of information. In: IEEE INFOCOM, pp. 1–6. IEEE Press, New York (2010)
4. Carzaniga, A., Papalini, M., Wolf, A.L.: Content-based publish/subscribe networking and information-centric networking. In: ACM SIGCOMM, pp. 56–61. ACM Press, New York (2011)
5. Zhang, L., Afanasyev, A., Burke, J., Jacobson, V., Clay, K., Crowley, P., Papadopoulos, C., Wang, L., Zhang, B.: Named data networking. ACM Comput. Commun. Rev. **44**(3), 66–73 (2014)
6. Ahlgren, B., Dannewitz, C., Imbrenda, C., Kutscher, D., Ohlman, B.: A survey of information-centric networking. IEEE Commun. Mag. **50**(7), 26–36 (2012)
7. Wang, L., Hoque, A.K.M.M., Yi, C., Alyyan, A., Zhang, B.: OSPFN: An OSPF based routing protocol for named data networking. Technical Report NDN-0003, NDN Project (2012)
8. DiBenedetto, S., Papadopoulos, C., Massey, D.: Routing policies in named data networking. In: ACM SIGCOMM, pp. 38–43. ACM Press, New York (2011)
9. Hoque, A.K.M.M., Amin, S.O., Alyyan, A., Zhang, B., Zhang, L., Wang, L.: NLSR: Named-data link state routing protocol. In: ACM SIGCOMM, pp. 15–20. ACM Press, New York (2013)
10. Kurose, J.: Information-centric networking: the evolution from circuits to packets to content. Comput. Netw. **66**, 112–120 (2014)
11. Gareth, T., Nishanth, S., Ruben, C.: A survey of mobility in information-centric networks. Commun. ACM **56**(12), 90–98 (2013)
12. Roos, S., Wang, L., Strufe, T., Kangasharju, J.: Enhancing compact routing in CCN with prefix embedding and topology-aware hashing. In: ACM Workshop on Mobility in the Evolving Internet Architecture, pp. 49–54. ACM Press, New York (2014)

13. Lee, J., Kim, D., Jang, M.W., Lee, B.J.: Proxy-based mobility management scheme in mobile content centric networking environment. In: IEEE International Conference on Consumer Electronics, pp. 595–596. IEEE Press, New York (2011)

14. Kim, D., Kim, J., Kim, Y., Yoon, H., Yeom, I.: Mobility support in content centric networks. In: ACM ICN, pp. 13–18. ACM Press, New York (2012)

15. Lv, J., Wang, X., Huang, M., Li, F., Li, K., Cheng, H.: Accomplishing information consistency under OSPF in general networks. In: IEEE International Conference on Parallel and Distributed Systems, pp. 278–285. IEEE Press, New York (2016)

16. Dressler, F., Akan, O.B.: Bio-inspired networking: from theory to practice. IEEE Commun. Mag. **48**(11), 176–183 (2010)

17. Dressler, F., Akan, O.B.: A survey on bio-inspired networking. Comput. Netw. **54**(6), 881–900 (2010)

18. Dressler, F., Suda, T., Carreras, I., Murata, M., Crowcroft, J.: Guest editorial bio-inspired networking. IEEE J. Sel. Areas Commun. **28**(4), 521–523 (2010)

19. Dixit, S., Sarma, A.: Advances in self-organizing networks. IEEE Commun. Mag. **43**(7), 76–77 (2005)

20. Dixit, S., Sarma, A.: Self-organization in networks today. IEEE Commun. Mag. **43**(8), 77–77 (2005)

21. Dorigo, M., Sttzle, T.: The ant colony optimization metaheuristic: algorithms, applications, and advances. In: Glover, F., Kochenberger, G.A. (eds.) Handbook of Metaheuristics. ISOR, vol. 57, pp. 250–285. Springer, Boston (2003). https://doi.org/10.1007/0-306-48056-5_9

22. Dorigo, M., Maniezzo, V., Colorni, A.: Ant system: optimization by a colony of cooperating agents. IEEE Trans. Syst. Man Cybern. Part B **26**(1), 29–41 (1996)

23. Lv, J., Wang, X., Huang, M.: ACO-inspired ICN routing mechanims with mobility support. Appl. Soft Comput. **58**, 427–440 (2017)

24. Hu, P., Chen, J.: Improved CCN routing based on the combination of genetic algorithm and ant colony optimization. In: International Conference on Computer Science and Network Technology, pp. 846–849. IEEE Press, New York (2013)

25. Eymann, J., Timm-Giel, A.: Multipath transmission in content centric networking using a probabilistic ant-routing mechanism. In: Pesch, D., Timm-Giel, A., Calvo, R.A., Wenning, B.-L., Pentikousis, K. (eds.) MONAMI 2013. LNICST, vol. 125, pp. 45–56. Springer, Cham (2013). https://doi.org/10.1007/978-3-319-04277-0_4

26. Li, C., Okamura, K., Liu, W.: Ant colony based forwarding method for content-centric networking. In: International Conference on Advanced Information Networking and Applications Workshops, pp. 306–311. IEEE Press, New York (2013)

27. Manome, S., Asaka, T.: Routing for content oriented networks using dynamic ant colony optimization. In: Asia-Pacific Symposium on Network Operations and Management, pp. 209–214. IEEE Press, New York (2015)

28. Huang, Q., Luo, F.: Ant colony optimization based QoS routing in named data networking. J. Comput. Methods Sci. Eng. **16**(3), 1–12 (2016)

29. Lv, J., Wang, X., Huang, M.: Ant colony optimization inspired ICN routing with content concentration and similarity relation. IEEE Commun. Lett. **21**(6), 1313–1316 (2017)

30. Lv, J., Wang, X., Ren, K., Huang, M., Li, K.: ACO-inspired information-centric networking routing mechanism. Comput. Netw. **126**, 200–217 (2017)

31. Shanbhag, S., Schwan, N., Rimac, I., Varvello, M.: SoCCeR: services over content-centric routing. In: ACM ICN, pp. 62–67. ACM Press, New York (2011)

Particle Swarm Optimization

Particle Swarm Optimization Based on Pairwise Comparisons

JunQi Zhang[1,2(✉)], JianQing Chen[1,2], XiXun Zhu[1,2], and ChunHui Wang[1,2]

[1] Department of Computer Science and Technology, Tongji University,
Shanghai, China
{zhangjunqi,1452307}@tongji.edu.cn
[2] Key Laboratory of Embedded System and Service Computing,
Ministry of Education, Shanghai, China

Abstract. Particle swarm optimization (PSO) is a widely-adopted optimization algorithm which is based on particles' fitness evaluations and their swarm intelligence. However, it is difficult to obtain the exact fitness evaluation value and is only able to compare particles in a pairwise manner in many real applications such as dose selection, tournament, crowdsourcing and recommendation. Such ordinal preferences from pairwise comparisons instead of exact fitness evaluations lead the traditional PSO to fail. This paper proposes a particle swarm optimization based on pairwise comparisons. Experiments show that the proposed method enables the traditional PSO to work well by using only ordinal preferences from pairwise comparisons.

Keywords: Particle swarm optimization · Pairwise comparisons
Evolutionary algorithms · Swarm intelligence

1 Introduction

Particle Swarm Optimization is an optimization method in swarm intelligence and was first proposed by Kennedy and Eberhart [5]. In the traditional PSO algorithm, a particle changes its velocity and position under the guidance of its own historical optimal position and the best position found so far by the whole swarm in order to achieve the global optimization. With characteristics of few parameters and easy implement, PSO has been applied to solve various optimization problems.

Shi and Eberhart [14] introduced a new parameter called inertia weight w to balance the global search ability and the local refinement. Besides, Clerc and Kennedy [3] analyzed w of how to control the convergence tendencies. Zhan et al. [16] presented an adaptive particle swarm optimization which consists of two main steps. First, perform a real-time evolutionary state estimation procedure to identify evolutionary state after evaluating the population distribution and particle fitness. Then, when the evolutionary state is classified as convergence speed, an elitist learning strategy is performed. Neri et al. [9] employed a

© Springer International Publishing AG, part of Springer Nature 2018
Y. Tan et al. (Eds.): ICSI 2018, LNCS 10941, pp. 125–131, 2018.
https://doi.org/10.1007/978-3-319-93815-8_13

probabilistic representation of the swarms behavior. In [7], Li et al. proposed a composite PSO algorithm called historical memory-based PSO (HMPSO) which uses an estimation of distribution algorithm to estimate and preserve the distribution information of particles' historical promising pbests. Each particle adopts the best candidate position of historical memory, particles' current pbests, and the swarm's gbest. Cheng and Jin [2] proposed a competitive swarm optimizer (CSO) introducing a pairwise competition mechanism where the particle that loses the competition will update its position by learning from the winner. Shen et al. [13] proposed a hierarchical learning bare-bones PSO (HLBPSO) using an archive to store the accepted infeasible solutions and auxiliary operations in order to help accept infeasible solutions to enter into the feasible region. Nitin et al. [12] presented a Dynamic-PSO (DPSO) which provides dynamicity to particles externally in such a manner that stagnated particles move towards potentially better unexplored region to maintain diversity. Qin et al. [10] proposed an inter-swarm interactive strategy which divides a swarm into a learning swarm and a learned swarm. The particles in the learning swarm learn from the experience of the learned swarm.

Nevertheless, it is difficult to obtain the exact fitness evaluation value but a preference from a pairwise comparison in many real applications such as dose selection [6], tournament [1], crowdsourcing [15] and recommendation [11]. Kpamegan and Flournoy [6] presented a class of up and down designs to identify the dose that maximizes the patients' success probability. Buhlmann and Huber [1] proposed ranking in tournaments using pairwise comparisons. Yi et al. [15] leveraged pairwise comparisons to present a crowdranking framework based on the theory of matrix completion for infering the ranking list of items. Lior and Kisilevich [11] presented a new, anytime preferences elicitation method that uses pairwise comparisons between items to create users' profiles. Jamieson and Nowak [4] embedded the objects in a d-dimensional Euclidean space and used pairwise comparisons to derive partial and full ranking.

Such ordinal preferences from pairwise comparisons instead of exact fitness evaluations lead the traditional PSO to fail. This paper proposes a particle swarm optimization based on pairwise comparisons. It derives the personal best position and the global best position from pairwise comparisons such that the traditional PSO can work.

The rest of the paper is organized as follows. Section 2 reviews the traditional PSO. In Sect. 3, Particle swarm optimization based on pairwise comparisons will be proposed to enable the conversion of traditional PSO to work based on pairwise comparisons. The experimental results on benchmark functions are presented in Sect. 4. Section 5 gives the conclusion and future work.

2   Standard Particle Swarm Optimization

PSO simulates social models such as birds flocking and fish schooling to solve optimization problems. In [14], Shi and Eberhart proposed a standard particle swarm optimization (SPSO). Each individual is modeled as a particle in an d-dimensional search space and represents a candidate solution to the problem.

Particles in the whole swarm are connected in a ring topology. Each particle consists of two vectors, position vector $X_i = [x_{i1}^t, x_{i2}^t, ...x_{id}^t]$ and velocity vector $V_i = [v_{i1}^t, v_{i2}^t, ...v_{id}^t]$ where $i \in \{1,2,...N\}$, N is the population size, d denotes the dimension of the solution space, t is the iteration number. The best solution of the ith particle found in the tth iteration is known as $pbest_i = [p_{i1}^t, p_{i2}^t, ...p_{id}^t]$ and the best solution found by all particles is called $gbest = [g_1^t, g_2^t, ...g_d^t]$. During the evolutionary procedure, particles update these two vectors under the guidance of the pbests and the best positions in their neighbors p_{gd}^t using the following equations:

$$v_{id}^{t+1} = wv_{id}^t + c_1 r_1 \left(pbest_{id}^t - x_{id}^t\right) + c_2 r_2 \left(p_{gd}^t - x_{id}^t\right) \tag{1}$$

$$x_{id}^{t+1} = x_{id}^{t+1} + v_{id}^{t+1} \tag{2}$$

where w is termed inertia weight to balance the global search ability and the local refinement and control the convergence tendencies [3]. c_1 and c_2 denote acceleration coefficients. c_1 represents the cognitive component and c_2 is the social component. As mentioned in [14], c_1 and c_2 is integer 2. r_1 and r_2 are random values ranging in $[0, 1]$. Its main procedure is presented in Algorithm 1.

Algorithm 1. SPSO

1: Initialize a group of particles (population size N), including positions and velocities
2: **while** (stop criterion not met) **do**
3:    **for** $i = 1$ to N **do**
4:       Evaluate the fitness value of each particle
5:       Compare each particle's fitness value with its *pbest*
6:       **if** the current fitness value is better **then**
7:          Update the *pbest*
8:       **end if**
9:    **end for**
10:    Update the *gbest*
11:    Update particles' velocities and positions according to Eqs. (1) and (2)
12: **end while**

---

3   PSO Based on Pairwise Comparisons

PSO cannot work without *pbest* and *gbest*. As a precondition of the traditional PSO, a specific fitness value is calculated via the evaluation function. Then the particle's current fitness value is compared with its *pbest*'s fitness value to update *pbest* and derive *gbest* which is the minimum of the updated *pbest*s. In the traditional PSO, it requires N times fitness evaluation totally in every iteration to obtain the fitness value. Based on these fitness values, *pbest*s and *gbest*s can be updated using Eqs. (1) and (2). So specific fitness value plays a significant role in the traditional PSO.

Nevertheless, it is difficult to obtain the exact fitness evaluation value but a preference from a pairwise comparison in many real applications such as dose selection, tournament, crowdsourcing and recommendation, where it is only able to compare particles in a pairwise manner. The outcome of the pairwise comparisons essentially represents pairwise preferences whether or not an particle is preferred to another one. In this paper, we propose an extension of SPSO based on pairwise comparisons for optimization (PC-SPSO), in which *pbest* and *gbest* are inferred from pairwise comparisons. In order to understand PC-SPSO, we give a definition and two algorithms as follows:

Algorithm 2. Getgbest(N, *pbest*, *gbest*)

Input: *pbests* of N particles in $\Re^d$, $pbest_1$, $pbest_2...pbest_N$
1: **for** $i = 1$ to N **do**
2:    **if** the *pbest* of ith particle is better than *gbest* **then**
3:        $gbest = X_i$
4:    **end if**
5: **end for**
Output: *gbest* of the whole swarm

Algorithm 3. PSO Based on Pairwise Comparisons

1: Initialization
2: $gbest = infinite$
3: **for** $i = 1$ to N **do**
4:    randomly initialize V_i and X_i
5:    $pbest_i = X_i$
6:    Getgbest $(N, pbest, gbest)$
7: **end for**
8: **while** (stop criterion not met) **do**
9:    /*pbest update*/
10:    **for** $i = 1$ to N **do**
11:        **if** $PC_i = 1$ **then**
12:            Update the pbest
13:        **end if**
14:    **end for**
15:    /*update the gbest*/
16:    Getgbest $(N, pbest, gbest)$
17:    Update the V_i and X_i according to Eqs. (1) and (2)
18: **end while**

Definition 1. *Let PC_i be a pairwise comparison between particle i and its pbest, $i \in \{1,2,...N\}$. The result is feedbacked by the environment and the following equation is executed:*

$$PC_i = \begin{cases} 1, & \text{if current particle is better than its pbest} \\ 0, & \text{otherwise.} \end{cases} \qquad (3)$$

Given position i, j, the outcome of the comparisons is feedbacked by the environment. If $PC_i = 1$, position i is preferred over position j. With the definition of PC_i, the pseudocode of PC-SPSO algorithm is summarized in Algorithms 2 and 3. In order to update $gbest$, it is compared with every particle's $pbest$ orderly and details are described in Algorithm 2. $pbest$ is updated according to the value of PC_i.

4   Experiment

In this section, the convergence curves of the proposed PC-SPSO on CEC2013 [8] benchmark functions are illustrated to verify the proposed method. We choose representative uni-modal f_1, multi-modal f_{12} and composition f_{23} test functions and the parameter settings are as follows:

(1) repeat times = 51 in each test function to obtain the mean results.
(2) the total number of the whole swarm $N = 50$ and they are connected with the ring topology.
(3) the inertia weight $w = 0.72984$.
(4) the acceleration coefficients $c_1 = c_2 = 1.49617$.
(5) the dimensions of all the test functions $d = 30$ (Fig. 1).

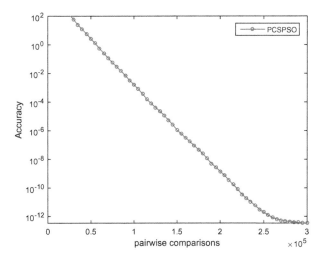

Fig. 1. On unimodal function f_1, as the number of pairwise comparisons increases, the accuracy converges to zero.

The result is shown in the figures. The x-axis represents the number of pairwise comparisons and the y-axis represents the accuracy which is the difference between the experiment fitness values and the actual fitness values (Figs. 2 and 3).

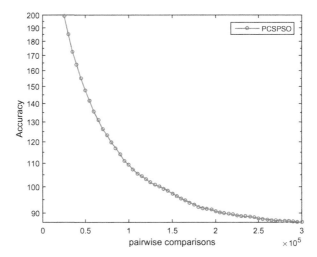

Fig. 2. The accuracy converges as the pairwise comparisons increases on multi-modal function f_{12}

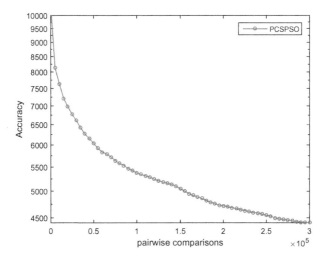

Fig. 3. As x increases, y converges to a constant value on composition function $f23$

5   Conclusion

In this paper, we introduce an extension of traditional PSO named PC-SPSO. A novel strategy is proposed using only ordinal preferences from pairwise comparisons to obtain *pbest* and *gbest* to guide the overall particles' directions when it is difficult to obtain the exact fitness evaluation value but a preference from a pairwise comparison in many real applications. The outcome of the pairwise comparisons essentially represents pairwise preferences whether or not an particle is preferred to another one. Experimental results carried out on benchmark functions show the convergence property of the proposed methods.

Our future work will focus on how to reduce the number of pairwise comparisons to obtain a satisfactory *gbest*. The applications of algorithms will also be considered in our future work.

References

1. Buhlmann, H., Huber, P.J.: Pairwise comparison and ranking in tournaments. Ann. Math. Stat. **34**(2), 501–510 (1963)
2. Cheng, R., Jin, Y.: A competitive swarm optimizer for large scale optimization. IEEE Trans. Cybern. **45**(2), 191–204 (2015)
3. Clerc, M., Kennedy, J.: The particle swarm - explosion, stability, and convergence in a multidimensional complex space. IEEE Trans. Evol. Comput. **6**(1), 58–73 (2002)
4. Jamieson, K.G., Nowak, R.D.: Active ranking using pairwise comparisons. In: Advances in Neural Information Processing Systems, pp. 2240–2248 (2011)
5. Kennedy, J., Eberhart, R.: Particle swarm optimization. In: Proceedings of IEEE International Conference on Neural Networks, 1995, vol. 4, pp. 1942–1948 (2002)
6. Kpamegan, E.E., Flournoy, N.: Up-and-down designs for selecting the dose with maximum success probability. Commun. Stat. Part C Seq. Anal. **27**(1), 78–96 (2008)
7. Li, J., Zhang, J.Q., Jiang, C.J., Zhou, M.C.: Composite particle swarm optimizer with historical memory for function optimization. IEEE Trans. Cybern. **45**(10), 2350–2363 (2015)
8. Liang, J.J., Runarsson, T.P., Mezura-Montes, E., Clerc, M., Suganthan, P.N., Coello, C.A.C., Deb, K.: Problem definitions and evaluation criteria for the CEC 2006 special session on constrained real-parameter optimization. Int. J. Comput. Assist. Radiol. Surg. (2) (2005)
9. Neri, F., Mininno, E., Iacca, G.: Compact particle swarm optimization. Inf. Sci. **239**(4), 96–121 (2013)
10. Qin, Q., Cheng, S., Zhang, Q., Li, L., Shi, Y.: Particle swarm optimization with interswarm interactive learning strategy. IEEE Trans. Cybern. **46**(10), 2238–2251 (2016)
11. Rokach, L., Kisilevich, S.: Initial profile generation in recommender systems using pairwise comparison. IEEE Trans. Syst. Man Cybern. Part C **42**(6), 1854–1859 (2012)
12. Saxena, N., Tripathi, A., Mishra, K.K., Misra, A.K.: Dynamic-PSO: an improved particle swarm optimizer. In: Evolutionary Computation, pp. 212–219 (2015)
13. Shen, Y., Chen, J., Zeng, C., Ji, B.: A novel constrained bare-bones particle swarm optimization. In: Evolutionary Computation, pp. 2511–2517 (2016)
14. Shi, Y., Eberhart, R.: A modified particle swarm optimizer, pp. 69–71 (1998)
15. Yi, J., Jin, R., Jain, S., Jain, A.K.: Inferring users preferences from crowdsourced pairwise comparisons: a matrix completion approach, pp. 208–212 (2013)
16. Zhan, Z.H., Zhang, J., Li, Y., Chung, S.H.: Adaptive particle swarm optimization. IEEE Trans. Syst. Man Cybern. Part B Cybern. **39**(6), 1362–1381 (2009)

Chemical Reaction Intermediate State Kinetic Optimization by Particle Swarm Optimization

Fei Tan[1(✉)] and Bin Xia[1,2]

[1] School of Life Sciences, Peking University, Beijing 100871, China
flyhighon@163.com
[2] College of Chemistry and Molecular Engineering, Peking University,
Beijing 100871, China

Abstract. Large biological molecules such as proteins associating to form multi-component complexes are attracting more and more research interests. The association reaction of the large biological molecules are closely related with associate rate and reaction intermediate states which are key to elucidate the reaction pathways as their kinetic and structural characteristics which shed lights on the reaction process and energy landscape. This paper proposes a novel method modelling the chemical reactions by using neural networks with the help of the predefined chemical reaction model, and then follows by using the typical particle swarm optimization algorithm to minimize the error between the output of neural networks and experimental data. Experiments are conducted to demonstrate the proposed method as a promising way dealing with this difficult task.

Keywords: Particle swarm optimization · Artificial neural networks
Intermediate state kinetics · Parameter optimization

1 Introduction

Association reactions between chemical or biological species often involve an intermediate state whose existence greatly expedite the efficiency of molecule association thus increasing the chemical or biological reaction speed [1].

Reaction intermediates, transition states, or sometimes called encounter complex along a reaction pathways refer to one or a set of configurations that possess rotational or translational correlations between the interacting species. The interactions between different subunits in a reaction intermediate might be native-like or near native-like and it does not necessarily corresponds to a local energy minimum or a species trapped in kinetic experiments [2].

In comparison to protein folding, structural and kinetic studies on intermediates and transient states on protein-protein association pathways are much less common mainly due to its low concentration and its fleeting existence [1].

© Springer International Publishing AG, part of Springer Nature 2018
Y. Tan et al. (Eds.): ICSI 2018, LNCS 10941, pp. 132–142, 2018.
https://doi.org/10.1007/978-3-319-93815-8_14

A much more general case is when experimental evidence provides only the kinetic and structural information of the native state which often exist as the dominant fraction and is much easier to detect using regular experimental tools. Kinetic or structural characteristics of the transitional state often demonstrate itself on experimentally measured data, for instance, a linear dependence of the observed association rate constant on reactant concentration indicates an absence of transitional state, while an hyperbolic dependence of reactant concentration signifies that the reaction is not a first order reaction and thus the involvement of possible transitional state [5]; 2D NMR spectrum of proteins might show a detenuation of peak intensity if the transitional state is involved in an intermediate exchange with the native state [1]. Then it is crucial to extract kinetic or structural information of the transitional state from the relatively scant experimental.

The main objective of this paper is to model the chemical reaction process and then use the particle swarm optimization algorithm to minimize the error between the output of neural networks for modelling the chemical reactions and experimental data. Based on the artificial neural networks and predefined chemical reaction model, this paper presents a novel model-based parameter extraction method to optimize the kinetic parameters associating with hidden reacting species with high efficiency and computational cost.

We introduce some basic knowledge about the chemical reaction simulation and model-based simulation in Sect. 2. Then we describe the proposed a neural networks based method for extracting the intermediate state kinetic parameters in Sect. 3. Some experimental results and discussions are given in Sect. 4. Finally, a concluding remark is given in Sect. 5.

2   Background

2.1   Diffusion and Reaction Encounter Complex

Molecule association from unbound components can be described using single or multi-step models, in multi-step models, an unstable encounter complex is formed through diffusion, in certain cases, the encounter complex evolve into an intermediate state that is a more stable species. The encounter complex and the intermediate state are the most unstable species in the reaction pathway, bonds in a intermediate or encounter complex are in the process of been constantly broken and remade. Experimental detection of the encounter complex and intermediate state has been done for some reactions, but for reactions, especially large biological reactions, when the approach of experimental measurement is limited, experimental detection of transient states might be extremely difficult. Therefore, computational methods aimed to describe the reaction environment and simulate the process of reaction emerges to track the course of molecule-molecule association.

2.2 Model-Based Simulation of Kinetic Parameters

Reaction models based on experimental evidence are beginning to be harness to accurately model the reaction process of association reactions and to simplify the complicated dynamic simulation of molecule association in an experimentally directed way.

Reaction models depicts the rate of reaction, the number of species participating in the reaction either in equation forms or in stochastic forms. Large scale reactions that involve large quantities of reactants are can be described by deterministic linear or non-linear ordinary differential equations for homogenous reaction space or partial differential equations for reactions partitioned into different compartments. Small scale association reaction that can be described by a limited number of molecules are more accurately simulated by stochastic simulation algorithms (SSA), chemical reaction models can be incorporated into both of the aforementioned simulation strategies based on existing experimental data.

Macroscopic deterministic reaction systems are often described by differential equations such as in case of single reactant

$$G\left(x, y\left(x\right), y(x)^{(1)}, ..., y(x)^{(n-1)}, y(x)^{(n)}\right) = 0 \tag{1}$$

or sets of differential equations when multiple reacting species is present

$$\begin{cases} G_1\left(x, y_1\left(x\right), y_1(x)^{(1)}, y_2\left(x\right)..., y_k\left(x\right), y_k(x)^{(1)}\right) = 0 \\ \vdots \\ G_k\left(x, y_1\left(x\right), y_1(x)^{(1)}, y_2\left(x\right)..., y_k\left(x\right), y_k(x)^{(1)}\right) = 0 \end{cases} \tag{2}$$

Some theoretical work has been done to understand the consequences of stochastic fluctuation of molecule concentration on molecular interactions, which form the basis of the majority of chemical or biological processes. In microscopic systems where only a small number of molecules are present, stochastic diffusion takes a crucial role; therefore, differential equations describing the behavior of molecules in such a system will take diffusion and the location of each particles into account. It has been shown experimentally that in some chemical or biological systems, stochasticity of reaction results in large variability in the reaction rate.

Take two freely diffusing reacting particles with a center to center distance r as example, $P(r, t)$ be the probability density of two particles to remain unbound and separated with a distance r at time t.

$$\frac{\partial p\left(r, t\right)}{\partial t} = D\frac{1}{r^{\omega-1}}\frac{\partial}{\partial r}\left(r^{\omega}\frac{\partial p\left(r, t\right)}{\partial r}\right) \tag{3}$$

The generalized form is when the space is divided into various compartments, and in compartment C_j, where the molecule X_{ij} denote a molecule species I in subvolume C_j, exemplifying the reaction as

$$n_{ij}X_{ij} + n_{kj}X_{kj} \rightarrow x_{ij}X_{ij} \tag{4}$$

where n_{ij} is the stoichiometry vector.

Modeling the reaction gives the reaction-diffusion master equation

$$\partial p\left(x,t\right)/\partial t = Mp\left(x,t\right) + Dp\left(x,t\right)/\partial t.$$
$$p\left(x,0\right) = \delta_{xx_0} \tag{5}$$

where M governs the reaction and D the diffusion.

$$Mp\left(x,t\right) = w_{rj}\left(x_j - n_r\right)p\left(x_1, ..., x_j - n_r, ..., x_K, t\right)$$
$$- w_{rj}\left(x_j\right)p\left(x,t\right)$$
$$Dp\left(x,t\right) = q^{(i)}\left(x_i - m^{(i)}\right)p\left(x_1, ..., x_i - m^{(i)}, ..., x_N, t\right) \tag{6}$$
$$- q^{(i)}x_{ik}p\left(x,t\right)$$

in which q_{jk} is the chemical reaction propensity function which is a measure of the reaction rate of each species proportional to its copy number. D is the diffusion rate constant and gamma the dimensionality.

Stochastic simulation algorithm (SSA) is used to model the chemical master equation. SSA is a procedure for numerically simulating the time evolution of a small scale, well-stirred, diffusion influenced chemically reacting system in which the reaction rate is subjected to stochastic variations. The most well-known and widely applied of which is developed by Gillespia and termed Gillespias Algorithm, the general principle of which is for chemical reactions of the form:

$$A + A \rightarrow C, A + B \rightarrow D. \tag{7}$$

The process of simulating the reaction numerically is as follows:

(1) Generate two random numbers r_1, r_2 uniformly distributed in $(0, 1)$.
(2) Compute the propensity functions of each reaction by $\alpha_1 = A(t)(A(t)-1)k_1$, $\alpha_2 = A(t)B(t)k_2$, $\alpha_3 = k_3$ and $\alpha_4 = k_4$. Compute $\alpha_0 = \alpha_1 + \alpha_2 + \alpha_3 + \alpha_4$.
(3) Here we determine the time when the next chemical reaction takes place as $t + \tau$ where $\tau = \frac{1}{\alpha_0} \ln\left[\frac{1}{r_1}\right]$
(4) Compute the number of molecules at time $t + \tau$ by
$A(t + \tau) = A(t) - 2, A(t) - 1, A(t) + 1, A(t)$
$B(t + \tau) = B(t) - 2, B(t) - 1, B(t) + 1, B(t)$
if $0 \le r_2 < \alpha_1/\alpha_0$; if $\alpha_1/\alpha_0 \le r_2 < (\alpha_1 + \alpha_2)/\alpha_0$; if $(\alpha_1 + \alpha_2)/\alpha_0 \le r_2 < (\alpha_1 + \alpha_2 + \alpha_3)/\alpha_0$; if $(\alpha_1 + \alpha_2 + \alpha_3)/\alpha_0 \le r_2 < 1$;

The step (4) offers the choice of which reaction occurs at time step t and the molecular number will be updated accordingly in the same step. However, despite of recent major improvements in the efficiency of the SSA, its drawback remains the inaccuracy of simulation results which is a common occurrence in experimental-data-independent computational simulations which is a direct consequence of the unpredictability of chemical or biological systems.

3 Proposed Method

3.1 Mathematical Modeling of Chemical or Biological Reactions

In this section, mathematical models of chemical or biological reactions are presented as differential equations. For systems where the reaction size is large enough that stochastic fluctuations in solvents or the copy number of critical reaction species have little effect on the macroscopic rate constants, Conventional Deterministic Reaction Rate equation (RRE) is sufficient to describe the reaction system. Depending on whether the reactants are partitioned into different spatial compartments, we categorize the RRE into ordinary differential equations and Partial Differential equations.

The method regards ordinary differential equations of the form that describe macroscopic reactions in which copy number of reactant are large enough and spatial variability is low. Most of the deterministic chemical Rate equations can be expressed in the form:

$$G\left(x, y\left(x\right), y(x)^{(1)}, ..., y(x)^{(n-1)}, y(x)^{(n)}\right) = 0, \ x \in D \tag{8}$$

where D designates a certain definition domain of x, y signifies the solution to be computed, $y^{(n)}$ denotes the nth order derivative of y.

The boundary conditions are defined as

$$\psi_i\left(x, y\left(x\right), y(x)^{(1)}, ..., y(x)^{(n-1)}, y(x)^{(n)}\right)\Big|_{x=t_i} = 0 \tag{9}$$

where t_i is any predefined points in domain D.

3.2 Neural Networks for Fitting Experimental Data and Solving Differential Equations

As a universal approximator, it is proposed that neural networks with appropriate architecture will be able to approximate any Borel measurable function to any desired precision [6,7]. Given the general form of the differential equations to be approximated are given above, here, we try to utilize a Feedforward Multilayer Perceptron (MLP) for fitting the given experimental data. An arbitrary continuous function y and its n-th order derivatives $\frac{d^n y}{dx^n}$ can be approximated by the feedforward MLP with multiple inputs, single output and single hidden layer with low variance and bias, which are given below.

$$y\left(x\right) = \sum_{i=1}^{m} \alpha_i f\left(w_i x + \beta_i\right) \tag{10}$$

$$\frac{d^n y}{dx^n} = \sum_{i=1}^{m} \alpha_i \frac{d^n}{dx^n} f\left(w_i x + \beta_i\right) \tag{11}$$

Where x is the independent variable, α_i, w_i, β_i are bounded real-valued adaptive parameters from the neural networks, m is the total number of hidden nodes and f is the activation function often taking the from of a sigmoid function

$$f\left(x\right) = \frac{1}{1 + e^{-x}} \tag{12}$$

Any given experimental data can be formulated with a linear combination of neural nodes, with an arbitrary number of nodes m. The adaptive parameters in the neural network can be modified by a search algorithm to account for the fitting of the experimental data.

3.3 Fitness Evaluation Function

The solution of the differential equation is incorporated into the fitness function. The fitness function contains two errors arising from the two subproblems. A linear combination of errors with certain biases from the differential equation and fitting of the neural network with experimental data form an unsupervised error function. The error to be minimized can be defined as the sum of the squared errors

$$e = e^1 + e^2 \tag{13}$$

or it can be expressed as an weighted error evaluation with minimization priority in either part of the error minimization according to the requirements.

$$e = (1 - \lambda)\, e^1 + \lambda e^2 \tag{14}$$

Where λ is the weight in the range of 0–1.

The weight factor puts emphasis on one error over the other, and offer more freedom in user coordination, this leads to a higher accuracy and better robustness. In the expression of e, e^1 is the error that originate from differential equations and can be expressed as

$$e^1 = \sum_{i=1}^{m} \left(G\left(x_i, y\left(x_i \right), y(x_i)^{(1)}, ..., y(x_i)^{(n-1)}, y(x_i)^{(n)} \right) \right)^2 \tag{15}$$

Where function G is the same as in Eq. 16, m is the total number of points in the definition domain of independent variable x.

The e^2 is an error arising from neural network data fitting of experimentally measured values with an expression in the form of

$$e^2 = (D\left(x_i \right) - N\left(x, p \right))^2 \tag{16}$$

where $N(x, p)$ is single output neural network with parameter p and n input units fed with variable vector x. $D(x_i)$ contains no adjustable parameters and is the experimental data vector. The weights vector p is adjusted and trained to adapt to the minimization problem.

In the minimization process, the parameters to be adapted in the minimization algorithms are just the parameters from the differential equations and the weights from the neural networks.

3.4   Global Minimization Search Algorithm

Our purpose is to use a global searching method to find a set of optimal parameters that best fit the experimental data and the chemical reaction derived differential equations. Here the typical particle swarm optimization (PSO) proposed by Eberhart and Kennedy in 1995 as a stochastic global optimization technique inspired from the behavior of particles or individuals in a swarm, is employed to solve this problem [8,9]. The main advantages of PSO algorithm are that it is simple in concepts, easy in implementation, stable in convergence and efficient computationally compared to other heuristic optimization techniques. In PSO algorithm, each individual of the swarm represents a possible solution in the optimization problem. The problem of finding a global optimum is turned into finding the optimum individual. Each individual or particle search in the problem space, and its measure of quality are its positions and velocities in an exploration space. The PSO algorithm initializes with each particle placed randomly within an exploration space, and then each particle searches the space with its positions and velocities updated iteratively according to previous local best $Lbest_i^{n-1}$ and its global best $Gbest_i^{n-1}$. The updating scheme are as follows:

$$V_i^j = \omega V_i^{j-1} + c_1 r_1 \left(Lbest_i^{n-1} - X_i^{j-1} \right) + c_2 r_2 \left(Gbest_i^{n-1} - X_i^{j-1} \right) \tag{17}$$

$$X_i^j = X_i^{j-1} + V_i^j \tag{18}$$

In the updating scheme, i is the number of the particle, j is the number of iteration, ω is the inertia weight, c_1 and c_2 defined by the authors as the local and global acceleration constant, r_1 and r_2 are random vector in the range of 0 and 1, X and V are positional and velocity vectors.

The velocities in PSO algorithm are updated according to Eq. 15, the first term is the velocity of the particle in previous iteration, the second term is the difference between the position of the particle and its previous local best position in the particles life history, the last term in the expression indicates the difference between the global best position of the of the particles and the ith particles present position. The more in the difference between the global best position and the position of the ith particle in iteration $n - 1$, the greater the change in the velocity of the particle in the next iteration, this difference will propagate itself to the particles position in the nth iteration.

The stopping criteria of PSO algorithm is when an user defined cutoff of the fitness value is reached by one of the particles of the swarm. Then the optimal parameters from the neural networks and the differential equations will be the outcomes of the PSO algorithms. The results can be used as references to future application and analysis.

The main steps of our application of neural networks and PSO in data fitting and parameter optimization process can be summarized as follows.

Step 1. Feedforward neural networks construction for experimental data fitting

Step 2. Constructing differential equations according to the chemical or biological reaction systems

Step 3. Fitness function construction by combining errors from data fitting and
differential equations

Step 4. PSO optimization of kinetic parameters

4   Experimental Results and Analysis

We have carried out our studies in different experimental conditions and have
measured the interconversion process of both monomers and dimers of $M^{Pro}-C$.
The experiments are done in $303K$, $306K$, $308K$ and $310K$, the overall interconversion rates are measured to be in increasing order. Elevated temperature
increases kinetic energy and translational velocities of particles in solutions,
enhancing the rate of particle collision, hence, increasing the temperature will
increase the overall association rate constant. However, intermediate states are
not detected directly by experimental measurement, but will the intermediate
state be affect in the same way by increasing temperature? Our method explicitly
deals with these kinds of problems.

We have carry out Neural Network Fitting of the dimeric species in our
program at various temperatures as shown in Fig. 1, Blue lines are experimentally measured dimeric concentration curves and colored lines with markers are
outcomes from NN, we can see an clear overlap of the lines and an minimum
systematic fitting error of around 10^{-3}, indicating the accuracy of the fitting
module in our program.

The intermediate state curve of WT $M^{Pro}-C$ in various temperature are
shown in Fig. 2, in which the intermediate state concentration are plotted as
a function of time (with unit in seconds). The values of the concentration of
intermediates are back-calculated from experimentally derived Neural Network
functions based on our predefined model.

Close inspection of the intermediate concentration curve indicates that
almost for all of the temperatures investigated, the intermediate concentration
is highest or almost the highest at the start of the interconversion process and
slowly reaches a low steady value with respect to time demonstrating that the
interconversion is approaching equilibrium. We also observed a high value in
intermediate state concentration at the start of the reaction and then a dive
in the concentration curve with respect to time, the shifts in intermediate concentration is caused by the interplay between the four pathways with its rate
constants denoted by k_a, k_b, k_c, and k_d. The highest point in intermediate state
concentration may mark the opportune time for experimental detection of this
elusive species. Judging from these result, increasing solution temperature, more
rapid thermodynamic motion affect the association rate constant and in turn
place its impact on the turnover rate of the intermediate state.

The intermediate concentration generally increases as temperature increases,
probably due to its faster conversion from monomers. Nevertheless, judging from
table (4), the conversion rate from the intermediate state to dimeric state WT

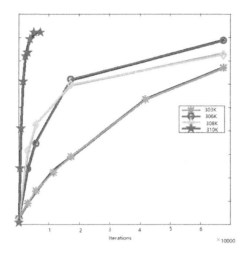

Fig. 1. Nerual Network Fitting of the dimeric species at various temperatures. The experimental curves are drawn as blue lines while nerual network curve are represented as colored lines interspersed with markers. 303K as green lines with flower markers, 306K with red lines and circular marker, 308K with cyan lines with diamond markers and purple lines represents 310K with star markers. (Color figure online)

$M^{Pro} - C$ also increases as temperature elevates, the general upshifting trend in intermediate concentration with incrementing temperature might be the another indication that the conversion from monomeric WT $M^{Pro} - C$ to dimers is reaction limited and thus increasing the reaction rate in the formation of intermediate state from monomers largely compensates the increase in diffusional encounters which works to reduce the concentration of the intermediate state.

As expected, the values of intermediate concentration is extremely low, approaching or below the current experimental detection limits of ordinary facilities such as Stop-Flow spectrometry, Nuclear Magnetic Resonance Spectroscopy, Electron Microscopy or crystallography, to make matter worse, the rapid shifting of the intermediate concentration and its final convergence to a extremely low steady value at equilibrium makes experimental detection even harder and thus the urgent need for theoretical and engineering prediction. The highest point in intermediate state concentration yielded from our program may mark the opportune time for experimental detection of this elusive species. Judging from these result, increasing solution temperature, more rapid thermodynamic motion affect the association rate constant and in turn place its impact on the turnover rate of the intermediate state.

The overall absolute error that combines the errors from Neural Network fitting and the deviations of the parameter-reconstructed reaction from the given models are given in Fig. 3, which shows the combined absolute errors obtained for $M^{Pro} - C$ systems in different temperature as PSO optimization progresses. As the number of iteration increases, the absolute errors decreases, first with a

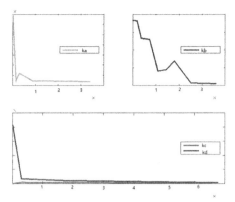

Fig. 2. Intermediate state curves as calculated from program-derive kinetic parameters of model 1. The meaning of each curve are indicated by its legend.

steep dive probably resulting from random global search in the parameter search space, and then with local adjustment which lead to a gradual reduction of the errors at the later part of the minimization process. Convergence is generally reached at 30000 iterations except for 303K, however, an acceptable error cutoff is already reached. Compromising execution time and performance, an iteration of 30000 is selected for all runs of our program.

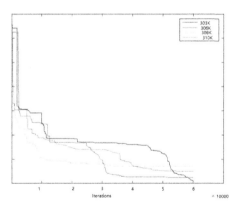

Fig. 3. The minimization of overall absolute error with the number of iteration. Different temperatures are represented by different thin colored lines, and the progression and the final convergence of total error are clearly observed in the figure. (Color figure online)

In summary, the convergence of total error is achieve at around iteration 30000 in PSO, while convergence of parameters is also achieved at 30000 iterations. Noticing that the optimized parameters of the kinetic equations reached convergence rapidly, without much random variations, meaning that the parameters are robust and stable in the optimization process undertaken by PSO. In neural network fitting of experimental data, fewer neural nodes in neural networks simplifies the network topology, reduces the amount of unknown parameters that went along with the neural networks, decreasing the possibility of overfitting. We reduced the number of nodes in the hidden layer to 5 to prevent overfitting while at the same time best maintaining the fitting capability of the neural networks.

The results of the optimum parameters yielded by our methods is obtained in the our experiments for both the wildtype $M^{Pro} - C$ and its mutants in various solution conditions. The outcome of the parameter values are the average of 10 repetitive runs of our program, with an variance in acceptable range. As was shown in the experiments, the values of the kinetic rate constant pertaining to the intermediate states of both the wild-type and the mutant protein in various experimental conditions are somewhat different, but the overall trends are generally the same with $k_b \gg k_c$, $k_a \gg k_d$, implying the lifetime of the intermediate state is transient, and due to the rapid turnover rate of the intermediate state, its quantity shall be dramatically low.

5   Conclusion

In this paper, a novel approach for predicting kinetic rate constants and reacting species concentration, which make use of the neural networks to model the chemical reaction and is optimized by using the typical swarm intelligence optimization algorithm, i.e., particle swarm optimization. The extensive experimental results have demonstrated the validation and effectiveness of our proposed approach in this paper.

References

1. Schreiber, G., Haran, G., Zhou, H.X.: Fundamental aspects of protein- protein association kinetics. Chem. Rev. **109**(3), 839–860 (2009)
2. Hartwell, L.H., Hopfield, J.J., Leibler, S., Murray, A.W.: From molecular to modular cell biology. Nature **402**, C47–C52 (1999)
3. Agbanusi, I.C., Isaacson, S.A.: A comparison of bimolecular reaction models for stochastic reaction-diffusion systems. Bull. Math. Biol. **76**(4), 922–946 (2014)
4. Northrup, S.H.: Diffusion-controlled ligand binding to multiple competing cell-bound receptors. J. Phys. Chem **92**(20), 5847–5850 (1988)
5. Martinez, H.L.: Kinetics of nonstationary, single species, bimolecular, diffusion-influenced irreversible reactions. J. Chem. Phys. **104**(7), 2692–2698 (1996)
6. Hornik, K., Stinchcombe, M., White, H.: Multilayer feedforward networks are universal approximators. Neural Netw. **2**(5), 359–366 (1989)
7. Tsoulos, I.G., Gavrilis, D., Glavas, E.: Solving differential equations with constructed neural networks. Neurocomputing **72**(10), 2385–2391 (2009)
8. Kennedy, J., Eberhart, R.: Particle swarm optimization. In: IEEE International Conference on Neural Networks, Perth, Australia, pp. 1942–1948 (1995)
9. Shi, Y.H. Eberhart, R.C.: A modified particle swarm optimizer. In: IEEE International Conference on Evolutionary Computation, Anchorage, USA, pp. 69–73 (1998)

Artificial Bee Colony Algorithms

A Hyper-Heuristic of Artificial Bee Colony and Simulated Annealing for Optimal Wind Turbine Placement

Peng-Yeng Yin[(⊠)] and Geng-Shi Li

National Chi Nan University, Nantou, Taiwan
`pyyin@ncnu.edu.tw`

Abstract. The ascending of quantity of CO_2 emissions is the main factor contributing the global warming which results in extremely abnormal weather and causes disaster damages. Due to intensive CO_2 pollutants produced by classic energy sources such as fossil fuels, practitioners and researchers pay increasing attentions on the renewable energy production such as wind power. Optimal wind turbine placement problem is to find the optimal number and placement location of wind turbines in a wind farm against the wake effect. The efficiency of wind power production does not necessarily grows with an increasing number of installed wind turbines. This paper presents a hyper-heuristic framework combining several lower-level heuristics with an artificial bee colony algorithm and a simulated annealing technique to construct an optimal wind turbine placement considering wake effect influence. Finally, we compare our approach with existing works in the literature. The experimental results show that our approach produces the wind power with a lower cost of energy.

Keywords: Micro-siting · Artificial bee colony · Simulated annealing
Hyper-heuristic · Wind turbine

1 Introduction

The climate change incurred by global warming has great impact on natural environment, and thus influencing human life. The ascending of quantity of CO_2 emissions is the main factor contributing the global warming which results in extremely abnormal weather and causes disaster damages. The use of renewable energy, such as solar and wind power, has become an important focus of social awareness. Wind power production is growing at the annual rate of about 30% in recent years, and it has been widely used in Europe, America, and Asia. As of end of June 2016, the leading Big Five countries for wind power production are China: 158 GW, United States: 74.7 GW, Germany: 47.4 GW, India: 27.2 GW and Spain: 23 GW [1]. Taiwan has abundant wind capacity due to its long coast line. However, 97.84% of Taiwan's energy supply in 2015 is imported and only 0.16% is generated from wind power (MOEA. http://www.moeaboe.gov.tw/). The wind capacity is under-explored and the development of new wind farms is beneficial to both economic growth and air pollutant reduction for Taiwan.

© Springer International Publishing AG, part of Springer Nature 2018
Y. Tan et al. (Eds.): ICSI 2018, LNCS 10941, pp. 145–152, 2018.
https://doi.org/10.1007/978-3-319-93815-8_15

Optimal wind turbine placement (OWTP) is an optimization problem to find the optimal number and placement location of wind turbines in a wind farm against the wake effect incurred by wind flow. The determined layout of the turbines in a wind farm is called *micro-siting*. Many optimization methods have been applied to solve the problem. Among them, genetic algorithm (GA) is the most prevalent one [2–5]. GA is an instance of metaheuristic algorithms which search beyond local optimality by enhancing global exploration capability based on computational intelligence. Other metaheuristic algorithms include ant colony optimization [6], particle swarm optimization [7], artificial bee colony [8], simulated annealing [9], to name a few.

Moreover, hyper-heuristic [10] is able to adapt to the characteristics of the given problem class. Hyper-heuristic framework deploys a problem-specific heuristic level and a global strategic level. The problem-specific heuristic level fosters several existing lower-level heuristics and the global strategic level selects the most appropriate heuristic to perform in a computation iteration. Hyper-heuristic is thus representing a class of heuristics instead of a single one. As the OWTP problem involves intensive matrix optimization which can be tackled by effective matrix-based lower-level heuristics and also due to the effective global exploration of artificial bee colony and simulated annealing, this paper proposes a hyper-heuristic algorithm with artificial bee colony and simulated annealing for optimal micro-siting of wind farms.

The remainder of this paper is organized as follows. Section 2 describes the model for calculation of wind power generation considering the wake effect, and review the hyper-heuristic optimization framework. Section 3 articulates the proposed hyper-heuristic algorithm. Section 4 describes the experimental results. Finally, Sect. 5 concludes this work.

2   Literature Review

2.1   Wind Energy Production Under Wake Effect

Given a wind farm divided into d × d grids, the center of each grid is a candidate location for placing a wind turbine to capture the wind energy. However, installing more wind turbines does not guarantee the maximal production efficiency because of the wake effect. The wake zone in a downstream wind depends on the terrain, wind direction, and surface roughness. The radius of the wake (r_1) caused by an upstream wind turbine increases linearly proportional to the downstream distance (D). The radius of the wake (r_2) at a downstream wind turbine is computed as follows.

$$r_2 = r_1 \left(\frac{1 - a}{1 - 2a} \right)^{\frac{1}{2}} \tag{1}$$

where a is the axial induction factor. Let v_0 be the mean wind speed without the wake effect and α be the entrainment constant which depends on the hub height (h) and surface roughness (z). The wind speed (v_i) at the downstream turbine with a distance (D) to its preceding turbine is estimated by

$$v_i = v_0 \left(1 - \left(\frac{2a}{1 + \alpha(D/r_2)} \right) \right) \tag{2}$$

$$\alpha = \frac{0.5}{\ln(h/z)} \tag{3}$$

If we assume there are n upstream turbines, the wind speed at a downstream wind turbine is therefore calculated as follows.

$$v_i = v_0 \left(1 - \left(\sum_{j=1}^{n} \left(1 - \frac{v_j}{v_0} \right)^2 \right)^{\frac{1}{2}} \right) \tag{4}$$

The yearly wind energy production by the wind farm with N_{WT} turbines considering the wake effect is given by

$$E = \sum_{k=1}^{N_{WT}} \int_{i \in S} \int_{j \in D} t_{ij} \xi v_k^3 \tag{5}$$

where t_{ij} is the time proportion in a year for the observed wind speed i and wind direction j described in probability distributions S and D and ξ is the constant for power conversion efficiency.

2.2   Hyper-Heuristic

Hyper-heuristic is an abstract-level algorithm framework which can select, combine, or generate more primitive heuristics to create an effective metaheuristic algorithm for the given type of problems [10, 11]. It works as follows. A set of lower-level heuristics for a particular class of problems are identified and implemented. These problems share some properties such as scheduling problems or allocation problems. A higher-level strategic methods including a heuristic selection (HS) method and a move acceptance (MA) method are designed. The HS is applied to select a lower-level heuristic to perform on the incumbent solution, and the MA is executed to evaluate the merit of the output and decides whether to accept the changed solution. Hyper-heuristic is an iterative learning process which learns the optimal strategy that selects the best lower-level heuristic to perform for different learning stages. As a result, hyper-heuristic can be thought of a heuristic for choosing heuristics, and it works in the heuristics space in contradiction to working in the solution space.

Hyper-heuristic algorithms have created several successful applications. Burke et al. [10] evaluates a hyper-heuristic approach for timetabling and rostering problems. The strategic-level hyper-heuristics selects low-level heuristics based on the reinforcement learning framework. A tabu list of heuristics is also maintained which prevents certain heuristics from being chosen at certain times during the search. Özcan et al. [11] proposes a timetabling hyper-heuristic framework which combines successive stages of heuristic selection and move acceptance. The heuristic selection is automatically controlled by the reinforcement learning technique, while the great deluge is employed to implement the acceptance function of the solution move.

3   Proposed Methods

In this section, we propose a hyper-heuristic algorithm of artificial bee colony and simulated annealing for resolving the OWTP problem. Our method is conceptualized in Fig. 1. Each of the components is described in the following sections.

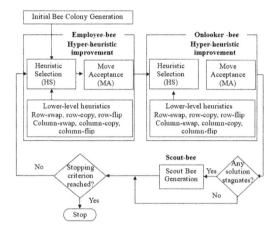

Fig. 1. Conceptual flowchart of the proposed method.

3.1   Artificial Bee Colony Optimization

The *artificial bee colony* (ABC) algorithm simulating the honeybee-foraging behavior to solve optimization problems [8]. We modify the ABC algorithm as follows. In each ABC iteration, the employed bee recalls its previously visited solution, from which a local search procedure is performed. We deploys a hyper-heuristic framework for implementing the local search procedure as shown in Fig. 1. The details of the developed hyper-heuristic will be noted. The onlooker bee selects a solution inhabited by an employ bee with a probability based on the quality estimate of the solution. It also conducts a local search (which is, again, implemented by a hyper-heuristic) to enhance the quality of the solution. The third type of search pattern is occasionally performed by the scout bee. When a solution whose quality fails to improve in a predefined number, called *limit*, of iterative steps, a scout bee is generated to find a new solution to replace the old one. The iterative procedure is repeated until a stopping criterion is met, and the best solution observed by all bees is output as the final solution. To cope with the micro-siting dimensions, all three types of bees employ the matrix form solution representation scheme as shown in Fig. 2. Considering a wind farm with 10×10 grids, a candidate micro-siting solution is represented by a binary matrix where entry value one indicates a wind turbine is placed at that location and entry value zero means no wind turbine is installed in that grid. The bee solutions are improved by matrix improvement lower-level heuristics which are provided in the hyper-heuristic framework as will be noted.

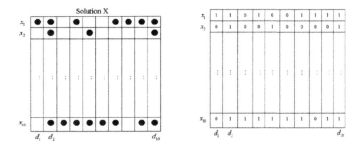

Fig. 2. Matrix form representation of a bee solution.

Two widely-used objectives for OWTP is the *cost of energy* (COE) and the *efficiency of production* (EOP), both are feasible for defining the fitness of a bee solution. The COE is defined as the monetary cost per unit of energy produced. In this paper, we employ a purchase-discount model for wind turbines as follows.

$$C = N_{WT} \left(\frac{2}{3} + \left(\frac{1}{3} \right) \left(e^{-0.00174 \, N_{WT}^2} \right) \right) \tag{6}$$

The purchase cost has an incentive term which is maximally one third off the turbine unit price. The COE is thus the purchase cost divided by the produced power,

$$\text{COE} = N_{WT} \left(\frac{2}{3} + \left(\frac{1}{3} \right) \left(e^{-0.00174 \, N_{WT}^2} \right) \right) \Bigg/ \sum_{k=1}^{N_{WT}} \int_{i \in S} \int_{j \in D} t_{ij} \zeta v_k^3 \tag{7}$$

The EOP is defined as the ratio between the production power with and without the wake effect. It reflects the appropriateness of the turbine placement in reducing the wind wake as much as possible. The EOP is computed as follows.

$$\text{EOP} = \sum_{k=1}^{N_{WT}} \int_{i \in S} \int_{j \in D} t_{ij} v_k^3 \Bigg/ \sum_{k=1}^{N_{WT}} \int_{i \in S} \int_{j \in D} t_{ij} v_0^3 \tag{8}$$

3.2   Hyper-Heuristic Improvement

Our hyper-heuristic framework has two layers. The problem-dependent layer consisting of a repository of lower-level heuristics (LLHs) and the problem-independent layer containing heuristic selection (HS) and move acceptance (MA) methods. A new bee solution is produced by applying HS to select one or more LLHs performing on the current solution. The MA method then makes the decision about whether to accept the new solution to replace the old one.

LLHs: As a micro-siting is represented as a matrix form (Fig. 2), a number of matrix improvement LLHs are implemented as follows.

- Row-swap LLH: Randomly select two rows from the current matrix solution. Swap the two rows to produce a new matrix.
- Row-copy LLH: Randomly select two rows from the current matrix solution. Copy one of the rows to replace the other. Replace the old matrix with the new one.
- Row-flip LLH: Randomly select one row from the current matrix solution. For each binary bit contained in the selected row, flip its bit value (from 0 to 1, or vice versa) with a mutation probability. Replace the old matrix with the new one.
- Column-swap/column-copy/column-flip: The three LLHs are similarly implemented but are performed in a column-wise fashion.

HS: The HS method selects one LLH with a probability proportional to the LLH's previous performance. Initially, all LLHs are assigned an equal probability. Once an LLH is selected and performed, the change in COE or EOP value (quality of the micro-siting) is used to update the LLH's probability. If the value is improved, the selection probability of the LLH is tuned up, and vice versa. Hence, the hyper-heuristic framework dynamically learns the optimal strategy for heuristic selection.

MA: The MA method decides to accept the newly produced matrix in a probabilistic way. We implement the *metropolitan criterion* introduced in simulated annealing [9] as our MA method. All improving solutions are selected. The worsening solutions are accepted with a probability determined by the metropolitan criterion with a probability $\exp(-\Delta/T)$ where T is the temperature parameter and Δ is the worsening amount in the fitness value.

4   Experimental Results

The simulations are conducted on well-known benchmark micro-siting problems introduced in Mosetti et al. [2] and Grady et al. [3]. The specifications of the problem instances follow the settings from the original papers for fair comparison where d = 10, TC = 0.88, H = 60 m, z = 0.3 m, and r_1 = 40 m.

4.1   Problem A

Problem A is a test case having multiple wind directions and multiple wind speeds. There are 36 wind directions with different occurrence probabilities. The wind speeds are 8, 12, and 17 m/s, respectively. The simulation results are tabulated in Table 1. We see that Mosetti method practiced a conservative energy production which yields a yearly power of 13460 with only 15 wind turbines installed. The EOP is 94.62%, the highest value among all methods. Both Grady and the proposed method installed 39 turbines in the wind farm, producing a power of 32038 and 33310, respectively. Therefore, the micro-siting produced by the proposed method is more robust against the wake effect than that produced by the Grady method. The COE obtained by the proposed method is the best among all compared approaches. The proposed method also outperforms the Grady method in obtaining a higher EOP.

Table 1. Simulation results with Problem A.

	Mosetti	Grady	Proposed method
E	13460	32038	33310
N_{WT}	15	39	39
C	13.3802	26.9217	26.8217
COE	0.000994	0.000840	0.000821
EOP (%)	94.62	86.62	90.45

4.2 Problem B

Problem B has the same wind conditions (multiple wind directions and multiple wind speeds) as Problem A, but adding land usage constraint. In the given wind farm, some parts of land cannot be placed turbines because of, such as, unstable terrains or undesirable high cost for installing turbines in swamp areas. Figure 3 shows the wind turbine layouts obtained by the proposed method. We observe that the wind turbines are positioned along the main wind direction (northwestern wind) and the land-constrained grids (shaded areas) are not used for turbine installation. The experimental result shows that the number of turbines installed by the proposed method is 27 which cost 20.5314 unit price. The produced power is 24649. The COE and EOP are 0.000833 and 84.65%, respectively.

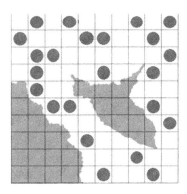

Fig. 3. Problem B: wind turbine layouts obtained by the proposed method.

5 Conclusions

In this paper we have proposed a hyper-heuristic framework with an artificial bee colony algorithm to construct an optimal wind turbine placement considering wake effect influence. The proposed hyper-heuristic contains two layers. The problem-dependent layer contains several lower-level heuristics (LLHs) which are matrix improvement methods particularly designed for the micro-siting matrix solution form. The problem-independent layer consists of a heuristic selection (HS) method and a move acceptance (MA) method. The HS selects a LLH to perform on a solution, and the MA decides whether to accept the move or not. Finally, we compare our approach with benchmark works in the literature. The experimental results show that our approach not only obtains a better production efficiency, but also produces the wind power with a lower cost of energy.

Acknowledgments. This research is partially supported by Ministry of Science and Technology of ROC, under Grant MOST 105-2410-H-260-018 -MY2.

References

1. World wind energy 2016 half-year report, World Wind Energy Association (WWEA). http://www.wwindea.org/
2. Mosetti, G., Poloni, C., Diviacco, B.: Optimization of wind turbine positioning in large wind farms by means of a genetic algorithm. Wind Eng. Ind. Aerodyn. **51**, 105–116 (1994)
3. Grady, S.A., Hussaini, M.Y., Abdullah, M.M.: Placement of wind turbines using genetic algorithms. Renewable Energy **30**, 259–270 (2005)
4. Emami, A., Noghreh, P.: New approach on optimization in placement of wind turbines within wind farm by genetic algorithms. Renewable Energy **35**, 1559–1564 (2010)
5. Chen, Y., Li, H., Jin, K., Song, Q.: Wind farm layout optimization using genetic algorithm with different hub height wind turbines. Energy Convers. Manag. **70**, 56–65 (2013)
6. Dorigo, M., Gambardella, L.: Ant colony system: a cooperative learning approach to the traveling salesman problem. IEEE Trans. Evol. Comput. **1**, 53–66 (1997)
7. Kennedy, J., Eberhart, R.C.: Particle swarm optimization. In: Proceedings of IEEE International Conference on Neural Networks IV, pp. 1942–1948 (1995)
8. Karaboga, D., Basturk, B.: A powerful and efficient algorithm for numerical function optimization: artificial bee colony (ABC) algorithm. J. Global Optim. **39**, 459–471 (2007)
9. Kirkpatrick, S., Vecchi, M.: Optimization by simulated annealing. Science **220**, 671–680 (1983)
10. Burke, E.K., Kendall, G., Soubeiga, E.: A tabu-search hyper-heuristic for timetabling and rostering. J. Heuristics **9**, 451–470 (2003)
11. Ozcan, E., Misir, M., Ochoa, G., Burke, E.K.: A reinforcement learning - great-deluge hyper-heuristic for examination timetabling. Int. J. Appl. Metaheuristic Comput. **1**, 39–59 (2010)

New Binary Artificial Bee Colony for the 0-1 Knapsack Problem

Mourad Nouioua[1,2], Zhiyong Li[1,2(✉)], and Shilong Jiang[3]

[1] The College of Computer Science and Electronic Engineering, Hunan University, Changsha, China
{mouradnouioua,zhiyong.li}@hnu.edu.cn
[2] Key Laboratory for Embedded and Network Computing of Hunan Province, Changsha, China
[3] PKU-HKUST Shenzhen-HongKong Institution, Shenzhen, China
jiangshilong03@126.com

Abstract. The knapsack problem is one of the well known NP-Hard optimization problems. Because of its appearance as a sub-problem in many real world problems, it attracts the attention of many researchers on swarm intelligence and evolutionary computation community. In this paper, a new binary artificial bee colony called NB-ABC is proposed to solve the 0-1 knapsack problem. Instead of the search operators of the original ABC, new binary search operators are designed for the different phases of the ABC algorithm, namely the employed, the onlooker and the scout bee phases. Moreover, a novel hybrid repair operator called (HRO) is proposed to repair and improve the infeasible solutions. To assess the performance of the proposed algorithm, NB-ABC is compared with two other existing algorithms, namely GB-ABC and BABC-DE, for solving the 0-1 knapsack problem. Based on a set of 15 0-1 high dimensional knapsack problems classified in three categories. the experimental results in view of many criteria show the efficiency and the robustness of the proposed NB-ABC.

Keywords: Binary optimization problem · 0-1 knapsack problem
Artificial bee colony

1 Introduction

The knapsack problem is a classical binary optimization problem in operational research which was demonstrated to be NP-Hard [1]. Although the knapsack problem is one of the old problems in combinatorial optimization, this problem still attracts the attention of many researchers on swarm intelligence and evolutionary computation community. This is mainly due to the possibility of modeling many real world optimization problems as knapsack problems. In other words, the application of the knapsack problem can be found in many areas including resource allocation [2], project selection [3], investment decision making problem [4] among others.

© Springer International Publishing AG, part of Springer Nature 2018
Y. Tan et al. (Eds.): ICSI 2018, LNCS 10941, pp. 153–165, 2018.
https://doi.org/10.1007/978-3-319-93815-8_16

The 0-1 knapsack problem is a very important variant of the knapsack problem which can be described as follows: given a knapsack with a capacity C and a set of D items where each item i ($i = 1, 2, ..., D$) has its own profit P_i and weight W_i, the main objective is to select a subset of items from the D items so that to maximize the total profit without exceeding the capacity C of the knapsack. Formally, the 0-1 knapsack problem is modeled as follows:

$$\begin{cases} \text{Maximize } \sum_{i=1}^{D} P_i * X_i \\ \text{Subject to } \sum_{i=1}^{D} W_i * X_i \leq C \end{cases} \tag{1}$$

where $X_i = 1$ if the item i is selected and $X_i = 0$ if the item i is not selected.

Due to the lack of efficiency of exact algorithms in case of high dimensional problems, alternative nature-inspired metaheuristic algorithms represent an important class of approximate methods that are widely used to solve different optimization problems including the 0-1 high dimensional knapsack problem.

Among a large set of recently developed nature-inspired metaheuristic algorithms, Artificial Bee Colony (ABC) is a simple and efficient optimization algorithm which is inspired from simulating the foraging behavior of bees [5]. ABC has been widely used to solve many optimization problems such as: numerical optimization problems [6], uncapacitated facility location problem [7], wireless sensor network [8], as well as the knapsack problem [9,10,12].

However, most of metaheuristic algorithms including ABC have been initially developed for continuous optimization problems. Thus, their original operators cannot be directly applied to binary optimization problems like the 0-1 knapsack problem. Indeed, to apply such algorithms to binary optimization problems, some modification techniques are required [13].

The ABC algorithm has been proposed for solving the 0-1 knapsack problem. *Liu et al.* [9] have proposed a binary discrete ABC named (BABC) where a round operator with a position clipping boundary condition (PCBC) have been used together to convert the real variables, obtained from using the original ABC equations, into binary variables.

Based on the genetic operators, *Ozturk et al.* [10] have developed a hybrid binary ABC named GB-ABC where the crossover and swap operators are used in the neighborhood searching mechanism instead of the original search equations. Besides, in order to perform the neighborhood searching mechanism, two different food sources are randomly selected. Then, the crossover followed by the swap operator are applied randomly between the current, the two chosen, the zero and the global best food sources to generate children and grand children food sources. The best solution among the produced food sources is selected as a neighborhood solution of the current food source.

Later, By using also a hybrid algorithm with the Differential Evolution (DE) [11], *Cao et al.* [12] recently developed a new modified ABC called (BABC-DE). A binary search operator which comprehensively considers the memory and neighbor information is designed in the employed bee phase. The binary swap mutation and the crossover operator of DE are used in the onlooker phase.

Although BABC-DE outperforms the other existing algorithms in solving the 0-1 knapsack problem, we show in this paper that its results can be further improved. To do so, we propose in this paper, a new modified binary artificial bee colony algorithm that we call NB-ABC to solve the 0-1 knapsack problem.

In the proposed algorithm NB-ABC, we develop new search mechanisms for the employed, the onlooker and the scout bee phases. Besides, new binary search operators using the well known Boolean operators such as OR, XOR and complement are developed to improve the exploitation and exploration capabilities of the algorithm. Furthermore, a hybrid strategy composed of two phases is adapted in order to repair and improve the unfeasible solutions.

In order to assess its performance, the proposed algorithm NB-ABC is compared with the two aforementioned recent algorithms designed for solving the 0-1 knapsack problem, namely GB-ABC and BABC-DE. The comparison is performed on a large set of 0-1 high dimensional knapsack instances including three kind of problems. The experimental study shows that globally, the results obtained by NB-ABC are better than those obtained by the other considered algorithms in terms of solutions quality, convergence as well as robustness.

The rest of this paper is organized as follows: Sect. 2 describes the details of the proposed method. In Sect. 3 we present and discuss the proposed experimental study. Finally, Sect. 4 concludes the paper and gives some perspectives for future work.

2   The Proposed NB-ABC Algorithm

Before detailing the different parts of the proposed algorithm, let us start by discussing the search equation used in the employed and onlooker phases of the standard ABC algorithm [5]. According to the search Eq. 2, the difference between the current solution X_i and the neighborhood solution X_k in a randomly selected variable j is calculated and multiplied by the parameter Φ which determines the magnitude and the direction of the perturbation. This perturbation is then added to the current food source solution X_i to obtain a new candidate solution V_i.

$$V_{ij} = X_{ij} + \Phi \times (X_{ij} - X_{kj}) \tag{2}$$

Semantically speaking, the new candidate solution is obtained by moving the old solution towards or away from another randomly selected solution. The direction (towards or away from) of the new candidate solution depends on the sign of the parameter Φ: If Φ is positive (resp. negative), the new candidate solution is located near (resp. away from) the randomly selected solution.

Based on this observation, new binary operators are developed in this paper instead of the search Eq. 2. The concept of movement is replaced here by either adding new items to the current solution or adding new items and removing some redundant items, which improves both exploitation and exploration abilities of the algorithm. Note that, the concept of magnitude cannot be applied in our study due to the nature of 0-1 knapsack problem where each variable is either

1 or 0. Moreover, unlike the original search equation of ABC in which only one variable is modified, the proposed binary operators can change more than one variable, depending on the chosen operators. Indeed, it has been observed that the modification of more than one variable speeds up the convergence of the algorithm.

2.1   Representation, Initialization and Evaluation of the Solutions

In NB-ABC, the colony (population) is composed of a set of food sources or solutions X_i, $i = (1, 2, ..., SN)$ where each solution $X_i = (X_{i1}, X_{i2}, ..., X_{iD})$ is a binary vector of length D. D is the dimension of the problem which corresponds to the number of items in the considered knapsack problem. The jth bit of the ith solution equals 1 (resp. 0) if the jth item is selected (resp. is not selected).

In addition to X_i, each solution has a fitness ($Profit_i$), a weight ($Weight_i$), a feasibility ($Feasibility_i$) and a variable named $trial_i$ which counts the number of consecutive times the solution X_i has not been improved.

At the initial stage, a set of food sources are randomly generated using the Bernoulli process as follows:

$$X_{ij}(0) = \begin{cases} 1, & \text{if } \alpha > 0.5 \\ 0, & \text{Otherwise} \end{cases} \quad (3)$$

where α is a random number in the range $[0, 1]$ and $j \in \{1, 2, ..., D\}$.

The fitness evaluation process is performed after each phase of NB-ABC in order to calculate the profit and the weight of each solution X_i as well as to check the feasibility of this solution. $Profit_i$ is simply the sum of profits of all items included in X_i. Similarly, $Weight_i$ is the sum of weights of all items included in this solution (see (4)). A solution X_i is infeasible if its weight is greater than the capacity of the knapsack.

$$[Profit_i, Weight_i] = [\sum_{j=1}^{D} P_j * X_j, \sum_{j=1}^{D} W_j * X_j] \quad (4)$$

where P_j and W_j represent the profit and weight of the jth item.

2.2   The Hybrid Repair Operator (HRO)

The operators used in the initialization as well as the three bee phases of NB-ABC may produce infeasible solutions. In order to repair and improve them, we introduce in NB-ABC a hybrid repair operator called (HRO) which includes two phases: greedy DROP phase and random ADD phase.

In the first phase, the selected items are sorted in terms of the ratio P_i/W_i in an increasing order. Then, a greedy selection is performed to take off items starting from that having the smallest ratio and so on until the capacity of the solution becomes smaller than the knapsack capacity. During the second phase, we randomly add to the knapsack some items from the unselected ones as long as the capacity of the knapsack is not exceeded. Note that DROP phase aims to make the solutions feasible while ADD phase improves the repaired solutions.

2.3   The Neighborhood Search Mechanism of NB-ABC

In the NB-ABC algorithm, new search operators are designed based on the similarity between the current solution and the selected neighbor solution. Firstly, each employed bee randomly selects a neighbor solution X_k from the colony. Then, a binary vector $V1_i$ is generated by using the following binary operator:

$$V1_i = (X_k \; AND \; (X_i \; XOR \; X_k)) \tag{5}$$

$V1_i$ gives all the items that are exclusively selected in the neighbor solution X_k of the current solution X_i. From this vector, two randomly selected items are added to the current solution to obtain a new candidate solution V_i.

In case of absence of exclusive items in X_k, two other binary vectors $V2_i$ and $V3_i$ are generated by using the following equation:

$$[V2_i, V3_i] = [\overline{(X_i \; OR \; X_k)}, (X_i \; AND \; X_k)] \tag{6}$$

Here, $V2_i$ contains all the items that are not selected in both solutions X_i and X_k while $V3_i$ contains all common items that are selected in both X_i and X_k.

A new candidate solution V_i is generated by randomly adding two items to the current solution X_i from the items of $V2_i$ and randomly taking out one item from the items of $V3_i$.

2.4   The Employed and Onlooker Bee Phases

During the employed bee phase, each employed bee performs the above neighborhood search mechanism on its attributed food source and produce a new food source X_k. After that, the new food source X_k is evaluated and repaired if it is infeasible. The profit of X_k is compared with the profit of X_i. If the new food source X_k is better than X_i, the employed bee moves to the new food source X_k. Otherwise, the employed bee keeps the food source X_k. Finally, the obtained solution and the best solution are compared.

After that, as in the original ABC [5], all the employed bees complete their search: they come back to the hive to share theirs fitness information with the onlooker bees. Each onlooker bee chooses a food source X_i based on a probability degree $Prob_i$ proportional to its profit $Profit_i$ using (7). After the selection of the food source, the same steps are applied as in the employed bees.

$$Prob_i = \frac{Profit_i}{\sum_{k=1}^{SN} Profit_k} \tag{7}$$

2.5   The Scout Bee Phase

The scout bee looks for a food source that has not been improved after several trials by comparing its value of the parameter $Trial$ with that of the parameter $Limit$ of the algorithm. The scout bee replaces this food source with a new randomly generated food source. In NB-ABC, a new mechanism is used for all the food sources that have not been improved. This mechanism involves the best food source in the scout bee process.

After randomly generating a new food source, the new food source is modified by taking out all the items that are selected both in this solution and in the best so far found solution. In order to define these items, we use the following binary operator:

$$NewX_{i1} = (X_i \; AND \; X_{best}) \tag{8}$$

where X_{best} denotes the best food source found so far.

Inversely, all the items that are not selected in the best food source and the new food source are added to the knapsack. These items are determined by the following binary operator:

$$NewX_{i2} = \overline{(X_i \; OR \; X_{best})} \tag{9}$$

The proposed scout bee phase operator allows us to generate new food sources that are significantly different from the best food source. These new generated food sources enable the algorithm to explore new search regions which improves the exploration ability of the algorithm.

2.6   Main Steps of NB-ABC for Solving 0-1 Knapsack Problem

The main steps of NB-ABC for solving 0-1 knapsack problem are given in Algorithm 1. After the random initialization of SN food sources (lines 1–11). The algorithm iteratively performs three consecutive phases: employed bee, onlooker bee and scout bee phases (lines 13–18) until the stopping criterion is met. Note that the stopping criterion used in NB-ABC is the maximum number of evaluation function FE_{max}.

3   Experimental Study

This section presents the results of evaluation of NB-ABC. NB-ABC has been compared with two other recent ABC based algorithms that are BABC-DE and GB-ABC, on a large set of 0-1 high dimensional knapsack problems.

All compared algorithms are implemented with MATLAB R2015a on the same PC with Intel(R) Core(TM) i5-2430M, 2.40 Ghz CPU, 4.00 GB RAM and Windows7 operating system.

3.1   General Setting of the Experiments

The proposed algorithm NB-ABC has only two parameters which are the population size $PopSize$ and the parameter $Limit$. The population size is fixed to 50 (i.e. The number of food sources $SN = PopSize/2 = 25$) for all knapsack problems. The parameter $Limit$ influences the frequency of the scout bee phase. After various simulations, we have found that 100 is a suitable value of this parameter for the high dimensional knapsack problems used in this study.

Algorithm 1. $NB\_ABC\_Algorithm$

Require: The food sources number SN, the maximum number of function evaluations
   FE_{max}, the parameter $Limit$.
Ensure: The best solution X_{best} with its profit Value $Profit_{best}$.
 1: $X_i = Initialization\_Phase(SN, D)$;
 2: **for** each bee $i = 1$ to SN **do**
 3:    $Trial_i \leftarrow 0$;
 4:    $Profit_i, Weight_i, Feasibility_i \leftarrow Fitness\_Evaluation\_Process(X_i)$; {Sect. 2.1}

 5:    **if** $(Feasibility_i == false)$ **then**
 6:       $Profit_i, Weight_i, Feasibility_i \leftarrow HRO(X_i)$; {Sect. 2.2}
 7:    **end if**
 8:    **if** $(Profit_i > Profit_{best})$ **then**
 9:       $X_{best} \leftarrow X_i; Profit_{best} \leftarrow Profit_i$; {Update X_{best}}
10:    **end if**
11: **end for**
12: $FE \leftarrow SN$;
13: **while** $FE <= FE_{max}$ **do**
14:    $X_i \leftarrow Employed\_Bee\_Phase(SN, X_i)$; {Sect. 2.4}
15:    $X_i \leftarrow Onlooker\_Bee\_Phase(SN, X_i)$;
16:    $FE \leftarrow FE + 2 \times SN$;
17:    $X_i \leftarrow Scout\_Bee\_Phase(SN, X_i, Limit)$; {Sect. 2.5}
18: **end while**
19: **Return** $X_{best}, Profit_{best}$.

The parameters of GB-ABC and BABC-DE are taken from their original papers: In BABC-DE [12], the number of food sources $SN = 25$, $Limit = 0.1 * SN * D$, w linearly decreases from 0.8 to 0.4 and $P_{cr} = 0.9$. For GB-ABC [10], the population size is $PopSize = 30$ and $Limit = 500$.

GB-ABC uses a penalty-based technique to deal with infeasible solutions. However, it has been shown that this technique is inefficient with large scale optimization problems. Thus, to correctly compare GB-ABC with the other algorithms, we have used in GB-ABC the same repair operator (HRO) used in the proposed NB-ABC. Moreover, in order to ensure a fair comparison, the same stopping criteria is used for all the compared algorithms which is the maximum number of function evaluations FE_{max}.

In the following experiments, each algorithm is run 50 time for each 0-1 knapsack problem. To asses the performance of each algorithm, we record the best, the worst and the average value of the best obtained solutions. We also record the standard deviation of the obtained solutions to evaluate the robustness of the algorithms. Finally, the obtained results are ranked based on the above criteria.

3.2   Comparison Results

In order to deeply evaluate the performance of the proposed NB-ABC, we perform the comparison between the algorithms on three different datasets used in

[12] and containing high dimensional (difficult) instances. The three datasets are randomly generated as follows:

Dataset1: Uncorrelated high dimensional 0-1 knapsack problems. This dataset contains 5 items from $kp1$ to $kp5$ with different dimensions. The values of weights W_i are randomly generated between 5 and 20 while the values of profits P_i are generated between 5 and 40.

Dataset2: Weakly related high dimensional 0-1 knapsack problems. This dataset contains 5 items from $kp6$ to $kp10$ with different dimensions. Each weight W_i is randomly generated between 5 and 20 while its corresponding profit P_i is chosen from the range $[W_i - 5, W_i + 5]$.

Dataset3: Strongly related high dimensional 0-1 knapsack problems. This dataset contains 5 items from $kp11$ to $kp15$. The value of each weight W_i is randomly chosen from 5 to 20 and its corresponding profit P_i equals $W_i + 5$.

For each knapsack problem kp_i, $i \in \{16, 17, \ldots, 30\}$, the capacity $C_i = 0.75 \times \sum_{j=1}^{D} W_i$. Note that the three datasets are created only once and used for all compared algorithms.

The results of comparison between NB-ABC, BABC-DE and GB-ABC are given in Tables 1, 2 and 3.

Table 1. The optimization results of algorithms NB-ABC, BABC-DE and GB-ABC for the uncorrelated high dimensional 0-1 knapsack problems

KP	Dim	FEmax	Algorithm	Mean	Best	Worst	StdDev	Rank
$kp1$	100	10000	NB-ABC	2087,02	2088	2087	0, 14	2
			BABC-DE	2087,16	2088	2085	1, 03	1
			GB-ABC	1916,44	2051	1677	115, 44	3
$kp2$	200	20000	NB-ABC	4127	4127	4127	0	2
			BABC-DE	4127,76	4128	4126	0, 59	1
			GB-ABC	3667,3	4089	3234	333, 96	3
$kp3$	500	20000	NB-ABC	10227,1	10228	10227	0, 3	1
			BABC-DE	10225,82	10228	10219	1, 73	2
			GB-ABC	8280,74	9333	8012	223, 01	3
$kp4$	1000	50000	NB-ABC	20325,92	20326	20325	0, 27	1
			BABC-DE	20324,14	20326	20315	1, 98	2
			GB-ABC	16145,9	16484	15703	187, 02	3
$kp5$	2000	50000	NB-ABC	40909	40909	40909	0	1
			BABC-DE	40900,14	40908	40861	8, 69	2
			GB-ABC	32019,26	32445	31390	266, 5	3
Average rank/Overall rank					1.4/1	1.6/2	3/3	

For the uncorrelated high dimensional 0-1 knapsack problems given in Table 1, we can remark that for the two first problems $kp1$ and $kp2$, BABC-DE outperforms NB-ABC and finds the best result whereas NB-ABC finds the best results on the three other problems ($kp3$ to $kp5$). GB-ABC can not outperform the other algorithms on any of the used 0-1 knapsack problems. Globally, we conclude that NB-ABC has better performance on solving the uncorrelated high dimensional than the other algorithms since it achieves the first overall rank.

From the results of the algorithms on solving the weakly related high dimensional 0-1 knapsack problems presented in Table 2, it is clear that the proposed NB-ABC obtains the best results on all problems of this dataset. Moreover, we can remark that the standard deviation of the proposed algorithm equals zero for all problems witch reflects the robustness and stability of NB-ABC on solving this kind of 0-1 knapsack problems.

Table 2. The optimization results of algorithms NB-ABC, BABC-DE and GB-ABC for the weakly related high dimensional 0-1 knapsack problems.

KP	Dim	FEmax	Algorithm	Mean	*Best*	*Worst*	StdDev	Rank
$kp6$	100	10000	NB-ABC	1108	1108	1108	0	1
			BABC-DE	1106,7	1108	1106	0,95	2
			GB-ABC	1022,12	1096	929	33,69	3
$kp7$	200	20000	NB-ABC	2179	2179	2179	0	1
			BABC-DE	2175,22	2179	2169	2,37	2
			GB-ABC	1912,9	2016	1816	50,64	3
$kp8$	500	20000	NB-ABC	5554	5554	5554	0	1
			BABC-DE	5543,5	5550	5535	3,94	2
			GB-ABC	4664,56	4793	4515	71,86	3
$kp9$	1000	50000	NB-ABC	10690	10690	10690	0	1
			BABC-DE	10662,16	10675	10640	7,58	2
			GB-ABC	8938,62	9245	8598	107,53	3
$kp10$	2000	50000	NB-ABC	21900	21900	21900	0	1
			BABC-DE	21827,52	21855	21800	11,94	2
			GB-ABC	18028,92	18377	17699	160,21	3
Average/Overall rank					1/1	2/2	3/3	

The comparison results on the strongly related high dimensional 0-1 knapsack problems presented in Table 3 demonstrates once again the efficiency of NB-ABC since it outperforms both BABC-DE and GB-ABC.

In addition to the performance measures shown in Tables 1, 2 and 3, the convergence speed is also an important criterion which should be observed. To

Table 3. The optimization results of algorithms NB-ABC, BABC-DE and GB-ABC for the strongly related high dimensional 0-1 knapsack problems.

KP	Dim	FEmax	Algorithm	Mean	Best	Worst	StdDev	Rank
$kp11$	100	10000	NB-ABC	1348	1348	1348	0	1
			BABC-DE	1342,9	1348	1338	2,57	2
			GB-ABC	1334,68	1348	1276	15,81	3
$kp12$	200	20000	NB-ABC	2704	2704	2704	0	1
			BABC-DE	2690,4	2699	2679	4,63	2
			GB-ABC	2628,82	2694	2470	60,98	3
$kp13$	500	20000	NB-ABC	6662,6	6663	6658	1,04	1
			BABC-DE	6617,66	6643	6578	13	2
			GB-ABC	6333,84	6558	6115	93,19	3
$kp14$	1000	50000	NB-ABC	13520,82	13526	13516	2,89	1
			BABC-DE	13434,7	13466	13381	19,37	2
			GB-ABC	12596,94	13035	12281	153,48	3
$kp15$	2000	50000	NB-ABC	27245,12	27251	27234	4,5	1
			BABC-DE	27062,06	27111	26986	31,55	2
			GB-ABC	25047,26	25398	24623	176,8	3
Average rank/Overall rank					1/1	2/2	3/3	

do so, the convergence curves of some 0-1 knapsack problems in particular runs are depicted in Fig. 1.

This figure shows that for $kp2$ and $kp7$, the convergence behaviors of NB-ABC and BABC-DE are very similar, which means that the two algorithms are very competitive on solving these problems. For $kp5$ and $kp10$, BABC-DE converges faster than NB-ABC at the beginning, but later, NB-ABC still constantly converges and surpasses BABC-DE. For $kp13$ and $kp15$, initially, BABC-DE and NB-ABC perform similarly. However, after a number of evaluations, the proposed NB-ABC algorithm outperforms BABC-DE and converges to better results.

Despite the stable behavior of GB-ABC in most of cases such as $kp5$, $kp10$, $kp13$ and $kp15$, its convergence is significantly slower that the two other algorithms.

To complete our experimental evaluation, the non parametric right-tailed Wilcoxon signed rank test is performed for NB-ABC against BABC-DE and GB-ABC. The non parametric Wilcoxon signed rank test [14] is a pairwise test that aims at determining whether significant differences exist between the averages of two samples. In our case, each sample is presented by the average of best results obtained by an algorithm over the 50 runs for problems $kp1$ to $kp15$.

Table 4 shows the results of the right-tailed Wilcoxon signed rank test for problems $kp1$ to $kp15$. R^+ is the sum of ranks in which NB-ABC outperforms

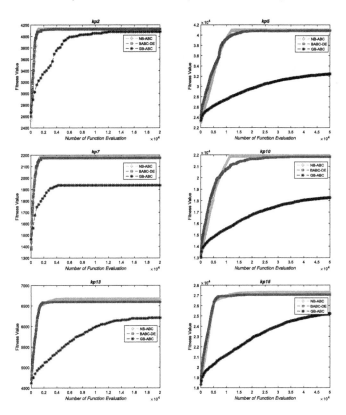

Fig. 1. Convergence curves of NB-ABC, BABC-DE and GB-ABC for kp2, kp5, kp7, kp10, kp13 and kp15

the other compared algorithm while R^- is the sum of ranks in which NB-ABC is outperformed by the other compared algorithm.

We can see that, NB-ABC obtains more R^+ than R^- compared with the two other algorithms (especially with GB-ABC). This means that NB-ABC often achieves better results than those obtained by GB-ABC. Moreover, the obtained $p-value$ is below 0.05 which allows us to reject the null hypothesis H_0 stating that the two compared algorithms have the same performance. Thus, we can conclude that NB-ABC is significantly better than BABC-DE and GB-ABC.

In summary, although the authors in [12] have demonstrated the effectiveness of BABC-DE comparing to several other algorithms used on their comparison, the above experiments show that our proposed algorithm NB-ABC can improve further the results obtained by BABC-DE. Indeed, on the one hand, the proposed mechanism search operator used on the employed and onlooker bee phases allows the algorithm to mainly improve the exploitation as well as the exploration as second objective. On the other hand, the scout bee phase improves the exploration ability of the algorithm by allowing it to visit new search regions.

Table 4. The results of right-tailed Wilcoxon signed rank test of NB-ABC against BABC-DE and GB-ABC ($\alpha = 0.05$) for $kp1$ to $kp15$.

NB-ABC vs.	R^+	R^-	$p - value$	H_0 Rejection
BABC-DE	117	3	1.52e−04	Yes
GB-ABC	120	0	3.05e−05	Yes

4   Conclusion and Future Works

In this paper, a new modified ABC-based algorithm called NB-ABC is developed to solve the 0-1 knapsack problem. In our proposal, new binary operators have been designed instead of the original search equations suitable for the continuous optimization problems but not for binary optimization ones.

The experimental results confirm the efficiency and robustness of our algorithm compared with GB-ABC and BABC-DE in view of several criteria.

Several orientations are opened for future work. First, we plan to deeply analyze the few cases where NB-ABC does not give the best results in order to improve it. Then, since the obtained results of NB-ABC are very interesting for 0-1 knapsack problem, we want to adapt it for solving other binary optimization problems issued from practical domains such as data mining and bioinformatics.

Acknowledgments. This work was partially supported by the National Natural Science Foundation of China (No. 61672215, U1613209).

References

1. Pisinger, D.: Where are the hard knapsack problems? Comput. Oper. Res. **32**, 2271–2284 (2005)
2. Reniers, G.L., Sörensen, K.: An approach for optimal allocation of safety resources: using the knapsack problem to take aggregated cost-efficient preventive measures. Risk Anal. **33**, 2056–2067 (2013)
3. Mavrotas, G., Diakoulaki, D., Kourentzis, A.: Selection among ranked projects under segmentation, policy and logical constraints. Eur. J. Oper. Res. **187**, 177–192 (2008)
4. Peeta, S., Salman, F.S., Gunnec, D., Viswanath, K.: Pre-disaster investment decisions for strengthening a highway network. Comput. Oper. Res. **37**, 1708–1719 (2010)
5. Karaboga, D.: An idea based on honey bee swarm for numerical optimization. Technical report-tr06, Erciyes University, Engineering Faculty, Computer Engineering Department (2005)
6. Karaboga, D., Basturk, B.: On the performance of artificial bee colony (ABC) algorithm. Appl. Soft Comput. **8**, 687–697 (2008)
7. Kiran, M.S.: The continuous artificial bee colony algorithm for binary optimization. Appl. Soft Comput. **33**, 15–23 (2015)
8. Ozturk, C., Karaboga, D., Gorkemli, B.: Probabilistic dynamic deployment of wireless sensor networks by artificial bee colony algorithm. Sensors **11**, 6056–6065 (2011)

9. Liu, W., Niu, B., Chen, H.N.: Binary artificial bee colony algorithm for solving 0-1 knapsack problem. Adv. Inf. Sci. Serv. Sci. **4**(22), 464–470 (2012)
10. Ozturk, C., Hancer, E., Karaboga, D.: A novel binary artificial bee colony algorithm based on genetic operators. Inf. Sci. **297**, 154–170 (2015)
11. Storn, R., Price, K.: Differential evolution-a simple and efficient heuristic for global optimization over continuous spaces. J. Global Optim. **11**, 341–359 (1997)
12. Cao, J., Yin, B., Lu, X., Kang, Y., Chen, X.: A modified artificial bee colony approach for the 0–1 knapsack problem. Appl. Intell. **48**, 1582–1595 (2017)
13. Banitalebi, A., Aziz, M.I.A., Aziz, Z.A.: A self-adaptive binary differential evolution algorithm for large scale binary optimization problems. Inf. Sci. **367**, 487–511 (2016)
14. Derrac, J., García, S., Molina, D., Herrera, F.: A practical tutorial on the use of nonparametric statistical tests as a methodology for comparing evolutionary and swarm intelligence algorithms. Swarm Evol. Comput. **1**, 3–18 (2011)

Teaching-Learning-Based Artificial Bee Colony

Xu Chen[1]([⊠]) and Bin Xu[2]

[1] School of Electrical and Information Engineering, Jiangsu University,
Zhenjiang 212013, Jiangsu, China
xuchen@ujs.edu.cn
[2] School of Mechanical Engineering, Shanghai University of Engineering Science,
Shanghai 201620, China

Abstract. This paper proposes a new hybrid metaheuristic algorithm called teaching-learning artificial bee colony (TLABC) for function optimization. TLABC combines the exploitation of teaching learning based optimization (TLBO) with the exploration of artificial bee colony (ABC) effectively, by employing three hybrid search phases, namely teaching-based employed bee phase, learning-based onlooker bee phase, and generalized oppositional scout bee phase. The performance of TLABC is evaluated on 30 complex benchmark functions from CEC2014, and experimental results show that TLABC exhibits better results compared with previous TLBO and ABC algorithms.

Keywords: Metaheuristic algorithm
Teaching learning based optimization · Artificial bee colony
Hybridization

1 Introduction

Metaheuristic search (MS) algorithms have received much attention regarding their potential as global optimization technique. Teaching learning based optimization (TLBO) [1] and artificial bee colony (ABC) [2] are two relative new MS algorithms. TLBO [3] is inspired by the teaching and learning process of a typical class, and it uses two operators namely teacher phase and a learner phase to search good solutions. ABC [2] is inspired by the intelligent foraging behavior of honey bees, and it uses three kinds of bees, namely employed bees, onlooker bees, and scout bees, to find good solutions. Both TLBO and ABC have aroused much interest in the last years and have been successfully applied to different kind of optimization problems [4–8].

Previous studies show that TLBO is good at exploitation [4], while ABC has a good exploration for global optimization [9]. However, a good search process needs to balance both exploration and exploitation; therefore, this paper proposes a hybrid teaching-learning-based artificial bee colony (TLABC) algorithm for global optimization. The proposed TLABC employs three hybrid search

© Springer International Publishing AG, part of Springer Nature 2018
Y. Tan et al. (Eds.): ICSI 2018, LNCS 10941, pp. 166–178, 2018.
https://doi.org/10.1007/978-3-319-93815-8_17

phases, namely teaching-based employed bee phase, learning-based onlooker bee phase, and generalized oppositional scout bee phase, which can efficiently combine the exploitation of TLBO with the exploration of ABC. TLABC is evaluated on 30 complex benchmark functions from CEC2014, and compared with eight well-established ABC and TLBO algorithms.

2   A Brief Introductions to TLBO and ABC

2.1   Teaching-Learning-Based Optimization

TLBO is a population-based optimization method which mimics the teaching and learning processes of a typical class [3]. The optimization process of TLBO is divided into two stages: teacher phase and learner phase.

In the teacher phase, the teacher provides knowledge to the learners to increase the mean result of the class. The learner with the best fitness in the current generation is identified as the teacher $x_{teacher}$, and the mean position is represented as $x_{mean} = \frac{1}{NP} \sum_{i=1}^{NP} x_i$. The position of each learner is updated by Eq. (1):

$$x_i^{new} = x_i^{old} + \boldsymbol{rand} \cdot (x_{teacher} - T_F \cdot x_{mean}) \qquad (1)$$

where x_i^{new} and x_i^{old} are the i-th learners new and old positions, respectively; $\boldsymbol{rand}$ is a random vector uniformly distributed within $[0,1]^D$; $T_F = round[1 + rand(0,1)]$ is the teacher factor; and its value is heuristically set to either 1 or 2. If x_i^{new} is better than x_i^{old}, x_i^{new} is accepted and flowed to learner phase, otherwise x_i^{old} is unchanged.

In the learner phase, each earner randomly interacts with other different learners to further improve his/her performance. Learner x_i randomly selects another learner $x_j (j \neq i)$ and the learning process can be expressed by Eq. (2):

$$x_i^{new} = \begin{cases} x_i^{old} + \boldsymbol{rand} \cdot (x_i - x_j), & \text{if } f(x_i) \leq f(x_j) \\ x_i^{old} + \boldsymbol{rand} \cdot (x_j - x_i), & \text{if } f(x_j) > f(x_i) \end{cases} \qquad (2)$$

2.2   Artificial Bee Colony

ABC is a swarm intelligence algorithm inspired on the foraging behavior of honey bee swarms [10]. It implements a cycle of the employed bee phase, onlooker bee phase and scout bee phase to search good solutions.

The ABC algorithm starts with randomly producing food sources:

$$x_{ij} = x_{\min,j} + (x_{\max,j} - x_{\min,j}) \cdot rand \qquad (3)$$

where $x_i = (x_{i1}, x_{i2}, \cdots, x_{iD})$, $i \in \{1, 2, \cdots, NP\}$ represents the i-th solution; $x_{\min,j}$ and $x_{\min,j}$ are the lower and upper bounds for the dimension j, respectively; $rand$ is a random real number in the range of $[0, 1]$. The fitness values of the food sources are then calculated as:

$$fit(x_i) = \begin{cases} \frac{1}{1+f(x_i)} & \text{if } f(x_i) \geq 0 \\ 1 + |f(x_i)| & \text{otherwise} \end{cases} \qquad (4)$$

where $f(\boldsymbol{x}_i)$ is the objective function value of $\boldsymbol{x}_i$.

In the employed bee phase, each employed bee performs a modification on the position of the food source by randomly selecting a neighboring food source. A new food source can be generated from the old food source $\boldsymbol{u}_i = (u_{i1}, u_{i2}, \cdots, u_{iD})$ as follows:

$$u_{ij} = x_{ij} + \psi \cdot (x_{ij} - x_{kj}) \tag{5}$$

where $k \in \{1, 2, \cdots, NP\}$ is randomly chosen index and must be different from i; ψ is a random number in the range $[-1, 1]$.

In the onlooker bee phase, an onlooker bee selects a food source to seek out ac-cording to the selection probability p, which is calculated as

$$p_i = \frac{fit(\boldsymbol{x}_i)}{\sum\limits_{i=1}^{SN} fit(\boldsymbol{x}_i)} \tag{6}$$

where fit is the fitness value of the solution, which is calculated as using Eq. (4). After the onlooker bee selects a food source $\boldsymbol{x}_s$ to seek out, a candidate food source position $\boldsymbol{u}_s = (u_{s1}, u_{s2}, \cdots, u_{sD})$ will be produced by using Eq. (5).

If the food source position of the employed bees cannot be further improved through a given number of steps (*limit*) in the ABC algorithm, this employed bee becomes a scout bee. The new random food source position (scout bee) will be generated from the Eq. (3).

The candidate solution is compared with the old one. If the new food source has a better quality than the old source, then the old source is replaced by the new one. Otherwise, the old source is retained.

3   Proposed Teaching-Learning-Based Artificial Bee Colony

TLBO is good at exploitation, but its exploration is relative poor for complex problems [4]. On the other hand, ABC has a good exploration for global optimization but poor at exploitation [9]. In order to balance the exploration and the exploitation during the searching process, this section proposes a hybrid teaching-learning artificial bee colony (TLABC) algorithm, which effectively combines the exploitation of TLBO with the exploration of ABC.

TLABC starts with initializing NP food sources $\boldsymbol{x}_i = (x_{i1}, \cdots, x_{ij}, \cdots, x_{iD})$, and calculates the fitness values using Eq. (4). Then it uses three hybrid search phases to find good solutions: (1) teaching-based employed bee phase, (2) learning-based onlooker bee phase, and (3) generalized oppositional scout bee phase. The details of these three phases are described as follows.

3.1   Teaching-Based Employed Bee Phase

In the teaching-based employed bee phase, each employed bee searches a new food source $\boldsymbol{u}_i = (u_{i1}, u_{i2}, \cdots, u_{iD})$ using a hybrid TLBO teaching strategy:

$$u_{i,d} = \begin{cases} x_{i,d}^{old} + rand_2 \cdot (x_{teacher,d} - T_F \cdot x_{mean,d}) & \text{if } rand_1 < 0.5 \\ x_{r1,d} + F \cdot (x_{r2,d} - x_{r3,d}) & \text{otherwise} \end{cases} \tag{7}$$

where r_1, r_2, and $r_3(r_1 \neq r_2 \neq r_3 \neq i)$ are integers randomly selected from $\{1, 2, \cdots, NP\}$; $d \in \{1, 2, \cdots, D\}$; $rand_1$ and $rand_2$ are two random numbers uniformly distributed within $[0, 1]$; and F is a scale factor in $[0, 1]$. If $\boldsymbol{u}_i$ is better than $\boldsymbol{x}_i$, then $\boldsymbol{u}_i$ is used to replace $\boldsymbol{x}_i$.

The hybrid TLBO teaching strategy using Eq. (7) can be viewed as a hybrid of basic teaching strategy of TLBO and mutation operator of differential evolution [11], and it is illustrated in Fig. 1.

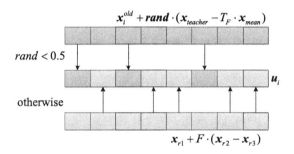

Fig. 1. Hybrid TLBO teaching strategy.

Remark 1: In the basic TLBO teaching strategy, all individuals use the same differential vector $(\boldsymbol{x}_{teacher} - T_F \cdot \boldsymbol{x}_{mean})$ to update the positions, so the diversity of the search directions is poor. By contrast, the hybrid TLBO teaching strategy uses a combination of TLBO teaching strategy and differential evolution mutation operator, which can improves the diversity of search directions greatly, and enhance the search ability of the proposed algorithm.

3.2   Learning-Based Onlooker Bee Phase

After the teaching-based employed bee phase, TLABC enters into the learning-based onlooker bee phase. In the learning-based onlooker bee phase, an onlooker bee selects a food source $\boldsymbol{x}_s$ to seek out according to the selection probability p, which is calculated using Eq. (6).

Then, the onlooker bee searches new food sources using the learning strategy of TLBO as follows:

$$\boldsymbol{u}_s = \begin{cases} \boldsymbol{x}_s + rand \cdot (\boldsymbol{x}_s - \boldsymbol{x}_j), & \text{if } f(\boldsymbol{x}_s) \leq f(\boldsymbol{x}_j) \\ \boldsymbol{x}_s + rand \cdot (\boldsymbol{x}_j - \boldsymbol{x}_s), & \text{if } f(\boldsymbol{x}_j) > f(\boldsymbol{x}_s) \end{cases} \tag{8}$$

where $j \in \{1, 2, \cdots, NP\}$ and $j \neq s$. If $\boldsymbol{u}_s$ is better than $\boldsymbol{x}_s$, then $\boldsymbol{u}_s$ is used to replace $\boldsymbol{x}_s$.

3.3   Generalized Oppositional Scout Bee Phase

After the learning-based onlooker bee phase, TLABC enters into the generalized oppositional scout bee phase. The generalized oppositional scout bee phase is proposed in [12], and it uses generalized opposition-based learning strategy [13] to enhance the basic scout bee phase. In this phase, if a food source $\boldsymbol{x}_i$ cannot be improved further for at least *limit* times, it is considered to be exhausted and would be abandoned. Then, a new random candidate solution $\boldsymbol{x}_i = (x_{i1}, \cdots, x_{ij}, \cdots, x_{iD})$ together with its generalized oppositional solution $\boldsymbol{x}_i^{GO} = (x_{i1}^{GO}, x_{i2}^{GO}, \cdots, x_{iD}^{GO})$ are generated using Eqs. (3) and (9) respectively.

$$x_{ij}^{GO} = k \cdot (a_j + b_j) - x_{ij} \tag{9}$$

where k is a random number in $[0, 1]$, and $a_j = \max\limits_{i}(x_{ij})$, $b_j = \min\limits_{i}(x_{ij})$.

The better solution between $\boldsymbol{x}_i$ and $\boldsymbol{x}_i^{GO}$ are used to replace the old exhausted food source:

$$\boldsymbol{x}_i = \begin{cases} \boldsymbol{x}_i, & \text{if } f(\boldsymbol{x}_i) \leq f(\boldsymbol{x}_i^{GO}) \\ \boldsymbol{x}_i^{GO}, & \text{if } f(\boldsymbol{x}_i) > f(\boldsymbol{x}_i^{GO}) \end{cases} \tag{10}$$

3.4   Framework of TLABC

Based on the three search phases described above, the framework of TLABC can be summarized in Fig. 2.

Remark 2: TLABC employs the three bee phases of ABC to search solutions, which is beneficial for global exploration. Meanwhile, TLABC uses the improved TLBO search equations and opposition-based learning strategy in the three bee phases, which is benefit for local exploitation. Therefore, it is hopeful that TLABC can provide a better balance between exploration and exploitation compared with the TLBO and ABC algorithms.

4   Experimental Results and Analysis

In this section, the proposed TLABC is evaluated on 30 benchmark functions from CEC2014 competition [14] and compared with well-established TLBO and ABC algorithms. The benchmark functions can be categorized into four groups: (1) G1: unimodal functions (F01–F03); (2) G2: simple multimodal functions (F04–F16); (3) G3: hybrid functions (F17–F22); and (4) G4: composition functions (F23–F30). More details for these functions can be found in [14]. The evaluation is performed under 30 variables, i.e., $D = 30$. The maximum number of functional evaluations $MaxFES = 10^4 \times D$ was used to terminate TLABC and the compared algorithms. All algorithms are run 30 times independently.

Algorithm 1. Teaching-learning-based artificial bee colony
1   **Stage 1: Initialization**
2   **For** each index $i = 1, 2, \cdots, NP$
3   Initialize the position of individual x_i using Eq. (3);;
4   Calculate the objective function value $f(x_i)$;
5   Calculate the fitness $fit(x_i)$ using Eq. (4);
6   Set $trial(i) = 0$ for each individual;
7   **End For**
8   **Stage 2: Teaching-based employed bee phase**
9   **For** each index $i = 1, 2, \cdots, NP$
10   Generate a new candidate solution u_i by hybrid TLBO teaching strategy using Eq.(7);
11   Calculate the objective function value $f(u_i)$;
12   Calculate the fitness value $fit(u_i)$ using Eq. (4);
13   Apply a greedy selection process between u_i and x_i to select the better one;
14   If solution x_i does not improve, $trial(i) = trial(i) + 1$, otherwise $trial(i) = 0$;
15   **End For**
16   **Stage 3: Learning-based on looker bee phase**
17   Calculate the selection probability p_i using Eq.(6);
18   **For** each index $i = 1, 2, \cdots, NP$
19   Select a solution x_s using the roulette method according to the probability p_i;
20   Generate a new candidate solution u_s by TLBO learning strategy using Eq.(8);
21   Calculate the objective function value $f(u_s)$
22   Calculate the fitness value $fit(u_s)$ using Eq. (4);
23   Apply a greedy selection process between u_s and x_s to select the better one.
24   If solution x_s does not improve, $trial(s) = trial(s) + 1$, otherwise $trial(s) = 0$.
25   **End For**
26   **Stage 4: Generalized oppositional scout bee phase**
27   **If** $\max(trial(i)) \geq \text{limit}$, **Then**
28   Generate a new random candidate solution x_i and its generalized oppositional solution x_i^{GO};
29   Replace the old x_i with the better one between the new x_i and x_i^{GO};
30   **End If**
31   **Stage 5: If the stop criterion is satisfied, stop and output the best solution achieved so far. Otherwise, return to Step 2.**

Fig. 2. Framework of TLABC.

4.1 Compared with TLBO Algorithms

TLABC is first compared with four well-known TLBO algorithms, they are basic TLBO [3], nonlinear inertia weighted TLBO (NIWTLBO) [15], TLBO with learning experience of other learners (LETLBO) [16], and generalized oppositional TLBO (GOTLBO) [5]. The parameters settings for TLABC and the compared TLBO algorithms are listed in Table 1.

Table 1. Parameter settings for TLABC and the compared TLBO algorithms

Algorithm	Parameter settings
TLBO	Population size $NP = 50$
NIWTLBO	$NP = 50$, inertia weight $w = 0 \sim 1.0$
LETLBO	$NP = 50$
GOTLBO	$NP = 50$, jumping rate $Jr = 0.3$
TLABC	$NP = 50$, $limit = 200$, scale factor $F = rand(0,1)$

Table 2 compares TLABC and the TLBO algorithms on four groups of benchmark functions. Following [17], each cell of the win-draw-loss table (see Table 2) consists of three numbers in $\alpha - \beta - \gamma$ style. In each triplet, α denotes the number of functions on the corresponding group which the TLABC performs statistically better than its competitor. The next number β shows how many times TLABC performs statistically similar its competitor. And, γ denotes the number of functions that TLABC performs statistically worse than its competitor. Note that in this table two algorithms are considered to be significantly different if the p-value of Wilcoxon rank-sum test is less than 0.05, and statistically similar otherwise.

Table 2. The win-draw-loss statistics results between TLABC and the compared TLBO algorithms

	TLBO	NIWTLBO	LETLBO	GOTLBO
G1	3-0-0	3-0-0	3-0-0	2-1-0
G2	9-2-2	9-2-2	7-3-3	8-3-2
G3	3-2-1	3-0-3	3-1-2	2-3-1
G4	5-2-1	3-2-3	6-2-0	1-2-5
Total	20-6-4	18-4-8	19-6-5	13-9-8

First, for unimodal functions F01–F03, TLABC performs significantly better than TLBO, NIWTLBO, and LETLBO on all 3 functions, and better than GOTLBO on 2 functions.

Second, for simple multimodal functions F04–F16, TLABC is significantly better than TLBO, NIWTLBO, and LETLBO on 9, 9, 7, and 8 functions, respectively. It is significantly worse than TLBO, NIWTLBO, and LETLBO on 2, 2, 3, and 2 functions, and similar to them on 2, 2, 3, and 3 functions, respectively.

Thirdly, for hybrid functions F17–F22, the performance of TLABC is better than TLBO, LETLBO and GOTLBO, while similar to NIWTLBO.

Finally, with regard to composition functions F23–F30, TLABC performs better than TLBO and LETLBO, similar to NIWTLBO, while worse than GOTLBO.

In summary, compared with the TLBO algorithms, TLABC shows the best overall performance on the unimodal functions, simple multimodal functions and hybrid functions. On composition functions, GOTLBO shows the best performance, TLABC and NIWTLBO the second. Based on the comparisons, it can be seen clearly that TLABC significantly improves the performance of TLBO on multimodal functions (i.e. the functions in Group 2). It should be attributed to the utilization of the three bee phases in TLABC, which is beneficial for the global exploration of TLABC. Meanwhile, the performance of TLABC is also very competitive on the other three group functions compared with TLBO algorithms.

4.2 Compared with ABC Algorithms

TLABC is also compared with four well-established ABC algorithms, they are basic ABC [2], gbest-guided ABC (GABC) [9], modified ABC(MABC) [18], and Gaussian bare-bones ABC (GBABC) [12]. The parameters settings for the TLABC and compared ABC algorithms are listed in Table 3.

Table 4 shows the win-draw-loss statistics results between TLABC and the compared ABC algorithms.

Table 3. Parameter settings for TLABC and the compared TLBO algorithms

Algorithm	Parameter settings
ABC	Population size $NP = 100$, $limit = 100$
GABC	$NP = 100$, $limit = 100$, $C = 1.5$
MABC	$NP = 100$, $limit = 100$, modification rate $MR = 0.4$, scaling factor $SF = 1$
GBABC	$NP = 100$, $limit = 100$, crossover rate $CR = 0.3$

Table 4. The win-draw-loss statistics results between TLABC and the compared ABC algorithms

	ABC	GABC	MABC	GBABC
G1	3-0-0	3-0-0	2-1-0	3-0-0
G2	3-2-8	3-2-8	5-2-6	3-2-8
G3	5-0-1	5-0-1	3-0-3	3-3-0
G4	7-0-1	6-2-0	5-2-1	4-3-1
Total	20-6-4	18-4-8	19-6-5	13-9-8

First, for unimodal functions F01–F03, TLABC performs significantly better than ABC, GABC, and GBABC on all 3 functions. TLABC performs significantly better than MABC on 2 functions, and similarly on 1 function.

Second, for simple multimodal functions F04–F16, the performance of TLABC is not very satisfactory. It performs worse than the other ABC.

Thirdly, for hybrid functions F17–F22, TLABC performs significant better than ABC, GABC, MABC, and GBABC on 5, 5, 3, and 3 functions, respectively. It is performs worse than ABC, GABC, MABC and GBABC on 1, 1, 3, and 0 functions, and similar to them on 0, 0, 0, and 3 functions, respectively.

Finally, with regard to composition functions F23–F30, TLABC shows the best performance on most of functions. It also outperforms the ABC algorithms on most of functions.

In summary, TLABC shows the best overall performance on the unimodal functions, hybrid functions, and composition functions. For the simple multi-modal functions, the performance of TLABC is not very satisfactory, but it also gets the best results on some multimodal functions.

From the comparisons, we can see that TLABC significantly improves the performance of ABC on unimodal functions (i.e. the functions in Group 1). This can be attributed to the use of the improved TLBO search equations and opposition-based learning strategy in TLABC, which enhances the global exploitation of TLABC. However, it sacrifices the exploration of the algorithm, as the performance of TLABC is not very satisfactory on simple multimodal functions compared with the ABC algorithms. Fortunately, TLABC achieves a very excellent performance on the hybrid functions and composition functions; therefore, the introduction of TLBO search equations and opposition-based learning strategy is useful for the overall performance enhancement of ABC.

4.3 Multiple-Problem Statistical Comparison

Table 5 shows the results of multiple-problem Wilcoxon test [19] between TLABC and the compared TLBO and ABC algorithms. It can be seen from the Table 5 that TLABC attains higher positive-ranks ($R+$) than negative-ranks ($R-$) compared with all the ABC and TLBO algorithms. This means that TLABC is overall better than the compared algorithms for all functions. Also, there are significant differences among TLABC, ABC, TLBO, NIWTLBO, LETLBO and GOTLBO when $\alpha = 0.05$ and $\alpha = 0.1$.

Table 5. Results of Multiple-problem Wilcoxon test between TLABC and the compared TLBO and ABC algorithms

	$R+$	$R-$	p-value	$\alpha = 0.05$	$\alpha = 0.1$
TLABC vs TLBO	375	60	3.32E-04	Yes	Yes
TLABC vs NIWTLBO	318	117	2.91E-02	Yes	Yes
TLABC vs LETLBO	331	104	1.29E-02	Yes	Yes
TLABC vs GOTLBO	328	107	1.57E-02	Yes	Yes
TLABC vs ABC	331	134	4.27E-02	Yes	Yes
TLABC vs GABC	311	154	1.09E-01	No	No
TLABC vs MABC	284	181	0.2	No	No
TLABC vs GBABC	256	209	0.2	No	No

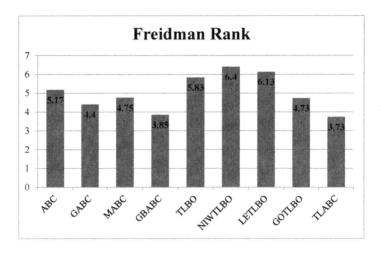

Fig. 3. Friedman rank of TLABC and the compared algorithms.

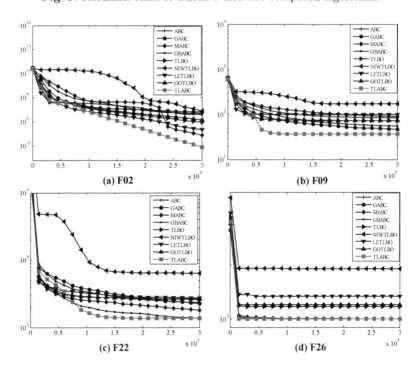

Fig. 4. Convergence graphs of TLABC and the compared algorithms on four typical functions.

Figure 3 shows the results of the Friedman rank test among TLABC and the compared algorithms. As shown in Fig. 3, TLABC gets the best rank, followed in order by GBABC, GABC, GOTLBO, MABC, ABC, TLBO, LETLBO, and NIWTLBO.

Figure 4 plots the Convergence graphs of TLABC and the compared algorithms on four typical functions F02, F09, F22, and F26. Overall, TLABC converge faster than the compared ABC and TLBO algorithms on these four functions.

5   Conclusion

Teaching learning based optimization (TLBO) and artificial bee colony (ABC) are two metaheuristic algorithms which have aroused great interests in recent years and have demonstrated their effectiveness on a wide variety of optimization problems. TLBO employs teaching and learning operators to search solutions, and its production operators are good at exploitation. ABC uses three search phases, namely employed bee phase, onlooker bee phase, and scout bee phase, to explore solutions. ABC is good at exploration; however, its exploitation ability is relative poor. In this paper, we have proposed a new hybrid algorithm named teaching-learning-based artificial bee colony (TLABC), which employs the teaching and learning operators of TLBO and the three bee search phases of ABC. The proposed TLABC is evaluated on the CEC2014 benchmark functions, and compared with previous eight well-known TLBO and ABC algorithms. Based on the experimental results, we can conclude that:

(1) TLABC significantly improves the performance of TLBO algorithms on multimodal functions. It should be attributed to the utilization of the three bee phases in TLABC, which is beneficial for the global exploration of TLABC.
(2) TLABC significantly improves the performance of ABC on unimodal functions. This can be attributed to the use of the improved TLBO search equations and opposition-based learning strategy in TLABC, which enhances the global exploitation of TLABC.
(3) TLABC can provide a better balance between exploration and exploitation compared with the TLBO and ABC algorithms. The overall performance of TLABC is better than all the compared TLBO and ABC algorithms on 30 CEC2014 benchmark functions, which demonstrates the superiority of the proposed hybrid algorithm.

Acknowledgements. This work was supported in part by Natural Science Foundation of Jiangsu Province (Grant No. BK 20160540), China Postdoctoral Science Foundation (Grant No. 2016M591783), and National Natural Science Foundation of China (Grant No. 61703268).

References

1. Rao, R.V., Savsani, V.J., Vakharia, D.: Teachinglearning-based optimization: a novel method for constrained mechanical design optimization problems. Comput. Aided Des. **43**, 303–315 (2011)
2. Karaboga, D., Basturk, B.: A powerful and efficient algorithm for numerical function optimization: artificial bee colony (ABC) algorithm. J. Global Optim. **39**, 459–471 (2007)
3. Rao, R., Savsani, V., Vakharia, D.: Teachinglearning-based optimization: an optimization method for continuous non-linear large scale problems. Inf. Sci. **183**, 1–15 (2012)
4. Zou, F., Wang, L., Hei, X., Chen, D., Yang, D.: Teachinglearning-based optimization with dynamic group strategy for global optimization. Inf. Sci. **273**, 112–131 (2014)
5. Chen, X., Yu, K., Du, W., Zhao, W., Liu, G.: Parameters identification of solar cell models using generalized oppositional teaching learning based optimization. Energy **99**, 170–180 (2016)
6. Yu, K., Wang, X., Wang, Z.: Constrained optimization based on improved teaching-learning-based optimization algorithm. Inf. Sci. **352**, 61–78 (2016)
7. Oliva, D., Cuevas, E., Pajares, G.: Parameter identification of solar cells using artificial bee colony optimization. Energy **72**, 93–102 (2014)
8. Xiang, Y., Peng, Y., Zhong, Y., Chen, Z., Lu, X., Zhong, X.: A particle swarm inspired multi-elitist artificial bee colony algorithm for real-parameter optimization. Comput. Optim. Appl. **57**, 493–516 (2014)
9. Zhu, G., Kwong, S.: Gbest-guided artificial bee colony algorithm for numerical function optimization. Appl. Math. Comput. **217**, 3166–3173 (2010)
10. Karaboga, D., Gorkemli, B., Ozturk, C., Karaboga, N.: A comprehensive survey: artificial bee colony (ABC) algorithm and applications. Artif. Intell. Rev. **42**, 21–57 (2014)
11. Das, S., Suganthan, P.N.: Differential evolution: a survey of the state-of-the-art. IEEE Trans. Evol. Comput. **15**, 4–31 (2011)
12. Zhou, X., Wu, Z., Wang, H., Rahnamayan, S.: Gaussian bare-bones artificial bee colony algorithm. Soft. Comput. **20**(3), 907–924 (2016)
13. Wang, H., Wu, Z., Rahnamayan, S., Liu, Y., Ventresca, M.: Enhancing particle swarm optimization using generalized opposition-based learning. Inf. Sci. **181**, 4699–4714 (2011)
14. Liang, J., Qu, B., Suganthan, P.: Problem definitions and evaluation criteria for the CEC 2014 special session and competition on single objective real-parameter numerical optimization. Zhengzhou University, Zhengzhou, China and Technical Report, Nanyang Technological University, Singapore, Computational Intelligence Laboratory (2013)
15. Wu, Z.-S., Fu, W.-P., Xue, R.: Nonlinear inertia weighted teaching-learning-based optimization for solving global optimization problem. Comput. Intell. Neurosci., 87 (2015)
16. Zou, F., Wang, L., Hei, X., Chen, D.: Teachinglearning-based optimization with learning experience of other learners and its application. Appl. Soft Comput. **37**, 725–736 (2015)
17. Kazimipour, B., Omidvar, M.N., Li, X., Qin, A.K.: A novel hybridization of opposition-based learning and cooperative co-evolutionary for large-scale optimization. In: IEEE Congress on Evolutionary Computation (CEC), pp. 2833–2840. IEEE (2014)

18. Akay, B., Karaboga, D.: A modified artificial bee colony algorithm for real-parameter optimization. Inf. Sci. **192**, 120–142 (2012)
19. Garca, S., Molina, D., Lozano, M., Herrera, F.: A study on the use of non-parametric tests for analyzing the evolutionary algorithms behaviour: a case study on the CEC2005 special session on real parameter optimization. J. Heuristics **15**, 617–644 (2009)

An Improved Artificial Bee Colony Algorithm for the Task Assignment in Heterogeneous Multicore Architectures

Tao Zhang[1,2], Xuan Li[1,2(✉)], and Ganjun Liu[1,2]

[1] School of Electrical and Information Engineering,
Tianjin University, Tianjin 300072, China
lixuantju@tju.edu.cn
[2] Texas Instruments DSP Joint Lab, Tianjin University, Tianjin 300072, China

Abstract. The Artificial Bee Colony (ABC) algorithm is a new kind of intelligent optimization algorithm. Due to the advantages of few control parameters, computed conveniently and carried out easily, ABC algorithm has been applied to solve many practical optimization problems. But the algorithm also has some disadvantages, such as low precision, slow convergence, poor local search ability. In view of this, this article proposed an improved method based on adaptive neighborhood search and the improved algorithm is applied to the task assignment in Heterogeneous Multicore Architectures. In the experiments, although the numbers of iteration decreases from 1000 to 900, the quality of solution has been improved obviously, and the times of expenditure is reduced. Therefore, the improved ABC algorithm is better than the original ABC algorithm in optimization capability and search speed, which can improve the efficiency of heterogeneous multicore architectures.

Keywords: Artificial bee colony algorithm · Task assignment
Neighborhood search

1 Introduction

Nowadays single core architectures is gradually replaced by multiple cores due to problems in obtaining further performance increases from single core processors [1]. Heterogeneous multicore architecture (HMA) is an integration of special purpose processing cores. The purpose of task assignment in HMA is to help system designers to get the best-performance and the lowest-cost design scheme in HMA [2]. Task assignment in HMA minimizes the execution time and consumed power of the target system [3] with certain constraint conditions.

Task assignment in HMA is an NP-hard problem [4]. Many heuristic algorithms have been applied to solve the NP-hard problem [5–8]. Due to the advantages of few control parameters, computed conveniently and carried out easily, ABC algorithm has been applied to solve many practical optimization problems [9], which have obtained preferable results.

ABC algorithm is based on swarm behavior, with the characteristics of integrity, relevance, dynamic and orderliness on systematics [10]. It can be evolved from

© Springer International Publishing AG, part of Springer Nature 2018
Y. Tan et al. (Eds.): ICSI 2018, LNCS 10941, pp. 179–187, 2018.
https://doi.org/10.1007/978-3-319-93815-8_18

disorder to order by self-organizing. Bees and bee colonies have feedback features at the same time [11]. Because it is limited by the way of evolution, there are still some disadvantages, such as low precision, slow convergence [12], poor local search ability [13–15]. In this paper, we describe the HMA as a model of a task assignment. The HMA are combined with two different cores. The original ABC algorithm is used in the model to achieve the DAG diagram corresponding to system tasks. Then an improved method based on adaptive neighborhood search is proposed to address the original ABC algorithm's disadvantages. Five DAG figures are generated randomly with TGFF [16] tools as a test set in order to compare the performance of the original and the improved ABC algorithms. The experimental results demonstrate that the improved ABC algorithm is more efficient.

2 Task Assignment Based on ABC

2.1 Bees Behavior

ABC simulates the co-operation, mutual coordination between individuals and groups in intelligent foraging and breeding behavior of bee swarms. They exchange information through dance and odor to finish foraging behavior. In a typical ABC algorithm, three types of artificial bees are considered as agents for solving an optimization problem, called employed bees, onlooker bees and scout bees. They have their own division or labor in foraging. The scout bees are responsible for investigation. The employed bees and onlooker bees are responsible for the exploitation of food sources. The bees maintained good coordination to achieve a better balance, and then completed the bee groups of foraging, reproduction and other behaviors.

2.2 Mathematical Model of the Artificial Bee Colony Algorithm

A system task is divided into a number of sub-tasks which can be completed by a combination of core A (represented by 0) and core B (represented by 1). When the two cores process the same task they consume different time and power. The coded information corresponding to the task assignment can be seen as an ordered set of binary numbers. The task assignment in HMA can be abstracted as a multi-objective combinatorial optimization problem in mathematics, to find a sub-optimal solution or the optimal solution under different constraints.

Bees can quickly find a better food source in foraging. Similarly, the task assignment can quickly find a better solution in the process. The correspondence among bee foraging behavior, mathematical model and task assignment is shown in Table 1.

Apparently, the more nodes there are, the more task assignment schemes. The number of schemes is growing at an exponential rate to the number of nodes. In a DAG, some tasks are completed by core A, the others are completed by core B. Figure 1 presents one scheme of the task assignments.

The best scheme from all the task assignment schemes is to be selected according to their fitness values and the probability to be searched. The maximum fitness food source is selected, which may be the optimal or suboptimal solution corresponding to

Table 1. The correspondence among Bee foraging behavior, mathematical model and task assignment

Bee foraging behavior	Mathematical model	Task assignment
All the food sources	All the solutions	All the Task assignment
The location of a food source	One solution	One Task assignment scheme
The best food source	The best solution	The best Task assignment scheme
The fitness of a food source	The quality of a solution	Performance of the system
Bees' foraging speed	Solutions' convergence rate	The speed of optimization capability

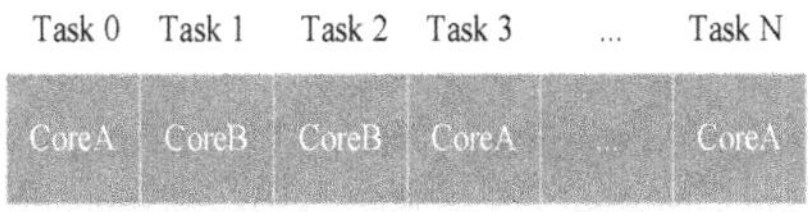

Task 0   Task 1   Task 2   Task 3   ...   Task N

| CoreA | CoreB | CoreB | CoreA | ... | CoreA |

Fig. 1. One scheme of the task assignments.

the best task assignment in HMA. The Eq. (1) is used to describe the best scheme of task assignment in HMA.

$$
\begin{cases}
Max\_fitness := \max(fitness[i]) \\
\displaystyle\sum_{j=0}^{N-1} T_j < Time\_Limit \\
s.t. \\
\displaystyle\sum_{j=0}^{N-1} Power_j < Power\_Limit
\end{cases}
\tag{1}
$$

Here $fitness(i)$ is the fitness value of i-th food source, T_j and $Power_j$ are the total time consuming and the total power consuming of the j-th node respectively. *Time_Limit* and *Power_Limit* are the maximum time and the maximum power limitations respectively.

2.3   Description of the Original ABC Algorithm

ABC is applied to solve the traveling salesman problem in literature [11]. The algorithm based on the mathematical model in Eq. (1) is applied to task assignment in HMA.

At first, the bees are equally divided into scout bees and onlooker bees. The scout bees search the food source and the food source in its neighborhood. If the fitness of its neighborhood position is greater than its fitness, then the location of i-th food source is substituted by the location of its neighborhood. Onlooker bees are sent according to the probability of each candidate food source to search food. The greater the probability is, the greater likelihood of neighborhood search is. If the fitness of the neighborhood position is greater than that of the current location, the current location is substituted by the location of its neighborhood.

When the time consumed by the neighborhood search is greater than the maximum limit time of food source, the food source is initialized. When its search time is greater than the global maximum limit, the worst food source is initialized. Every bit of coding information (0 or 1) is selected probably in the initialization.

At last the optimal or suboptimal food source searched is recorded. The information coding corresponds to the best scheme of task assignment in HMA. In original ABC algorithm, scout bees and onlooker bees finish their neighborhood search by updating one bit of information coding randomly, such as 0 (1) is updated as 1 (0). So the information update of food source is implemented.

3 The Analysis and Improvement of ABC Algorithm

3.1 The Shortcoming of the Original ABC Algorithm

In ABC algorithm, food source is updated through replacing the sub-optimal position by optimal position. The food-searching process is equivalent to the process of finding the optimal solution to task assignment in HMA.

When the initial position of the food source is far away from the optimal food source, there is a big difference between the encoded information of them. The method mentioned above will be very low efficiency. Obviously, the convergence rate will be lower and the method will increase the number of invalid iterative search. It is a broader range and high-discrete solution space. Finding the optimal solution is a continuous iteration and selection process. Therefore, in order to improve the optimization capability and reduce the time overhead, invalid iterations should be avoided or minimized.

3.2 The Improvement of ABC Algorithm

In view of the deficiencies of the original ABC algorithm, the efficiency of ABC algorithm is improved from the aspects of invalid iteration and neighborhood search strategy.

The Improvement of Neighborhood Search Strategy

When neighborhood search iteration is less than the constraint condition, the neighborhood search strategy updates one bit of the coded information in an iteration. On the contrary, when neighborhood search iterations exceed the constraint condition, but the fitness of the corresponding food source cannot be improved, then, the neighborhood search strategy is changed to update several bits of the coded information in an iteration.

Function named Search_Neighbourfood_Strategy_Improved([i]) is used to updates the coded information of the food source randomly. The pseudo-code is as follows (Table 2):

Table 2. The pseudo-code of the new neighborhood search program for the i-th food source.

Function: Search_Neighbourfood_Strategy_Improved([i])
begin
/*update several bits of the coded information to realize the neighborhood search*/
1    $X_{i,neighbour\_location:=Update\_nbits}(X_{i,old\_location})$;
/*The location of neighborhood food source is assigned to the current food source*/
$X_{i,old\_location} := X_{i,neighbour\_location}$;
2   **end**

Here, $X_{i,old\_location}$ is the information coding of the i-th food's current location, $X_{i,neighbour\_location}$ is the information coding of the i-th food source's neighborhood.

The Improvement of Calculating the Worst Food Source

During later iteration, all of the current food sources are approaching the final result. The worst food source is re-coded according the best food source's current location instead of initialize the worst food source. Several bits of the best food source's current location are kept and the remaining bits are re-coded. The pseudo-code is as follows (Table 3):

Table 3. The pseudo-code of generating a new solution.

Function: SendScoutBees_new([i])
begin
/*update several bits of the coded information to realize the neighborhood search*/
1    $X_{neighbour\_location} := update\_nbits(X_{best\_location})$;
/*The location of neighborhood food source is assigned to the new food source*/
$X_{new\_location} := X_{neighbour\_location}$;
2   **end**

Here, $X_{best\_location}$ is the information coding of the current best food source's location, $X_{neighbour\_location}$ is the information coding of the current best food source's neighborhood, $X_{new\_location}$ is the information of the new solution.

4   Experimental Results and Analysis

Algorithms in this paper are implemented in C-language and tested on a computer with Intel core i5-4460 and 8 GB RAM. The running environments consists of Windows 10 and Microsoft Visual Studio 2013 Ultimate. In the experiment we set population size as 15. Food sources number is equal to 0.5 * population size. The number of initial time scout bees is equal to the follow bee, which scale is equal to 0.5 * population size.

Five DAGs generated randomly with TGFF tool are regarded as a sample set to compare the test results of the original ABC algorithm and the improved ABC (I-ABC) algorithms. The parameter settings are shown in Table 4.

Table 4. Parameter settings

Parameters	Values
CoreA execution time	[392 ms, 450 ms]
CoreA consumed power	[25 w, 35 w]
CoreB execution time	[72 ms, 84 ms]
CoreB consumed power	[264 w, 336 w]

The comparison results between the ABC and the I-ABC algorithms are shown in Table 5.

Table 5. Comparison results between the ABC and the I-ABC algorithms

Nodes	Algorithm	Iterations	Optimal solution	The worst solution	Average solution	Average consumed power	Average execution time
30	ABC	1000	1590.1074	1911.0752	**1801.8261**	5970.2704	0.2317 s
30	I-ABC	900	1238.3132	1163.5138	**1418.6363**	5962.4877	0.2214 s
52	ABC	1000	1618.9009	2471.8289	**2116.6482**	1053.5813	1.5177 s
52	I-ABC	900	1493.8208	2072.0464	**1629.4947**	1055.6977	1.4246 s
75	ABC	1000	1791.9229	2784.7266	**2337.8188**	1544.2631	6.1917 s
75	I-ABC	900	1660.3372	2356.6123	**1914.4037**	1551.2477	5.8043 s
102	ABC	1000	2104.1284	3092.9399	**2600.3895**	2066.0012	13.6863 s
102	I-ABC	900	1968.8102	2662.5608	**2221.5824**	2090.9569	12.9610 s
132	ABC	1000	2708.5594	3218.9221	**2934.5233**	2905.2343	34.2272 s
132	I-ABC	900	2701.4824	3028.0132	**2835.6697**	2998.8134	32.6838 s

To illustrate the effectiveness of the I-ABC algorithm, its performances are shown in Figs. 2 and 3.

According to the comparison in Table 5, Figs. 2 and 3, data could be analyzed from the following three aspects:

The Local Search Ability: Although the number of iterations is reduced from 1000 to 900, the optimal solution of the improved algorithm is not only not worse, even better than that of the original algorithm. It is more obvious for the case of 52 nodes. From 30 nodes to 132 nodes, the quality of the solution increases about the 21.27%, 23.02%, 18.11%, 14.57%, 3.37% respectively. Meanwhile the time-consumed is reduced, and the power-consumed is the similar. Therefore, the I-ABC algorithm shows better local search ability.

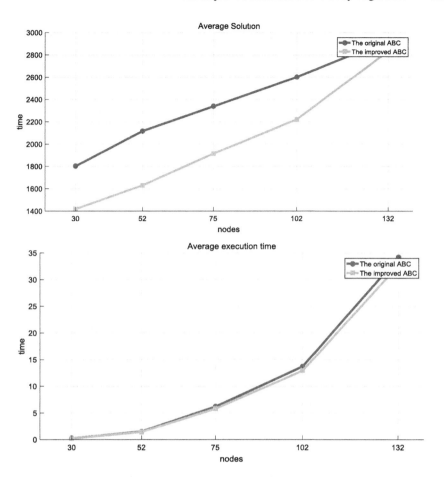

Fig. 2. Comparison of two algorithms over the average solution and the average execution time.

The Solution Accuracy: The D-value between the worst solution and the optimal solution in the I-ABC algorithm is reduced obviously. The final solution is also reduced significantly. For the case of 132 nodes, the final solution reduced about 3.5%, so the algorithm's accuracy is improved.

The Convergence Speed: When the consumed power is substantially the same, the improved algorithm can reduce the average execution time of the task.

From what we have been discussed above, we can get a conclusion that the precision of optimal solution of the I-ABC algorithm is higher than that of the original ABC algorithm, and the average execution time is reduced. The I-ABC algorithm is more efficient.

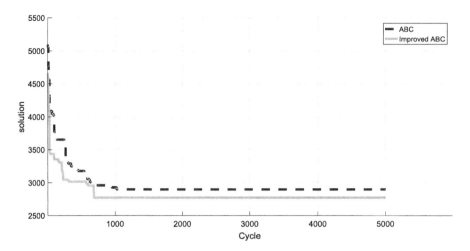

Fig. 3. Comparison results between the ABC and the I-ABC algorithms (132 nodes).

5   Conclusion

ABC algorithm has the features of less parameter and strong robustness, for which it is used in task assignment in HMA. Based on the original ABC algorithm, the neighborhood search scheme is proposed to solve the problems of low precision, slow convergence and poor local search ability. The experimental result shows that, in the case of less iterations, the I-ABC algorithm reduces the task execution time, and in case that the power-consumed obeys the restrictive conditions, the I-ABC algorithm reduces average solution with reduced numbers of iteration. D-value between the worst solution and the optimal solution is also reduced. The task assignment in HMA could be more efficient with the I-ABC algorithm.

References

1. Ya-Shu, C., Chiang Liao, H., Ting-Hao, T.: Online real-time task scheduling in heterogeneous multicore system-on-a-chip. IEEE Trans. Parallel Distrib. Syst. **24**(1), 118–130 (2013)
2. Hayashi, A., Wada, Y., Watanabe, T., Sekiguchi, T., Mase, M., Shirako, J., Kimura, K., Kasahara, H.: Parallelizing compiler framework and API for power reduction and software productivity of real-time heterogeneous multicores. In: Cooper, K., Mellor-Crummey, J., Sarkar, V. (eds.) LCPC 2010. LNCS, vol. 6548, pp. 184–198. Springer, Heidelberg (2011). https://doi.org/10.1007/978-3-642-19595-2_13
3. Fred, A.B., Daniel, J.S., Landon, P.C.: The impact of dynamically heterogeneous multicore processors on thread scheduling. IEEE Micro **28**(3), 17–25 (2018)
4. Jing, L., Kenli, L., Dakai, Z., et al.: Minimizing cost of scheduling tasks on heterogeneous multicore embedded systems. ACM Trans. Embed. Comput. Syst. **16**(2), 1–25 (2016)
5. Lanying, L., Yan-bo, S.: New Genetic algorithm and simulated annealing integration of Hardware/Software partitioning. Comput. Eng. Appl. **46**(28), 73–76 (2010)

6. Jianliang, Y., Manmam, P.: Hardware/Software partitioning algorithm based on wavelet mutation binary particle swarm optimization. In: 3rd International Conference on Communication Software and Networks, pp. 347–359. IEEE (2011)
7. Ahmed, U., Khan, G.N.: Embedded system partitioning with flexible granularity by using a variant of tabu search. In: Canadian Conference on Electrical and Computer Engineering, pp. 2073–2076. IEEE (2004)
8. Hai, Y., Xiao-ya, F., Sheng-bing, Z., et al.: A guiding function based greedy partitioning algorithm for dynamically reconfigurable systems. In: 8th International Conference on Solid-State and Integrated Circuit Technology, pp. 2009–2012. IEEE (2007)
9. Dengxu, H., Ruimin, J., Shaotang, S.: An article bee colony optimization algorithm guided complex method. In: 5th International Symposium on Computational Intelligence and Design, pp. 348–351. IEEE (2012)
10. Wei, Z., Jing, L., Jian-chao, Z.: Artificial bee colony algorithm and its application in combinatorial optimization. J. Taiyuan Univ. Sci. Technol. **1**, 108–112 (2010)
11. Li, L., Cheng, Y., Tan, L., Niu, B.: A discrete artificial bee colony algorithm for tsp problem. In: Huang, D.-S., Gan, Y., Premaratne, P., Han, K. (eds.) ICIC 2011. LNCS, vol. 6840, pp. 566–573. Springer, Heidelberg (2012). https://doi.org/10.1007/978-3-642-24553-4_75
12. Jun, L., Qian, W.: A modified artificial bee colony algorithm based on converge-onlookers approach for global optimization, pp. 10253–10262. Applied Mathematics & Computation, 219(20) (2010)
13. Guopu, Z., Sam, K.: Gbest-guided artificial bee colony algorithm for numerical function optimization. Appl. Math. Comput. **217**(7), 3166–3173 (2010)
14. Wang, H., Liu, J., Wang, Q.: Modified artificial bee colony algorithm for numerical function optimization. Comput. Eng. Appl. **48**(19), 36–39 (2012)
15. Bai, L., Li-gang, G., Wen-lun, Y.: An improved artificial bee colony algorithm based on balance-evolution strategy for unmanned combat aerial vehicle path planning. Sci. World J. **2014**(1), 95–104 (2014)
16. Dick, R.P., Rhodes, D.L., Wolf, W.: TGFF: task graphs for free. In: Proceedings of the Sixth International Workshop on Hardware/Software Codesign, (CODES/CASHE 1998), pp. 97–101. IEEE (1998)

.

Genetic Algorithms

Solving Vehicle Routing Problem Through a Tabu Bee Colony-Based Genetic Algorithm

Lingyan Lv[1], Yuxin Liu[1], Chao Gao[1(✉)], Jianjun Chen[1], and Zili Zhang[1,2(✉)]

[1] School of Computer and Information Science, Southwest University,
Chongqing 400715, China
{cgao,zhangzl}@swu.edu.cn
[2] School of Information Technology, Deakin University,
Locked Bag 20000, Geelong, VIC 3220, Australia

Abstract. Vehicle routing problem (VRP) is a classic combinatorial optimization problem and has many applications in industry. Solutions of VRP have significant impact on logistic cost. In most VRP models, the shortest distance is used as the objective function, which is not the case in many real-word applications. To this end, a VRP model with fixed and fuel cost is proposed. Genetic algorithm (GA) is a common approach for solving VRP. Due to the premature issue in GA, a tabu bee colony-based GA is employed to solve this model. The improved GA has three characteristics that differentiate from other similar algorithms: (1) The maximum preserved crossover is proposed, to protect the outstanding sub-path and avoid the phenomenon that two identical individuals cannot create new individuals; (2) The bee evolution mechanism is introduced. The optimal solution is selected as the queen-bee and a number of outstanding individuals are as the drones. The utilization of excellent individual characteristics is improved through the crossover of queen-bee and drones; (3) The tabu search is applied to optimize the queen-bee in each generation of bees and improve the quality of excellent individuals. Thus the population quality is improved. Extensive experiments were conducted. The experimental results show the rationality of the model and the validity of the proposed algorithm.

Keywords: Vehicle routing problem · Genetic algorithm
Bee colony algorithm · Tabu search

1 Introduction

The Vehicle Routing Problem (VRP) [11], introduced by Dantzig and Ramser in 1959, is defined as follows: some routes are made, in which vehicles can pass through a series of points in an orderly manner under the certain constraints, to achieve some optimization, such as the shortest distance, minimum cost and other targets. Reasonable vehicle routing can reduce the logistics

© Springer International Publishing AG, part of Springer Nature 2018
Y. Tan et al. (Eds.): ICSI 2018, LNCS 10941, pp. 191–200, 2018.
https://doi.org/10.1007/978-3-319-93815-8_19

costs and enhance the competitiveness of enterprises. Therefore, the VRP has drawn widespread attention from the scholars. We elaborate the existing research results from two aspects of the VRP models and its solution algorithms.

The analysis of relevant literature shows that most of the VRP models take the shortest distance as the objective function, which ignores the fuel consumption, load rate and other related factors. For example, the shortest distance is considered as the objective function [2,10]; A VRP model with the lowest carbon emissions is proposed in [9]; The literature [12] optimizes the vehicle fixed-cost without the fuel-cost. Such VRP models are different from the actual situations.

For solving the route optimization problems such as Traveling Salesman Problem (TSP) [6] and VRP, bionic algorithms are widely used, such as the Genetic Algorithm (GA) [13], the Ant Colony (ACO) algorithm [3,8,14] and the Simulated Annealing (SA) [1] algorithm. Among them, GA is used most frequently due to the high concurrency and fantastic local search ability. However, the traditional GA also has some drawbacks [7], such as the premature issue and individual degradation, which affects the global optimization ability and convergence speed, leading to that it can only be used for small-scale VRP models. Generally, the distribution of enterprises is large and the optimization result of vehicle routing directly affects the logistics cost. Therefore, it is necessary to optimize the traditional GA to improve the performance for solving large-scale VRP models.

A VRP model with the fixed-cost and fuel-cost is built in this study to reduce the logistics costs based on the above analysis. Further, a tabu bee colony-based genetic algorithm is proposed to solve the VRP model. The proposed algorithm is novel in three aspects. First, the maximum preserved crossover is put forward, to protect the outstanding sub-path which would be destroyed in traditional crossover and avoid the phenomenon that two identical individuals cannot produce new individuals. Second, the bee evolution mechanism is introduced in this paper. The optimal solution is selected as the queen-bee and a number of outstanding individuals are chosen as the drones. The utilization of excellent individual characteristics is improved through the crossover of queen-bee and drones. Finally, the tabu search [4] is applied, to optimize the queen bee in each generation of bees and improve the quality of the excellent individuals, so as to improve the population quality.

2   Mathematical Model of VRP

Most of the existing VRP models take the shortest distance as the objective function, and do not address the fuel consumption, cost and other related factors, which is different from the real situations. Addressing on this issue, a VRP model with the fixed-cost and fuel-cost is constructed in this paper.

The proposed VRP model can be described as follows: Let $G = (V, E)$ be a graph where $V = 0, 1, ..., n$ is a vertex set, and vertex 0 represents a depot, while the remaining vertices correspond to customers; c_{ij} is the linear distance between customer i and j; Q is the vehicle capacity; q_i is the demand of customer.

Given the following variables:

$$x_{ijk} = \begin{cases} 1, \text{ the vehicle } k \text{ moves from customers } i \text{ to } j. \\ 0, \text{ otherwise} \end{cases} \qquad (1)$$

$$y_{ik} = \begin{cases} 1, \text{ the delivery for customer } i \text{ is done by the vehicle k.} \\ 0, \text{ otherwise} \end{cases} \qquad (2)$$

The total fuel-cost can be calculated as formula (3):

$$C = s_i[e_1 + p_i(e_2 - e_1)] = e_1 s_i + s_i p_i(e_2 - e_1) \qquad (3)$$

Where, e_1, e_2 are the no-load fuel-cost and the full-load fuel-cost of vehicle respectively, s_i is the total distance.

$$C_{min} = \sum_{i=0}^{L}\sum_{j=0}^{L}\sum_{k=1}^{m} c_{ij} x_{ijk} e_1 + \sum_{i=0}^{L}\sum_{j=0}^{L}\sum_{k=1}^{m} c_{ij} x_{ijk} p_{ijk}(e_2 - e_1) \qquad (4)$$

$$F_{all} = \sum_{k=1}^{m} y_{0k} F \qquad (5)$$

F is the fixed-cost of each vehicle, then the objective function can be described as follows:

$$Z_{min} = \sum_{i=0}^{L}\sum_{j=0}^{L}\sum_{k=1}^{m} c_{ij} x_{ijk} e_1 + \sum_{i=0}^{L}\sum_{j=0}^{L}\sum_{k=1}^{m} c_{ij} x_{ijk} p_{ijk}(e_2 - e_1) + \sum_{k=1}^{m} y_{0k} F \qquad (6)$$

Subject to:

$$p_{ijk} = \frac{(\sum_{j=1}^{L} q_j y_{jk} - \sum_{i=1}^{j-1} q_i y_{ik})}{q} \qquad (7)$$

$$\sum_{i=1}^{L} q_i y_{ik} \leq Q, k = 1, 2, ..., m \qquad (8)$$

$$\sum_{k=1}^{m} y_{ik}, i = 1, 2, ..., L \qquad (9)$$

$$\sum_{j=1}^{L} x_{0jk} = m \qquad (10)$$

$$\sum_{i=1}^{L} x_{ijk} = y_{ik}, j = 1, 2..., L, k = 1, 2, ..., m \qquad (11)$$

$$\sum_{j=1}^{L} x_{ijk} = y_{ik}, i = 1, 2..., L, k = 1, 2, ..., m \qquad (12)$$

$$x_{ijk}(x_{ijk} - 1) = 0 \tag{13}$$

$$y_{ik}(y_{ik} - 1) = 0 \tag{14}$$

Equation (4) represents the total vehicle fuel-cost; Eq. (5) represents the total fixed-cost of the all vehicles departing from the depot; Eq. (6) is the objective function of the problem; Eq. (7) represents the vehicle load rate from customer i to customer j; Eq. (8) is the constraint of loading capacity; Eq. (9) is the vehicle constraint; Eq. (10) makes sure the number of vehicles can meet the customers' demands; Eqs. (11) and (12) are the constraints between customer and corresponding vehicle; Eqs. (13) and (14) mean x_{ijk}, y_{ik} are both integer variables.

3   Tabu Bee Colony-Based Genetic Algorithm

In this paper, a tabu bee colony-based genetic algorithm is proposed to solve the VRP model. The proposed algorithm is novel in three aspects. First, the maximum preserved crossover is put forward, to protect the outstanding sub-path which would be destroyed in traditional crossover and avoid the phenomenon that two identical individuals cannot produce new individuals. Second, the bee evolution mechanism is introduced in this paper. The optimal solution is selected as the queen-bee and a number of outstanding individuals are chosen as the drones. The utilization of excellent individual characteristics is improved through the crossover of queen-bee and drones. Finally, the tabu search is applied, to optimize the queen bee in each generation of bees and improve the quality of the excellent individuals, so as to improve the population quality.

The tabu bee colony-based genetic algorithm is designed as follows:

(1) Chromosome coding: The natural number encoding is used to express each solution as the form $(0, i_1, i_2, ..., i_e, 0, i_f, ..., i_k, 0, i_p, ..., i_n, 0)$, where 0 represents the distribution center, and i_j means the customer j in sub-path i.
(2) Initial population: The customers' permutation is randomly generated, in which 0 is inserted at the beginning and the end, and $m - 1$ 0 are inserted in the middle according to the constraints (m is the number of sub-paths, given by the algorithm). This step would be repeated until the initial population of size N is generated.
(3) Fitness function: The objective function Eq. (6) is selected as a fitness function to calculate the individual fitness values in the population.
(4) Select operator: The individuals are sorted according to their fitness values. The best individual is selected as the queen-bee and optimized by the tabu search operator. And a number of outstanding individuals are selected as drones by roulette options. The sector is divided to make the excellent individuals enter the next generation more possibly.
(5) Tabu operator: The Eq. (6) is considered as the objective function, and the queen-bee is the initial solution. In order to search for a better solution space, four operators are used: reversal operator, 1-0 exchange, 2-opt exchange and 3-opt exchange.

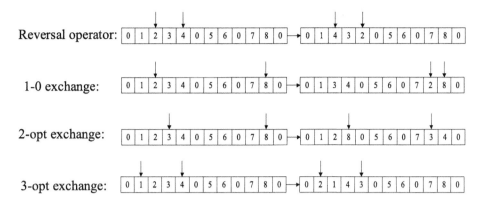

Fig. 1. Illustration of the tabu search operator

(a) Reversal operator: Some parts of one sub-path are reversed, it is an internal exchange of lines. As shown in Fig. 1, the sub path 234 is reversed to 432.

(b) 1-0 exchange: One customer is removed to another sub-path. For example, the customer 2 is inserted between customer 7 and 8 in Fig. 1, which belongs to the exchange between lines.

(c) 2-opt exchange: Two points in two sub-paths are selected to exchange the tails of them, just as shown in Fig. 1.

(d) 3-opt exchange: Four continuous customers (i, i+1, j, j+1) are exchanged to (i+1, i, j+1, j). As shown in Fig. 1, 1234 are changed to 2143.

(6) Maximum preserved crossover operator: Two same father individuals cannot generate new individual and good sub-path would be destroyed in traditional crossover. A new crossover operator is proposed in this paper. As shown in Fig. 2, the sub-path with the highest load rate is selected and moved to the top of the temporary string. Then the customers that are same as the temporary one are deleted. The remaining customers' permutations are transformed into the path form, and these sub-pathes are merged to complete the crossover operator.

(7) Mutation operator: As shown in Fig. 3, two non-0 codes are randomly selected to exchange their bits to produce a new path.

(8) Bee evolution mechanism: The optimal individual is used to assist population evolution so as to improve the utilization of excellent characteristics, and operated as follows:

(a) According to the above steps, population A and B of size N have been generated, after that, queen-A and queen-B are selected and optimized by tabu operator.

(b) Two random numbers r_a and r_b between (0, 1) are generated that $r_a + r_b = 1$, and $N/2r_a$ and $N/2r_b$ drones are selected from population A and B.

(c) Queen-A and queen-B cross with corresponding drones respectively, to form a new population C of size N.

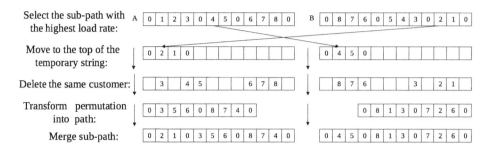

Fig. 2. Illustration of the crossover operator

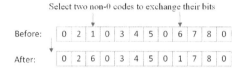

Fig. 3. Illustration of the mutation operator

(d) The population C is mutated to generate a new population D, and the corresponding queen-D is selected and optimized.

(e) Queen-A, queen-B and queen-D are admitted to compete. The best individual is selected as the queen of the new generation, and group D, is the new population. The above steps would be repeated until the iteration is over and then output the optimal solution.

4 Simulation Experiments

4.1 Datasets

This paper uses the distribution network with 30 nodes in [5] to estimate the rationality of the VRP model and the performance of the proposed Tabu Bee Colony-based Genetic Algorithm (TBCGA). The coordinates and demands of the nodes are shown in Table 1. The standard Genetic Algorithm (GA) [5], Tabu Search (TS) algorithm [5], Cloud Adaptive Genetic Algorithm (CAGA) [5] and TBCGA are selected to run 20 times based on the above dataset. Then we get the optimal solution, the worst solution, mean value and other factors from the results. Next we analyze the efficiency and stability of the algorithm. Experiment parameters are set as Table 2.

4.2 Experimental Analysis

The details of the optimal solution obtained based on our proposed algorithm are described in Table 3. In this table, the first column is the capacity of the vehicle.

Table 1. Demands and coordinates of synthetic dataset.

No.	Demands/t	Coordinates/KM	No.	Demands/t	Coordinates/KM	No.	Demands/t	Coordinates/KM
1	1.8	(2,83)	11	0.6	(64,16)	21	1	(40,11)
2	2.7	(73,63)	12	2.2	(9,98)	22	0.9	(17,37)
3	3.4	(85,100)	13	0.8	(12,43)	23	1.8	(70,75)
4	1.3	(41,70)	14	1	(52,53)	24	3.9	(52,4)
5	0.3	(4,36)	15	0.4	(25,61)	25	2.3	(81,91)
6	0.8	(44,36)	16	4	(72,47)	26	1.6	(87,22)
7	3.5	(13,10)	17	0.1	(90,28)	27	2.3	(34,40)
8	1.7	(19,40)	18	1	(18,75)	28	3.2	(85,58)
9	1	(10,66)	19	1.5	(43,3)	29	3.1	(9,93)
10	0.7	(15,87)	20	0.8	(55,5)	30	2.1	(68,98)

Table 2. Experiment parameters.

Parameters	Value	Interpretation	Parameters	Value	Interpretation
Q	8t	The vehicle capacity	E1	0.56 yuan/(km.t)	The full-load oil cost
E2	0.56 yuan/(km.t)	The full-load oil cost	F	100 yuan/time	Fixed-cost of vehicle
N	100	Population size	C	50	Iteration

Table 3. The optimal solution in proposed algorithm.

Load	Path	Mileage /KM	Oil cost /yuan	To-cost /yuan	Load-rate %	To-cost /yuan
8t	0-6-27-15-9-1-18-0	141.95	131.48	231.48	91.25	1515.00
	0-25-3-30-0	129.63	135.20	235.20	97.5	
	0-4-10-29-12-0	129.61	123.89	223.89	91.25	
	0-8-22-13-5-7-0	136.62	130.95	230.95	90	
	0-2-28-23-0	94.11	92.13	192.13	96.25	
	0-21-19-24-20-11-0	112.01	117.94	217.94	97.5	
	0-14-16-17-26-0	103.77	83.41	183.41	83.75	

The second column lists the sub-path of the best solution. The third to fifth columns provide the mileage, load-rate, and oil-cost of each sub-path respectively. The sixth column presents the all-cost which is the sum of the vehicle fixed-cost and the oil-cost. The last column gives the total cost required for the entire solution. As shown in Table 3, the distance of the sub-path 0-2-28-23-0 is the shortest, but its total cost is not the least. Similarly, the sub-path 0-6-27-15-9-1-18-0 has the longest distance, however it doesn't have the highest cost. Consequently, the distance of path is not the decisive factor of cost. The model which takes the shortest distance as the objective function can not

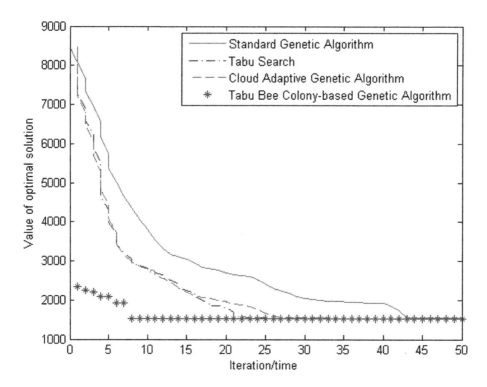

Fig. 4. The iteration of optimal solution

always get the least cost. Thus the VRP model with the fixed-cost and fuel-cost is more consistent with the actual distribution.

Next we use the GA, TS, CAGA and TBCGA to simulate based on the above instance, and compare the convergence of the optimal solutions obtained from each algorithm, to validate the performance of the TBCGA. The results are shown in Fig. 4.

In Fig. 4, all the GA, TS and CAGA are trapped in local optimal solutions compared to the TBCGA. And the solution of the TBCGA is the best, which means that the TBCGA has the strongest global optimization ability. The TBCGA gets the optimal solution in eighth generation, and the GA, TS and CAGA converge in about the 43rd, the 22nd, and the 26th generation. The converge speed from fast to slow are the TBCGA, TS, CAGA and the GA algorithm. Thus, the TBCGA performs better than other algorithms. Further, in order to validate the stability of our proposed algorithm, we use GA, TS, CAGA and TBCGA to run 20 times based on the above instance, to count the optimal solution, the worst solution, the mean value and other indicators. The results are shown in Table 4.

In Table 4, all the optimal solutions of GA, TS and CAGA are 1560.41 yuan, but the optimal solution of TBCGA is 1515.00 yuan, which is obviously more competitive. For the worst solution, the one of GA is 5632.85 yuan, the one of TS

Table 4. Demands and coordinates of synthetic dataset.

Algorithm	The optimal solution in proposed algorithm					
	Optimal solution /yuan	The worst solution /yuan	Mean value	Run time/s	Success rate/%	Average number iters/time
SGA	1560.41	5632.85	2654.38	12.2	15	52.31
TS	1560.41	4562.21	2156.43	32.5	12	26.42
CAGA	1560.41	3245.23	1685.62	8.9	48	33.26
TBCGA	1515.00	1615.44	1568.88	10.1	52	15.67

is 4562.21 yuan, the one of CAGA is 3245.23 yuan, which all have a big difference with their corresponding optimal solutions. But the worst solution in TBCGA is 1615.44 yuan, closing to the optimal value. This shows that our proposed algorithm is more stable and there is less fluctuation between the obtained values. The mean value obtained from TBCGA is also superior to the others. The time required for our algorithm is also relatively small. In addition, for the success-rate and the average iterations, our algorithm also outperforms other algorithms. The simulation results demonstrate that the proposed algorithm TBCGA performs better than the compared algorithms in terms of the global optimization ability, convergence speed and the stability of algorithm.

5 Conclusion

In this paper, we study the vehicle routing problem, and establish a VRP model with vehicle fixed-cost and oil-cost. We propose a Tabu Bee Colony-based Genetic Algorithm for solving the VRP model. The simulation results indicate that the proposed algorithm is competitive in terms of the quality of the solutions found, convergence speed and the stability of algorithm. However, there are some deficiencies in this study, mainly reflected in the following two points: (1) The runtime of our algorithm is not the shortest; (2) The VRP models with the same type of vehicles may result in the waste of resources, due to the differences between vehicle capacity and customer demands. Next, we will focus on how to shorten the algorithm runtime and study the VRP models with multiple vehicles to better simulate the realistic distribution.

Acknowledgments. This work is supported by the Fundamental Research Funds for the Central Universities (No. XDJK2016A008), CQ CSTC (No. cstc2015gjhz40002), Chongqing Graduate Student Research Innovation Project (No. CYB16064) and CCF-DiDi bigData Joint Lab. Dr. Chao Gao and Prof. Zili Zhang are the corresponding authors of this paper.

References

1. Afifi, S., Dang, D.-C., Moukrim, A.: A simulated annealing algorithm for the vehicle routing problem with time windows and synchronization constraints. In: Nicosia, G., Pardalos, P. (eds.) LION 2013. LNCS, vol. 7997, pp. 259–265. Springer, Heidelberg (2013). https://doi.org/10.1007/978-3-642-44973-4_27

2. Feng, L., Ong, Y.S., Lim, M.H., Tsang, I.W.: Memetic search with interdomain learning: a realization between CVRP and CARP. IEEE Trans. Evol. Comput. **19**(5), 644–658 (2015)

3. Hidayat, S., Nurpraja, C.: Efficient distribution of toy products using ant colony optimization algorithm. In: IOP Conference Series: Materials Science and Engineering, vol. 277, p. 012046. IOP Publishing (2017)

4. Jia, H., Li, Y., Dong, B., Ya, H.: An improved tabu search approach to vehicle routing problem. Procedia-Soc. Behav. Sci. **96**, 1208–1217 (2013)

5. Jie, J., Xu, W., Xianlong, G.: Research on capacitated vehicle routing problem with cloud adaptive genetic algorithm. J. Chongqing Univ. **8**, 006 (2013)

6. Laporte, G., Asef-Vaziri, A., Sriskandarajah, C.: Some applications of the generalized travelling salesman problem. J. Oper. Res. Soc. **47**(12), 1461–1467 (1996)

7. Liang, M., Gao, C., Zhang, Z.: A new genetic algorithm based on modified physarum network model for bandwidth-delay constrained least-cost multicast routing. Nat. Comput. **16**(1), 85–98 (2017)

8. Liu, Y., Gao, C., Zhang, Z., Lu, Y., Chen, S., Liang, M., Tao, L.: Solving NP-hard problems with physarum-based ant colony system. IEEE/ACM Trans. Comput. Biol. Bioinf. **14**(1), 108–120 (2017)

9. MirHassani, S., Mohammadyari, S.: Reduction of carbon emissions in VRP by gravitational search algorithm. Manage. Environ. Qual. Int. J. **25**(6), 766–782 (2014)

10. Mohammed, M.A., Ghani, M.K.A., Hamed, R.I., Mostafa, S.A., Ahmad, M.S., Ibrahim, D.A.: Solving vehicle routing problem by using improved genetic algorithm for optimal solution. J. Comput. Sci. **21**, 255–262 (2017)

11. Pillac, V., Gendreau, M., Guéret, C., Medaglia, A.L.: A review of dynamic vehicle routing problems. Eur. J. Oper. Res. **225**(1), 1–11 (2013)

12. Xiao, Y., Zhao, Q., Kaku, I., Xu, Y.: Development of a fuel consumption optimization model for the capacitated vehicle routing problem. Comput. Oper. Res. **39**(7), 1419–1431 (2012)

13. Yusuf, I., Baba, M.S., Iksan, N.: Applied genetic algorithm for solving rich VRP. Appl. Artif. Intell. **28**(10), 957–991 (2014)

14. Zhang, Z., Gao, C., Liu, Y., Qian, T.: A universal optimization strategy for ant colony optimization algorithms based on the Physarum-inspired mathematical model. Bioinspir. Biomimetics **9**(3), 036006 (2014)

Generation of Walking Motions for the Biped Ascending Slopes Based on Genetic Algorithm

Lulu Gong[✉], Ruowei Zhao, Jinye Liang, Lei Li, Ming Zhu,
Ying Xu, Xiaolu Tai, Xinchen Qiu, Haiyan He, Fangfei Guo,
Jindong Yao, Zhihong Chen, and Chao Zhang[✉]

Translational Medical Center for Stem Cell Therapy and Institute
for Regenerative Medicine, Shanghai East Hospital, Shanghai Key Laboratory
of Signaling and Disease Research, School of Life Sciences and Technology,
Tongji University, Shanghai 200092, China
{lulugong, zhangchao}@tongji.edu.cn

Abstract. This study aims to generate the optimal trajectories for the biped walking up sloping surfaces after ensuring the minimum energy consumption by using genetic algorithm (GA) and motion/force control scheme. During optimization, the step length, the maximum height of swing foot and walking speed were optimized with the seven-link biped model. The impactless bipedal walking was investigated for walking on the ground level and slopes with different gradients, respectively. The results showed that the biped consumed more energy when the optimal walking speed increased for walking on the same slopes. There were no great differences in optimal step length when the biped changed the walking speed. The results showed that the proposed approach is able to generate optimal gaits for the biped simply by changing boundary conditions with GA.

Keywords: Biped · Genetic algorithm · Optimization · Slope
Impactless

1 Introduction

The biped robots are required to have humanlike walking pattern to adapt to complicated environment like walking on flat terrain, negotiating stairs, going upslope and downslope. That is, the biped should have the ability to maintain stability and consume minimum energy during walking.

As one kind of special locomotion patterns, impactless walking ensures the feet contact the floors with zero velocity for the whole walking cycle [1]. Gong and Schiehlen [2] and Gong [3] have reported that the motion/force control scheme can be used effectively to generate stable walking for the biped walking on slopes and stairs. Haq et al. studied the impactless walking gaits of the 7-link planar bipedal robot and proposed that locking the knee and increasing springs of different joints could decrease the energy consumption [4].

Due to the advantages of efficiency and being robust, genetic algorithm (GA) was frequently adopted in many researches as the global optimization method. GA was used

© Springer International Publishing AG, part of Springer Nature 2018
Y. Tan et al. (Eds.): ICSI 2018, LNCS 10941, pp. 201–209, 2018.
https://doi.org/10.1007/978-3-319-93815-8_20

to optimize the angle trajectories for the bipedal level ground walking and going up-stairs based on Consumed Energy (CE) and Torque Change (TC) by Capi et al. [5]. Cardenas-Maciel et al. [6] generated periodic motions for a numerical investigation case of a 3 degrees of freedom (DOFs) biped robot while ensuring minimal energy. Lim et al. [7] proposed the real-coded genetic algorithms (RCGA) to generate various three-dimensional (3D) optimal locomotion trajectories for biped robots ascending and descending stairs. Safa et al. [8] investigated the passive bipedal locomotion on a series of parallel local slopes, and found that adding feet and an upper body could increase the maximum stable speed and the stability of the biped robot. An time-efficient and force-resisting control strategy were used to control the joint motors of a walking biped robot based on GA and the linear interpolation technique by Kim et al. [9].

This study proposes an optimization method in generating optimal trajectories for the biped walking up different slopes via the combination of the motion/force control scheme and GA. This paper is organized as follows. Section 2 introduces the 7-link planar biped model. Section 3 briefly explains the process and parameters of GA and definition of cost function. Simulations and comparisons of the biped walking up slopes with different gradients at different speeds are demonstrated in Sect. 4. Section 5 makes some concluding remarks of this study.

2   Biped Motion Analysis for Ascending Slopes

2.1   Dynamics of the 7-Link Planar Biped Model

In this study, a planar 7-link biped robot was investigated to walk up the slopes with different gradients ensuring the dynamic balance. Figure 1 demonstrates the schematic view of the 7-link biped model going up slopes, which was used in our previous study [3]. The biped robot has two thighs, two shanks, two feet and one head-arms-trunk (HAT). Table 1 lists the physical parameters of the biped [3]. It is assumed that one complete gait cycle is composed of two phases, the single support phase (SSP) and double support phase (DSP).

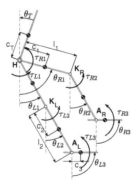

Fig. 1. Schematic view of the 7-link biped model [3].

Table 1. The parameters of the biped model [3].

Parameter	$k = 1$	$k = 2$	$k = 3$
m_k	5.3 kg	2.25 kg	0.5 kg
J_k	$0.08 \text{ kg} \cdot \text{m}^2$	$0.09 \text{ kg} \cdot \text{m}^2$	$0.006 \text{ kg} \cdot \text{m}^2$
l_k	0.3 m	0.35 m	–
c_k	0.07 m	0.145 m	0.05 m
m_T	14.8 kg	–	–
J_T	$0.9 \text{ kg} \cdot \text{m}^2$	–	–
c_T	0.2 m	–	–

For an autonomous multibody system with n DOFs, the vector $y \in R^n$ can define the n position coordinates. The equation of the "flying" biped can be written as

$$M(y)\ddot{y} = h(\dot{y}, y) + B^T \tau \tag{1}$$

where $y = [y_1 \cdots, y_n]^T$ and $M(y)$ represents the inertia matrix; $h(\dot{y}, y)$ is the applied and centrifugal forces; B is the control input matrix; τ represent the control troques/forces. The equations of motions of the 7-link biped model were generated by using the software Neweul-M^2 [10].

The "flying" biped has nine DOFs and six control inputs. For the walking biped, there are 6 DOFs in the SSP and 3 DOFs in the DSP, respectively. During SSP, there are 3 rheonomic constraints (motion constraints) on the upper body and 3 rheonomic constraints (motion constraints) on the lifting leg. While during DSP, there are 3 rheonomic constraints (motion constraints) on upper body and 3 scleronomic constraints (force constraints) on the hind leg (trailing leg). Therefore, the control strategy for the whole process of walking is the mixture of motion control and force control.

The specified motion is investigated to ensure the feet contact with the ground with zero velocities during the whole process of walking, which is regarded as impactless walking.

The motions of equations for the walking biped are the same with our previous study [3], which can be defined as:

$$M\ddot{y} = h + B^T \tau + C_b^T \lambda_b + C_c^T \lambda_c, \tag{2}$$

$$C_c(\dot{y}, y, t)\ddot{y} + C_{c0}(\dot{y}, y, t) = 0. \tag{3}$$

In this case, λ_b represent the specified reactions of constraints; $C_c^T \lambda_c$ are the reaction forces of constraints; $C_b = \partial \phi_b / \partial y$ and $C_c = \partial \phi_c / \partial y$ where ϕ_b are rheonomic constraints of SSP and ϕ_c are scleronomic constraints of DSP.

The next step is to calculate the control torques/forces τ with:

$$\tau = \left(D_c B^T \right)^{-1} D_c \left(M\ddot{y} - h - C_b^T \lambda_b \right) \tag{4}$$

where D_c is the orthogonal complement matrix to matrix C_c.

Then, the reactions of constraints λ_c can be calculated by

$$\lambda_c(\dot{y}, y, t) = -\left(C_c M^{-1} C_c^T\right)^{-1}\left[C_{c0} + C_c M^{-1}\left(h + B^T \tau + C_b^T \lambda_b\right)\right], \qquad (5)$$

where $C_{c0}(\dot{y}, y, t) = -\left(\dot{C}_c \dot{y} + d/dt(\partial \phi_c / \partial t)\right)$.

2.2   Constraints of the Biped Model

The constraints ϕ_a are the trajectories the position of hip joint and the orientation of HAT,

$$\phi_a = \begin{bmatrix} x_H - x_{Hn}(t) \\ y_H - (h_0 + x_H \cdot tan\gamma) \\ \theta_T \end{bmatrix} = 0. \qquad (6)$$

Constraints ϕ_b and ϕ_c represent the trajectories of left and right lower limb joints,

$$\phi_{b,c} = \begin{bmatrix} x_H + l_1 sin\theta_{i1} + l_2 sin\theta_{i2} - x_{Ai} \\ y_H - l_1 cos\theta_{i1} - l_2 cos\theta_{i2} - y_{Ai} \\ \theta_{i3} - (\pi/2 + \gamma) \end{bmatrix} = 0, \qquad (7)$$

where $i = R\,or\,L$; x_{Ai} and y_{Ai} represent the coordinates of the ankle joints; γ is the gradient of the slopes.

3   Optimization Strategy of Genetic Algorithm (GA)

3.1   GA Process

Being robust and able to finding global solutions, genetic algorithms (GAs) are widely used in many optimization problems. Based on natural selection and natural genetic principles, the GA operates via several processes, that is initialization, evaluation, selection, reproduction, replacement and termination.

During the initialization stage, a set of candidate individuals is generated randomly, which is called as population. In the evaluation stage, the objective function is used to evaluate each candidate individual. The fittest individuals are selected by survival-of-fittest mechanism based on the values of the evaluation at the selection stage. These fittest individuals are often called parents. The reproduction stage is to generate new individuals by the application of genetic operations including crossover and mutation. The first genetic operation, crossover, can create new individuals with information of two parents. These new individuals serve as the offspring population. Then, the diversity in the population is produced by changing the value of one parameter in the individual via mutation. In the replacement stage, the original parental population are replaced by the new offspring population in this stage. The whole process is called one generation (GN), and can be repeated in an iterative manner.

The termination of the iterations is decided by the terminating conditions.

3.2   GA Parameters

In the presented approach, GA is adopted to search for optimal step lengths (s), the maximum height from the current sloping surface of swing foot (h_A) and walking velocities for the biped ascending different slopes. The initial population is 10. Single-point crossover and discrete mutation operator are used. The crossover ratio and mutation ratio are set as 0.9 and 0.02, respectively. The maximum of generations (*GNmax*) is defined as 1000. The GA process switches to the termination stage, when the number of generation equals to *GNmax* or when the value of the objective function does not change for 10 conservative generations. Figure 2 shows the whole process of GA.

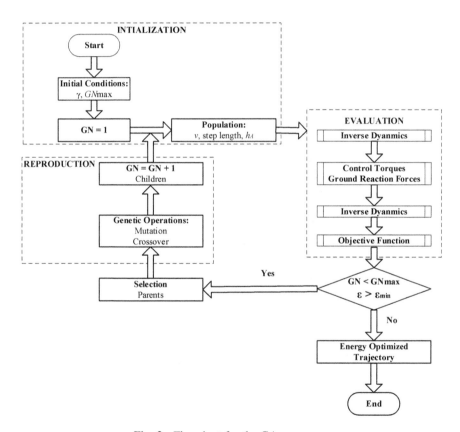

Fig. 2. Flowchart for the GA processes.

3.3   Cost Function

The cost function is used to evaluate energy efficiency of the joint trajectories during one step. It is important to minimize the energy consumption in the design of a biped robot and generation of the locomotion pattern. The sum of the work by the six lower limb joints is the energy consumption of the system. For one joint, the work can be defined as

$$W(t) = \int_{t_0}^{t_1} |\mu_m \omega| dt, \qquad (8)$$

where t is the time, μ_m represent the control torques of six lower limb joints and ω are the relative angular velocities of six joints. The period of one step equals to the duration from t_0 to t_1. The total energy cost for one step can be obtained by adding the work by six joints. The actuator and transmission efficiency are not included in the mechanical power output. The mechanical power output is defined as $P = |\mu_m \omega|$.

Specific resistance (ε) has been used as the index to evaluate the performance of legged vehicles [11]. The specific resistance can be obtained with the mechanical power, P, the biped weight, mg and walking speed, v, as

$$\varepsilon(v) = \frac{P(v)}{mgv}. \qquad (9)$$

In this study, the objective function depends on the minimized specific resistance (ε_{min}).

4 Simulation Results

We investigated the bipedal walking on level ground ($0°$) and up slopes with the gradients of $3°$, $6°$, $9°$ and $12°$ at different walking speeds, respectively. During optimization, the range of parameters: step length (s), the maximum height from the current sloping surface of the swing foot (h_A), slow walking speed (v_s), normal walking speed (v_n) and fast walking speed (v_f) were varied in the ranges of (0.1 m, 0.4 m), (0.05 m, 0.15 m), (0.4 m/s, 0.6 m/s), (0.6 m/s, 0.8 m/s) and (0.8 m/s, 1.0 m/s), respectively. Generally, GA yielded the optimal values between 30 generations to 85 generations.

All the optimal values for the biped walking up slopes were obtained by calculating ε_{min}. Figure 3 showed the optimal consumed energy and step length against the gradient of the slope (γ). Figure 3(a) demonstrated that the minimal energy consumption was ascendant with the increase of γ. And ε_{min} increased when the optimal walking speed enhanced. As showed in Fig. 3(b), walking velocity didn't have obvious influences on the optimal step length (s). While the optimal step length decreased when γ increased. All the values of h_A were close to the lower boundary for the biped walking on different slopes at different speed. The optimal minimal walking velocities were also nearly the same with the lower boundary which was defined before.

Figure 4 depicted the stick diagrams of the biped walking on flat terrain and different slopes at the optimal fast speed.

Figure 5 plotted the ankle joint trajectories of the biped walking on slopes with gradient of $6°$ and $12°$ at slow speed, normal speed and fast speed, respectively.

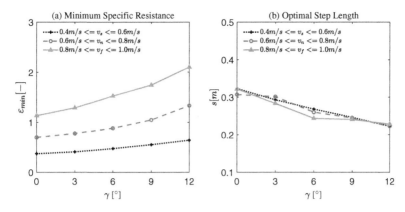

Fig. 3. Optimal data for the biped walking up different slopes vs. γ: (a) minimum specific resistance (ε_{min}); (b) optimal step length (s).

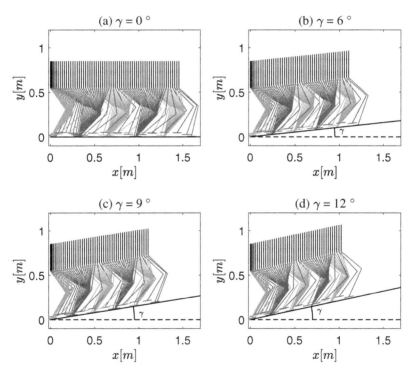

Fig. 4. Stick diagrams of the biped walking at optimal fast speed: (a) on the flat terrain; (b) on the slope with the gradient of 6°; (c) on the slope with the gradient of 9°; (d) on the slope with the gradient of 12°.

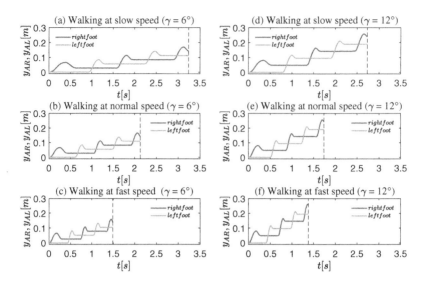

Fig. 5. Ankle joint trajectories of the biped: (a) walking up the slope with the gradient of 6° at slowing speed; (b) walking up the slope with the gradient of 6° at normal speed; (c) walking up the slope with the gradient of 6° at fast speed; (d) walking up the slope with the gradient of 12° at slow speed; (e) walking up the slope with the gradient of 12° at normal speed; (f) walking up the slope with the gradient of 12° at fast speed.

5   Conclusions

Simulation results show that GA is able to generate the optimal trajectories of the impactless bipedal walking on the slopes. There are great differences in energy consumption for the biped walking at different speeds. It has been observed that biped consumed more energy when walking at faster speed. There were no obvious differences in optimal step length when walking speed changed. The rise of slope gradients can result in the decline of the optimal step length for the biped ascending slopes. These conclusions confirm the validity and effectiveness to generate various optimal gaits of the biped simply by appropriately altering some of the boundary conditions.

Acknowledgments. The author Lulu Gong would like to express her sincerely appreciation to Prof. Werner Schiehlen of University of Stuttgart for his talent and valuable guidance, which made the successful completion of this work possible. This work was supported by the National Science Foundation of China (Grant No. 11402176, 81570760, and 31771283), the National Key Research and Development Program of China (Grant No. 2017YFA0103900, 2017YFA0103902, and 2017YFA0103904), Ministry of Science and Technology of China (Grant No. 2016ZY05001905 & 2017ZY050105); One Thousand Youth Talents Program of China to CZ; The Program for Professor of Special Appointment (Eastern Scholar) at Shanghai Institutions of Higher Learning (No. A11323 to CZ); The Shanghai Rising-Star Program (Grant No. 15QA1403600); and the Fundamental Research Funds for the Central Universities of Tongji University to Lulu Gong and Chao Zhang.

References

1. Blajer, W., Schiehlen, W.: Walking without impacts as a motion/force control problem. Trans. ASME J. Dyn. Syst. Measure. Control **114**, 660–665 (1992)
2. Gong, L., Schiehlen, W.: Impactless biped walking on a slope. Theor. Appl. Mech. Lett. **3**, 013002 (2013)
3. Gong, L.: Impactless biped walking on stairs. In: ASME 2013 International Design Engineering Technical Conferences and Computers and Information in Engineering Conference (IDETC/CIE 2013). American Society of Mechanical Engineers (2013)
4. Haq, A., Aoustin, Y., Chevallereau, C.: Compliant Joints Increase the Energy Efficiency of Bipedal Robot. World Scientific Publ Co Pte Ltd, Singapore (2012)
5. Capi, G., Nasu, Y., Barolli, L., Mitobe, K., Takeda, K.: Application of genetic algorithms for biped robot gait synthesis optimization during walking and going up-stairs. Adv. Robot. **15**, 675–694 (2001)
6. Cardenas-Maciel, S.L., Castillo, O., Aguilar, L.T.: Generation of walking periodic motions for a biped robot via genetic algorithms. Appl. Soft Comput. **11**, 5306–5314 (2011)
7. Lim, I.-S., Kwon, O., Park, J.H.: Gait optimization of biped robots based on human motion analysis. Robot. Autonom. Syst. **62**, 229–240 (2014)
8. Safa, A.T., Mohammadi, S., Hajmiri, S.E., Naraghi, M., Alasty, A.: How local slopes stabilize passive bipedal locomotion? Mech. Mach. Theory **100**, 63–82 (2016)
9. Kim, Y.J., Lee, J.Y., Lee, J.J.: A balance control strategy for a walking biped robot under unknown lateral external force using a genetic algorithm. Int. J. Humanoid Rob. **12**, 37 (2015)
10. Kurz, T., Eberhard, P., Henninger, C., Schiehlen, W.: From Neweul to Neweul-M2: symbolical equations of motion for multibody system analysis and synthesis. Multibody Sys. Dyn. **24**, 25–41 (2010)
11. Schiehlen, W.: Energy-optimal design of walking machines. Multibody Sys. Dyn. **13**, 129–141 (2005)

On Island Model Performance for Cooperative Real-Valued Multi-objective Genetic Algorithms

Christina Brester[1,2(✉)], Ivan Ryzhikov[1,2], Eugene Semenkin[1],
and Mikko Kolehmainen[2]

[1] Siberian State University of Science and Technology, Krasnoyarsk, Russia
christina.brester@gmail.com, {ryzhikov-88,
eugenesemenkin}@yandex.ru
[2] University of Eastern Finland, Kuopio, Finland
mikko.kolehmainen@uef.fi

Abstract. Solving a multi-objective optimization problem results in a Pareto front approximation, and it differs from single-objective optimization, requiring specific search strategies. These strategies, mostly fitness assignment, are designed to find a set of non-dominated solutions, but different approaches use various schemes to achieve this goal. In many cases, cooperative algorithms such as island model-based algorithms outperform each particular algorithm included in this cooperation. However, we should note that there are some control parameters of the islands' interaction and, in this paper, we investigate how they affect the performance of the cooperative algorithm. We consider the influence of a migration set size and its interval, the number of islands and two types of cooperation: homogeneous or heterogeneous. In this study, we use the real-valued evolutionary algorithms SPEA2, NSGA-II, and PICEA-g as islands in the cooperation. The performance of the presented algorithms is compared with the performance of other approaches on a set of benchmark multi-objective optimization problems.

Keywords: Multi-objective optimization · Real-valued genetic algorithm
Island model cooperation

1 Introduction

Multi-objective optimization problems (MOPs) are quite essential in Decision-Making Theory because the decision-making process is in most cases related to a few criteria which could contradict one another. These problems differ from single-objective optimization problems since the goal is to find a good approximation of the Pareto front. In this study, we consider the widest class of optimization problems called *black box optimization problems* (BBOPs). There are many problems which might be reduced to BBOPs and whose objective functions can only be evaluated and, in general, there is no information about these functions and their mathematical properties.

Evolutionary algorithms (EAs) and particularly genetic algorithms (GAs) with different schemes and modifications are the most common search heuristics to solve

© Springer International Publishing AG, part of Springer Nature 2018
Y. Tan et al. (Eds.): ICSI 2018, LNCS 10941, pp. 210–219, 2018.
https://doi.org/10.1007/978-3-319-93815-8_21

complex BBOPs, and so these algorithms are also useful and efficient in solving MOPs. In this study, we present real-valued modifications of three widely used multi-objective genetic algorithms (MOGA): the Strength Pareto Evolutionary Algorithm 2 (SPEA2) [1], the Non-Sorting Genetic Algorithm II (NSGA-II) [2], and the Preference-Inspired Co-Evolutionary Algorithm with goal vectors (PICEA-g) [3]. The effectiveness of these algorithms has been shown on benchmark and real problems in many studies [4–6].

Despite the recent development of a wide range of novel effective MOGAs, according to the No Free Lunch theorem, a particular algorithm performs well on a specific class of problems. There are some combinations of settings which make an algorithm more efficient in solving a particular problem. In many cases, "adaptation" for a problem can be achieved by meta-heuristics [7], in particular, by the use of coevolution: different algorithms solve the same problem and share computational resources and information about a search space. In addition, there is also a hypothesis that a cooperation of algorithms allows the benefits of each algorithm to be kept and this cooperation may even outperform the algorithms included in it [8–10]. We propose using an island model cooperation wherein each algorithm works independently from the others and after a certain number of iterations, the algorithms exchange their best solutions. The proposed approach has been applied in various problems and there are results proving its high performance [11, 12].

In this study, we consider a number of implementations of the island model algorithm and vary the cooperation settings to provide a deeper analysis of their influence on the algorithm performance. We investigate two island models: *homogeneous*, i.e. the cooperation of similar algorithms, and *heterogeneous*, the cooperation of distinct algorithms. Other important factors of the island model cooperation, which are also under investigation, are the migration rate (interval) and the migration set cardinality. The MOPs solved are taken from the CEC 2009 competition and the results obtained are compared with the results of other EA-based approaches.

2 Multi-objective Genetic Algorithm for Real-Valued Problems

2.1 Problem Statement

We consider MOPs on a real-valued search space, so we need to find a solution of the following extremum problem:

$$X^* = \{x^* : \nexists x \in R^n \to F(x) \succ F(x^*)\}, \tag{1}$$

where X^* is a set of non-dominated solutions, n is a dimensionality of a search space, an objective vector-function $F(\cdot) : R^n \to R^m$ and m is the number of criteria. Here, the operator $\succ$ has the following meaning (in the case of minimization):

$$x, y \in R^n, x \succ y \Leftrightarrow \exists i \leq m : F_i(x) < F_i(y), \forall j \neq i : F_j(x) \leq F_j(y). \qquad (2)$$

The minimization MOP can be defined as follows:

$$x \in R^n, i = \overline{1, m}, F_i(x) \rightarrow \min. \qquad (3)$$

While solving (3), our goal is to find an approximation of the Pareto front. The main feature of MOPs is that we do not need to find a precise non-dominated solution, but a set of solutions that portrays the Pareto front well. In those cases when we know the Pareto front, Inverted Generational Distance (IGD) [13] can be used to estimate the solution quality:

$$\rho_{IGD}\left(X^*, \widehat{X}\right) = \frac{1}{|X^*|} \cdot \sum_{i=1}^{|X^*|} \min_{j=1, |\widehat{X}|} \|x_i^* - \widehat{x}_j\|, \qquad (4)$$

Here $\widehat{X}$ is the found approximation of the Pareto front and X^* is the true Pareto front (1). The Euclidean distance is used as the norm. In this study, to investigate the algorithm performance, we involve ten unconstrained real-valued MOPs (seven problems with two objectives and three problems with three objectives) from the CEC 2009 competition [13], where the true Pareto front is given for each problem. Therefore, it is possible to estimate the closeness of the found solution to the true Pareto front by (4) and, thus, to estimate the algorithm performance based on this metric.

2.2   Proposed Algorithms

While designing MOGAs, researchers develop some specific mechanisms aimed at getting a representative Pareto front approximation. This front estimation should portray the peculiarities of the true front thoroughly. To achieve this purpose, in the MOGA scheme special fitness assignment strategies (usually, based on the Pareto dominance idea), diversity preservation techniques and elitism have been incorporated.

The algorithms used in our study are implemented according to their original schemes. GAs typically operate with binary chromosomes [14]. However, this binary solution representation often leads to a decrease in the algorithm performance on real-valued optimization problems. Therefore, in our study, we implement real-coded MOGAs and incorporate into their schemes particular genetic operators which can deal with real-valued strings.

To select effective solutions for the offspring generation, we apply tournament selection, which compares solutions based on their fitness values assigned according to the scheme of a particular MOGA. The tournament size is equal to 7.

As a crossover operator, we use uniform (discrete) crossover. Each offspring gene is chosen from the chromosomes of the selected parents with equal likelihood. In our experiments, the number of parents is 2.

In the mutation operator, we implement the next scheme [15]:

$$x'_k = \begin{cases} x_k + \sigma_k \cdot (b_k - a_k) \text{ with probability } p_m, \\ x_k \text{ with probability } 1 - p_m \end{cases}, \tag{5}$$

with

$$\sigma_k = \begin{cases} (2 \cdot rand)^{\frac{1}{\eta+1}} - 1 & \text{if } rand < 0.5 \\ 1 - (2 - 2 \cdot rand)^{\frac{1}{\eta+1}} & \text{otherwise} \end{cases}, \tag{6}$$

where rand is a uniformly random number [0, 1]. There are two control parameters: the mutation rate $p_m = 1/n$ and the distribution index η is equal to 1.0. a_k and b_k are the lower and upper bounds of the k-th variable in the chromosome.

The main idea of the island model cooperation is that each algorithm is an isolated island fulfilling the search independently. In some iterations (generations), islands exchange some individuals. Here we denote the migration rate as m_r and the cardinality of the migration set is m_c. In the proposed modification, the migration set replaces the worst individuals in each island population. Here, "worst" denotes the worst individuals in the population in the sense of fitness values, which are evaluated differently for MOGAs, according to their fitness assignment strategies. The final approximation is obtained by merging together all the populations and archives (if there are any), sorting solutions with Fast Non-Dominated Sorting (taken from NSGA-II) and then selecting a certain number of the best solutions.

The island heuristic can be implemented in two different ways: as a homogeneous cooperation or as a heterogeneous one. In this paper, we consider both variants based on the algorithms given above. The homogeneous cooperation includes a number of islands working as one of the following MOGAs: SPEA-2, NSGA-II or PICEA-g, whereas the heterogeneous cooperation consists of all three of these algorithms.

We take the following parameters by default: $m_c = 30$, $m_r = 30$, the subpopulation size is $l_i = \frac{600}{n_i}$, where n_i is the number of islands and the number of generations is 500.

3 Proposed Algorithm Performance Analysis

According to the rules of the CEC 2009 competition, for each algorithm run 300 000 objective vector-function evaluations might be performed. We perform 30 independent program launches for each algorithm with particular settings on every problem.

3.1 Parameter Influence Analysis

Island Type. In this part, we consider the different structures of island algorithms. First, we apply the homogeneous model with three parallel islands (SPEA2 – SPEA2 – SPEA2, NSGA-II – NSGA-II – NSGA-II, PICEA-g – PICEA-g – PICEA-g). Then, we compare the cooperative modifications with their original versions. In Fig. 1, we

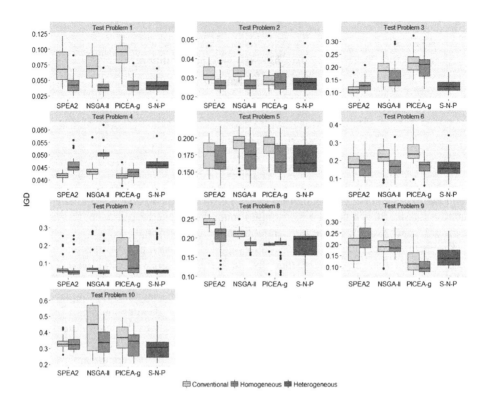

Fig. 1. IGD metric values of homogeneous and heterogeneous algorithms. (Color figure online)

present the IGD values obtained with conventional algorithms (blue boxplots) and their cooperative homogeneous modifications (green boxplots).

Furthermore, we include three different MOGAs in one heterogeneous cooperation (SPEA2 – NSGA-II – PICEA-g). The results of this experiment might also be found in Fig. 1 (purple boxplots "S-N-P").

Based on the experimental results, we may conclude that the island cooperation allows us to outperform the conventional algorithms which are in the cooperation. This happens for most of the considered problems. Another conclusion is that the heterogeneous cooperation often outperforms homogeneous ones in the sense of the median and minimum IGD values. Moreover, for some test problems homogeneous cooperative MOGAs or even their conventional versions give better results.

However, we may note that for Test Problems 3, 7, 8, 9 and 10, conventional MOGAs as well as their homogeneous cooperative versions provide us with essentially different results. This proves that an arbitrary choice of the MOGA may lead to a deterioration of the solution quality. Meanwhile, the heterogeneous cooperation allows us to obtain IGD values which are comparable with the results of the best MOGA for the problem.

Migration Rate. Next, for the heterogeneous cooperation we vary the migration rate (interval) $m_r = 10, 30, 50, 100$, having the constant migration size $m_c = 30$.

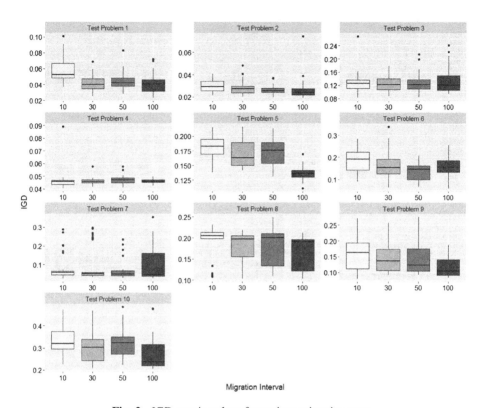

Fig. 2. IGD metric values for various migration rates.

The results obtained are given in Fig. 2. This examination proves that the migration rate affects the IGD metric. For most of the test problems, the IGD value dramatically decreases when the migration rate increases. This fact can be observed by the median and minimum value of the IGD metric. At the same time, we can see that there is a difference in IGD variances for migration rates equal to 50 and 100: there might be a good migration rate value in between, so this requires further investigation.

Migration Size. Moreover, for the heterogeneous MOGA we also vary the migration set cardinality (size) $m_c = 2, 10, 30, 50, 100$ ($m_r = 30$). The results for all the problems are given in Fig. 3.

Figure 3 show that for diverse migration set cardinalities, the IGD values differ insignificantly. Here we should refer to the dependency between the migration set cardinality and the migration rate as well as the population size. All these parameters should be considered together and it might be so that for 200 individuals in each subpopulation, the migration occurs quite often ($m_r = 30$), so all these m_c values work in a similar way.

The Number of Islands. Finally, we investigate the number of islands: 3, 6 and 9 for both homogeneous and heterogeneous cooperation. The results obtained are presented in Fig. 4.

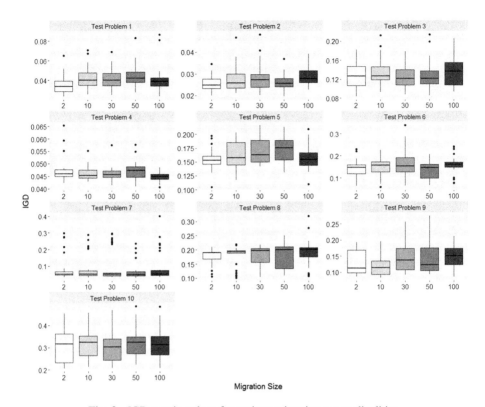

Fig. 3. IGD metric values for various migration set cardinalities.

In this series of experiments, we set the following parameter values: for the 3-island cooperation $m_c = 30$, $l_i = 200$, $m_r = 30$; for the 6-island cooperation $m_c = 15$, $l_i = 100$, $m_r = 30$; for the 9-island cooperation $m_c = 5$, $l_i = 66$, $m_r = 30$.

The results given in Fig. 4 reveal that for Test Problems 5, 6, 7, 8 and 10, cooperative MOGAs with different numbers of islands provide us with very similar results. However, due to the parallel work of islands, one algorithm run requires much less computational time if the cooperation has more islands. Therefore, from this perspective, 9-island cooperation seems to be more beneficial.

Nevertheless, we should admit that for different problems, increasing and decreasing the number of islands works almost in an opposite way (Test Problems 1 and 4).

In addition to these parameters, various schemes of interaction between the islands should be analysed because in this study we implement only a fully connected topology (each island sends its best solutions to all the other ones and as a response it receives solutions from other islands).

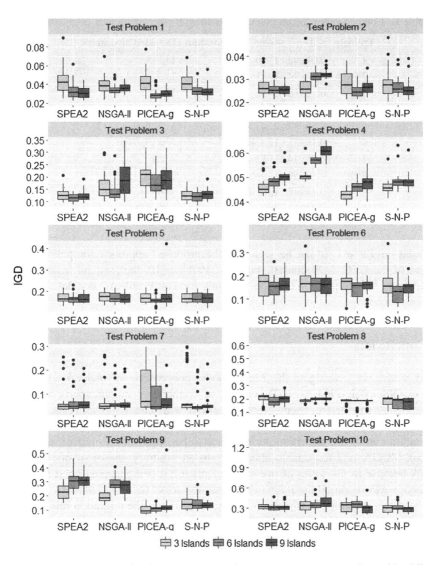

Fig. 4. IGD metric values for homogeneous and heterogeneous cooperation with different numbers of islands.

3.2   Overall Rating

Finally, we compare the results of the 3-island heterogeneous MOGA having default parameters with the winners of the CEC 2009 competition based on the averaged IGD values. The results are given in Table 1, where the CEC winners are denoted as follows: MOEAD – 1, GDE3 – 2, MOEADGM – 3, MTS – 4, LiuLiAlgorithm – 5, DMOEADD – 6, NSGAIILS – 7, OWMOSaDE – 8, ClusteringMOEA – 9, AMGA – 10, MOEP – 11, DECMOSA-SQP – 12, OMOEAII – 13.

Table 1. Comparison of the proposed approach with other algorithms (problems 1–5).

Problem	IGD	Winning algorithms	Defeated algorithms
1	0.04192	1–10	11–13
2	0.02834	1–11	13
3	0.12315	1–12	13
4	0.04598	2, 4–6, 10–12	1, 3, 7–9, 13
5	0.16959	2, 4, 5, 10, 13	1, 3, 6–9, 11, 12
6	0.16325	1, 4, 6, 9–13	2, 3, 5, 7, 8
7	0.09744	1–13	–
8	0.17850	1, 4–8, 10	2, 3, 9, 11–13
9	0.14448	1, 2, 4–8, 10, 12	3, 9, 11, 13
10	0.31011	4	1–3, 5–13

Based on Table 1, it can be seen that the proposed approach competes with the winners of the CEC 2009 contest. For Test Problem 10, the 3-island heterogeneous MOGA takes second place in this top-list. Only for Test Problem 7 is it defeated by all the CEC winners.

4   Conclusion

In this study, we investigate the island model cooperation of real-valued MOGAs (SPEA2, NSGA-II, PICEA-g). Two types of cooperative modifications, which are homogeneous and heterogeneous, are compared with conventional versions of the algorithms considered. Based on this comparison, we conclude that the island model cooperation allows the algorithm performance to be improved. Moreover, the heterogeneous MOGA is a reasonable alternative to an arbitrary choice of one particular MOGA because in the series of our experiments it has demonstrated good reliability.

Then, we have varied the main control parameters of the island model cooperation and found that its structure (the included algorithms) and the migration rate affect the algorithm performance to a greater extent. Furthermore, the number of islands is also a crucial parameter because the computational time reduces sufficiently when the number of islands increases.

Further study is related to implementing modern effective MOGAs, which should be included in the island model cooperation, and developing different schemes of the interaction between the islands. It is also important to investigate the cross-parameter influence on the performance of the cooperative MOGA, especially such parameters as the migration rate and the migration set cardinality for each particular solution exchange scheme.

Acknowledgements. This research is supported by the Russian Foundation for Basic Research within project No 16-01-00767.

References

1. Zitzler, E., Laumanns, M., Thiele, L.: SPEA2: improving the strength pareto evolutionary algorithm for multiobjective optimization. In: Evolutionary Methods for Design Optimisation and Control with Application to Industrial Problems, EUROGEN 2001, vol. 3242, no. 103, pp. 95–100 (2002)
2. Deb, K., Pratap, A., Agarwal, S., Meyarivan, T.: A fast and elitist multiobjective genetic algorithm: NSGA-II. IEEE Trans. Evol. Comput. **6**(2), 182–197 (2002)
3. Wang, R.: Preference-inspired co-evolutionary algorithms. A thesis submitted in partial fulfillment for the degree of the Doctor of Philosophy, University of Sheffield, p. 231 (2013)
4. Stringer, J., Lamont G., Akers, G.: Radar phase-coded waveform design using MOEAs. In: WCCI 2012 IEEE World Congress on Computational Intelligence (2012). https://doi.org/10.1109/cec.2012.6256554
5. Jiang, Sh., Yang, Sh.: A strength pareto evolutionary algorithm based on reference direction for multi-objective and many-objective optimization. IEEE Trans. Evol. Comput. (2017). https://doi.org/10.1109/TEVC.2016.2592479
6. Guliashki, V., Kirilov, L., Genova, K.: An interactive evolutionary algorithm for multiple objective integer problems. Int. J. Inf. Technol. Secur. **5**(2), 45–54 (2013)
7. Brester, Ch., Ryzhikov, I., Semenkin, E.: Restart operator for multi-objective genetic algorithms: implementation, choice of control parameters and ways of improvement. Int. J. Inf. Technol. Secur. **9**(4), 25–36 (2017)
8. Whitley, D., Rana, S., Heckendorn, R.B.: Island model genetic algorithms and linearly separable problems. In: Corne, D., Shapiro, Jonathan L. (eds.) AISB EC 1997. LNCS, vol. 1305, pp. 109–125. Springer, Heidelberg (1997). https://doi.org/10.1007/BFb0027170
9. Alba, E.: Parallel Metaheuristics: A New Class of Algorithms. Wiley, Hoboken (2005). https://doi.org/10.1002/0471739383
10. Van Veldhuizen, D.A., Zydallis, J.B., Lamont, G.B.: Considerations in engineering parallel multiobjective evolutionary algorithms. IEEE Trans. Evol. Comput. **7**(2), 144–173 (2003). https://doi.org/10.1109/TEVC.2003.810751
11. Brester, Ch., Ryzhikov, I., Semenkin, E.: Multi-objective optimization algorithms with the island metaheuristic for effective project management problem solving. Organizacija (J. Manag. Inf. Syst. Hum. Resour.) **50**(4), 364–373 (2017)
12. Ryzhikov, I., Brester, Ch., Semenkin, E.: Multi-objective dynamical system parameters and initial value identification approach in chemical disintegration reaction modelling. In: Proceedings of the 14th International Conference on Informatics in Control, Automation and Robotics (ICINCO 2017), vol. 1, pp. 497–504 (2017). https://doi.org/10.5220/0006431504970504
13. Zhang, Q., Zhou, A., Zhao, S., Suganthan, P. N., Liu, W., Tiwari, S.: Multi-objective optimization test instances for the CEC 2009 special session and competition. Technical report CES-487, University of Essex and Nanyang Technological University (2008)
14. Brester, Ch., Semenkin, E.: Cooperative multi-objective genetic algorithm with parallel implementation. In: Tan, Y., Shi, Y., Buarque, F., Gelbukh, A., Das, S., Engelbrecht, A. (eds.) ICSI 2015. LNCS, vol. 9140, pp. 471–478. Springer, Cham (2015). https://doi.org/10.1007/978-3-319-20466-6_49
15. Liu, M., Zou, X., Chen, Y., Wu, Z.: Performance assessment of DMOEA-DD with CEC 2009 MOEA competition test instances. In: 2009 IEEE Congress on Evolutionary Computation (2009). https://doi.org/10.1109/cec.2009.4983309

Differential Evolution

Feature Subset Selection Using a Self-adaptive Strategy Based Differential Evolution Method

Ben Niu[1], Xuesen Yang[1], Hong Wang[1(✉)], Kaishan Huang[1], and Sung-Shun Weng[2]

[1] College of Management, Shenzhen University, Shenzhen 518060, China
ms.hongwang@gmail.com
[2] Department of Information and Finance Management,
National Taipei University of Technology, Taipei, Taiwan

Abstract. Feature selection is a key step in classification task to prune out redundant or irrelevant information and improve the pattern recognition performance, but it is a challenging and complex combinatorial problem, especially in high dimensional feature selection. This paper proposes a self-adaptive strategy based differential evolution feature selection, abbreviated as SADEFS, in which the self-adaptive elimination and reproduction strategies are used to introduce superior features by considering their contributions in classification under historical records and to replace the poor performance features. The processes of the elimination and reproduction are self-adapted by leaning from their experiences to reduce search space and improve classification accuracy rate. Twelve high dimensional cancer micro-array benchmark datasets are introduced to verify the efficiency of SADEFS algorithm. The experiments indicate that SADEFS can achieve higher classification performance in comparison to the original DEFS algorithm.

Keywords: Feature selection · Differential evolution · Self-adaptive strategy
Roulette wheel method

1 Introduction

Pattern recognition plays a crucial role in the recognition of patterns and regularities in data mining [1]. An example of pattern recognition is classification. In classification tasks, the unknown samples are assigned to one of a given set of classes based on the training data. Dataset contains information that are either redundant or irrelevant [2], which needs a pre-processing step to remove some features without losing much information thus enhance the performance of classification and decrease the training time.

Feature selection methods can be generally divided into two groups: the wrappers and the filters [3]. Wrapper methods require the learning model to evaluate subsets of features which allows, unlike filter approaches, to select the possible relevant features and eliminate useless features for classification. Evolutionary computation (EC),

© Springer International Publishing AG, part of Springer Nature 2018
Y. Tan et al. (Eds.): ICSI 2018, LNCS 10941, pp. 223–232, 2018.
https://doi.org/10.1007/978-3-319-93815-8_22

inspired by the nature evolution of species, includes a series of global search techniques [4–7]. However, in the existing era of large data mining, the dimension of features can be large e.g. some cancer micro-array data where there are many thousands of features, and a few tens to hundreds of samples. Therefore, it's a challenge to find a promising feature subset from such tens of thousands of features. All the algorithms still suffer formulation of feature subset from original features.

Roulette has been successfully applied to feature selection, especially in evolutionary algorithms. Al-Ani et al. [8] proposed a method to reduce the search space using a set of wheels that involve distributing the features, but it do not take into account of combination among features because all the features are divided into several wheels. To prevent the same feature repeatedly appeared in a feature subset, Al-Ani et al. [9] put forward a simple yet efficient DE based real number optimizer method using a repair mechanism is used. However, it didn't take into account the features that had never appeared in the wheel. To address this issue, float-number optimizer has been wildly studied since it is a simple operation. The literatures [10, 11] utilized float-number optimizer based on differential evolution algorithm to solve the feature selection problem. Their main contribution was to calculate the distribution of features and supplied in classification task by using roulette wheels.

In this paper, more suitable solutions will be reorganized to replace the elimination subsets and match different searching evolutionary phases. All the features associated with corresponding parameters will be separately evaluated. The main contributions of this paper are: (1) Self-adapted strategy is utilized to judge the opportunity for new feature access. (2) The self-adapted strategy is embedded in the population to enhance the effectiveness of feature subsets.

The remaining paper is organized as follows. The original differential evolution and related work are reviewed in Sect. 2. The proposed improvement strategy is described in detail in Sect. 3. Experiment on cancer micro-array benchmark datasets and experimental results are given in Sect. 4. Finally, Sect. 5 provides the conclusions and future work.

2   Related Algorithms

2.1   Differential Evolution

A population of NP individuals each of D-dimensional float number in the gth generation is a NP $\times$ D vector that can be represented as: $\overrightarrow{X}_{i,j}(g)$, where $i = 0, 1, \ldots,$ NP -1 and i indicates i-th individual in the population, $j = 1, 2, \ldots,$ D where j represents the dimension of the population. In feature selection, where NP denotes the number of subset, and D indicates the number of feature in each subset. Firstly, the initial population is generated as [12].

$$X_{i,j}(g) = X_{jmin} + rand \times (X_{jmax} - X_{jmin}), i = 0 \, to \, NP - 1, j = 1 \, to \, D \qquad (1)$$

where X_{jmax} (X_{jmin}) refers the maximum (minimum) space bound.

Mutation is the crucial step in differential evolution algorithm, mainly used to generate new individual which named mutant vector, several mutation schemes were pointed out such as DE/rand/1, DE/rand/1/bin, DE/best/1 and DE/target-to-best/1 [13], The most classical one is DE/rand/1, which choose three parent vectors and they different from each other, one (i.e. $X_{r1,j}$) is use to add the other two weighted difference vectors (i.e. $X_{r2,j}$ and $X_{r3,j}$) in Eq. (2) [12].

$$V_{i,j}(g) = X_{r1,j}(g) + F \times (X_{r2,j}(g) - X_{r3,j}(g)) \tag{2}$$

where $F \in (0,1)$ denotes the *weighting factor* that controls the rate in the process of population. Three individuals are chosen randomly to generate the new individual.

The next step is crossover phase, crossover operation is used to generate trial vector $U_{i,j}(g)$ from the pair of corresponding vector: target vector $X_{i,j}(g)$ and mutant vector $V_{i,j}(g)$ according to a certain probability [12].

$$U_{i,j}(g) = \begin{cases} X_{i,j}(g), & \text{if } rand_j(0,1) \leq CR \text{ or } j = j_{rand} \\ V_{i,j}(g), & \text{otherwise} \end{cases} \tag{3}$$

where $CR \in [0,1]$, represents the probability of the crossover operation and it may influence the exploration and exploitation of optimization.

Compared with the target vector and the trial vector, the best one will be chosen for the next generation. Here is the selection operation [12]:

$$X_{i,j}(g+1) = \begin{cases} X_{i,j}(g), & \text{if } fit(X_{i,j}(g)) \leq fit(U_{i,j}(g)) \\ U_{i,j}(g), & \text{otherwise} \end{cases} \tag{4}$$

where *fit* is the fitness value refers to the classification error rate in feature selection and calculate by classifier (e.g. K-Nearest Neighbor classifier in this paper).

2.2 Roulette Mechanism

DE is a real number optimizer instead of a binary version, after rounding off each float number or modifying phenomenon of over bounds, the same number will appear in an individual, and which is not allowed in feature selection. Thus the roulette mechanism is used to calculate the superior features. For each feature, a cost weighting is introduced to calculate the probabilities called *distribution factor*, represents its distribution. The *distribution factor* of the feature f_i is calculated as follows [8]:

$$W(i) = c \times \frac{PD_j}{ND_j + PD_j} + \frac{NF - DNF}{NF} \times (1 - \frac{ND_j + PD_j}{\max(ND_j + PD_j)}) \tag{5}$$

where $c \in (0,1)$ is a control parameter, PD_j represents frequency that feature j has been appeared in the individuals with its fitness function values below the average. ND_j

represents frequency that feature j has been appeared in individuals with the fitness function value above the average. *NF* denotes the number of total features. *DNF* is a desire number of features. As seen in the equation, $W(i)$ reflects the importance of features to be selected. Then a relative difference is applicated to update $W(i)$ according to the following equation [8]:

$$T = (W_{g+1} - W_g) \times W_{g+1} + W_g \qquad (6)$$

where g and $g+1$ indicates the current and next generations.

The above equation provides higher weights to features if they perform better in the next iteration compare with the current one. Next add some sort of randomness, which could give appropriate emphasis to unseen features [8].

$$T = T - 0.5 \times rand \times (1 - T) \qquad (7)$$

The *distribution factors* of features not only appear in roulette but also outside the roulette are updated in each iteration, particularly, the value of *distribution factor* will be smaller within the features outside the roulette.

3   The Proposed Algorithm

In the last chapter, we got a very important factor: *distribution factor* which will be applied in our proposed strategies. After the repair step, elimination mechanism is used to delete those individuals who do not perform well within the current generation. Only eliminate the worse individuals is not logical because feature selection is a combinatorial optimization problem and there may exist potential superior features in the worse performance feature subset. Thus an elimination weight index was proposed to take into consideration of the influence by two factors: fitness value and distribution factor. The mechanisms of elimination and reproduction are used in several algorithms [14, 15], but they have not applied to the DE algorithm. Firstly, all the features are divided into three parts, the details of the division are showed below.

- *Part* 1: features appeared in the roulette and perform well in current generation
- *Part* 2: features appeared in the roulette and perform worse in current generation
- *Part* 3: features did not appear in the roulette of current generation

The performance of the features contributing to the combination individuals can be evaluated according to the fitness value, i.e. classification error rate. Particularly, it is allowed that the same feature appear in both Part 1 and Part 2. And all the features are divided into two subsets by another way, the details of the division are showed below.

- *Subset* 1: features whose *distribution factor* larger than the mean value
- *Subset* 2: features whose *distribution factor* lower than the mean value

WR denotes the scale of non-excellent individuals within *Part 2* as follows:

$$WR = \frac{N_{um}^i}{DNF} \tag{8}$$

where i represents the pool performance individual. N_{um}^i is the number of intersection features between *Part 2* and *Subset II* for i^{th} individual. *DNF* is the desire number of features. Elimination weight index of the individual i within the current generation g is calculated as follows:

$$EW_i = \alpha \times fit + (1 - \alpha) \times \frac{WR}{\max(WR)} \tag{9}$$

where $\alpha \in (0, 1)$ is the control parameter. In classification task, α could be larger than 0.5 thus $\alpha > (1 - \alpha)$, i.e. the classification accuracy is more important than the distribution factor. By sorting elimination weight index from large to small, from the above two equations, the feature subsets which perform worse and contain bigger proportion of non-excellent features are more probability to be chosen to eliminate.

To improve the performance of the solutions and maintain the population exploration properties in the early stages of the search. After the elimination step, the potential features will be chosen to reproduce new individuals from candidate-features pool. Historical memory cumulative is taken into account so as those features who perform well in several generations or in different individuals have greater probability to enter the pool of candidate-features. The index values are updated after each elimination in the gth iteration according to the following scheme, while:

- Feature belongs to *Part 1*, the index values for reproduction is incremented by β.
- Feature belongs to *Part 2*, the index values for reproduction is decremented by β.
- Feature belongs to *Part 3*, the index values for reproduction remain unchanged.

The reproduction index of the feature f_i, abbreviated as *RI*, within the current generation g is calculated as follows:

$$RI(g + 1) = \begin{cases} RI(g) + \beta, & if\, f_i \in Part\, 1 \\ RI(g) - \beta, & if\, f_i \in Part\, 2 \\ RI(g), & otherwise \end{cases} \tag{10}$$

Pseudo-code: (SADEFS)

---

01 Input: dataset for training and testing: *Tr* and *Te*; number of features to be selected D;

02 Initialization: Dim, population, fitness calculation, max iteration, LP , etc.

03 Optimization process:

04 For k = 1: max iteration

05   For j = 1: Number of individuals

06   Adapt the population using Eqs.(2–4)

07   Repair the population (refer to Eqs.(5–7))

08   if iteration< LP

09   Eliminate the individuals of population using Eqs.(8-9)

10   For i = 1 : Number of features

11   Obtain the value *RI* and sort them

12   end

13   Reproduction: Adapt the population using Eq.(10)

14   end

15   end

16 end

17 Output: classification accuracy and its corresponding selected feature vector.

Adaptive rules use the feedback from search procedure to obtain better feature subset. The probability of the reproduction operation of this feature in the next iterations should be adequately high, depending on the value of *RI*. The value of *RI* to each feature is initialized as the same value, i.e., all features have the equal probability to be chosen. In particular, the importance of unless features will be lower than unseen features after updating index. The number of learning iteration within the elimination and reproduction operation hereby named learning period (LP, e.g. LP = 50 while max iteration = 100).

4 Benchmark Tests and Experimental Results

To validate the SADEFS, we use several high dimensional cancer micro-array benchmark datasets, which have often been used to test feature selection method in the literature, Table 1 represents the detail information of the datasets. The basic parameters setting for both DEFS and SADEFS are the same, that is, the population size n is set to be 50, and the maximum number of iterations is 100. The parameters for SADEFS: LP = 50, $RI = 0.5$, $\beta = 0.1$, $\alpha = 0.6$, $c = 0.5$.

Table 1. Datasets for feature selection.

Datasets	Features	Class	Samples
Colon	2000	2	62
Leukemia (ALLAML)	7129	2	72
9_Tumors	5726	9	60
11_Tumors	12,533	11	174
14_Tumors	15,009	26	308
Brain_Tumor1	5920	5	90
Brain_Tumor2	10,367	4	50
SRBCT	2309	4	83
Leukemia1	5328	3	72
Leukemia2	11,225	3	72
Prostate_Tumor	10,509	2	102
Lung_Cancer 1	12,600	5	203
DLBCL	5470	2	77

The average results of DEFS and SADEFS with 30 times running are minutely shown on Fig. 1. The red dotted line and the blue line are the means of classification accuracy of 30 times' running for SADEFS and DEFS, respectively.

In previous research, DEFS had proved the better performance compare with some FS algorithm, such as PSOFS, GAFS, ANTFS [8]. For each figure, the classification accuracy rate (%) is used to denotes the performance of feature selection algorithms. Results prove that SADEFS has the priority performance on some datasets e.g. 9_Tumors, Brain_Tumor1, Lung_Cancer and 11_Tumors, within other datasets just perform a litter better because DEFS has reached very high classification accuracy rate (nearly 100%).

According to these information, SADEFS is more effective or equal to select the significant feature subset. Because in these datasets, the search space will be very large, effectively identify who are the most promising features, which leads to compose the superior feature subset. The learning period parameter LP may influence the result of optimization. So dataset 9_Tumors is used to investigate the impact of parameter LP on SADEFS algorithm. Table 2 shows the experimental results. The SADEFS algorithm runs 30 times with five different learning periods LP of 10, 30, 50, 70, and 90. The bold type is used to underline the best of all feature subset obtain the global optimum with different LPs. Most of the best performance solution appear at LP = 50 or LP = 70, the parameters near this range (LP = 50) seem more logical for controlling a balance between the exploration and the exploitation.

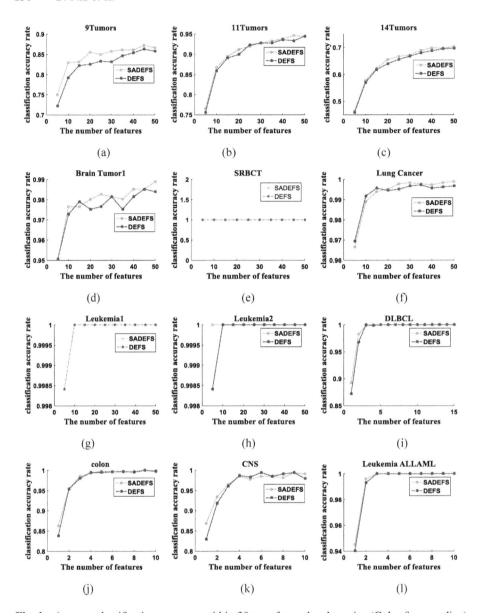

Fig. 1. Average classification accuracy within 30 runs for each subset size (Color figure online)

Table 2. Different LPs parameter optimization results

LP	Number of features									
	5	10	15	20	25	30	35	40	45	50
10	0.7463	0.8074	0.8241	**0.8667**	0.8463	0.8518	**0.8722**	0.8444	0.8667	0.8518
30	0.7333	0.8056	0.8315	0.8426	0.8426	0.8444	0.8593	0.8481	0.8648	0.8685
50	**0.7500**	**0.8296**	0.8315	0.8555	0.8500	0.8574	0.8611	**0.8611**	**0.8722**	0.8667
70	0.7407	0.8185	**0.8333**	0.8352	**0.8741**	**0.8592**	0.8611	0.8481	0.8518	**0.8704**
90	0.7407	0.8093	**0.8333**	0.8518	0.8333	0.8370	0.8574	0.8370	0.8518	0.8500

5   Conclusion and Future Work

In this study, a novel self-adaptive population updating strategy with differential evolution (DE) algorithm was proposed, which can reduce the exhaustive search by eliminating some useless features and introducing most suitable feature. As evolution proceeds, certain features in different solutions always perform well and keep effective information associating with other features when searching through different regions. The self-adaptive elimination and reproduction strategies are used to select the superior features to replace the poor performance features according to their contribution in classification performance in historical records.

Acknowledgment. This work is partially supported by The National Natural Science Foundation of China (Grants Nos. 71571120, 71471158, 61472257), Natural Science Foundation of Guangdong Province (2016A030310074), NTUT-SZU Joint Research Program (2018003), and Project supported by GDHVPS 2016.

References

1. Bishop, C.M.: Pattern Recognition and Machine Learning. Information Science and Statistics, p. 049901. Springer, New York (2006)
2. Bermingham, M.L., Pongwong, R., Spiliopoulou, A., Hayward, C., Rudan, I., Campbell, H.: Application of high-dimensional feature selection: evaluation for genomic prediction in man. Sci. Rep. **5**, 10312 (2015)
3. Guyon, I., Elisseeff, A.: An introduction to variable and feature selection. J. Mach. Learn. Res. **3**(6), 1157–1182 (2003)
4. Khushaba, R.N., Al-Ani, A., AlSukker, A., Al-Jumaily, A.: A combined ant colony and differential evolution feature selection algorithm. In: Dorigo, M., Birattari, M., Blum, C., Clerc, M., Stützle, T., Winfield, A.F.T. (eds.) ANTS 2008. LNCS, vol. 5217, pp. 1–12. Springer, Heidelberg (2008). https://doi.org/10.1007/978-3-540-87527-7_1
5. Bidi, N., Elberrichi, Z.: Feature selection for text classification using genetic algorithms. In: International Conference on Modelling, Identification and Control, pp. 806–810. IEEE (2017)
6. Rashno, A., Nazari, B., Sadri, S., Saraee, M.: Effective pixel classification of mars images based on ant colony optimization feature selection and extreme learning machine. Neurocomputing **226**(C), 66–79 (2017)

7. Chen, Q., Zhang, M., Xue, B.: Feature selection to improve generalization of genetic programming for high-dimensional symbolic regression. IEEE Trans. Evol. Comput. **21**(5), 792–806 (2017)
8. Al-Ani, A., Alsukker, A., Khushaba, R.N.: Feature subset selection using differential evolution and a wheel based search strategy. Swarm Evol. Comput. **9**, 15–26 (2013)
9. Khushaba, R.N., Al-Ani, A., Al-Jumaily, A.: Feature subset selection using differential evolution and a statistical repair mechanism. Expert Syst. Appl. **38**(9), 11515–11526 (2011)
10. Bharathi, P.T., Subashini, P.: Differential evolution and genetic algorithm based feature subset selection for recognition of river ice types. J. Theoret. Appl. Inf. Technol. **67**(1), 254–262 (2014)
11. Masood, A., Al-Jumaily, A.: Adaptive differential evolution based feature selection and parameter optimization for advised SVM classifier. In: Arik, S., Huang, T., Lai, W.K., Liu, Q. (eds.) ICONIP 2015. LNCS, vol. 9489, pp. 401–410. Springer, Cham (2015). https://doi.org/10.1007/978-3-319-26532-2_44
12. Storn, R., Price, K.: Differential evolution – a simple and efficient heuristic for global optimization over continuous spaces. J. Global Optim. **11**(4), 341–359 (1997)
13. Qin, A.K., Huang, V.L., Suganthan, P.N.: Differential evolution algorithm with strategy adaptation for global numerical optimization. IEEE Trans. Evol. Comput. **13**(2), 398–417 (2009)
14. Wang, H., Niu, B.: A novel bacterial algorithm with randomness control for feature selection in classification. Neurocomputing **228**, 176–186 (2017)
15. Shi, Y.: Brain storm optimization algorithm. In: Tan, Y., Shi, Y., Chai, Y., Wang, G. (eds.) ICSI 2011. LNCS, vol. 6728, pp. 303–309. Springer, Heidelberg (2011). https://doi.org/10.1007/978-3-642-21515-5_36

Improved Differential Evolution
Based on Mutation Strategies

John Saveca[1], Zenghui Wang[1(✉)], and Yanxia Sun[2]

[1] Department of Electrical and Mining Engineering,
University of South Africa, Johannesburg 1710, South Africa
Johnsaveca80@gmail.com, wangzengh@gmail.com
[2] Department of Electrical and Electronic Engineering Science,
University of Johannesburg, Johannesburg 2092, South Africa
sunyanxia@gmail.com

Abstract. Differential Evolution (DE) has been regarded as one of the excellent optimization algorithm in the science, computing and engineering field since its introduction by Storm and Price in 1995. Robustness, simplicity and easiness to implement are the key factors for DE's success in optimization of engineering problems. However, DE experiences convergence and stagnation problems. This paper focuses on DE convergence speed improvement based on introduction of newly developed mutation schemes strategies with reference to DE/rand/1 on account and tuning of control parameters. Simulations are conducted using benchmark functions such as Rastrigin, Ackley and Sphere, Griewank and Schwefel function. The results are tabled in order to compare the improved DE with the traditional DE.

Keywords: Differential Evolution · Convergence speed · Mutation scheme
Control parameters

1 Introduction

Differential Evolution (DE) has received much attention from various researchers and research institutions since its inception by Storn and Price two decades ago. DE's recognition involves its robustness, simplicity, speed and reliability to convergence to true optimum when solving an optimization problem. DE has gained much more success in series of benchmark academic competitions, black box global optimization competitions and real world optimization applications, leading to a big interest from both researchers and practitioners [6, 8]. Like other Evolutionary Algorithms (EA), DE uses a population based stochastic search method instead of complex mathematical operation [5]. By characteristics, DE is identified as an efficient and reliable global optimizer for different optimization fields such as constrained and unconstrained optimization, multimodal optimization and multi-objective optimization [6]. Despite DE algorithm being regarded as one of the best reliable and efficient EA method for solving optimization problems, it also has its own limitations. DE experiences stagnation, which in return deteriorates its performance. The occurrence of stagnation causes the algorithm not to get better solutions from the candidate solutions that are newly created, even though the

© Springer International Publishing AG, part of Springer Nature 2018
Y. Tan et al. (Eds.): ICSI 2018, LNCS 10941, pp. 233–242, 2018.
https://doi.org/10.1007/978-3-319-93815-8_23

diversity of the population remains [5]. Chances of stagnation occurrence depend on the availability of number of different potential trial vectors and their survival chances in the following generations [5]. In this paper, DE improvement is proposed, based on modification of mutation schemes and tuning of control parameters. The research will look to improve DE's convergence speed without experiencing stagnation. The improved DE will be used to optimize power quality in smart. Unlike Genetic Algorithm optimizing process which is affected by crossover function, in DE, mutation function plays a significant role during optimization [7]. DE's general notation is denoted as DE/X/Y/Z, where X indicates the mutation vector, Y indicated the number of difference vectors used and Z indicates the exponential or binomial crossover scheme [7]. As reported by [8], Differential mutation contains two parts, selection of base vector and summing of the difference vectors. The rest of the paper is organized as follows: Sect. 2 discusses background of the classical DE, evolutionary functions and mutation function schemes. Section 3 discusses the Improved DE algorithm formation and formulas. Section 4 gives the methodology to be followed during the experiment of DE improvement. Section 5 gives the results of the experiment and the discussion of the results. Section 6 gives the conclusion of the research.

2 Differential Evolution

Differential Evolution (DE) algorithm is one of the stochastic population-based evolutionary optimization algorithm that forms random search and optimization procedures by following natural evolutionary principles. Its term DE is due to existence of a special type of difference vector, as explained in [1]. During optimization, DE preserves candidate solutions population and creates new candidate solutions by combination of existing candidate solutions according to their simple formulae. The best candidate solution with better fitness on the optimization problem is kept close by [2]. DE uses three evolutionary functions during problem optimization, being mutation function, crossover function and selection function. Mutation function randomly generates variations to existing individuals to present new information into the population. The functioning creates mutation vectors vi, g at each generation g, based on the population of the current parent $\{X1,i,0 = (x1,i,0, x2,i,0, x3,i,0, \ldots, xD,i,0)|i = 1, 2, 3, \ldots, N\}$

$$DE/rand/1 \quad vi, = Xr0, + Fi(Xr1, -Xr2,) \tag{1}$$

$$DE/current\text{-}to\text{-}rest/1 \quad vi, = Xi, + Fi(Xbest, -Xi,) + Fi(Xr1, -Xr2,) \tag{2}$$

$$DE/best/1 \quad vi, = Xbest, + Fi(Xr1, -Xr2,) \tag{3}$$

where,

$r0$, $r1$, $r2$ = different integers uniformly chosen from the set $\{1, 2, \ldots, N\}\backslash\{i\}$,
$Xr1, -Xr2,$ = different vector to mutate the parent,
$Xbest,$ = best vector at the current generation,
Fi = mutation factor which ranges on the interval (0, 1+).

The crossover function performs an exchange of information between different individuals in the current population. The final trial vector is formed by binomial crossover operation.

$$u_{i,g} = \left(u_{1,i,g}, u_{2,i,g}, \ldots, u_{D,i,g} \right) \tag{4}$$

$$u_{j_{..}} = \begin{cases} vj, i, g \ldots \ldots \text{ if } randj\,(0,1) \leq CRi \text{ or } j = jrand \\ xj, i, g \ldots \ldots \ldots \text{ otherwise} \end{cases} \tag{5}$$

where,

randj (a, b) = uniform random number on the interval (a, b) and newly generated for each j,

jrand = *jrandiant* $(1, D)$ = integer randomly chosen from 1 to D and newly generated for each i.

The selection function passes a driving force towards the most favorable point by preferring individuals of better fitness. The selection operation selects the better one from the parent vector Xi, and the trial vector ui, according to their fitness values $f(\cdot)$ [3].

$$X_{i,+1} = \begin{cases} ui, g \ldots \ldots \text{ if } f\,(ui, g) < Xi, g \\ Xi, g \ldots \ldots \ldots \ldots \ldots \text{ otherwise} \end{cases} \tag{6}$$

Unlike other evolutionary algorithms, DE requires selection of only three control parameters, namely, Population Size (PS), Mutation Factor (F) and Crossover rate (Cr). According to [4], number of iterations (Iter$_{max}$) is not considered a control parameter, since some stopping criteria is need on the simulation. However, it is very helpful to have an estimation number of iterations in order to prevent a very long running time of the program. Mutation factor F value that can be selected ranges from 0.1 to 2.0 while the Crossover rate value ranges from 0.1 to 1.0. Population size is determined by the Dimensionality D of the objective function, where the values from 5D to 10D are suggested. However, the values are extended from 2D up to 40D [4].

3   Improved Differential Evolution

For DE improvement, two factors have been considered, the first being tuning of control parameters to get the suitable combination to be used on a selected mutation scheme. In this case the selected mutation scheme is DE/rand/1. DE/rand/1 is the most commonly used scheme due to its simplicity and fast convergence during optimization of the problem. The second factor is modification of selected mutation scheme. Three modifications schemes are developed by taking Mutation Factor F into account on mutation formula. As reported by [9], it is mutation that separates one DE strategy from another. Mutation is responsible for expansion and exploration of the search space in order to obtain the optimum solution for a given optimization problem, by combining different parameter vectors in such a way that a new population vector, termed donor vector is generated [1]. F is responsible for the amplification of the differential variation [1–10]. In this modification, F will also be used to amplify the base vector $Xr0$ in order to explore much wider search space for better optimum solution. For the first modification, the individual vector $Xr0$ is squired and divided by mutation factor F as shown in the formula. The formula will be named DE/Modi/1

$$DE/Modi/1 \quad vi, = (Xr0)^2, \div Fi + Fi(Xr1, -Xr2,) \tag{7}$$

where,

$r0, r1, r2$ = different integers uniformly chosen from the set $\{1, 2, \ldots, N\}\backslash\{i\}$,
$Xr1, -Xr2,$ = different vector to mutate the parent,
$Xr0,$ = base vector,
Fi = mutation factor which ranges on the interval $(0, 1+)$.

On the second modification, the parent vector is multiplied by the mutation factor F. In this case the individual vector is not squired as shown in the next formula. The formula will be named DE/Modi/2

$$DE/Modi/2 \quad vi, = Fi \times Xr0, + Fi(Xr1, -Xr2,) \tag{8}$$

The third and final modification involves three factors applied to the individual vector. First it is squired as done on the first modification, secondly it is multiplied by the mutation factor, thirdly, it is divided by 2 as shown in the formula. The formula will be named DE/Modi/3

$$DE/Modi/3 \quad vi, = Fi \times (Xr0)^2 \div 2 + Fi(Xr1, -Xr2,) \tag{9}$$

4 Methodology

The following steps, which are also shown in Fig. 1, were taken during simulation of the DE improvement by means of control parameter tuning and mutation scheme modification. The following benchmark functions were used to during simulation of the experiment, Rastrigin function, Ackley function, Sphere Function, Griewank Function. Schwefel Function, Bukin Function. SumPower Function and SumSquare Function. DE/rand/1 is selected for the experiment.

Step 1: DE/rand/1 pseudo-code is done on matlab and Setting of control parameters is done in the following manner, the constant parameters: D = 2, PS = 50, I_-max = 200. The varying parameters: F = [0.1–2.0], Cr = [0.1–1.0].
Step 2: Each benchmark function mentioned above is tested by varying F and C from 0.1 to 2.0 and from 0.1 to 1.0 respectively in order to determine the perfect set of values that makes a fast convergence on the optimization process.
Step 3: The determined set values of F and C are then used in the three modified mutation schemes without being varied. In this case the determined set Combination values of F/C are 0.2/0.2, 0.2/0.3, 0.2/0.5, 0.2/0.7, 0.2/0.9, 0.1/0.9, 0.4/0.9, 0.6/0.9

and 0.8/0.9. The results of all the convergence of all the above mentioned bench-mark functions during F/C combination are tabled and will be compared with the results of convergence that are obtained on the modified mutation schemes.

Step 4: The original mutation scheme DE/rand/1 formula is modified according to the above mentioned mutation schemes modifications. The control parameters on the modified mutation schemes are, F = 0.2, 0.1, 0.4, 0.6 and 0.8, C = 0.9, 0.2, 0.3, 0.5, 0.7 and 0.9, D = 2, PS = 50, I_max = 200.

Step 5: All the benchmark functions are simulated for convergence speed for DE/Modi/1, DE/Modi/2 and DE/Modi/3. The results are tabled and compared with the results of DE/rand/1.

Step 6: Statistical data and time complexity will be determined.

Following is the pseudo-code for DE with one of the modified mutation scheme DE/Modi/3.

```
Set NP, C, F, parameters
initialize population p= {x₁, x₂, x₃...xₘ}, x₁ ∈ D
repeat
for i=1 to NP do
      Generate MxN matrix
      for m=1:M
        for n=1:N
           X(m,n)=X_min(n)+rand()*(X_max(n)-X_min(n));
        end
      end
    generate a new mutant vector
    y = (xᵣ₁)²*Fₓ/2+ Fₓ *(xᵣ₂ −Xᵣ₃)
                   if f(y) < f(x) then inert y into the new generation
                      else insert x into new generation
                   end
    end
until stopping criteria
```

Fig. 1. DE/Modi/3 pseudo-code.

5   Results and Discussion

Follows are the results obtained during simulation of the five benchmark functions. All simulations are ran up maximum of 200 iterations. All simulations are run according to the following parameters: I_max = 200 iterations, D = 2, PS = 50 and F/C combina-tion = 0.2/0.2, 0.2/0.3, 0.2/0.5, 0.2/0.7, 0.2/0.9, 0.1/0.9, 0.4/0.9, 0.6/0.9 and 0.8/0.9.

Following are the results of DE/rand/1 strategy as shown in Figs. 2, 3, 4, 5, 6 and Table 1.

From the above results of DE/rand/1, it can be noticed that most functions con-vergence becomes more strong after 63 iterations. For Griewank function, the

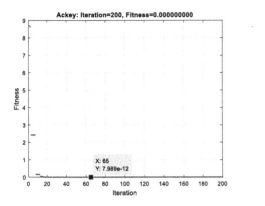

Fig. 2. Ackley's fitness vs iterations using DE/rand/1.

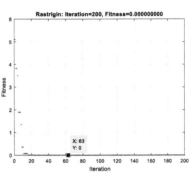

Fig. 3. Rastrigin's fitness vs iterations using DE/rand/1

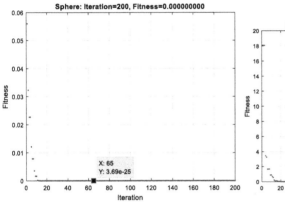

Fig. 4. Sphere's fitness vs iterations using DE/rand/1.

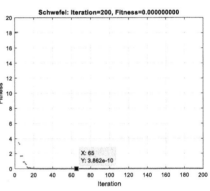

Fig. 5. Schwefel's fitness vs iterations using DE/rand/1.

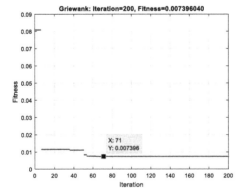

Fig. 6. Griewank's fitness vs iterations using DE/rand/1.

Table 1. DE/rand/1 results

Benchmark function	DE/rand/1	
	Iterations	Fitness
Ackley	65	7.989e−12
Rastrigin	63	0
Sphere	65	3.69e−25
Schwefel	65	3.862e−10
Griewank	71	0.007396

convergence is not much strong as it generates the fitness of 0.007396 after 71 iterations. Therefore it means Griewank function will require more generations in order for it to have a strong convergence of fitness zero (0) or close to zero (0).

Follows are the results of DE/Modi/1 strategy as shown in Figs. 7, 8, 9, 10, 11 and Table 2.

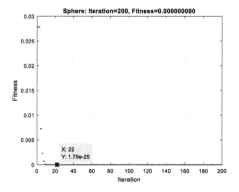

Fig. 7. Ackley's fitness vs iterations using DE/Modi/1.

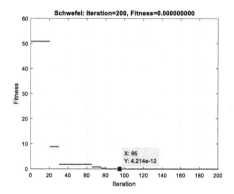

Fig. 8. Rastrigin's fitness vs iterations using DE/Modi/1

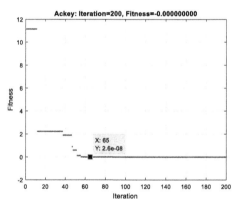

Fig. 9. Sphere's fitness vs iterations using DE/Modi/1.

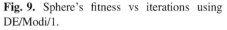

Fig. 10. Schwefel's fitness vs iterations using DE/Modi/1.

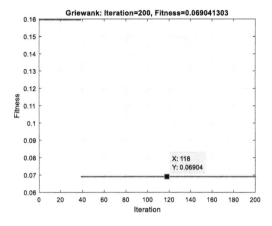

Fig. 11. Griewank's fitness vs iterations using DE/Modi/1.

Table 2. DE/Modi/1 results

Benchmark function	DE/Modi/1	
	Iterations	Fitness
Ackley	65	2.6e−08
Rastrigin	39	0
Sphere	22	1.79e−25
Schwefel	95	4.214e−12
Griewank	118	0.06904

From the above results of DE/Modi/1, it can be noticed that the convergence of the strategy is slightly slow for Ackley function. For Griewank, the convergence turns to be very weak and slow compared to classical DE strategy. For Schwefel function the convergence is robust but extremely slow compared to DE/Rand/1 strategy. The convergence speed improved for Rastrigin and Sphere functions.

Table 3 is the results of DE/Modi/2 strategy.

Table 3. DE/Modi/2 results

Benchmark function	DE/Modi/2	
	Iterations	Fitness
Ackley	17	1.863e−11
Rastrigin	14	0
Sphere	19	1.04e−28
Schwefel	18	6.02e−11
Griewank	21	0

From the results obtained from DE/Modi/2, it can be noticed that convergence speed robustness of all the functions has improved compared to both above strategies DE/Rand/1 and DE/Modi/1. In this strategy, Griewank function is able to reach a robust convergence.

Table 4 is the results obtained from DE/Modi/3 strategy.

Table 4. DE/Modi/3 results

Benchmark function	DE/Modi/3	
	Iterations	Fitness
Ackley	16	2.538e−11
Rastrigin	12	0
Sphere	15	1.189−26
Schwefel	24	4.09e−13
Griewank	29	0

From the results of DE/Modi/3, it can be noticed that there is a slight change of convergence speed between DE/Modi/2 and DE/Modi/3. Convergence speed for Ackley and Rastrigin function slightly improved compared to DE/modi/2, while for Sphere, Schwefel and Griewank function, convergence speed slightly dropped compared to DE/Modi/2.

6   Conclusion

Based on the above results, it has been noticed that DE/Modi/1 results lack robustness and convergence speed, making just 41.67% of best convergence time. For DE/Modi/3 it can be noticed that improvement is achieved compared to classical DE/Rand/1 with a percentage of 81.94% of the best convergence time. DE/Modi/2 achieved the best results with 84.72% of best convergence time compared to all other modified strategies on this paper with best convergence speed and strong convergence. On the other hand F/C combination of 0.1/0.9 produced fast and robust convergence during the DE/Modi2 and DE/Modi3 simulation session, making it the best Mutation Factor/Crossover Rate combination for the DE/Modi2 and DE/Modi3 mutation strategies. It can be concluded that DE convergence speed has been improved through modified strategies DE/Modi2 and DE/Modi/3 with F/C combination of 0.1/0.9. The modified mutation strategies DE/Modi2 and DE/Modi/3 with F/C combination of 0.1/0.9 can be used in future due to their robust convergence, fast and effective convergence speed and ability to optimize other functions that classical DE/rand/1 is not able to optimize to minimum optimal point such as Griewank and Bukin function.

Acknowledgments. This research is supported partially by South African National Research Foundation Grants (No. 112108 and 112142), and South African National Research Foundation Incentive Grant (No. 95687), Eskom Tertiary Education Support Programme Grants (Z. Wang, Y. Sun), Research grant from URC of University of Johannesburg.

References

1. Chattopadhyay, S., Sanyal, S.K., Chandra, A.: Comparison of various mutation schemes of differential evolution algorithm for the design of low-pass FIR filter, pp. 809–814 (2011)
2. Sagoo, S.: Array failure correction using different optimization techniques, MTech thesis (2016)
3. Ganbavale, M.P.: Differential evolution using matlab. Birla Institute of Technology and Science, Pilani, Hyderabad Campus (2014)
4. Penunuri, F., Cab, C., Tapia, J.A., Zambrano-Arjona, M.A.: A study of the classical differential evolution control parameters. Swarm Evol. Comput. **26**, 86–96 (2015)
5. Zheng, L.M., Zhang, S.X., Tang, K.T., Zheng, S.Y.: Differential evolution powered by collective information. Inf. Sci. **399**, 13–29 (2017)
6. Wu, G., Shen, X., Chen, H., Lin, A., Suganthan, P.N.: Ensemble of differential evolution variants. Inf. Sci. **423**, 172–186 (2017)
7. Thangaraj, R., Pant, M., Abraham, A.: New mutation schemes for differential evolution algorithm and their application to the optimization of directional over-current relay settings. Appl. Math. Comput. **216**, 532–544 (2010)
8. Opara, K., Arabas, J.: Comparizon of mutation strategies in differential evolution-a probabilistic perspective. Swarm Evol. Comput. **338**, 1–37 (2017)
9. Tayal, D., Gupta, C.: A new scaling factor for differential evolution optimization. In: National Conference on Communication Technologies & Its Impact on Next Generation Computing CTNGC2012 Proceedings, IJCA, pp. 1–5 (2012)
10. Sarker, R.A., Elsayed, S.M., Ray, T.: Differential evolution dynamic parameters section for optimization problems. IEEE Trans. Evol. Comput. **18**, 689–707 (2014)

Applying a Multi-Objective Differential Evolution Algorithm in Translation Control of an Immersed Tunnel Element

Qing Liao and Qinqin Fan[✉]

Logistics Research Center, Shanghai Maritime University,
Shanghai 201306, China
forever123fan@163.com

Abstract. Translation control of an immersed tunnel element under the water current flow is a typical optimization problem, which always emphasizes on short duration and high translation security. Various optimization approaches have been proposed to address this issue in previous works, but most of them take only one objective into consideration. Thus, it is solved as a single objective optimization problem. However, the translation control of the immersed tunnel element usually involves two or more conflicting objectives in actual situation. It's necessary to convert the translation control problem into a multi-objective optimization problem to obtain effective solutions. Therefore, a recently proposed multi-objective differential evolution algorithm is employed to solve the problem in the present work. The translation model of the immersed tunnel element is introduced with three sub-objectives. Results indicate that a multi-objective differential evolution algorithm can provide a set of non-dominated solutions for assisting decision makers to complete the translation of the immersed tunnel element according to different targets and changing environment.

Keywords: Tunnel element · Multi-objective optimization
Differential evolution algorithm

1 Introduction

Compared with traditional transport engineering, an immersed tunnel has been widely used since it can effectively shorten transport time and improve operation efficiency [1].

Numerous studies related to the immersed tunnel project have studied on the tug towing process and focused on the stability of tug. Sinibaldi and Bulian [2] carried out a numerical bifurcation analysis by a 4-degree of freedom nonlinear dynamical system for determining the system equilibrium when a relevant parameter is revised. The results indicate that the wind direction and speed significantly influence the response of the system. Moreover, a potentially dangerous fishtailing phenomenon will happen when stable equilibrium solutions do not exist. Bao [3] stated that the movement and control of large vessels are generally affected by the pushing positions of tugs.

© Springer International Publishing AG, part of Springer Nature 2018
Y. Tan et al. (Eds.): ICSI 2018, LNCS 10941, pp. 243–250, 2018.
https://doi.org/10.1007/978-3-319-93815-8_24

Fitriadhy et al. [4] measured wind effects and obtained course stability regions of the towed barge when the length of towing line and the angle or speeds of wind varied.

Works about translation of the immersed tunnel also involve varieties of models. Not only tug towing forth but also the environment concerned is measured in each optimization model. Wang [5] applied model test and numerical simulation to the immersed tunnel transportation to obtain a variety of towing plans for the Hong Kong Zhuhai Macao Bridge project. Moreover, a few comparative analysis approaches are used to achieve the optimal scheme. Therefore, the towing resistance can be obtained under a specific translation velocity. For assessing the hydrodynamic characteristics of surroundings encountered in transit, Zhu et al. [6] used numerical simulation method to track its variation range in line with various parameters. The results shows that the change of the free-board and nearby waves both have impacts on the coefficients. Lu et al. [7] investigated the environmental and geological conditions which were tightly connected to the towing resistance of the immersed tunnel elements and searched calculation methods of wind, wave and current resistance. It turned out that the water depth and the angle between element and flow could directly affect the resistance. Li et al. [8] introduced the immersed tunnel transportation problem in mathematical description with working tugboats numbers, surplus towing force and the floating speed, and designed the WLIPPSO method to solve the optimization problem. At last, a better translation control plan was obtained.

Some interesting parts have also been investigated till now. Lin [9] employed a set of physical models to analyze the motion and dynamic response of sinking tunnel elements under different flow conditions. The results indicated that mooring ropes' tension force increased with high wave height. Wu and Xie [10] adopted the finite element software ANASYS to analyze tube tunnel. Based on the actual project data, the environment interaction relations of tunnel elements were studied and the theoretical calculation was carried out in order to provide the reference for later tube tunnel design.

Based on the aforementioned introductions, it can be found that the works related to translation of the immersed tunnel element are rare in literature. Not to mention the fact that the translation control of the immersed tunnel element is an optimization problem. In Ref. [8], although a particle swarm optimization (PSO) is used to solve this problem, a single objective optimization is considered. However, there are always two or more conflicting objective functions in the translation control of the immersed tunnel element. In other words, the translation control of the immersed tunnel element is a multi-objective optimization problem. To solve this problem, a recently proposed multi-objective differential evolution algorithm (i.e., multi-objective differential evolution with performance-metric-based self-adaptive mutation operator (MODE-PMSMO)) is used in the present work. Results indicate that the MODE-PMSMO is able to provide a set of non-dominated solutions for helping decision makers to finish the translation of the immersed tunnel element. Additionally, it is easy for decision makers to select a suitable solution for dealing with uncertain disturbances.

2 MODE-PMSMO Applied to Optimize the Translation Control Problem of the Immersed Tunnel Element

2.1 Translation Control of the Immersed Tunnel Element

In this section, the translation model of the immersed tunnel element is introduced. It is composed of translation velocity of the immersed tunnel element, resistance of the immersed tunnel element translation and resultant force and resultant moment of the tugs. The objective function for the translation control of the immersed tunnel element can be defined as follows:

$$F(x) = \left[\min\{-v_1\}, \min\left\{ \sum_{i=1}^{N} (F_i - F_{i,\max}) \right\}, \min\left\{ \sum_{i=1}^{N} |(F_{i,\max} - F_i) - F_{\text{mean}}| \right\} \right]^T. \quad (1)$$

s.t.

$$\begin{cases} v_{1,\min} \leq v_1 \leq v_{1,\max} \\ F_{1,\min} \leq F_1 \leq F_{1,\max} \\ F_{2,\min} \leq F_2 \leq F_{2,\max} \\ F_{3,\min} \leq F_3 \leq F_{3,\max} \\ \alpha_{1,\min} \leq \alpha_1 \leq \alpha_{1,\max} \\ \alpha_{2,\min} \leq \alpha_2 \leq \alpha_{2,\max} \\ \alpha_{3,\min} \leq \alpha_3 \leq \alpha_{3,\max} \\ \alpha_{4,\min} \leq \alpha_4 \leq \alpha_{4,\max} \\ \alpha_{5,\min} \leq \alpha_5 \leq \alpha_{5,\max} \\ \alpha_{6,\min} \leq \alpha_6 \leq \alpha_{6,\max} \end{cases}$$

where v_1 is the velocity of the immersed tunnel element relative to the shore, F_i is the towing force of the i-th tug, α_i is the angle of the positive x-axis counter clockwise to the towing force F_i, and N is the quantity of the tugs. $F_{i,\max}$ and $F_{i,\min}$ are the maximal and minimum towing force of the i_{th} tug, respectively, F_{mean} is the mean value of the surplus towing force of all tugs, and $v_{1,\min}$ and $v_{1,\max}$ are the lower and upper limits of v_1, respectively.

2.2 Methods of the MODE-PMSMO

It's been well known that the performance of differential evolution algorithm is sensitive to strategies and parameter settings. To further improve the performance of multi-objective DE, Fan et al. [11] proposed the MODE-PMSMO. In the MODE-PMSMO algorithm, a suitable mutation operator can be automatically selected based on a modified performance metric. The flowchart of the MODE-PMSMO is shown in Fig. 1. Furthermore, more detailed descriptions can refer to Ref. [11].

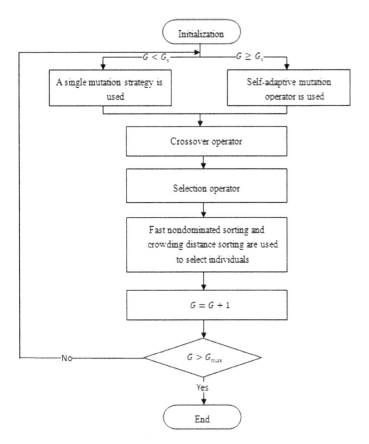

Fig. 1. The flowchart of the MODE-PMSMO

3   Case Study

According to the translation model of the immersed tunnel element presented in Sect. 2, the MODE-PMSMO [11] is employed to obtain a set of optimal operation conditions. Both advantage and disadvantage of each optimal operation condition is observed.

In the current experiment, the MODE-PMSMO is used to solve the translation control problem of the immersed tunnel element in Hong Kong Zhuhai Macao bridge project. Then, the number of tugs is set to be 6 in the present study. The population size of the MODE-PMSMO is set to be 100. The maximum number of function evaluations is set to be 30,000. Moreover, the parameter settings in translation model of the immersed tunnel element are shown in Table 1. The upper and lower limits of variables in Eq. (1) are shown in Table 2.

Four PF from four different views are plotted in Fig. 2. Figure 2(a) shows the PF obtained by MODE-PMSMO on three objectives. Figure 2(b) exhibits that the translation velocity of the immersed tunnel element increases with decreasing the total

Table 1. Parameter settings in translation model of the immersed tunnel element

Immersed tunnel element			Floating pontoon				Seawater	Current velocity
Length (L)	Width (B)	Draft (d)	Length (L_p)	Draft (d_p)	Width (B_p)	Width (B'_p)	Density (ρ)	v_0
m	m	m	m	m	m	m	kg/m^3	knots
180	37.95	11.1	40.2	6.2	7.2	56.4	1025	2

Tug								
G1,G2			G3,G4			G5,G6		
Power	Main engine speed	$F_{i,\max}$	Power	Main engine speed	$F_{i,\max}$	Power	Main engine speed	$F_{i,\max}$
Hp	r/min	ton	Hp	r/min	ton	Hp	r/min	ton
6800	750	56	5200	750	50	4000	750	43
θ_1	Current direction (θ_0)							
Deg.	Deg.							
0	17							

Table 2. Upper and lower limits of variables

Optimized variables	Lower	Upper
v_1(knots)	0	6.623
F_1(kN)	0	46 * 9.8
F_2(kN)	0	46 * 9.8
F_3(kN)	0	40 * 9.8
α_1(Deg.)	−75	165
α_2(Deg.)	−165	75
α_3(Deg.)	35	255
α_4(Deg.)	105	325
α_5(Deg.)	15	350
α_6(Deg.)	15	350

surplus towing force, thus decision makers should strike a balance between the translation velocity and the total surplus towing force based on different conditions. From Fig. 2(c), it can be observed that high translation velocity is difficult to guarantee the trade-off of the surplus towing force of each tug. Also, Fig. 2(d) indicates that large total surplus of towing force can achieve a good balance to the surplus towing force of each tug. Based on the above observations, it can be concluded that the translation velocity is inversely proportional to the total surplus towing force, and large total surplus of towing force is beneficial to implement the trade-off of the surplus towing force of each tug. Additionally, two boundary points (i.e., S1 and S2) shown in Fig. 2 (b) are selected from the achieved PF. S1 denotes the total surplus towing force is

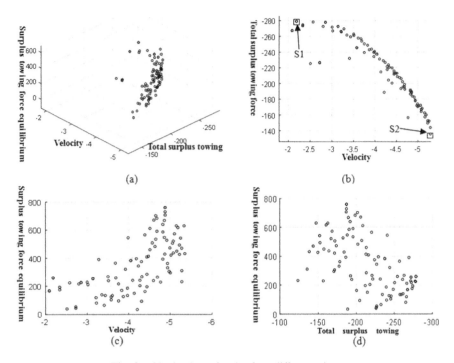

Fig. 2. Obtained *PF* for the four different views

Table 3. Towing force and angle of each tug for S1

Tug No.	Towing force (kN)	Angle (deg.)
1	89.87	−58.49
2	1.99	3.35
3	3.67	186.59
4	0.14	257.25
5	122.78	249.21
6	18.98	198.24

Table 4. Towing force and angle of each tug for S2

Tug No.	Towing force (kN)	Angle (deg.)
1	404.88	−5.44
2	326.78	−13.63
3	60.16	40.25
4	342.62	324.64
5	122.78	50.51
6	286.43	3.42

maximal while the translation velocity is minimal. S2 represents the translation velocity is the fastest, but the total surplus towing force is minimal. The detailed results of two points are summarized in Tables 3 and 4. It can be observed from Table 3 that, to ensure the large total surplus of towing force, tugs 1, 5, and 6 play an important role in the translation of the immersed tunnel element, whereas tugs 2, 3, and 4 can be used as a standby tug to deal with changing environment or uncertain disturbance. Table 4 indicates that, to achieve high translation velocity, tugs 1, 2, 4, and 6 should provide greater towing force to the immersed tunnel element, and tugs 3 and 5 can provide relatively small towing force.

4 Conclusion

In this paper, the translation problem of the immersed tunnel element is converted into a multi-objective optimization problem, which is solved by a recently proposed multi-objective differential evolution algorithm, i.e., MODE-PMSMO. In the case study, the parameter settings of the model are collected from Hong Kong Zhuhai Macao bridge project. The simulation results show that the MODE-PMSMO can provide a set of non-dominated solutions for helping decision makers and improve the transportation efficiency. Moreover, decision makers can select another solution when operating environment change dramatically.

Acknowledgment. We express our appreciation to the volume editor and reviewers for their constructive suggestions and comments on the earlier versions of the paper. This work was supported by the National Nature Science Foundation of china (No. 61603244). Here we would like to express our gratitude to them.

References

1. Fu, Q.G.: Development and prospect of immersed tunnels. China Harbour Eng. **6**, 53–58 (2004). (in Chinese)
2. Sinibaldi, M., Bulian, G.: Towing simulation in wind through a nonlinear 4-DOF model: bifurcation analysis and occurrence of fishtailing. Ocean Eng. **88**, 366–392 (2014)
3. Bao, W.M.: Application of harbor operational tugs in maneuvering large vessels in port. Navig. Chin. **4**, 23–26 (2006). (in Chinese)
4. Fitriadhy, A., Yasukawa, H., Koh, K.K.: Course stability of a ship towing system in wind. Ocean Eng. **64**, 135–145 (2013)
5. Wang, H.F.: The Resistance Research and the Schematic Study of Immersed Tube Transport at Sea. Eng. M. Dissertation, Dalian University of Technology (2015). (in Chinese)
6. Zhu, et al.: Numerical simulation of the hydrodynamic characteristics of the immersed tube tunnel in tugging. J. Beijing Jiaotong Univ. **34**, 5 (2010). (in Chinese)
7. Lu, et al.: An analytical study on the hydraulic resistance for the immersed tunnel elements during transportation for the project of Hong Kong-Zhuhai- Macao Bridge. In: the World Tunnel Congress (WTC)/39th General Assembly of the International-Tunneling-and-Underground-Space-Association (ITA), pp. 778–785. Swiss Tunneling Soc, Geneva, Switzerland (2013)

8. Li, et al.: Translation control model and optimization method of immersed tube under action of water flow. J. Traffic Transp. Eng. **16**, 10 (2016). (in Chinese)
9. Lin, L.Y.: Experimental Investigation on the Motion and Dynamic Response of Tunnel Element in the process of Immersing. Eng. M. Dissertation, Dalian University of Technology (2013). (in Chinese)
10. Wu, Y.K., Xie, Y.L.: Research on tube tunnels by three-dimensional finite element software ANASYS. J. Xian Univ. Sci. Technol. **34**, 6 (2014). (in Chinese)
11. Fan, Q.Q., Wang, W.L., Yan, X.F.: Multi-objective differential evolution with performance-metric-based self-adaptive mutation operator for chemical and qbiochemical dynamic optimization problems. Appl. Soft Comput. **59**, 33–44 (2017)

Path Planning on Hierarchical Bundles with Differential Evolution

Victor Parque[1,2(✉)] and Tomoyuki Miyashita[1]

[1] Waseda University, 3-4-1 Okubo, Shinjuku-ku, Tokyo 169-8555, Japan
parque@aoni.waseda.jp
[2] Egypt-Japan University of Science and Technology,
Borg El Arab, Alexandria 21934, Egypt

Abstract. Computing hierarchical routing networks in polygonal maps is significant to realize the efficient coordination of agents, robots and systems in general; and the fact of considering obstacles in the map, makes the computation of efficient networks a relevant need for cluttered environments. In this paper, we present an approach to compute the minimal-length hierarchical topologies in polygonal maps by Differential Evolution and Route Bundling Concepts. Our computational experiments in scenarios considering convex and non-convex configuration of polygonal maps show the feasibility of the proposed approach.

Keywords: Route bundling · Hierarchical network design
Minimal trees

1 Introduction

Over the last decade research on Internet of Things and collaborative robots has made clear that optimal and robust routing in networks are significant to realize the effective coordination and communication of multi-agent systems; and the fact of having obstacles over the map, makes the computation of collision-free routing a relevant need in cluttered environments [3, 14, 41–43].

Research in route planning has its origins in the mid 60's, and since the seminal work of Lozano-Perez in 1979 [19], the problem has been extensively studied in the literature. For recent reviews, see [22, 38]. Often, collision-free trajectories are computed considering the optimality of navigation in the free space. And well-known methods such as RRT [16, 17] and PRM [15] guarantee probabilistic completeness, while RRT* guarantees asymptotic optimality. Also, approaches based on sampling and optimization with gradient-based approaches are used, such as CHOMP, STOMP, and TrajOpt. However, these methods are sensitive to initial conditions (initial trajectory). Also, path planning based on geometric information has been argued to be accurate [1, 4, 7, 18, 34], in which finding optimal origin-destination is usually based on the triangulation of the free space. Also, online and approximation approaches have been proposed as well, e.g. the Potential Field method [2], and the Cell Decomposition method

© Springer International Publishing AG, part of Springer Nature 2018
Y. Tan et al. (Eds.): ICSI 2018, LNCS 10941, pp. 251–260, 2018.
https://doi.org/10.1007/978-3-319-93815-8_25

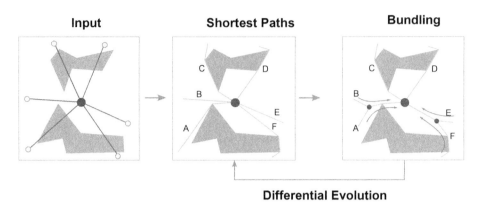

Fig. 1. Basic concept of the proposed approach

[11]. Furthermore, heuristic approaches have been used to achieve optimality of routes in the global sense, and examples include nature inspired approaches such as Neural Networks [8,36], Genetic Algorithms [6], Differential Evolution [26,31,32,40,44] and Particle Swarm Optimization (PSO) [21,45].

Being related to the *Steiner tree* problem, path planning on hierarchical bundles is key to allow efficient distribution and communication of sparsely distributed nodes. Having started in the 30's [39], the *Steiner tree* problem was popularized in the 40's [35]. In practical settings, the Obstacle-Avoiding Rectilinear Steiner (OARST) given n nodes in a polygonal map has received recent attention in VLSI systems [3,14,41–43]; and there exists a polynomial-time approximation of the more general Obstacle-Avoiding Steiner Tree (OAST) with $O(nlog^2n)$ (n is number of terminals and obstacle vertices) [23]. However, the exhaustive study of global optimization and gradient-free approaches on Minimum Steiner Trees in polygonal maps has received little attention.

Other related works to path planning on hierarchical bundles involve the edge bundling in network visualization [5,10,12,13,37], the path bundling in bipartite networks [26,29,32], and the minimal trees in n-star networks with fixed roots [33]. However, path planning considering minimal Steiner trees and flexible root configuration has received little examination in the literature.

In this paper, in order to fill the above gaps, we propose an approach to compute minimal trees given n points with a star topology and flexible configuration of the root, wherein the goal is to generate topologically compact and minimal trees being free of clutter and easy to visualize. The basic idea of our approach, depicted by Fig. 1, is to allow routes to be bundled by using a hierarchical configuration, and optimize the location of the root by Differential Evolution. Our results by using a diverse set of polygonal map configurations show the feasibility to compute minimal trees in the plane.

In the rest of this article, after describing the key components in our proposed approach, we discuss our findings though our computational experiments, and finally summarize our insights and future work.

2   Path Planning on Hierarchical Bundles

The basic outline of our algorithm is depicted by Fig. 1, in the following we briefly describe the key components and dynamics.

2.1   Preliminaries

The *input* in our algorithm is the set of terminal nodes V and a polygonal map P; and the *output* is a tree layout aiming at minimizing the total tree length, while not only preserving connectivity from the root r towards the nodes in the terminal set V, but also avoiding the obstacles in map P.

2.2   Shortest Paths

The route r is known a-priori and its location is an interior point of the convex hull of V. The shortest paths are computed from the root r towards each node in the terminal V by using the A* algorithm with visibility graphs, rendering the set ρ of *shortest routes* from the source r to each terminal node in V.

2.3   Route Bundling

Then, shortest routes are clustered by the hierarchical agglomerative approach with complete and Euclidean metric, which renders a *dendogram* $\mathbf{Z} = [z_{ij}] \in \mathbb{R}^{|\rho| \times 2}$ denoting the ordering of path bundling in which the rows of the matrix $\mathbf{Z}$ are configured in ascending order, with *similar* (*different*) routes being located first (last). For clustering and similarity computation, the distance between two routes is computed by the following metric:

$$d(\rho_i, \rho_j) = \left(\sum_{k=1}^{SP} ||\rho_i^k - \rho_j^k||^2 \right) \cdot \left(cos^{-1} \left(\frac{\mathbf{a_i}.\mathbf{a_j}}{|\mathbf{a_i}||\mathbf{a_j}|} \right) \right), \tag{1}$$

where $\rho_i \in \rho$, ρ_i^k is the k-th sampled point along the route ρ_i, SP is the number of equally-separated interpolated points along the route ρ_i, and $\mathbf{a_i} = \rho_i^{end} - \rho_i^{init}$ in which $\rho_i^{init}, \rho_i^{end} \in \mathbb{R}^2$ are the *starting* and the *end* coordinates of the route ρ_i, respectively. The main rationale of using the above distance metric is due to its key benefit of measuring not only *piecewise gaps* (due to difference in topology), but also *orientation gaps* (due to arbitrariness of location of end nodes). Furthermore, note that the above distance metric is able to be computed under parallelization schemes, bringing benefits in scalability for large-scale path planning applications.

By using the order of the *dendogram* (hierarchical clustering), routes are bundled by a nature-inspired approach which considers the *merging*, the *expansion* and the *shrinkage* of leaves [33]. The bundle process is executed in *bottom-up* approach (from terminal nodes to root), followed by a *top-down* approach (from root to terminal nodes), which ensures co-adaptation while searching for optimal topologies.

– *Merging* occurs when the anchoring node x is far from the root r, yet close to either routes u or v. Farness of node x to r, and closeness of x to u, v is computed by $\ell(x, r) > \delta_1$ and $D(r, u, v) < \delta_2$, respectively, where:

$$D(r, u, v) = min(\ell(r, u), \ell(r, v)), \tag{2}$$

where $\ell(x, w)$ is the length of the *shortest route* from node x to node w along the polygonal map P. The role of using the user-defined thresholds δ_1 and δ_2 is to allow flexibility and granularity when designing and generating minimal trees: smaller (larger) values of $\delta_1(\delta_2)$ creates more (less) intermediate nodes x, thus the global tree length is expected to be small (large). Then the *farthest* leaf (u or v) is merged to the *closest* one (u or v), in which the *closest* leaf is computed by the following metric:

$$closest = \begin{cases} u, & \text{for } \ell(x, u) < \ell(x, v) \\ v, & \text{for } \ell(x, u) > \ell(x, v) \end{cases} \tag{3}$$

As a natural consequence, the *farthest* node is the opposite of the above.
– *Expansion* occurs when the anchoring node x is *far* from the root r, and *far* from leaves u, v.
– *Shrinkage* occurs either when the tree has a single leaf, or when the anchoring node x is *close* to the root r and *close* to either u or v.

The above bundling operations are guided by the *dendogram* **Z**; in which some of the edges of the T are compounded and some intermediate nodes are inserted due to the *expand* operation. Note that tree operations are performed recursively.

2.4   Optimizing the Root of Trees

The root in the tree T is allowed to be flexible, and its location is optimized by minimizing:

$$J(T, r) = \sum_{s \in leaves(T)} \ell(r, s), \tag{4}$$

where r is the root of tree T. Note that the above definition is *recursive*. Due to the nature of handling obstacles with arbitrary geometry, the optimization of the above cost function is realized by Differential Evolution with Neighborhood and Convex Encoding [26, 32], which is used due to its advantages to not only balance the *exploration* and the *exploitation* while searching for the optimal location of the root, but also to render feasible root coordinates by using a triangular encoding, which allows to sample obstacle-avoiding coordinates in polygonal maps efficiently.

3   Computational Experiments

In order to evaluate the performance of our proposed path bundling algorithm, we performed computational experiments in diverse scenarios.

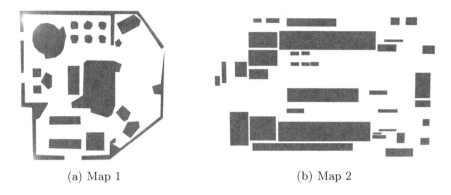

(a) Map 1   (b) Map 2

Fig. 2. Polygonal maps

3.1   Settings

Our computing environment was an Intel i7-4930K @ 3.4 GHz, Matlab 2016a. To evaluate our approach in diverse scenarios, we used polygonal maps with convex and non-convex polygonal configurations, as shown by Fig. 2 [9,20]. Also, for each configuration, 5 independent runs for path planning in origin-destination pairs consisting of 20 edges in a star-topology was performed. The main motivation of using the above is due to our foci on scenarios being close to indoor environments, where complexity is controlled by the convexity and the configuration of the polygonal map.

As for parameters in Differential Evolution, we used: probability of crossover $CR = 0.5$, scaling factor $\alpha = \beta = |ln(U(0,1))/2|$, population size with 10 individuals, neighborhood ratio $\eta = 0.2$, and termination criterion is 5000 function evaluations. The main reason of using crossover probability $CR = 0.5$ is to give the same importance to the sampling with historical search vectors, and with local and global interpolations. The scaling factors α, β allow to search in small steps when computing the self-adaptive directions. Furthermore, small values of population size and neighborhood factor enable efficient sampling within the local neighborhood [32]. Fine tuning of the above is out of our scope.

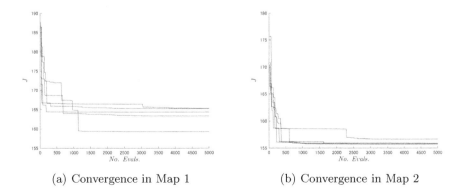

(a) Convergence in Map 1   (b) Convergence in Map 2

Fig. 3. Convergence over different Maps

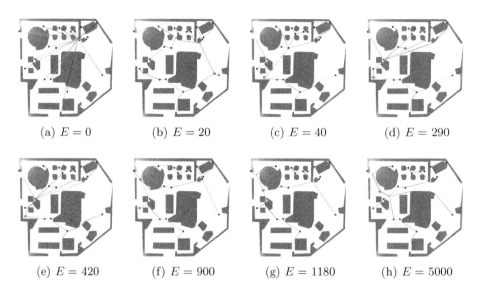

(a) $E = 0$ (b) $E = 20$ (c) $E = 40$ (d) $E = 290$

(e) $E = 420$ (f) $E = 900$ (g) $E = 1180$ (h) $E = 5000$

Fig. 4. Convergence examples in Map 1 after E function evaluations.

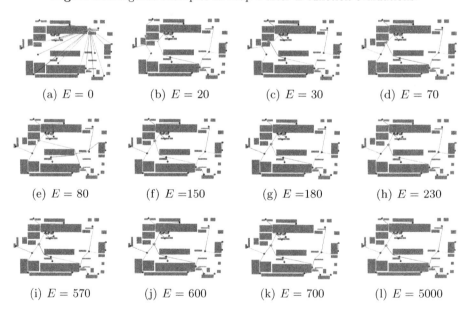

(a) $E = 0$ (b) $E = 20$ (c) $E = 30$ (d) $E = 70$

(e) $E = 80$ (f) $E = 150$ (g) $E = 180$ (h) $E = 230$

(i) $E = 570$ (j) $E = 600$ (k) $E = 700$ (l) $E = 5000$

Fig. 5. Convergence examples in Map 2 after E function evaluations.

3.2   Results

In order to show the learning performance of our proposed approach, Fig. 3 shows the convergence behaviour as a function of the number of evaluations over independent runs. By observing Fig. 3, we can confirm that computing minimal trees becomes possible within a 1000–1500 function evaluations.

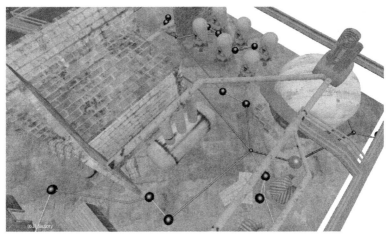

(a) Minimal Tree in Map 1

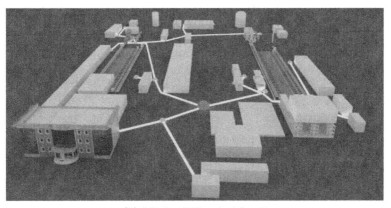

(b) Minimal Tree in Map 2

Fig. 6. Minimal trees.

Also, in order to show the evolvability performance of our proposed approach, Figs. 4 and 5 show the elite solutions generating the path planners in hierarchical bundles after E function evaluations. Here $E = 0$ denotes the input (as portrayed by the basic concept in Fig. 1), and $E = 5000$, denotes the converged solution. By looking at the generated topologies in Figs. 4 and 5, we can observe that it is possible to compute the optimal location of the roots (which is different from the initial solution), and that larger changes in topology occur at earlier stages of the learning algorithm. We believe this fact occurs due to the highly explorative (exploitative) nature in earlier (later) generations, which induces in large (small) changes in the nature of the topology of minimal trees. Finally, to visualize deployment, Fig. 6 shows the generated topologies of the minimal trees in their respective environments [9,20].

We believe that our obtained results are building blocks to further advance path planning in hierarchical networks in the presence of polygonal obstacles. Investigating the learning performance with canonical encodings in directed graphs [28] and undirected graphs [24], the use of concurrency concepts in networks [30] and in exploration-exploitation [25], as well as the formation of modules in hierarchical bundles by succinct subset partitions [27] are in our agenda.

4   Conclusion

We proposed a method to compute hierarchical networks in polygonal maps given n points configured in an n-star topology with flexible root location. The basic idea of our approach is based on path bundling to find minimal trees while avoiding obstacles, and evolution to compute the optimal location of the roots in the minimal tree. Our computational experiments involving convex and non-convex polygonal map scenarios confirm the feasibility to compute obstacle-avoiding minimal trees, and the efficiency to converge to optimal solutions within 1000–1500 function evaluations. In our future work, we aim at exploring the learning performance of minimal topologies by using succinct encodings of graphs, concurrency and combinatorial subset formation. We believe our approach may find uses in Operations Research, Communications and Multi-Agent Systems.

References

1. Chazelle, B.: A theorem on polygon cutting with applications. In: Proceedings of 23rd IEEE Symposium on Foundations of Computer Science, pp. 339–349 (1982)
2. Chiang, H.T., Malone, N., Lesser, K., Oishi, M., Tapia, L.: Path-guided artificial potential fields with stochastic reachable sets for motion planning in highly dynamic environments, pp. 2347–2354, May 2015
3. Chow, W., Li, L., Young, E., Sham, C.: Obstacle-avoiding rectilinear Steiner tree construction in sequential and parallel approach. Integr. VLSI J. **47**, 105–114 (2014)
4. Cormen, T., Leiserson, C., Rivest, R.: Introduction to Algorithms. MIT Press, Cambridge (1993)
5. Cui, W., Zhou, H., Qu, H., Wong, P.C., Li, X.: Geometry-based edge clustering for graph visualization. IEEE Trans. Visual. Comput. Graph. **14**, 1277–1284 (2008)
6. Davoodi, M., Panahi, F., Mohades, A., Hashemi, S.N.: Clear and smooth path planning. Appl. Soft Comput. **32**, 568–579 (2015)
7. Dijkstra, E.W.: A note on two problems in connexion with graphs. Numerische Mathematik **1**, 269–271 (1959)
8. Duan, H., Huang, L.: Imperialist competitive algorithm optimized artificial neural networks for UCAV global path planning. Neurocomputing, **125**, 166–171 (2014). Advances in Neural Network Research and Applications Advances in Bio-Inspired Computing: Techniques and Applications
9. exedesign: Factory. http://www.blendswap.com/blends/view/55233
10. Gansner, E.R., Hu, Y., North, S., Scheidegger, C.: Multilevel agglomerative edge bundling for visualizing large graphs. In: IEEE Pacific Visualization Symposium, pp. 187–194 (2011)

11. Ghita, N., Kloetzer, M.: Trajectory planning for a car-like robot by environment abstraction. Robot. Auton. Syst. **60**(4), 609–619 (2012)
12. Holten, D.: Hirerarchical edge bundles: visualization of adjacency relations in hierarchical data. In: IEEE Pacific Visualization Symposium, pp. 187–194 (2006)
13. Holten, D., van Wijk, J.J.: Force-directed edge bundling for graph visualization. In: Eurographics, Symposium on Visualization (2009)
14. Jing, T.T., Hu, Y., Feng, Z., Hong, X., Hu, X., Yan, G.: A full-scale solution to the rectilinear obstacle-avoiding Steiner problem. Integr. VLSI J. **41**, 413–425 (2008)
15. Kavraki, L.E., Svestka, P., Latombe, J.C., Overmars, M.H.: Probabilistic roadmaps for path planning in high-dimensional configuration spaces. IEEE Trans. Robot. Autom. **12**(4), 566–580 (1996)
16. LaValle, S.M.: Rapidly-exploring random trees: a new tool for path planning. Technical report. Computer Science Department, Iowa State University (TR 98–11)
17. LaValle, S.M., Kuffner Jr., J.J.: Rapidly-exploring random trees: progress and prospects (2000)
18. Lee, D.T., Preparata, F.P.: Euclidean shortest paths in the presence of rectilinear barriers. Networks **14**(3), 393–410 (1984)
19. Lozano-Pérez, T., Wesley, M.A.: An algorithm for planning collision-free paths among polyhedral obstacles. Commun. ACM **22**(10), 560–570 (1979)
20. LWP23D: Game map: Factory. https://www.blendswap.com/blends/view/81600
21. Mac, T.T., Copot, C., Tran, D.T., Keyser, R.D.: A hierarchical global path planning approach for mobile robots based on multi-objective particle swarm optimization. Appl. Soft Comput. **59**, 68–76 (2017)
22. Mohanan, M., Salgoankar, A.: A survey of robotic motion planning in dynamic environments. Robot. Auton. Syst. **100**, 171–185 (2018)
23. Müller-Hannemann, M., Tazari, S.: A near linear time approximation scheme for Steiner tree among obstacles in the plane. Comput. Geom. Theory Appl. **43**, 395–409 (2010)
24. Parque, V., Kobayashi, M., Higashi, M.: Bijections for the numeric representation of labeled graphs. In: IEEE International Conference on Systems, Man and Cybernetics, pp. 447–452 (2014)
25. Parque, V., Kobayashi, M., Higashi, M.: Searching for machine modularity using Explorit. In: IEEE International Conference on Systems, Man and Cybernetics, pp. 2599–2604 (2014)
26. Parque, V., Miura, S., Miyashita, T.: Optimization of route bundling via differential evolution with a convex representation. In: 2017 IEEE International Conference on Real-time Computing and Robotics (RCAR), pp. 727–732, July 2017
27. Parque, V., Miyashita, T.: On k-subset sum using enumerative encoding. In: IEEE International Symposium on Signal Processing and Information Technology, pp. 81–86 (2016)
28. Parque, V., Miyashita, T.: On succinct representation of directed graphs. In: IEEE International Conference on Big Data and Smart Computing, pp. 199–205 (2017)
29. Parque, V., Kobayashi, M., Higashi, M.: Optimisation of bundled routes. In: 16th International Conference on Geometry and Graphics, pp. 893–902 (2014)
30. Parque, V., Kobayashi, M., Higashi, M.: Neural computing with concurrent synchrony. In: Loo, C.K., Yap, K.S., Wong, K.W., Teoh, A., Huang, K. (eds.) ICONIP 2014, Part I. LNCS, vol. 8834, pp. 304–311. Springer, Cham (2014). https://doi.org/10.1007/978-3-319-12637-1_38
31. Parque, V., Miura, S., Miyashita, T.: Computing path bundles in bipartite networks. In: 7th International Conference on Simulation and Modelling Methodologies, Technologies and Applications, pp. 422–427, Madrid, Spain (2017)

32. Parque, V., Miura, S., Miyashita, T.: Route bundling in polygonal domains using differential evolution. Robot. Biomimetics **4**(1), 22 (2017)
33. Parque, V., Miyashita, T.: Bundling n-Stars in polygonal maps. In: 29th IEEE International Conference on Tools with Artificial Intelligence, 6–8 November, Boston, USA (2017)
34. Hart, P.E., Nilsson, N.J., Raphael, B.: A formal basis for the heuristic determination of minimum cost paths. IEEE Trans. Syst. Sci. Cybern. **4**(2), 100–107 (1968)
35. Robbins, H., Courant, R.: What is Mathematics?. Oxford University Press, Oxford (1941)
36. Šter, B.: An integrated learning approach to environment modelling in mobile robot navigation. Neurocomputing **57**, 215–238 (2004). New Aspects in Neurocomputing: 10th European Symposium on Artificial Neural Networks 2002
37. Selassie, D., Heller, B., Heer, J.: Divided edge bundling for directional network data. IEEE Trans. Visual. Comput. Graph. **17**(12), 2354–2363 (2011)
38. Souissi, O., Benatitallah, R., Duvivier, D., Artiba, A., Belanger, N., Feyzeau, P.: Path planning: a 2013 survey. In: Proceedings of 2013 International Conference on Industrial Engineering and Systems Management (IESM), pp. 1–8, October 2013
39. Vojtěch, J., Kössler, M.: O minimálních grafech, obsahujících n daných bodů. Časopis pro pěstování matematiky a fysiky **063**(8), 223–235 (1934)
40. Wang, M., Luo, J., Fang, J., Yuan, J.: Optimal trajectory planning of free-floating space manipulator using differential evolution algorithm. Adv. Space Res. **61**(6), 1525–1536 (2018)
41. Winter, P.: Euclidean Steiner minimal trees with obstacles and Steiner visibility graphs. Discrete Appl. Math. **47**, 187–206 (1993)
42. Winter, P., Zachariasen, M., Nielsen, J.: Short trees in Polygons. Discrete Appl. Math. **118**, 55–72 (2002)
43. Zhang, H., Ye, D., Guo, W.: A heuristic for constructing a rectilinear Steiner tree by reusing routing resources over obstacles. Integr. VLSI J. **55**, 162–175 (2016)
44. Zhang, X., Chen, J., Xin, B., Fang, H.: Online path planning for UAV using an improved differential evolution algorithm. IFAC Proc. Vol. **44**(1), 6349–6354 (2011). 18th IFAC World Congress
45. Zhang, Y., Gong, D.W., Zhang, J.H.: Robot path planning in uncertain environment using multi-objective particle swarm optimization. Neurocomputing **103**, 172–185 (2013)

Fireworks Algorithm

Accelerating the Fireworks Algorithm with an Estimated Convergence Point

Jun Yu[1(✉)], Hideyuki Takagi[2], and Ying Tan[2,3]

[1] Graduate School of Design, Kyushu University, Fukuoka 815-8540, Japan
takagi@design.kyushu-u.ac.jp
[2] Faculty of Design, Kyushu University, Fukuoka 815-8540, Japan
[3] School of Electronics Engineering and Computer Science,
Peking University, Beijing 100871, China

Abstract. We propose an acceleration method for the fireworks algorithms which uses a convergence point for the population estimated from moving vectors between parent individuals and their sparks. To improve the accuracy of the estimated convergence point, we propose a new type of firework, the *synthetic firework*, to obtain the correct of the local/global optimum in its local area's fitness landscape. The synthetic firework is calculated by the weighting moving vectors between a firework and each of its sparks. Then, they are used to estimate a convergence point which may replace the worst firework individual in the next generation. We design a controlled experiment for evaluating the proposed strategy and apply it to 20 CEC2013 benchmark functions of 2-dimensions (2-D), 10-D and 30-D with 30 trial runs each. The experimental results and the Wilcoxon signed-rank test confirm that the proposed method can significantly improve the performance of the canonical firework algorithm.

Keywords: Fireworks algorithm · Estimated convergence point
Synthetic individuals · Acceleration

1 Introduction

The fireworks algorithm (FWA) [1], as a new member of swarm intelligence algorithms inspired by the explosion of real fireworks, has attracted much attentions in academia and industry. It simulates explosions repeatedly to implement local search points (sparks) around a specific point (firework) and evolves towards the optimal solution. Many improved versions of FWA have been proposed. The enhanced FWA (EFWA) [2] improves the corresponding operations of the original FWA and can achieve a better performance. Dynamic FWA (dynFWA) [3] uses a dynamic explosion amplitude for the current best firework to tune the search range more intelligently. An amplitude reduction strategy and local optima-based selection strategy [4] were also proposed to improve the performance of FWA obviously. Although many new ideas and mechanisms have been

© Springer International Publishing AG, part of Springer Nature 2018
Y. Tan et al. (Eds.): ICSI 2018, LNCS 10941, pp. 263–272, 2018.
https://doi.org/10.1007/978-3-319-93815-8_26

introduced to FWA to develop new variations, little attention was given to the generated sparks, which therefore offer a potential new direction for research.

Using gradient information has always been a very hot topic full of potential. Many practitioners have tried to build and use gradients to accelerate convergence. For example, [5] estimates the natural gradient for the exponential family based on regularized linear regression. In addition, [6] proposes an alternative way to compute search directions by exploiting neighborhood information. In this paper, we introduce a new type of firework, the synthetic firework. Using gradient information derived from the generated sparks, we can gain an understanding about the direction of local evolution on the fitness landscape. This local gradient information is then used to estimate a convergence point for the fireworks population.

The main objective of this paper is to use the estimated convergence point as an elite individual to accelerate FWA by substituting it for the worst firework individual in next generation if its fitness is better. The secondary one is to analyze the applicability of the proposed strategy, and introduce some topics which are open to discussion.

We introduce the framework of canonical FWA in Sect. 2.1 and a method for estimating the convergence point in Sect. 2.2. New types of fireworks are described in detail in Sect. 3. We evaluate them by comparing them with the original FWA using 20 benchmark functions of 3 different dimensions in Sect. 4. Finally, we discuss the experimental evaluations in Sect. 5 and conclude in Sect. 6.

2   Related Research

2.1   Fireworks Algorithm

Real fireworks are launched into the sky, and many sparks are generated around the fireworks. The explosion process of a firework can be viewed as a local search around a specific point. FWA simulates this explosion process iteratively to find the optimal solution. Figure 1 illustrates the process of FWA, which consists principally of three operations: explosion, mutation and selection [1].

Since there are some limitations in classic FWA and its performance is also not very prominent among all its subsequent variants, such as EFWA and

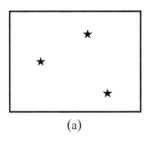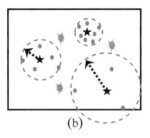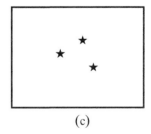

| (a) | (b) | (c) |

Fig. 1. The search process of FWA. (a) fireworks are generated, (b) sparks are created around each firework, and mutation points are also generated, (c) new fireworks are created in the next generation using the sparks from (b). Steps (b) and (c) are iterated until the termination condition is satisfied.

dynFWA, we employ the more powerful EFWA [2] as our baseline algorithm and combine it with our proposed strategy. The EFWA introduces five major improvements into conventional FWA to improve its performance. For details on these improvements, refer to [2].

2.2   Method for Estimating the Convergence Point for a Population

The convergence point for the moving vectors between parent individuals and their offspring in the next EC search generation can be calculated mathematically [7,8]. Let us begin by defining symbols. a_i and c_i in the Fig. 2 are the i-th parent individual and its offspring individual, respectively ($a_i, c_i \in \mathbb{R}^d$). The i-th moving vector is defined as the direction vector, $b_i = c_i - a_i$. The unit direction vector of the b_i is given as $b_{0i} = b_i/||b_i||$, i.e. $b_{0i}^T b_{0i} = 1$.

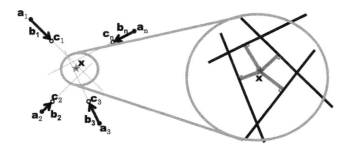

Fig. 2. The moving vector b_i ($= c_i - a_i$) is calculated from a parent individual a_i and its offspring c_i in the d-dimensional searching space. The $\star$ mark is the convergence point for these moving vectors.

Let $x \in \mathbb{R}^d$ be the point that is the nearest to the n extended directional line segments, $a_i + t_i b_i$ ($t_i \in R$). The *nearest*, means that the total distance from x to the n extended directional line segments, $J(x, \{t_i\})$ in Eq. (1), becomes the minimum. We may insert an orthogonality condition, Eq. (2), into Eq. (1) and thus remove t_i.

$$J(x, \{t_i\}) = \sum_{i=1}^{n} ||a_i + t_i b_i - x||^2 \tag{1}$$

$$b_i^T(a_i + t_i b_i - x) = 0 \quad \text{(orthogonal condition)} \tag{2}$$

The $\hat{x}$ that minimizes the total distance in the Eq. (1) is obtained by partially differentiating each element of x and setting them equal 0. Finally, the convergence point $\hat{x}$ is given by Eq. (3), where I_d is the unit matrix.

$$\hat{x} = \left\{ \sum_{i=1}^{n} \left(I_d - b_{0i} b_{0i}^{\mathrm{T}} \right) \right\}^{-1} \left\{ \sum_{i=1}^{n} \left(I_d - b_{0i} b_{0i}^{\mathrm{T}} \right) a_i \right\} \tag{3}$$

3   Proposed Method

We introduce a new kind of firework, named the synthetic firework, to make full use of the many generated sparks, which are otherwise only involved in the selection operation and then destroyed. The synthetic fireworks and fireworks of the current generation form many moving vectors which can be used to estimate a convergence point that is expected to locate near the global optimum. The estimated point is regarded as an elite individual and replaces the worst individual from the next generation if its fitness is better.

The method for calculating the synthetic fireworks is as follows. Each firework and its generated sparks form a subgroup, and we can construct many vectors between the firework and its generated sparks. If the firework is worse than one of the generated sparks, this vector's direction is considered to be promising. Otherwise, its antipode is used to calculate a synthetic firework. There are many methods to evaluate the potential of these directions. In this paper, we simply use the fitness difference between the endpoint and the start point of a vector to evaluate it. Thus, the larger the fitness difference is, the higher will be the weight of the vector. In order to not increase the number of fitness evaluations, we only calculate the antipode for a firework which is lacking a fitness evaluation if the antipodal direction is to be used. The fitness difference of the original vector is roughly used to evaluate the used antipodal direction. Finally, a synthetic firework can be roughly calculated by weighting those vectors with Eq. 4 in each firework group. Figure 3 illustrates how a synthetic firework is thus formed.

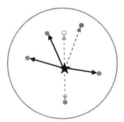

Fig. 3. A synthetic firework is generated from a firework and its generated sparks. The black five-pointed star and the red solid points represent the firework and its generated sparks, respectively. The presence of a red hollow circle means that the antipode has been used. The purple solid point is the synthetic firework obtained by weighting these vectors. (Color figure online)

$$v^i = \sum_{j=1}^{m} \frac{f(x^i) - f(s_j^i)}{\sum_{i=1}^{n} \|(f(x^i) - f(s_j^i))\|} * (s_j^i - x^i) + x^i \tag{4}$$

Where x^i and s^i_j represent the i-th firework and its j-th generated spark or antipodal point. v^i is the i-th synthetic firework of the i-th firework group; m is the number of generated sparks of the i-th firework; $f()$ is a fitness function.

We can obtain new synthetic fireworks up to the population of the current firework generation. Since we do not increase the number of fitness evaluations and a new synthetic firework is expected to be better than the firework belonging to its subgroup, we will not evaluate the synthetic fireworks. A moving vector is calculated from the current firework to the newly generated synthetic firework in each subgroup, and the convergence point is estimated using these moving vectors with the estimation method described in the Sect. 2.2. Algorithm 1 outlines the flow of EFWA using our proposed strategy.

Algorithm 1. The framework for the fireworks algorithm using our proposed strategy. Steps 11 to 16 are from our proposal.

 1: Initialize n fireworks randomly.
 2: Evaluate the fitness of each firework.
 3: **while** the termination condition is not satisfied **do**
 4:    Generate explosion sparks around each firework.
 5:    Use Gaussian mutation to obtain Gauss sparks.
 6:    **if** sparks are generated outside the search area **then**
 7:       Use a mapping rule to bring them back into the area.
 8:    **end if**
 9:    Evaluate the fitness of each generated spark.
10:    Select n fireworks for the next generation from the generated sparks and the current fireworks.
11:    Calculate the synthetic fireworks for each subgroup.
12:    Obtain moving vectors using the synthetic fireworks and the current fireworks.
13:    Estimate a convergence point.
14:    **if** the estimated convergence point is better than the worst firework in the next generation **then**
15:       Replace the worst firework with the estimated point.
16:    **end if**
17: **end while**
18: end of program.

Note that our proposed strategy does not change the structure of the original FWA when it is combined with other fireworks algorithms. It simply uses the fireworks and the generated sparks to build local gradient information, then uses this to estimate a convergence point to accelerate convergence.

4   Experimental Evaluations

We use 20 benchmark functions from the CEC2013 benchmark test suite [9] in our evaluations, which is designed for real parameter single-objective optimization. Table 1 shows their types, characteristics, variable ranges, and optimum fitness values. These landscape characteristics include shifted, rotated, global on bounds, unimodal and multi-modal. We test them with 3 dimensional settings: $D = 2$, 10 and 30. We select EFWA [2] as our test baseline and combine it with our proposal for this experiment using parameters as described in Table 2, where the definition of the symbols can be found in the original literature [1,2].

For fair evaluations, we evaluate convergence against the number of fitness calls rather than generations. We test each benchmark function with 30 trial runs in 3 different dimensional spaces. We apply the Wilcoxon signed-rank test on the fitness values at the stop condition, i.e. the maximum number of fitness calculations, and compare EFWA with (EFWA + our proposed method). Table 3 shows the result of these statistical tests.

Table 1. Benchmark function: Uni = unimodal, Multi = multimodal.

No.	Types	Characteristics	Ranges	Optimum fitness value
F_1	Uni	Sphere function	$[-100, 100]$	-1400
F_2		Rotated high conditioned elliptic function		-1300
F_3		Rotated bent cigar function		-1200
F_4		Rotated discus function		-1100
F_5		Different powers function		-1000
F_6	Multi	Rotated Rosenbrock's function	$[-100, 100]$	-900
F_7		Rotated Schaffers function		-800
F_8		Rotated Ackley's function		-700
F_9		Rotated Weierstrass function		-600
F_{10}		Rotated Griewank's function		-500
F_{11}		Rastrigin's function		-400
F_{12}		Rotated Rastrigin's function		-300
F_{13}		Non-continuous rotated Rastrigin's function		-200
F_{14}		Schwefel's function		-100
F_{15}		Rotated Schwefel's function		100
F_{16}		Rotated Katsuura function		200
F_{17}		Lunacek BiRastrigin function		300
F_{18}		Rotated Lunacek BiRastrigin function		400
F_{19}		Expanded Griewank's plus Rosenbrock's function		500
F_{20}		Expanded Scaffer's F_6 function		600

Table 2. Parameter setting of EFWA.

Parameters	Values
# of fireworks for 2-D, 10-D and 30-D search	5
# of sparks m	50
# of Gauss mutation sparks,	5
constant parameters	$a = 0.04$ $b = 0.8$
Maximum amplitude A_{max}	40
stop condition; MAX_{NFC}, for 2-D, 10-D, and 30-D search	1,000, 10,000, 40,000
Dimensions of benchmark functions, D	2, 10, and 30
# of trial runs	30

Table 3. Statistical test results of the Wilcoxon signed-rank test for average fitness values of 30 trial runs of the proposal (EFWA + our proposed method) and conventional method (EFWA) at the stop condition, MAX_{NFC}. $A \gg B$ and $A > B$ mean that A is significant better than B with significant levels of 1% and 5%, respectively. $A \approx B$ means that although A is better than B, there is no significant difference between them.

$Func.$	2-D	10-D	30-D
f_1	proposal $\gg$ EFWA	proposal $\gg$ EFWA	proposal $\gg$ EFWA
f_2	proposal $\approx$ EFWA	proposal $\gg$ EFWA	proposal $\gg$ EFWA
f_3	proposal $\approx$ EFWA	proposal $>$ EFWA	proposal $>$ EFWA
f_4	EFWA $\approx$ proposal	proposal $\approx$ EFWA	proposal $\approx$ EFWA
f_5	proposal $\gg$ EFWA	proposal $\gg$ EFWA	proposal $\gg$ EFWA
f_6	proposal $\approx$ EFWA	EFWA $\approx$ proposal	proposal $\approx$ EFWA
f_7	proposal $>$ EFWA	EFWA $\approx$ proposal	proposal $\approx$ EFWA
f_8	proposal $\approx$ EFWA	EFWA $\approx$ proposal	proposal $\approx$ EFWA
f_9	EFWA $\approx$ proposal	EFWA $\approx$ proposal	EFWA $\approx$ proposal
f_{10}	proposal $>$ EFWA	proposal $\gg$ EFWA	proposal $\gg$ EFWA
f_{11}	proposal $\approx$ EFWA	proposal $\gg$ EFWA	proposal $\gg$ EFWA
f_{12}	EFWA $\approx$ proposal	proposal $\approx$ EFWA	proposal $\approx$ EFWA
f_{13}	proposal $\approx$ EFWA	proposal $\approx$ EFWA	proposal $\approx$ EFWA
f_{14}	proposal $\approx$ EFWA	proposal $>$ EFWA	proposal $\gg$ EFWA
f_{15}	proposal $\approx$ EFWA	proposal $\approx$ EFWA	EFWA $\approx$ proposal
f_{16}	EFWA $\approx$ proposal	proposal $\approx$ EFWA	proposal $\approx$ EFWA
f_{17}	proposal $\gg$ EFWA	proposal $\gg$ EFWA	proposal $\gg$ EFWA
f_{18}	proposal $>$ EFWA	proposal $\approx$ EFWA	EFWA $\approx$ proposal
f_{19}	proposal $\approx$ EFWA	proposal $\approx$ EFWA	proposal $\gg$ EFWA
f_{20}	proposal $\approx$ EFWA	proposal $\approx$ EFWA	EFWA $\approx$ proposal

5   Discussions

Most fireworks algorithm variants mainly use their computational resources for generating sparks, but the information from these sparks is not fully used. In our experimental evaluations, the total number of generated sparks was 10 times of that of the fireworks. It is clearly productive to consider how these many sparks can be used efficiently. We introduced a new type of firework, called the synthetic firework, to explore local gradient information on the fitness landscape. Thanks to the use of multiple vectors in each subgroup, the synthetic firework also has a certain anti-noise property, as its calculation cancels noise from the directions of the various moving vectors. This can help to improve the precision of the estimated convergence point. In any case, the proposed method increases each generation's fitness calculations by only one - so we can say that it is a low risk, high return strategy.

What potential still remains for our proposed firework, the synthetic firework? Although we have used only the fitness difference between the two endpoints of a moving vector to evaluate it, we think that not only these fitness differences but also their lengths should be considered to understand the local gradient information more accurately, yielding further improvements in the estimate. Additionally, there are many other ways to weight moving vectors and increase the precision of the estimated convergence point. As an example, the fitness value at the beginning point or the end point of a moving vector can be used to evaluate it, which means that the lower the distance from the optimal area, the higher the weight given. A precise way of obtaining reasonable weights for the vectors is also a potential discussion topic.

We would like to point out that the new type of firework introduced can be used to speed up convergence. In this paper, we used synthetic fireworks to estimate a convergence point without evaluating their fitness. They have the potential to act as a new guide for individuals, helping move them toward a preferable evolutionary direction rather than random exploration. The new synthetic fireworks can be introduced into a population to improve the diversity and reduce selection pressure. How to use them reasonably is also a potential discussion topic.

We also performed an extra experiment to investigate the fitness of synthetic fireworks. We compared the synthetic firework with the firework individual belonging to its same subgroup. The experimental results show that in the early stages, synthetic fireworks are better than fireworks individuals, while the probability of a better synthetic firework decreases as the convergence progresses. For optimization problems with different characteristics, it seems reasonable to use a different method for assigning weights when creating the synthetic fireworks. Perhaps different optimization stages could use different weighting methods to obtain better synthetic fireworks. Summarizing the relationship between weighting method and optimization problem is thus also a potential topic for study.

From the results of the statistical tests, we find that the proposed method is beneficial for unimodal optimization problems ($f_1 - f_5$), while the performance on low-dimensional multimodal optimization problems is not obvious. This may be because the basic estimation method, which is clearly effective for unimodal optimization problems, is not always valid for multimodal problems where the moving vectors go toward different local optima. Further, the number of moving vectors is small (in this case, the number is 5), and even on some multimodal optimization problems, it is less than the number of peaks. Regardless, the proposed strategy does not show any deleterious effect. [10] confirmed the effectiveness of using an extra individual pool to preserve outstanding individuals from past generations and using this pool, instead of the current generation, to estimate convergence points. For the next stage, using past searching individuals to increase the number of moving vectors, and combining it with the clustering method may allow us to extend our proposal to multimodal optimization problems.

6   Conclusion

We propose a new kind of fireworks which uses the generated sparks to efficiently estimate a convergence point which can act as an elite individual to accelerate the fireworks algorithm. The controlled experiments confirm that the proposed strategy can significantly improve the performance of conventional EFWA, and the higher the dimension, the more obvious the effect.

In future work, we will further study the proposed synthetic fireworks and use them to beneficially guide the evolution of the population. Additionally, it is suggested that we can further improve the accuracy of the estimated point by using historical information to better understand the fitness landscape.

Acknowledgment. This work was supported in part by Grant-in-Aid for Scientific Research (JP15K00340) and the Natural Science Foundation of China (NSFC) under grant no. 61673025.

References

1. Tan, Y., Zhu, Y.: Fireworks algorithm for optimization. In: Tan, Y., Shi, Y., Tan, K.C. (eds.) ICSI 2010, Part I. LNCS, vol. 6145, pp. 355–364. Springer, Heidelberg (2010). https://doi.org/10.1007/978-3-642-13495-1_44
2. Zheng, S.Q., Janecek, A., Tan, Y.: Enhanced fireworks algorithm. In: IEEE Congress on Evolutionary Computation, Cancun, Mexico, pp. 2069–2077, June 2013
3. Zheng, S.Q., Janecek, A., Li, J.Z., Tan, Y.: Dynamic search in fireworks algorithm. In: IEEE Congress on Evolutionary Computation, Beijing, China, pp. 3222–3229, July 2014
4. Yu, J., Takagi, H.: Acceleration for fireworks algorithm based on amplitude reduction strategy and local optima-based selection strategy. In: International Conference on Swarm Intelligence, Fukuoka, Japan, pp. 477–484, July 2017
5. Luigi, M., Matteo, M.: Robust estimation of natural gradient in optimization by regularized linear regression. In: 1st International SEE Conference on Geometric Science of Information, Paris, France, pp. 861–867, August 2013

6. Schtze, O., Alvarado, S., Segura, C., Landa, R.: Gradient subspace approximation: a direct search method for memetic computing. Soft Comput. **21**(21), 6331–6350 (2017)
7. Murata, N., Nishii, R., Takagi, H., Pei, Y.: Estimation methods of the convergence point of moving vectors between generations. In: Japanese Society for Evolutionary Computation Symposium 2014, Hatsukaichi, Japan, pp. 210–215, December 2014. (in Japanese)
8. Murata, N., Nishii, R., Takagi, H., Pei, Y.: Analytical estimation of the convergence point of populations. In: 2015 IEEE Congress on Evolutionary Computation, Sendai, Japan, pp. 2619–2624, May 2015
9. Liang, J.J., Qu, B.Y., Suganthan, P.N., Alfredo, G.H.: Problem definitions and evaluation criteria for the CEC 2013 special session on real-parameter optimization (2013). http://al-roomi.org/multimedia/CEC_Database/CEC2013/RealParameterOptimization/CEC2013_RealParameterOptimization_TechnicalReport.pdf
10. Yu, J., Takagi, H.: Estimation of the convergence points of a population using an individual pool. In: 10th International Workshop on Computational Intelligence and Applications, Hiroshima, Japan, pp. 67–72, November 2017

Discrete Fireworks Algorithm for Clustering in Wireless Sensor Networks

Feng-Zeng Liu[1,2(✉)], Bing Xiao[1], Hao Li[1], and Li Cai[1]

[1] Air Force Early-Warning Academy, Wuhan 430019, China
fengzeng_liu@126.com, xb_sky@126.com, snk.poison@163.com,
caili20080808@163.com
[2] Academy of Information and Communication,
National University of Defense Technology, Wuhan 430010, China

Abstract. Grouping the sensor nodes into clusters is an approach to save energy in wireless sensor networks (WSNs). We proposed a new solution to improve the performance of clustering based on a novel swarm intelligence algorithm. Firstly, the objective function for clustering optimization is defined. Secondly, discrete fireworks algorithm for clustering (DFWA-C) in WSNs is designed to calculate the optimal number of clusters and to find the cluster-heads. At last, simulation is conducted using the DFWA-C and relevant algorithms respectively. Results show that the proposed algorithm could obtain the number of clusters which is close to the theoretical optimal value, and can effectively reduce energy consumption to prolong the lifetime of WSNs.

Keywords: Clustering · Discrete fireworks algorithm · Optimization
WSNs

1 Introduction

WSNs enable the reliable monitoring of a variety of environments for both civil and military applications [1]. Usually, sensor nodes in the network are energy-constrained and hard to get charged. To save energy and prolong the lifetime of network, various protocols and approaches are designed for communication between sensors and base stations. Grouping the sensor nodes into clusters is one of them, which could effectively manage the network energy and enhance the overall stability of the networks [2]. In order to obtain better performance, determining the number of cluster-heads and selecting appropriate sensor nodes as the cluster-heads are important in the process of clustering [3]. Thus, evolutionary algorithms are applied for solving this WSNs clustering optimization problem, such as SAA (Simulated Annealing Algorithm) [4], PSO (Particle Swarm Optimization) [5], ACA (Ant Colony Algorithm) [6], etc.

In 2010, a swarm intelligence algorithm named fireworks algorithms (FWA) was proposed [7], and received increasing attention in recent years due to its

© Springer International Publishing AG, part of Springer Nature 2018
Y. Tan et al. (Eds.): ICSI 2018, LNCS 10941, pp. 273–282, 2018.
https://doi.org/10.1007/978-3-319-93815-8_27

advanced performance for optimization and successful application in dealing with complex optimization problems [8–11]. FWA shows its potential capacity for solving clustering optimization in WSNs. However, the published literature of this application are rare and hard to find.

As a consequence, this paper focuses on clustering in WSNs based on discrete fireworks algorithm. Mathematical formulation of clustering optimization in WSNs is built using first order radio model. DFWA-C is designed to find optimized cluster-head nodes. To validate the performance of the proposed DFWA-C, comparison simulations are conducted with exploiting the algorithms of DFWA-C, Direct [1], LEACH [1] and HEED [12] respectively. Results show that DFWA-C is effective and obviously outperform the other algorithms in lifetime and remaining energy of WSNs.

2   Formulation of Clustering in WSNs

WSNs contain hundreds or thousands of sensor nodes and are deployed in broad area. The amount of data produced by the nodes is transmitted to base stations and provided to end-users. To complete these work, clustering-based routing protocols are designed to reduce energy dissipation in WSNs [13]. Aiming to minimize the energy consumption, optimization in clustering can improve the performance of routing protocols.

2.1   WSNs Model

In this work, we use the WSNs model proposed in [1,4], which has the following features.

- The base station is fixed and has unlimited energy.
- All the nodes in the network are homogeneous and energy-constrained.
- Every node has the capacity of data fusion, and the location information of itself.
- Every node could be the cluster-head or the member-node, which is decided by the base station and, a node can only be in one cluster.

The set of nodes in WSN is $C = \{c_1, c_2, \ldots, c_N\}$, where N is the number of Nodes. The set of cluster-heads is $C_H = \{ch_1, ch_2, \ldots, ch_K\}$, where K is the number of clusters or cluster-heads. Absolutely $C_H \in C$, $K \leq N$. How to find the best K and choose C_H from C is the clustering optimization problem. During the lifetime of WSNs, there are many rounds and C_H is reselected in every round.

2.2   Energy Consumption Model

Energy consumption in WSNs is computed based on first order radio model [1], which assumes the radio dissipates E_{elec} to run the transmitter or receiver circuitry and ϵ_{amp} for the transmit amplifier. Energy consumption of sending l bits to a node whose distance is d meters is,

$$E_{Tx}(l, d) = l * E_{elec} + l * \epsilon_{amp} * d^2 \tag{1}$$

and energy consumption of receiving l bits is,

$$E_{Rx}(l, d) = l * E_{elec} \tag{2}$$

2.3   Objective Function

Reducing network energy consumption in every round will prolong the lifetime of WSNs. Therefore, minimizing the energy consumption is the principal goal of optimization. Assume l bits are sent by every node in one round and, there are K clusters. In one cluster, the cluster-head node receive data from every member node, fuse the received data and sensed data itself to l bits. Then, the cluster-head node send them to base station. The total energy consumption in one cluster is E_{CLU},

$$
\begin{aligned}
E_{CLU} &= E_{MEM} + E_{CH} \\
&= \sum_{i=1}^{K_m}(l * E_{elec} + l * \epsilon_{amp} * d_i^2) \\
&\quad + (K_m * l * E_{elec} + l * E_{elec} + l * \epsilon_{amp} * d_{CHtoBS}^2)
\end{aligned}
\tag{3}
$$

where E_{MEM} and E_{CH} are the energy consumed by member nodes and cluster-head node in one round. K_m is the number of member nodes in the cluster. d_i is the distance between member node i and cluster-head node. d_{CHtoBS} is the distance between cluster-head node and base station. For the whole network, the total energy consumption E_{TOT} in one round is sum of E_{CLU},

$$E_{TOT} = \sum_{i=1}^{K} E_{CLU}^i \tag{4}$$

E_{TOT} varies with K and C_H. Let 0–1 array $X = (x_1, x_2, \ldots, x_N)$ be the uniform representation of K and C_H, where,

$$x_i = \begin{cases} 1 & \text{if } c_i \in C_H \\ 0 & \text{otherwise} \end{cases} \tag{5}$$

To minimize the total energy consumption, the objective function of optimization is,

$$minf(X) = E_{TOT}(X) \tag{6}$$

where $E_{TOT}(X)$ is the total energy consumption under the cluster-head selection array X. When the optimal X is found, the cluster-heads are obtained. Then, all the nodes are divided in to different clusters based on the shortest distance from the cluster-heads.

2.4   Optimal Number of Clusters

Theoretically, there exists the optimal number of clusters, which can be used to verify the performance of optimization algorithms. Suppose the N sensor nodes are evenly deployed in the square area with length of L_A meters and, the energy consumption model is based on first order radio model, the optimal number of clusters [5] is,

$$K_{opt} = L_A * \sqrt{N\epsilon_{amp}/2\pi(\epsilon_{amp}d_{toBS}^2 - E_{elec})} \tag{7}$$

where d_{toBS} is the mean distance between the cluster-head nodes and base station.

3   Discrete Fireworks Algorithm for Clustering

FWA is a novel swarm intelligence algorithm which is inspired by observing fireworks explosion. In FWA, two types of explosion (search) processes are employed to keep the balance between global search capacity and local search capacity, that make FWA excellent in convergence speed and global solution accuracy. The solution space of clustering in WSNs is discrete. Therefore, FWA is redesigned to discrete fireworks algorithm for discrete space.

3.1   Design of DFWA-C

In DFWA-C, location of element (fireworks or sparks) i is set to $X_i = (x_1^i, x_2^i, \ldots, x_N^i)$ as defined above, whose value space is discrete. For each generation of explosion, M fireworks are set off in M locations. After explosion and mutation of fireworks, the locations of sparks are obtained. All the locations are evaluated by Eq. 6, for example, gorgeous degree (value of objective function) of element i is $Y_i = f(X_i)$. If the optimal location is found, the algorithm stops. Otherwise, M locations are selected from the current sparks and fireworks for the next generation of explosion. Three operators (explosion, mutation and selection) are the key parts in DFWA-C.

Explosion Operator. Sparks are produced by the fireworks explosion, which are viewed as searching process around specific point. Usually, high-quality firework may be close to the optimal location, that it is proper to utilize more sparks to search the local area around the firework. In the contrast, low-quality firework may be far from the optimal location. Thus, few sparks should be generated from the firework and the explosion radius should be larger. The number of sparks generated by fireworks i is defined as follows,

$$S_i = round\left(S_{def} \bullet \frac{f_{max} - f(X_i) + \varepsilon}{\sum_{i=1}^{M}(f_{max} - f(X_i)) + \varepsilon}\right) \tag{8}$$

where S_{def} is a parameter controlling the total number of sparks. f_{max} is the maximum value of objective function among the M fireworks, and ε is an infinitely small constant to avoid zero-division-error. To avoid overwhelming effects, the value range of S_i is set to be $[S_{min}, S_{max}]$, which is a default parameter.

The Amplitude of explosion for firework i is an integer that denotes the number of changed dimensions in X_i, and is defined as follows,

$$A_i = ceil \left(A_{def} \bullet \frac{f(X_i) - f_{min} + \varepsilon}{\sum_{i=1}^{M}(f(X_i - f_{min}) + \varepsilon)} \right) \tag{9}$$

where A_{def} is the maximum amplitude that is set default. f_{min} is the minimum value of objective function among the M fireworks.

Let $X_{i,j} = (x_{i,j}^1, x_{i,j}^2, \ldots, x_{i,j}^N)$ denote the location of the j spark generated by fireworks i. The procedure of producing $X_{i,j}$ is described as follows,

Step1. Generate the integer r from 1 to N randomly.
Step2. Generate the interval length l_r from 1 to A_i randomly.
Step3. Let the downward index $r_d = r$, and the upward index $r_u = r + l_r$. If $r + l_r > N$ then $r_u = N$.
Step4. The value of $X_{i,j}$ is set as,

$$x_{i,j}^k = \begin{cases} 1 - x_i^k & \text{if } r_d \le k \le r_u \\ x_i^k & \text{otherwise} \end{cases} \tag{10}$$

Mutation Operator. To keep the diversity of sparks, mutation operator is designed to generate mutation sparks which are able to escape from the local location. Firstly, M_g mutation fireworks are selected randomly. Secondly, mutation dimitions are selected randomly from N dimensions. Then, let $\hat{X}_i = (\hat{x}_i^1, \hat{x}_i^2, \ldots, \hat{x}_i^N)$ denote the location of mutation sparks generated by mutation fireworks i,

$$\hat{x}_i^k = \begin{cases} 1 & \text{if } g_i^k > 1 \text{ and } x_i^k \in DS \\ 0 & \text{if } g_i^k \le 1 \text{ and } x_i^k \in DS \\ x_i^k & \text{if } x_i^k \notin DS \end{cases} \tag{11}$$

where DS is the dimension space. g_i^k is a gaussian random number generated by $N(1,1)$.

Selection Operator. The candidate fireworks set Θ consists of fireworks, explosion sparks and mutation sparks. M fireworks are selected from set Θ for the next generation explosion. The current element which has the best location evaluated by the objective function is kept. And the left $M - 1$ elements are selected based on their distances to each other. The generous distance of X_i and X_j is defined as follows,

$$D(X_i, X_j) = \sum_{k=1}^{N} V_{i,j}^k \tag{12}$$

where

$$V_{i,j}^k = \begin{cases} 1 & \text{if } x_i^k \neq x_j^k \\ 0 & \text{if } x_i^k = x_j^k \end{cases} \qquad (13)$$

The probability of selecting element i from Θ is defined as

$$p(X_i) = \frac{\sum_{j \in \Theta} D(X_i, X_j)}{\sum_{j \in \Theta} \left(\sum_{k \in \Theta} D(X_k, X_j) \right)} \qquad (14)$$

3.2   Framework of DFWA-C

In order to obtain optimal clusters in WSN, N sensor nodes are coded into a 0–1 array which represents whether the node is chosen as cluster-head. Meanwhile, the array indicates the location of firework in the discrete fireworks algorithm. In DFWA-C, M fireworks are set off in M locations randomly at beginning. Then, explosion sparks and mutation sparks are generated and evaluated by the objective function. M fireworks are selected for the next generation until the optimization is achieved. Framework of DFWA-C is depicted as Fig. 1.

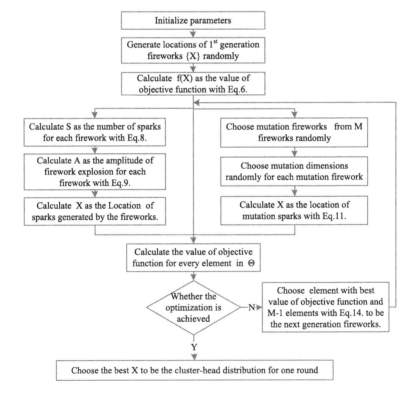

Fig. 1. Flow chart of DFWA-C

4   Simulations and Analysis

To investigate the performance of proposed DFWA-C, we conducted simulations with respect to number of clusters and lifetime of WSNs. The simulated area is 150 m × 150 m. Base station is supposed to be at the center of the area, and sensor nodes scatter in the area randomly. The parameters of WSNs are set as follow: $l = 200$ bit, $E_{elec} = 50 \times 10^{-6}$ J/bit, $\epsilon_{amp} = 100 \times 10^{-9}$ J/(bit × m^2), the initial energy of every sensor node is 10 J. The parameters of DFWA-C are set as follow: $M = 50$, $S_{def} = 50$, A_{def} is set to the same as the dimension of firework location, $M_g = 10$. Then, Simulations run in the Matlab R2014a on Intel(R) Core(TM) i5-3470 @3.2 GHz under Windows 7 environment.

4.1   Number of Clusters

The size of WSNs is set to 100, 200, 300, and 400 respectively. To eliminate random errors, 30 WSNs are generated at each size and, simulation runs 100 times for each WSN. Number of clusters K is calculated by DFWA-C. The optimal number of clusters K_{opt} is calculated by Eq. 7. The mean values are shown in Table 1. Results show that deviations between K and K_{opt} always exist. This is because K_{opt} is obtained under the ideal conditions that nodes are evenly distributed. However, all the deviations are less than 10%. It shows that the proposed algorithm could obtain the cluster number which is close to the theoretical optimal value.

Table 1. Comparison of cluster number

Size of WSNs	d_{toBS}	K	K_{opt}
100	59.14	10.40	10.93
200	57.37	16.86	16.02
300	55.41	21.97	20.44
400	54.70	26.04	23.97

4.2   Lifetime and Energy Consumption of WSNs

To evaluate energy consumption, we conduct network running simulation, and compare with the algorithms of Direct, LEACH and HEED. The size of WSNs is 100. To eliminate random errors, 30 WSNs are generated and, simulaition runs 100 times for each WSN. In order to improve the computational efficiency, the number of generations in DFWA-C is set to a fixed value of 30. Suppose the lifetime of WSNs are the time when 50% nodes fail. The run results are shown in Figs. 2 and 3. In Fig. 2, the lifetime of WSNs based on DFWA-C is 258, as a comparison, the lifetime of WSNs based on other algorithms is less than 230. In Fig. 3, the energy consumption among the four algorithms have little difference at beginning. However, the gap grows with time steps. After 200 time

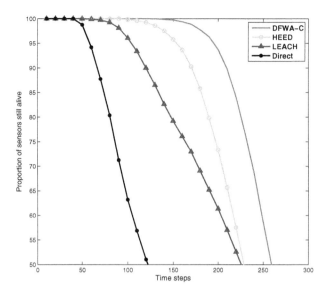

Fig. 2. Lifetime of WSNs

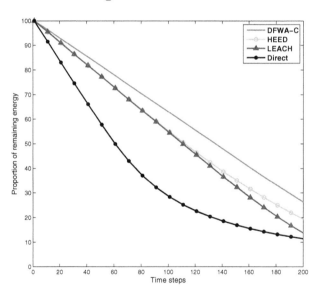

Fig. 3. Energy consumption

steps, remaining energy of WSNs based on Direct, LEACH and HEED are less than 20%. Remaining energy of WSNs based on DFWA-C still has 26%. Results show that proposed DFWA-C could effectively reduce energy consumption and prolong the lifetime of WSNs.

5   Conclusion

In this paper, we described DFWA-C, a novel swarm intelligence algorithm that optimize the number of clusters and find the proper cluster-heads in WSNs. 0–1 array is designed to indicate whether the node is chosen as cluster-head, and is also the location of firework. Then the objective function for clustering optimization is proposed based on the array. Three operators (explosion operator, mutation operator, and selection operator) are given to obtain the optimal location of firework. At last, simulations are conducted to evaluate the performance of proposed algorithm. Results show that the DFWA-C outperforms the Direct, LEACH and HEED algorithms on reducing energy consumption and prolonging the lifetime of WSNs. In future, we will keep improving the proposed algorithm, especially on the computational complexity when the size of WSNs increases.

Acknowledgments. This work is supported by National Natural Science Foundation of China under Grant No. 61502522.

References

1. Heinzelman, W.R., Chandrakasan, A.P., Balakrishnan, H.: Energy-efficient communication protocol for wireless microsensor networks. In: 33rd Hawaii International Conference on System Science, pp. 3005–3014 (2000)
2. Low, C.P., Fang, C., Ng, J.M., Ang, Y.H.: Efficient load-balanced clustering algorithms for wireless sensor networks. Comput. Commun. **31**, 750–759 (2008)
3. Abbasi, A.A., Younis, M.: A survey on clustering algorithms for wireless sensor networks. Comput. Commun. **30**, 2826–2841 (2007)
4. Heinzelman, W.R., Chandrakasan, A.P., Balakrishnan, H.: An application-specific protocol architecture for wireless microsensor networks. IEEE Trans. Wirel. Commun. **1**(4), 660–670 (2002)
5. Su, J.S., Guo, W.Z., Yu, C.L., Chen, G.L.: Fault-tolerance clustering algorithm with load-balance aware in Wireless sensor network. Chin. J. Comput. **37**(2), 445–456 (2014)
6. Liao, F.B., Zhang, W.M.: Uneven clustering routing protocol for wireless sensor networks based on improved ant colony algorithm. Comput. Meas. Contr. **25**(04), 147–152 (2017)
7. Tan, Y., Zhu, Y.: Fireworks algorithm for optimization. In: Tan, Y., Shi, Y., Tan, K.C. (eds.) ICSI 2010. LNCS, vol. 6145, pp. 355–364. Springer, Heidelberg (2010). https://doi.org/10.1007/978-3-642-13495-1_44
8. Tan, Y., Zheng, S.Q.: Recent advance in fireworks algorithm. CAAI Trans. Intell. Syst. **9**(5), 516–528 (2014)
9. Majdouli, M.A.E., Imrani, A.A.E.: Discrete Fireworks algorithm for single machine scheduling problems. Int. J. Appl. Metaheuristic Comput. **7**(3), 24–35 (2016)
10. Tan, Y.: Fireworks Algorithm. A Novel Swarm Intelligence Optimization Method. Springer, Heidelberg (2015). https://doi.org/10.1007/978-3-662-46353-6
11. Xue, J.J., Wang, Y., Li, H., Xiao, J.: Discrete fireworks algorithm for aircraft mission planning. In: Tan, Y., Shi, Y., Niu, B. (eds.) ICSI 2016, LNCS. Lecture Notes in Computer Science, vol. 9712, pp. 544–551. Springer, Cham (2016). https://doi.org/10.1007/978-3-319-41000-5_54

12. Younis, O., Fahmy, S.: Heed: a hybrid, energy-efficient, distributed clustering approach for ad-hoc sensor networks. IEEE Trans. Mob. Comput. **3**(4), 660–669 (2004)
13. Albath, J., Thakur, M., Madria, S.: Energy constraint clustering algorithms for wireless sensor networks. Ad Hoc Netw. **11**, 2512–2525 (2013)

Bare Bones Fireworks Algorithm
for Capacitated p-Median Problem

Eva Tuba[1(✉)], Ivana Strumberger[1], Nebojsa Bacanin[1], and Milan Tuba[2]

[1] Faculty of Informatics and Computing, Singidunum University, Belgrade, Serbia
tuba@ieee.org
[2] Department of Mathematical Sciences, State University of Novi Pazar,
Novi Pazar, Serbia

Abstract. The p-median problem represents a widely applicable problem in different fields such as operational research and supply chain management. Numerous versions of the p-median problem are defined in literature and it has been shown that it belongs to the class of NP-hard problems. In this paper a recent swarm intelligence algorithm, the bare bones fireworks algorithm, which is the latest version of the fireworks algorithm is proposed for solving capacitated p-median problem. The proposed method is tested on benchmark datasets with different values for p. Performance of the proposed method was compared to other methods from literature and it exhibited competitive results with possibility for further improvements.

Keywords: Capacitated p-median · Optimization · Metaheuristics
Bare bones fireworks algorithm · Swarm intelligence

1 Introduction

The p-median problem was firstly introduced to mathematically define problems that are of the great importance, especially in operational research. It describes the facility location problem which can be used in telecommunication and industrial applications, transportation, distribution and many others. The facility location problem refers to the situations where different objects of interest such as hospitals, emergency ambulances, gas stations, antennas and more need to be placed in such a way to optimally cover certain area. Besides p-median problem, facility location problems can be described in different ways. Variety of the problem definitions exist since it represents rather important theoretical and practical problem.

The p-median is commonly used for solving facility location problem. It is defined as a problem of placing the p facilities (medians) so that the overall distance between n demanding points and the nearest facilities is the minimal. Besides this basic definition of the p-median problem, several other versions exist. Uncapacitated p-median problem [1] is the basic version, while the capacitated p-median [2] represents extended version where each facility has the limited

© Springer International Publishing AG, part of Springer Nature 2018
Y. Tan et al. (Eds.): ICSI 2018, LNCS 10941, pp. 283–291, 2018.
https://doi.org/10.1007/978-3-319-93815-8_28

capacity for serving the demand points. Continuous p-median used in [3] considers continuous space for placing the facilities rather then predefined possible positions.

The p-median problem has been proved to be NP-hard [4], which means that deterministic methods cannot solve it, at least not within the acceptable amount of time. Instead of exact, deterministic methods, for NP-hard optimization problems different approximative methods have been used. One of most used group of approximative methods during the last two decades are nature inspired metaheuristics, especially swarm intelligence algorithms. Swarm intelligence algorithms try to find a solution of the optimization problem by imitating behavior of different swarms in the nature, e.g. bee food gathering, elephant herding, ant colony path finding, etc. Very simple agents in term of the operations that they can perform, when communicate between themselves and use the collective knowledge, can demonstrate impressive intelligence. Among the earliest swarm intelligence algorithms are particle swarm optimization (PSO) [5] and ant colony optimization (ACO) [6]. Due to the fact that the idea of imitating phenomena from the nature achieved impressive results in solving hard optimization problems, researchers proposed numerous swarm intelligence algorithms with the aim to solve the problems even more efficiently. These algorithms were widely explored and applied to the problems from various fields. For example, firefly algorithm [7] was applied to support vector machine parameter tuning problem [8], constrained mean-variance portfolio optimization problem [9], wireless sensor networks node localization [10], elephant herding optimization algorithm [11,12] was used for image processing [13], unmanned aerial vehicle path planning [14], brain storm optimization algorithm [15] was improved [16] and applied to problems such as target covering by drones [17], robot path planning [18], bat algorithm [19] applied to support vector machine parameters tuning [20], extreme learning machine optimization [21], and many others.

Since p-median problem is an NP-hard optimization problem, swarm intelligence and other nature inspired algorithms were used for solving it. In [3] genetic algorithm was combined with particle swarm optimization for solving continuous p-median problem. Inverse p-median problem where demands and coordinates of customers should be adjusted according to the predetermined positions of p facilities, was solved by the firefly algorithm in [22]. Artificial bee colony algorithm improved by randomized local search was proposed for positive/negative p-median problem in [23].

In this paper, one of the newest versions of the fireworks algorithm, bare bones fireworks algorithm (BBFWA) was adjusted and used to solve capacitated p-median problem. Based on the extensive search of the literature it can be concluded that no version of the fireworks algorithm was used for solving this problem.

The rest of the paper is structured as follows. In Sect. 2 mathematical model of the capacitated p-median problem is defined. In Sect. 3 history of the fireworks algorithm and the proposed bare bones fireworks algorithm are presented. Simulation results are shown in Sect. 4 and finally, in Sect. 5 conclusion and suggestion for further research are given.

2 Mathematical Formulation of the p-Median Problem

Mathematical model of the capacitated p-median problem is defined as follows. Demanding points v_i where $i = 1, 2, \ldots, n$ are points in the two dimensional space. They are also potential places for p medians or facilities. Each point v_i has demands of c_i where again $i = 1, 2, \ldots, n$. The shortest distance between points i and j is denoted as $d_{i,j}$ and it represents the Euclidean distance between two points in the plane.

Next, we denoted variable y_{ij} that represents if the demanding point v_i is satisfied by the facility j:

$$y_{ij} = \begin{cases} 1 & \text{if demand of point } i \text{ is satisfied from facility } j \\ 0 & otherwise \end{cases} \tag{1}$$

Capacitated p-median problem is defined by the model given below:

$$\text{minimize } \sum_{i=1}^{n} \sum_{j=1}^{p} d_{ij} y_{ij} \tag{2}$$

subject to

$$\sum_{j=1}^{n} y_{ij} = 1 \quad \text{for } i = 1, 2, \ldots, n \tag{3}$$

$$\sum_{i=1}^{n} x_i = p \tag{4}$$

$$y_{ij} \le x_j \quad \text{for } i, j = 1, 2, \ldots, n \tag{5}$$

$$\sum_{i=1}^{n} c_i y_{ij} \le k_j \quad \text{for } j = 1, 2, \ldots, n \tag{6}$$

$$x_i \in \{0, 1\} \quad \text{for } i = 1, 2, \ldots, n \tag{7}$$

$$y_{ij} \in \{0, 1\} \quad \text{for } i = 1, 2, \ldots, n, \ j = 1, 2, \ldots, p \tag{8}$$

Function 2 is the objective function, sum of distances between demand vertex and corresponding facilities. Equations (3–8) represent constraints. Equation (3) refers to the constrain that each customer can use only one facility. The Eq. (4) limits the number of placed facilities to be p. Equation (5) ensures that each facility can be assigned only to the vertex where is facility. Constraint given by Eq. (6) keeps the number of demands equal or lower to the facility capacity. The last constrains defined by Eqs. (7) and (8) represent the variable domain.

In this paper we propose adjusted bare bones fireworks algorithm for solving this NP-hard optimization problem.

3   Bare Bones Algorithm for Capacitated p-Median Problem

Bare bones fireworks algorithm (BBFWA) is one of the newest versions of the fireworks algorithm (FWA) that was originally proposed in 2010 by Tan and Zhu [24]. BBFWA was proposed in 2018 by Li and Tan [25]. Fireworks algorithm was inspired by the explosion of fireworks. When explode, fireworks produce sparks and in the BBFWA (and all other versions of the FWA) sparks represent potential solutions, while firework's position represents the best solution among the sparks from the previous iteration.

Fireworks algorithm evolved in the last eight years. Drawbacks of the each version were noticed and eventually removed. The first improved version, named enhanced fireworks algorithm, was proposed in 2013 [26]. Next year, in 2014, dynamic search in fireworks [27] and adaptive fireworks were presented [28]. A year later, in 2015, fireworks with covariance mutation [29] was implemented, after which a cooperative framework for fireworks algorithm was proposed in [30]. Guided fireworks algorithm (GFWA) was the previous version presented in 2017 [31]. Bare bones fireworks is the simplest version so far, but very efficient. It was tested on standard benchmark functions and compared to previous versions. It obtained the best results for all test functions.

Since 2010, when the original FWA was presented, FWA and its later version were applied to various real world optimization problems. In [32], it was used for solving constrained portfolio optimization. Original FWA was used for parameter tuning of local-concentration model for spam detection in [33]. Enhanced FWA was applied to wireless sensor networks location problem in [34]. Multilevel image thresholding problem was solved by FWA in [35]. Guided FWA was proposed for solving image registration problem in [37] and JPEG quantization table selection in [38].

As mentioned before, BBFWA is rather simple for implementation, but very powerful optimization algorithm. Contrarily to the previous version, in the BBFWA one firework and fixed number of sparks are used. In each iteration the best solution is saved and in the next iteration, N solutions are generated around it. Exploration and exploitation are implemented by regulating the size of the space around the best solution where the new solutions are generated. If the best solution in the current generation was not improved, window size is reduced in order to better search the promising area in the next iteration. On the other hand, if better solution was found, it means that the search space still is not searched enough, thus the window size is increased. Pseudo code of the BBFWA is given in Algorithm 1.

In Algorithm 1, Lb and Ub are lower and upper boundaries of the search space, respectively. Vector x saves the best solution found at that moment, while $f(x)$ is the objective function. Solutions s_i, $i = 1, 2, \ldots, n$ are uniformly generated around the best solution, i.e. in the hyper-rectangle bounded by $x - A$ and $x + A$, where parameter A determines the size of the hyper-rectangle. If the best solution was not improved, at the end of one iteration, parameter A is multiplied by constant $C_a > 1$, i.e. increased. On the other hand, if the best solution does

Algorithm 1. Bare bones fireworks algorithm [25]

Sample $x \sim U(Lb, Ub)$
Evaluate $f(x)$
$A = Ub - Lb$
repeat
  for $i = 1$ to N **do**
    Sample $s_i \sim U(x - A, x + A)$
    Apply mapping operator to s_i
    Evaluate $f(s_i)$
  end for
  if $\min\limits_{i=1,2,\ldots,N}(f(s_i)) < f(x)$ **then**
    $x = \mathrm{argmin}(f(s_i))$
    $A = C_a A$
  else
    $A = C_r A$
  end if
until maximal iteration number is reached
return x

---

not change, parameter A is decreased by multiplying it by constant $C_r < 1$. At the beginning, $A = Ub - Lb$.

In this paper we used the BBFWA for solving p-median problem.

Dimension of input vector is equal to $2 * p$, the number of facilities that need to be set multiplied by the dimension of the search space (which is in this paper 2). Search range was set to the minimal and maximal coordinates of the demand points, i.e. $[\min(x_i), \max(x_i)]$ where $i = 1, 2$.

Since for this problem the best solution can be the same for large number of consecutive iterations, we limited incrementation of the parameter A so that it cannot be larger then its initial value, $Ub = Lb$.

4   Experimental Results

The proposed algorithm was implemented in Matlab version R2016b. All experiments were performed on Intel ® Core™ i7-3770K CPU at 4 GHz, 8 GB RAM computer with Windows 10 Professional OS.

Parameters were set based on the several experiments. It was noticed that the solutions space needs to be widely searched. Parameters determined to be the best in the original paper where the BBFWA was proposed [25], were not adequate for the considered problem. Mentioned fact resulted by larger values for parameters C_a and C_r. In other words, if the better solution is found, size of the hyper-rectangle around the best solution is increased by factor 1.4 while in case when no better solution is found, search space around the best solution is reduced by factor 0.8. In order to compare the results with the method proposed in [39], we set the population size and the maximal iteration number to $N = 100$ and $maxIter = 50{,}000$, same as in [39].

Our proposed method was compared with genetic algorithm (GA) for continuous capacitated p-median problem proposed in [40]. In [40] parallel genetic algorithm was proposed and tested on 3 real instances $sjc3b$, $sjc4a$ and $sjc4b$ from [41]. Test examples $sjc4a$ and $sjc4b$ have 402 demand nodes that need to be covered by 30 and 40 facilities, respectively. Dataset $sjc3b$ has 300 demand nodes and 30 facilities. The optimal solutions for this data sets are known. For each test set, the proposed BBFWA was run 10 times. We reported the results same way as in [40], confidence interval of percentage difference between the average and the best solution obtained in 10 runs from the optimal solution. Confidence level was 95%. Also, standard deviations were reported. Results obtained by the proposed BBFWA and results from [40] are presented in Table 1.

Table 1. Comparison of our proposed algorithm and the method proposed in [40]

Inst.	n	p	opt	GAklas1		BBFWA	
				Average	Best	Average	Best
sjc3b	300	30	40635.90	0.1692% ± 0.0623%	0.0000%	0.1511% ± 0.0471%	0.0000%
sjc4a	402	30	61925.51	0.3435% ± 0.1377%	0.0329%	0.2384% ± 0.1193%	0.0121%
sjc4b	402	40	52458.02	0.2794% ± 0.0620%	0.0716%	0.2019% ± 0.0494%	0.0665%

It can be seen in Table 1 that our proposed BBFWA outperformed parallel genetic algorithm in all cases in terms of the average, standard deviation and the best found solution in 10 runs. For the first test set, $sjc3a$, both algorithms were able to find the optimal solution at least once in 10 runs. Our proposed BBFWA on average was making 0.1511% error, while genetic algorithm was worse with the error 0.1692%. For the second dataset, our proposed BBFWA was finding better solution in all runs which resulted with average error 0.2384 ± 0.1193 compared to the genetic algorithm that obtained average 0.3435 ± 0.1377. For this dataset the standard deviation is the largest which means that the rather different solutions were found in 10 runs.

Additionally, we compared our results with the genetic algorithm proposed in [42] where five test sets from OR-Library [43] were used. Comparison of the results is shown in Table 2.

The proposed BBFWA again outperformed the genetic algorithm. Both algorithms found the optimal solution in at least one run for datasets $pmed9$, $pmed12$ and $pmed13$. For instances $pmed10$ and $pmed11$, our proposed BBFWA was able to find optimal solutions while the genetic algorithm was not. For the dataset $pmed10$, the proposed BBFWA found on average significantly better solutions while for the other instances the difference was not so large. In all cases, the proposed method outperformed the genetic algorithm. Considering these results and the ones from the previous examples, we can conclude that the BBFWA has good qualities for solving p-median problem.

Table 2. Comparison of the proposed BBFWA and GA proposed in [42]

Inst.	n	p	pt	Best solution		Average solution	
				GA	BBFWA	GA	BBFWA
pmed9	50	5	715	715	715	715.6	**715.0**
pmed10	50	5	829	837	829	838.0	**830.2**
pmed11	100	10	1006	1009	1006	1010.5	**1007.2**
pmed12	100	10	966	966	966	966.9	**966.4**
pmed13	100	10	1026	1026	1026	1028.0	**1026.0**

5   Conclusion

Novel version of the fireworks algorithm, bare bones fireworks algorithm, was proposed for solving NP-hard optimization p-median problem. In this paper, capacitated p-median problem was considered. The proposed method was compared to other algorithms from the literature. Optimal solutions were achieved for all tests which was not the case with genetic algorithm based methods proposed in literature. Further work can include dynamic adjustment of the BBFWA parameters that can additionally improve convergence speed.

Acknowledgment. This research is supported by the Ministry of Education, Science and Technological Development of Republic of Serbia, Grant No. III-44006.

References

1. Martí, R., Corberán, A., Peiró, J.: Scatter search for an uncapacitated p-hub median problem. Comput. Oper. Res. **58**, 53–66 (2015)
2. Herda, M., Haviar, M., et al.: Hybrid genetic algorithms with selective crossover for the capacitated p-median problem. Cent. Eur. J. Oper. Res. **25**, 651–664 (2017)
3. Borah, S., Dewan, H.: A hybrid PSO model for solving continuous p-median problem. In: Prasath, R., O'Reilly, P., Kathirvalavakumar, T. (eds.) MIKE 2014. LNCS (LNAI), vol. 8891, pp. 178–188. Springer, Cham (2014). https://doi.org/10.1007/978-3-319-13817-6_19
4. Kariv, O., Hakimi, S.L.: An algorithmic approach to network location problems. II: the p-medians. SIAM J. Appl. Math. **37**, 539–560 (1979)
5. Eberhart, R., Kennedy, J.: A new optimizer using particle swarm theory. In: Proceedings of the Sixth International Symposium on Micro Machine and Human Science, pp. 39–43. IEEE (1995)
6. Dorigo, M., Gambardella, L.M.: Ant colonies for the travelling salesman problem. Biosystems **43**, 73–81 (1997)
7. Yang, X.-S.: Firefly algorithms for multimodal optimization. In: Watanabe, O., Zeugmann, T. (eds.) SAGA 2009. LNCS, vol. 5792, pp. 169–178. Springer, Heidelberg (2009). https://doi.org/10.1007/978-3-642-04944-6_14
8. Tuba, E., Mrkela, L., Tuba, M.: Support vector machine parameter tuning using firefly algorithm. In: 26th International Conference Radioelektronika, pp. 413–418. IEEE (2016)

9. Bacanin, N., Tuba, M.: Firefly algorithm for cardinality constrained mean-variance portfolio optimization problem with entropy diversity constraint. Sci. World J. 1–16 (2014). Aritcle ID: 721521

10. Tuba, E., Tuba, M., Beko, M.: Two stage wireless sensor node localization using firefly algorithm. In: Yang, X.-S., Nagar, A.K., Joshi, A. (eds.) Smart Trends in Systems, Security and Sustainability. LNNS, vol. 18, pp. 113–120. Springer, Singapore (2018). https://doi.org/10.1007/978-981-10-6916-1_10

11. Wang, G.G., Deb, S., Gao, X.Z., Coelho, L.D.S.: A new metaheuristic optimisation algorithm motivated by elephant herding behaviour. Int. J. Bio-Inspir. Comput. **8**, 394–409 (2016)

12. Tuba, E., Capor-Hrosik, R., Alihodzic, A., Jovanovic, R., Tuba, M.: Chaotic elephant herding optimization algorithm. In: IEEE 16th World Symposium on Applied Machine Intelligence and Informatics (SAMI), pp. 213–216. IEEE (2018)

13. Tuba, E., Alihodzic, A., Tuba, M.: Multilevel image thresholding using elephant herding optimization algorithm. In: Proceedings of 14th International Conference on the Engineering of Modern Electric Systems (EMES), pp. 240–243 (2017)

14. Alihodzic, A., Tuba, E., Capor-Hrosik, R., Dolicanin, E., Tuba, M.: Unmanned aerial vehicle path planning problem by adjusted elephant herding optimization. In: 25th Telecommunications Forum (TELFOR), pp. 804–807 (2017)

15. Shi, Y.: Brain storm optimization algorithm. In: Tan, Y., Shi, Y., Chai, Y., Wang, G. (eds.) ICSI 2011. LNCS, vol. 6728, pp. 303–309. Springer, Heidelberg (2011). https://doi.org/10.1007/978-3-642-21515-5_36

16. Tuba, E., Dolicanin, E., Tuba, M.: Chaotic brain storm optimization algorithm. In: Yin, H., Gao, Y., Chen, S., Wen, Y., Cai, G., Gu, T., Du, J., Tallón-Ballesteros, A.J., Zhang, M. (eds.) IDEAL 2017. LNCS, vol. 10585, pp. 551–559. Springer, Cham (2017). https://doi.org/10.1007/978-3-319-68935-7_60

17. Tuba, E., Capor-Hrosik, R., Alihodzic, A., Tuba, M.: Drone placement for optimal coverage by brain storm optimization algorithm. In: Abraham, A., Muhuri, P.K., Muda, A.K., Gandhi, N. (eds.) HIS 2017. AISC, vol. 734, pp. 167–176. Springer, Cham (2018). https://doi.org/10.1007/978-3-319-76351-4_17

18. Dolicanin, E., Fetahovic, I., Tuba, E., Capor-Hrosik, R., Tuba, M.: Unmanned combat aerial vehicle path planning by brain storm optimization algorithm. Stud. Inform. Control **27**, 15–24 (2018)

19. Yang, X.S.: A new metaheuristic bat-inspired algorithm. Stud. Computat. Intell. **284**, 65–C74 (2010)

20. Tuba, E., Tuba, M., Simian, D.: Adjusted bat algorithm for tuning of support vector machine parameters. In: IEEE Congress on Evolutionary Computation (CEC), pp. 2225–2232. IEEE (2016)

21. Alihodzic, A., Tuba, E., Tuba, M.: An upgraded bat algorithm for tuning extreme learning machines for data classification. In: Proceedings of the Genetic and Evolutionary Computation Conference Companion, pp. 125–126. ACM (2017)

22. Alizadeh, B., Bakhteh, S.: A modified firefly algorithm for general inverse p-median location problems under different distance norms. OPSEARCH **54**, 618–636 (2017)

23. Jayalakshmi, B., Singh, A.: A hybrid artificial bee colony algorithm for the p-median problem with positive/negative weights. OPSEARCH **54**, 67–93 (2017)

24. Tan, Y., Zhu, Y.: Fireworks algorithm for optimization. In: Tan, Y., Shi, Y., Tan, K.C. (eds.) ICSI 2010. LNCS, vol. 6145, pp. 355–364. Springer, Heidelberg (2010). https://doi.org/10.1007/978-3-642-13495-1_44

25. Li, J., Tan, Y.: The bare bones fireworks algorithm: a minimalist global optimizer. Appl. Soft Comput. **62**, 454–462 (2018)

26. Zheng, S., Janecek, A., Tan, Y.: Enhanced fireworks algorithm. In: IEEE Congress on Evolutionary Computation, pp. 2069–2077. IEEE (2013)
27. Zheng, S., Janecek, A., Li, J., Tan, Y.: Dynamic search in fireworks algorithm. In: IEEE Congress on Evolutionary Computation (CEC), pp. 3222–3229. IEEE (2014)
28. Li, J., Zheng, S., Tan, Y.: Adaptive fireworks algorithm. In: 2014 IEEE Congress on Evolutionary Computation, pp. 3214–3221. IEEE (2014)
29. Yu, C., Tan, Y.: Fireworks algorithm with covariance mutation. In: IEEE Congress on Evolutionary Computation (CEC), pp. 1250–1256. IEEE (2015)
30. Zheng, S., Li, J., Janecek, A., Tan, Y.: A cooperative framework for fireworks algorithm. IEEE/ACM Trans. Comput. Biol. Bioinform. **14**, 27–41 (2015)
31. Li, J., Zheng, S., Tan, Y.: The effect of information utilization: Introducing a novel guiding spark in the fireworks algorithm. IEEE Trans. Evol. Comput. **21**, 153–166 (2017)
32. Bacanin, N., Tuba, M.: Fireworks algorithm applied to constrained portfolio optimization problem. In: IEEE Congress on Evolutionary Computation (CEC 2015), pp. 1242–1249 (2015)
33. He, W., Mi, G., Tan, Y.: Parameter optimization of local-concentration model for spam detection by using fireworks algorithm. In: Tan, Y., Shi, Y., Mo, H. (eds.) ICSI 2013. LNCS, vol. 7928, pp. 439–450. Springer, Heidelberg (2013). https://doi.org/10.1007/978-3-642-38703-6_52
34. Arsic, A., Tuba, M., Jordanski, M.: Fireworks algorithm applied to wireless sensor networks localization problem. In: IEEE Congress on Evolutionary Computation (CEC), pp. 4038–4044. IEEE (2016)
35. Tuba, M., Bacanin, N., Alihodzic, A.: Multilevel image thresholding by fireworks algorithm. In: Proceedings of the 25th International Conference Radioelektronika, pp. 326–330 (2015)
36. Tan, Y.: Implementation of fireworks algorithm based on GPU. In: Tan, Y. (ed.) Fireworks Algorithm, pp. 227–243. Springer, Heidelberg (2015). https://doi.org/10.1007/978-3-662-46353-6_14
37. Tuba, E., Tuba, M., Dolicanin, E.: Adjusted fireworks algorithm applied to retinal image registration. Stud. Inform. Control **26**, 33–42 (2017)
38. Tuba, E., Tuba, M., Simian, D., Jovanovic, R.: JPEG quantization table optimization by guided fireworks algorithm. In: Brimkov, V.E., Barneva, R.P. (eds.) IWCIA 2017. LNCS, vol. 10256, pp. 294–307. Springer, Cham (2017). https://doi.org/10.1007/978-3-319-59108-7_23
39. Rabie, H.M., El-Khodary, I.A., Tharwat, A.A.: Particle swarm optimization algorithm for the continuous p-median location problems. In: 10th International Computer Engineering Conference (ICENCO), pp. 81–86. IEEE (2014)
40. Herda, M.: Parallel genetic algorithm for capacitated p-median problem. Procedia Eng. **192**, 313–317 (2017)
41. Lorena, L.A., Senne, E.L.: A column generation approach to capacitated p-median problems. Comput. Oper. Res. **31**, 863–876 (2004)
42. Herda, M.: Combined genetic algorithm for capacitated p-median problem. In: 16th IEEE International Symposium on Computational Intelligence and Informatics (CINTI), pp. 151–154. IEEE (2015)
43. Beasley, J.E.: OR-library: distributing test problems by electronic mail. J. Oper. Res. Soc. **41**, 1069–1072 (1990)

Bacterial Foraging Optimization

Differential Structure-Redesigned-Based Bacterial Foraging Optimization

Lu Xiao[1], Jinsong Chen[2], Lulu Zuo[1(✉)], Huan Wang[3],
and Lijing Tan[4]

[1] College of Management, Shenzhen University, Shenzhen 518060, China
ghllu.zuo@gmail.com
[2] Department of Information Management,
National Yunlin University of Science and Technology,
Douliu, Yunlin 64002, Taiwan
[3] The Graduate School of Business Administration,
Meiji University, Tokyo, Japan
taoxueshi2020@gmail.com
[4] College of Management, Shenzhen Institute of Information Technology,
Shenzhen 518172, China

Abstract. This paper proposes an improved bacterial forging optimization with differential tumble, perturbation, and cruising mechanisms, abbreviated as DPCBFO. In DPCBFO, the differential information between the population and the optimal individual is used to guide the tumble direction of the bacteria. The strategy of perturbation is employed to enhance the global search ability of the bacteria. While a new cruising mechanism is proposed in this study to improve the possibility of searching for the optimal by comparing the current position with the others obtained in the next chemotaxis steps. In addition, to reduce the computation complexity, the vectorized parallel evaluation is applied in the chemotaxis process. The performance of the proposed DPCBFO is evaluated on eight well-known benchmark functions. And the simulation results illustrate that the proposed DPCBFO achieves the superior performance on all functions.

Keywords: Bacterial forging optimization · Differential tumble
Cross perturbation · Cruising mechanism

1 Introduction

Inspired by the social behavior in the biological system, swarm intelligent optimization algorithms are proposed by many scientists, such as particle swarm optimization algorithm (PSO), ant colony optimization (ACO) and Artificial fish school algorithm (AFSA). Recently, inspired by the foraging behavior of the E. coli bacteria, bacterial foraging optimization (BFO) [1] was first proposed as a new swarm intelligent algorithm. Due to the superior efficiency in dealing with real-world optimization problems (e.g. face recognition problem [2], feature selection problem [3] and vehicle routing problem [4]), BFO has attracted the attention of researchers from different fields.

However, due to the fixed step size and a lack of information communication between bacterial individuals, premature convergence and higher computational

© Springer International Publishing AG, part of Springer Nature 2018
Y. Tan et al. (Eds.): ICSI 2018, LNCS 10941, pp. 295–303, 2018.
https://doi.org/10.1007/978-3-319-93815-8_29

complexity are the main shortcomings in the original BFO. So many improved versions of BFO were proposed to address these two issues. These improved algorithms are classified into two categories. Based on the adaptive chemotaxis step, one category is to choose the local optimal and global optimal in the entire process. According to the current and best positions of bacteria, a new improved version of BFO [5] adaptively adjusted chemotaxis step and obtained the superior performance on some benchmark functions. In [6], combining some strategies (i.e. bacterial chemotaxis method, communication mechanism and adaptive foraging strategy), a new bacterial colony foraging (BCF) was proposed to improve the convergence performance. In order to improve exploration and exploitation abilities, the unit length of the chemotaxis step was adjusted according to the swarm information and the gravitational search method in the effective bacterial foraging optimization (EBFO) [7]. The other category focuses on increasing communication between bacteria by introducing a new method to the original BFO. Aiming at obtaining lower computational complexity and maintaining the critical search capability, a general loop strategy was employed to substitute the nested loop and eliminate the reproduction step in the modified BFO [8]. The multi-level thresholding approach is introduced in the modified BFO [9] for enhancing the convergence performance. In addition, a novel modification of BFO [10] with new designed chemotaxis and conjugation strategies was proposed to address the shortcoming of premature convergence. Though many modified version of BFO has been developed in recent years, the premature convergence and higher computational complexity are still the major problems.

In this paper, based on three mechanisms (i.e. differential tumble, cross perturbation and cruising mechanism), a new modified version of BFO is proposed to enhance the convergence performance and reduce the computational complexity. Differential tumble method is developed and embedded in the chemotaxis process to improve the convergence speed. In order to enhance the population diversity, cross perturbation mechanism is introduced in the proposed DPCBFO algorithm. In addition, cruising mechanism is used for bacterial to obtain the optimal foraging. Compared with two algorithms (genetic algorithm and BFO), the new proposed combination algorithm is tested on eight benchmark functions.

The rest of organized as follows. Section 2 briefly describes the BFO algorithm. In Sect. 3, the novel DPCBFO algorithm is shown in detail. Section 4 gives experimental results of the simulations on benchmark functions. Finally, the conclusion is presented in Sect. 5.

2 Original BFO Algorithm

BFO [1], a recent stochastic search evolutionary algorithm, is first proposed by Passino, which has three steps in the process, including chemotaxis, reproduction, and elimination & dispersal.

Chemotaxis: Bacteria move toward food by swimming or tumbling of flagella. The bacteria can swim a few steps in a particular direction and then start to tumble, which is beneficial for find the optimal food.

Reproduction: Based on evaluating the fitness function as the health standard, the least healthy half of bacteria die and the other healthier bacteria is reproduced in the same location. Hence, the population of bacteria is constant.

Elimination & dispersal: Bacteria will undergo dramatic changes as the environment changes. When the environment is constant, the bacteria will change as the food decreases.

In addition, BFO also has the characteristics of the cluster. Bacteria can find their own way of foraging, and receive the signals from others. Meanwhile, bacteria keep a safe distance between each other to ensure their living space. Therefore, the foraging behavior of each bacterium in BFO is influenced by two factors: one is its own behavior and the other is the information transmitted by other bacteria.

3   The Proposed DPCBFO Algorithm

Based on the differential, perturbation, and cruising mechanism, the proposed algorithm is described in details as follows.

3.1   Differential Tumbling Mechanism

In the original BFO algorithm, the movements of bacteria are randomly generated. Although it is an appropriate simulation of E. coli, it brings out some disadvantages, e.g. low convergence rate, poor search performance.

Inspired by mutation method of the individual in differential evolution (DE) [11], a new method of the chemotactic step is proposed based on the optimal position. The direction of swimming is obtained by subtracting each bacterial position from the optimal bacterial position. So the bacteria will be distributed around the optimal position. In this way, it makes the algorithm explore more optimal values near the current optimal position. The new optimal value is taken as the center of the next-generation distribution. This strategy will facilitate the convergence rate. The overall process can be modeled as:

$$\Phi_i = C_i \cdot \left(K_1 \cdot \left(X_{best,G} - X_{r,G} \right) + K_2 \cdot \left(X_{best,G} - X_{i,G} \right) \right) \tag{1}$$

where C_i is the chemotactic step size. K indicates a vector, is a random number between 0 to 1. K_1 and K_2 are two different random numbers of K. D is the dimension of the problem. G is the current number of iterations. $X_{best,G}$ is the optimal position in the current generation. r means the random integer in the range of [1, NP] and i means particle ordinal. NP is the swarm size of bacteria.

3.2   Cross Perturbation Mechanism

In original BFO, tumbling can be seen as a perturbation before the bacteria swim. However, the degree of original tumbling perturbation is too severe, which will lead to poor search performance.

In DPCBFO, after calculating the direction of tumbling, the current population will be perturbed by the direction (i.e. the position of the bacteria was superimposed by the cross perturbation formula with the corresponding tumbling direction). Inspired by crossover operator of DE, a novel equation is proposed as follows.

$$x_{i,G}^j = \begin{cases} x_{i,G}^j + \phi_{i,G}^j & if\,(rand_i^j \le CR) \\ x_{i,G}^j & otherwise \end{cases} \quad j = 1, 2, \ldots, D \qquad (2)$$

Based on the position vector, i.e. $X_{i,G} = \left\{ x_{i,G}^1, x_{i,G}^2, \ldots, x_{i,G}^D \right\}$, we select partial vector parameter values from the tumbling direction to being superimposed on the original value of x in the cross-perturbation formula. CR means the crossover probability in the range from 0 to 1. $\Phi_{i,G} = \left\{ \phi_{i,G}^1, \phi_{i,G}^2, \ldots, \phi_{i,G}^D \right\}$ means the position vector of tumbling direction i. $rand_i^j$ is a random number between 0 to 1. If $rand_i^j$ is smaller than CR or equal to it, $x_{i,G}^j$ will replace by the sum of $x_{i,G}^j$ and $\phi_{i,G}^j$. Otherwise, $x_{i,G}^j$ remains constant. We can control the degree of perturbation by changing the value of CR. The softness of perturbation is ensured if making tumbling vector parameter $\phi_{i,G}^j$ as a perturbation value. So it will not break up the trend of search optimal, and avoid to get into premature convergence.

3.3 Cruising Mechanism and Chemotactic Algorithm Structure Improvement

The slow convergence speed is the key problem in BFO algorithm. Low convergence speed is accounted for the larger numbers of cycles performed in the iterations. In each iteration, the chemotactic step needs to evaluate multiple positions. Therefore, a novel mechanism – Cruising method, is proposed to obtain the optimal solution. It allows bacteria to traverse all position according to the parameters of swimming times and the direction of swimming. Then bacteria return to the optimal position in the process (Fig. 1).

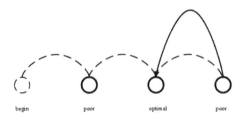

begin   poor   optimal   poor

Fig. 1. The diagram of cruising mechanism

The advantage of cruising mechanism is that the bacteria will not stop like the original BFO when it encounters a bad point. It will continue to travel completely and get the optimal point of the entire path. The experiment makes bacteria be trapped into local optima in a low possibility. At the same time, due to the fixed number of swims, the running speed will be improved by using parallel computing.

Based on the vectorizable parallel computing of cruising mechanism, the algorithm structure of the chemotactic step is improved. As shown in Fig. 2, the left is the chemotaxis operation of BFO, and the right is the chemotaxis operation of DPCBFO.

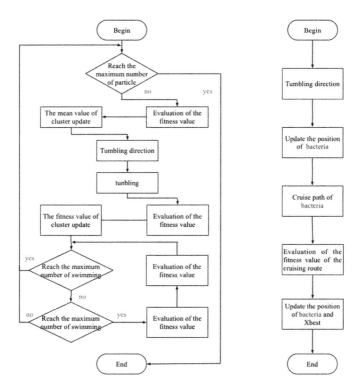

Fig. 2. The comparison of BFO chemotaxis structure and DPCBFO chemotaxis structure

In the original BFO, there are three fitness evaluations within the chemotaxis step (pre-cruise evaluation, after-cruise evaluation, and swimming evaluation). In cruising mechanism of DPCBFO, the update point is selected by using greedy way. Therefore, the above three assessments can be regarded as swimming times and incorporated into the evaluation of the fitness value of the cruising route. With the swimming parameters N_s controlling, the procedure calls the function of evaluation only once in the entire chemotaxis. And, we simplify all kinds of loops and the cluster mechanism in the chemotactic algorithm, due to the vectorized parallel computing.

4   Experiment

In order to compare DPCBFO with the original BFO and genetic algorithm (GA), the performance of DPCBFO is evaluated on eight benchmark functions in this section.

4.1   Benchmark Function and Parameters Setting

To evaluate the performance of DPCBFO, eight well-known benchmark functions [12] is used in this paper, including Sphere F1, Schwefel F2, Rosenbrock F3, Sum of different power F4, Rastrigin F5, Sin F6, Ackley F7 and Quartic F8. In order to enhance the probability of finding the optimal value from the beginning, the asymmetric initialization method [13] is used in this proposed algorithm. Among these eight functions, F1–F4 are unimodal functions and F5–F8 are multimodal functions. The optimal value is 0. All functions have the dimension of 30.

N_{re} means the number of replication in the elimination & dispersal step. T_{ed} means the length of elimination & dispersal. N_s is the swimming times of bacteria per round. The population of all algorithms is 50. The maximum number of iterations is 5000. Each function runs 30 times. The parameters of GA and BFO all come from the literature [14]. Detailed parameters of BFO: migration times $N_{ed} = 2$, chemotaxis times $N_c = 100$, swimming times $N_s = 4$, size of swimming step $C = 0.1$ and migration probability $P_{ed} = 0.25$. To satisfy 5000 iterations, N_{re} is set to 25. The parameters setting of DPCBFO is shown in Table 1.

Table 1. Parameters setting

Function	T_{ed}	N_{re}	P_{ed}	CR	C	N_s
Sphere	5000	1	0.4	0.5	0.5	4
Schwefel	5000	1	0.4	0.5	0.5	4
Rosenbrock	50	2	0.4	0.01	0.5	4
Sum of different power	5000	1	0.4	0.5	0.5	4
Rastrigin	50	2	0.4	0.01	0.5	4
Sin	50	2	0.4	0	0.5	4
Ackley	50	2	0.4	0	0.5	4
Quartic	50	2	0.4	0	0.5	4

4.2   Experimental Result and Analyses

Table 2 displays the simulation results of the comparative algorithms (i.e. DPCBFO, BFO, and GA). On each function, the optimal value of the three algorithms is marked as bold. The convergence curves of the comparative algorithms are shown in Fig. 3. As shown in Table 2, the proposed algorithm obtains the superiority on both unimodal function and multimodal functions in terms of convergence speed and convergence performance.

The proposed algorithm is a variant of BFO, the performance of the new framework is tested with a similar experimental setting. In the experiment, the optimal value can be

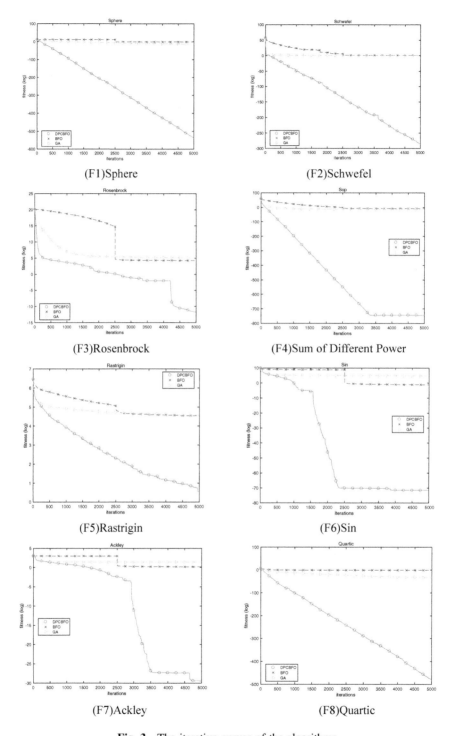

(F1)Sphere

(F2)Schwefel

(F3)Rosenbrock

(F4)Sum of Different Power

(F5)Rastrigin

(F6)Sin

(F7)Ackley

(F8)Quartic

Fig. 3. The iterative curves of the algorithms

Table 2. The experimental results of the benchmark functions

Function	Result	DPCBFO	BFO	GA
Sphere	Mean	**4.592E−234**	3.988E−01	2.898E−06
	SD	**0.000E+00**	7.165E−03	3.028E−12
	Time	**0.86**	14.13	2.31
Schwefel	Mean	**4.887E−125**	3.171E+00	1.726E+00
	SD	**3.834E−248**	2.932E−01	6.085E−01
	Time	**0.95**	13.58	2.64
Rosenbrock	Mean	**7.552E−06**	6.843E+01	1.633E+02
	SD	**4.173E−10**	8.103E+01	1.947E+04
	Time	**1.18**	17.26	3.12
Sum of different power	Mean	**4.900e−324**	3.954E−04	2.813E−07
	SD	**0.000E+00**	5.049E−08	2.531E−14
	Time	**1.83**	28.85	6.30
Rastrigin	Mean	**1.758E+00**	9.407E+01	9.722E+01
	SD	**2.027E+00**	3.534E+02	1.576E+03
	Time	**1.10**	13.25	2.65
Sin	Mean	**8.202E−32**	3.233E−01	1.310E+02
	SD	**4.761E−62**	5.189E−03	3.525E+03
	Time	**1.37**	15.76	3.54
Ackley	Mean	**1.435E−13**	1.184E+00	4.109E+00
	SD	**3.748E−26**	4.688E−02	7.549E−01
	Time	**1.18**	13.78	2.92
Quartic	Mean	**2.293E−209**	2.261E−01	1.627E−15
	SD	**0.000E+00**	3.653E−03	3.100E−29
	Time	**1.93**	14.45	3.12

found without being copied or migrated in unimodal function. And in multimodal functions, frequent copying and migration within a small period are required to enhance the population diversity and optimal point. At the same time, the convergence rate will have an obvious improvement in unimodal function with the participation of CR. Although we set CR to 0 in some multimodal function, other CR values that are set to only 0.01 have a very large effect.

5   Conclusions

In order to verify the optimization capabilities of the proposed DPCBFO algorithm, eight well-known benchmark functions are used to test its performance. The results illustrate that DPCBFO has the best performance and computational performance. And it is significantly better than the original BFO. In DPCBFO, we use the differential tumbling direction formula to deal with the problem of low efficiency in the original formula. The cross-perturbation mechanism reduces the possibility of falling into local optimum. And the parallel computing based on the cruising mechanism greatly reduces the running time of the algorithm. Different functions are designed different parameter styles, so the establishment of adaptive parameter control mechanism is the future research direction.

Acknowledgment. This work is partially supported by The National Natural Science Foundation of China (Grants No. 61472257), Natural Science Foundation of Guangdong Province (2016A030310074). Lu Xiao and Jinsong Chen contributed equally to this paper and shared the first authorship.

References

1. Passino, K.M.: Biomimicry of bacterial foraging for distributed optimization and control. IEEE Control Syst. **22**(3), 52–67 (2002)
2. Panda, R., Naik, M.K.: A novel adaptive crossover bacterial foraging optimization algorithm for linear discriminant analysis based face recognition. Appl. Soft Comput. **30**(C), 722–736 (2015)
3. Chen, Y.P., Li, Y., Wang, G., Zheng, Y.F., Xu, Q., Fan, J.H., et al.: A novel bacterial foraging optimization algorithm for feature selection. Expert Syst. Appl. Int. J. **83**(C), 1–17 (2017)
4. Tan, L., Lin, F., Wang, H.: Adaptive comprehensive learning bacterial foraging optimization and its application on vehicle routing problem with time windows. Nat. Comput. **151**(3), 1208–1215 (2015)
5. Tan, L.J., Yi, W.J., Yang, C., Feng, Y.Y.: Adaptive structure-redesigned-based bacterial foraging optimization. In: Huang, D.-S., Jo, K.-H. (eds.) ICIC 2016. LNCS, vol. 9772, pp. 897–907. Springer, Cham (2016). https://doi.org/10.1007/978-3-319-42294-7_80
6. Chen, H., Niu, B., Ma, L., Su, W., Zhu, Y.: Bacterial colony foraging optimization. Nat. Comput. **137**(2), 268–284 (2014)
7. Zhao, W., Wang, L.: An effective bacterial foraging optimizer for global optimization. Inf. Sci. **329**, 719–735 (2015)
8. Niu, B., Liu, J., Wu, T., Chu, X.H., Wang, Z.X., Liu, Y.M.: Coevolutionary structure-redesigned-based bacterial foraging optimization. IEEE/ACM Trans. Comput. Biol. Bioinform. **PP** (99), 1 (2017)
9. Tang, K., Xiao, X., Wu, J., Yang, J., Luo, L.: An improved multilevel thresholding approach based modified bacterial foraging optimization. Appl. Intell. **46**(1), 1–13 (2017)
10. Yang, C., Ji, J., Liu, J., Yin, B.: Bacterial foraging optimization using novel chemotaxis and conjugation strategies. Inf. Sci. Int. J. **363**(C), 72–95 (2016)
11. Mallipeddi, R., Suganthan, P.N., Pan, Q.K., Tasgetiren, M.F.: Differential evolution algorithm with ensemble of parameters and mutation strategies. Appl. Soft Comput. **11**(2), 1679–1696 (2011)
12. Niu, B., Liu, J., Zhang, F., Yi, W.: A cooperative structure-redesigned-based bacterial foraging optimization with guided and stochastic movements. In: Huang, D.-S., Jo, K.-H. (eds.) ICIC 2016. LNCS, vol. 9772, pp. 918–927. Springer, Cham (2016). https://doi.org/10.1007/978-3-319-42294-7_82
13. Niu, B.: Bacterial Colony Optimization and Bionic Management. Science Press (2014)
14. Wang, H., Zuo, L., Liu, J., Yang, C., Li, Ya., Baek, J.: A comparison of heuristic algorithms for bus dispatch. In: Tan, Y., Takagi, H., Shi, Y., Niu, B. (eds.) ICSI 2017. LNCS, vol. 10386, pp. 511–518. Springer, Cham (2017). https://doi.org/10.1007/978-3-319-61833-3_54

An Algorithm Based on the Bacterial Swarm and Its Application in Autonomous Navigation Problems

Fredy Martínez[1]([✉])[iD], Angelica Rendón[1], and Mario Arbulú[2]

[1] District University Francisco José de Caldas, Bogotá D.C, Colombia
fhmartinezs@udistrital.edu.co, avrendonc@correo.udistrital.edu.co
[2] Corporación Unificada Nacional de Educación Superior, Bogotá D.C, Colombia
mario_arbulu@cun.edu.co
http://www.udistrital.edu.co

Abstract. Path planning is a very important problem in robotics, especially in the development of Automatic Guided Vehicles (AGVs). These problems are usually formulated as search problems, so many search algorithms with a high level of intelligence are evaluated to solve them. We propose a navigation algorithm based on bacterial swarming from a simplified model of bacterium that promises simple designs both at the system level and at the agent level. The most important feature of the algorithm is the inclusion of bacterial Quorum Sensing (QS), which reduces the convergence time, which is the major disadvantage of the scheme. The results in both simulation and real prototypes show not only stability but higher performance in convergence speed, showing that the strategy is feasible and valid for decentralized autonomous navigation.

Keywords: Artificial bacterium · Autonomous · Path planning
Quorum Sensing

1 Introduction

One of the objectives of autonomous robotics is the development of AGVs [8]. These vehicles allow the autonomous transport of cargo along more or less pre-defined routes between a point of origin and a target point. It is desirable in these tasks that the vehicle be autonomous, find its destination regardless of its current position, and solve problems caused by obstacles on the path. In addition, depending on the environment and type of cargo, it is ideal to have swarms of these vehicles. This type of activity is of great importance in industrial automation schemes, since it allows the design of intelligent warehouses, the implementation of flexible manufacturing systems, and considerably reduce production times and costs [2,3].

Path planning is one of the key problems to be solved in the operation of these autonomous vehicles [6,10]. This problem focuses specifically on finding a

© Springer International Publishing AG, part of Springer Nature 2018
Y. Tan et al. (Eds.): ICSI 2018, LNCS 10941, pp. 304–313, 2018.
https://doi.org/10.1007/978-3-319-93815-8_30

safe route from the current position of the robot vehicle to the final target position, intelligently dodging obstacles in the environment, and according to some motion policy that contemplates performance conditions and safe movement. Path planning problems can be divided into two categories according to the characteristics of the environment: static environments (do not change during robot navigation) and dynamic environments (change during navigation task).

The majority of AGV's researches contemplate static and generally observable environments, which allows the mapping of the environment and the design of the route in an off-line way, to then instruct the movement to the robots [5]. However, in real industrial environments the environments are usually dynamic, with continuous movements of people and equipment. There are different documented cases in which biological systems efficiently solve this type of problems, one of these schemes is observed in the interaction between bacteria [9, 11].

Self-assembly processes are responsible for the generation of order in nature [4]. They involve components at different scales, such as molecules, cells, organisms, communities, ecosystems and weather systems. These interactions between elements of relatively simple structure can be analyzed, modeled and replicated in the design of artificial systems. One of these systems is the bacterial communities. As biological organisms bacteria have a very simple structure, their behavior can be described from local interactions between organisms and with the environment, and as a system they have proven to be very successful in very adverse conditions [1].

In the biological model, the cell-cell communication is performed through the exchange of chemical molecules called auto inducers. This mechanism, called Quorum Sensing (QS), allows bacteria to monitor their environment for the presence of other bacteria, and thus, to respond to fluctuations in the number and/or species present. That means, coordinate collective behavior in bacteria under environment conditions [7].

During operation of this mechanism, the concentration of the signal molecule reflects the number of bacterial cells in a particular area. The detection of a threshold concentration, a molecular signal, indicates that the population has reached the quorum, i.e., is ready to perform a specific collective behavior. This means that QS is a mechanism used by bacteria to activate phenotypic changes in the population, i.e., to coordinate gene-expression.

This research proposes a different design scheme inspired by this mechanism of gene expression control, mechanism which is dependent on cell density, and that allows to coordinate the navigation of a swarm of robots by means of indications in the environment (landmarks), and local communication between robots. The tasks to be carried out by robots are modeled as behaviours that are expressed by the organism according to population density and a control policy. That is, robots contain code equivalent to gene expression, which is responsible for social behaviors of independent cells using extracellular signals.

The paper is organized as follows. In Sect. 2 presents a description of the problem. Section 3 describes the proposed strategy and a general design outline for basic navigation tasks. Section 4 introduces some results obtained with the proposed strategy. Finally, conclusion and discussion are presented in Sect. 5.

2 Problem Statement

The multi-agent model adopted for artificial systems design is composed of a set of artificial bacteria or agents. This set of agents, and their interactions, reflect the dynamics that will solve the problems. All agents are identical in design. Nevertheless, to solve tasks, each of them undergoes certain behavior inside the system along the time.

A bacterium is a pair

$$V = (f, p) \tag{1}$$

where f is a nonnegative integer $(f \in \mathbb{Z}^+)$ that indicates the amount of neighboring bacteria in contact, and p is a point in q-dimensional space $(p \in \mathbb{R}^q)$.

The population density is evaluated using the distance between bacteria. Let:

$$d_{ij} = d(V_i, V_j) \tag{2}$$

as the distance between bacteria V_i and V_j, which is calculated by any appropriate norm. A bacterial population is defined as a nonempty set of bacteria.

$$W_0 = \{V_1, V_2, V_3, \cdots, V_m\} \tag{3}$$

with non-zero distance among bacteria:

$$d_{ij} \neq 0, \qquad \forall i, j \quad , \quad i \neq j \tag{4}$$

A group of bacteria is characterized by the parameter T, the quorum threshold, it is the parameter defining whether or not it has reached the quorum. The principle of the algorithm based on QS is the grouping of agents. Agents are grouped into different areas of the environment according to local readings and their genome that follows some search criteria. Since the proposed model considers only local interactions, and that the goal of the design focuses on the coordination of the movement of the agents, the QS mechanism should facilitate the movement of agents in the environment towards areas with sufficient population, reflecting the decisions of many agents.

The system is composed of the n agents (n artificial bacteria) as a continuous system, whose dynamics can be described by differential equations. The agents in this system, all identical in design, experience at any instant a behavior l of a set l_a of possible behaviors of the agents. Furthermore, each agent is always performing a behavior at any given time. The variables in these differential equations indicate the size of the bacterial population that belongs to each of these behaviors.

In particular, considering the circumstances under which bacteria can be grouped, and that the intensity of this grouping is who allows to find a solution,

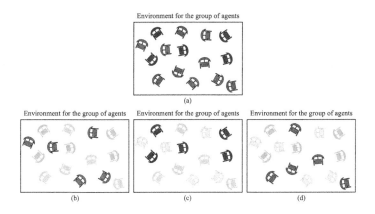

Fig. 1. System and agents with three different behaviors. (a) System composed of a group of agents (bacteria) in a three-stage process ($a = 3$), (b) system agents running behavior l_1, (c) system agents running behavior l_2, and (d) system agents running behavior l_3.

we propose a general three-stage model ($a = 3$). The additional intermediate stage should facilitate the population changes (Fig. 1).

Groups of agents at a given time experiencing the same behavior (any of the a behaviors). Therefore, the system can be analyzed as consisting of groups of agents characterized by a common behavior of a set of behaviors l_a.

The model for this system is hybrid, the different agent behaviors are triggered by certain events (event-based). The set of agents, each with a continuous dynamic $\boldsymbol{X}_a$, switches between different behaviors during the development of the task. The group of agents simultaneously experiencing the same behavior, it also has a continuous collective behavior, so the system also has a continuous dynamic $\boldsymbol{X}_p$. When changing behavior one or more system agents (with discrete control mode determined by $\boldsymbol{L}_a$), changes the system as well (with discrete control mode determined by $\boldsymbol{L}_p$).

This means that the behavior space of the system is divided into a set $\boldsymbol{L}_p$ of l_a regions. The state of the system H_p is therefore defined by the values of the continuous variables of the system $\boldsymbol{X}_p$ and the discrete control mode determined by $\boldsymbol{L}_p$ (Fig. 2).

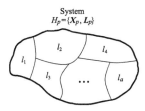

Fig. 2. System and its fractions characterized by their behavior.

Each of these population fractions is characterized by a set of differential equations with state variables (vectors) denoted by:

$$x_i \quad / \quad i = 1, 2, 3, \cdots, b \tag{5}$$

A set of dimension b (the number of grouping areas defined by the agents in the system) that allows to describe the dynamics of the a different behaviors. The hybrid system then can be described as:

$$
\begin{aligned}
H_p &= \{\boldsymbol{X}_p, \boldsymbol{L}_p\} \\
\boldsymbol{X}_p &\subset \mathbb{R}^b \\
l_a &\subset \boldsymbol{L}_p
\end{aligned}
\tag{6}
$$

The algorithm does not intend to explicitly define the position of the robots. On the contrary, it looks to abstract the information from the environment to reduce the complexity in the design of the path. These features ensure navigation in environments with obstacles, even when they are in motion. It also eliminates the problem of impossible movements for the robot, since the dynamics of the robot is not part of the model. This allows the normal differences between robots, and even the use of radically different robots. Also, the problem of controller design is independent of the number of robots, which promises scalability to large groups and system functionality against the failure of a few of them.

3   Methodology

The research proposes the system as a three-stage process of individual behaviors. These three basic behaviors are: (1) Reproduction, (2) Exploration, and (3) Virulence.

The first behavior, *Reproduction*, allows to activate the robot in the environment. The last behavior, *Virulence*, must be the robot's final behavior when it finds the target area. The second behavior, *Exploration*, should help to find potential grouping areas. The principle of the algorithm based on QS is the grouping of agents. Agents are grouped into different areas of the environment according to local readings and their genome (internal code) that follows some search criteria. The areas with the highest number of agents must show virulence and will correspond navigation task solution. These population sizes are then the most important variables in the model.

The population size of each of these fractions is characterized by a continuous variable in the following way:

- R Agents whose behavior is reproduction.
- X_i Agents whose behavior is exploration in the area i of a total of b areas in the environment.
- Z_i Agents whose behavior is virulence in the area i of a total of b areas in the environment.

When agents begin to explore and activate their virulence, they begin to group in different areas of the environment (a total of b areas). This increases the number of system variables, where i indicates the grouping area of the agents. When the agents are reproducing there is no grouping.

The reproduction is the first behavior for all bacteria. After an artificial agent is enabled on the system (R), it begins to take local information but without activating its virulence (X_i), to finally activate its virulence when the quorum is fulfilled (Z_i). The activation or virulence of agents that are exploring the environment starts when $Z_i = T$, the quorum threshold. Both explorers and virulent can switch to new areas of the environment if the local information indicates that they are in areas of higher performance (according to the task). This is the most important part of the process, because it gives the opportunity to each agent individually to find the best solution.

This parallel navigation structure allows that the explorers consider different areas of the environment before gathering around some of them. Thus, when a quorum is reached, the agents begin to become virulent according to the best option for each of them. The flow chart of Fig. 3 shows the rules by which agents interact with each other and with the environment to meet the goal.

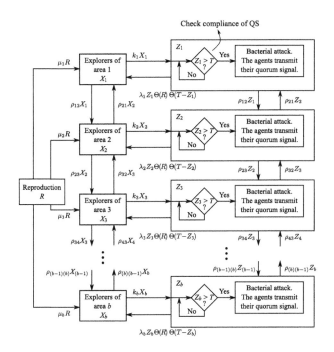

Fig. 3. Flowchart for the proposed dynamic of bacterial QS.

4   Results

The strategy was evaluated in different simulations and real platforms. In a first simulated case we designed a simple navigation task. Let us think in an environment with four high performance areas (for example, meeting areas with some interesting variable: temperature, noise, light, humidity, ...) denoted by the points p_1, p_2, p_3 and p_4. Among these points, we will assume that p_1, p_2 and p_4 have a similar performance (local maxima, the variable is higher than the average values of the environment, but not the maximum), while point p_3 has a superior performance (global maximum, the variable has the maximum value in the environment). Under these conditions, we expect that the agents are distributed in the environment and navigate initially grouped around these four points. But then, they must migrate to the point of higher performance p_3.

We assume for simplicity that for the initial selection of the four areas do not exist favoritism criteria, i.e.:

$$\mu_1 = \mu_2 = \mu_3 = \mu_4 = \mu$$
$$\lambda_1 = \lambda_2 = \lambda_3 = \lambda_4 = \lambda \tag{7}$$

The migration process is based solely on the performance of the areas detected by the agents (ρ and k calculation) and the QS. Accordingly, the system of equations can be written as ecu. (8).

$$\dot{R} = -4\mu R$$
$$\dot{X}_1 = \mu R + \lambda Z_1 \Theta(R) \Theta(T - Z_1) - \rho_{12}X_1 + \rho_{21}X_2 - k_1 X_1$$
$$\dot{X}_2 = \mu R + \lambda Z_2 \Theta(R) \Theta(T - Z_2) - \rho_{23}X_2 + \rho_{32}X_3 + \rho_{12}X_1 - \rho_{21}X_2 - k_2 X_2$$
$$\dot{X}_3 = \mu R + \lambda Z_3 \Theta(R) \Theta(T - Z_3) - \rho_{34}X_3 + \rho_{43}X_4 + \rho_{23}X_2 - \rho_{32}X_3 - k_3 X_3$$
$$\dot{X}_4 = \mu R + \lambda Z_4 \Theta(R) \Theta(T - Z_4) + \rho_{34}X_3 - \rho_{43}X_4 - k_4 X_4 \tag{8}$$
$$\dot{Z}_1 = k_1 X_1 - \rho_{12}Z_1 + \rho_{21}Z_2 - \lambda Z_1 \theta(R) \Theta(T - Z_1)$$
$$\dot{Z}_2 = k_2 X_2 - \rho_{23}Z_2 + \rho_{32}Z_3 + \rho_{12}Z_1 - \rho_{21}Z_2 - \lambda Z_2 \theta(R) \Theta(T - Z_2)$$
$$\dot{Z}_3 = k_3 X_3 - \rho_{34}Z_3 + \rho_{43}Z_4 + \rho_{23}Z_2 - \rho_{32}Z_3 - \lambda Z_3 \Theta(R) \theta(T - Z_3)$$
$$\dot{Z}_4 = k_4 X_4 + \rho_{34}Z_3 - \rho_{43}Z_4 - \lambda Z_4 \Theta(R) \Theta(T - Z_4)$$

Each agent must determine the value of the coefficients from local interactions between agents and with the environment. For this test will be assumed the following values:

$$
\begin{array}{ll}
\mu = 0.01 & \rho_{34} = 0.001 \\
\lambda = 0.03 & \rho_{43} = 0.01 \\
\rho_{12} = 0.001 & k_1 = 0.01 \\
\rho_{21} = 0.001 & k_2 = 0.01 \\
\rho_{23} = 0.01 & k_3 = 0.02 \\
\rho_{32} = 0.001 & k_4 = 0.01
\end{array} \tag{9}
$$

These values agree with the characteristics described for this example (higher value for ρ_{23}, ρ_{43} and k_3). Figures 4, 5 and 6 show the results. We simulate the system with an initial population of 300 agents in reproduction and a quorum threshold of $T = 10$. Figure 4 shows how this population is rapidly reduced by activating the other two behaviors (almost 10% over the first 50 min). In Fig. 5 is shown as explorers agents increase in the four areas. While growth is similar in all four cases, we can appreciate more agents in area 3 (blue curve). Finally, in Fig. 6 is shown as increasing the virulent agents in the four regions. Initially, the agents increase in all four cases. However, in areas 1, 2 and 4 the number of agents decreases after about 200 to 300 min, while in area 3 (blue curve) the number of agents always increases. These curves show the migration of agents to the area 3.

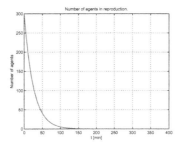

Fig. 4. Macro model simulation for a simple grouping task $(T = 10)$ - Reproduction.

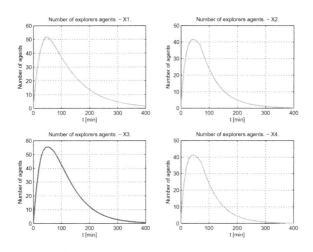

Fig. 5. Macro model simulation for a simple grouping task $(T = 10)$ - Exploration. (Color figure online)

With a quorum threshold of $T = 10$ the four areas achieve to activate the QS at some point (area three at 25 min, area one at 43 min, area two at 68 min

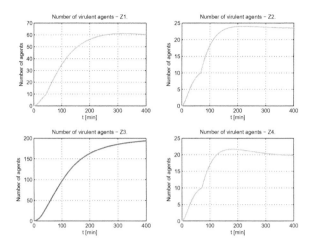

Fig. 6. Macro model simulation for a simple grouping task ($T = 10$) - Virulence. (Color figure online)

and area four at 73 min). Upon reaching a population of 10 agents, in four cases there was an increase in the rate of population growth. With a quorum threshold of $T = 60$, only area three activates the QS at 137 min. In the latter case, the population of virulent agents in two and four areas never exceeds 10 agents, and in the area one reaches up to 18 agents.

In experimental tests we evaluate the behaviors on a 45 cm × 61 cm robot equipped with a set of nine infrared sensors (each with a range of 0.2 to 0.8 m). From the signals of the infra-red sensors the robot determines the proximity to other robots or obstacles in the environment. Once this information is identified, the robot establishes its behavior, following the navigation policies of the model.

5   Conclusions

In this paper we propose a navigation scheme for robot swarms that mimics the behavior of bacterial QS. The navigation scheme is supported in robot grouping, which can be oriented to specific navigation tasks through landmarks in the environment that the robot can identify locally. Grouping, and therefore navigation is accelerated according to the number of agents in an area. In the cases analyzed, it is clear how the size of the quorum threshold affects QS. The variation in the value of T directly affects the characteristics of the population growth in each of the areas. Small values of T allow virulent agents to reach the QS and increase their bacterial population in local minima, but they do not exceed the local maximum. In this case, the grouping is also faster. With large values of T, the QS tends to be expressed only in the global maximum, but the process takes a little longer. In both cases, the QS helps to find the global maximum (more virulent bacteria gather at the area of higher performance).

Acknowledgments. This work was supported by the District University Francisco José de Caldas and Corporación Unificada Nacional de Educación Superior. The authors thank the research group ARMOS for the evaluation carried out on prototypes of ideas and strategies.

References

1. Adamou, A., Gueroui, A., Labraoui, N., Omer, B., Titouna, C., Damakoa, I.: Adaptive scheme for collaborative mobile sensing in wireless sensor networks: bacterial foraging optimization approach. In: IEEE 27th Annual Inter. Symposium on Personal, Indoor, and Mobile Radio Communications (PIMRC 2016), pp. 1–6 (2016)
2. Hazza, M., Nabila, A., Yulian, E., Hatem, A.: Empirical study on AGV guiding in indoor manufacturing system using color sensor. In: 5th International Symposium on Computational and Business Intelligence (ISCBI 2017), pp. 125–128 (2017)
3. Iwamura, K., Chen, J., Tanimizu, Y., Sugimura, N.: A study on transportation processes of autonomous distributed AGV based on social force model. In: International Symposium on Flexible Automation (ISFA), pp. 206–209 (2016)
4. Jones, G., King, P., Morgan, H., Planque, M., Zauner, K.: Autonomous droplet architectures. Artif. Life **21**(2), 195–204 (2015)
5. Li, G., Yang, Y., Zhao, F., Zhou, Y.: An improved differential evolution based artificial fish swarm algorithm and its application to AGV path planning problems. In: 36th Chinese Control Conference (CCC 2017), pp. 2556–2561 (2017)
6. Martínez, F., Acero, D.: Robótica Autónoma: Acercamientos a algunos problemas centrales. CIDC, Distrital University Francisco José de Caldas (2015). ISBN 9789588897561
7. Martínez, F.H., Delgado, J.A.: Hardware emulation of bacterial quorum sensing. In: Huang, D.-S., Zhao, Z., Bevilacqua, V., Figueroa, J.C. (eds.) ICIC 2010. LNCS, vol. 6215, pp. 329–336. Springer, Heidelberg (2010). https://doi.org/10.1007/978-3-642-14922-1_41
8. Oleari, F., Magnani, M., Ronzoni, D., Sabattini, L., Cardarelli, E., Digani, V., Secchi, C., Fantuzzi, C.: Improving AGV systems: integration of advanced sensing and control technologies. In: IEEE International Conference on Intelligent Computer Communication and Processing (ICCP 2015), pp. 257–262 (2015)
9. Padilha, F., Subtil, M., Fabro, J., Schneider, A.: Trajectory planning in dynamic environments for an industrial AGV, integrated with fuzzy obstacle avoidance. In: 12th Latin American Robotics Symposium (LARS) and 3rd Brazilian Symposium on Robotics (LARS-SBR 2015), pp. 347–352 (2015)
10. Pia, M., Marcello, A., Pedroncelli, G., Ukovich, W.: A software tool for the decentralized control of agv systems. In: International Conference on Control, Decision and Information Technologies (CoDIT 2016), pp. 478–483 (20016)
11. Rendón, A.: Evaluación de estrategia de navegación autónoma basada en comportamiento reactivo para plataformas robóticas móviles. Tekhnê **12**(2), 75–82 (2015)

Artificial Immune System

Comparison of Event-B and B Method: Application in Immune System

Sheng-rong Zou[✉], Chen Wang, Si-ping Jiang, and Li Chen

College of Information Engineer, Yangzhou University,
Yangzhou 225127, China
srzou@qq.com

Abstract. The increasing scale and complex of software makes it difficult to ensure the correctness and consistency of the software, therefore, formal methods emerge and are gradually recognized by industry. Event-B and B method are two formal system languages based on set theory and predicate logic. By comparing the advantages and disadvantages of the Event-B and B method, combining with the case and rewriting requirements from the aspects of environment, function and properties, we use the Event-B to establish the abstract model of immune system and refine it step by step according to the refinement strategy until validating the model. The immune system is a typical large and high-complexity model involving many cytokines and immune responses. Taking immune system model as an example, this paper discusses how to apply the Event-B mothed to this systems from the perspective of the above functions.

Keywords: Event-B · B method · Immune system · Formal modeling

1 Introduction

Formal method [1] has strict mathematical definition, rigorous reasoning and increasingly sophisticated tools, gradually recognized by the industry circles, especially in high-security and real time control system. Modeling and verifying the system by the method is an effective way to eliminate the potential danger, and is the prerequisite for the correct design and development of the system. For example, the Paris metro [2] is modeled using the B method, and there are many cases [3, 4] in China that explicitly indicate the need to use formal method when passing industry certification. The formal methods mentioned are Z method, B method and Event-B. The B method and the Event-B are the most widely used, while the Event-B is the simplification of the B method and draws the advantages of other formal methods.

2 Comparison of Event-B and B Method

2.1 Definition and Advantages of B Method

B method [5], as a formal method, can provide an unambiguous, consistent and accurate description of the system, which makes the system more reliable and accurate.

Y. Tan et al. (Eds.): ICSI 2018, LNCS 10941, pp. 317–326, 2018.
https://doi.org/10.1007/978-3-319-93815-8_31

The B method is analyzed by mathematical method, and avoids the inconsistency and completeness in the requirements design process. It also makes the requirements specification, design and abstract model in the system development process under a unified mathematical framework. B machine includes variables, invariant and operation, which can describe the system from two aspects: static behavior and dynamic behavior [6].

2.2   Event-B Method

Event-B [7] is formal method of system-level modeling and analysis. Key features of it are the use of set theory as a modelling notation, the use of refinement to represent system at different abstraction levels, and the use of mathematical proof to verify consistency between refinement levels [8].

First of all, the Event-B model is composed of a state. The state is represented by some constants and variables, the constants are connected by some axioms, variables are connected by some invariants, and axioms and invariants are expressed by the set theory expression; Secondly, the Event-B model is composed of many events, an Event is composed of Guards and Actions, Guards represent the enabling condition of the event, Actions represent the way in which the state is modified by the event, and Guards and Actions are expressed in the set theory.

Event-B model consists of machine and context. Machine contains the dynamic structure of the system model which includes variables, invariants and events, context contains the static structure of the system model which contains constants and axioms. These is a Sees relationship between them. There is an extension relationship between contexts, and the extending context can quote the parameters in the extended context, and this is also true in the machines [9]. Also, the machine can quote the parameters in the context it sees (see Fig. 1).

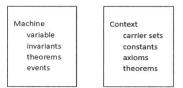

Fig. 1.   The model component of Event-B.

Here are some of the advantages of the Event-B method:

- Event-B separates the Machine from the Context, reduces complexity, facilitates management, and helps to correctly understand the concepts of abstraction and refinement, which is the correct way to construct software.
- The Event-B can be started from the state diagram. In the Machine, a State machine [10] is represented by a state diagram, and the relationship between two states is a transfer representing Event. These two states respectively represents the precondition and post-conditions of the Event. The current condition starts when the Guards are satisfied, until the post-conditions are satisfied. The Event is modified by Actions.

- In the Event-B translation process, the transition rules are mature, which can be implemented only with a state diagram, and that Event-B is generally more suitable for the real-time control system.
- Event-B model is easier to refine, and it supports the formalized model of different refinement levels, so that each abstract machine has its appropriate scale.
- Event-B is proved more convenient. The state is defined by a variable, and it guarantees that the invariant is true regardless of the value of the variable. Most of the theorem proving can be done automatically by relevant tools, reducing the difficulty of proving.

2.3   The Comparison of Two Methods

From what has been discussed above, we draw the following conclusions (see Table 1).

Table 1. Comparison of Event-B and B method.

	B method	Event-B
Basics	Set theory, first order logic [5]	Set theory, predicate logic [7], increase context and event drivers depending on the environment requirements
Modeling	The static property and dynamic behavior are described by variable, invariant, operation, etc.	The static property and dynamic behavior are described separately and can be started by state [9]
Refinement	Using a gradual approach to enrich the model, the most elaborate model will be automatically translated into program	Support for different elaboration levels, elaborate model layer by layer, also apply to large, complex systems with fragile environments. [11]
Proof	Most of the corresponding certification obligations are automatically generated according to the model statute	Most of the statues can be automatically proved, the method can support the automatic generation of proof obligation, and provide the automatic proof and manual proof statistics

From the above introduction and comparison of the two methods we can see that Event-B method has more advantages compared with the method B, and with the strong support of commercial tools, it has been widely used in industry.

3   Immune System Based on Event-B

The development method based on Event-B starts from requirements [12]. The refinement strategy is built on the basis of describing the requirements specification and extracting the corresponding abstract functions, properties and context requirements.

Then we make a formal modeling and validate the model. If the model is correct, the state and event of the abstract machine can be further refined and supplemented until the model meets all requirements, and finally the verification result of the complete model is obtained (see Fig. 2).

Fig. 2. The overall architecture of Event-B development method.

This section takes the immune system model [13] as an example to illustrate the use of the Event-B method in the development of real-time control system. The system uses the Rodin tool platform [14, 15] which is an open toolset. Rodin is developed based on Eclipse, and the plug-in mechanism of Eclipse enables it to continuously extend functionality, among which UML-B [16] is one of Rodin's plug-ins. This plug-in is a graphical formalized modeling notation, it provides an additional complement to the Event-B model in the form of classes and state machines, UML-B tool generates the Event-B model corresponding to the UML-B development, and then we using the Rodin tool to perform and prove the obligations associated with the Event-B model.

3.1 Requirements Specification

Immune cells play a role in removing foreign bodies when they invade the body [17, 18]. The immune process is mediated by T cells. T cells begin to increase and differentiate after being stimulated by antigens, and turn into effector T cells. When the same antigen enters the body again, the effector T cells have direct killing effect to the antigen. As we can see from the above requirements description, the main participants in this system have antibodies, antigens and T cells.

There are six cell use-cases in the immune system, which are instruction, growth, regrowth, proliferate, collide and kill. The use-cases before the collision are the first four, and all use cases are included after the collision.

3.2 Establish the Initial Model

First, the initial model of the immune system is established through the above six use cases, and an initial model of the immune system that do not collide is established at this level of abstraction. The requirements description is shown below (see Table 2).

On the basis of this requirement description, we define the Context and Machine.

The Definition of Context. We create a static part of the immune system's initial model called Context_CELL, in which we define the type cell to describe the cell class, and all other cells inherit the cell class. We define constant nonageMaxHp to represent the maximum life value in the nonage period, constant matureMaxHp to represent the maximum life value in the mature period, constant initialHp to represent the initial health value, constant grow to represent growth value, constant regrow to represent regrowth value, constant growTime and regrowTime to represent the point at which growth values increase, constant splitCellNum to represent an increase in the number of cells.

Table 2. Requirements description for the initial model.

Model CELL	Requirements description
Req1.1	Antigen cells enter the immune system
Req1.2	Some cells enter the nonage stage and begin to grow
Req1.3	The cells reach mature stage and continue to grow to the split stage
Req1.4	The cell divides during the period of split, and the new divided cells enter the immature stage, and then turn to Req1.2

The Definition of Machine. We create a dynamic part of the immune system's initial model called Machine_Cell, and reference Context_Cell. The definition variable HP represents the cell's life value, cellNum represents the number of cells, and time represents the time of cell movement.

The state Machine function of UML-B is used in Machine. State machines may be attached to classes, to states of another statemachine or simply at the Machine level. The transitions of a state machine represent events with the additional behavior associated with the change of state defined by the transition. That is, the event can only occur when the instance is in the source state and, when it fires, the instance changes to the target state.

The four use-cases that are designed when the requirements are not refined are expressed in this state machine. The state diagram is shown below (see Fig. 3).

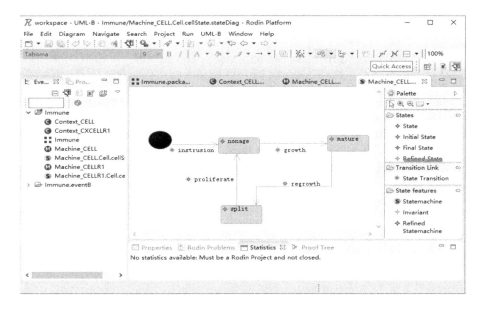

Fig. 3. State diagram of initial modeling

Each transformation in the state machine represents an event, which is modified by the Guards and Actions. The description of events and transformations is as follows:

1. The cells enter the immune system and begin to transition from the initial state to the nonage state, we set the initial value for cells.

```
Instruction = InitialState1 -> nonage:
Action1: hp(self) := initialHp;
```

2. The cells are transformed from nonage state into mature state. The life value is between zero and the maximum life value of the nonage stage. Every period of time the value of life increases by a certain amount. The Guards for growth restrain Req1.2.

```
growth = nonage -> mature:
Guard1: cellState(self) = nonage
Guard2: hp(self) > 0
Guard3: hp(self) < nonageMaxHp
Guard4: time(self) mod growTime = 0
Action1: hp(self) = hp(self) + grow
```

3. The cells are transformed from mature state into split state. The life value is between the maximum life value of the nonage period and the maximum life value of the mature stage. Every period of time the value of life increases by a certain amount. The Guards for growth restrain Req1.3.

```
regrow = mature -> split:
Guard1: cellState(self) = mature
Guard2: hp(self) < matureMaxHp
Guard3: time(self) mod regrowTime = 0
Action1: hp(self) = hp(self) + regrow
```

4. The cells are transformed from split state into nonage state. When the cell's life value is greater than or equal to the maximum life value of the mature stage, it begins to divide, and the cells produced by the division are the nonage stage cells, and the cell's life value is restored to the initial value. The Guards for proliferate restrain Req1.4, which ensures that the division is done in the mature state.

```
proliferate = split -> nonage:
Guard1: cellState(self) = split
Guard2: hp(self) >= matureMaxHp
Action1: cellNum(self) = cellNum(self) + splitCellNum
Action2: hp(self) = initialHp
```

3.3   Refinement of the Model

This section refines the initial model, adds the collision module on the basis of CELL, and introduces the loss of life value and recovery of life value. The requirements description of the refinement is described below (see Table 3).

Table 3. Refinement of initial model.

Model CELLR1	Requirements description
Req2.1	Antigen cells enter the immune system
Req2.2	Some cells enter the nonage stage and begin to grow, the value of life increases gradually over time, and the cells do not collide temporarily
Req2.3	The cells reach mature stage, the value of life increases gradually over time; the cell starts to collide, and the life value is lost when the collision occurs; if the cell life value is less than or equal to zero, the cell dies
Req2.4	The cell divides during the period of split, and the new divided cells enter the immature stage, and then turn to Req2.2

First, we create Context_CELLR1 to inherit Context_CELL. Then, we add constant otherAttack to indicate the attack value of the other cell in the collision, thisDef to indicate the defensive value of the cell itself during a collision, selfResume to indicate the cell's own recovery value, disMin to indicate the minimum distance between two cells, and lifecycle to indicate the loss value in the cell's lifecycle transformation.

In the refinement of the event, Machine_CELLR1 is created to refine Machine_-CELL, where Machine_CELLR1 can quote Context_CELLR1. In Machine_CELLR1, the variable dis is defined to describe the distance between the cells, and when the distance is less than or equal to the minimum distance, it represents a collision between the cells. Continuing to use HP, cellNum, and time in Machine_CELL.

In the refinement of the state machine, we add collision and kill events. The state diagram is shown below (see Fig. 4).

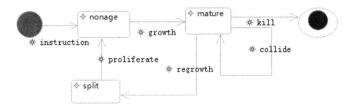

Fig. 4. Refinement of the state diagram for the initial modeling

The added events and transitions are described as follows:

1. The cells are in mature state, when the distance between the two cells is less than the minimum distance, the cells collide, and the current value of cells change. The Guards for collide restrain Req2.3, and it ensures that the collision is carried out in mature state and that the distance between the cells should be minimized.

```
Collide = mature->mature:
Guard1: cellState(self) = mature
Guard2: dis(self) ≤ disMin
Action1: hp(self) = hp(self) - otherAttack + thisDef -
lifecycle
```

2. The state of the cell is transformed from mature to death, when the cell life value is less than or equal to zero, the cell dies and clears the cell. The Guards for kill restrain Req2.4.

```
kill = mature->FinalState1:
Guard1: cellState(self) = mature
Guard2: hp(self) ≤ 0
```

We can see from the above that, the state diagram maps each instance to its state. In this paper, the translation to Event-B is described using the disjoint sets representation. The generated Event-B machine for CELLR1 is show in the Rodin screenshot of Fig. 5. Each Event-B statement is preceded by it label which describes it purpose.

```
INVARIANTS
    dis_type:    dis ∈ Cell → N not theorem
EVENTS
    INITIALISATION:    not extended ordinary
    THEN
        Cell_init:    Cell = ø
        hp_init:      hp = ø
        cellNum_init: cellNum = ø
        time_init:    time = ø
        dis_init:     dis = ø
        cellState_init: cellState = ø
    END

    instruction:    not extended ordinary
    REFINES
        instrusion
    ANY
        self    constructed instance of class Cell
    WHERE
        self_type:  self ∈ Cell_SET \ Cell not theorem
    THEN
        Cell_constructor:   Cell = Cell ∪ {self}
        cellState_enterState_nonage:   cellState(self) = nonage
        instruction_Action1:   hp(self) = initialHp
    END

    growth: not extended ordinary
    REFINES
        growth
    ANY
        self    contextual instance of class Cell
    WHERE
        self_type:  self ∈ Cell not theorem
```

Fig. 5. Generated Event-B specification of CELLR1

3.4   Proof of the Model

Through the refinement, the immune system model has been established, the following is the use of strict mathematical justification to ensure the correctness of the model, only when all the proof obligations of the model are correct can the correctness of model be expressed [19]. The Rodin platform provides automatic verification tools for model verification and simplifies the tedious process of certification. All the models for the immune system were constructed using the UML-B tool and corresponding Event-B machines were generated. All the proof obligations (POs) for the two machines were generated and proved using the Rodin tool provers [20]. The total number of proof obligations (POs) is 46 in which all of them are proved automatically. The results are shown in the figure below (see Fig. 6).

Element Name	Total	Auto	Manual	Reviewed	Undischarged
Immune.eventB	46	19	0	0	27
Context_CXCELL	0	0	0	0	0
Context_CXCELLR1	0	0	0	0	0
Machine_CELLR1_implicitContext	0	0	0	0	0
Machine_CELL_implicitContext	0	0	0	0	0
Machine_CELL	30	13	0	0	17
Machine_CELLR1	16	6	0	0	10

Fig. 6. The proof results of the model.

4   Conclusion

In the above article, we briefly introduced the Event-B, B methods and their advantages and disadvantages, also analyzed and compared them from several aspects and summarized them. From the summary, it can be seen that the Event-B is more advantageous than the B method. The case of the immune system proves that the formalized method based on the Event-B is reliable and effective, and this technique and method can improve the quality of the early model. We use the refinement to represent systems at different abstraction levels and the mathematical proof to verify consistency between refinement levels. In the specific usage scenario, Event-B technology is used to analyze and model, so as to facilitate the communication, modification and confirmation of the final model.

References

1. Wing, J.M.: A specifier's introduction to formal methods. IEEE Comput. **23**(9), 8–24 (1990)
2. Abrial, J.R.: Formal methods: the becoming practice. J. Univ. Comput. Sci. **13**(5), 619–628 (2007)
3. Shi, J., Zhu, L., Fang, H.: A hardware resource oriented binary intermediate language. In: Proceedings of 2012 17th International Conference on Engineer of Complex Computer Systems (ICECCS 2012), pp. 211–219 (2012)

4. Lei, Y., Hu, X., Chen, Y.: Formal model of vehicle on-board controller system based on Event-B. Digital Technol. Appl. **2012**(8), 13 (2012)
5. Abrial, J.R.: The B-book: Assigning Programs to Meanings. Cambridge University Press, Cambridge (1996)
6. Schneider, S.: The B-Method: An Introduction. Palgrave, Hampshire (2001)
7. Abrial, J.R.: Modeling in Event-B: System and Software Engineering. Cambridge University Press, Cambridge (2010)
8. Hallerstede, S.: On the Purpose of Event-B Proof Obligations. Formal Aspects Comput. **23**(1), 133–150 (2011)
9. Li, M.: Formal software engineering teaching based on Event-B method and rodin. Comput. Eng. Sci. **38**(1), 143–145 (2016)
10. OMG: UML 2.1.2 Superstructure Specification (2007). http://www.omg/org/cgibin/docs/formal/2007-11-02.pdf
11. Event-B (2014). http://www.event-b.org
12. Zhang, Y., Guo, J., Zhu, X.: Modeling and development of multi-application smart cards based on Event-B. Comput. Eng. Sci. **36**(10), 1943–1951 (2014)
13. Zou, S., Zhu, Y., Du, Z.: Influenza immune model based on agent. J. Nanjing Univ. (Eng. Technol. Ed.) **15**(3), 50–54 (2015)
14. Rodin Platform and Plug-in Installation (2011). http://www.event-b.org/install.html
15. Abrial, J.R., Leino, R.: Mini-course around Event-B and Rodin: hypervisor (2010). http://research.microsoft.com/apps/video/default.aspx?id=151665
16. Snook, C., Butler, M.: UML-B and Event-B: an integration of languages and tools. In: The 9th IASTED International Conference on Software Engineer. ACTA Press (2008)
17. Mo, H., Zuo, X.: Artificial Immune System. Science Press, Beijing (2009)
18. Zou, S.: Formally specifying T cell cytokine networks with B method. In: Zhang, J., He, J.-H., Fu, Y. (eds.) CIS 2004. LNCS, vol. 3314, pp. 385–390. Springer, Heidelberg (2004). https://doi.org/10.1007/978-3-540-30497-5_60
19. Qiao, L., Yang, M., Tan, Y., Pu, G., Yang, H.: Formal verification of memory management system in spacecraft using Event-B. J. Softw. **28**(5), 1204–1220 (2017)
20. Abrial, J.-R., Butler, M., Hallerstede, S., Voisin, L.: An open extensible tool environment for event-B. In: Liu, Z., He, J. (eds.) ICFEM 2006. LNCS, vol. 4260, pp. 588–605. Springer, Heidelberg (2006). https://doi.org/10.1007/11901433_32

A Large-Scale Data Clustering Algorithm Based on BIRCH and Artificial Immune Network

Yangyang Li[✉], Guangyuan Liu, Peidao Li, and Licheng Jiao

Key Laboratory of Intelligent Perception and Image Understanding of Ministry of Education of China, International Research Center for Intelligent Perception and Computation, School of Artificial Intelligence, Xidian University, Xi'an 710071, China
yyli@xidian.edu.cn

Abstract. This paper describes a large-scale data clustering algorithm which is a combination of Balanced Iterative Reducing and Clustering using Hierarchies Algorithm (BIRCH) and Artificial Immune Network Clustering Algorithm (aiNet). Compared with traditional clustering algorithms, aiNet can better adapt to non-convex datasets and does not require a given number of clusters. But it is not suitable for handling large-scale datasets for it needs a long time to evolve. Besides, the aiNet model is very sensitive to noise, which greatly restricts its application. Contrary to aiNet, BIRCH can better process large-scale datasets but cannot deal with non-convex datasets like traditional clustering algorithms, and requires the cluster number. By combining these two methods, a new large-scale data clustering algorithm is obtained which inherits the advantages and overcomes the disadvantages of BIRCH and aiNet simultaneously.

Keywords: Large-scale · Clustering · Immune network · BIRCH
AiNet

1 Introduction

As an unsupervised data analysis technique, cluster analysis has been applied in Data Mining, Pattern Recognition, Image Segmentation and so on, whose goal is to determine the intrinsic grouping in a set of unlabeled data with no or poor prior knowledge. K-means [1] and Fuzzy C-means (FCM) [2, 3] are the most classic ones. Besides, Genetic Algorithm (GA) [4], Particle Swarm Optimization (PSO) [5], Multi-Objective Algorithm [6], hierarchical methods [7] and density-based methods [8] are also applied in cluster analysis.

Traditional clustering algorithms cannot well handle non-convex datasets because clusters are represented by cluster centers. So kernel method [9], Spectral method (SC) [10] and Principal Component Analysis (PCA) [11] are introduced to improve the performance but still do not solve the problem fundamentally. However, the Artificial Immune Network Clustering Algorithm [12, 13] can discover clusters of arbitrary shape and represent them via a number of network nodes without providing the cluster number. One of the most famous Artificial Immune Network models, aiNet [12], takes

© Springer International Publishing AG, part of Springer Nature 2018
Y. Tan et al. (Eds.): ICSI 2018, LNCS 10941, pp. 327–337, 2018.
https://doi.org/10.1007/978-3-319-93815-8_32

data points as antigens, simulates the process of antibody cloning and selection in biological immune system to build an antibody network.

With the data size increasing exponentially, it is difficult for traditional algorithms to process this kind of large-scale data. Balanced Iterative Reducing and Clustering using Hierarchies (BIRCH) [14] and Clustering Using Representatives (CURE) [15] are just designed to deal with the clustering problem of large database.

Although aiNet can handle non-convex datasets and does not require the cluster number, it needs a long time to converge when handling large-scale datasets. In order to produce the advantages of aiNet to cluster large-scale data, a two-step clustering method combining the advantages and overcoming their shortcomings of BIRCH and aiNet is proposed in this paper. First, a rough partition of the large-scale dataset will be obtained by BIRCH. It divides the original dataset into small uniform pieces. Then, the result will be gotten by clustering those pieces by aiNet.

The rest of the paper is organized as follows. Section 2 introduces the aiNet clustering algorithm, BIRCH algorithm and some related work. Section 3 describes the algorithm, BIRCH_aiNet we proposed in detail. Comparison experiments with BIRCH [14], Inverse Weighted K-means Online Algorithm V2 (IWKO2) [18] and Online FCM (OFCM) [19] are shown in Sect. 4 and conclusions in Sect. 5.

2   Related Work and AiNet Clustering Algorithm

In this section, we firstly present an overview of basic concepts and mechanisms of the cluster analysis, then introduce aiNet and BIRCH algorithm and finally briefly describe the advantages and disadvantages of them.

2.1   Clustering Analysis

Given a $X = \{x_1, x_2, \ldots, x_n\}, x_i \in \Re^d, i = \{1, 2, \ldots, N\}$, X is the dataset having N patterns $x_1, x_2, \ldots, x_N$, and d is the dimension. Cluster analysis is to partition this dataset into k disjoint clusters $C = \{C_1, C_2, \ldots, C_k\}$. And we expect patterns from the same cluster are as similar as possible and those from different clusters differ as much as possible.

2.2   AiNet Clustering Algorithm

Artificial Immune Network (aiNet) [12] was proposed by de Castro, which simulates the process that the antigen (Ag) invades antibody (Ab) network in vertebrate immune systems. It views data points in the dataset as antigens, which invade and stimulate the immune network to produce antibodies. In the process, it will carry out immune operations such as clone reproduction, affinity maturation and network suppression to dynamically adjust the network structure until it converges. Finally, a network reflecting the structure of the dataset will be generated. Because of the scale of the network node set is much smaller than that of the original dataset, so it greatly reduces the redundancy of the data. Figure 1 is the pseudo-code of aiNet.

Procedures:

1. Initialize Ab set and following parameters: δ_s (suppression threshold), δ_d (natural death threshold), n (number of best-matching cells taken for each Ag_j), N (clone number multiplier), ζ (the rate of affinity maturation) and r (the rate of eliminated cells).

2. At each iteration step, do:

2.1 For each $Ag_j, j = \{1, 2, ..., N_{Ag}\}$, do:

2.1.1 Calculate its affinity $f_{i,j}, i = \{1, 2, ..., N_{Ab}\}$ to all $Ab_i, f_{i,j} = 1/D_{i,j}$, $D_{i,j} = \| Ab_i - Ag_j \|$;

2.1.2 Select the subset $Ab_{\{n\}}$ composed of the n highest affinity antibodies;

2.1.3 Clone each antibody in $Ab_{\{n\}}$ based on their affinity $f_{i,j}$, and generate a set C of its clones: the higher the affinity, the larger clone size for each of the n selected antibodies (we can use Equation (1) to generate the total clone size Nc for each cell in $Ab_{\{n\}}$);

$$N_c = \sum_{i=1}^{n} round(N - D_{i,j} \cdot N) \qquad (1)$$

2.1.4 Apply Equation (2) to each individual in C, and generate a mutated set C^*;

$$C_k^* = C_k + \alpha_k \cdot (Ag_j - C_k); \alpha \propto 1/f_{i,j}; k = \{1, ..., N_c\} \qquad (2)$$

2.1.5 Calculate the affinity $d_{k,j} = 1/D_{k,j}$ between Ag_j and every element of C^*: $D_{k,j} = \| C_k^* - Ag_j \|$;

2.1.6 Re-select $\zeta\%$ of the antibodies with highest $d_{k,j}$ from C^*, and put them into the memory cell matrix M_j;

2.1.7 Apoptosis: eliminate those memory cells in M_j whose affinity $D_{k,j} > \delta_d$;

2.1.8 Calculate the affinity $S_{i,k}$ among the memory cells: $S_{i,k} = \| M_{j,i} - M_{j,k} \|$, $\forall i, k$;

2.1.9 Clonal suppression: clear those memory cells whose $S_{k,j} < \delta_s$;

2.1.10 $M \leftarrow [M; M_j]$;

2.2 Calculate the affinity among all the memory cells from M: $S_{i,k} = \| M^i - M^k \|$, $M^i \in M, M^k \in M, \forall i, k$;

2.3 Network suppression: eliminate the memory cells in M whose $S_{i,k} < \delta_s$;

2.4 Randomly generate a few antibodies to replace the r% of the worst individuals in M: $Ab \leftarrow [M; Ab_{new}]$;

3. Test the stopping criterion: if the stop criterion is met, output Ab; otherwise turn to Step 2.

Fig. 1. The Pseudo code of aiNet.

The stopping criterion: We can stop iterating applying any of the following criteria:

1. When it reaches the maximum number of iterations;
2. When the network reaches a pre-defined number of cells;
3. When the average error between all the antigens and the network nodes exceeds a pre-specified threshold;
4. If its average error rises after consecutive iterations.

When the process terminates, we will get the network node set. As Fig. 2 shows, Fig. 2(a) is the distribution of an artificial dataset, and Fig. 2(b) is the network nodes produced by aiNet. We can find that the node set has the same structure as the original one but it is much smaller. So aiNet can reduce the redundancy of the data greatly.

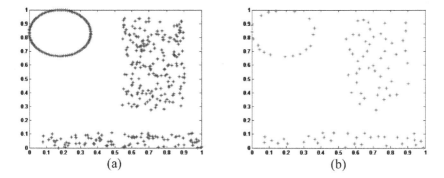

(a)   (b)

Fig. 2. Original dataset and its structure: a. original dataset, b. network nodes produced by aiNet

After getting the node set, we firstly get the Minimum Spanning Tree (MST) of the network. Then calculate the length of each edge of the MST and display them in a bar graph. Then we can find that the length of two edges of the MST is far longer than others. The dataset will be divided into three parts and cluster analysis is accomplished via cutting these two edges of the MST.

2.3   BIRCH Clustering Algorithm

BIRCH [14] is a hierarchical clustering algorithm designed for large-scale database. It adopted the idea of the Sequential Processing method [16, 17] which allows to process the data point one by one, and reduces memory requirements of the algorithm.

Cluster Feature (CF) and Cluster Feature Tree (CF Tree) are the cores of BIRCH. CF Tree, including many CFs, is a high-balanced tree representing the division of the dataset. These CFs form a CF Tree according to the hierarchical relationship. And the bottom CF, called minicluster, represents a mini cluster of the dataset.

Given a dataset $\vec{O} = \{\vec{o}_1, \vec{o}_2, \ldots, \vec{o}_n\}, \vec{o}_i \in \Re^d, i = \{1, 2, \ldots, N\}$, then CF is defined as:

$$CF = (N, \overline{LS}, \overline{SS}) \tag{3}$$

Where $\overline{LS} = \sum_{i=1}^{N} \vec{o}_i$ represents the linear sum of all data points, and $\overline{SS} = \sum_{i=1}^{N} \vec{o}_i^2$ is the quadratic sum. Via CF, we can obtain the following statistics:

(1). The center of CF: $\overrightarrow{X_O} = \dfrac{\sum_{i=1}^{N} \overrightarrow{X_i}}{N}$

(2). The radius of CF: $R = \left(\dfrac{\sum_{i=1}^{N} (\overrightarrow{X_i} - \overrightarrow{X_O})^2}{N}\right)^{1/2}$

(3). The distance between two CFs: $D_{12} = \left(\dfrac{\sum_{i=1}^{N_1} \sum_{j=N_1+1}^{N_1+N_2} (\overrightarrow{X_i} - \overrightarrow{X_j})^2}{N_1 N_2}\right)^{1/2}$

(4). The formula to merge two CFs:

$$CF = CF_1 + CF_2 = (N_1 + N_2, \overrightarrow{LS_1} + \overrightarrow{LS_2}, \overrightarrow{SS_1} + \overrightarrow{SS_2})$$

The process of building a CF Tree:

Step 1: Set the parameters: Branching factor (B) and Threshold (T). Then initialize an empty CF as the root node, randomly choose a data point and put it in this CF;

Step 2: Randomly choose a data point and wrap it into a new CF (CF-new), and calculate the distance between it and other existing CFs using formula (4)

$$D_{12} = \left(\dfrac{\sum_{i=1}^{N_1} \sum_{j=N_1+1}^{N_1+N_2} (\overrightarrow{X_i} - \overrightarrow{X_j})^2}{N_1 N_2}\right)^{1/2} \tag{4}$$

Where $\overrightarrow{X_i}$ and $\overrightarrow{X_j}$ represent the points of two different CFs;

Step 3: Choose a CF (CF-close) which is the closest to CF-new, and determine whether the value D is less than the Threshold (T): if so, turn to Step 4; otherwise insert CF-new into the CF Tree and turn to Step 5;

Step 4: Determine if the number of children in CF-close is less than Branching factor (B): if so, merge CF-new and CF-close; otherwise turn to Step 5;

Step 5: First merge CF-new and CF-close to form a new CF, then divide the new CF (CF-merge) into two sub-CFs. The procedures are as follows: Find two children which are the farthest in CF-merge, then take either of them as the seed node of each sub-CF respectively and divide CF-merge into two small clusters based on the closest criteria, finally wrap them into two CFs and insert the two new CFs into the Tree. Note that we also need to check whether we have to split the parent as well up to the root, if so, do the same as Step 5;

Step 6: Check whether all the points of the original dataset have been scanned: if so, output the CF Tree; otherwise, turn to Step 2.

BIRCH can generate the result by scanning the dataset only once and has good performance in suppressing noise. But it can only process spherical dataset and requires the cluster number.

2.4   The Advantages and Disadvantages of AiNet and BIRCH

Cluster Analysis is a complex problem in Data Ming, and there doesn't exist a clustering algorithm suitable for all kinds of datasets. Without exception, aiNet and BIRCH also have this problem.

From Table 1, it is obvious that the advantages and disadvantages of them are mutually complementary. So it's logical to design a new algorithm by combining them.

Table 1. The advantages and disadvantages of aiNet and BIRCH

aiNet algorithm	BIRCH algorithm
Advantages:	**Advantages:**
1. Don't need to give the cluster number;	1. Low time and space complexity;
2. Suitable for non-convex datasets;	2. Strong ability of suppressing noise;
Disadvantages:	**Disadvantages:**
1. Need a long running time;	1. Need to give the cluster number;
2. Sensitive to noise;	2.Not suitable for non-convex datasets;

3   Large-Scale Data Clustering Algorithm Based on BIRCH and Artificial Immune Network

By combining aiNet and BIRCH, we designed a large-scale data clustering algorithm which inherits their advantages and overcome their shortcomings. Firstly, it builds a CF Tree by BIRCH, which makes the algorithm possess the ability of processing large-scale datasets and restraining noise. Then, the miniclusters produced by BIRCH will be processed by aiNet in order to deal with non-convex datasets. The procedures are as below:

Step 1: Coarse division: use BIRCH to scan the dataset and build a CF Tree;

Step 2: Denoising: clear those low-density miniclusters;

Step 3: aiNet Learning: use aiNet to process the miniclusters and get the network node set;

Step 4: Generate Minimum Spanning Tree (MST): generate a MST by linking the network nodes;

Step 5: MST Separation: separate the MST by cutting those edges whose weight is significantly larger than that of others;

Step 6: Result: divide the original dataset according to the MST separation.

4 Experimental Results

In order to test the performance of BIRCH_aiNet, we compare it with some representative large-scale data clustering algorithms, such as BIRCH [14], IWKO2 (Inverse Weighted K-means Online Algorithm V2) [18] and OFCM (Online FCM) [19]. Among these algorithms, IWKO2 is the serial form of an improved K-means algorithm. It introduces the concept of weight to address the problem of K-means, the sensitivity to initial conditions. Meanwhile, a serial transformation is applied in the algorithm to reduce its space complexity. OFCM is a partitioning method based on FCM, which divides the original dataset into many subsets, utilizes FCM to process every subset and combines them to obtain the result. The simulation has been carried out on a 2.7 GHz AMD Athlon(TM) PC with 2G RAM by programming with Matlab. And 20 independent runs were performed on each test problem.

4.1 Test Dataset

We chose 2 artificial datasets and 4 real world datasets, UCI datasets[1], whose basic characteristics are shown in Table 2.

Table 2. Description of the datasets

Dataset		Number of samples	Dimension	The cluster number
Artificial dataset	En_data3	1010000	2	3
	En_sticks	1034000	2	4
UCI dataset	Skin_Nonshin	245057	3	2
	Covertype	581012	54	7
	Shuttle	43500	9	7
	Magic04	19020	10	2

En_data3 and En_sticks, based on two small-scale ones, data3 and sticks, are large-scale artificial datasets which have more than one million samples. So their distributions are the same as data3 and sticks. In addition, to test the algorithm's ability of anti-noise, 1% of noise samples are added in the datasets (shown in Fig. 3). We tested these two datasets for the following reasons: (1) if the algorithm could process those datasets whose samples are more than one million; (2) if the algorithm could suppress the interference of noise; (3) if the algorithm could deal with non-convex datasets.

---

[1] http://www.ics.uci.edu/~mlearn/MLRepository.html.

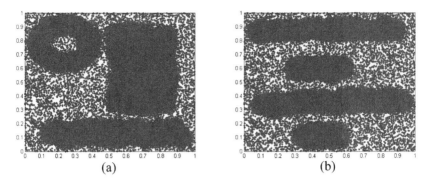

Fig. 3. Two large-scale artificial datasets: a. En_data3, b. En_sticks

4.2   Experimental Results and Analysis

The main parameters of each algorithm are as follows: the Branching Factor of BIRCH was set to 3000, and the Threshold was 0.01 except Magic04 and Covertype. The Thresholds of Magic04 and Covertype were set to 0.1 and 0.3 respectively. The iteration times of IWKO2 and OFCM were 20, and the cluster number was also provided and remaining parameters can be referred in [18, 19]. The input algorithm, BIRCH, was set as the same as BIRCH. As for the output algorithm, suppression threshold (σ_s) and natural death threshold (σ_s) of aiNet were marked in the result.

The clustering result is shown by Clustering Accuracy (CA) [20] defined as:

$$CA = \frac{\sum_{i=1}^{k} n_i}{n} \tag{5}$$

Where n is the size of the dataset, and n_i is the number of points correctly divided into the ith cluster. CA is in the interval of [0,1] and a large value means a good result.

Table 3 shows the results of the four compared algorithms on six datasets and each result is the mean value of 20 independent experiments.

Table 3. The Clustering accuracy

Dataset	CA(%)			
	BIRCH	IWKO2	OFCM	BIRCH_aiNet(σ_d, σ_s)
En_data3	89.71	89.33	91.32	**97.32 (0.01, 0.04)**
En_sticks	71.08	69.61	79.55	**100 (0.01, 0.04)**
Skin_Nonshin	49.34	51.42	51.70	**72.87 (0.03, 0.04)**
Covertype	16.82	19.04	14.09	**26.36 (0.3, 05)**
Shuttle	50.4	47.11	40.06	**83.16 (0.01, 0.1)**
Magic04	46.18	43.74	58.36	**64.45 (0.2, 0.4)**

It is obvious that BIRCH has the same result as IWKO2 on two artificial datasets, and the result is a little worse than OFCM. It illustrates that fuzzy clustering algorithms are more stable than traditional hard clustering algorithms. But BIRCH_aiNet can correctly divide almost all the points on these two datasets and its Clustering Accuracy is much higher than that of other five algorithms. The reason is that the two artificial datasets are not spherical and the first three algorithms have poor performances on these datasets, which proves our algorithm can well process non-convex datasets. Figure 4 shows two scatter grams of the network nodes generated by aiNet on two artificial datasets. It is noticeable that the network node set has the same distribution as the original dataset and the noise points were also well suppressed.

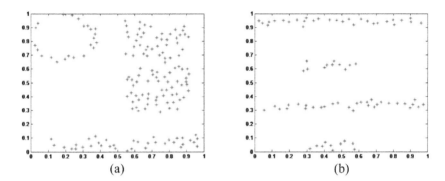

Fig. 4. Network nodes of two datasets generated by Aritficial Immune Network: a. En_data3, b. En_sticks

BIRCH, IWKO2 and OFCM almost had the same result on UCI datasets. On Covertype, IWKO2 performed better than BIRCH and OFCM; While on Shuttle, BIRCH won; and on Magic04, OFCM got the best result among the three algorithms. They three all have their own advantages, but there are no essential differences between them. Our algorithm obtained the best result on all UCI datasets.

To test the stability of every algorithm, the statistical results of BIRCH, IWKO2, OFCM and BIRCH_aiNet on En_sticks, Skin_NonSkin, Shuttle and Magic04 are shown. Figure 5 shows the statistical CA values of four algorithms of 20 independent runs. Box plots were utilized to display the distribution of these samples. In a notched box plot, the notches represent a robust estimation of the uncertainty about the medians for box-to-box comparison. The boxes have lines at the lower quartile, median, and upper quartile. The whiskers are lines extending from each end of the boxes to show the extent of the remaining data. Outliers are data with values beyond the ends of the whiskers. Symbol '+' denotes outliers. The four plots present the results of the above four clustering algorithms, BIRCH, IWKO2, OFCM and BIRCH_aiNet, to process four datasets, En_sticks, Skin_Nonshin, Shuttle and Magic04, respectively.

Figure 5 shows our algorithm obtained the highest CA and had stronger stability on En_sticks and Shuttle. Although OFCM appeared to be the most stable, its CA was lower than that of our algorithm. BIRCH and IWKO2 had more outliers because they are hard clustering algorithms and more easily fall into local optima.

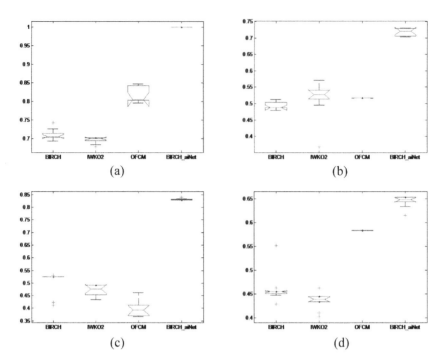

Fig. 5. Statistical CA values of four algorithms on four datasets: a. plotbox-En_sticks, b. plotbox-Skin_Nonshin, c. plotbox-Shuttle, d. plotbox-Magic04

5   Conclusions

This paper presented a large-scale data clustering algorithm based on BIRCH and aiNet. It used BIRCH as the input algorithm to improve its capability of anti-noise and aiNet was employed as the output algorithm to process complex datasets. So this measure overcomes the disadvantages and retains the advantages of them, which results in the good performance of our new algorithm on complex large-scale datasets.

Acknowledgment. This work was supported by the National Natural Science Foundation of China under Grant 61772399, Grant U170126, Grant 61773304, Grant 61672405 and Grant 61772-400, the Program for Cheung Kong Scholars and Innovative Research Team in University Grant IRT_15R53, the Fund for Foreign Scholars in University Research and Teaching Programs (the 111 Project) Grant B07048, and the Major Research Plan of the National Natural Science Foundation of China Grant 91438201.

References

1. Hartigan, J.A., Wong, M.A.: A K-Means clustering algorithm. Appl. Statis. **28**(1), 100–108 (1979)
2. Dunn, J.C.: A fuzzy relative of the ISODATA process and its use in detecting compact well-separated clusters. J. Cybern. **3**(3), 32–57 (1974)
3. Bezdek, J.C.: Pattern Recognition with Fuzzy Objective Function Algorithms. Plenum Press, New York (1981)
4. Maulik, U., Bandyopadhyay, S.: Genetic algorithm-based clustering technique. Pattern Recogn. **33**(9), 1455–1465 (2004)
5. Das, S., Abraham, A., Konar, A.: Automatic kernel clustering with a Multi-Elitist particle swarm optimization algorithm. Pattern Recogn. Lett.-PRL **29**(5), 688–699 (2008)
6. Handl, J., Knowles, J.D.: Multi-objective clustering and cluster validation. In: Jin, Y. (ed.) Multi-Objective Machine Learning, vol. 16. Springer, Heidelberg (2006). https://doi.org/10.1007/3-540-33019-4_2
7. Fred, A.L.N., Leitao, Y.M.N.: Partitional vs hierarchical clustering using a minimum grammar complexity approach. In: Ferri, F.J., Iñesta, J.M., Amin, A., Pudil, P. (eds.) Advances in Pattern Recognition. SSPR/SPR 2000, vol. 1876. Springer, Heidelberg, pp. 193–202 (2000). https://doi.org/10.1007/3-540-44522-6_20
8. Nanni, M., Pedreschi, D.: Time-Focused clustering of trajectories of moving objects. J. Intell. Inf. Syst. **27**(3), 267–289 (2006)
9. Girolami, M.: Mercer kernel-based clustering in feature space. IEEE Trans. Neural Netw. **13**(3), 780–784 (2002)
10. Ng, A.Y,, Jordan, M.I., Weiss, Y.: On spectral clustering: analysis and an algorithm. In: Neural Information Processing Systems, pp. 849–856 (2001)
11. Martínez, A.M, Kak, A.C.: PCA versus LDA. IEEE Trans. Pattern Anal. Mach. Intell.-PAMI **23**(2), 228–233 (2009)
12. de Castro, L.N., Von, Z.F.J.: aiNet: an artificial immune network for data analysis. In: Data Mining: A Heuristic Approach, pp. 231–259 (2001)
13. Timmis, J., Neal, M.: A Resource Limited Artificial Immune System for Data Analysis. Research and Development in Intelligent Systems XVII, pp. 19–32, December 2000
14. Zhang, T., Ramakrishnan, R., Livny, M.: BIRCH: an efficient data clustering method for very large databases. In: Proceedings of ACM SIGMOD Conference, Montreal, Canada, pp. 103–114 (1996)
15. Greensmith, J., Aickelin, U., Cayzer, S.: Introducing dendritic cells as a novel immune-inspired algorithm for anomaly detection. In: The 4th International Conference on Artificial Immune Systems (ICARIS 2005), Banff, Alberta, Canada (2005)
16. Richard, O.D.: Sequential k-Means clustering (2008). http://www.cs.princeton.edu/courses/archive/fall08/cos436/Duda/C/sk_means.html
17. Richard, O.D., Peter, E.H., David, G.S.: Pattern Classification, 2nd edn. China Machine Press, Beijing (2004)
18. Barbakh, W., Fyfe, C.: Online clustering algorithms. Int. J. Neural Syst. **18**(3), 185–194 (2008)
19. Havens, T.C., Bezdek, J.C., Leckie, C., et al.: Fuzzy c-means algorithms for very large data. IEEE Trans. Fuzzy Syst. **20**(6), 1130–1146 (2012)
20. Handl, J., Knowles, J.: An evolutionary approach to multiobjective clustering. IEEE Trans. Evol. Comput. **11**(1), 56–76 (2007)

Hydrologic Cycle Optimization

Hydrologic Cycle Optimization Part I: Background and Theory

Xiaohui Yan[1] and Ben Niu[2(✉)]

[1] School of Mechanical Engineering, Dongguan University of Technology, Dongguan 523808, China
[2] College of Management, Shenzhen University, Shenzhen 518060, China
drniuben@gmail.com

Abstract. A novel Hydrologic cycle Optimization (HCO) is proposed by simulating the natural phenomena of the hydrologic cycle on the earth. Three operators are employed in the algorithm: flow, infiltration, evaporation and precipitation. Flow step simulates the water flowing to lower areas and makes the population converge to better areas. Infiltration step executes neighborhood search. Evaporation and precipitation step could keep diversity and escape from local optima. The proposed algorithm is verified on ten benchmark functions and applied to a real-world problem named Nurse Scheduling Problem (NSP) with several comparison algorithms. Experiment results show that HCO performs better on most benchmark functions and in NSP than the comparison algorithms. In Part I, the background and theory of HCO are introduced firstly. And then, experimental studies on benchmark and real world problems are given in Part II.

Keywords: Hydrologic cycle optimization · Swarm intelligence
Computing intelligence

1 Introduction

Optimization problems are kind of problems we unusually encountered in both engineering and numerical calculation. Recently, many population-based algorithms are proposed as the classic operation approaches. However, they are restricted and perform not well in solving complex optimization problems. These population-based algorithms include some evolutionary algorithms, such as Genetic Algorithm (GA) [1], Genetic Programming (GP) [2], Swarm Intelligence algorithms inspired by animal colonies (Particle Swarm Optimization (PSO) [3], Artificial Bee Colony (ABC) algorithm [4], Bacterial Foraging Optimization (BFO) [5]), and some other heuristic algorithms, such as Fireworks Algorithm (FWA) [6] and Brain Storm Optimization (BSO) [7].

Generally, when we use population-based algorithms to solve an optimization problem, we unusually consider the objective function as a multi-dimension objective space. And the individuals in the population-based algorithms are points in the space. In each different algorithm, we use different evolution rules to control these points move to better areas (areas with better fitness). By the iteration of selecting the superior and eliminating the inferior, these points may converge near to the optimal point finally

© Springer International Publishing AG, part of Springer Nature 2018
Y. Tan et al. (Eds.): ICSI 2018, LNCS 10941, pp. 341–349, 2018.
https://doi.org/10.1007/978-3-319-93815-8_33

and the result is subsequently obtained. This process in very visual in a three-dimensional figure (with one objective and two decision variables): Individuals will move towards lower positions (for minimization problems) and gathered to global or local optima.

There is a saying in an ancient Chinese poetry: 'all rivers run east into the sea'. As in China, the elevation is higher in the western area and lower in the eastern area in general. Most of rivers will run east as the terrain reason. In fact, the water most converged into the lowest place, the ocean, by the cyclical process. This is similar with the optima searching process mentioned above. Inspired by this phenomenon and the similarity, we decide to develop an optimization algorithm according to the hydrologic cycle process.

In 2012, Eskandar proposed a water cycle algorithm called WCA [8], which has raised wide attention of scholars. In this paper, we analyze the hydrologic cycle process and its main factors firstly. Then, a novel hydrologic cycle optimization algorithm is proposed under the model, which abbreviated as HCO. As a new and independent algorithm proposed, the difference between HCO and WCA is analyzed in this paper. Each operator of HCO is also simulated to demonstrate its effect. To verify optimization ability of the proposed algorithm, we test it on a set of benchmark functions and a real-world problem with several other well-known optimization algorithms. The results show that the proposed algorithm outperformed than the other algorithms on most benchmark functions and the nurse scheduling problem. The comparison and application will be given in part II.

Part I of the paper is organized as followed. In Sect. 2, the hydrologic cycle model and its main factors are introduced. In Sect. 3, the HCO algorithm is proposed and its operators are described in detail. In Sect. 4, we discuss the difference between HCO and WCA. The effect of three operators are simulated and analyzed in Sect. 5. Finally, conclusions are drawn in Sect. 6.

2 Hydrologic Cycle Model

Water is the most abundant natural material on the surface of the earth. It covers more than 71 percent of the earth's surface. The state of water in the earth includes solid, liquid and gas. Most of the water on earth exists in the atmosphere, ground, lakes, rivers and oceans. As a common but important ecological phenomenon on the earth, hydrologic cycle was firstly studied by Perot and Mariotte early in 16 century.

Hydrologic cycle refers to the water in the earth, move from one place to another by a series of physical processes, such as evaporation, precipitation, infiltration, surface flow and underground flow, and so on, while the total water keep balance [9]. For example, water in the ocean may be vaporized to water vapor by absorbing energy of the sun. Then, it could be transported to the land as a cloud. And finally, it falls onto the mountains or rivers by precipitation such as rainfall [10]. The simplified model of the hydrologic cycle is shown in Fig. 1.

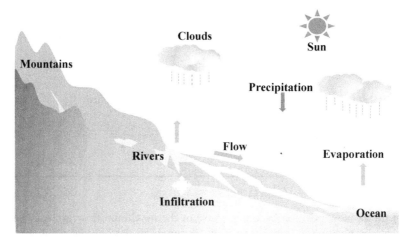

Fig. 1. Simple model of hydrologic cycle

3 Hydrologic Cycle Optimization Algorithm

As described above, the core factors of hydrologic cycle model mainly contain evaporation, precipitation, flow and infiltration. Based on the simplified model and these factors, we proposed our hydrologic cycle optimization algorithm. In HCO, it mainly contains three steps: flow, permeation, evaporation and precipitation.

3.1 Flow

Flow is the main reason that water will move and gather to lower areas. It is also one of the most important phenomena in the hydrologic cycle on land. In our HCO algorithm, flow is also the core operator. It provides the core evolutionary motivation.

In the optimization problems to be solved, there is no "gravity" exist, so we need to set up some rules to simulate the water flow to lower areas. As the gradient information is unknown, we let each individual try to move towards another individual which its fitness is better (lower position) to test whether it is a gradient descent direction. If the potential position newly produced is worse than the original position, the trial is regarded as a failure. The new position is abandoned and it will stay at the original position. And once the new position is better, it may find a descent direction. Then it will move towards the direction several times till the direction becomes worse or the maximum flow times is reached. The maximum flow times is a parameter which controls the maximum move times in one flow step and avoids premature. In the algorithm, we named it *maxFT*. The pseudo code of flow step is given in Table 1.

It should be mentioned that, in each flow step, for the individuals with best fitness, there is no better position for reference. So for these (maybe only one) best individuals, we select another individual from the population randomly as the flow direction. The rest procedure is the same as above: If the new position is better, it flows towards the

Table 1. Pseudo code of flow step of HCO

For each individual X_i in the population

 Select another individual X_j which its fitness is better than X_i randomly

$$X_{try} = X_i + (X_j - X_i).* rand(1, Dimension)$$

 While the new position is better && max flow times not reached

$$X_i = X_{try}$$

  Flow another time using the equation above

 End

End

---

direction till the new position becomes worse or the maximum flow times is reached. And if the new position is worse than itself, it remain in the original position.

3.2   Infiltration

In the flow step. It is difficult to find a gradient descent direction for the best individual. And this situation is also existing at the late stage of the searching process. Individuals may converge to local optima and hard to find better positions. This phenomenon also exists in the hydrologic cycle in nature. Water may gather in some lakes or other low-lying areas and hard to flow to other areas as it is at the local lowest place. Though the water can't move to another place by flowing, it can move by some other physical processes, such as infiltration or evaporation. Infiltration is especially common for groundwater. Unlike the surface flow, the movement of groundwater is more slowly and multi-dimensional. Besides on gravity, it is also related to the properties of molecular force, heat, vegetation and void spaces of soil. In infiltration process of groundwater, water might move downward to the underground rivers. It might also move horizontally, or even move upward by syphon of soil or vegetation. Though this circulation process is extremely slow and taking a long time, it is still an important part of the hydrologic cycle.

For above reason, we use infiltration as the second operator of HCO. In this step, water individual can move and search its neighborhood even it can't find a gradient descent direction. This is helpful for both exploiting the neighborhood and escaping the local optima. In infiltration step, for each individual, we select another individual randomly as a neighbor, and select some dimensions randomly preparing to execute a neighborhood search. Then modify the selected dimensions towards or away from the neighbor. The pseudo code of infiltration step of HCO is given in Table 2.

In this part, we didn't use the greedy selection. Which means the position of the individuals may become worse. This step could maintain the diversity of the population in some degree.

Table 2. Pseudo code of infiltration step of HCO

For each individual X_i in the population
Select another individual X_j randomly
Select *sd* dimensions randomly to form a vector *SD*
$$X_{i,SD} = X_{i,SD} + (X_{i,SD} - X_{j,SD}) \cdot 2 * (rand(1, sd) - 0.5)$$
End

3.3   Evaporation and Precipitation

Evaporation and precipitation play an important role in the hydrologic cycle. It is the main way that water changes its state and moves to another place far away. It is also the core motivation that water could be transported from low-lying areas such as oceans and lakes to high attitude areas such as mountains. In our HCO algorithm, we use this operator to keep diversity and escape from local optima.

In evaporation and precipitation step, each water individual will be evaporated by a probability, which is controlled by a parameter called ⟦ P⟧ _eva. And if an individual is evaporated, it will be precipitated to another position by two alternative rules: first, it will be precipitated to a random position in the searching space; second, it will be precipitated to a neighborhood position of best position so far. In the current version of the algorithm, the neighborhood position is generated using Gauss mutation. The pseudo code of evaporation and precipitation step of HCO is given in Table 3.

Table 3. Pseudo code of evaporation and precipitation step of HCO

For each individual X_i in the population
　IF rand<P_{eva}.
　IF rand<0.5
　　Move X_i to another position randomly
　Else
　　Move X_i to neighborhood of best position so far using Gauss mutation
　End
　End
End

Just like the rainfall may occur on both the land and the ocean, we use the above two rules to simulate these two kinds of phenomenon. The first rule could enhance the diversity greatly and avoid trapping in local optima. And the second rule could enhance the local exploitation ability near the optima. For convenience, the probabilities of the two rules are the same in the current algorithm.

4   Difference Between HCO and WCA

As it has mentioned above, there are much similarities between HCO and WCA. They are both inspired by the water cycle on the earth. However, as two different algorithms, they have essential differences.

First, in WCA, individuals are divided into three different roles: sea, rivers and stream. In each iteration, individuals are given their roles according to their finesses [11]. And the role of may be transferred in these thee roles. In our HCO algorithm, all individuals are the same role just like PSO algorithm. Each individual presents part of water in the current position. Compared with WCA, HCO is simpler for understanding and coding.

Second, WCA algorithm mainly focus on the converge process of water. In each step, stream converge to rivers, rivers converge to sea. In HCO algorithm, there are another important step: infiltration. Infiltration is a common phenomenon existed in nature. It plays an important role especially in groundwater cycle. The infiltration step enhances the local search ability of HCO, and could avoid premature in some degree.

Third, in WCA, it uses parameter C as the moving step. The position updating equation is absolute distance based [12]. It's another parameter $dmax = 1e - 16$. The proper parameter setting is important to the optimization ability. For different problems with different scale, it may hard to set the values. In our HCO, position updating equation is relative distance based. It could adapt to different problems.

Performance comparison between HCO and WCA will be given in part II.

5   Simulating and Testing the Effect to Operators of HCO

5.1   Flow Operator

Flow is the core operator of HCO. It makes the population converge to better areas. In the first experiment, we use flow operator only. Infiltration, Evaporation and precipitation are not used. Figure 2 shows the location changes of waters on function under this situation.

It is clear that the water individuals gather rapidly as the iteration increases. All individuals gather near in the optima position at about iteration 16, just seen in Fig. 2 (d). The simulation demonstrates that the population will converge to better position under flow operator.

5.2   Infiltration Operator

Although the flow step make the population converge to better areas, it also may lead the population to premature. Figure 3 shows the location changes of water individuals on powers function. (a) and (b) are only use flow operator. (c) and (d) use both flow and infiltration operator. In Fig. 2 (d), all points look like to overlap with each other as the scale of axes. Actually, they may be like Fig. 3(a) if we enlarge the scale. As in flow step, each individual move to another individual with better position, if we only use this operator, individuals will only gather to best current position and hard to execute global search. There is no trap-escaping mechanism. And the results may stop improving, just like in Fig. 3(b).

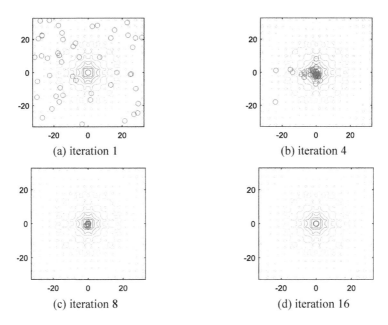

Fig. 2 Location changes of water individuals with only flow operator on ackley function

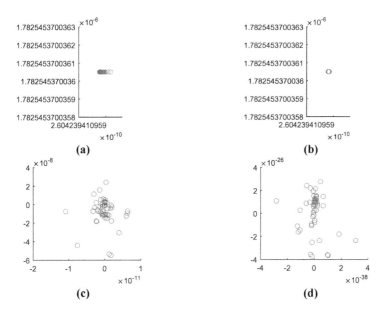

Fig. 3. Location changes of water individuals on powers function

Infiltration operator is a good supplement. In infiltration, individual moves to random neighbor. Though the position of an individual may change worse, it enhances the diversity and won't make the population too near together. Just like Fig. 3(c) and (d), the optimization result could continue improved.

In general, infiltration operator can keep diversity and avoid premature.

5.3   Evaporation and Precipitation Operator

As mentioned above, infiltration operator could keep diversity in some degree. However, it is a local search strategy essentially. We can see that though the points didn't overlap with each other in Fig. 3(c) and (d), they still gather in a tiny space. Once the population gather in a local optima. It still has no chance to escape. A global search approach must be introduced. In HCO algorithm, we introduce evaporation and precipitation operator to enhance the global searching ability. Water individuals can be moved to random place in the searching space by a pre-determined probability. Figure 4 shows the effect of evaporation and precipitation operator: a few individuals jump to far away while most of the individuals gather near the optima.

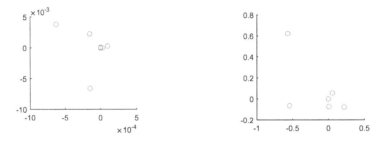

Fig. 4. Location changes of water individuals with evaporation and precipitation operator on powers function

Evaporation and precipitation operator could keep the diversity of population further more. With this operator, the population could escape the local optima easily.

6   Conclusion

In this paper, a novel hydrologic cycle optimization algorithm is proposed by simulating the natural phenomenon of the hydrologic cycle on the earth. Three operators are used in HCO: flow, infiltration, evaporation and precipitation. In flow step, water individual flows and converge to better areas. In infiltration step, neighborhood search is applied to avoid losing the dynamics of evolution. In evaporation and precipitation step, individuals will be evaporated and move to random place or near the current optima in the searching area. This operator could keep diversity and escape from local optima.

In part I, the background and theory of HCO are given. The hydrologic cycle phenomena and simple model on the earth is analyzed. Under the model, our HCO is proposed. The difference of HCO and another algorithm inspired by water cycle, WCA is drawn. And then, the effects of the three operators are tested and analyzed.

In part II, we compared the optimization ability of HCO with four other algorithms on ten benchmark functions. Nurse Scheduling Problem (NSP) is also applied to test its optimization ability on real-world problem. The experiments show that HCO performed best on most functions and got a better solution in NSP than the comparison algorithms.

However, as a newly proposed algorithm, it has still much work to do. It performed not well on two valley-shaped functions. The optimization ability for current version of HCO is not sufficient compared with some recent variation algorithm. We will continue to test and improve the model and algorithm in future work.

Acknowledgement. This work is supported by the National Natural Science Foundation (Grant No. 61703102, 71571120), Natural Science Foundation of Guangdong (Grant No. 2015A0303 10274, 2015A030313649), and Project of Department of Education of Guangdong Province (No. 2015KQNCX157). And the authors are very grateful to the anonymous reviewers for their valuable suggestions and comments to improve the quality of this paper.

References

1. Holland, J.: Genetic algorithms. Sci. Am. **267**(1), 66–72 (1992)
2. Koza, J.R., Poli, R.: Genetic programming. Search Methodologies, 127–164 (2005)
3. Kennedy J., Eberhart R.C.: Particle swarm optimization. In: Proceedings of the 1995 IEEE International Conference on Neural Networks, vol. 4, pp. 1942–1948 (1995)
4. Karaboga, D., Akay, B.: A comparative study of artificial bee colony algorithm. Appl. Math. Comput. **214**(1), 108–132 (2009)
5. Passino, K.M.: Biomimicry of bacterial foraging for distributed optimization and control. IEEE Control Syst. Mag. **22**, 52–67 (2002)
6. Tan, Y., Zhu, Y.: Fireworks algorithm for optimization. In: Tan, Y., Shi, Y., Tan, K.C. (eds.) ICSI 2010. LNCS, vol. 6145, pp. 355–364. Springer, Heidelberg (2010). https://doi.org/10. 1007/978-3-642-13495-1_44
7. Shi, Y.: Brain storm optimization algorithm. In: Tan, Y., Shi, Y., Chai, Y., Wang, G. (eds.) ICSI 2011. LNCS, vol. 6728, pp. 303–309. Springer, Heidelberg (2011). https://doi.org/10. 1007/978-3-642-21515-5_36
8. Eskandar, H., Sadollah, A., Bahreininejad, A., et al.: Water cycle algorithm – a novel metaheuristic optimization method for solving constrained engineering optimization problems. Comput. Struct. **110–111**(10), 151–166 (2012)
9. Schlesinger, W.H., Bernhardt, E.S.: The global water cycle. In: Biogeochemistry (Third Edition), pp. 399–417. Academic Press, Boston (2013). Chap. 10
10. White, J.: A closer look: the hydrologic cycle. Calif. Agric. **419**(2), 191–198 (2012)
11. Sadollah, A., Eskandar, H., Kim, J.H.: Water cycle algorithm for solving constrained multi-objective optimization problems. Appl. Soft Comput. **27**, 279–298 (2015)
12. Niu, B., Fan, Y., Zhao, P., Xue, B., Li, L., Chai, Y.: A novel bacterial foraging optimizer with linear decreasing chemotaxis step. In: 2nd International Workshop on Intelligent Systems and Applications, pp. 1–4. Institute of Electrical and Electronics Engineers (IEEE), Wuhan (2010)

Hydrologic Cycle Optimization Part II: Experiments and Real-World Application

Ben Niu[1], Huan Liu[1], and Xiaohui Yan[2(✉)]

[1] College of Management, Shenzhen University, Shenzhen 518060, China
[2] School of Mechanical Engineering, Dongguan University of Technology,
Dongguan 523808, China
yxhsunshine@gmail.com

Abstract. A novel Hydrologic Cycle Optimization (HCO) is proposed by simulating the natural phenomena of the hydrologic cycle on the earth. Three operators are employed in the algorithm: flow, infiltration, evaporation and precipitation. Flow step simulates the water flowing to lower areas and makes the population converge to better areas. Infiltration step executes neighborhood search. Evaporation and precipitation step could keep diversity and escape from local optima. The proposed algorithm is verified on ten benchmark functions and applied to a real-world problem named Nurse Scheduling Problem (NSP) with several comparison algorithms. Experiment results show that HCO performs better on most benchmark functions and in NSP than the other algorithms. In Part I, the background and theory of HCO are introduced firstly. And then, experimental studies on benchmark and real world problems are given in Part II.

Keywords: Hydrologic cycle optimization · Swarm Intelligence
Application · Nurse scheduling problem

1 Introduction

Optimization problems are kind of problems we unusually encountered in both engineering and numerical calculation. Recently, many population-based algorithms are proposed as the classic operation approaches. However, they are restricted and perform not well in solving complex optimization problems. These population-based algorithms include some evolutionary algorithms, such as Genetic Algorithm (GA) [1], Genetic Programming (GP) [2], Swarm Intelligence algorithms inspired by animal colonies (Particle Swarm Optimization (PSO) [3], Artificial Bee Colony (ABC) algorithm [4], Bacterial Foraging Optimization (BFO) [5]), and some other heuristic algorithms, such as Fireworks Algorithm (FWA) [6] and Brain Storm Optimization (BSO) [7].

There is a saying in an ancient Chinese poetry: 'all rivers run east into the sea'. As in China, the elevation is higher in the western area and lower in the eastern area in general. Most of rivers will run east as the terrain reason. In fact, the water most converged into the lowest place, the ocean, by the cyclical process. This is similar with the optima searching process mentioned above. Inspired by this phenomenon and the

© Springer International Publishing AG, part of Springer Nature 2018
Y. Tan et al. (Eds.): ICSI 2018, LNCS 10941, pp. 350–358, 2018.
https://doi.org/10.1007/978-3-319-93815-8_34

similarity, we decide to develop an optimization algorithm according to the hydrologic cycle process.

In 2012, Eskandar proposed a water cycle algorithm called WCA [8], which has raised wide attention of scholars. In this paper, we analyze the hydrologic cycle process and its main factors firstly. Then, a novel hydrologic cycle optimization algorithm is proposed under the model, which abbreviated as HCO. As a new and independent algorithm proposed, the difference between HCO and WCA is analyzed in this paper. Each operator of HCO is also simulated to demonstrate its effect. To verify the performance of the proposed algorithm, we test it on a set of benchmark functions and a real-world problem with several other well-known optimization algorithms. The results show that the proposed algorithm outperformed than the other algorithms compared on most benchmark functions and the nurse scheduling problem. The comparison and application will be given in part II.

Part II of this paper is structured as follows. In Sect. 2, the proposed HCO and other four comparison algorithms are tested on ten benchmark functions. Results are presented and discussed. In Sect. 3, the HCO is applied to solve the nurse scheduling problem with other comparison algorithms. Finally, conclusions of Part II are presented in Sect. 4.

2 Experiments

In this section, the performance of HCO is tested on ten unconstrained benchmark functions. Several classic algorithms are employed for comparison, including WCA, PSO [9], GA and a variation of BFO algorithm, Modified Bacterial Foraging Optimization (MBFO) [10]. Due to the similarity between flow operator in HCO and chemotaxis step in BFO, MBFO is also selected to compare with our proposed HCO.

2.1 Benchmark Functions

The benchmark functions for our tests are listed in Table 1. Among these functions, f_1 and f_2 are unimodal functions with independent variables. They are bowl-shaped. f_3–f_6 are unimodal functions with dependent variables. f_3 and f_4 are plate-shaped. f_5 and f_6 are valley-shaped. f_7 and f_8 are multimodal functions with independent variables. f_9 and f_{10} are multimodal functions with dependent variables. All these functions are widely adopted by many researchers to test the optimization ability of their algorithms [11, 12].

In our experiments, we tested algorithms on these benchmark functions with a dimension of 20. To compare these algorithms fairly, we use the maximum number of function evaluations (FEs) as the termination criterion in our tests. It is also used in many other works [13, 14]. The FEs is setting as 100000 in our test.

2.2 Parameters Settings

The population sizes S of all algorithms are set as 50. In HCO, the maximum flow times *maxFT* is 3. Evaporation probability P_{eva} is 0.1. All the control parameters for the involved comparison algorithms are set to be default of their original literatures.

Table 1. Benchmark functions

Function		Formulation	Type	Variable ranges	$f(x^*)$
f_1	Powers	$f(x) = \sum_{i=1}^{n} \lvert x_i \rvert^{i+1}$	UI	$[-1, 1]^n$	0
f_2	Sumsquares	$f(x) = \sum_{i=1}^{n} i x_i^2$	UI	$[-10, 10]^n$	0
f_3	Zakharov	$f(x) = \sum_{i=1}^{n} x_i^2 + \left(\sum_{i=1}^{n} 0.5 i x_i\right)^2 + \left(\sum_{i=1}^{n} 0.5 i x_i\right)^4$	UD	$[-5, 10]^n$	0
f_4	Schwefel2.22	$f(x) = \sum_{i=1}^{n} \lvert x_i \rvert + \prod_{i=1}^{n} \lvert x_i \rvert$	UD	$[-10, 10]^n$	0
f_5	Dixon_Price	$f(x) = (x_i - 1)^2 + \sum_{i=2}^{n} i\left(2 x_i^2 - x_{i-1}\right)^2$	UD	$[-10, 10]^n$	0
f_6	Rosenbrock	$f(x) = \sum_{i=1}^{n-1} \left(100\left(x_i^2 - x_{i+1}\right)^2 + (1 - x_i)^2\right)$	UD	$[-15, 15]^n$	0
f_7	Schwefel	$f(x) = 418.9829 n - \sum_{i=1}^{n} \left(x_i \sin\left(\sqrt{\lvert x_i \rvert}\right)\right)$	MI	$[-500, 500]^n$	0
f_8	Rastrigin	$f(x) = \sum_{i=1}^{n} \left(x_i^2 - 10\cos(2\pi x_i) + 10\right)$	MI	$[-10, 10]^n$	0
f_9	Ackley	$f(x) = 20 + e - 20 e^{\left(-0.2\sqrt{\frac{1}{D}\sum_{i=1}^{D} x_i^2}\right)} - e^{\left(\frac{1}{D}\sum_{i=1}^{D} \cos(2\pi x_i)\right)}$	MD	$[-32.768, 32.768]^n$	0
f_{10}	Griewank	$f(x) = \frac{1}{4000}\left(\sum_{i=1}^{D} x_i^2\right) - \left(\prod_{i=1}^{D} \cos\left(\frac{x_i}{\sqrt{i}}\right)\right) + 1$	MD	$[-600, 600]^n$	0

In MBFO, $Nc = 50$, $Ns = 4$, $Nre = 4$, $Ned = 10$, $Pe = 0.25$, $\lambda = 1.04$, the initial step size $Cs = 0.1(Ub\text{-}Lb)$, where Lb and Ub refer the lower bound and upper bound of the variables of the problems. In PSO algorithm, ω decreased from 0.9 to 0.7. $C1 = C2 = 2.0$. $Vmin = 0.1 \times Lb$, $Vmax = 0.1 \times Ub$. In GA, Pc is 0.95 and Pm is 0.1. In WCA, $Nsr = 4$, $dmax = 1e\text{-}16$.

2.3   Results and Statistical Analysis

Results of the five algorithms on the benchmark functions are listed in Table 2. Best values of these algorithms on each benchmark function are marked as bold. Convergence plots of the algorithms are shown in Fig. 1.

HCO obtained the best mean values on seven of all ten functions. It is obvious that HCO performed much better than other four comparison algorithms on Powers, Sumsquares, Schwefel2.22, Ackley and Griewank, which could be seen in Fig. 1. On these five benchmark functions, both the convergence speed and accuracy are much better than comparison algorithms. Especially at the end stage of the algorithm, it still maintains excellent convergence trend while other algorithms slow down their convergence speed. On Griewank function, HCO performed best on all five algorithms though its final mean value is not that distinct. However, the Min value equals zero, which denotes that it could find global optima in some runtimes.

On Dixon_Price and Rosenbrock function, all algorithm didn't perform well. It has mentioned above these two functions are unimodal functions and have no local optima. All algorithms trapped and barely improved after 5000 FEs. The final results obtained by HCO are a little worse than WCA and PSO. On two multimodal independent variable-functions, all algorithm didn't perform well neither. On Schwefel function, the results obtained by GA are a little better than HCO. On Rastrigin function, most algorithms trapped into local optima while HCO obtained well results in some runtimes: though the mean value is not very good, the min value is acceptable. And the

Table 2. Results obtained by HCO, MBFO, PSO, GA and WCA

		HCO	MBFO	PSO	GA	WCA
Powers	Mean	**3.7016E-37**	4.0119E-09	1.7294E-17	5.1447E-03	4.0180E-30
	Std	**1.1695E-36**	1.2019E-08	3.1250E-17	4.0542E-03	1.0373E-29
	Min	**5.3919E-52**	5.6070E-13	6.7939E-20	9.7543E-04	5.3039E-36
	Max	**3.6985E-36**	3.8204E-08	8.5247E-17	1.5543E-02	3.2952E-29
Sumsquares	Mean	**5.1304E-25**	1.2199E+01	9.8584E-03	4.7217E+01	1.6447E-20
	Std	**1.0731E-24**	2.0548E+01	3.9476E-03	2.0118E+01	5.1203E-20
	Min	**6.1772E-29**	5.6495E-05	5.6492E-03	1.6060E+01	1.7583E-23
	Max	**3.0061E-24**	6.6103E+01	1.6082E-02	7.7512E+01	1.6217E-19
Zakharov	Mean	1.2322E-04	1.2449E+02	5.8891E+01	4.0113E+02	**7.9534E-09**
	Std	1.0867E-04	5.3491E+01	6.5056E+01	7.5368E+01	**9.3902E-09**
	Min	8.1818E-06	5.8390E+01	2.8912E-02	2.5678E+02	**1.2332E-09**
	Max	3.9409E-04	1.8146E+02	1.8165E+02	5.0564E+02	**2.8489E-08**
Schwefel2.22	Mean	**3.9429E-24**	2.7964E-02	2.5281E-01	8.9493E+00	1.0564E-07
	Std	**5.6621E-24**	1.7066E-02	2.2667E-01	1.7111E+00	3.3294E-07
	Min	**3.2804E-27**	6.3887E-03	9.4537E-02	6.1432E+00	4.8396E-13
	Max	**1.6339E-23**	5.6358E-02	8.5706E-01	1.1179E+01	1.0532E-06
Dixon_Price	Mean	1.1104E+00	3.8571E+01	**7.8473E-01**	9.4929E+01	6.6667E-01
	Std	1.2158E+00	4.2162E+01	**1.0083E-01**	4.3812E+01	1.8892E-08
	Min	**6.6667E-01**	6.6669E-01	6.7377E-01	5.6328E+01	**6.6667E-01**
	Max	4.5537E+00	1.3319E+02	9.4180E-01	1.8785E+02	**6.6667E-01**
Rosenbrock	Mean	**3.0646E+01**	6.0635E+02	4.6866E+01	1.3061E+03	4.7282E+01
	Std	**1.8369E+01**	8.4787E+02	3.1384E+01	6.0339E+02	3.2017E+01
	Min	2.0566E+01	1.5426E+01	2.6358E+01	5.2035E+02	**7.6594E+00**
	Max	**8.2560E+01**	2.1822E+03	1.1366E+02	2.4317E+03	8.8487E+01
Schwefel	Mean	3.0330E+03	3.0845E+03	6.3314E+03	**1.0780E+03**	3.6994E+03
	Std	5.4843E+02	5.7164E+02	8.5847E+02	**4.0631E+02**	6.2497E+02
	Min	**1.8955E+03**	2.0733E+03	4.6592E+03	6.1976E+02	2.7909E+03
	Max	3.8184E+03	3.8909E+03	7.6603E+03	**1.8282E+03**	4.3276E+03
Rastrigin	Mean	**1.0509E+01**	1.4878E+01	6.9609E+01	1.5907E+02	9.0654E+01
	Std	6.8835E+00	**5.2404E+00**	1.5393E+01	3.6817E+01	2.7678E+01
	Min	**2.4213E+00**	7.2997E+00	5.0816E+01	9.2285E+01	5.7727E+01
	Max	**2.4522E+01**	2.2891E+01	9.6671E+01	2.3057E+02	1.4029E+02
Ackley	Mean	**8.1878E-12**	1.3821E-02	1.8124E+00	1.9700E+01	3.1922E-01
	Std	**1.9798E-11**	7.1328E-03	3.4190E-01	6.3694E-01	9.9788E-01
	Min	**2.2204E-14**	4.1141E-03	1.3425E+00	1.8866E+01	2.8495E-10
	Max	**6.4209E-11**	2.1115E-02	2.4979E+00	2.0578E+01	3.1591E+00
Griewank	Mean	1.9717E-03	9.1016E-01	1.0035E-01	5.5634E+00	2.6971E-02
	Std	4.3158E-03	7.5480E-01	4.9980E-02	1.9504E+00	2.6539E-02
	Min	**0.0000E+00**	7.3105E-02	2.4494E-02	3.8840E+00	2.2204E-15
	Max	**1.2321E-02**	2.1680E+00	1.9885E-01	1.0693E+01	8.3109E-02

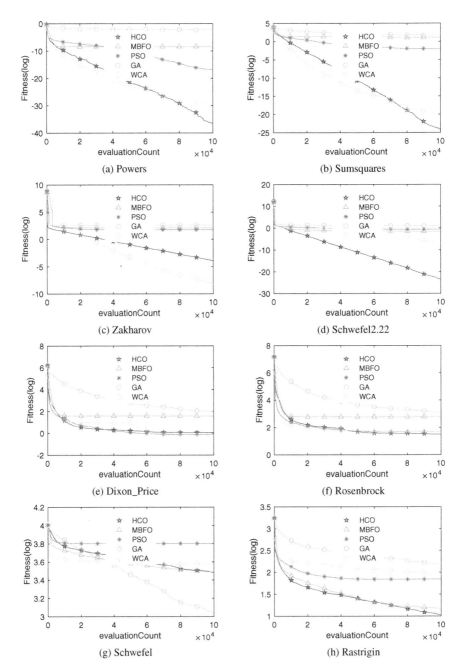

Fig. 1. Convergence plots of HCO, MBFO, PSO, GA and WCA algorithms on ten benchmark functions

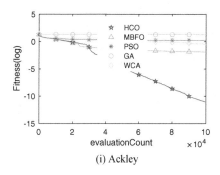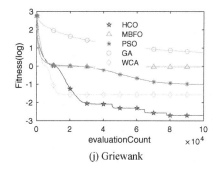

(i) Ackley   (j) Griewank

Fig. 1. (*continued*)

convergence trend is nice at the end stage of the algorithm, seen in Fig. 1(h). In general, HCO shows well optimization ability and performs best among the five algorithms on most benchmark functions.

3   Real-World Application

In this section, the proposed algorithm is applied to solve Nurse Scheduling Problem in order to test the performance of our algorithm in real-world application.

3.1   Nurse Scheduling Problem

Nurse Scheduling Problem (NSP) can be described as creating schedules by assigning the nurses to specific shifts in specific time periods. In this paper, the model of NSP [15] can be constructed as follows:

(i) Objective function

$$\min f(x) = \sum_{i=1}^{nn}\sum_{j=1}^{sk}\sum_{k=1}^{ss}\sum_{d=1}^{sd} x_{i,j,k,d} * w_{j,k} + c * \sum_{j=1}^{sk}\sum_{k=1}^{ss}\sum_{d=1}^{sd} m_{j,k,d} \tag{1}$$

Where nn is the number of nurses; sk is the number of skill types; ss is the number of shift types; sd is the number of total days in scheduling cycle; $x_{i,j,k,d}$ represents that Nurse i with skill type j is assigned on day d in shift type k; $w_{j,k}$ is the wage of nurses with skill type j in shift type k; c denotes punishment coefficients and $m_{j,k,d}$ is the number of nurses with skill type j that do not satisfy demands on day d in shift type k.

(ii) Hard constraints

$$\sum_{k=1}^{ss} x_{i,j,k,d} = 1 \quad i = 1,2,\dots nn; \; j = 1,2,\dots,sk; \; d = 1,2,\dots,sd \tag{2}$$

$$x_{i,j,3,d} + x_{i,j,1,d+1} \leq 1 \quad i = 1,2,\ldots,nn; j = 1,2,\ldots,sk; d = 1,2,\ldots,sd-1 \quad (3)$$

$$lp \leq \sum_{d=1}^{sd} x_{i,j,k,d} \leq up \quad i = 1,2,\ldots,nn; j = 1,2,\ldots,sk; k = 1,2,\ldots,ss \quad (4)$$

where lp and up represent the nurse's lower limit and upper limit of work shifts, respectively.

(iii) Soft constraint

$$\sum_{i=1}^{nn} x_{i,j,k,d} \geq h_{i,j,k,d} \quad j = 1,2,\ldots,sk; k = 1,2,\ldots,ss; d = 1,2,\ldots,sd-1 \quad (5)$$

where $h_{i,j,k,d}$ is the minimum coverage demands of a hospital on day d, in shift type k and for skill type j nurses.

3.2 Experiments

(i) Encoding

In HCO, each individual representing a potential scheduling solution for nn nurses can be constructed as an array of $1 * nn$. This array is consist of nn matrices of size $ss * sd$, which is shown below (Fig. 2).

$$POP = \left[\begin{pmatrix} 1 & \cdots & 0 \\ \vdots & \ddots & \vdots \\ 0 & \cdots & 1 \end{pmatrix} \begin{pmatrix} 1 & \cdots & 0 \\ \vdots & \ddots & \vdots \\ 0 & \cdots & 1 \end{pmatrix} \begin{pmatrix} 1 & \cdots & 0 \\ \vdots & \ddots & \vdots \\ 0 & \cdots & 1 \end{pmatrix} \cdots \begin{pmatrix} 1 & \cdots & 0 \\ \vdots & \ddots & \vdots \\ 0 & \cdots & 1 \end{pmatrix} \right]$$
$$\underbrace{}_{nn}$$

Fig. 2. The combination of each individual

(ii) Experiment settings

In Sect. 2, we found that WCA and PSO algorithms perform well on some benchmark functions. Therefore, in the NSP experiment, the competitive two algorithms are chosen as comparison algorithms. The number of nurse is 11, including 5 juniors, 4 middles and 2 seniors. The hospital's minimum coverage demand is generated randomly. Therefore, the parameters in NSP model are set as: $nn = 11$, $sk = 3$, $ss = 4$ (morning shift, afternoon shift, night shift and free shift), $sd = 7$, $c = 1000$.

The population sizes S of all algorithms are 50 and the number of iterations is 10000. Each algorithm ran 10 times. Other parameters in HCO, WCA and PSO are the same as the settings in Sect. 2.

(iii)   Results and analyses

Table 3 presents the numerical results of the mean value and standard deviation for each algorithm. Figure 3 shows the convergence characteristics for the three algorithms.

As shown in Table 3 and Fig. 3, compared with the two other algorithms, HCO has a stronger global search ability and obtains better solutions in NSP.

Table 3. Numerical results obtained by the three algorithms

Algorithm	HCO	WCA	PSO
Mean	**4.49E+03**	4.71E+03	4.68E+03
Std.	3.33E+01	1.27 E+02	**2.65E+01**

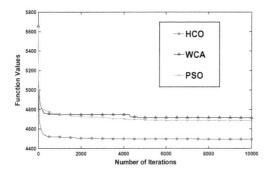

Fig. 3. Convergence curve of the three algorithms

4   Conclusion

In Part II of this paper, to verify the optimization ability of the proposed HCO, we tested it on ten classic benchmark functions. WCA, PSO, GA and a variation of BFO algorithm-MBFO are employed for comparison. The results show that HCO performs best on seven functions of all ten. And on six among that, the superiority is distinct, which indicates the good performance of HCO. Moreover, HCO and other comparison algorithms are applied to solve the nurse scheduling problem. The experimental results show that HCO acquires better solutions than other comparison algorithms for NSP.

In the future, we will continue to improve model of HCO to enhance its performance and may apply it to other real-world applications, like portfolio selections, feature selections etc.

Acknowledgement. This work is supported by the National Natural Science Foundation (Grant Nos. 71571120, 61703102), Natural Science Foundation of Guangdong (Grant Nos. 2015A030310274, 2015A030313649), Project of Guangdong Province Universities and Colleges Pearl River Scholar Funded Scheme 2016, and Project of Department of Education of Guangdong Province (No. 2015KQNCX157).

References

1. Holland, J.: Genetic algorithms. Sci. Am. **267**(1), 66–72 (1992)
2. Koza, J.R., Poli, R.: Genetic programming. In: Burke, E.K., Kendall, G. (eds.) Search Methodologies, pp. 127–164. Springer, Boston (2005). https://doi.org/10.1007/0-387-28356-0_5
3. Kennedy, J., Eberhart, R.C.: Particle swarm optimization. In: Proceedings of the 1995 IEEE International Conference on Neural Networks, vol. 4, pp. 1942–1948 (1995)
4. Karaboga, D., Akay, B.: A comparative study of Artificial Bee Colony algorithm. Appl. Math. Comput. **214**(1), 108–132 (2009)
5. Passino, K.M.: Biomimicry of bacterial foraging for distributed optimization and control. IEEE Control Syst. Mag. **22**, 52–67 (2002)
6. Tan, Y., Zhu, Y.: Fireworks algorithm for optimization. In: Tan, Y., Shi, Y., Tan, K.C. (eds.) ICSI 2010. LNCS, vol. 6145, pp. 355–364. Springer, Heidelberg (2010). https://doi.org/10.1007/978-3-642-13495-1_44
7. Shi, Y.: Brain storm optimization algorithm. In: Tan, Y., Shi, Y., Chai, Y., Wang, G. (eds.) ICSI 2011. LNCS, vol. 6728, pp. 303–309. Springer, Heidelberg (2011). https://doi.org/10.1007/978-3-642-21515-5_36
8. Eskandar, H., Sadollah, A., Bahreininejad, A., et al.: Water cycle algorithm – a novel metaheuristic optimization method for solving constrained engineering optimization problems. Comput. Struct. **110–111**(10), 151–166 (2012)
9. Kennedy, J.: Particle swarm optimization. In: Sammut, C., Webb, G.I. (eds.) Encyclopedia of Machine Learning, pp. 760–766. Springer, Boston (2011). https://doi.org/10.1007/978-0-387-30164-8
10. Yan, X., Zhang, Z., Guo, J., Li, S., Zhao, S.: A modified bacterial foraging optimization algorithm for global optimization. In: Huang, D.-S., Bevilacqua, V., Premaratne, P. (eds.) ICIC 2016. LNCS, vol. 9771, pp. 627–635. Springer, Cham (2016). https://doi.org/10.1007/978-3-319-42291-6_62
11. Ma, L., Zhu, Y., Zhang, D., Niu, B.: A hybrid approach to artificial bee colony algorithm. Neural Comput. Appl. **27**(2), 387–409 (2016)
12. Niu, B., Fan, Y., Zhao, P., Xue, B., Li, L., Chai, Y.: A novel bacterial foraging optimizer with linear decreasing chemotaxis step. In: 2nd International Workshop on Intelligent Systems and Applications, pp. 1–4. Institute of Electrical and Electronics Engineers (IEEE), Wuhan (2010)
13. Liang, J.J., Qin, A.K., Suganthan, P.N., Baskar, S.: Comprehensive learning particle swarm optimizer for global optimization of multimodal functions. IEEE Trans. Evol. Comput. **10**(3), 281–295 (2006)
14. Ma, L., Zhu, Y., Liu, Y., Tian, L., Chen, H.: A novel bionic algorithm inspired by plant root foraging behaviors. Appl. Soft Comput. **37**(C), 95–113 (2015)
15. Niu, B., Wang, C., Liu, J., Gan, J., Yuan, L.: Improved bacterial foraging optimization algorithm with information communication mechanism for nurse scheduling. In: Huang, D.-S., Jo, K.-H., Hussain, A. (eds.) ICIC 2015. LNCS, vol. 9226, pp. 701–707. Springer, Cham (2015). https://doi.org/10.1007/978-3-319-22186-1_69

Other Swarm-based Optimization Algorithms

Multiple Swarm Relay-Races
with Alternative Routes

Eugene Larkin[1][(✉)], Vladislav Kotov[1], Aleksandr Privalov[2],
and Alexey Bogomolov[1]

[1] Tula State University, 300012 Tula, Russia
elarkin@mail.ru, vkotov@list.ru,
a.v.bogomolov@gmail.com
[2] Tula State Pedagogical University, 300026 Tula, Russia
privalov.61@mail.ru

Abstract. Competition of swarms, every of which performs a conveyor cooperation of units, operated in physical time, is considered. Such sort of races objectively exists in economics, industry, defense, etc. It is shown, that natural approach to modeling of multiple relay-race with alternative routes is M-parallel semi-Markov process. Due to alternation there are multiple arks in the graph, represented the structure of semi-Markov process. Notion «the space of switches» is introduced. Formulae for calculation the number of routes in the space of switches, stochastic and time characteristics of wandering through M-parallel semi-Markov process are obtained. Conception of distributed forfeit, which depends on stages difference of swarm units, competed in pairs, is proposed. Dependence for evaluation of total forfeit of every participant is obtained. It is shown, that sum of forfeit may be used as optimization criterion in the game strategy optimization task.

Keywords: Relay-race · M-parallel semi-Markov process · Stage
Route · Evolution · Distributed forfeit

1 Introduction

One of ways of unit cooperation in swarm is the conveyor interaction, in which second swarm unit continue to process object of job (data, part of mechanism etc.) immediately after previous unit finishes its part of job. A conveyor cooperation objectively exists in economics, industry, defense, etc. As a rule, the swarm does not operate separately, but in concurrency [1–4] with other swarms, which have conveyor organization too. Conveyor organization of swarms may be represented as overcoming the distance, which is divided onto stages [5]. Let us demand, that efficiency of distance overcoming depends not only on overall winning the race, but on winning or losing stages of distance. If stages are pre-determined, there is the only parameter, namely the time distribution law, which participant can vary and control. In such a way, there is the trivial solution of winning problem - to run distance stages with the greatest possible speed [6, 7]. Such solution is acceptable for a swarm, whose units have sufficient resources to maintain high speed of running distance stages. If it has not, swarm unit tries to find asymmetric response, which leads to the final point of the distance, but along the alternative route. For an external observer selection of route by swarm unit occurs randomly, so model of running the distance on alternative routes should be the stochastic one [8, 9]. The availability of alternative generates premises for an emergence of game situations, in which one can to manage not only by the stage passing time, but also by probabilities (for gamer adversary) or by periodicity (for gamer itself) of rout selection. Those team which can evaluate the benefits and losses from choice of this or that distance route, may construct the optimal strategy of relay-races game for winning the competition as a whole.

Approaches for forecasting of benefits and losses of relay-races games are currently known insufficiently, that explains necessity and relevance of the investigations in this domain.

2   The Structure and the Model of Alternative Route Relay-Race

The chart of relay-races with alternative routes is shown on the Fig. 1. Nodes of the graph represent the relay points, arcs of the graph represent alternative routes.

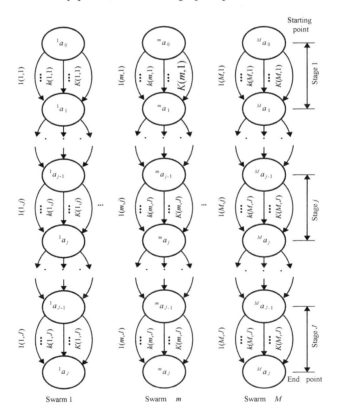

Fig. 1. Relay-races with alternative routes

The following assumptions are made below [5]:

- in relay-races participate M swarms;
- swarms operate independently of each other;
- swarms should to overcome the distance in the real physical time;
- the distance is divided onto J stages, and every stage is overcame by one unit of the swarm, so quantity of stages is equal to quantity units in the swarm;
- the j-th stage of m-th swarm includes K(m, j) routs;
- after finishing j-th stage by j-th unit of the m-th swarm (j + 1)-th unit may choose one of $K(m, j + 1)$ possible routes of the (j + 1)-th stage;
- first units start their first stages at once;
- time of passing of routes by units is a random one and is defined with accuracy to density;
- after completion of j-th stage by j-th unit (j + 1)-th unit starts (j + 1)-th stage without a lag;
- winning or losing of a stage competition is understood as completion the stage the first or not the first;
- winner's forfeit is distributed in time and depends on difference of stages and routes, which pass winner and loser.

Model of multiple alternative route relay-races may be performed as M-parallel semi-Markov process [7–10]

$$\mu = \{A, \boldsymbol{h}(t)\} \tag{1}$$

where t - is the time; A - set of states; $\boldsymbol{h}(t)$ - is the semi-Markov matrix;

$$A = \bigcup_{m=1}^{M} {}^{m}A, \ {}^{m}A \cap {}^{n}A = \emptyset, \text{ when } m \neq \mathbf{n}. \tag{2}$$

$$^{m}A = \{{}^{m}a_0, \ldots, {}^{m}a_j, \ldots, {}^{m}a_J\}. \tag{3}$$

$^{m}a_0, \ 1 \leq m \leq M$ - are the starting states of the M-parallel process; $^{m}a_J, \ 1 \leq m \leq M$- are the absorbing states of the M-parallel process;

$$\boldsymbol{h}(t) = \begin{bmatrix} {}^{1}\boldsymbol{h}(t) & \cdots & \mathbf{0} & \cdots & \mathbf{0} \\ & & \cdots & & \\ & & {}^{m}\boldsymbol{h}(t) & & \\ & & \cdots & & \\ \mathbf{0} & \cdots & \mathbf{0} & \cdots & {}^{M}\boldsymbol{h}(t) \end{bmatrix}. \tag{4}$$

t - is the time; $^{m}\boldsymbol{h}(t)$- is the m-th semi-Markov matrix [8] of size $(J+1) \times (J+1)$; $\mathbf{0}$ - is the zero matrix of size $(J+1) \times (J+1)$.

In its turn m-th semi-Markov matrix $^m\boldsymbol{h}(t)$ of size $J \times J$ is as follows:

$$^m\boldsymbol{h}(t) = \left[^m\boldsymbol{h}_{j,l}(t)\right].\tag{5}$$

where $^m\boldsymbol{h}_{j,l}(t)$ - is the vector-element of $^m\boldsymbol{h}(t)$, disposed on the intersection of j-th row and l-th column;

$$^m\boldsymbol{h}_{j,l}(t) = \begin{cases} ^m\boldsymbol{h}_{j+1}(t), & \text{when } 0 \leq j \leq J-1; \\ 0, & \text{otherwise}; \end{cases}\tag{6}$$

$$^m\boldsymbol{h}_j(t) = \left[h_{1(m,j)}(t), \ldots, h_{k(m,j)}(t), \ldots, h_{K(m,j)}(t)\right].\tag{7}$$

$$h_{k(m,j)}(t) = p_{k(m,j)}(t)f_{k(m,j)}(t).\tag{8}$$

$$p_{k(m,j)} = \int_0^\infty h_{k(m,j)}(t)\,dt.\tag{9}$$

$p_{k(m,j)}$ - is the probability of choice of $k(m,j)$ route by j-th unit of m-th swarm; $f_{k(m,j)}(t)$ - is the time density of overcoming $k(m,j)$ route by j-th unit of m-th swarm; $p_{k(m,J)} = 0$, $f_{k(m,j)}(t) = \lim_{\tau \to \infty} \delta(t-\tau)$, $1 \leq m \leq M$.

Increment of numeration of j in (6) is due to the fact that initial values of j nominate numbers of semi-Markov process states, output values of j nominate numbers of stages of the distance or swarm units.

Let us consider the switch from $^m a_j$ to $^m a_j$ by any route in semi-Markov process [11–13]

$$^m\mu = \{^m A, ^m\boldsymbol{h}(t)\}.\tag{10}$$

Due to the fact, that all possible switches compile the full group of incompatible events, time density of the process $^m\mu$ residence in the state $^m a_j$ is as follows [14]:

$$^m f_j(t) = \sum_{k(m,j)=1}^{K(m,j)} h_{k(m,j)}(t).\tag{11}$$

$$\sum_{k(m,j)=1}^{K(m,j)} p_{k(m,j)} = 1.\tag{12}$$

Let us select from all possible routes of wandering through the process $^m\mu$ route as follows:

$$s_{l(m)} = [k(m,1), \ldots, k(m,j), \ldots, k(m,J)].\tag{13}$$

Common number of selected routes is equal to

$$K(m) = \prod_{j=1}^{J} K(m,j).$$
(14)

Weighted time density of wandering from the state $^{m}a_0$ till the state $^{m}a_J$ through the selected route is as follows:

$$h_{k(m)}(t) = L^{-1} \left[\prod_{j=1}^{J} L\left[h_{k(m,j)}(t)\right] \right].$$
(15)

Probability of remaining the process on the route (13) may be evaluated as follows:

$$p_{k(m)} = \int_{0}^{\infty} h_{k(m)}(t)\, dt = \prod_{j=1}^{J} p_{k(m,j)}.$$
(16)

Pure time density of wandering from the state $^{m}a_0$ till the state $^{m}a_J$ through the selected route is as follows:

$$f_{k(m)}(t) = \frac{h_{k(m)}(t)}{p_{k(m)}}.$$
(17)

Time density of wandering from the state $^{m}a_0$ till the state $^{m}a_J$ on any possible arbitrary route (13) is as follows:

$$^{m}f_{\Sigma}(t) = \sum_{k(m)=1}^{K(m)} h_{k(m)}(t).$$
(18)

3 Common Formulae for Evolution Parameters

Let us extract from every semi-Markov process $^{m}\mu$ route (13). When there are wanderings through selected routes, switches in processes compete between them. The result of competition is the combination of stages, occupied by corresponding swarm units at a current time. All possible combination may be obtained as Cartesian product of sets (13)

$$S_{l(w)} = \overset{M}{\underset{m=1}{\overset{C}{\prod}}} {}^m s_{l(w)} = \{[k(1,0), \ldots, k(m,0), \ldots, k(M,0)], \ldots, \tag{19}$$

$$[k(1,j), \ldots, k(m,j), \ldots, k(M,j)], \ldots, [k(1,J), \ldots, k(m,J), \ldots, k(M,J)]\}.$$

where $\overset{C}{\prod}$ - is the sign of group Cartesian product.

Cartesian product gives M-dimensional space $S_{l(w)}$ of states.

Process of switches begins from the state $\mathbf{S}_b = [k(1,0), \ldots, k(m,0), \ldots, k(M,0)] = [0, \ldots, 0, \ldots, 0]$ and ends at the state $\mathbf{S}_e = [k(1,J), \ldots, k(m,J), \ldots, k(M,J)] = [J, \ldots, J, \ldots, J]$. Common number of states is equal to $(J+1)^M$. Wandering through the space $S_{l(w)}$ has the character of evolution, in which after every switch only one element of vector S may increase on unit. Sequence of switches generates the trajectory of switches. Common quantity of switches is equal to $R = JM$.

Common quantity of switch trajectories grows fast in dependence of number of stages and swarms (R. Bellman's "curse of dimensionality" [17]). To define common quantity of switch trajectories let us link digit «1» with increment on the first co-ordinate and digit «2» with increment on the second co-ordinate of two-dimensional, $J_1 \times J_2$, space of switches. Let us find the $(J_1 \times J_2)$-th Cartesian degree of the set $\{1, 2\}$ and gather all vectors, which include J_1 «ones» and J_2 «twos» into one set. Cardinality of this set is equal to J_1 -th binomial coefficient, i.e.

$$Q_{J_1, J_2} = \frac{(J_1 + J_2)!}{J_1! \cdot J_2!}. \tag{20}$$

Let us divide set of «twos» onto subset of J_2 «twos» and subset of J_3 «threes», find the $(J_1 \times J_2 + J_3)$-th Cartesian degree of the set $\{1, 2, 3\}$ and gather all vectors, which include J_1 «ones», J_2 «twos» and J_2 «threes» into one set. Then common number of switch trajectories in 3 dimensional space may be find as follows:

$$Q_{J_1, J_2, J_3} = \frac{(J_1 + J_2 + J_3)! \cdot (J_2 + J_3)!}{J_1! \cdot (J_2 + J_3)! \cdot J_2! \cdot J_3!} = \frac{(J_1 + J_2 + J_3)!}{J_1! \cdot J_2! \cdot J_3!}.$$

In common case

$$Q_{J_1, \ldots J_M} = \frac{\left(\sum\limits_{m=1}^{M} J_m\right)!}{\prod\limits_{m=1}^{M} J_m!}. \tag{21}$$

When $J_1 = \ldots = J_m = \ldots = J_M = J$,

$$Q_J^M = \frac{(MJ)!}{(J!)^M}.$$ (22)

For evaluation of stochastic and time characteristics of M-parallel semi-Markov process evolution let us consider the common case, when time intervals between switches are determined with densities $g_1(t), \ldots, g_m(t), \ldots, g_M(t)$. In such a case time density till the first switch is defined as

$$g_w(t) = \sum_{m=1}^{M} \tilde{g}_{wm}(t) = \sum_{m=1}^{M} g_m(t) \prod_{\substack{\alpha=1 \\ \alpha \neq m}}^{M} [1 - G_\alpha(t)].$$ (23)

Where $g_{wm}(t)$ - is the weighted density of time of winning the m-th density; $G_{...}(t) = \int_0^t g_{...}(\tau) d\tau$ - is the distribution function; α - is an auxiliary index.

Probability of the m-th density winning and pure density of the m-th density winning are equal, correspondingly:

$$\pi_{wm} = \int_0^\infty \tilde{g}_{wm}(t) dt; \quad g_{wm} = \frac{\tilde{g}_{wm}(t)}{\pi_{wm}}.$$ (24)

Next formula, necessary for relay-races simulation, is the dependence for waiting time density. If from competing processes $g_\alpha(t)$ and $g_\beta(t)$ wins the process $g_\beta(t)$, it waits until $g_\alpha(t)$ will be completed the stage. Waiting time is as follows [3, 5]:

$$g_{\beta \to \alpha}(t) = g_\beta(t) \to_\alpha (t) \frac{\eta(t) \int_0^\infty g_\beta(\tau) g_\alpha(t+\tau) d\tau}{\int_0^\infty G_\beta(t) dG_\alpha(t)}.$$ (25)

where $\eta(t)$ - is the Heaviside function; α, β - are auxiliary indices.

With use of formulae obtained may be formed recursive procedure of relay-race evolution analysis.

4   Recursive Procedure of Evolution Analysis

Recursive character of evolution follows from competitive character of choice of a switch direction in the space $S_{l(w)}$. For build up the recursive procedure let us to introduce auxiliary time density $^r g_{j(m)}(t)$, where r - is the common number of switches during evolution; j - is the stage under consideration; m - is the number of swarm (number of semi-Markov process).

Table 1. Recursive procedure

r	S	Densities
0	$0, ..., 0, ..., 0, ..., 0$	$f_{k(1,1)}, ..., f_{k(m,1)}, ..., f_{k(n,1)}, ..., f_{k(M,1)}$ $^0g_{1(1)}, ..., {}^0g_{1(m)}, ..., {}^0g_{1(n)}, ..., {}^0g_{1(M)}$
1	$0, ..., 0, ..., 1, ..., 0$	$^0g_{1(n)\to1(1)}, ..., {}^0g_{1(n)\to1(m)}, ..., f_{k(n,2)}, ..., {}^0g_{1(n)\to1(M)}$ $^1g_{1(1)}, ..., {}^1g_{1(m)}, ..., {}^1g_{2(n)}, ..., {}^1g_{1(M)}$
2	$0, ..., 1, ..., 1, ..., 0$	$^1g_{2(m)\to2(1)}, ..., f_{k(m,2)}, ..., {}^1g_{2(m)\to2(n)}, ..., {}^1g_{2(m)\to2(M)}$ $^2g_{1(1)}, ..., {}^2g_{2(m)}, ..., {}^2g_{2(n)}, ..., {}^2g_{1(M)}$
		...
r-1	$j(1), ..., j(m), ...,$ $j(n), ..., j(M)$	... $^{r-1}g_{j(1)}, ..., {}^{r-1}g_{j(m)}, ..., {}^{r-1}g_{j(n)}, ..., {}^{r-1}j_{i(M)}$
r	$j(1), ..., j(m), ...,$ $j(n), ..., j(M)+1$	$^{r-1}g_{j(M)\to j(1)}, ..., {}^{r-1}g_{j(M)\to j(m)}, ..., {}^{r-1}g_{j(M)\to j(n)}, ..., f_{k(M,j+1)}$ $^rg_{j(1)}, ..., {}^rg_{j(m)}, ..., {}^rg_{j(n)}, ..., {}^rg_{j(M)+1}$
...	...	...
R-2	$J(1), ..., J(m),.$ $..., J(n)$-2$, ..., J(M)$	... $^{R-2}g_{J(n)-1}$
R-1	$J(1), ..., J(m), ..., J(n)-1, ...,$ $J(M)$	$f_{k(n,J)}$ $^{R-1}g_{J(n)-1}$
R	$J(1), ..., J(m) ..., J(n), ...,$ $J(M)$	Relay-race is over

Recursive procedure for one of realization of switch trajectory is shown in the Table 1.

On the first phase of recursion (no switches are made) original time densities $f_{k(1,1)}$, ..., $f_{k(m,1)}$, ..., $f_{k(n,1)}$, ..., $f_{k(M,1)}$ compete between them. To formalize competition description next substitution should be done:

$$^0g_{1(m)} := f_{k(m,1)}, \ 1 \le m \le M \tag{26}$$

After winning in competition one of swarm, f.e. n-th, as it is shown in the Table 1, when $r = 1$, time densities, which participate at the next phase are defined as follows:

$$^1g_{j(m)}(t) := \begin{cases} f_{k(n,2)}(t), \ j := 2 \\ \text{when } n\text{-th process wins, } m = n; \\ ^0g_{1(n)\to1(m)}(t) = {}^0g_{1(n)}(t) \to {}^0g_{1(m)}(t), \\ j := 1 \text{ when } m\text{-th process lost, } m \neq n, \end{cases} \tag{27}$$

where $^0g_{1(n)}(t) \to {}^0g_{1(m)}(t)$ - is the operation, defined as (26).

Probability of winning the first unit of n-th swarm is defined with formulae (23), (24), which for the case under consideration are as follows:

$$\pi_{w1(n)}\left(q_J^M\right) = \int_0^\infty {}^0g_{1(n)}(t) \prod_{\substack{\alpha=1 \\ \alpha \neq n}}^M \left[1 - {}^0G_{1(\alpha)}(t)\right] dt. \tag{28}$$

On the r-th phase of recursion (r switches were made) time densities ${}^{r-1}g_{j(1)}, \ldots,$ ${}^{r-1}g_{j(m)}, \ldots, {}^{r-1}g_{j(n)}, \ldots, {}^{r-1}g_{j(M)}$ compete between them. After winning in competition one of swarm, f.e. M-th, as it is shown in the Table 1, time densities, which participate at the next phase, are becoming as follows:

$$
{}^r g_{j(m)}(t) := \begin{cases}
f_{k(M,j+1)}(t), \; j := j+1, \\
\text{when } M\text{-th process wins}, \; m = M; \\
{}^{r-1}g_{j(M) \to j(m)}(t) = {}^{r-1}g_{j(M)}(t) \to {}^{r-1}g_{j(m)}(t) \\
j := j \text{ when } m\text{-th process lost}, \; m \neq M.
\end{cases} \tag{29}
$$

Probability of winning the j-th unit of M-th swarm is defined with formulae (23), (24), which for the case under consideration are as follows:

$$\pi_{wj(M)}\left(q_J^M\right) = \int_0^\infty {}^r g_{j(n)}(t) \prod_{\substack{\alpha=1 \\ \alpha \neq M}}^M \left[1 - {}^r G_{j(\alpha)}(t)\right] dt. \tag{30}$$

On the last, $(R-1)$-th stage there is no competition, and time between switches is defined as ${}^{R-1}g_{J(n)}(t)..$ In the case, shown in the Table 1, ${}^{R-1}g_{J(n)}(t) := f_{k(n,J)}(t)$; $\pi_{wJ(n)}\left(q_J^M\right) = 1$.

5 Evaluation of Effectiveness of Alternative Relay-Race Strategy

Quite natural for evaluation of effectiveness is the model, in which

- the pairs of swarms, f.e. m-th and n-th are considered;
- swarm unit, which gets a stage with higher number, acquires from swarm unit, who gets a stage with lower number, a forfeit;
- forfeit is defined as distributed payment $c_{k(m,j),k(n,i)}(t)$, value of which depends on time, difference of stages and selected routs.

Let us extract from common evolution, m-th and n-th swarms and tabulate it in the Table 2. This gives s-th

Table 2. Evolution m-th and n-th swarms

r	S	Densities	r	S	Densities
0	0, 0	$f_{k(m,1)}, f_{k(n,1)},$ $^0g_{1(m)}, {}^0g_{1(n)}$	$r+1$	$j(m)+1, j(n)$	$f_{k(m,J+1)}, {}^{r+1}g_{j(m)\to j(n)}$ $^{r+1}g_{j(m)+1}, {}^{r+1}g_{j(n)}$
1	0, 1	$^0g_{1(m)\to1(n)}, f_{k(n,2)}$ $^1g_{0(m)}, {}^1g_{2(n)}$			...
			$R-2$	$J(m), J(n)$	... $^{R-2}g_{J(m)}, {}^{R-2}g_{J(n)}$
2	1, 1	$f_{k(m,2)}, {}^1g_{1(m)\to2(n)}$	$R-1$	$J(m), J(n)+1$	$^{R-2}g_{J(n)\to J(m)}$ $^{R-1}g_{J(m)}$
		...			
r	$i(m),$ $i(n)$	... $^rg_{j(m)}, {}^rg_{j(n)}$	R	$J(m)+1, J(n)+1$	Relay-race is over

Analysis of evolution shows that situation, which change conditions of forfeit payments emerges from winning of one of participant and lasts till the next switch. If after r switches densities $^rg_{i(m)}(t)$ and $^rg_{i(n)}(t)$ compete, then common sum of forfeit on the stage is as follows [3, 5]:

$$^rC_{k(m,j),k(n,i)}\left(q_J^M\right) = \begin{cases} \dfrac{\int_0^\infty {}^rg_{j(m)}(t)\left[1-{}^rG_{j(n)}(t)\right]c_{k(m,j),k(n,i)}(t)\,dt}{\int_0^\infty {}^rg_{j(m)}(t)\left[1-{}^rG_{j(n)}(t)\right]dt}, & \begin{array}{l}\text{when}\\ \text{wins}\\ \text{swarm } m;\end{array} \\[2em] \dfrac{\int_0^\infty {}^rg_{j(m)}(t)\left[1-{}^rG_{i(m)}(t)\right]c_{k(n,i),k(m,j)}(t)\,dt}{\int_0^\infty {}^rg_{j(n)}(t)\left[1-{}^rG_{i(m)}(t)\right]dt}, & \begin{array}{l}\text{when}\\ \text{wins}\\ \text{swarm } n,\end{array} \end{cases}$$
(31)

where q_J^M - is the number of evolution variant (selected switch trajectory).

Cost of pair competition on the q_J^M-th switching trajectory is as follows:

$$C_{k(m,j),k(n,i)}\left(q_J^M\right) = \sum_{r=1}^{2J} {}^rC_{k(m,j),k(n,i)}\left(q_J^M\right).$$
(32)

The probability of emergence of q_J^M-th trajectory is as follows:

$$\pi_{k(m,j),k(n.i)}\left(q_J^M\right) = \prod_{r=1}^{2J} \pi_w(r).$$
(33)

where $\pi_w(r)$ - is the probability of proper direction choice on the switching trajectory.

Common cost of paired (m-th and n-th swarms) relay-race on the pre-determined, $k(m)$-th and $k(n)$-th routes is as follows:

$$C_{k(m),k(n)} = \sum_{q_J^M=1}^{Q_J^M} \pi_{k(m,j),k(n.i)}\left(q_J^M\right) C_{k(m,j),k(n.i)}\left(q_J^M\right). \tag{34}$$

With use (16) common cost of competition on the mentioned route pair is as follows:

$$C_{m,n} = \sum_{k(n)=1}^{K(n)} \sum_{k(m)=1}^{K(m)} p_{k(m)} p_{k(n)} C_{k(m),k(n)}. \tag{35}$$

Cost $C_{m,n}$ is the forfeit, which in pair competition n-th swarm pays to m-th swarm. To define all forfeits, which swarms «not m-th» pay to m-th swarm one should to summarize $C_{m,n}$ by n:

$$C_{m\Sigma} = \sum_{\substack{n=1, \\ n \neq m}}^{M} C_{m,n},\ 1 \leq m \leq M. \tag{36}$$

Formula (36) may be used as a criterion of optimization of m-th swarm behavior strategy in alternative route relay-race games. In this case possible routs, probabilities and time characteristics of other swarms may be defined through observation of partner's activity. Own, m-th swarm routs, probabilities and time characteristics are optimization variables. Methods of optimization task solving may be adopted from the game theory.

6 Example

For verification of the method operation of the swarm with the structure, shown on the Fig. 2, was considered

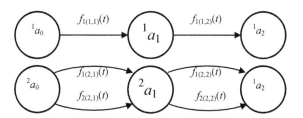

Fig. 2. Structure of the swarm

Time densities of passing the stages by the first swarm are

$$f_{1(1,1)}(t) = f_{1(1,2)}(t) = \delta(t-1). \tag{37}$$

which corresponds to the rigid schedule of stages overcoming. Time densities of passing the stages by the second swarm are

$$f_{1(2,1)}(t) = f_{1(2,2)}(t) = \begin{cases} \frac{1}{0,2} & \text{when } |t-1| \leq 0,1; \\ 0 & \text{otherwise;} \end{cases} \tag{38}$$

$$f_{2(2,1)}(t) = f_{2(2,2)}(t) = \begin{cases} -50t+56,65 \\ \quad \text{when } 0,933 \leq t \leq 1,133; \\ 0 & \text{otherwise;} \end{cases} \tag{39}$$

Expectations of (37), and (38) are equal to 1, just alike the expectation of (36). Value of forfeit is proportional to the time, and equal for all combinations of stages number difference, i.e. $C = 1 \cdot t$.

When second swarm choice "first-first" routes, calculated sum of forfeit, which first swarm gets from the second swarm, is equal to zero due to the symmetry of densities (37), (38) with respect to expectations. When second swarm choice "second-second" routes, due to the asymmetry of densities (39), calculated sum of forfeit, which the first swarm gets from the second swarm, is equal to 0.0042 despite of expectations equality in (37) and (39). So when scheduling, first swarm should take into account aftereffect caused by (39), which does not compensate by low probabilities of proper situation emerging.

7 Conclusion

Working out the model of alternative route relay-race opens new page in the game theory because competition evolve in real physical time. Every stage may be won or lost by swarm unit and all swarms have possibilities of choice one of possible rout, as it is in a real life.

Further investigation in this area should be directed to finding more tight links of proposed method with classical game theory and use typical optimal game strategies [18] in concurrency with partner swarms. Also it is possible of working out radically new strategies, oriented only on the use with the model of multiple alternative route relay-races.

The research was carried out within the state assignment of the Ministry of Education and Science of Russian Federation (No 2.3121.2017/PCH).

References

1. Heymann, M.: Concurrency and discrete event control. IEEE Control Syst. Mag. **10**, 103–112 (1990)
2. Chatterjee, K., Jurdziński, M., Henzinger, T.A.: Simple stochastic parity games. In: Baaz, M., Makowsky, J.A. (eds.) CSL 2003. LNCS, vol. 2803, pp. 100–113. Springer, Heidelberg (2003). https://doi.org/10.1007/978-3-540-45220-1_11
3. Ivutin, A.N., Larkin, E.V.: Simulation of concurrent games. Bull. South Ural State Univ. Ser. Math. Model. Program. Comput. Softw. Chelyabinsk **8**(2), 43–54 (2015)
4. Valk, R.: Concurrency in communicating object petri nets. In: Agha, Gul A., De Cindio, F., Rozenberg, G. (eds.) Concurrent Object-Oriented Programming and Petri Nets. LNCS, vol. 2001, pp. 164–195. Springer, Heidelberg (2001). https://doi.org/10.1007/3-540-45397-0_5
5. Larkin, E.V., Ivutin, A.N., Kotov, V.V., Privalov, A.N.: Simulation of relay-races. Bull. South Ural State Univ. Math. Model. Program. Comput. Softw. **9**(4), 117–128 (2016)
6. Mark, S.: Squillante stochastic analysis and optimization of multiserver systems. In: Ardagna, D., Zhang, L. (eds.) Run-Time Models for Self-managing Systems and Applications. Mathematic Subject Classification, pp. 1–25. Springer, Basel (2010). https://doi.org/10.1007/978-3-0346-0433-8_1
7. Larkin, E.V., Ivutin, A.N.: Estimation of latency in embedded real-time systems. In: 3rd Mediterranean Conference on Embedded Computing (MECO 2014), Budva, Montenegro, pp. 236–239 (2014)
8. Korolyuk, V., Swishchuk, A.: Semi-Markov Random Evolutions. Springer, Dordrecht (1995). https://doi.org/10.1007/978-94-011-1010-5. 309 p.
9. Iverson, M.A., Ozguner, F., Follen, G.J.: Run-time statistical estimation of task execution times for heterogeneous distributed computing. In: Proceedings of 5th IEEE International Symposium on High Performance Distributed Computing, pp. 263–270 (1996)
10. Limnios, N., Swishchuk, A.: Discrete-time semi-Markov random evolutions and their applications. Adv. Appl. Probab. **45**(1), 214–240 (2013)
11. Markov, A.A.: Extension of the law of large numbers to dependent quantities. Izvestiia Fiz.-Matem. Obsch. Kazan Univ., 2nd Ser., pp. 135–156 (1906)
12. Bielecki, T.R., Jakubowski, J., Niewęgłowski, M.: Conditional Markov chains: properties, construction and structured dependence. Stoch. Process. Their Appl. **127**(4), 1125–1170 (2017)
13. Janssen, J., Manca, R.: Applied Semi-Markov processes. Springer, Boston (2006). https://doi.org/10.1007/0-387-29548-8. 310 p.
14. Larkin, E., Ivutin, A., Kotov, V., Privalov, A.: Semi-Markov modelling of commands execution by mobile robot. In: Ronzhin, A., Rigoll, G., Meshcheryakov, R. (eds.) ICR 2016. LNCS (LNAI), vol. 9812, pp. 189–198. Springer, Cham (2016). https://doi.org/10.1007/978-3-319-43955-6_23
15. Bauer, H.: Probability Theory, 523 p. Walter de Gruyter, Berlin (1993)
16. Shiryaev, A.N.: Probability. Springer, New York (1996). https://doi.org/10.1007/978-1-4757-2539-1. 611 p.
17. Bellman, R.E.: Dynamic Programming. Dover Publications, Inc., New York (2003). 339 p.
18. Myerson, R.B.: Game Theory. Harvard University Press, Cambridge (1997). 568 p.
19. Goetz, B., Peierls, T.: Java Concurrency in Practice. Addison Wesley, Reading (2006). 403 p.

Brain Storm Optimization with Multi-population Based Ensemble of Creating Operations

Yuehong Sun[1,2(✉)], Ye Jin[1], and Dan Wang[1]

[1] School of Mathematical Sciences, Nanjing Normal University,
Nanjing 210023, China
05234@njnu.edu.cn
[2] Jiangsu Key Laboratory for NSLSCS, Nanjing Normal University,
Nanjing 210023, China

Abstract. Brain storm optimization (BSO) algorithm is a novel swarm intelligence algorithm. Inspired by differential evolution (DE) with multi-population based ensemble of mutation strategies (MPEDE), a new variant of BSO algorithm, called brain storm optimization with multi-population based ensemble of creating operations (MPEBSO), is proposed in this paper. There are three equally sized smaller indicator sub-populations and one much larger reward subpopulation. BSO algorithm is used to update individuals in every subpopulation. At first, each creating operation has one smaller indicator subpopulation, in which different mutation strategy is used to add noise instead of the Gaussian random strategy. After every certain number of generations, the larger reward subpopulation will be adaptively assigned to the best performing creating operation with more computational resources. The competitive performance of the proposed MPEBSO on CEC2005 benchmark functions is highlighted compared with DE, MPEDE, and other four variants of BSO.

Keywords: Brain storm optimization · Multi-population
Ensemble of creating operations

1 Introduction

Brain Storm Optimization (BSO) algorithm is a novel swarm intelligence algorithm which is inspired by the human brainstorming process [1]. More and more attentions have been paid to the improvement and application of BSO algorithm. Shi [2] presented BSO and verified the effectiveness of it by two benchmark functions. The grouping operator and the creating operator of BSO were modified by Zhan [3] in 2012. A quantum-behaved brain storm optimization (QBSO) [4] was given in 2014, which improved the diversity of population and used the global information. Cao et al. [5] described an improved BSO with differential evolution strategy (BSODE) in 2015, in which the differential evolution (DE) strategy and

© Springer International Publishing AG, part of Springer Nature 2018
Y. Tan et al. (Eds.): ICSI 2018, LNCS 10941, pp. 374–383, 2018.
https://doi.org/10.1007/978-3-319-93815-8_36

a new step size are introduced. In 2016 a BSO algorithm with re-initialized the bad ideas and adaptive step size (IRGBSO) [6] was given by Mohammed El-Abd. Later he put forward the global-best BSO algorithm (GBSO) [7] by introducing a global-best version combined with per-variable updates and fitness-based grouping to improve the performance of BSO in 2017.

In this paper, we propose a brain storm optimization with multi-population based ensemble of creating operation (MPEBSO). The mutation and crossover from DE are imbedded in the creating operation to avoid premature and generate better ideas. Also, the scaling factor F in mutation strategy and the crossover rate CR in crossover strategy are learned from the technique proposed in differential evolution with multi-population based ensemble of mutation strategies (MPEDE) [8].

The rest of the paper is organized as follows. The basic BSO and DE algorithms are briefly introduced in Sect. 2. The proposed MPEBSO algorithm is described in Sect. 3. The numerical experiments and results are shown in Sect. 4. The last section is major conclusions and future research directions of this paper.

2 Two Basic Algorithms

2.1 Brain Storm Optimization

The BSO algorithm originates from the human brainstorming process. As stated in literature [1,2], a potential solution to the problem is named an idea in BSO. The BSO algorithm consists of clustering, replacing, and creating operations.

Clustering operation is responsible for gathering all similar ideas together. During each generation, all ideas are clustered into M clusters by some clustering method. The best idea in each cluster is selected as the cluster center.

Replacing operation of cluster center is also known as disrupting operation. It means that a cluster is randomly chosen and replaced with a newly generated idea with a probability of $p_{replace}$ to improve searching capability.

In the process of creating operation, a new idea can be generated based on one or two ideas according to a probability of p_{one} at first. Then, the corresponding probabilities $p_{one-center}$ and $p_{two-center}$ are used to choose ideas from the cluster center(s) or the random idea(s) in the cluster(s). The selecting operation is defined as follows:

$$X_{selected} = \begin{cases} X_i, & \text{one cluster} \\ rand * X_{i_1} + (1 - rand) * X_{i_2} & \text{two clusters} \end{cases}, \quad (1)$$

where $rand$ is a random value between 0 and 1. Then, $X_{selected}$ is updated as

$$X_{new} = X_{selected} + \xi * normrnd(0, 1), \quad (2)$$

where $normrnd$ is the Gaussian distribution with mean 0 and variance 1 to add noise to the idea $X_{selected}$, and ξ in (3) is an adjusting factor slowing the convergence speed down

$$\xi = rand * logsig(\frac{0.5 * iteration_{max} - iteration_{current}}{k}), \tag{3}$$

where $logsig$ is a logarithmic sigmoid transfer function; $iteration_{max}$ is the maximum iteration number; $iteration_{current}$ represents the number of the current iteration; and k is the slope of the $logsig$ function.

2.2 Differential Evolution

Differential evolution [9] is an efficient global optimization algorithm. In the process of DE, firstly, two individuals are selected from the parents to generate the difference vector; Secondly, another individual added to the difference vectors can generate the new individual; Then, the new individual generates a new offspring by crossover operation; Finally, selection operation is performed between the parent and offspring individuals, and the eligible individual are kept to the next generation.

In basic DE algorithm, the mutation vector is defined as "DE/rand/1":

$$V_i^g = X_{r_1}^g + F * (X_{r_2}^g - X_{r_3}^g), \tag{4}$$

where g is the generation number, and the indices r_1, r_2 and r_3 are mutually exclusive integers randomly chosen from 1 to N. F is a mutation scaling factor which affects the differential variation between two individuals.

In order to increase the diversity of the population, crossover operation is introduced to generate offspring individual U_i at the kth generation:

$$U_i^g = \begin{cases} V_i^g, & \text{if } rand \leq CR \\ X_i^g & \text{otherwise} \end{cases}, \tag{5}$$

where CR is a parameter of crossover rate.

3 The Improved Algorithm: MPEBSO

We introduce an ensemble of multiple creating operations into the brain storm optimization. The new creating operations change the noise in Eq. (2) in the original BSO. The whole population is dynamically divided into three indicator subpopulations (with equal and relatively smaller sizes) and one relatively big sized reward subpopulation at each generation. Every creating operation is randomly assigned with an indicator subpopulation. The best performing creating operation obtains the reward subpopulation after every certain generations with the most computation resources.

3.1   Three Different Creating Operations

It was show in MPEDE [8] that different mutation strategies are required for a DE variant to solve various optimization problems efficiently. Furthermore, even for the same problem, the most suitable strategies at different stages of the evolutionary process may be different. Therefore, it is crucial that the most suitable creating operation must be picked out during the evolution process of MPEBSO. Different from basic BSO, three strategies are used to add noise to the idea $X_{selected}$ in (1), and the corresponding creating operations are described in (6)–(8). The first creating operation is derived from the mutation strategy "current-to-pbest/1" [8]:

$$X_{new} = X_{selected} + F * (X_{pbest} - X_{selected} + X_{r_1} - \tilde{X}_{r_2}), \qquad (6)$$

where F is the mutation scaling factor generated through the parameter adaptive approach in MPEDE; X_{pbest} is the best idea in the population; X_{r_1} is randomly chosen from the corresponding subpopulation; $\tilde{X}_{r_2}$ is an individual in an archive. The "current-to-pbest/1" with an archive performs well in solving complex optimization problems by introducing more diversity in the mutation operation [10]. After the mutation, crossover operation in (5) is performed on X_{new}. The parameter CR is also generated by the parameter adaptive approach in MPEDE.

The second creating operation originates from the mutation strategy "current-to-rand/1" [8] which is excellent in solving rotated problems with its rotation-invariant [11]:

$$X_{new} = X_{selected} + K * (X_{r_1} - X_{selected}) + F * (X_{r_2} - X_{r_3}) \qquad (7)$$

where X_{r_1}, X_{r_2} and X_{r_3} are different ideas in the corresponding subpopulation, and K is a rand number between 0 and 1. This creating operation is applied without the aid of crossover operation.

The third creating operation is borrowed from the idea differential strategy (IDS) in MBSO [3], which is proved to be better than the original Gaussian random strategy:

$$X_{new} = X_{selected} + F * (X_{r_1} - X_{r_2}). \qquad (8)$$

After the mutation, the crossover operation is also performed on X_{new} as in the first creating operation.

Three creating operations above use the difference between ideas. At first, the ideas are different from each other. So, the difference is large and the ideas which is newly generated can increase the diversity in the early stage. At the later stage of the brainstorming process, the difference may be smaller which means that the interference is also smaller to help update the ideas.

3.2   Multi-population Based Creating Operation Ensemble Approach

Inspired by MPEDE, the multi-population based creating operation ensemble approach is proposed here. The whole population P is segmented into four sub-populations randomly in each generation. Three indicator subpopulations which have the same size and relatively small scale are P_1, P_2, and P_3. One reward subpopulation is P_4 that has the relatively large scale. Suppose the size of P is N, and the size of P_j is N_j. μ_j is the proportion of P_j in P, and $\mu_1 = \mu_2 = \mu_3$.

At the very start, three creating operations randomly obtain P_1, P_2 and P_3 respectively. P_4 is assigned to one of the creating operations. With the evolution of the algorithm, after every gr (a predefined number) generations, the best performing creating operation is picked out. In the next gr generations, the best performing creating operation will obtain the reward subpopulation P_4 which means it has more computational resources. Picking out the best performing creating operation is equivalent to selecting the biggest ratio of $\frac{\Delta f_j}{\Delta FES_j}$, where the Δf_j is the cumulative improvement of the objective function value that comes with the jth creating operation, and ΔFES_j is the function evaluations consumed by the jth creating operation during the previous gr generations. The above procedure is performed periodically with the parameter gr. The existence of subpopulation is intended to provide sufficient computational resources for each creating operation. The pseudo code of MPEBSO are listed in Fig. 1.

4   Experimental Results

Comparing the proposed MPEBSO with QBSO [4], BSODE [5], IRGBSO [6], GBSO [7], DE [9], and MPEDE [8], the experimental results of benchmark functions with 30 decision variables in CEC05 [12] are given under the same machine with an Intel 3.20 GHz CPU, 8 GB memory, and the operating system is Windows 7 with MATLAB 9.0 (R2016a). The common parameters of all BSO variants are set as: $M = 5$, $p_{replace} = 0.2$, $p_{one} = 0.8$, $p_{one-center} = 0.4$, and $p_{two-center} = 0.5$. All other parameters are consistent with the correspond references. The additional parameters of MPEBSO is set as: $N = 250$, $\mu_1 = \mu_2 = \mu_3 = 0.2$, $\mu_4 = 0.4$, and $gr = 20$. All functions in CEC05 have different optimal values $f(x^*)$. We set the maximum function evaluations as 300000. Each algorithm runs independently 50 times on all benchmark functions. The mean results (Mean) and the standard deviation (Std) of each algorithm are recorded with the format of $f(x) - f(x^*)$ in Tables 1 and 2. The best results are highlighted in boldface. Rank records the performance-rank of seven algorithms for dealing with each benchmark function according to their mean results. The total rank for each algorithm is defined according to their mean rank values over 25 benchmark problems. The number of (1st/2nd/7th) is counted for each algorithm.

MPEBSO algorithm

1:Input paramenters: N, gr, M, $MaxG$ and μ_j, j=1, 2, 3, 4;
2:Set Δf_j=0, ΔFES_j=0 and $N_j = \mu_j * N$, j=1, 2, 3, 4;
3:Initialize P randomly distributed in the solution space;
4:Randomly divide P into P_1, P_2, P_3 and P_4 according to their sizes;
5:Randomly select a subpopulation P_j, $j \in \{1, 2, 3\}$ and combine P_j with P_4;
6:Let $P_j = P_j \cup P_4$ and $N_j = N_j + N_4$;
7:Set $g = 0$;
8:**While** $g \leq MaxG$ **do**
9:     $g = g + 1$;
10:    **For** $j = 1 : 3$
11:       Calculate $CR_{i,j}$ and $F_{i,j}$ for each individual X_i in P_j
12:       by formula (15) $\sim$ (18) in Sect. 4.2 in Ref. [8] ;
13:       Cluster N_j ideas in P_j into M clusters;
14:       Randomly choose a cluster center in P_j and replace it with
15:       a randomly generated idea with a probability of $P_{replace}$;
16:       **For** $l = 1 : N_j$
17:          **If** $rand < P_{one}$
18:             Randomly select one cluster in P_j
19:             **If** $rand < P_{one-center}$
20:                Select the cluster center as $X_{selected}$
21:             **Else**
22:                Select an idea in this cluster as $X_{selected}$
23:             **End If**
24:          **Else**
25:             Randomly select two clusters in P_j
26:             **If** $rand < P_{two-center}$
27:                Select the centers of two clusters in P_j and combine them as $X_{selected}$
28:             **Else**
29:                Select an idea in two clusters respectively and combine them as $X_{selected}$
30:             **End IF**
31:          **End If**
32:       **End For**
33:       Execute jth creating operation and crossover operation over the subpopulation P_j;
34:    **End For**
35:    **For** $i = 1 : N$
36:       **If** $f(X_{i,g}) \leq f(U_{i,g})$
37:          $X_{i+1,g} = X_{i,g}$;
38:       **Else**
39:          $X_{i+1,g} = U_{i,g}$; $\Delta f_j = \Delta f_j + f(X_{i,g}) - f(U_{i,g})$;
40:       **End If**
41:    **End For**
42:    $P = \bigcup_{j=1,2,3} P_j$;
43:    **If** $\mathrm{mod}(g, gr) == 0$
44:       $k = \underset{1 \leq j \leq 3}{argmax}(\frac{\Delta f_j}{gr * N_j})$
45:    **End If**
46:    $\Delta f_j = 0$, j=1, 2, 3;
47:    Randomly divide P into P_1, P_2, P_3 and P_4;
48:    Let $P_k = P_k \cup P_4$ and $N_k = N_k + N_4$;
49: **End While**

Fig. 1. The pseudo code of the MPEBSO algorithm

Table 1. Results of benchmark functions in CEC05 with 30 variables(f_1–f_{13})

Functions	Criteria	QBSO	BSODE	IRGBSO	GBSO	MPEBSO	DE	MPEDE
f_1	Mean	1.18E−02	**0.00E+00**	**0.00E+00**	**0.00E+00**	**0.00E+00**	**0.00E+00**	**0.00E+00**
	Std	7.80E−03	**0.00E+00**	**0.00E+00**	**0.00E+00**	**0.00E+00**	**0.00E+00**	**0.00E+00**
	Rank	7	1	1	1	1	1	1
f_2	Mean	5.32E+02	2.95E−04	1.83E−03	1.45E−02	**0.00E+00**	3.63E−05	9.49E−27
	Std	4.12E+02	2.35E−04	1.28E−03	7.36E−03	**0.00E+00**	4.66E−05	3.45E−26
	Rank	7	4	5	6	1	3	2
f_3	Mean	3.15E+06	6.62E+05	5.98E+05	1.31E+06	2.26E+04	3.85E+05	**2.04E+02**
	Std	1.40E+06	4.20E+05	2.87E+05	5.64E+05	1.81E+04	2.44E+05	**6.53E+02**
	Rank	7	5	4	6	2	3	1
f_4	Mean	1.40E+04	1.62E−01	2.37E−02	6.54E−01	2.15E−06	1.66E−02	**6.21E−16**
	Std	3.80E+03	2.02E−01	2.37E+03	6.79E−01	7.48E−06	2.25E−02	**2.83E−15**
	Rank	7	5	4	6	2	3	1
f_5	Mean	6.77E+03	1.43E+03	3.76E+01	2.19E+02	3.87E+00	6.86E−01	**1.11E−05**
	Std	2.02E+03	4.62E+02	1.75E−02	1.27E+02	1.25E+01	5.47E−01	**2.97E−05**
	Rank	7	6	4	5	3	2	1
f_6	Mean	4.47E+02	9.01E+02	9.92E+02	2.28E+02	**1.12E+00**	1.98E+00	1.19E+00
	Std	5.29E+02	1.67E+03	2.01E+01	6.34E+02	1.82E+00	**1.63E+00**	3.15E+00
	Rank	5	6	7	3	1	3	2
f_7	Mean	2.50E−01	1.08E−02	**7.09E−04**	3.86E−03	1.07E−02	4.70E+03	2.96E−03
	Std	1.10E−01	8.96E−03	**2.65E−03**	7.61E−03	1.26E−02	0.00E+00	4.15E−03
	Rank	7	6	1	3	4	6	2
f_8	Mean	2.11E+01	2.13E+01	2.13E+01	2.12E+01	**2.09E+01**	**2.09E+01**	2.10E+01
	Std	6.12E−02	8.06E−02	8.79E−02	6.67E−02	**4.46E−02**	4.47E−02	5.11E−02
	Rank	3	6	6	5	1	1	3
f_9	Mean	3.11E+01	4.00E+01	2.81E+01	4.98E−01	3.70E+00	1.18E+02	**0.00E+00**
	Std	9.72E+00	9.80E+00	5.71E+00	7.17E−01	7.59E+00	2.83E+01	**0.00E+00**
	Rank	5	6	4	2	3	7	1
f_{10}	Mean	1.16E+02	3.42E+01	2.52E+01	2.20E+01	**2.19E+01**	1.77E+02	2.45E+01
	Std	2.58E+01	7.46E+00	6.46E+00	**5.59E+00**	6.82E+00	1.12E+01	6.46E+00
	Rank	6	4	3	2	1	7	5
f_{11}	Mean	2.97E+01	3.93E+01	2.71E+00	**8.49E−01**	1.64E+01	3.90E+01	1.67E+01
	Std	3.82E+00	1.41E+00	2.11E+00	1.45E+00	3.20E+00	**9.94E−01**	7.11E+00
	Rank	5	7	2	1	3	6	4
f_{12}	Mean	3.07E+04	1.22E+05	1.38E+04	5.17E+03	4.56E+03	2.26E+03	**1.23E+03**
	Std	1.16E+04	7.44E+04	1.51E+04	5.10E+03	5.94E+03	2.75E+03	**1.67E+03**
	Rank	6	7	5	4	3	2	1
f_{13}	Mean	4.74E+00	3.76E+00	3.30E+00	1.91E+00	**1.68E+00**	1.52E+01	1.96E+00
	Std	4.33E−01	8.61E−01	5.24E−01	2.72E−01	3.24E−01	1.08E+00	**1.94E−01**
	Rank	6	5	4	2	1	7	3

The proposed MPEBSO algorithm outperforms the others on 9 out of 25 benchmark problems, including two unimodal functions (f_1, f_2), three basic multimodal functions (f_6, f_8, and f_{10}), one expanded multimodal function (f_{13}), and three hybrid composition functions (f_{18}, f_{24}, and f_{25}). MPEBSO is the second performing algorithm on five functions (f_3, f_4, f_{16}, f_{17}, and f_{19}). It can be observed that MPEBSO algorithm has no worst performance on any benchmark function and ranks first over other comparative algorithms expect MPEDE.

Table 2. Results of benchmark functions in CEC05 with 30 variables(f_{14}–f_{25})

Functions	Criteria	QBSO	BSODE	IRGBSO	GBSO	MPEBSO	DE	MPEDE
f_{14}	Mean	1.28E+01	1.29E+01	1.03E+01	**1.01E+01**	1.12E+01	1.32E+01	1.25E+01
	Std	3.65E−01	5.97E−01	8.26E−01	1.03E+00	6.61E−01	1.76E−01	**3.41E−01**
	Rank	5	6	2	1	3	7	4
f_{15}	Mean	3.56E+02	3.74E+02	3.48E+02	**3.32E+02**	3.52E+02	4.00E+02	4.00E+02
	Std	1.24E+02	8.29E+01	9.65E+01	5.57E+01	8.21E+01	**4.08E+01**	7.07E+01
	Rank	4	5	2	1	3	6	6
f_{16}	Mean	2.08E+02	2.05E+02	1.64E+02	1.61E+02	1.16E+02	2.09E+02	**4.77E+01**
	Std	1.44E+02	1.75E+02	1.70E+02	1.66E+02	1.63E+02	4.07E+01	**1.74E+01**
	Rank	6	5	4	3	2	7	1
f_{17}	Mean	2.06E+02	9.35E+01	2.11E+02	1.19E+02	8.42E+01	2.29E+02	**5.48E+01**
	Std	1.44E+02	7.70E+01	1.91E+02	1.32E+02	1.01E+02	3.17E+01	**3.16E+01**
	Rank	5	3	6	4	2	7	1
f_{18}	Mean	9.18E+02	9.05E+02	**9.04E+02**	9.04E+02	9.04E+02	9.04E+02	9.04E+02
	Std	7.05E+00	1.90E+00	**2.24E−01**	3.56E+01	1.13E+00	8.57E−01	6.31E−01
	Rank	7	6	1	1	1	1	1
f_{19}	Mean	9.15E+02	9.05E+02	9.04E+02	9.04E+02	9.04E+02	**9.03E+02**	9.04E+02
	Std	6.61E+00	4.95E+00	**2.36E−01**	4.00E+01	1.01E+00	5.13E−01	3.09E−01
	Rank	7	6	2	2	2	1	1
f_{20}	Mean	9.13E+02	**8.98E+02**	8.99E+02	9.04E+02	9.04E+02	9.04E+02	9.04E+02
	Std	3.66E+01	2.54E+01	2.07E+01	2.95E+01	1.06E+00	8.08E−01	**3.51E−01**
	Rank	7	1	2	3	3	3	3
f_{21}	Mean	5.89E+02	1.02E+03	5.76E+02	**5.00E+02**	5.12E+02	**5.00E+02**	**5.00E+02**
	Std	2.35E+02	3.85E+00	1.56E+02	**0.00E+00**	0.00E+00	**0.00E+00**	7.06E−14
	Rank	7	6	5	1	4	1	1
f_{22}	Mean	9.48E+02	8.33E+02	**8.17E+02**	8.79E+02	8.72E+02	8.78E+02	8.56E+02
	Std	4.45E+01	3.14E+01	2.08E+01	2.57E+01	2.06E+01	**1.47E+01**	1.52E+01
	Rank	7	2	1	6	4	5	3
f_{23}	Mean	6.04E+02	1.02E+03	5.59E+02	**5.34E+02**	5.50E+02	5.50E+02	**5.34E+02**
	Std	1.90E+02	9.15E+00	8.08E+01	3.52E−04	8.06E+01	8.06E+01	**2.90E−13**
	Rank	6	7	5	1	3	3	1
f_{24}	Mean	2.53E+02	8.17E+02	**2.00E+02**	2.00E+02	2.00E+02	2.00E+02	2.00E+02
	Std	2.04E+02	1.21E+01	**0.00E+00**	0.00E+00	0.00E+00	0.00E+00	2.90E−14
	Rank	6	7	1	1	1	1	1
f_{25}	Mean	2.18E+02	**2.10E+02**	8.48E+02	2.20E+02	**2.10E+02**	1.64E+03	**2.10E+02**
	Std	7.56E+00	**2.46E−01**	3.16E+02	4.18E+01	8.98E−01	4.07E+00	3.35E−01
	Rank	4	1	6	5	1	7	1
Mean rank		5.96	4.92	3.48	3	2.2	4	2.08
Total rank		7	6	4	3	2	5	1
1st/2nd/7th		0/0/11	3/1/4	5/5/1	8/4/0	9/5/0	6/2/7	13/4/0

Figures 2(a) and (b) illustrates the convergence performance of five BSO variants. Figures 2(c) and (d) illustrates the convergence performance of MPEBSO, DE and MPEDE. The horizontal axis is the number of function evaluations (FES), and the vertical axis is the function values over one independent run. The convergence speed and precision of MPEBSO is slightly inferior to MPEDE, but it is obviously superior to DE and other four variants of BSO.

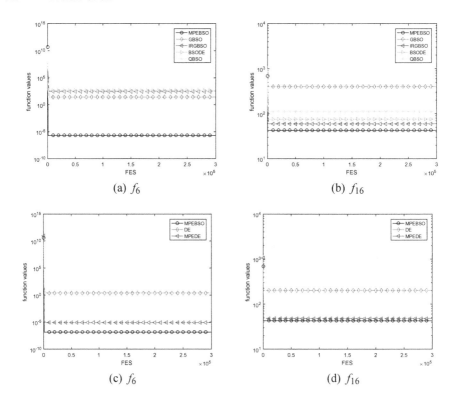

Fig. 2. Comparison of convergence for MPEBSO and other comparison algorithms

5 Conclusion

Inspired by the MPEDE algorithm, we proposed a novel MPEBSO algorithm, in which a multi-population based approach was utilized to realized a dynamic ensemble of creating operations. In essence, this was the combination of BSO algorithm and DE algorithm. The mutation and the crossover were used to add noise instead of the Gaussian random strategy in basic BSO. The final simulation results showed that this change promoted the convergence speed and accuracy of MPEBSO. In the near future, we expect the creating operations can be effectively improved and more new BSO variants can be applied to the real-world optimization problems.

Acknowledgments. This research is partly supported by Humanity and Social Science Youth foundation of Ministry of Education of China (Grant No. 12YJCZH179), the Natural Science Foundation of the Jiangsu Higher Education Institutions of China (Grant No. 16KJA110001), the National Natural Science Foundation of China (Grant No. 11371197), the Foundation of Jiangsu Key Laboratory for NSLSCS (Grant No. 201601). The authors thank the anonymous reviewers for providing valuable comments to improve this paper, and add special thanks to Professor Mohammed El-Abd and Cao zijian for providing the source codes of the comparative algorithms (GBSO, IRGBSO, BSODE).

References

1. Shi, Y.: An optimization algorithm based on brainstorming process. Int. J. Swarm Intell. Res. **2**, 35–62 (2011)
2. Shi, Y.: Brain storm optimization algorithm. In: Tan, Y., Shi, Y., Chai, Y., Wang, G. (eds.) ICSI 2011. LNCS, vol. 6728, pp. 303–309. Springer, Heidelberg (2011). https://doi.org/10.1007/978-3-642-21515-5_36
3. Zhan, Z., Zhang, J., Shi, Y., Liu, H.: A modified brain storm optimization. In: Proceedings of the 2012 IEEE Congress on Evolutionary Computation, Brisbane, Australia, pp. 1969–1976 (2012)
4. Duan, H., Li, C.: Quantum-behaved brain storm optimization approach to solving loneys solenoid problem. IEEE Trans. Magn. **51**, 1–7 (2015)
5. Cao, Z., Wang, L., Hei, X., Shi, Y., Rong, X.: An improved brain storm optimization with differential evolution strategy for applications of ANNs. Math. Probl. Eng. **2015**, 1–18 (2015)
6. El-Abd, M.: Brain storm optimization algorithm with re-initialized ideas and adaptive step size. In: Proceedings of the 2016 IEEE Congress on Evolutionary Computation, Vancouver, Canada, pp. 2682–2686 (2016)
7. El-Abd, M.: Global-best brain storm optimization algorithm. Swarm Evol. Comput. **37**, 27–44 (2017)
8. Wu, G., Malipeddi, R., Suganthan, P.N., Wang, R., Chen, H.: Differential evolution with multi-population based ensemble of mutation strategies. J. Inf. Sci. **329**, 329–345 (2016)
9. Storn, R., Price, K.: Differential evolution - a simple and efficient heuristic for global optimization over continuous spaces. J. Global. Optim. **11**, 341–359 (1997)
10. Zhang, J., Sanderson, A.C.: JADE: adaptive differential evolution with optional external archive. IEEE Trans. Evol. Comput. **13**, 945–958 (2009)
11. Das, S., Abraham, A., Chakraborty, U.K., Konar, A.: Differential evolution using a neighbourhood based mutation operator. IEEE Trans. Evol. Comput. **13**, 526–553 (2009)
12. Suganthan, P.N., Hansen, N., Liang, J.J., Deb, K., Chen, Y.-P., Auger, A., Tiwari, S.: Problem Definitions and Evaluation Criteria for the CEC 2005 Special Session on Real-Parameter Optimization, KanGAL Report #2005005. IIT Kanpur, India (2005)

A Novel Memetic Whale Optimization Algorithm for Optimization

Zhe Xu[1,2], Yang Yu[2], Hanaki Yachi[2], Junkai Ji[2], Yuki Todo[3],
and Shangce Gao[2(✉)]

[1] School of Computer Information and Engineering,
Changzhou Institute of Technology, Changzhou 213032, Jiangsu, China
[2] Faculty of Engineering, University of Toyama, Toyama, Japan
`gaosc@eng.u-toyama.ac.jp`
[3] Faculty of Electrical and Computer Engineering, Kanazawa University,
Kanazawa-shi 920-1192, Japan

Abstract. Whale optimization algorithm (WOA) is a newly proposed search optimization technique which mimics the encircling prey and bubble-net attacking mechanisms of the whale. It has proven to be very competitive in comparison with other state-of-the-art metaheuristics. Nevertheless, the performance of WOA is limited by its monotonous search dynamics, i.e., only the encircling mechanism drives the search which mainly focus the exploration in the landscape. Thus, WOA lacks of the capacity of jumping out the of local optima. To address this problem, this paper propose a memetic whale optimization algorithm (MWOA) by incorporating a chaotic local search into WOA to enhance its exploitation ability. It is expected that MWOA can well balance the global exploration and local exploitation during the search process, thus achieving a better search performance. Forty eight benchmark functions are used to verify the efficiency of MWOA. Experimental results suggest that MWOA can perform better than its competitors in terms of the convergence speed and the solution accuracy.

Keywords: Evolutionary computation
Whale optimization algorithm · Chaos · Local search
Memetic computing · Optimization

1 Introduction

In recent years, metha-heuristic algorithms, e.g., particle swarm optimization [1,2], differential evolution [3–5], gravitational search algorithm [6–9], artificial bee colony algorithm [10], ant colony optimization [11,12], fireworks algorithm [13,14], brain storm optimization [15–17], whale optimization algorithm (WOA) [18] have attracted more and more interests due to its flexibilities in a wide successful applications including optimization, prediction, classification, data mining, internet of things, etc. The famous No-Free-Lunch theorems [19] demonstrate that there is no such an algorithm which can outperform the others for all

© Springer International Publishing AG, part of Springer Nature 2018
Y. Tan et al. (Eds.): ICSI 2018, LNCS 10941, pp. 384–396, 2018.
https://doi.org/10.1007/978-3-319-93815-8_37

problems, thus further indicating that the hybridization of different algorithms seems to be promising for improving the performance of algorithms [20–25]. However, the issues of how to combine two or more different algorithms to achieve a better performing hybrid algorithm which significantly outperforms its component algorithms still remain very challenging.

In the literature, several frameworks have been proposed to combine different algorithms for construct a hybrid and high-performing algorithm, e.g., in a parallel manner [26], a cascade manner [27], an ensemble strategy [28], and a memetic combination manner [29]. In this study, we propose a novel algorithm by hybridizing the whale optimization algorithm (WOA) with chaotic local search in a memetic combination manner.

WOA is a group-swarm intelligence technique applied algorithms. It mimics hunting behavior of humpback whales to update the location of populations for finding the optimal in search space. In exploration phase, humpback whales will search for the prey which in WOA is considered as the potential solution and encircle them. After that, other search agents will enhance their search movements and update their positions according to the location of potential solution. In the exploitation phase which aims for improving the solution quality by searching the neighborhood of potential solution, the humpback whales will use a search method called bubble-nets attacking method. This method has two searching approaches: one is called shrinking encircling mechanism; the other is spiral updating position. The two approaches, each has a probability of 50% to be chosen for updating the positions of search agents. This choice mechanism makes sure that search agents will keep their diversity in the whole search phase. Although WOA has good search performance but still can't avoid sticking into local optima and has inferior solution quality.

On the other hand, chaos is a universal character of nonlinear dynamic systems and it is apparently an irregular motion, seemingly unpredictable random behavior which can be exhibited by a deterministic nonlinear system in deterministic conditions [30]. Because of ergodicity and randomicity, a chaotic system changes randomly but eventually goes through every state of the search space if the time duration is long enough. A chaotic local search is generated based the chaotic systems.

For alleviating the inherent local optimal solutions trapping problem, the memetic combination strategy is used in this study to combine chaotic local search with WOA. The memetic combination strategy is considered as a union of population-based global search and local improvements which are inspired by Darwinian principles of natural evolution and Dawkins f notion of a meme [31]. The effectiveness of the hybrid algorithm relies on the use of WOA for globally rough exploration and chaotic local search for locally fine improvements. To testify the performance of the proposed memetic whale optimization algorithm (MWOA), 23 widely used numerical test functions and 25 CEC2005 benchmark functionsare tested. Experimental results show that MWOA can perform better than WOA and other competitors in terms of the convergence speed and the solution accuracy.

2 Brief Description of Traditional WOA

As we know, whale is the biggest mammal in this world. Although they are big, they have high intelligence quotient to guarantee the superb hunting skills which include encircling prey and bubble-net attacking method. That is why researchers can get the inspiration from humpback whales to create the whale optimization algorithm [18]. The WOA has two main phases: exploration phase and exploitation phase. In the latter phase, two hunting skills called encircling prey and bubble-net attacking method are designed for improving the solution quality by searching the neighborhood of the global best agent so far. Here is the introduction about encircling prey and bubble-net attacking method.

2.1 Encircle Prey

Humpback whales will take an encirclement action to approach the location of prey which is supposed as the global best agent so far in WOA, and other agents will update their locations according towards it. The behavior is as follows: $\vec{D} = |\vec{C}\vec{X^*}(t) - \vec{X}(t)|$, $\vec{X}(t + 1) = \vec{X^*}(t) - \vec{A}\vec{D}$, where $\vec{X^*}(t)$ is the global best agent so far, t is the current iteration, $\vec{A}$ and $\vec{C}$ are coefficient vectors, $\vec{X}$ is the position vector, and $\vec{X^*}$ in each iteration will be replaced if a better solution appears. And coefficient vectors are defined as follow: $\vec{A} = 2\vec{a}\,\vec{r} - \vec{a}$, $\vec{C} = 2\vec{r}$, where $\vec{a}$ is linearly decreased from 2 to 0 by the lapse of iteration (in both exploration and exploitation phases) and $\vec{r}$ is a random vector and $\vec{r} \in [0, 1]$. Otherwise $p \leq 0.5$, the encircling prey and the exploration phase called search for prey will be chosen according to the lapse of time.

2.2 Bubble-Net Attacking Method (Exploitation Phase)

For explaining this behavior of humpback whales, two methods are designed as in the following.

Shrinking encircling mechanism: As Eq. (2) shows, $\vec{A}$ is decreased as well as $\vec{a}$ is linearly decreased from 2 to 0. If the value of $\vec{A}$ is in $[-1, 1]$, search agent will appear in the place between position of original agent and global best agent so far.

Spiral updating position: This method calculates the distance between whale position (X,Y), and global best agent so far (X^*, Y^*), then using a spiral equation to simulate the helical structure of humpback whale movement. The equation is as follows:

$$\vec{X}(t + 1) = \vec{D'}(e^{bl}) \cos{(2\pi l)} + \vec{X^*}(t) \tag{1}$$

where $\vec{D'} = |\vec{X^*}(t) - \vec{X}(t)|$ represents the distance between ith whale and the prey (global best agent so far), b is a constant for defining the shape of the logarithmic spiral, and l is a random number in $[-1, 1]$.

For mimicking the simultaneous behavior that humpback whales move toward the prey with shrinking circle and spiral-shaped path, WOA assumes that each method has a probability of 50% to be chosen into the optimization process. The mathematical model is as followed:

$$\overrightarrow{X}(t+1) = \begin{cases} \overrightarrow{X^*}(t) - \overrightarrow{A}\,\overrightarrow{D}, & if\ p < 0.5 \\ \overrightarrow{D'}(e^{bl})\cos(2\pi l) + \overrightarrow{X^*}(t), & if\ p \geq 0.5 \end{cases} \tag{2}$$

where p is a random number in $[0, 1]$. However as we know, it is far from enough that an optimization algorithm only has exploitation phase. Hence, besides the exploitation phase, WOA also has exploration phase which uses a random dynamic method to keep the diversity of population and avoid premature convergence.

2.3 Search for Prey (Exploration Phase)

Instead of the limitation in Eq. (2) which depends on the value of $\overrightarrow{A}$ in $[-1, 1]$, here in exploration phase, while $\overrightarrow{A}$ with the random values greater than 1 or less than -1 will explore the space far away from the global best agent so far. To be different from the exploitation phase, WOA choose a random agent instead of the global best to generate a new one. And the model which will urge WOA to implement global search is shown as follows: $\overrightarrow{D} = |\overrightarrow{C}\overrightarrow{X}_{rand} - \overrightarrow{X}|$, $\overrightarrow{X}(t+1) = \overrightarrow{X}_{rand} - \overrightarrow{A}\,\overrightarrow{D}$, where $\overrightarrow{X}_{rand}$ is a random position vector (a random whale) chosen from the current population.

As the method mentioned above, $\overrightarrow{a}$ is linearly decreased from 2 to 0, making $\overrightarrow{A}$ in $[-2, 2]$, depends on the value of $\overrightarrow{A}$, WOA will randomly switch into exploration or exploitation phase. This ensures WOA having a superior search ability.

3 Memetic Whale Optimization Algorithm (MWOA)

In this study, 12 different chaotic maps are used to perform the chaotic local search. These chaotic maps [8] include Logistic map, PWLCM, Singer map, Sine map, Gaussian map, Tent map, Bernoulli map, Chebyshev map, Circle map, Cubic map, Sinusoidal map, and ICMIC. The details of these chaotic maps can

Table 1. Success memory.

Index	Chaotic map 1	Chaotic map 2	...	Chaotic map J
1	$ns_{1,T-LI}$	$ns_{2,T-LI}$	...	$ns_{k,T-LI}$
2	$ns_{1,T-LI+1}$	$ns_{2,T-LI+1}$	...	$ns_{k,T-LI+1}$
...	...	...	...	...
LI	$ns_{1,T-1}$	$ns_{2,T-1}$	...	$ns_{k,T-1}$

Table 2. Failure memory.

Index	Chaotic map 1	Chaotic map 2	...	Chaotic map J
1	$ns_{1,T-LI}$	$ns_{2,T-LI}$	...	$ns_{k,T-LI}$
2	$ns_{1,T-LI+1}$	$ns_{2,T-LI+1}$	...	$ns_{k,T-LI+1}$
...	...	...	...	...
LI	$ns_{1,T-1}$	$ns_{2,T-1}$	...	$ns_{k,T-1}$

be refer to [8]. In the proposed MWOA, with respect to each current global best agent X_g, one chaotic map is selected from 12 chaotic maps according to the probability learned from a success rate and a failure rate which are calculated from a success memory and a failure memory. We previously set a learning iteration (LI) of which number is 50. In these previous iterations, chaotic maps are randomly selected like it in MWOA-R but the distinction is the result will be marked in the success and failure memory depending on this chaotic local search is successful or not. The method is used on the current global best agent X_g to generate a new agent $X_{g'}$ for comparing the fitness of kth chaotic map to decide whether X_g would be taken the place of by $X_{g'}$. If X_g has been replaced, we call it a success and plus one in the success memory while other chaotic maps will get 0. Otherwise plus one in the failure memory and the same for other chaotic maps. Here is the success memory Table 1 and failure memory Table 2.

If iteration number is over 50, the first column of Tables 1 and 2 will be removed to make space for the newest one. At the first, each chaotic map can be chosen at an equal probability $1/J$. When the memory started to be recorded, the probabilities of which chaotic map to be chosen will be renew after each record. It is calculated by:

$$p_{j,T} = \frac{S_{j,T}}{\sum_{j=1}^{T} S_j, T} \tag{3}$$

$$S_{j,T} = \frac{\sum_{t=T-LI}^{T-1} ns_{j,t}}{\sum_{t=T-LI}^{T-1} ns_{j,t} + \sum_{t=T-LI}^{T-1} nf_{j,t}} + \varepsilon \tag{4}$$

where $j = 1, 2, ..., 12; T > LI$. $p_{j,T}$ denotes the probability of each chaotic map can be selected. $\sum_{t=T-LI}^{T-1} ns_{j,t}$ calculates the total number of $j - th$ chaotic map successfully generates a new agent which can replace the current global best agent X_g. $\sum_{t=T-LI}^{T-1} nf_{j,t}$ is the total number of the new agents which can not replace the current global best agent. Equation (4) calculates the success rate and $\varepsilon = 0.01$ is for avoiding a null one. It is obvious that the chaotic map with higher success rate will has a higher chance to be selected to generate new agents.

The selected chaotic map is to generated a turbulence for the current global best solution X_g in the population. It is aimed to perform a local improvement for X_g according to

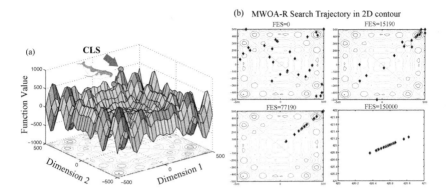

Fig. 1. (a) 3D graph of the multimodal function F8 in 2D; (b) The 2-dimensional sketch of the search trajectory for the multimodal function F8.

$$X_{g'}^j(k) = X_g(k) + r(ub - lb)(z(j) - 0.5) \tag{5}$$

where $j = 1, 2, ..., 12$ stands for the number of each single chaotic map, ub and lb are the upper bound and lower boundary respectively. $z(j)$ is a chaotic variable generated by jth chaotic map. $r \in (0, 1)$ is chaotic search radius. It should be noticed that if the acquired value of $X_{g'}^j(k)$ in Eq. (5) locates out of the search neighborhood $[X_g - r(ub - lb), X_g + r(ub - lb)]^n$, these values will be reset to the closest boundary value. In this range, the current global best agent is labeled as X_g, chaotic local search visits the candidate agent $X_g(k) = X_g^1(k), ...X_g^d(k), ...X_g^n(k), k = 1, 2, ...$, where k denotes the iteration number and n is the dimension. In each iteration, chaotic local search will search all dimensions of X_g in turn to generate a new agent $X_{g'}(k)$. It should be noted that the proposed MWOA using the above described success- rate-based selection of chaotic maps is denoted as MWOA-M. Alternatively, the two variants of MWOA where the probability $p_{j,T}$ of each chaotic map to be selected is generated uniformly and equally to be 1 is called MWOA-R and MWOA-P, respectively. In addition, only a single chaotic map is used in the framework of MWOA for all used 12 maps is called MWOA-1, MWOA-2, ..., MWOA-12 sequentially.

After each chaotic local search, if the fitness of the new agent $X_{g'}^j(k)$ is better than current global best fitness value, $X_{g'}^j(k)$ will replace $X_g(k)$ to get into next iteration. And we call it is a successful local search. By the lapse of iteration, it is more efficient to narrow the search radius as: $r = \rho r$ where ρ is a shrinking parameter which equals to 0.988.

4 Experiments

In the experimental period, we use benchmark functions and real world problems to compare the performance between WOA and MWOAs. We choose 23 mostly used numerical functions which are divided into unimodal and multimodal functions, where unimodal functions test the convergence speed of optimization algorithms and multimodal functions can check out whether optimization algorithms can avoid sticking into local optimal or not. The numerical functions can intuitively show the improvements in search ability compared with WOA. Figure 1(a) illustrates the property of multimodal F8. Then we also use 25 CEC2005 composite benchmark functions [32]. Because they are rotated and shifted so that the problem of optimal usually lying at the center or boundary of search range can be solved. Also hybrid composition functions can maximize the embodiment of search ability. It should be pointed out that we perform a contrast experiment by using a uniform distribution in [0, 1] and a standard normal distribution with mean 0 and variance 1 to compare the difference between chaotic sequences and random sequences and test the effect of chaos. The local search using uniform distribution is called WOA-UD, and the other is named WOA-ND.

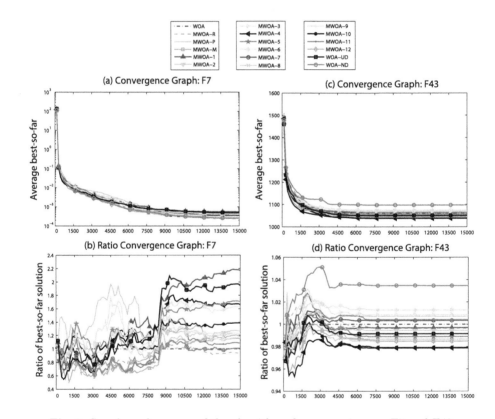

Fig. 2. Search performance of the algorithms for comparison on F7 and F43.

The population size is 30, and FES is set to $D*5000$, while D is the dimension of test function. Each function will be tested for 30 independent runs and their statistical data are listed blow from the Tables 4 and 5. We use $r = r * \rho$ (where r is set to 0.00001 and ρ is 0.988) as a common shrinking search radius in MWOAs.

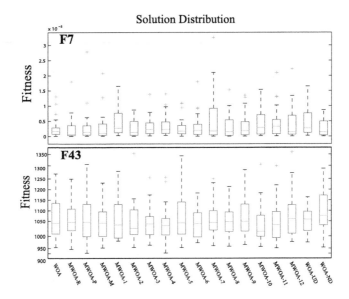

Fig. 3. Box-and-whisker diagrams of F7 and F43.

Table 3. Average Rankings of the algorithms based on Friedman test.

Algorithm	Ranking (F1–F48)	Ranking (F24–F48)	p-value (F1–F48)	p-value (F24–F48)
WOA	10	10.14	0.006826	0.026969
MWOA-R	**7.05**	**6.80**	-	-
MWOA-P	11.19	11.68	0.000148	0.00123
MWOA-M	9.09	8.82	0.060991	0.180969
MWOA-1	8.95	8.66	0.081905	0.218018
MWOA-2	9.63	8.52	0.018222	0.254662
MWOA-3	9.22	9.52	0.046782	0.071646
MWOA-4	10.01	9.6	0.006633	0.06369
MWOA-5	8.71	8.26	0.128541	0.33359
MWOA-6	10.41	11.1	0.002084	0.004403
MWOA-7	9.53	9.54	0.022904	0.069584
MWOA-8	8.97	9.36	0.078602	0.089999
MWOA-9	9.97	10.22	0.007439	0.023516
MWOA-10	9.93	11.18	0.008333	0.003723
MWOA-11	9.33	8.76	0.036312	0.194273
MWOA-12	9.25	8.46	0.043701	0.27161
WOA-UD	9.75	9.96	0.013295	0.03637
WOA-ND	10.02	10.42	0.006444	0.016512

In Tables 4 and 5, the best value of each function is bolded for clarity. In each function, best value belongs to MWOAs rather than conventional WOA. And mostly concentrated on MWOA-R, MWOA-P and MWOA-M.

Table 4. Experimental results of benchmark functions (F1–F24) using traditional WOA, MWOA-S, MWOA-R, MWOA-P, CGSA-M, WOA-UD and WOA-ND.

Algorithm	F1	F2	F3	F4	F5	F6
WOA	0.00E+00 ± 0.00E+00	0.00E+00 ± 0.00E+00	8.18E+02 ± 1.37E+03	1.81E+01 ± 2.72E+01	2.52E+01 ± 3.12E-01	7.76E-05 ± 3.40E-05
MWOA-R	0.00E+00 ± 0.00E+00	0.00E+00 ± 0.00E+00	5.14E+02 ± 6.41E+02	1.19E+01 ± 2.12E+01	2.52E+01 ± 4.54E-01	7.22E-05 ± 2.93E-05
MWOA-P	0.00E+00 ± 0.00E+00	0.00E+00 ± 0.00E+00	2.28E+03 ± 3.48E+03	1.64E+01 ± 2.47E+01	2.58E+01 ± 3.20E-01	2.45E-04 ± 1.15E-04
MWOA-M	0.00E+00 ± 0.00E+00	0.00E+00 ± 0.00E+00	6.55E+02 ± 1.04E+03	**1.06E+01 ± 1.82E+01**	2.54E+01 ± 4.52E-01	8.36E-05 ± 2.69E-05
MWOA-1	0.00E+00 ± 0.00E+00	0.00E+00 ± 0.00E+00	**3.65E+02 ± 5.56E+02**	1.73E+01 ± 2.48E+01	2.53E+01 ± 3.07E-01	8.04E-05 ± 4.04E-05
MWOA-2	0.00E+00 ± 0.00E+00	0.00E+00 ± 0.00E+00	9.18E+02 ± 1.57E+03	1.64E+01 ± 2.31E+01	2.52E+01 ± 3.92E-01	8.62E-05 ± 3.30E-05
MWOA-3	0.00E+00 ± 0.00E+00	0.00E+00 ± 0.00E+00	4.47E+02 ± 6.02E+02	1.43E+01 ± 2.14E+01	2.51E+01 ± 3.79E-01	8.03E-05 ± 4.38E-05
MWOA-4	0.00E+00 ± 0.00E+00	0.00E+00 ± 0.00E+00	8.95E+02 ± 7.85E+02	1.85E+01 ± 2.28E+01	2.52E+01 ± 3.51E-01	8.62E-05 ± 3.48E-05
MWOA-5	0.00E+00 ± 0.00E+00	0.00E+00 ± 0.00E+00	5.96E+02 ± 7.46E+02	1.61E+01 ± 2.25E+01	2.52E+01 ± 2.78E-01	8.08E-05 ± 3.13E-05
MWOA-6	0.00E+00 ± 0.00E+00	0.00E+00 ± 0.00E+00	9.86E+02 ± 1.27E+03	1.92E+01 ± 2.68E+01	2.52E+01 ± 4.00E-01	7.70E-05 ± 3.15E-05
MWOA-7	0.00E+00 ± 0.00E+00	0.00E+00 ± 0.00E+00	4.28E+02 ± 6.88E+02	1.49E+01 ± 2.37E+01	**2.51E+01 ± 3.20E-01**	7.81E-05 ± 2.82E-05
MWOA-8	0.00E+00 ± 0.00E+00	0.00E+00 ± 0.00E+00	6.17E+02 ± 8.65E+02	1.62E+01 ± 2.78E+01	2.52E+01 ± 2.96E-01	7.89E-05 ± 3.27E-05
MWOA-9	0.00E+00 ± 0.00E+00	0.00E+00 ± 0.00E+00	6.76E+02 ± 1.22E+03	1.75E+01 ± 2.60E+01	2.53E+01 ± 4.00E-01	**7.19E-05 ± 3.17E-05**
MWOA-10	0.00E+00 ± 0.00E+00	0.00E+00 ± 0.00E+00	5.13E+02 ± 7.97E+02	1.37E+01 ± 1.88E+01	2.52E+01 ± 3.10E-01	7.56E-05 ± 3.87E-05
MWOA-11	0.00E+00 ± 0.00E+00	0.00E+00 ± 0.00E+00	8.10E+02 ± 9.65E+02	1.87E+01 ± 2.23E+01	2.51E+01 ± 3.35E-01	8.32E-05 ± 3.48E-05
MWOA-12	0.00E+00 ± 0.00E+00	0.00E+00 ± 0.00E+00	7.13E+02 ± 8.48E+02	1.84E+01 ± 2.10E+01	2.52E+01 ± 3.02E-01	7.23E-05 ± 2.68E-05
WOA-UD	0.00E+00 ± 0.00E+00	0.00E+00 ± 0.00E+00	5.40E+02 ± 7.46E+02	1.36E+01 ± 2.14E+01	2.52E+01 ± 3.19E-01	7.98E-05 ± 3.78E-05
WOA-ND	0.00E+00 ± 0.00E+00	0.00E+00 ± 0.00E+00	6.02E+02 ± 8.32E+02	1.65E+01 ± 2.62E+01	2.53E+01 ± 4.52E-01	7.95E-05 ± 3.23E-05

	F7	F8	F9	F10	F11	F12
WOA	2.53E-04 ± 3.02E-04	-1.22E+04 ± 7.30E+02	0.00E+00 ± 0.00E+00	3.14E-15 ± 1.98E-15	1.65E-03 ± 6.34E-03	2.25E-04 ± 1.17E-03
MWOA-R	**2.36E-04 ± 3.72E-04**	-1.20E+04 ± 9.00E+02	**0.00E+00 ± 0.00E+00**	2.66E-15 ± 1.81E-15	**0.00E+00 ± 0.00E+00**	**1.21E-05 ± 5.10E-06**
MWOA-P	3.07E-04 ± 5.26E-04	-1.22E+04 ± 8.14E+02	3.79E-15 ± 1.44E-14	3.02E-15 ± 1.77E-15	9.66E-04 ± 3.69E-03	4.40E-05 ± 2.20E-05
MWOA-M	2.90E-04 ± 4.39E-04	**-1.23E+04 ± 3.86E+02**	0.00E+00 ± 0.00E+00	2.90E-15 ± 2.02E-15	3.79E-04 ± 2.08E-03	1.84E-04 ± 9.31E-04
MWOA-1	5.50E-04 ± 8.13E-04	-1.21E+04 ± 1.01E+03	0.00E+00 ± 0.00E+00	3.14E-15 ± 2.18E-15	3.71E-04 ± 2.03E-03	1.58E-05 ± 1.85E-05
MWOA-2	3.20E-04 ± 3.83E-04	-1.17E+04 ± 1.46E+03	3.79E-15 ± 1.44E-14	3.38E-15 ± 2.12E-15	1.80E-03 ± 5.65E-03	2.95E-04 ± 1.54E-03
MWOA-3	2.94E-04 ± 3.68E-04	-1.20E+04 ± 1.09E+03	0.00E+00 ± 0.00E+00	3.85E-15 ± 2.65E-15	0.00E+00 ± 0.00E+00	5.51E-05 ± 2.30E-04
MWOA-4	4.21E-04 ± 4.27E-04	-1.21E+04 ± 8.52E+02	0.00E+00 ± 0.00E+00	3.97E-15 ± 2.42E-15	7.05E-04 ± 3.86E-03	1.42E-05 ± 7.45E-06
MWOA-5	4.32E-04 ± 4.80E-04	-1.20E+04 ± 1.34E+03	0.00E+00 ± 0.00E+00	3.73E-15 ± 2.54E-15	4.61E-04 ± 2.53E-03	1.55E-05 ± 7.34E-06
MWOA-6	4.12E-04 ± 4.95E-04	-1.23E+04 ± 7.94E+02	0.00E+00 ± 0.00E+00	3.97E-15 ± 2.42E-15	9.15E-04 ± 3.56E-03	1.22E-05 ± 4.83E-06
MWOA-7	4.93E-04 ± 4.80E-04	-1.21E+04 ± 7.96E+02	1.89E-15 ± 1.04E-14	3.97E-15 ± 2.59E-15	2.37E-03 ± 7.83E-03	4.46E-04 ± 2.37E-03
MWOA-8	2.56E-04 ± 2.53E-04	-1.25E+04 ± 1.60E+02	0.00E+00 ± 0.00E+00	3.49E-15 ± 2.46E-15	1.06E-03 ± 4.11E-03	2.20E-04 ± 1.14E-03
MWOA-9	3.11E-04 ± 3.00E-04	-1.23E+04 ± 4.56E+02	3.79E-15 ± 2.08E-14	3.73E-15 ± 2.36E-15	1.21E-03 ± 3.74E-03	2.24E-04 ± 1.15E-03
MWOA-10	3.51E-04 ± 3.43E-04	-1.23E+04 ± 4.83E+02	1.89E-15 ± 1.04E-14	3.73E-15 ± 2.36E-15	8.56E-04 ± 4.69E-03	2.01E-04 ± 1.03E-03
MWOA-11	2.75E-04 ± 2.95E-04	-1.22E+04 ± 9.73E+02	1.89E-15 ± 1.04E-14	3.26E-15 ± 2.35E-15	1.69E-03 ± 5.50E-03	1.29E-05 ± 5.18E-06
MWOA-12	3.00E-04 ± 3.86E-04	-1.20E+04 ± 9.42E+02	0.00E+00 ± 0.00E+00	3.73E-15 ± 2.17E-15	1.35E-03 ± 4.20E-03	5.80E-04 ± 3.09E-03
WOA-UD	4.93E-04 ± 4.80E-04	-1.22E+04 ± 7.57E+02	0.00E+00 ± 0.00E+00	2.78E-15 ± 2.03E-15	1.76E-03 ± 5.54E-03	1.66E-05 ± 2.48E-05
WOA-ND	2.56E-04 ± 2.53E-04	-1.23E+04 ± 6.57E+02	0.00E+00 ± 0.00E+00	2.78E-15 ± 2.03E-15	1.14E-03 ± 4.37E-03	9.95E-04 ± 5.36E-03

	F13	F14	F15	F16	F17	F18
WOA	4.31E-03 ± 2.01E-02	0.00E+00 ± 0.00E+00	0.00E+00 ± 0.00E+00	0.00E+00 ± 0.00E+00	0.00E+00 ± 0.00E+00	0.00E+00 ± 0.00E+00
MWOA-R	2.77E-03 ± 4.95E-03	0.00E+00 ± 0.00E+00	0.00E+00 ± 0.00E+00	0.00E+00 ± 0.00E+00	0.00E+00 ± 0.00E+00	0.00E+00 ± 0.00E+00
MWOA-P	4.84E-03 ± 6.04E-03	0.00E+00 ± 0.00E+00	0.00E+00 ± 0.00E+00	0.00E+00 ± 0.00E+00	0.00E+00 ± 0.00E+00	0.00E+00 ± 0.00E+00
MWOA-M	6.58E-03 ± 1.87E-02	0.00E+00 ± 0.00E+00	0.00E+00 ± 0.00E+00	0.00E+00 ± 0.00E+00	0.00E+00 ± 0.00E+00	0.00E+00 ± 0.00E+00
MWOA-1	**1.70E-03 ± 3.77E-03**	0.00E+00 ± 0.00E+00	0.00E+00 ± 0.00E+00	0.00E+00 ± 0.00E+00	0.00E+00 ± 0.00E+00	0.00E+00 ± 0.00E+00
MWOA-2	2.65E-03 ± 4.90E-03	0.00E+00 ± 0.00E+00	0.00E+00 ± 0.00E+00	0.00E+00 ± 0.00E+00	0.00E+00 ± 0.00E+00	0.00E+00 ± 0.00E+00
MWOA-3	6.85E-03 ± 1.80E-02	0.00E+00 ± 0.00E+00	0.00E+00 ± 0.00E+00	0.00E+00 ± 0.00E+00	0.00E+00 ± 0.00E+00	0.00E+00 ± 0.00E+00
MWOA-4	5.65E-03 ± 1.79E-02	0.00E+00 ± 0.00E+00	0.00E+00 ± 0.00E+00	0.00E+00 ± 0.00E+00	0.00E+00 ± 0.00E+00	0.00E+00 ± 0.00E+00
MWOA-5	2.10E-03 ± 4.12E-03	0.00E+00 ± 0.00E+00	8.18E+02 ± 0.00E+00	0.00E+00 ± 0.00E+00	0.00E+00 ± 0.00E+00	0.00E+00 ± 0.00E+00
MWOA-6	4.67E-03 ± 8.95E-03	0.00E+00 ± 0.00E+00	0.00E+00 ± 0.00E+00	0.00E+00 ± 0.00E+00	0.00E+00 ± 0.00E+00	0.00E+00 ± 0.00E+00
MWOA-7	2.86E-03 ± 4.77E-03	0.00E+00 ± 0.00E+00	0.00E+00 ± 0.00E+00	0.00E+00 ± 0.00E+00	0.00E+00 ± 0.00E+00	0.00E+00 ± 0.00E+00
MWOA-8	2.20E-03 ± 4.17E-03	0.00E+00 ± 0.00E+00	0.00E+00 ± 0.00E+00	0.00E+00 ± 0.00E+00	0.00E+00 ± 0.00E+00	0.00E+00 ± 0.00E+00
MWOA-9	4.21E-03 ± 8.85E-03	0.00E+00 ± 0.00E+00	0.00E+00 ± 0.00E+00	0.00E+00 ± 0.00E+00	0.00E+00 ± 0.00E+00	0.00E+00 ± 0.00E+00
MWOA-10	3.13E-03 ± 4.95E-03	0.00E+00 ± 0.00E+00	0.00E+00 ± 0.00E+00	0.00E+00 ± 0.00E+00	0.00E+00 ± 0.00E+00	0.00E+00 ± 0.00E+00
MWOA-11	1.04E-02 ± 3.63E-02	0.00E+00 ± 0.00E+00	0.00E+00 ± 0.00E+00	0.00E+00 ± 0.00E+00	0.00E+00 ± 0.00E+00	0.00E+00 ± 0.00E+00
MWOA-12	3.08E-03 ± 6.76E-03	0.00E+00 ± 0.00E+00	0.00E+00 ± 0.00E+00	0.00E+00 ± 0.00E+00	0.00E+00 ± 0.00E+00	0.00E+00 ± 0.00E+00
WOA-UD	3.53E-03 ± 5.12E-03	0.00E+00 ± 0.00E+00	0.00E+00 ± 0.00E+00	0.00E+00 ± 0.00E+00	0.00E+00 ± 0.00E+00	0.00E+00 ± 0.00E+00
WOA-ND	3.11E-03 ± 5.64E-03	0.00E+00 ± 0.00E+00	0.00E+00 ± 0.00E+00	0.00E+00 ± 0.00E+00	0.00E+00 ± 0.00E+00	0.00E+00 ± 0.00E+00

	F19	F20	F21	F22	F23	F24
WOA	0.00E+00 ± 0.00E+00	0.00E+00 ± 0.00E+00	0.00E+00 ± 0.00E+00	0.00E+00 ± 0.00E+00	0.00E+00 ± 0.00E+00	5.90E+00 ± 3.63E+00
MWOA-R	0.00E+00 ± 0.00E+00	0.00E+00 ± 0.00E+00	0.00E+00 ± 0.00E+00	0.00E+00 ± 0.00E+00	0.00E+00 ± 0.00E+00	**1.97E+00 ± 2.89E+00**
MWOA-P	0.00E+00 ± 0.00E+00	0.00E+00 ± 0.00E+00	0.00E+00 ± 0.00E+00	0.00E+00 ± 0.00E+00	0.00E+00 ± 0.00E+00	4.56E+00 ± 1.71E+00
MWOA-M	0.00E+00 ± 0.00E+00	0.00E+00 ± 0.00E+00	0.00E+00 ± 0.00E+00	0.00E+00 ± 0.00E+00	0.00E+00 ± 0.00E+00	5.17E+00 ± 2.28E+00
MWOA-1	0.00E+00 ± 0.00E+00	0.00E+00 ± 0.00E+00	0.00E+00 ± 0.00E+00	0.00E+00 ± 0.00E+00	0.00E+00 ± 0.00E+00	8.84E+00 ± 1.42E+01
MWOA-2	0.00E+00 ± 0.00E+00	0.00E+00 ± 0.00E+00	0.00E+00 ± 0.00E+00	0.00E+00 ± 0.00E+00	0.00E+00 ± 0.00E+00	8.26E+00 ± 1.04E+01
MWOA-3	0.00E+00 ± 0.00E+00	0.00E+00 ± 0.00E+00	0.00E+00 ± 0.00E+00	0.00E+00 ± 0.00E+00	0.00E+00 ± 0.00E+00	8.06E+00 ± 9.17E+00
MWOA-4	0.00E+00 ± 0.00E+00	0.00E+00 ± 0.00E+00	0.00E+00 ± 0.00E+00	0.00E+00 ± 0.00E+00	0.00E+00 ± 0.00E+00	6.57E+00 ± 6.30E+00
MWOA-5	0.00E+00 ± 0.00E+00	0.00E+00 ± 0.00E+00	8.18E+02 ± 0.00E+00	0.00E+00 ± 0.00E+00	0.00E+00 ± 0.00E+00	6.98E+00 ± 1.12E+01
MWOA-6	0.00E+00 ± 0.00E+00	0.00E+00 ± 0.00E+00	0.00E+00 ± 0.00E+00	0.00E+00 ± 0.00E+00	0.00E+00 ± 0.00E+00	9.55E+00 ± 2.04E+01
MWOA-7	0.00E+00 ± 0.00E+00	0.00E+00 ± 0.00E+00	0.00E+00 ± 0.00E+00	0.00E+00 ± 0.00E+00	0.00E+00 ± 0.00E+00	5.84E+00 ± 2.56E+00
MWOA-8	0.00E+00 ± 0.00E+00	0.00E+00 ± 0.00E+00	0.00E+00 ± 0.00E+00	0.00E+00 ± 0.00E+00	0.00E+00 ± 0.00E+00	8.58E+00 ± 1.25E+01
MWOA-9	0.00E+00 ± 0.00E+00	0.00E+00 ± 0.00E+00	0.00E+00 ± 0.00E+00	0.00E+00 ± 0.00E+00	0.00E+00 ± 0.00E+00	8.82E+00 ± 1.30E+01
MWOA-10	0.00E+00 ± 0.00E+00	0.00E+00 ± 0.00E+00	0.00E+00 ± 0.00E+00	0.00E+00 ± 0.00E+00	0.00E+00 ± 0.00E+00	1.03E+01 ± 2.01E+01
MWOA-11	0.00E+00 ± 0.00E+00	0.00E+00 ± 0.00E+00	0.00E+00 ± 0.00E+00	0.00E+00 ± 0.00E+00	0.00E+00 ± 0.00E+00	7.40E+00 ± 5.78E+00
MWOA-12	0.00E+00 ± 0.00E+00	0.00E+00 ± 0.00E+00	4.83E+02 ± 0.00E+00	0.00E+00 ± 0.00E+00	0.00E+00 ± 0.00E+00	5.61E+00 ± 3.53E+00
WOA-UD	0.00E+00 ± 0.00E+00	0.00E+00 ± 0.00E+00	0.00E+00 ± 0.00E+00	0.00E+00 ± 0.00E+00	0.00E+00 ± 0.00E+00	9.92E+00 ± 1.60E+01
WOA-ND	0.00E+00 ± 0.00E+00	0.00E+00 ± 0.00E+00	0.00E+00 ± 0.00E+00	0.00E+00 ± 0.00E+00	0.00E+00 ± 0.00E+00	8.54E+00 ± 1.35E+01

Table 5. Experimental results of benchmark functions (F25–F48) using traditional WOA, MWOA-S, MWOA-R, MWOA-P, MWOA-M, WOA-UD and WOA-ND.

Algorithm	F25	F26	F27	F28	F29	F30
WOA	6.45E+04 ± 1.18E+04	3.81E+07 ± 1.78E+07	1.61E+05 ± 5.85E+04	1.99E+04 ± 4.53E+03	7.47E+04 ± 1.37E+05	4.81E+03 ± 6.45E+01
MWOA-R	**5.71E+04 ± 9.73E+03**	3.89E+07 ± 1.73E+07	1.56E+05 ± 4.66E+04	1.82E+04 ± 4.71E+03	8.06E+04 ± 9.59E+04	4.80E+03 ± 6.47E+01
MWOA-P	6.19E+04 ± 1.04E+04	5.16E+07 ± 2.45E+07	1.63E+05 ± 4.31E+04	1.95E+04 ± 4.36E+03	1.81E+05 ± 1.78E+05	4.79E+03 ± 6.91E+01
MWOA-M	6.25E+04 ± 9.05E+03	3.40E+07 ± 1.51E+07	1.59E+05 ± 3.47E+04	1.80E+04 ± 3.92E+03	7.49E+04 ± 9.18E+04	4.80E+03 ± 6.75E+01
MWOA-1	6.51E+04 ± 1.22E+04	3.36E+07 ± 1.43E+07	**1.42E+05 ± 3.72E+04**	1.82E+04 ± 5.17E+03	6.68E+04 ± 1.11E+05	4.80E+03 ± 6.58E+01
MWOA-2	5.99E+04 ± 1.08E+04	3.51E+07 ± 1.77E+07	1.63E+05 ± 5.02E+04	1.90E+04 ± 4.02E+03	**5.57E+04 ± 3.97E+04**	4.82E+03 ± 5.59E+01
MWOA-3	6.38E+04 ± 1.10E+04	3.91E+07 ± 1.85E+07	1.46E+05 ± 4.83E+04	1.94E+04 ± 2.98E+03	6.19E+04 ± 1.09E+05	4.79E+03 ± 6.79E+01
MWOA-4	6.26E+04 ± 1.01E+04	3.88E+07 ± 1.76E+07	1.52E+05 ± 5.41E+04	**1.77E+04 ± 3.38E+03**	1.07E+05 ± 2.45E+05	4.79E+03 ± 6.77E+01
MWOA-5	6.31E+04 ± 1.17E+04	3.46E+07 ± 1.17E+07	1.51E+05 ± 4.52E+04	1.92E+04 ± 4.81E+03	1.01E+05 ± 1.65E+05	4.81E+03 ± 6.61E+01
MWOA-6	6.46E+04 ± 1.07E+04	4.02E+07 ± 1.89E+07	1.63E+05 ± 4.55E+04	1.93E+04 ± 3.85E+03	1.68E+05 ± 3.87E+05	4.79E+03 ± 6.57E+01
MWOA-7	6.36E+04 ± 1.16E+04	3.49E+07 ± 1.58E+07	1.51E+05 ± 3.43E+04	2.03E+04 ± 4.43E+03	1.09E+05 ± 2.51E+05	4.80E+03 ± 6.76E+01
MWOA-8	6.48E+04 ± 1.52E+04	**3.34E+07 ± 1.80E+07**	1.57E+05 ± 4.28E+04	1.94E+04 ± 3.87E+03	8.69E+04 ± 1.47E+05	**4.78E+03 ± 6.57E+01**
MWOA-9	6.29E+04 ± 1.06E+04	3.96E+07 ± 1.89E+07	1.76E+05 ± 6.64E+04	1.96E+04 ± 3.57E+03	6.88E+04 ± 7.27E+04	4.79E+03 ± 6.36E+01
MWOA-10	6.75E+04 ± 1.18E+04	4.00E+07 ± 1.50E+07	1.59E+05 ± 5.23E+04	1.91E+04 ± 4.58E+03	8.33E+04 ± 1.24E+05	4.81E+03 ± 6.77E+01
MWOA-11	6.34E+04 ± 1.24E+04	3.46E+07 ± 1.56E+07	1.51E+05 ± 3.43E+04	2.07E+04 ± 4.19E+03	6.58E+04 ± 5.24E+04	4.80E+03 ± 6.76E+01
MWOA-12	6.23E+04 ± 1.21E+04	3.48E+07 ± 1.30E+07	1.52E+05 ± 4.27E+04	1.90E+04 ± 4.20E+03	1.66E+05 ± 2.24E+05	4.81E+03 ± 6.19E+01
WOA-UD	6.15E+04 ± 1.20E+04	3.55E+07 ± 1.43E+07	1.58E+05 ± 5.05E+04	2.04E+04 ± 4.99E+03	7.79E+04 ± 1.06E+05	4.80E+03 ± 6.67E+01
WOA-ND	6.15E+04 ± 1.15E+04	3.78E+07 ± 1.67E+07	1.59E+05 ± 5.21E+04	1.86E+04 ± 3.94E+03	7.55E+04 ± 1.00E+05	4.80E+03 ± 6.57E+01

Algorithm	F31	F32	F33	F34	F35	F36
WOA	2.08E+01 ± 1.09E-01	2.26E+02 ± 4.23E+01	4.78E+02 ± 9.21E+01	3.65E+01 ± 2.65E+00	1.50E+05 ± 1.05E+05	2.20E+01 ± 8.39E+00
MWOA-R	**2.08E+01 ± 1.05E-01**	**2.15E+02 ± 4.61E+01**	4.26E+02 ± 7.14E+01	3.65E+01 ± 2.68E+00	1.42E+05 ± 1.17E+05	2.17E+01 ± 6.32E+00
MWOA-P	2.08E+01 ± 8.56E-02	2.25E+02 ± 3.87E+01	4.62E+02 ± 8.35E+01	3.72E+01 ± 2.80E+00	2.12E+05 ± 1.48E+05	2.22E+01 ± 5.10E+00
MWOA-M	2.08E+01 ± 7.57E-02	2.31E+02 ± 4.14E+01	4.46E+02 ± 8.46E+01	3.76E+01 ± 2.62E+00	1.75E+05 ± 1.22E+05	2.38E+01 ± 7.05E+00
MWOA-1	2.08E+01 ± 1.04E-01	2.27E+02 ± 3.47E+01	**3.95E+02 ± 9.43E+01**	3.74E+01 ± 2.96E+00	**1.16E+05 ± 7.63E+04**	2.30E+01 ± 6.60E+00
MWOA-2	2.08E+01 ± 1.19E-01	2.29E+02 ± 3.66E+01	4.03E+02 ± 1.06E+02	3.73E+01 ± 3.00E+00	1.17E+05 ± 7.36E+04	2.17E+01 ± 4.63E+00
MWOA-3	2.08E+01 ± 1.04E-01	2.36E+02 ± 4.44E+01	4.31E+02 ± 9.77E+01	3.73E+01 ± 2.52E+00	1.24E+05 ± 9.72E+04	2.32E+01 ± 6.36E+00
MWOA-4	2.08E+01 ± 9.73E-02	2.25E+02 ± 4.88E+01	4.48E+02 ± 8.53E+01	3.78E+01 ± 2.65E+00	1.32E+05 ± 1.16E+05	2.31E+01 ± 5.39E+00
MWOA-5	2.08E+01 ± 8.57E-02	2.24E+02 ± 4.81E+01	4.44E+02 ± 1.16E+02	3.69E+01 ± 2.79E+00	1.68E+05 ± 8.07E+04	2.28E+01 ± 5.05E+00
MWOA-6	2.08E+01 ± 1.14E-01	2.24E+02 ± 5.18E+01	4.04E+02 ± 8.37E+01	3.72E+01 ± 2.93E+00	1.79E+05 ± 1.29E+05	2.12E+01 ± 3.97E+00
MWOA-7	2.08E+01 ± 8.01E-02	2.33E+02 ± 3.86E+01	4.31E+02 ± 8.33E+01	3.70E+01 ± 2.84E+00	1.37E+05 ± 1.25E+05	**2.11E+01 ± 5.12E+00**
MWOA-8	2.08E+01 ± 1.20E-01	2.27E+02 ± 3.39E+01	4.17E+02 ± 1.07E+02	3.75E+01 ± 2.01E+00	1.81E+05 ± 1.08E+05	2.30E+01 ± 5.71E+00
MWOA-9	2.08E+01 ± 1.14E-01	2.23E+02 ± 3.31E+01	4.30E+02 ± 8.95E+01	**3.64E+01 ± 3.44E+00**	1.41E+05 ± 7.41E+04	2.36E+01 ± 4.98E+00
MWOA-10	2.08E+01 ± 9.49E-02	2.28E+02 ± 3.98E+01	4.52E+02 ± 1.03E+02	3.69E+01 ± 3.51E+00	1.90E+05 ± 1.56E+05	2.35E+01 ± 6.57E+00
MWOA-11	2.08E+01 ± 9.75E-02	2.32E+02 ± 3.87E+01	4.33E+02 ± 8.27E+01	3.73E+01 ± 2.17E+00	1.42E+05 ± 1.30E+05	2.12E+01 ± 5.24E+00
MWOA-12	2.08E+01 ± 1.12E-01	2.23E+02 ± 4.42E+01	4.31E+02 ± 7.25E+01	3.67E+01 ± 2.29E+00	1.53E+05 ± 8.57E+04	2.30E+01 ± 5.33E+00
WOA-UD	2.08E+01 ± 1.13E-01	2.31E+02 ± 4.22E+01	4.29E+02 ± 8.41E+01	3.71E+01 ± 3.18E+00	1.54E+05 ± 1.14E+05	2.16E+01 ± 7.04E+00
WOA-ND	2.08E+01 ± 1.16E-01	2.39E+02 ± 4.79E+01	4.52E+02 ± 8.45E+01	3.81E+01 ± 2.48E+00	1.43E+05 ± 8.44E+04	2.17E+01 ± 6.09E+00

Algorithm	F37	F38	F39	F40	F41	F42
WOA	1.35E+01 ± 2.94E-01	7.02E+02 ± 1.99E+02	5.03E+02 ± 8.67E+01	5.65E+02 ± 1.16E+02	**1.02E+03 ± 8.14E+01**	1.06E+03 ± 8.45E+01
MWOA-R	1.35E+01 ± 2.18E-01	6.82E+02 ± 1.71E+02	4.72E+02 ± 9.64E+01	**5.37E+02 ± 7.99E+01**	1.04E+03 ± 9.40E+01	1.04E+03 ± 7.33E+01
MWOA-P	1.34E+01 ± 3.67E-01	7.15E+02 ± 1.97E+02	4.78E+02 ± 1.01E+02	5.59E+02 ± 8.56E+01	1.06E+03 ± 8.31E+01	1.08E+03 ± 8.23E+01
MWOA-M	1.34E+01 ± 3.37E-01	6.59E+02 ± 2.09E+02	4.68E+02 ± 9.19E+01	5.60E+02 ± 1.13E+02	1.04E+03 ± 8.43E+01	1.03E+03 ± 8.10E+01
MWOA-1	1.35E+01 ± 3.24E-01	6.98E+02 ± 2.25E+02	**4.51E+02 ± 7.06E+01**	5.67E+02 ± 8.58E+01	1.02E+03 ± 5.41E+01	1.04E+03 ± 9.04E+01
MWOA-2	1.34E+01 ± 3.09E-01	**6.29E+02 ± 1.94E+02**	4.87E+02 ± 1.35E+02	5.85E+02 ± 1.16E+02	1.08E+03 ± 1.01E+02	1.04E+03 ± 5.79E+01
MWOA-3	1.34E+01 ± 3.60E-01	7.28E+02 ± 1.78E+02	4.91E+02 ± 1.10E+02	5.50E+02 ± 8.95E+01	1.05E+03 ± 7.16E+01	1.04E+03 ± 8.53E+01
MWOA-4	1.34E+01 ± 2.82E-01	6.90E+02 ± 1.93E+02	5.03E+02 ± 1.32E+02	5.51E+02 ± 9.28E+01	1.07E+03 ± 1.11E+02	1.07E+03 ± 9.83E+01
MWOA-5	1.34E+01 ± 3.33E-01	7.33E+02 ± 1.75E+02	4.51E+02 ± 9.37E+01	5.54E+02 ± 7.74E+01	1.06E+03 ± 8.28E+01	**1.02E+03 ± 7.71E+01**
MWOA-6	1.35E+01 ± 3.60E-01	6.72E+02 ± 2.10E+02	4.75E+02 ± 8.48E+01	5.54E+02 ± 1.11E+02	1.06E+03 ± 8.87E+01	1.06E+03 ± 9.47E+01
MWOA-7	1.35E+01 ± 3.35E-01	6.97E+02 ± 2.20E+02	4.91E+02 ± 1.12E+02	5.63E+02 ± 8.19E+01	1.05E+03 ± 8.53E+01	1.05E+03 ± 8.47E+01
MWOA-8	1.34E+01 ± 4.17E-01	7.06E+02 ± 1.81E+02	4.76E+02 ± 1.06E+02	5.54E+02 ± 8.70E+01	1.03E+03 ± 7.54E+01	1.07E+03 ± 7.80E+01
MWOA-9	1.34E+01 ± 3.44E-01	7.44E+02 ± 2.13E+02	4.54E+02 ± 8.59E+01	5.79E+02 ± 1.44E+02	1.05E+03 ± 7.68E+01	1.08E+03 ± 1.02E+02
MWOA-10	1.34E+01 ± 2.92E-01	7.20E+02 ± 1.88E+02	4.68E+02 ± 9.40E+01	5.47E+02 ± 9.48E+01	1.06E+03 ± 8.64E+01	1.08E+03 ± 1.04E+02
MWOA-11	1.35E+01 ± 3.18E-01	7.12E+02 ± 2.16E+02	4.79E+02 ± 1.15E+02	5.46E+02 ± 1.52E+02	1.05E+03 ± 7.44E+01	1.06E+03 ± 8.90E+01
MWOA-12	**1.33E+01 ± 3.73E-01**	6.64E+02 ± 2.13E+02	5.03E+02 ± 1.10E+02	5.78E+02 ± 1.13E+02	1.02E+03 ± 7.42E+01	1.09E+03 ± 1.06E+02
WOA-UD	1.34E+01 ± 2.40E-01	7.55E+02 ± 1.62E+02	4.79E+02 ± 1.06E+02	5.49E+02 ± 8.97E+01	1.05E+03 ± 8.02E+01	1.04E+03 ± 8.41E+01
WOA-ND	1.35E+01 ± 2.67E-01	7.20E+02 ± 1.85E+02	4.54E+02 ± 7.76E+01	5.52E+02 ± 8.02E+01	1.04E+03 ± 9.52E+01	1.04E+03 ± 9.84E+01

Algorithm	F43	F44	F45	F46	F47	F48
WOA	1.06E+03 ± 1.03E+02	1.26E+03 ± 1.48E+02	1.22E+03 ± 8.79E+01	1.27E+03 ± 6.85E+01	1.34E+03 ± 8.98E+01	1.63E+03 ± 5.64E+00
MWOA-R	1.06E+03 ± 8.30E+01	1.24E+03 ± 1.50E+02	1.23E+03 ± 1.03E+02	1.27E+03 ± 6.70E+01	**1.34E+03 ± 9.97E+01**	**1.63E+03 ± 5.32E+00**
MWOA-P	1.07E+03 ± 1.02E+02	1.29E+03 ± 4.84E+01	1.26E+03 ± 1.36E+02	1.27E+03 ± 1.05E+02	1.36E+03 ± 9.98E+01	1.63E+03 ± 5.41E+00
MWOA-M	**1.04E+03 ± 7.68E+01**	1.24E+03 ± 1.19E+02	1.25E+03 ± 1.13E+02	1.27E+03 ± 4.95E+01	1.38E+03 ± 6.12E+01	1.63E+03 ± 7.13E+00
MWOA-1	1.06E+03 ± 7.74E+01	1.27E+03 ± 5.12E+01	1.23E+03 ± 1.05E+02	1.29E+03 ± 4.76E+01	1.36E+03 ± 6.04E+01	1.63E+03 ± 4.71E+00
MWOA-2	1.05E+03 ± 8.08E+01	1.26E+03 ± 5.31E+01	**1.19E+03 ± 9.88E+01**	1.27E+03 ± 8.37E+01	1.36E+03 ± 5.47E+01	1.63E+03 ± 5.09E+00
MWOA-3	1.07E+03 ± 9.46E+01	1.23E+03 ± 1.60E+02	1.22E+03 ± 1.16E+02	1.29E+03 ± 4.97E+01	1.36E+03 ± 9.09E+01	1.63E+03 ± 5.37E+00
MWOA-4	1.04E+03 ± 8.58E+01	1.27E+03 ± 4.18E+01	1.21E+03 ± 9.60E+01	1.28E+03 ± 5.75E+01	1.37E+03 ± 6.36E+01	1.63E+03 ± 6.25E+00
MWOA-5	1.05E+03 ± 9.48E+01	1.20E+03 ± 2.12E+02	1.21E+03 ± 1.30E+02	1.25E+03 ± 7.60E+01	1.38E+03 ± 7.02E+01	1.63E+03 ± 5.24E+00
MWOA-6	1.07E+03 ± 1.01E+02	1.29E+03 ± 5.74E+01	1.24E+03 ± 9.46E+01	1.28E+03 ± 4.43E+01	1.36E+03 ± 8.65E+01	1.63E+03 ± 4.03E+00
MWOA-7	1.06E+03 ± 9.44E+01	1.25E+03 ± 4.68E+01	1.24E+03 ± 1.00E+02	**1.25E+03 ± 6.96E+01**	1.36E+03 ± 9.83E+01	1.63E+03 ± 4.49E+00
MWOA-8	1.05E+03 ± 9.12E+01	**1.20E+03 ± 2.35E+02**	1.23E+03 ± 9.01E+01	1.29E+03 ± 4.53E+01	1.36E+03 ± 1.09E+02	1.63E+03 ± 6.19E+00
MWOA-9	1.04E+03 ± 6.91E+01	1.26E+03 ± 1.01E+02	1.25E+03 ± 1.37E+02	1.27E+03 ± 5.09E+01	1.38E+03 ± 4.62E+01	1.63E+03 ± 5.94E+00
MWOA-10	1.04E+03 ± 7.97E+01	1.24E+03 ± 1.06E+02	1.24E+03 ± 9.53E+01	1.27E+03 ± 7.04E+01	1.36E+03 ± 5.49E+01	1.63E+03 ± 5.03E+00
MWOA-11	1.06E+03 ± 1.08E+02	1.23E+03 ± 1.96E+02	1.22E+03 ± 9.91E+01	1.27E+03 ± 5.93E+01	1.35E+03 ± 7.85E+01	1.63E+03 ± 7.14E+00
MWOA-12	1.04E+03 ± 7.46E+01	1.24E+03 ± 1.62E+02	1.21E+03 ± 7.99E+01	1.29E+03 ± 4.08E+01	1.36E+03 ± 1.02E+02	1.63E+03 ± 6.21E+00
WOA-UD	1.05E+03 ± 6.07E+01	1.26E+03 ± 1.54E+02	1.23E+03 ± 9.56E+01	1.34E+03 ± 6.90E+01	1.36E+03 ± 8.15E+01	1.63E+03 ± 6.06E+00
WOA-ND	1.10E+03 ± 9.45E+01	1.28E+03 ± 4.77E+01	1.22E+03 ± 1.18E+02	1.27E+03 ± 9.41E+01	1.38E+03 ± 7.84E+01	1.63E+03 ± 5.27E+00

To more precisely assess the performance of each algorithm, Friedman test is proposed as a statistical analysis method to rank each one according to their search results. The Friedman test is a nonparametric statistical analysis method. It is used to test the performance between different groups. The group with better performance will get lower rank in each benchmark function. In our experiment, Friedman test is used to assess test functions separately.

Table 3 summarizes the average rank each algorithm obtained in total 48 benchmark test functions (from F1–F48) and independently lists the results of CEC2005 benchmark functions (from F24–F48) because of the difficulty. Based on this table, it is obvious that our proposed algorithms MWOA-R gets the top rank in both all functions and CEC2005 test functions. It means that MWOA-R outperforms MWOA-S and conventional WOA and testifies that the method of randomly implement chaos into local search is a effective improvement and worth developing in our following researches.

The convergence graphs of F3, F6, F43 and F47 are exhibited in Fig. 2. The upper side is the average best-so-far solutions, and the lower side is the ratio of the best-so-far solutions by the number of function evaluations. Two kinds of convergence graphs can directly exhibit convergence speed between conventional WOA and MWOAs. These graphs show the performance of MWOA-R is much better than others. This point also can be seen from the boxplots in Fig. 3.

Table 3 also exhibits the p-values when MWOA-R is considered as the control algorithm to compare with the rest of the algorithms. Under the condition of considering $\alpha = 0.5$, MWOA-R is better than $13/17$ algorithms from F1–F48 and is better than $7/17$ algorithms from F24–F48.

When considering $\alpha = 0.1$, MWOA-R can perform better than $16/17$ algorithms from F1–F48 and perform better than $11/17$ algorithms from F24–F48.

All these statistical analysis results can demonstrate that MWOA-R is the most promising and the most competitive and can outperform the conventional WOA with no doubt.

5   Conclusions

In our paper, we combine chaos with conventional meta-heuristic algorithm WOA to yield a new improved version of WOA, called MWOA. Main conclusions drawn from the experiments: As in Friedman test, MWOA-R gets the top rank among all the tested algorithms, the combination of multiple chaos has been verified considerable methods to enhance the performance of chaotic local search. Most single chaos embedded MWOAs perform better than conventional WOA and it indicates that chaotic local search can improve the performance of WOA.

Acknowledgements. This research was partially supported by JSPS KAKENHI Grant Number 17K12751, 15K00332 (Japan).

References

1. Engelbrecht, A.P.: Fundamentals of Computational Swarm Intelligence. Wiley, Chichester (2006)
2. Yu, H., Xu, Z., Gao, S., Wang, Y., Todo, Y.: PMPSO: a near-optimal graph planarization algorithm using probability model based particle swarm optimization. In: 2015 IEEE International Conference on Progress in Informatics and Computing (PIC), pp. 15–19. IEEE (2015)
3. Das, S., Suganthan, P.N.: Differential evolution: a survey of the state-of-the-art. IEEE Trans. Evol. Comput. **15**(1), 4–31 (2011)
4. Gao, S., Wang, Y., Wang, J., Cheng, J.J.: Understanding differential evolution: a poisson law derived from population interaction network. J. Comput. Sci. **21**, 140–149 (2017)
5. Shi, Q., Chen, W., Jiang, T., Shen, D., Gao, S.: Handling multiobjectives with adaptive mutation based ε-dominance differential evolution. In: Tan, Y., Shi, Y., Buarque, F., Gelbukh, A., Das, S., Engelbrecht, A. (eds.) ICSI 2015. LNCS, vol. 9140, pp. 523–532. Springer, Cham (2015). https://doi.org/10.1007/978-3-319-20466-6_55
6. Ji, J., Gao, S., Wang, S., Tang, Y., Yu, H., Todo, Y.: Self-adaptive gravitational search algorithm with a modified chaotic local search. IEEE Access **5**, 17881–17895 (2017)
7. Gao, S., Vairappan, C., Wang, Y., Cao, Q., Tang, Z.: Gravitational search algorithm combined with chaos for unconstrained numerical optimization. Appl. Math. Comput. **231**, 48–62 (2014)
8. Song, Z., Gao, S., Yu, Y., Sun, J., Todo, Y.: Multiple chaos embedded gravitational search algorithm. IEICE Trans. Inf. Syst. **100**(4), 888–900 (2017)
9. Li, S., Jiang, T., Chen, H., Shen, D., Todo, Y., Gao, S.: Discrete chaotic gravitational search algorithm for unit commitment problem. In: Huang, D.-S., Jo, K.-H. (eds.) ICIC 2016. LNCS, vol. 9772, pp. 757–769. Springer, Cham (2016). https://doi.org/10.1007/978-3-319-42294-7_67
10. Karaboga, D.: Artificial bee colony algorithm. Scholarpedia **5**(3), 6915 (2010)
11. Gao, S., Wang, Y., Cheng, J., Inazumi, Y., Tang, Z.: Ant colony optimization with clustering for solving the dynamic location routing problem. Appl. Math. Comput. **285**, 149–173 (2016)
12. Gao, S., Wang, W., Dai, H., Li, F., Tang, Z.: Improved clonal selection algorithm combined with ant colony optimization. IEICE Trans. Inf. Syst. **91**(6), 1813–1823 (2008)
13. Tan, Y., Zhu, Y.: Fireworks algorithm for optimization. In: Tan, Y., Shi, Y., Tan, K.C. (eds.) ICSI 2010. LNCS, vol. 6145, pp. 355–364. Springer, Heidelberg (2010). https://doi.org/10.1007/978-3-642-13495-1_44
14. Zheng, S., Li, J., Janecek, A., Tan, Y.: A cooperative framework for fireworks algorithm. IEEE/ACM Trans. Comput. Biol. Bioinform. **14**(1), 27–41 (2017)
15. Shi, Y.: Brain storm optimization algorithm. In: Tan, Y., Shi, Y., Chai, Y., Wang, G. (eds.) ICSI 2011. LNCS, vol. 6728, pp. 303–309. Springer, Heidelberg (2011). https://doi.org/10.1007/978-3-642-21515-5_36
16. Wang, Y., Gao, S., Yu, Y., Xu, Z.: The discovery of population interaction with a power law distribution in brain storm optimization. Memetic Comput. (2017). https://doi.org/10.1007/s12293-017-0248-z
17. Yu, Y., Gao, S., Cheng, S., Wang, Y., Song, S., Yuan, F.: CBSO: a memetic brain storm optimization with chaotic local search. Memetic Comput. (2017). https://doi.org/10.1007/s12293-017-0247-0

18. Mirjalili, S., Lewis, A.: The whale optimization algorithm. Adv. Eng. Softw. **95**, 51–67 (2016)
19. Wolpert, D.H., Macready, W.G.: No free lunch theorems for optimization. IEEE Trans. Evol. Comput. **1**(1), 67–82 (1997)
20. Grosan, C., Abraham, A.: hybrid evolutionary algorithms: methodologies, architectures, and reviews. In: Abraham, A., Grosan, C., Ishibuchi, H. (eds.) Hybrid Evolutionary Algorithms. SCI, vol. 75, pp. 1–17. Springer, Heidelberg (2007). https://doi.org/10.1007/978-3-540-73297-6_1
21. Prosser, P.: Hybrid algorithms for the constraint satisfaction problem. Comput. Intell. **9**(3), 268–299 (1993)
22. Liao, T.W.: Two hybrid differential evolution algorithms for engineering design optimization. Appl. Soft Comput. **10**(4), 1188–1199 (2010)
23. Kao, M.Y., Ma, Y., Sipser, M., Yin, Y.: Optimal constructions of hybrid algorithms. J. Algorithms **29**(1), 142–164 (1998)
24. Gao, S., Tang, Z., Dai, H., Zhang, J.: A hybrid clonal selection algorithm. Int. J. Innov. Comput. Inf. Control **4**(4), 995–1008 (2008)
25. Wang, S., Aorigele, Liu, G., Gao, S.: A hybrid discrete imperialist competition algorithm for fuzzy job-shop scheduling problems. IEEE. Access **4**, 9320–9331 (2016)
26. Juang, C.F.: A hybrid of genetic algorithm and particle swarm optimization for recurrent network design. IEEE Trans. Syst. Man Cybern. Part B (Cybern.) **34**(2), 997–1006 (2004)
27. Gong, Y.J., Li, J.J., Zhou, Y., Li, Y., Chung, H.S.H., Shi, Y.H., Zhang, J.: Genetic learning particle swarm optimization. IEEE Trans. Cybern. **46**(10), 2277–2290 (2016)
28. Tasgetiren, M.F., Suganthan, P.N., Pan, Q.K.: An ensemble of discrete differential evolution algorithms for solving the generalized traveling salesman problem. Appl. Math. Comput. **215**(9), 3356–3368 (2010)
29. Hart, W.E., Krasnogor, N., Smith, J.E.: Recent advances in memetic algorithms, vol. 166. Springer, Heidelberg (2005). https://doi.org/10.1007/3-540-32363-5
30. Kellert, S.H.: In the wake of chaos: unpredictable order in dynamical systems. University of Chicago press (1994)
31. Liu, B., Wang, L., Jin, Y.H.: An effective pso-based memetic algorithm for flow shop scheduling. IEEE Trans. Syst. Man Cybern. Part B (Cybern.) **37**(1), 18–27 (2007)
32. Suganthan, P.N., Hansen, N., Liang, J.J., Deb, K., Chen, Y.P., Auger, A., Tiwari, S.: Problem definitions and evaluation criteria for the CEC 2005 special session on real-parameter optimization. KanGAL report 2005005, p. 2005 (2005)

Galactic Gravitational Search Algorithm for Numerical Optimization

Sheng Li[1], Fenggang Yuan[2], Yang Yu[2], Junkai Ji[2], Yuki Todo[3], and Shangce Gao[2(✉)]

[1] College of Computer Science and Technology, Taizhou University,
Taizhou 225300, Jiangsu, China
[2] Faculty of Engineering, University of Toyama, Toyama, Japan
gaosc@eng.u-toyama.ac.jp
[3] Faculty of Electrical and Computer Engineering,
Kanazawa University, Kanazawa-shi 920-1192, Japan

Abstract. The gravitational search algorithm (GSA) has proven to be a good optimization algorithm to solve various optimization problems. However, due to the lack of exploration capability, it often traps into local optima when dealing with complex problems. Hence its convergence speed will slow down. A clustering-based learning strategy (CLS) has been applied to GSA to alleviate this situation, which is called galactic gravitational search algorithm (GGSA). The CLS firstly divides the GSA into multiple clusters, and then it applies several learning strategies in each cluster and among clusters separately. By using this method, the main weakness of GSA that easily trapping into local optima can be effectively alleviated. The experimental results confirm the superior performance of GGSA in terms of solution quality and convergence in comparison with GSA and other algorithms.

Keywords: Gravitational search algorithm
Clustering-based learning strategy
Population-based intelligent algorithm

1 Introduction

Meta-heuristic algorithms have developed dramatically in the past few decades. They generally increase speed by sacrificing the optimality, accuracy, or completeness of solutions, so they are faster and more efficient in solving problems than traditional methods. Meta-heuristic algorithms are often used to solve computationally complex problems with clear simplifications and methods. They can produce solutions on their own and their goal is to find a solution that is the closest to the optimum within a reasonable time frame. Some well-known meta-heuristic algorithms contains particle swarm optimization (PSO) [17], genetic algorithms (GA), artificial neural networks, and so on. These algorithms have drawn more and more attention since they have been proposed. Nature-inspired

© Springer International Publishing AG, part of Springer Nature 2018
Y. Tan et al. (Eds.): ICSI 2018, LNCS 10941, pp. 397–409, 2018.
https://doi.org/10.1007/978-3-319-93815-8_38

optimization algorithms [15] constitute an important branch of meta-heuristic algorithms and they have been developed a lot in these years. Most of the meta-heuristic algorithms (such as PSO, brain storm optimization [14,18], gravitational search algorithm (GSA) [11] and firefly algorithm) belong to this branch.

GSA which is firstly proposed in 2009 has exhibited great performance due to its strong search ability. It is a swarm intelligent algorithm based on the law of gravity [8]. It reveals that there is an attractive force between any two objects, and this force is proportional to their masses and inversely proportional to the square of the distance between them. In GSA, each candidate solution is treated as a single object. In each iteration, objects attract each other under the force of gravity and exchange information with each other. Then objects update their positions by moving randomly to the areas previously visited by others. The Object with higher quality (representing better candidate solutions) are more attractive, and make others move toward them, resulting in faster convergence speed and better optimal solutions. However, it is undeniable that GSA still has some inherent drawbacks. For example, it can easily fall into local optima, which means that it is difficult to get better solutions in the subsequent search phases. Exploration requires an algorithm that searches extensively for the optimal solution, and exploitation requires algorithms to search locally in the current space. They are conflicting, which means emphasizing one will sacrifice the other. How to maintain the proper balance between exploration and exploitation has become a critical issue for all optimization algorithms [3–6,12]. In this work, we apply a clustering-based learning strategy [1] to the GSA to improve its exploration capability and maintain a good balance with subsequent exploitation capability. In the clustering-based learning strategy, a cluster construction is used to divide the whole population into several clusters, an intra-galaxy learning strategy is devoted to evolving individuals to move toward heavier objects (i.e., better solutions), and inter-galaxy learning strategy is implemented to realize information exchanges among different clusters. By doing so, the information exchanges among clusters are controlled, assuring to some extent that the population diversity can be maintained. Experiment is conducted based on 23 traditional benchmark functions and 25 CEC2005 test functions. Simulation results suggest that the proposed GGSA can perform better GSA and other algorithms in terms of solution quality and convergence speed.

This paper is structured as follows. In Sects. 2, the basic concepts of GSA and clustering-based learning strategy (CLS) are introduced, respectively. In Sect. 3, we introduce the improved GSA with CLS, which is defined as galactic gravitational search algorithm (GGSA). In Sect. 4, experiments and results are exhibited. The general conclusions and plans will be presented in Sect. 5.

2   Gravitational Search Algorithm

GSA is a newly developed stochastic search algorithm based on the law of gravity and mass interactions. This is a method that simulates mass interactions when searching for multidimensional spaces under the influence of gravitation. In GSA, all objects attract each other by the power of gravity, which forces them to move globally to the objects with greater masses.

We assume there are K objects, and define the position of the ith object by: $X_i = (x_i^1, ..., x_i^d, ..., x_i^n)$ for $i = 1, 2, ..., K$, where x_i^d represents the position of the ith object in the dth dimension. n is the dimension of the search space.

The force acting on the object i from the object j at iteration t is defined as below:

$$F_{ij}^d(t) = G(t)\frac{M_{pi}(t) \times M_{aj}(t)}{R_{ij}(t) + \varepsilon})(x_j^d(t) - x_i^d(t)), \tag{1}$$

where M_{pi} is the passive gravitational mass of the object i. M_{aj} denotes the active gravitational mass of the object j. $G(t)$ indicates the current gravitational constant. ε is a small constant to avoid the null value. $R_{ij}(t)$ is the Euclidean distance between the objects i and j. It is defined as $R_{ij}(t) = \|X_i(t), X_j(t)\|_2$.

The total force acting on the object i in the dth dimension is the sum of the dth components of the forces from all other objects. To assign a stochastic characteristic to GSA, we add a random weight to all forces that from all other objects, thus the total force F_i^d can be defined as

$$F_i^d(t) = \sum_{j=1}^{N} rand_j F_{ij}^d(t), \ j \neq i \tag{2}$$

where $rand_j$ is a random variable in the interval $[0, 1]$.

Hence the acceleration $a_i^d(t)$ of the object i at iteration t, and in dimension dth is expressed as $a_i^d(t) = \frac{F_i^d(t)}{M_{ii}(t)}$, where M_{ii} is the inertial mass of the object i. The next velocity and position of object i at iteration $t+1$ are calculated as $v_i^d(t+1) = rand_i \times v_i^d(t) + a_i^d(t)$, $x_i^d(t+1) = x_i^d(t) + v_i^d(t+1)$, where v_i^d denotes the current velocity of object i, x_i^d is the current position of object i, $rand_i$ represents a random variable in the interval $[0, 1]$, which is utilized to provide a random characteristic to the search.

The gravitational constant G is initialized at the beginning and decreases over time to adjust the search accuracy.

In other words, G is a function of the initial value G_0 and iteration t: $G(t) = G_0 e^{-\alpha \frac{t}{T}}$, where G_0 denotes the initial value of G. α is a constant value. T represents the maximum iteration.

Gravitational and inertial masses are calculated by fitness values. Objects with heavier masses mean stronger attractive force. This means that the better objects are more attractive and move more slowly. Assuming that the gravitational and inertial masses are equal, the map of fitness can be used to calculate the value of masses. We use the following equation to update the gravitational and inertial mass: $M_{ai} = M_{pi} = M_{ii} = M_i$, $i = 1, 2, ..., N$, $m_i(t) = \frac{fit_i(t) - worst(t)}{best(t) - worst(t)}$, $M_i(t) = \frac{m_i(t)}{\sum_{j=1}^{N} m_j(t)}$, where $fit_i(t)$ is the fitness value of the object i at iteration t. $best(t)$ and $worst(t)$ are the best and worst fitness values of the object i, respectively.

For a minimization problem, $worst(t)$ and $best(t)$ are defined as $best(t) = \min_{j \in \{1,...,N\}} fit_j(t)$ and $worst(t) = \max_{j \in \{1,...,N\}} fit_j(t)$.

Reducing the number of objects in the equation over time is a way to achieve a good balance between exploration and exploitation. Therefore, we suggest only a set of objects that with greater masses can apply the force to others. However, we need to exercise caution when using this policy, as this may reduce the exploration capacity while increase the exploitation capacity.

To avoid trapping into local optima, the exploration must be used at the beginning of the algorithm. Exploration must fade out and exploitation must fade in during with the convergent procedure. In order to improve the performance of GSA via controlling exploration and exploitation, only the *Kbest* agents will attract the others. *Kbest* is a function of time in which the initial value K_0 declines over time. In this way, all objects release the force at the beginning. *Kbest* decreases linearly as time goes, and only one object can leave and apply force to the others at the end of the convergent procedure. Therefore, Eq. (2) can be modified as: $F_i^d(t) = \sum_{j \in Kbest, j \neq 1} rand_j F_{ij}^d(t)$, where *Kbest* is the set of first K objects with the best fitness values and heaviest masses.

3   Galactic Gravitational Search Algorithm (GGSA)

As we mentioned before, GSA has the following drawbacks: (1) easily fall into the local optimum; (2) lack of the initial exploration capability which can lead to slow convergence; (3) exploration capacity is insufficient which can lead to fail to get the optimal solutions.

In this work, we apply a clustering-based learning strategy to the initial population of GSA. It can improve the exploration capability of the initial population and maintain the diversity of information among the populations. Good balance can be maintained between exploration and exploitation capabilities of GSA at the same time.

We define the improved GSA with CLS as galactic gravitational search algorithm (GGSA) and the principle of GGSA is shown in Fig. 1.

In GSA, information among objects transfer with each other via the gravitational forces, hence, objects could constantly approach the optimal solution through cooperation and competition in search space.

However, the exchanges of information among individuals in the initial stage of the algorithm can not be fully utilized. Too many redundant searches lead to inefficient search ability of the algorithm. In order to improve the search efficiency, we need to assign more effective information to some representative individuals to increase their influence. In this section, we will introduce a method called clustering-based learning strategy (CLS) [1] that could promote the exchange rate of information between individuals to further enhance the performance of GSA. CLS is divided into three parts: cluster construction, intra-galaxy learning strategy and inter-galaxy learning strategy.

3.1 Galaxy Construction

In this research, we utilize the K-means clustering algorithm [7,9] which is widely known as one of the most commonly used clustering methods to make the cluster construction. K-means clustering algorithm divides a set of n objects into K clusters which is an input parameter, and makes objects have high similarity within the same cluster while objects have low similarity in different clusters. The steps of K-means clustering are shown as below:

(1) K individuals are randomly selected as the initial seed, and the initial segmentation is established by using the initial seed as the center of mass in the initial cluster.
(2) Each individual is assigned to the nearest centroid to form a cluster.
(3) Keep the number of clusters unchanged. Recalculate the new centroid for each cluster based on the Euclidean distance.
(4) Repeat steps (2) and (3) until the change of the clusters stops or the stopping condition is met.

In K-means clustering algorithm, clustering similarity is based on the mean value of the objects which can be regarded as the "center of gravity" in the cluster. Initial population of GSA are divided into K clusters, just like the stars in the sky are divided into their own galaxies. Thus we call the combination of GSA and K-means clustering algorithm as galactic gravitational search algorithm (GGSA).

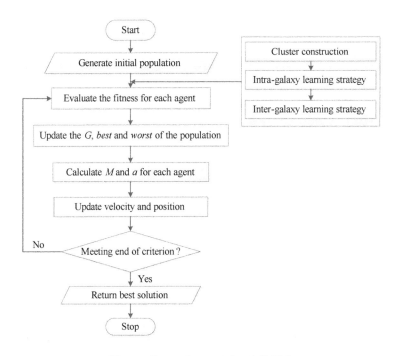

Fig. 1. General principle of GGSA.

In GGSA, each cluster is regarded as galaxy and each object is considered as a star in the galaxy.

3.2   Intra-galaxy Learning Strategy

This section explains the learning mechanism used within the galaxy which is called intra-galaxy learning strategy. Stars in the same galaxy exhibit similar status and behavior to improve their performance. Therefore, it would be beneficial to enhance the search capabilities of GGSA by enhancing the information exchange rate between the stars within the galaxy. The way to share valid information via strengthening internal exchange within galaxies has proven to be an effective interaction mode for optimization problems. Interaction of information is operated through the following two steps.

Galactic Replacement Operator: In each galaxy, compare the fitness of the galactic center with the worst star and replace the worst star with the galactic center if the fitness of galactic center is better than the fitness of the worst star.

Internal Learning Operator: Each star exchanges information with the best stars in the same galaxy, hence a trial star is produced through a learning operation (note that the details of the learning process will be given later). After that, one-on-one survivor selection is used between each star and the corresponding trial star. The best stars in each galaxy have the most valuable information, so the best stars are chosen to exchange information with each star in the galaxy. In this way, each star can get more useful information from better stars apart from the best star in each galaxy. Therefore, they can have a greater possibility of moving to a more suitable space promising with better solutions.

3.3   Inter-galaxy Learning Strategy

This section explains the learning mechanisms of exchanging information among galaxies which is called inter-galaxy learning strategy. As different galaxies are concentrated in different parts of the search space, the search can be directed to more promising search areas by combining the valid information of each galaxy. The combination about the valid information of different galaxies has proven to be an effective way to explore the search space. This learning strategy consists of two steps: exterior learning operator and global learning operator.

Exterior Learning Operator: Each galaxy is represented by the best star in the galaxy, then exchanges information with the global best star of all galaxies to generate a trial star. The reason for this step is that the global best star is closest to the most promising areas of the search space, hence each galaxy can quickly move toward more promising areas by exploiting the information from the global best star. This step is similar to the internal learning operator described in the previous section.

Global Learning Operator: The global best star interacts with all galactic centroids. The goal is that the global best star can synthesize those information for better performance because the centroid of all galactic centroids integrates information from the entire population.

In the two operators above, the test stars are generated through the learning operation and one-on-one survivor selections are made between each star and the corresponding trial star. In addition, the inter-cluster learning strategy conducting after the intra-cluster learning strategy can effectively prevent the loss of population diversity.

3.4   Learning Operation

In the two learning strategies described above, the exchange of information takes place through a learning operation that determines the way in which information is obtained from better objects.

Firstly, a uniformly random number $R \in (0,1)$ is generated. $rand(0.5, 1)$ represents a uniformly distributed random number in $(0.5, 1)$ and the test subject is generated in a region between $0.5 * (S_b + S_i)$ and S_i or its symmetry region according to R is less than 0.5 or not to maintain the diversity of the population. In this way, vector differences and perturbations are the same around a better star. Therefore, the learning process has the characteristic of being rotationally invariant.

4   Experiments and Results

To evaluate the performance of GGSA, we choose 48 benchmark functions which are consisted of the most commonly used 23 standard benchmark functions and CEC2005 benchmark function suit.

4.1   Experiment with 23 Standard Benchmark Functions

In this section, we express the experiments and results that employed with 23 standard benchmark functions [16].

We compared the experimental results of GGSA, GA, PSO and original GSA. The results obtained from the 23 standard benchmark functions are shown in Table 1, where *best* represents the best-so-far solution of 30 independent runs and *mean* is the average solution. For the same test function, we use the red font to label out the best solution of the four algorithms. The experimental results obtained of GGSA are significantly better than the other three algorithms.

To verify this conclusion, we performed Wilcoxon rank-sum test [2] on the experimental results.

The Wilcoxon test result on the experimental results above is shown in Table 2, and the p-value is 1.1683E-5 which means the performance of GGSA is far superior to that of GSA.

Table 1. Experimental results of 23 standard benchmark functions

		GA	PSO	GSA	GGSA
F1	Best	9.6732E+00	1.1100E−04	6.5369E−17	5.7638E − 17
	Mean	2.3159E+01	2.3000E−03	1.2064E−16	1.1559E − 16
F2	Best	7.1230E−01	6.7800E−03	3.1680E − 08	3.2595E−08
	Mean	1.1123E+00	2.0021E+00	5.6314E−08	5.2552E − 08
F3	Best	3.9578E+02	1.3977E + 02	2.6443E+02	1.6462E+02
	Mean	5.6168E+02	4.1145E + 02	5.1558E+02	5.1005E+02
F4	Best	9.4512E+00	5.4789E+00	9.5779E − 09	1.1052E−08
	Mean	1.1673E+01	8.2144E+00	1.6790E+00	9.3929E − 01
F5	Best	5.4487E+02	8.2199E+01	2.6009E+01	2.3921E + 01
	Mean	1.1101E+03	3.7000E+05	4.8754E+01	3.2823E + 01
F6	Best	4.1165E+00	6.1200E−03	0.0000E + 00	0.0000E + 00
	Mean	2.4032E+01	9.0000E − 04	6.6667E−02	6.6667E−02
F7	Best	4.3100E−02	2.9800E−02	3.1676E−02	2.4149E − 02
	Mean	5.6700E−01	4.1200E − 02	6.0760E−02	5.5661E−02
F8	Best	−1.2000E + 04	−1.0600E+04	−3.5455E+03	−3.8695E+03
	Mean	−1.2000E + 04	−9.9800E+03	−2.5046E+03	−2.7293E+03
F9	Best	3.7689E + 00	3.5542E+01	1.8904E+01	1.5919E+01
	Mean	5.9876E + 00	5.5126E+01	2.7129E+01	2.7063E+01
F10	Best	1.3425E+00	3.4000E−03	4.8418E − 09	5.1384E−09
	Mean	2.1458E+00	8.9000E−03	7.9794E−09	7.8681E − 09
F11	Best	1.0479E+00	6.0000E − 04	3.3832E+00	3.0885E+00
	Mean	1.1578E+00	1.2300E − 02	8.5573E+00	7.8041E+00
F12	Best	1.3900E−02	6.0000E−04	4.6969E−19	4.3708E − 19
	Mean	5.6200E − 02	2.3450E−01	1.9735E−01	1.4285E−01
F13	Best	2.5100E−02	1.3400E − 31	6.9852E−18	3.6849E−18
	Mean	8.7200E−02	3.1100E − 18	1.7005E−01	8.3418E−02
F14	Best	9.9800E−01	9.9800E−01	9.9800E−01	9.9800E − 01
	Mean	9.9800E−01	9.9800E−01	4.6128E+00	3.9174E + 00
F15	Best	1.1000E−03	3.0700E−04	9.8339E − 04	1.3091E−03
	Mean	4.0000E−03	2.8000E − 03	4.1833E−03	3.3619E−03
F16	Best	−1.0313E+00	−1.0316E + 00	−1.0316E + 00	−1.0316E + 00
	Mean	−1.0313E+00	−1.0316E + 00	−1.0316E + 00	−1.0316E + 00
F17	Best	3.9790E−01	3.9790E−01	3.9789E − 01	3.9789E − 01
	Mean	3.9960E−01	3.9790E−01	3.9789E − 01	3.9789E − 01
F18	Best	3.0000E+00	3.0000E + 00	3.0000E + 00	3.0000E + 00

(*continued*)

Table 1. (*continued*)

		GA	PSO	GSA	GGSA
	Mean	5.7500E+00	3.0000E + 00	3.0000E + 00	3.0000E + 00
F19	Best	−3.8628E+00	−3.8628E+00	−3.8628E+00	−3.8628E+00
	Mean	−3.8627E+00	−3.8628E + 00	−3.8628E + 00	−3.8628E + 00
F20	Best	−3.3220E + 00	−3.3220E+00	−3.3220E+00	−3.3220E+00
	Mean	−3.3098E + 00	−3.2369E+00	−3.3220E+00	−3.3220E+00
F21	Best	−1.0153E+01	−1.0153E+01	−1.0153E+01	−1.0153E + 01
	Mean	−5.6605E+00	−5.7496E+00	−7.4498E+00	−7.9121E + 00
F22	Best	−1.0403E+01	−1.0403E+01	−1.0403E+01	−1.0403E + 01
	Mean	−7.3421E+00	−9.1118E+00	−1.0303E+01	−1.0368E + 01
F23	Best	−1.0536E+01	−1.0536E+01	−1.0536E+01	−1.0536E + 01
	Mean	−9.7634E+00	−9.7364E+00	−1.0276E+01	−1.0536E + 01

Table 2. Results obtained by the Wilcoxon test for algorithm GGSA

VS	R^+	R^-	p-value	$\alpha = 0.05$
GSA	265.5	10.5	1.1683E−5	YES

Some convergence charts are shown in Fig. 2. The green line represents the convergence curve of GGSA, and the red dotted line represents the convergence curve of GSA. Obviously, GGSA converges faster than GSA and can find better solutions in the search space.

Box-and-whisker chart of some of the 23 standard benchmark functions are displayed in Fig. 3. The top line represents the maximum solution, The bottom line represents the minimum solution, The upper edge of the box represents the value of three quarters. The lower edge of the box represents a quarter-value. The red line represents the median line. The closer the upper and lower bounds

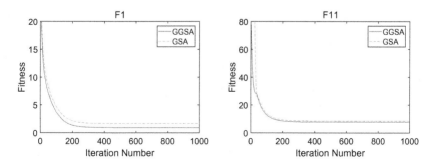

Fig. 2. Convergence charts of F1 and F11 in 23 benchmark functions.

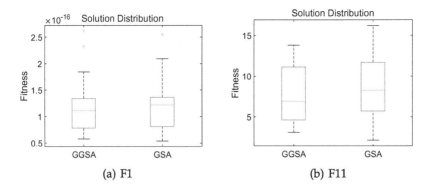

Fig. 3. Box-and-whisker charts of F1 and F11 in 23 standard benchmark functions.

of the box, the more stable the result of the solution is. At the same time, the lower the position of the box, the better the solution is. It can be seen from the chart that the convergence of GGSA is more stable and better than GSA.

4.2   Experiment of CEC2005 Benchmark Functions

In this section, we utilize the CEC2005 composite benchmark functions [13] to test the performance of GGSA. Firstly, a brief introduction to the CEC2005 composite benchmark functions is made. Function F_1 to F_5 are shifted unimodal functions; Function F_6 to F_{12} are multimodal basic functions; Function F_{13} and F_{14} are multimodal expanded functions. Function F_{15}-F_{25} are hybrid composition functions. The user-defined parameters are set as follows: the population size (N) is set to be 100, the dimension of functions is 30, the maximum number of iterations (1500) is chosen as the stopping criteria. The algorithm executes independently on each test function for 30 times.

A contrast on the experimental results of GGSA, whale optimization algorithm (WOA) [10] and original GSA is shown in Table 3, where *mean* represents the average solution of 30 independent runs and Std is the Standard deviation. As the same, we highlight the best results in red font. The result of the Wilcoxon test is shown in Table 4. It is obvious that the experimental results of GGSA are much better than those of the WOA and the original GSA.

We also displayed some convergence charts and box-whisker charts in Figs. 4 and 5. The conclusions of those charts also demonstrate the convergence stability and the capability to find better solutions of GGSA.

Table 3. Experimental Results of CEC2005

	WOA		GSA		GGSA	
	Mean	Std	Mean	Std	Mean	Std
F1	−4.44E+02	9.86E+00	−4.50E+02	1.49E−14	−4.50E + 02	1.49E−14
F2	6.01E+04	9.74E+03	1.44E+04	9.36E+02	1.43E + 04	1.25E+03
F3	3.67E+07	1.30E+07	1.09E+07	4.31E+06	9.58E + 06	2.15E+06
F4	1.43E+05	4.58E+04	5.09E+04	8.00E+03	4.53E + 04	5.32E+03
F5	1.78E+04	3.54E+03	1.62E+04	1.21E+03	1.59E + 04	1.39E+03
F6	6.24E+04	1.07E+05	3.93E + 04	7.03E+04	1.29E+05	1.91E+05
F7	4.57E+03	5.41E+01	1.10E+04	2.98E+02	1.06E + 04	2.37E+02
F8	−1.19E + 02	9.80E−02	−1.20E+02	8.30E−02	−1.20E+02	7.67E−02
F9	−1.19E+02	4.58E+01	−2.86E+02	4.87E+00	−2.88E + 02	5.48E+00
F10	8.27E+01	8.79E+01	−3.00E + 02	4.46E+00	−3.00E+02	5.95E+00
F11	1.26E+02	2.13E+00	9.01E + 01	2.27E−01	9.01E+01	2.88E−01
F12	1.48E+05	9.46E+04	9.94E+03	1.02E+04	9.19E + 03	6.18E+03
F13	−1.09E+02	5.17E+00	−1.21E+02	1.37E+00	−1.21E + 02	1.35E+00
F14	−2.87E + 02	2.52E−01	−2.86E+02	1.66E−01	−2.86E+02	1.75E−01
F15	7.81E+02	2.07E+02	4.20E + 02	3.98E−05	4.20E+02	4.11E−05
F16	5.70E+02	8.48E+01	3.41E + 02	2.16E+02	3.58E+02	2.18E+02
F17	6.63E+02	8.51E+01	4.68E+02	2.52E+02	3.51E + 02	2.26E+02
F18	1.05E+03	9.62E+01	9.46E+02	5.48E+01	9.27E + 02	7.24E+01
F19	1.05E+03	9.21E+01	9.60E+02	4.20E+01	9.46E + 02	6.24E+01
F20	1.04E+03	7.12E+01	9.46E+02	5.58E+01	9.45E + 02	5.46E+01
F21	1.58E+03	1.46E+02	1.03E+03	2.88E+02	1.01E + 03	2.76E+02
F22	1.57E+03	8.93E+01	1.26E + 03	9.97E+00	1.26E+03	1.18E+01
F23	1.61E+03	1.21E+02	9.46E + 02	2.23E+02	1.01E+03	2.77E+02
F24	1.58E+03	1.24E+02	4.60E+02	1.27E−12	4.60E + 02	1.19E−12
F25	1.89E + 03	5.09E+00	1.92E+03	7.64E+00	1.92E+03	7.20E+00

Table 4. Results obtained by the Wilcoxon test for GGSA

VS	R^+	R^-	p-value	$\alpha = 0.05$
WOA	276.5	48.5	1.3746E−3	YES
GSA	242.5	82.5	3.069E−2	YES

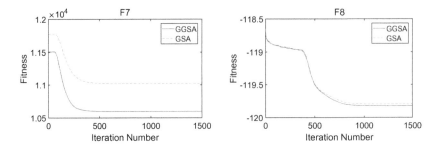

Fig. 4. Convergence charts of F1 and F11 in CEC2005.

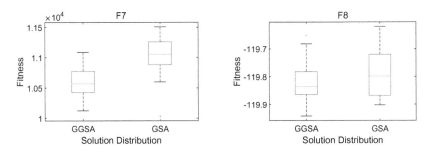

Fig. 5. Box-and-whisker charts of F7 and F8 in CEC2005.

5   Conclusions

This paper mainly applies a clustering-based learning mechanism in GSA algorithm to make up for the shortcomings of GSA. Both the Wilcoxon's rank-sum test and the statistical test results confirm that our improvements acting on the GSA are effective and more competitive than the original GSA. This result indicates that the combination of GSA with the clustering-based learning method is an alternative modification to enhance the search ability of GSA, meanwhile help it maintain population diversity during the convergent procedure. Furthermore, it gives an inspiration that the clustering-based learning method can be applied to solve dynamic and multi-objective problems in our future research.

Acknowledgment. This research was partially supported by Taizhou Science and Technology Support Social Development Project (Guidance) under No. 201701 and JSPS KAKENHI Grant Number 17K12751, 15K00332 (Japan).

References

1. Cai, Y., Wang, J., Yin, J.: Learning-enhanced differential evolution for numerical optimization. Soft Comput. **16**(2), 303–330 (2012)
2. Derrac, J., García, S., Molina, D., Herrera, F.: A practical tutorial on the use of nonparametric statistical tests as a methodology for comparing evolutionary and swarm intelligence algorithms. Swarm Evol. Comput. **1**(1), 3–18 (2011)

3. Gao, S., Song, S., Cheng, J., Todo, Y., Zhou, M.: Incorporation of solvent effect into multi-objective evolutionary algorithm for improved protein structure prediction. IEEE/ACM Trans. Comput. Biol. Bioinf. (2017). https://doi.org/10.1109/TCBB.2017.2705094

4. Gao, S., Todo, Y., Gong, T., Yang, G., Tang, Z.: Graph planarization problem optimization based on triple-valued gravitational search algorithm. IEEJ Trans. Electr. Electron. Eng. **9**(1), 39–48 (2014)

5. Gao, S., Vairappan, C., Wang, Y., Cao, Q., Tang, Z.: Gravitational search algorithm combined with chaos for unconstrained numerical optimization. Appl. Math. Comput. **231**, 48–62 (2014)

6. Gao, S., Wang, Y., Wang, J., Cheng, J.: Understanding differential evolution: a Poisson law derived from population interaction network. J. Comput. Sci. **21**, 140–149 (2017)

7. Hartigan, J.A., Wong, M.A.: Algorithm as 136: a k-means clustering algorithm. J. R. Stat. Soc. Ser. C (Appl. Stat.) **28**(1), 100–108 (1979)

8. Ji, J., Gao, S., Wang, S., Tang, Y., Yu, H., Todo, Y.: Self-adaptive gravitational search algorithm with a modified chaotic local search. IEEE Access **5**, 17881–17895 (2017)

9. Kanungo, T., Mount, D.M., Netanyahu, N.S., Piatko, C.D., Silverman, R., Wu, A.Y.: An efficient k-means clustering algorithm: analysis and implementation. IEEE Trans. Pattern Anal. Mach. Intell. **24**(7), 881–892 (2002)

10. Mirjalili, S., Lewis, A.: The Whale optimization algorithm. Adv. Eng. Softw. **95**, 51–67 (2016)

11. Rashedi, E., Nezamabadi-Pour, H., Saryazdi, S.: GSA: a gravitational search algorithm. Inf. Sci. **179**(13), 2232–2248 (2009)

12. Song, Z., Gao, S., Yu, Y., Sun, J., Todo, Y.: Multiple chaos embedded gravitational search algorithm. IEICE Trans. Inf. Syst. **100**(4), 888–900 (2017)

13. Suganthan, P.N., Hansen, N., Liang, J.J., Deb, K., Chen, Y.P., Auger, A., Tiwari, S.: Problem definitions and evaluation criteria for the CEC 2005 special session on real-parameter optimization. KanGAL report 2005005 (2005)

14. Wang, Y., Gao, S., Yu, Y., Xu, Z.: The discovery of population interaction with a power law distribution in brain storm optimization. Memetic Comput. (2017). https://doi.org/10.1007/s12293-017-0248-z

15. Yang, X.S.: Nature-Inspired Optimization Algorithms. Elsevier, Amsterdam (2014)

16. Yao, X., Liu, Y., Lin, G.: Evolutionary programming made faster. IEEE Trans. Evol. Comput. **3**(2), 82–102 (1999)

17. Yu, H., Xu, Z., Gao, S., Wang, Y., Todo, Y.: PMPSO: a near-optimal graph planarization algorithm using probability model based particle swarm optimization. In: IEEE International Conference on Progress in Informatics and Computing (PIC), pp. 15–19. IEEE (2015)

18. Yu, Y., Gao, S., Cheng, S., Wang, Y., Song, S., Yuan, F.: CBSO: a memetic brain storm optimization with chaotic local search. Memetic Comput. (2017). https://doi.org/10.1007/s12293-017-0247-0

Research Optimization on Logistic Distribution Center Location Based on Improved Harmony Search Algorithm

Xiaobing Gan[1], Entao Jiang[1], Yingying Peng[2], Shuang Geng[1(✉)], and Mijat Kustudic[1]

[1] Shenzhen University, Shenzhen, China
gracegeng0303@163.com
[2] Lancaster University, Lancaster, UK

Abstract. Logistics distribution center are important logistics nodes and the choice of locations are critical management decisions. This study addresses a logistics distribution center location problem that aims at determining the location and allocation of the distribution centers. Considering the characteristic and complexity of problem, we propose an improved harmony search algorithm, in which we employ a novel way of improvising new harmony. The improved algorithm is compared with genetic algorithm, particle swarm optimization, generalized particle swarm optimization, and classical harmony search algorithm in solving a simulated distribution center location problem. Experiment results show that the improved algorithm can solve the logistics distribution center problem with more stable convergence speed and higher accuracy.

Keywords: Optimization · Logistics distribution center location
Harmony search algorithm

1 Introduction

In recent years, with the rapid development of social economy and economic globalization, the logistics industry has been paid more attention and become an important industry for economic development [1, 2]. As the node of logistics network, distribution center connecting between the upriver supply points and the downriver requirement points, play a role of connecting link between the preceding and the following in the whole logistics system [3, 4]. Reasonable location selection for distribution centers determines the transport cost, inventory cost, customer satisfactions, and overall efficacy and reliability of the logistic system. Therefore, how to design a logistic distribution center location and allocation strategy has been a hot spot which many service providers and academic researchers have paid their attention to.

Logistics distribution center location problem consists of two sub-problems: the location and allocation. The location problem focuses on the selections of locations of distribution centers. The allocation problem aims to allocate the distribution center to corresponding customers in order to satisfy the customer demand of product. During the location and allocation arrangement process, the distance cost should be minimized.

© Springer International Publishing AG, part of Springer Nature 2018
Y. Tan et al. (Eds.): ICSI 2018, LNCS 10941, pp. 410–420, 2018.
https://doi.org/10.1007/978-3-319-93815-8_39

Studies on selecting logistics distribution center location have proposed many methods, which can be divided into two groups: qualitative analysis [5–7] and quantitative analysis [8, 9]. Quantitative analysis involves gravity method [8] and integer programming [9], but gravity method is not applicable to discrete problems, and integer programming cannot solve the problem well, which size is larger. Qualitative analysis consists of fuzzy evaluation [7] and computational intelligence, etc. Fuzzy evaluation method is not objective. Computational intelligence method involving genetic algorithm [10], particle swarm optimization [11], solve the complex optimization combination problem well. Inspired by the study that harmony search algorithm (HS) can be used in solving discrete problem [12], we propose an improved harmony search algorithm (IHS) to solve logistics distribution center location problem.

The rest of this paper is organized as follows: the model of logistics distribution center location is described in Sect. 2. A brief description for harmony search algorithm is presented in Sect. 3. The improved harmony search algorithm is proposed in Sect. 4. Section 5 designs simulation experiments. Finally, Sect. 6 discusses the conclusions.

2 The Model of Logistics Distribution Center Location

Logistics center location model [11] is non-convex and non-smooth nonlinear programming model with the complex constraints. Base on minimizing the total charge of the distribution system, the problem of logistics distribution center location is to solve the locations of centers and the allocations of service demands. To facilitate the formulation and resolution of the problem, the following assumptions are set as underpinnings of the model:

(1) The inventory of each distribution center needs to meet all demands of the requirement points that the distribution center serves;
(2) Each requirement point can only be supplied by one distribution center;
(3) The demand for each requirement point and the location of the requirement points are already known;
(4) The total cost will not be considered other expense besides the cost of delivery.

The model parameters are defined as follow:

(1) N: The number of requirement points;
(2) M: The number of the distribution centers;
(3) W_i: The demand quantity of the requirement point;
(4) d_{ij}: The distance from requirements point i to the nearest distribution center j;
(5) Z_{ij}: 0–1 variables. When it is 1, the requirement point i is supplied by the distribution center j, otherwise, $Z_{ij} = 0$;
(6) D: the upper distance for the new distribution center to the requirement points which serviced by it.

Based on above assumptions, the model for distribution center location-allocation selects the distribution center from the potential set and distributes items to the customers. The objective function below aims to minimize the total cost of delivery from distribution centers from to requirement points:

$$F = \min \sum_{i \in N} \sum_{j \in M} d_{ij} W_i Z_{ij}$$

Subject to

For the requirement point i the goods can only be delivered from one distribution center set M_i:

$$\sum_{j \in M} Z_{ij} = 1, i \in N \tag{1}$$

The demand of customer is distributed by the potential distribution center:

$$Z_{ij} \leq r_j, \quad j \in M_i \tag{2}$$

The number of the distribution centers is equal to Q:

$$\sum_{j \in M_i} r_j = Q \tag{3}$$

The distributive scope should not exceed D:

$$d_{ij} \leq D \tag{4}$$

Z_{ij} and r_j are 0–1 variables. When r_j is 1, point j is chosen as the distribution center;

$$Z_{ij} \in \{0, 1\}, r_j \leq \{0, 1\} \tag{5}$$

3   The Basic Harmony Search Algorithm

Geem and Kim (2001) first proposed the harmony search algorithm [13]. Harmony search algorithm is a simulation of the musical performance when musicians play all the instruments to gain the better harmony. The steps of the basic harmony search algorithm are as follows:

Step 1: Initializing the optimization problem and algorithm parameters.

First, the optimization problem is defined as follows:

$$Minimize f(x)$$

Subject to $Lx_i \leq x_i \leq Ux_i, \forall i \in \{1, 2, \ldots, N\}$

The parameters are assigned in this step, including Harmony memory size (HMS), Harmony memory (HM), Harmony memory considering rate (HMCR), Pitch adjusting rate (PAR), and the maximum iteration (T).

Step 2: Create an initial Harmony Memory (HM).

The HM matrix is initialized by many randomly generated solution vectors as the HMS.

$$HM = \begin{bmatrix} X^1 \\ X^2 \\ \vdots \\ X^{HMS} \end{bmatrix} = \begin{bmatrix} x_1^1 & x_2^1 & \cdots & x_N^1 \\ x_1^2 & x_2^2 & \cdots & x_N^2 \\ \vdots & \vdots & \cdots & \vdots \\ x_1^{HMS} & x_2^{HMS} & \cdots & x_N^{HMS} \end{bmatrix}$$

Step 3: Improvise a new harmony.

A new harmony denoted as $x' = [x_1' x_2' \ldots x_{N-1}' x_N']$ is improvised by applying these three rules: memory consideration, pitch adjustment, and random selection. For example, $x_{new}(j)$ will be generated from the j th of HM if a random number rand() in the range of [0,1] is smaller than HMCR. Otherwise, $x_{new}(j)$ will be generated by a random selection. Then, each variable $x_{new}(j)$ will be determined if it needs to be adjusted. If a new random number rand() in the range of [0,1] is smaller than PAR, the variable $x_{new}(j)$ will be adjusted. $LB(j)$ and $UB(j)$ are the lower and upper bounds of the decision variable $x(j)$.

$$if(rand1() < HMCR)$$
$$x_{new}(j) = x_\alpha(j)$$
$$if(rand2() < PAR)$$
$$x_{new}(j) = x_{new}(j) \pm rand() \times BW$$
$$else$$
$$x_{new}(j) = LB(j) + rand() \times (UB(j) - LB(j))$$

Where $\alpha \in (1, 2, \ldots, HMS)$, $x_\alpha(j)$ is selected from HM.

Step 4: Update the harmony memory.

If the new harmony is better than the worst on in harmony memory, the new harmony would be added into the harmony memory and the worst one in harmony would be removed.

Step 5: Check the termination criterion.

If the algorithm runs to the maximum iteration, the algorithm is stopped and return the best harmony vector X_{Best} in the HM. Otherwise, return to Step 2 (Fig. 1).

4 The Improved Harmony Search Algorithm

4.1 The Solution Representation

The problem of logistics distribution center location consists of two problems; the locations of centers and the allocations of service demands. Figure 1 shows the solution representation of the example of the six positions coordinates of three centers and the allocation of thirty requirement points.

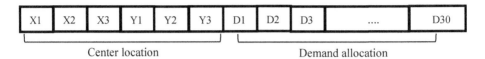

Fig. 1. Vector solution for the logistics distribution center.

We use x_1, x_2, x_3, y_1, y_2, y_3 to present the locations of three centers and use three integers, "1", "2" and "3" to represent which of the three centers supply for the requirement points.

4.2 Improvement

In basic HS algorithm, each variable $x_{new}(j)$ of the new harmony is improvised from the $x_\alpha(j)$ in the HM or randomly and undergoes a pitch adjustment with a probability of PAR if it is updated by the memory consideration. Good fitness value in the HS algorithm indicates that proper distribution centers location and allocation scheme of the service demand is achieved which lead to less transportation cost collectively.

The way of improvising the new harmony is improved by the following method. During each iteration, with a probability of HMCR, the new harmony X_{new} is selected from harmonies in HM and adjusted as: $X_{new} = X_\alpha + rand() * BW$. After the harmony memory consideration is finished, if the random number $rand2()$ is smaller than PAR, adjust the best harmony as: $X_\ell = X_{best} + rand() * BW$ and calculate the fitness value of X_ℓ. If the fitness value of X_ℓ is less than the fitness value of X_{best}, the new harmony X_{new} is adjusted as: $X_{new} = X_\ell$.

$$\text{if } (rand1() < HMCR)$$
$$X_{new} = X_\alpha + rand() * BW$$
$$\text{if } (rand2() < PAR)$$
$$X_\ell = X_{best} + rand() * BW$$
$$\text{if } Fitness\,(X_\ell) < Fitness\,(X_{best})$$
$$X_{new} = X_\ell$$
$$else$$
$$X_{new} = LB + rand() \times (UB - LB)$$

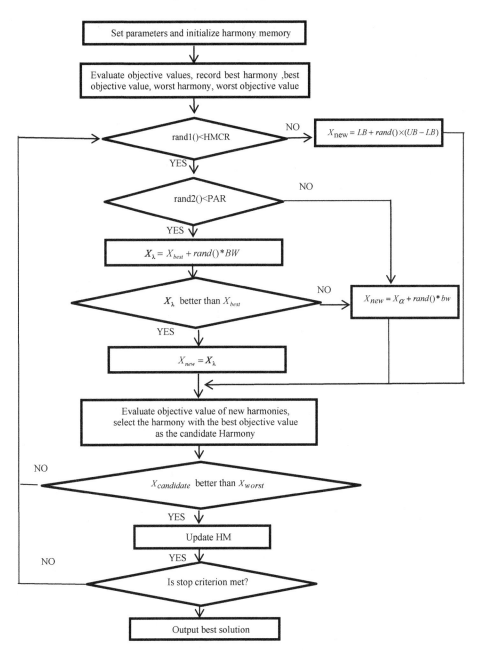

Fig. 2. The chart of the proposed IHS.

Besides the improvement of improvising new harmony, algorithm need to obtain the current optimum as quickly as possible ($X_{best} \in HM$) in early iterations, and to explore the global optimum in late iterations. Therefore, the HMCR and PAR is designed to gradually reduce from large value to small value as iteration go on. Calculation function for HMCR and PAR is described as follows:

$$HMCR = HMCR_{\text{max}} \times \left(\frac{HMCR_{\text{min}}}{HMCR_{\text{max}}}\right) \wedge \left(\frac{t}{T\text{max}}\right)$$

$$PAR = PAR_{\text{max}} - (PAR_{\text{max}} - PAR_{\text{min}}) \times \left(\frac{t}{T\text{max}}\right)$$

In the meantime, IHS algorithm increases number of new harmonies. Improvising more new harmonies can not only obtain the current optimum, but also explore the global optimum.

4.3   Algorithm Description and Flowchart

Based on the above analysis, the procedures of the proposed IHS are depicted in Fig. 2 and summarized as follows:

Step1: Initialize related parameters such as Harmony memory size HMS, maximum Harmony memory considering rate $HMCR_{\text{max}}$, minimum Harmony memory considering rate $HMCR_{\text{min}}$, maximum Pitch adjusting rate PAR_{max}, minimum Pitch adjusting rate PAR_{min}, and the maximum iteration T.

Step2: Create an initial Harmony Memory HM. The HM matrix is initialized by many randomly generated solution vectors as the HMS.

Step3: Improvising some new harmonies. With a probability of HMCR, the new harmony is selected from harmonies in HM and adjusted as: $X_{new} = X_\alpha + rand() * BW$. If the random number is smaller than PAR, adjust the best harmony as: $X_\ell = X_{best} + rand() * BW$ and calculate the fitness value of X_ℓ. If the fitness value of X_ℓ is less than the fitness value of X_{best}, the new harmony X_{new} is adjusted as: $X_{new} = X_\ell$.

Step4: Compare and obtain the candidate harmony. Calculate the fitness value of new harmonies, and choose the least one as the candidate harmony $X_{candidate}$.

Step5: Compare $X_{candidate}$ and X_{worst} of the HM. If $X_{candidate} < X_{worst}$, update HM.

Step6: If the iteration is equal to maximum iteration T, export X_{best} of the algorithm, stop the algorithm. Otherwise, go back to Step3.

5   Numerical Experiments

To evaluate the performance of the proposed IHS algorithm, simulation setting is designed as: distribution centers location will be ascertained in the area of 100×100 based on demand and distance of 30 sampling points. We adopt MATLAB R2017a to program, and compare the improved harmony search algorithm, basic harmony search algorithm, genetic algorithm, particle swarm optimization algorithm and improved PSO called GPSO [14]. All the data sampling points are described as Table 1.

Table 1. Location and demand of requirement points.

i	(u_i, v_i)	W_i	i	(u_i, v_i)	W_i	i	(u_i, v_i)	W_i
1	(9,91)	35	11	(25,95)	31	21	(20,66)	34
2	(26,31)	47	12	(76,93)	48	22	(56,43)	38
3	(78,28)	38	13	(85,76)	30	23	(92,59)	47
4	(8,12)	36	14	(75,56)	42	24	(79,9)	42
5	(39,42)	44	15	(63,26)	35	25	(89,87)	39
6	(11,26)	37	16	(42,23)	41	26	(54,91)	44
7	(10,64)	32	17	(37,87)	52	27	(62,67)	48
8	(89,40)	46	18	(48,63)	33	28	(31,54)	36
9	(8,47)	34	19	(32,75)	42	29	(18,45)	30
10	(22,17)	39	20	(18,82)	40	30	(67,85)	41

5.1 Parameter Settings

As for IHS algorithm, we test different parameters through experiments, and conclude the parameters as follows: the harmony memory size is 20, the maximum iterations is 400, the number of new harmonies is 5, maximum Harmony memory considering rate $HMCR_{max} = 0.99$, minimum Harmony memory considering rate $HMCR_{min} = 0.6$, maximum Pitch adjusting rate $PAR_{max} = 0.2$, and minimum Pitch adjusting rate $PAR_{min} = 0.05$.

Parameters settings of HS, GPSO, PSO and GA are displayed as follows: In the basic HS algorithm, $HMCR = 0.9$, $PAR = 0.25$. In GPSO, $c_1 = c_2 = 2$, $\omega = 0.2$, $t_{max} = 2$, $t_{min} = 0.7$, $N = 20$. In PSO, $c_1 = c_2 = 2$, $\omega = 0.2$, $N = 20$. In GA, the crossover probability is 0.5, the mutation probability is 0.1, and population size is 20.

5.2 Conclusion Analysis

5.2.1 Comparison the Optimal Value

As shown in Table 2, the optimal value of the IHS algorithm is 3.32×10^4 and it decreases about 10.27% compared with the optimal value of the basic HS algorithm. It also decreases about 14.21% and 13.76% compared with GA and GPSO. Iteration number in Table 2 means the first iteration when the best fitness value was obtained.

Table 2. The comparison of algorithms.

Algorithm name	The best fitness value	Average fitness value	Iteration number
IHS	3.32×10^4	3.45×10^4	240
HS	3.70×10^4	3.74×10^4	260
GA	3.87×10^4	3.93×10^4	150
PSO	4.11×10^4	3.98×10^4	20
GPSO	3.85×10^4	3.71×10^4	50

5.2.2   Comparison the Average Optimal Value and the Convergence Speed

Since the GPSO and GA algorithm easily fall into local optimization and form immature convergence, the average values of GA and GPSO running 30 times are 3.93×10^4 and 3.71×10^4, and the average value of IHS running 30 times is 3.45×10^4. The average value of IHS decreases about 12.21% compared with the GA algorithm, and it decreases about 7% compared with the GPSO algorithm. Thus, IHS can save cost of transportation, indicating that the algorithm is efficient.

The change of the optimal fitness of the IHS algorithm, GPSO algorithm, PSO algorithm and genetic algorithm can be seen from Fig. 3, and the IHS algorithm has the highest accuracy. From Fig. 4, we also see the change of the average fitness of the four compared algorithms, and the IHS algorithm has the most stable convergence and is not easy to fall into local optimization and form immature convergence.

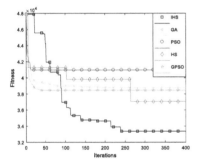

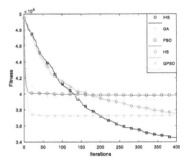

Fig. 3. The comparison of best fitness value.

Fig. 4. The comparison of the average fitness value.

As shown in Fig. 5, the logistics distribution center location is (37.888, 72.486), (21.941, 23.852), (72.661, 50.303) obtained by the IHS algorithm, the distribution center located in (37.888, 72.486) can supply the demand for ten requirement points (1, 7, 11, 17, 19, 20, 21, 26, 28, 30), the distribution center located in (21.941, 23.852)

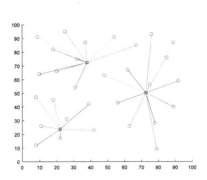

Fig. 5. Logistics distribution center location.

can supply the demand for eight requirement points (2, 4, 5, 6, 9, 10, 16, 29), and the distribution center located in (72.661, 50.303) can supply the demand for twelve requirement points (3, 8, 12, 13, 14, 15, 18, 22, 23, 24, 25, 27).

For the above results, the distribution center location method based on IHS can not only determine the optimal distribution center, but also optimize structure of the logistics network.

6 Conclusion

This paper presents an improved harmony search algorithm to address the logistics distribution center location problem. In the proposed approach, a new way of improvising the new harmony improves the ability of global optimum exploration and stable convergence of harmony search algorithm. To verify the performance of IHS, the experiments have been carried out. The results demonstrate that IHS is more effective than basic HS, GA, PSO, an GPSO on solving the logistics distribution center location problem.

Acknowledgement. This work is supported by the Guangdong Provincial Science and Technology Plan Project (No. 2013B040403005) and Youth Creative Talents Project (2015KQNCX138).

References

1. Gu, W., Foster, K., Shang, J.: Enhancing market service and enterprise operations through a large-scale GIS-based distribution system. Expert Syst. Appl. **55**, 157–171 (2016)
2. Yang, L., et al.: Logistics distribution centers location problem and algorithm under fuzzy environment. J. Comput. Appl. Math. **208**(2), 303–315 (2007)
3. Zhang, S., et al.: Swarm intelligence applied in green logistics: a literature review. Eng. Appl. Artif. Intell. **37**, 154–169 (2015)
4. Jayaram, J., Avittathur, B.: Green supply chains: a perspective from an emerging economy. Int. J. Prod. Econ. **164**, 234–244 (2015)
5. Tu, C.-S., et al.: Applying an AHP -QFD conceptual model and zero-one goal programming to requirement-based site selection for an airport cargo logistics center. Int. J. Inf. Manag. Sci. **21**(4), 407–430 (2010)
6. Kuo, M.S.: Optimal location selection for an international distribution center by using a new hybrid method. Expert Syst. Appl. **38**(6), 7208–7221 (2011)
7. Esnaf, S., Kucukdeniz, T.: A fuzzy clustering-based hybrid method for a multi-facility location problem. J. Intell. Manuf. **20**(2), 259–265 (2009)
8. Zhou, Y., Peng, F., Wang, G.: A study on the dynamic characteristics of the drive at center of gravity (DCG) feed drives. Int. J. Adv. Manuf. Technol. **66**, 325–336 (2013)
9. Manzini, R., Gamberi, M., Regattieri, A.: Applying mixed integer programming to the design of a distribution logistic network. Int. J. Ind. Eng. Theory Appl. Pract. **13**(2), 207–218 (2006)
10. Wen-Jun, F.U., et al.: Application of improved genetic algorithm in logistics distribution. J. Yanan Univ. **33**(1), 19–21 (2014)

11. Hua, X., Hu, X., Yuan, W.: Research optimization on logistics distribution center location based on adaptive particle swarm algorithm. Optik – Int. J. Light Electron Opt. **127**(20), 8443–8450 (2016)
12. Zini, H., Elbernoussi, S.: Minimizing makespan in hybrid flow shop scheduling with multiprocessor task problems using a discrete harmony search. In: IEEE International Conference on Computational Intelligence and Virtual Environments for Measurement Systems and Applications. IEEE, pp. 177–180 (2017)
13. Zong, W.G., Kim, J.H., Loganathan, G.V.: A new heuristic optimization algorithm: harmony search. Simul. Trans. Soc. Model. Simul. Int. **76**(2), 60–68 (2016)
14. Garcíagonzalo, E., Fernándezmartínez, J.L.: A brief historical review of particle swarm optimization (PSO). J. Bioinform. Intell. Control. **1**(1), 3–16 (2012)

Parameters Optimization of PID Controller Based on Improved Fruit Fly Optimization Algorithm

Xiangyin Zhang[1,2,3]($\boxtimes$), Guang Chen[1,2,3], and Songmin Jia[1,2,3]

[1] Faculty of Information Technology,
Beijing University of Technology, Beijing, China
xy_zhang@bjut.edu.cn
[2] Beijing Key Laboratory of Computational Intelligence
and Intelligent System, Beijing, China
[3] Engineering Research Center of Digital Community,
Ministry of Education, Beijing, China

Abstract. Fruit fly optimization algorithm (FOA) is a novel bio-inspired technique, which has attracted a lot of researchers' attention. In order to improve the performance of FOA, a modified FOA is proposed which adopts the phase angle vector to encoded the fruit fly location and brings in the double sub-swarms mechanism. This new strategies can enhance the search ability of the fruit fly and helps find the better solution. Simulation experiments have been conducted on fifteen benchmark functions and the comparisons with the basic FOA show that θ-DFOA performs better in terms of solution accuracy and convergence speed. In addition, the proposed algorithm is used to optimization the PID controller, and the promising performance is achieved.

Keywords: Fruit fly optimization algorithm (FOA) · Double sub-swarms
PID controller

1 Introduction

Inspired by the food finding behavior of fruit flies, fruit fly optimization algorithm (FOA) was recently proposed by Pan [1]. As a novel bio-inspired technique, FOA has attracted a lot of researchers' attention and has been successfully applied to solve the optimization problems in various areas, including the semiconductor final testing scheduling problem [2], general regression neural network optimization [3, 4], parameter tuning for proportional-integral-derivative controllers [5, 6], UAV path planning [7], multidimensional knapsack problem [8], identification of dynamic protein complexes [9], and so on.

However, the basic FOA still has the drawback that easily traps into the local optimal or premature in the complicated optimization problems. In order to improve the search efficiency and global search ability of the basic FOA, several improved versions of FOA are proposed by researchers [2, 6, 8, 10–13]. Yuan et al. [13] employed the

© Springer International Publishing AG, part of Springer Nature 2018
Y. Tan et al. (Eds.): ICSI 2018, LNCS 10941, pp. 421–431, 2018.
https://doi.org/10.1007/978-3-319-93815-8_40

behavior of multiple fruit fly swarms and proposed the multi-swarm fruit fly optimization algorithm (MFOA), in which several sub-swarms move independently in the search space at the same time and local behavior rules between sub-swarms are also designed. Pan et al. [11] introduced a new control parameter to adjust the search scope around the fruit fly swarm location adaptively as well as a new solution generating method to enhance the accuracy and convergence rate, and presented the improved fruit fly optimization (IFFO) algorithm.

In this paper, the novel phase angle-encoded fruit fly optimization algorithm with double sub-swarms (θ-DFOA) is proposed and the PID controller based on θ-DFOA is designed as well. In θ-DFOA, double sub-swarms lead the evolution process of the fruit flies in order to enhance the balance of FOA in terms of the exploitation and exploration ability, while the phase angle-based encoded strategy for fruit fly locations helps to achieve the high performance in the convergence process. Numerical simulation results illustrate that θ-DFOA is not only superior to the basic FOA in solving the Benchmark functions, but also more powerful in parameter tuning for the PID controller.

The rest of this paper is organized as follows. Overview of the basic FOA is described in Sect. 2. Section 3 presents the improved FOA with the detailed modified strategies. Numerical experiment comparisons on the Benchmark functions are provided in Sect. 4. In Sect. 5, the proposed method is used to optimization the PID controller. Section 6 concludes with a brief summary of this paper finally.

2 Fruit Fly Optimization Algorithm

The FOA is a novel bio-inspired algorithm firstly put forward in 2011 [1]. The inspiration of FOA is that fruit flies are superior to other species in terms of olfactory and visual senses. When looking for the food, the fruit fly can use its olfactory organ to sense various odors floating in the air, and use its visual organ to spot the food and the locations of other fruit flies. The food searching process of fruit flies is illustrated as Fig. 1.

FOA randomly generates a fruit fly swarm's initial location. Then, each fruit fly is assigned the random direction and distance for following movement. As the food location is unknown, the distance to the origin is estimated. After they arrive at the new positions, the algorithm can find the best position with the results of calculation and judgment. Repeating this process and FOA can finally get the optimal solution. Compared with existing bio-inspired algorithms, FOA is much simpler to implement [7], which only takes several lines to code the core part in any programming language.

STRUCTURE OF FOA

/* Initialization */

1   Set the generation counter $NC = 0$, the number of fruit flies as M_{pop}, and randomly initialize the fruit fly swarm's location as $[X_{axis}, Y_{axis}]$.

/* Iterative search */

2   **while** termination criteria is not satisfied **do**

3   Generation counter $NC = NC + 1$

/* Search using osphresis */

4   **for** $i = 1 : M_{pop}$ **do**

5   Generate the random direction and distance, and
             $X_i = X_{axis} + random$, $Y_i = Y_{axis} + random$

6   Compute the distance to the origin: $D_i = \sqrt{X_i^2 + Y_i^2}$

7   Calculate the judged value of smell concentration: $S_i = 1/D_i$

8   Evaluate the smell concentration judge function (also called fitness function) to get the smell concentrations: $Smell_i = f(S_i)$

9   **end for**

/* Search using vision */

10   Select the fruit fly that has the best smell concentration: $index = \arg\max(Smell_i)$

11   **if** $[X_{index}, Y_{index}]$ has the better smell than $[X_{axis}, Y_{axis}]$, **then** The fruit fly uses vision to fly towards the location: $X_{axis} = X_{indes}$ and $Y_{axis} = Y_{indes}$

12   **end while**

Fig. 1. Procedure of FOA.

3 Improved FOA

The proposed θ-DFOA adopts the phase angle vector to encoded the fruit fly location and brings in the double sub-swarms mechanism to enhance the search ability of the olfactory organ of the fruit fly.

(1) *Phase angle-encoded location*

In the original FOA, the location of the fruit fly is determined by the X-axis and Y-axis coordinates, and the smell concentration judgement corresponds to the decision variable of the problem solved. The mapping $S = 1/\sqrt{X^2 + Y^2}$ from the location to the decision variable is evidently not the one-one mapping, because the four different locations $(\pm X, \pm Y)$ map to the same solution. Even if the fruit flies achieve the optimal solution finally, the fruit flies actually do not converge to the same location. To overcome this drawback, the improved FOA denotes the fruit fly location as a phase angle vector $\mathbf{\Theta} = [\theta_1, \theta_2, \cdots, \theta_D]$, where each phase angle $\theta_j \in [-\pi/2, \pi/2]$. Set $f : [-\pi/2, \pi/2]^D \rightarrow [\mathbf{S}_{min}, \mathbf{S}_{max}]$ as the one-one mapping from the phase angle vector to the decision variable in the search space, where $\mathbf{S}_{min} = [S_{min,1}, S_{min,2}, \cdots, S_{min,D}]$ and $\mathbf{S}_{max} = [S_{max,1}, S_{max,2}, \cdots, S_{max,D}]$ are the lower and upper boundaries of the search space, respectively. In this paper, the following sinusoidal function is adopted to compute the smell concentration judgement **S** (decision variable of the problem) of the location $\mathbf{\Theta}$ for the fruit fly, as follows

$$\mathbf{S} = f(\mathbf{\Theta}) = ((\mathbf{S}_{\max} - \mathbf{S}_{\min}) \sin \mathbf{\Theta} + \mathbf{S}_{\max} + \mathbf{S}_{\min})/2 \tag{1}$$

The above transformation is a monotonic increasing function. Given any one angle in the phase angle space, there is one and only one decision variable in the solution space corresponding to the angle, and vice versa.

(2) *Initialization of fruit fly swarm*

In the initial phase of θ-DFOA, the phase angle-encoded location of the i–th fruit fly, denoted as the vector $\mathbf{\Theta}_i = [\theta_{i,1}, \theta_{i,2}, \cdots, \theta_{i,D}]$, is randomly generated within $[-\pi/2, \pi/2]$, as follows

$$\theta_{i,j} = random(-\pi/2, \pi/2), j = 1, 2, \cdots, D \tag{2}$$

where $random()$ is the random number uniformly distributed within the range. Then, evaluate and compute the smell concentration $Smell_i$ for each $\mathbf{\Theta}_i$. Find the best and the worst smell concentration $Smell_{best}$, $Smell_{worst}$, as well as the corresponding phase angle $\mathbf{\Theta}_{best}^g$ and $\mathbf{\Theta}_{worst}^g$. Unlike the basic FOA, the improved FOA has two sub-swarms, namely the best fruit fly swarm with the phase angle location $\mathbf{\Theta}_{best}^g$ and the worst fruit fly swarm with the phase angle location $\mathbf{\Theta}_{worst}^g$.

(3) *Double sub-swarm mechanism for the osphresis-based search*

When the fruit flies execute the osphresis-based foraging in the g-th iteration, the fruit fly individual firstly compute its distance to the best and the worst fruit fly swarms, respectively. If the fruit fly is closer to the best fruit fly swarm than to the worst fruit fly swarm, then it randomly generates the new phase angle location $\theta_{i,j}^g$ around the best swarm location $\theta_{best,j}^g$ within the interval $[-R^g, R^g]$ for each j. If the fruit fly is closer to the worst fruit fly swarm than to the best fruit fly swarm, then it randomly re-initializes the new phase angle location $\theta_{i,j}^g$ within $[-\pi/2, \pi/2]$ for each j. The improved osphresis-based searching process is as follows

$$\theta_{i,j}^g = \begin{cases} \theta_{best,j}^g + random(-R^g, R^g) & \|\mathbf{\Theta}_i^g - \mathbf{\Theta}_{best}^g\| \leq \|\mathbf{\Theta}_i^g - \mathbf{\Theta}_{worst}^g\| \\ random(-\pi/2, \pi/2) & \text{otherwise} \end{cases} \tag{3}$$

In the evolution process, the fruit flies are far from the optimum solution in the early searching phase, and thus, the search radius should be suitably large to enhance the exploiting capability to the unknown territory in the decision space. Then, in the later iterations, the fruit flies are close to the optimum solution, and thus, the search radius should be reduced to improve the exploring capability to the better solutions.

Therefore, the proposed θ-DFOA changes the search radius dynamically with the iteration number is computed as follows

$$R^g = \frac{\pi}{2} \text{logsig}(10 \cdot (0.5 - g/G_{\max})) \tag{4}$$

(4) *Vision-based foraging search*

The vision-based foraging search of the θ-DFOA is also a greedy selection process for the optimal individual. Firstly, evaluate and compute the smell concentration $Smell_i^g$ for each new generated Θ_i^g through the osphresis-based search phase. Then, select the best Θ_b^g with the minimum smell concentration where $b = \arg\min(Smell_i^g)$ and the worst Θ_w^g with the maximum smell concentration where $w = \arg\max(Smell_i^g)$. Then, compare Θ_b^g, Θ_w^g with the current two fruit fly swarm location Θ_{best}^g, Θ_{worst}^g. If Θ_b^g has the lower smell concentration than Θ_{best}^g, the best fruit fly swarm updates the current location and flies to the new location Θ_b^g. While if Θ_w^g has the upper smell concentration

---

STRUCTURE OF Θ-DFOA

/* Initialization */

1   Set the generation counter $g = 0$, the number of fruit flies as M_{pop}. Randomly initialize the phase angle for each fruit flies as Θ_i^0, $i=1, ..., M_{\text{pop}}$, within $[-\pi/2, \pi/2]$, and compute the smell concentration $Smell_i$. Select the best phase angle Θ_{best} with $Smell_{\text{best}}$ and the worst phase angle Θ_{worst} with $Smell_{\text{best}}$.

/* Iterative search */

2   **while** termination criteria is not satisfied **do**

3   Set $g = g + 1$, and compute the search radius $R^g = \pi/2 \cdot \text{logsig}(10 \cdot (0.5 - g/G_{\max}))$.

/* Search using osphresis */

4   **for** $i = 1 : M_{\text{pop}}$ **do**

5   Compute the distance from Θ_i^g to Θ_{best} and Θ_{worst}, respectively.

6   Generate the new phase angle according to

$$\theta_{i,j}^g = \begin{cases} \theta_{\text{best},j}^g + random(-R^g, R^g) & \|\Theta_i^g - \Theta_{\text{best}}^g\| \leq \|\Theta_i^g - \Theta_{\text{worst}}^g\| \\ random(-\pi/2, \pi/2) & \text{otherwise} \end{cases}$$

7   Calculate the judged value of smell concentration:
$$S_{i,j}^g = ((S_{\max,j} - S_{\min,j})\sin\theta_{i,j}^g + S_{\max,j} + S_{\min,j})/2$$

8   Evaluate the smell concentration judge function (also called fitness function) to get the smell concentrations: $Smell_i = f(S_i)$.

9   **end for**

/* Search using vision */

10   Select the best and the worst fruit flies that has the minimum and maximum smell concentration: $b = \arg\min(Smell_i)$, and $w = \arg\max(Smell_i)$

11   **if** $Smell_b < Smell_{\text{best}}$, **then** the best fruit fly swarm updates its location as $\Theta_{\text{best}} = \Theta_b$

12   **if** $Smell_w > Smell_{\text{worst}}$, **then** the worst fruit fly swarm updates its location as $\Theta_{\text{worst}} = \Theta_w$

13   **end while**

14   /* Output */ Decode and output the best solution.

Fig. 2. Procedure of θ-DFOA.

than Θ^g_{worst}, the worst fruit fly swarm updates the current location and flies to the new location Θ^g_w. Otherwise, the two fruit fly swarm will remain at the current location and begin to the next iteration calculation. The vision-based foraging process can be expressed as follows

$$\Theta^{g+1}_{best} = \begin{cases} \Theta^g_b, & Smell^g_b \leq Smell^g_{best} \\ \Theta^g_{best}, & otherwise \end{cases} \text{ and } \Theta^{g+1}_{worst} = \begin{cases} \Theta^g_w, & Smell^g_w \geq Smell^g_{worst} \\ \Theta^g_{worst}, & otherwise \end{cases}$$

(5)

where $Smell^g_{best}$ and $Smell^g_{worst}$ is the smell concentration of the two fruit fly swarm location Θ^g_{best} and Θ^g_{worst}, respectively.

The implementation procedure of our proposed θ-DFOA is as follows (Fig. 2):

4 Experimental Comparison on Benchmark Functions

In order to validate the effectiveness of θ-DFOA, fifteen benchmark functions are tested, including unimodal, multimodal and composition functions. All of these benchmark functions are difficult minimization problems and the information are listed the second and third columns in Table 1. The tests are implemented on a computer with Intel(R) Core(TM) i3 3.07 GHz CPU, 4 GB memory, and Window 7. Both the FOA

Table 1. Statistical results for various methods ($\mu \pm \sigma$ (best)) on Benchmark functions.

	Dim.	Range	FOA	θ-DFOA
f_1	2	[−100,100]	$-0.99 \pm 3.40 \times 10^{-3}$ (−0.99)	$-0.99 \pm 3.30 \times 10^{-3}$ (−1.00)
f_2	10	[−100,100]	596.01 ± 179.69 (53.57)	-209.13 ± 0.22 (−209.56)
f_3	10	[−100,100]	830.30 ± 189.50 (551.00)	1.30 ± 0.57 (0.00)
f_4	10	[−100,100]	869.05 ± 205.07 (463.89)	1.47 ± 0.25 (1.04)
f_5	10	[−32,32]	9.91 ± 0.97 (7.32)	1.08 ± 0.44 (0.62)
f_6	10	[−5.12, 5.12]	10.07 ± 2.01 (6.45)	0.01 ± 0.0035 (0.0087)
f_7	10	[−100,100]	2.64 ± 0.24 (2.12)	2.47 ± 0.36 (1.76)
f_8	10	[−10,10]	248.48 ± 78.40 (126.57)	4.27 ± 6.08 (1.84)
f_9	10	[−1,1]	-0.97 ± 0.0098 (−0.98)	$-1.00 \pm 1.30 \times 10^{-5}$ (−1.00)
f_{10}	10	[−600,600]	8.15 ± 1.58 (3.48)	0.91 ± 0.12 (0.69)
f_{11}	10	[−1,1]	$3.21 \times 10^{-4} \pm 3.07 \times 10^{-5}$ (5.36×10^{-4})	$1.75 \times 10^{-7} \pm 1.37 \times 10^{-7}$ (1.52×10^{-8})
f_{12}	10	[−10,10]	3.56 ± 0.51 (2.63)	0.47 ± 0.26 (0.06)
f_{13}	10	[−1.28,1.28]	0.08 ± 0.02 (0.02)	$3.9 \times 10^{-3} \pm 2.5 \times 10^{-3}$ (6.75×10^{-4})
f_{14}	10	[−5.12,5.12]	38.77 ± 4.99 (26.76)	26.89 ± 14.12 (5.69)
f_{15}	10	[−10,10]	$4.1 \times 10^4 \pm 1.87 \times 10^4$ (1.76×10^4)	$1.09 \times 10^4 \pm 1.22 \times 10^4$ (1.03×10^3)

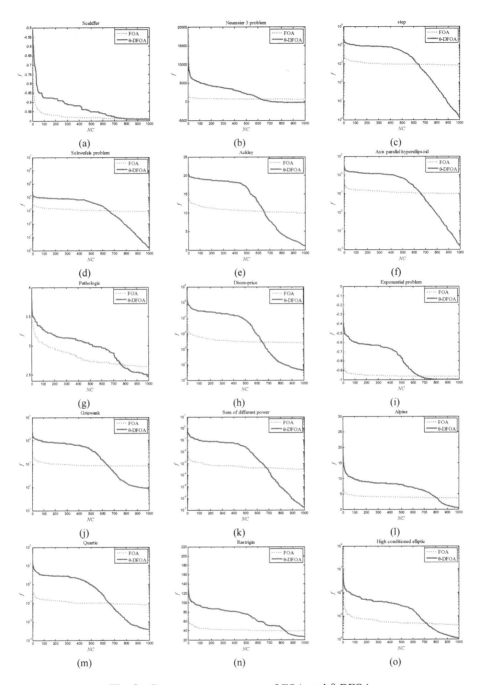

Fig. 3. Convergence progresses of FOA and θ-DFOA.

and θ-DFOA algorithms are coded using the Matlab-2009a, and no commercial algorithm tools are used. Due to the randomness nature of swarm intelligence algorithms, the two tested algorithms are run 50 times independently for each function and the statistical results are used for the performance evaluation and comparison. The main parameters of the proposed θ-DFOA and the basic FOA are set as maximum number of iteration $G_{max} = 100$, and the population size $M_{pop} = 40$.

Table 1 reports summary statistics for the optimum values found by the two FOA algorithms for all Benchmark functions after 50 independent runs. It compares the best values (best), the mean values (μ), and the standard variance (σ) of the solutions found. For all functions, the results show that the proposed θ-DFOA algorithm performs better than the basic FOA algorithm. The θ-DFOA algorithm gets the smallest variance over the simulations. The simulation results show that the double sub-swarm based osphresis search brings solutions with much higher accuracy to the optimization problem. The convergence curves of the average best function values are displayed in Fig. 3. It can be seen that, the basic FOA achieve the faster convergence speed and the smaller cost than θ-DFOA in the early iterations. However, in the later iterations that the basic FOA comes to the stagnation, θ-DFOA still shows the ability to search better solutions. The searching range R of θ-DFOA decreases with the increase of the iterations, which contributes to improve the local search ability near the optimal solution and leads to the improved global convergence of θ-DFOA.

5   θ-DFOA for PID Controller

The PID controller are the most common type of controllers by far, because of its simple structure, strong robustness and high reliability [11, 12]. PID control system is widely used in process control and motion control, particularly, in deterministic control system with mathematical model. In the following section, we apply the proposed θ-DFOA to the parameter tuning for the PID controller.

In the PID controller, the output variable $e(t) = r(t) - y(t)$ represents the tracking error between the desired output value $r(t)$ and the actual output value $y(t)$. According to the error signal $e(t)$, the PID controller computes the sum of the proportional, the integral and the derivative of this error signal, and inputs it to the controlled object. The PID controller can be written as

$$u(t) = K_P(e(t) + K_I \int_0^t e(t)dt + K_D \frac{de(t)}{dt} \tag{6}$$

where K_P, K_I and K_D are the proportional gain, the integral gain and the derivative gain, respectively.

With the PID controller and the controlled object, the dynamic performance of the control system can be obtained. Therefore, the cost function is defined as follows:

$$J = w_1 \cdot \sigma + w_2 \cdot t_s + w_3 \cdot \int_0^t |e| \, dt \tag{7}$$

where the overshoot of the control system is $\sigma = |y_p - r|/r \times 100\%$, where y_p is the peak value of the output signal. The rise time of the control system t_s is defined as the minimum time when the output reaches and does not exceed the 5% error band. The accumulated absolute error is $e = r(t) - y(t)$. w_1, w_2 and w_3 are weight coefficients.

To verify the efficiency of the proposed θ-DFOA in parameter tuning for the PID controller, comparison experiment between FOA and θ-DFOA is provided. Consider the following second-order system with the transfer function

$$G(s) = \frac{s + 10}{s^2 + 5s + 10} \tag{8}$$

The tuning parameters include K_P, K_I and K_D, which means the optimization problem is three-dimensional and $D = 3$. Set the population size of the θ-DFOA and FOA as $M_{pop} = 30$, and the maximum number of iteration as $G_{max} = 50$. Figure 4 shows the evolution process of the cost function, as well as the response curves of the closed-loop system. Table 2 shows the PID parameters obtained by θ-DFOA and FOA after 50 iterations.

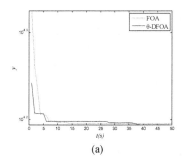
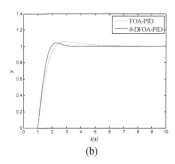

(a)   (b)

Fig. 4. Comparison between FOA and θ-DFOA in the PID controller parameter tuning.

Table 2. Results of the PID controller parameter tuning.

	K_P	K_I	K_D	J_{best}
FOA	6.99	3.14	3.67	1.57×10^4
θ-DFOA	9.99	2.99	3.79	1.56×10^4

From the above simulation result, it illustrates that θ-DFOA has the better performance and faster convergence speed compared with the basic FOA in PID parameters tuning problem. The θ-DFOA gets the best value after the 100 iterations, but FOA falls into the local minimum. Therefore, θ-DFOA can search the optimal parameters more quickly and efficiently than the basic FOA. The time response curves show that the overshoot obtained by θ-DFOA is lower than that of FOA, while the rise time of the θ-DFOA is also lower than that of the basic FOA. The θ-DFOA based PID controller creates the very perfect step response of the system, indicating that the θ-DFOA is better than FOA for parameters optimization of the PID controller.

6 Conclusion

In this paper, a novel component design is proposed to modify the basic FOA algorithm. In order to improve the performance of FOA, the proposed θ-DFOA adopts the phase angle vector to encoded the fruit fly location and brings in the double sub-swarms mechanism to enhance the search ability of the olfactory organ of the fruit fly. This new strategy helps the basic algorithm find a better solution, which results in high accurate solution and fast convergence speed. Simulation experiments have been conducted on fifteen benchmark functions. Comparisons with the basic FOA show that θ-DFOA performs better in terms of solution accuracy and convergence speed. The proposed θ-DFOA is also used to optimization the PID controller, and the promising performance is achieved. In the future research, we will conduct more theoretical and experimental research works on FOA to further improve its performance and its applications.

Acknowledgement. This work is supported by National Natural Science Foundation of China (No. 61703012 and 61563011), Beijing Natural Science Foundation (No. 4182010), and the BJUT Promotion Project on Intelligent Manufacturing (No. 040000546317552).

References

1. Pan, W.T.: A new fruit fly optimization algorithm: taking the financial distress model as an example. Knowl.-Based Syst. **26**, 69–74 (2012)
2. Zheng, X.L., Wang, L., Wang, S.Y.: A novel fruit fly optimization algorithm for the semiconductor final testing scheduling problem. Knowl.-Based Syst. **57**, 95–103 (2014)
3. Lin, S.M.: Analysis of service satisfaction in web auction logistics service using a combination of fruit fly optimization algorithm and general regression neural network. Neural Comput. Appl. **22**(3–4), 783–791 (2013)
4. Li, H.Z., Guo, S., Li, C.J., Sun, J.Q.: A hybrid annual power load forecasting model based on generalized regression neural network with fruit fly optimization algorithm. Knowl.-Based Syst. **37**, 378–387 (2013)
5. Sheng, W., Bao, Y.: Fruit fly optimization algorithm based fractional order fuzzy-PID controller for electronic throttle. Nonlinear Dyn. **73**(1–2), 611–619 (2013)
6. Arya, Y., Kumar, N.: BFOA-scaled fractional order fuzzy PID controller applied to AGC of multi-area multi-source electric power generating systems. Swarm Evol. Comput. **32**, 202–218 (2017)
7. Zhang, X.Y., Jia, S.M., Li, X.Z., Jian, M.: Design of the fruit fly optimization algorithm based path planner for UAV in 3D environments. In: Proceedings of 2017 IEEE International Conference on Mechatronics and Automation, pp. 381–386. IEEE, Takamatsu (2017)
8. Meng, T., Pan, Q.K.: An improved fruit fly optimization algorithm for solving the multidimensional knapsack problem. Appl. Soft Comput. **50**, 79–93 (2017)

9. Yuan, X.F., Liu, Y.M., Xiang, Y.Z., Yan, X.G.: Parameter identification of BIPT system using chaotic-enhanced fruit fly optimization algorithm. Appl. Math. Comput. **268**, 1267–1281 (2015)
10. Kanarachos, S., Griffin, J., Fitzpatrick, M.E.: Efficient truss optimization using the contrast-based fruit fly optimization algorithm. Comput. Struct. **182**, 137–148 (2017)
11. Pan, Q.K., Sang, H.Y., Duan, J.H., Gao, L.: An improved fruit fly optimization algorithm for continuous function optimization problems. Knowl.-Based Syst. **62**, 69–83 (2014)
12. Mitić, M., Vuković, N., Petrović, M., Miljković, Z.: Chaotic fruit fly optimization algorithm. Knowl.-Based Syst. **89**, 446–458 (2015)
13. Yuan, X.F., Dai, X.S., Zhao, J.Y., He, Q.: On a novel multi-swarm fruit fly optimization algorithm and its application. Appl. Math. Comput. **233**, 260–271 (2014)

An Enhanced Monarch Butterfly Optimization with Self-adaptive Butterfly Adjusting and Crossover Operators

Gai-Ge Wang[1]([⊠]), Guo-Sheng Hao[2], and Zhihua Cui[3]

[1] Department of Computer Science and Technology,
Ocean University of China, Qingdao 266100, China
gaigewang@gmail.com, gaigewang@163.com
[2] School of Computer Science and Technology,
Jiangsu Normal University, Xuzhou, Jiangsu, China
guoshenghaoxz@tom.com
[3] Complex System and Computational Intelligence Laboratory,
Taiyuan University of Science and Technology, Taiyuan 030024, Shanxi, China
zhihua.cui@hotmail.com

Abstract. After studying the behavior of monarch butterflies in nature, Wang *et al.* proposed a new promising swarm intelligence algorithm, called monarch butterfly optimization (MBO), for addressing unconstrained optimization tasks. In the basic MBO algorithm, the fixed butterfly adjusting rate is used to carry out the butterfly adjusting operator. In this paper, the self-adaptive strategy is introduced to adjust the butterfly adjusting rate. In addition, the crossover operator that is generally used in evolutionary algorithms (EAs) is used to further improve the quality of butterfly individuals. The two optimization strategies, self-adaptive and crossover operator, are combined, and then self-adaptive crossover operator is proposed. After incorporating the above strategies into the basic MBO algorithm, a new version of MBO algorithm, called Self-adaptive Monarch Butterfly Optimization (SaMBO), is put forward. Also, few studies of constrained optimization has been done for MBO research. In this paper, in order to verify the performance of our proposed SaMBO algorithm, the proposed SaMBO algorithm is further benchmarked by 21 CEC 2017 constrained optimization problems. The experimental results indicate that the proposed SaMBO algorithm outperforms the basic MBO and other five state-of-the-art metaheuristic algorithms.

Keywords: Monarch butterfly optimization · Migration operator
Butterfly adjusting operator · Self-adaptive · Constrained benchmark problems

1 Introduction

In our daily life, we are striving for maximum profit and minimum cost when tackling all kinds of problems. These problems can be mathematically modelled into maximum/minimum problems, which can be further solved by various optimization techniques. Most researchers and engineers divide these optimization techniques into two

© Springer International Publishing AG, part of Springer Nature 2018
Y. Tan et al. (Eds.): ICSI 2018, LNCS 10941, pp. 432–444, 2018.
https://doi.org/10.1007/978-3-319-93815-8_41

categories: the traditional optimization methods and modern metaheuristic algorithms [1]. The former has the strict process and will generate the same results under the same conditions; while the latter based on random distribution only provides a loose framework and different runs will generate different results even under the same conditions. Because the modern metaheuristic algorithms can address more complicated problems well that are difficult to be solved by the traditional methods, a huge number of researchers from the various walks of life pay more and more attention to metaheuristic algorithms. The metaheuristic algorithms largely involves the following optimization techniques: evolutionary computation [2], swarm intelligence, and artificial neural network [3]. Among different kinds of metaheuristic algorithms, swarm intelligence (SI) algorithms [4] are one of the most representative paradigms.

Since particle swarm optimization (PSO) with the inspiration of bird flock [5–9] is proposed in 1995, several scholars start to study the phenomena and laws of nature, and they have designed various swarm intelligence algorithms, such as harmony search [10, 11], artificial bee colony [12, 13], cuckoo search [14–19], fireworks algorithm [20], bat algorithm (BA) [21–24], earthworm optimization algorithm [25], elephant herding optimization [26–28], moth search algorithm [29, 30], biogeography-based optimization [31–33], firefly algorithm [34–36], krill herd [37–42], and MBO [43]. Except the theoretical researches, these swarm intelligence algorithms have been successfully used to various complicated engineering problems, such as floorplanning [44, 45], dynamic vehicle routing [46], data clustering [47], prediction of pupylation sites [48], target assessment [49, 50], Knapsack [51], gesture segmentation [52], test-sheet composition [53], economic load dispatch [54, 55], unit commitment [56], IIR system identification [57], shape design [58], and path planning [59]. Among these swarm intelligence algorithms (SIs), MBO [43] is one of the most promising SIs.

After studying the life habits of monarch butterflies in North America, Wang *et al.* [43] developed a novel promising SI-based optimization approach, called Monarch Butterfly Optimization (MBO). In MBO, all the butterflies are respectively located at Land 1 and Land 2, and they independently update their positions through butterfly adjusting operator and migration operator in a parallel manner. Subsequently, they will share their information by combining these butterflies located at Land 1 and Land 2.

However, in MBO, the butterfly adjusting operator was implemented with the fixed butterfly adjusting rate (*BAR*) [43]. This updating way failed to extract the information from the optimization process, leading to slow convergence on certain difficult optimization problems. In this paper, the butterfly adjusting rate (*BAR*) will be updated as the optimization process of MBO evolves. As a critical component of evolutionary algorithms (EAs), crossover operator, has a significant effect on the performance of EAs. Also, in our current work, crossover operator will be introduced to further improve the quality of butterfly individuals after implementing butterfly adjusting operator. The self-adaptive strategy is used to update the crossover rate, and then a self-adaptive crossover operator is proposed. After incorporating these optimization strategies into the basic MBO algorithm, a new variant of MBO namely Self-adaptive Monarch Butterfly Optimization (SaMBO), is proposed. Though many scholars proposed several improved MBO algorithms, they are just tested by the unconstrained functions. Different with most previous work, 21 CEC 2017 constrained functions are applied to verify the effectiveness of our proposed SaMBO algorithm. The experimental results indicate that the proposed SaMBO approach has better performance than the basic MBO algorithm and five other metaheuristic algorithms in most cases. This also implies the self-adaptive strategy and crossover operator can efficiently improve the performance of MBO when addressing constrained optimization problems.

The rest of this paper is structured as follows. Section 2 review the related work of the basic MBO algorithm. Section 3 provides the framework of the basic MBO method, followed by the description of the self-adaptive and crossover operator in Sect. 4. Also, the main steps of SaMBO algorithm is given in Sect. 4. Subsequently, SaMBO is benchmarked by 21 CEC 2017 constrained functions in Sect. 5. In Sect. 6, some concluding remarks as well as scope for further work is provided.

2   Related Work

Though monarch butterfly optimization algorithm [43] has been proposed only three years, many scholars have worked on MBO algorithm. In this section, some of the most representative work regarding MBO are summarized and reviewed.

Yi *et al.* [60] proposed a quantum inspired MBO called QMBO, by incorporating quantum computation into MBO. In QMBO, the worst butterflies are updated by quantum operators. The UCAV path planning problem is modeled into an optimization problem, and then its optimal path can be obtained by QMBO. Feng *et al.* [61] presented a binary MBO (BMBO) method, which is to address the 0-1 knapsack problem. In BMBO, each butterfly was represented as a two-tuple string. Several individual allocation techniques and a novel repair operator were applied. Wang *et al.* [62] put forward a variant of MBO method in combination with two optimization strategies namely GCMBO. In GCMBO, self-adaptive crossover (SAC) operator and greedy strategy are utilized to improve its search ability. Feng *et al.* [63] combined the chaos theory with MBO, and then proposed a chaotic MBO (CMBO). In CMBO, in order to tune two main operators, the best chaotic map is selected from 12 maps. Worst individuals are improved by Gaussian mutation operator. Ghanem and Jantan [64] combined ABC with elements from MBO, namely Hybrid ABC/MBO (HAM). HAM used an updated butterfly adjusting operator that is considered as a mutation operator to share information with the employee bees in ABC. Feng *et al.* [65] proposed a kind of multi-strategy MBO for discounted 0-1 knapsack problem. In MMBO, neighborhood mutation and Gaussian perturbation are utilized. Feng *et al.* [66] combined MBO with 7 kinds of DE mutation strategies based on intrinsic mechanism of MBO and the character of DE operator. Migration operator is replaced by DE operator. DEMBO solved 30 typical discounted 0-1 knapsack problem. Feng *et al.* [67] presented a generalized opposition-based learning (OBL) [68] MBO with Gaussian perturbation namely OMBO, in which OBL is used on half individuals. 15 large-scale 0-1 KP cases from 800 to 2000 dimensions are used. Chen *et al.* [69] proposed a variant of MBO by a greedy strategy to solve dynamic vehicle routing problems. The proposed algorithm only accept better individuals than before. Also, a later perturbation is to make a trade-off between global and local search. Faris *et al.* [70] modified the position updating strategy used in MBO, in which both the previous solutions and butterfly with the best fitness up to now are utilized. Furthermore, it is applied to train neural networks.

Though many scholars have made several in-depth studies of MBO from different aspects. In MBO, the butterflies in Land 1 are updated by butterfly adjusting operator with the fixed butterfly adjusting rate, leading to failing to find the final optima for certain difficult functions, while here, the self-adaptive strategy is introduced to update butterfly adjusting rate during the whole optimization process. Also, the crossover operator and self-adaptive strategy are cooperatively to update the butterflies in Land 1. The detailed description of the proposed algorithm will be provided as follows.

3   Monarch Butterfly Optimization

In MBO, the number of butterflies located at Land 1 and Land 2 are calculated according to the parameter p, which are NP_1 (ceil($p * NP$)) and NP_2 ($NP - NP_1$), respectively. The butterflies located at Land 1 and Land 2 can be called Subpopulation 1 (SP 1) and Subpopulation 2 (SP 2), respectively. NP is the population size while p is the ratio of butterflies in SP 1. The butterfly individuals in SP 1 is updated by migration operator, which can be given as [43]

$$x_{i,k}^{t+1} = x_{r_1,k}^{t} \tag{1}$$

where $x_{r_1,k}^{t}$ is the kth element of x_{r_1}. Butterfly r_1 is randomly selected from SP 1. If $r \leq p$, $x_{i,k}^{t+1}$ is generated by Eq. (1). If $r > p$, $x_{r_1,k}^{t}$ is generated by

$$x_{i,k}^{t+1} = x_{r_2,k}^{t} \tag{2}$$

where $x_{r_2,k}^{t}$ is the kth element of x_{r_2}, and butterfly r_2 is randomly selected from SP2.

For all the elements in butterfly j, if $rand \leq p$, it can be updated as [43]

$$x_{j,k}^{t+1} = x_{best,k}^{t} \tag{3}$$

where $x_{j,k}^{t+1}$ indicates the kth element of x_j at generation $t + 1$; $x_{best,k}^{t}$ indicates the kth element of the fittest butterfly x_{best}. If $rand > p$, it can be updated as

$$x_{j,k}^{t+1} = x_{r_3,k}^{t} \tag{4}$$

where $x_{r_3,k}^{t}$ is the kth element of x_{r_3}. Here, $r_3 \in \{1, 2, \ldots, NP_2\}$.

Under this condition, if $rand > BAR$, it can be further updated as follows [43].

$$x_{j,k}^{t+1} = x_{j,k}^{t+1} + \alpha \times (dx_k - 0.5) \tag{5}$$

4   SaMBO Algorithm

Though MBO is one of the relatively newest swarm intelligence algorithms, which is just proposed in 2015 [43], several scholars have carried out many in-depth studies. Many improved MBO algorithms have been proposed, and they have been used to successfully address various engineering problems. However, the butterflies in Land 1 is updated by butterfly adjusting operator with the fixed butterfly adjusting rate. In our present work, self-adaptive strategy and crossover operator are introduced to improve the performance of the basic MBO algorithm, and then a new variant of MBO algorithm namely SaMBO will be proposed. The detailed description of SaMBO algorithm will be given below.

4.1   Self-adaptive Strategy

As mentioned before, the butterfly adjusting operator is implemented with the fixed butterfly adjusting rate (BAR). Here, BAR is updated as the MBO evolves by introducing a self-adaptive strategy, which can be updated as

$$BAR = BAR_0 + (1 - BAR_0) \times t/t_{max} \tag{6}$$

where BAR_0 is initial butterfly adjusting rate; t and t_{max} are the current and maximum generation, respectively.

From Eq. (6), we can see, BAR is changed during the whole optimization process in the range $[BAR_0, 1]$. This indicates that less and less butterflies will be updated by Eq. (5), which has played smaller and smaller important role as MBO evolves.

4.2   Crossover Operator

As we aware, crossover operator and mutation operator are two of the most important operators in EAs. In the current work, the crossover operator will be introduced to further improve the quality of butterfly individuals generated by butterfly adjusting operator. In order to provide a clear description, the butterfly generated by Eqs. (3)–(5) is called x_{j1}^{t+1}. For the sake of fully exploiting the information of SP 2, an updated crossover operator is designed and further used to generate another new butterfly individual x_{j2}^{t+1}, which can be expressed as:

$$x_{j2}^{t+1} = x_j^t \times Cr + x_{j1}^{t+1} \times (1 - Cr) \tag{7}$$

where x_j^t is the original butterfly in SP 2, and Cr is crossover rate. Here, a self-adaptive strategy is used to adjust Cr, which can be represented as follows:

$$Cr = 0.8 + 0.2 \times \frac{f(x_j^t) - f(x_{best})}{f(x_{worst}) - f(x_{best})} \tag{8}$$

where $f(x_j^t)$ is the fitness of butterfly j in SP2; x_{best} and x_{worst} are the best and the worst butterfly in SP1 and SP2 with fitness of $f(x_{best})$ and $f(x_{worst})$, respectively. From Eq. (8), Cr is changed during the whole optimization process in the range of [0.2, 0.8].

Subsequently, the better butterfly individual will be considered as the newly-generated butterfly individual $x_{j,new}^{t+1}$ for the next generation, which can be given as

$$x_{j,new}^{t+1} = \begin{cases} x_{j1}^{t+1}, & f(x_{j1}^{t+1}) < f(x_{j2}^{t+1}) \\ x_{j2}^{t+1}, & f(x_{j2}^{t+1}) < f(x_{j1}^{t+1}) \end{cases} \tag{9}$$

where $f(x_{j1}^{t+1})$ and $f(x_{j2}^{t+1})$ are fitness of the butterfly x_{j1}^{t+1} and x_{j2}^{t+1}, respectively.

After incorporating the self-adaptive strategy and crossover operator mentioned above into the butterfly adjusting operator, an updated butterfly adjusting operator is proposed. The main steps of the updated butterfly adjusting operator can be given in Algorithm 1.

Algorithm 1   Updated butterfly adjusting operator

Begin

    for $j = 1$ to NP_2 (for all butterflies in SP 2) **do**

        Calculate the butterfly adjusting rate by Eq. (6);

        for $k = 1$ to D (all the elements in jth butterfly) **do**

            Randomly generate *rand*;

            if *rand* $\leq$ *p* **then**

                Generate $x_{j1,k}^{t+1}$ by Eq. (3).

            else

                Randomly select a butterfly in SP 2; Generate $x_{j1,k}^{t+1}$ by Eq. (4).

            end if

        end for k

        Generate x_{j2}^{t+1} by performing crossover operator as shown in Eq. (7).

        Generate $x_{j,new}^{t+1}$ by Eq. (9).

    end for j

End.

After incorporating the updated butterfly adjusting operator into MBO, SaMBO is proposed, and its main description is given as Algorithm 2.

Algorithm 2   SaMBO algorithm

Begin

Step 1: Initialization. Set the generation counter $t = 1$; initialize the population P; set t_{max}, NP_1, and NP_2, S_{Max}, p, $peri$, and initial butterfly adjusting rate BAR_0.

Step 2: Fitness evaluation. Evaluate each butterfly according to its position.

Step 3: While $t < t_{max}$ do

Divide butterflies into two subpopulations (SP 1 and SP 2).

for $i=1$ to NP_1 (for all butterflies in SP 1) **do**

Generate $x_{i,k}^{t+1}$ by performing migration operator as Section 3.1.

end for i

for $j= 1$ to NP_2 (for all butterflies in SP 2) **do**

Generate $x_{j,new}^{t+1}$ as Algorithm 1.

end for j

Evaluate the butterfly population.

Step 4: end while

Step 5: Output the best solution.

End.

5   Simulation Results

In this section, the effectiveness of the proposed SaMBO algorithm is fully investigated on 21 constrained benchmark functions, as shown in Table 1. In Table 1, D is the number of decision variables ($D = 30$), I is the number of inequality constraints, and E is the number of equality constraints. More detailed information regarding 21 constrained benchmark functions can be found in [71]. In order to get a fair comparison, all the implementations are carried out under the same conditions [11, 72]. For MBO and SaMBO, the parameters are set below: $S_{max} = 1.0$, $BAR_0 = (\sqrt{2} - 1)/2$, $t_{max} = 50$, $peri = 1.2$, $p = 5/12$, and $NP = 50$. For others, their parameters are the same with [43].

In essence, all the metaheuristic algorithms are based on stochastic distribution, therefore, in order to remove the influence of randomness, fifty independent runs are performed. In the following experiments, the optimal solution for each test problem is highlighted in **bold** font. After fifty implementations, the mean values obtained by seven metaheuristic algorithms are recorded in Table 2.

Table 1. Details of 21 constrained benchmark functions.

	Search range	Type of objective	Number of constraints	
			E	I
C01	$[-100, 100]D$	Non separable	0	1, Separable
C02	$[-100, 100]^D$	Non separable, Rotated	0	1, Non separable, rotated
C03	$[-100, 100]^D$	Non separable	1, Separable	1, Separable
C04	$[-10, 10]^D$	Separable	0	2, Separable
C05	$[-10, 10]^D$	Non separable	0	2, Non separable, rotated
C06	$[-100, 100]^D$	Separable	2, Non separable	0
C07	$[-10, 10]^D$	Separable	2, Non separable	0
C08	$[-100, 100]^D$	Separable	2, Non separable	0
C09	$[-100, 100]^D$	Separable	1, Non separable	1, Non separable
C10	$[-100, 100]^D$	Separable	0	2, Separable
C11	$[-100, 100]^D$	Non separable	0	3, Separable
C12	$[-100, 100]^D$	Separable	1	1
C13	$[-100, 100]^D$	Non separable	1, Non separable	1, Separable
C14	$[-100, 100]^D$	Separable	1	2, Non separable
C15	$[-100, 100]^D$	Rotated	0	2, Rotated
C16	$[-100, 100]^D$	Rotated	0	3, Rotated
C17	$[-100, 100]^D$	Rotated	1, Rotated	1, Rotated
C18	$[-100, 100]^D$	Rotated	1, Rotated	1, Rotated
C19	$[-100, 100]^D$	Rotated	1, Rotated	1, Rotated
C20	$[-100, 100]^D$	Rotated	1, Rotated	1, Rotated
C21	$[-100, 100]^D$	Rotated	1, Rotated	2, Rotated

From Table 2, it can be observed that, for Mean function values, SaMBO has the absolute advantage over MBO algorithm and other five metaheuristic algorithms on seventeen benchmarks (C01–C06, C10–C16, and C18–C21). While for other metaheuristic algorithms, MBO performs the best on three constrained benchmark functions (C07, C08, and C09), while BA can successfully get the best function value on only one constrained function (C17). From Table 2, we can see, self-adaptive strategy and crossover operator can improve significantly the search ability of the basic MBO algorithm.

Table 2. Mean function values obtained by SaMBO and other six metaheuristic algorithms.

	BA	ES	HS	MBO	PBIL	PSO	SaMBO
C01	1.13E5	7.81E4	7.09E4	5.88E4	6.80E4	5.62E4	**4.63E4**
C02	1.24E5	8.04E4	6.75E4	6.76E4	6.79E4	5.61E4	**4.02E4**
C03	1.62E5	8.78E4	8.00E4	6.62E4	6.84E4	6.00E4	**4.62E4**
C04	795.00	970.90	804.30	459.40	827.20	576.30	**291.00**
C05	3.38E6	3.76E6	2.04E6	1.04E6	1.81E6	7.97E5	**2.35E5**

(continued)

Table 2. (*continued*)

	BA	ES	HS	MBO	PBIL	PSO	SaMBO
C06	1.07E3	1.06E3	1.05E3	986.10	1.04E3	1.04E3	**974.60**
C07	9.55	8.18	7.19	**1.12**	4.56	6.72	1.88
C08	1.06E3	1.05E3	1.04E3	**996.60**	1.03E3	1.03E3	1.00E3
C09	8.01E3	8.28E3	8.87E3	**7.44E3**	7.95E3	8.82E3	7.47E3
C10	6.49E4	4.88E4	4.62E4	1.97E4	4.93E4	2.47E4	**1.28E4**
C11	2.92E10	1.86E10	1.71E10	5.46E9	1.70E10	5.27E9	**2.21E9**
C12	87.82	81.82	79.11	64.50	76.81	64.97	**58.53**
C13	18.59	12.95	13.07	7.18	13.34	7.66	**3.78**
C14	6.94E4	4.86E4	4.79E4	2.35E4	4.90E4	2.50E4	**1.11E4**
C15	2.33E5	1.65E5	1.58E5	1.08E5	1.62E5	9.04E4	**5.18E4**
C16	3.46E11	2.27E11	2.07E11	1.25E11	2.17E11	8.03E10	**2.59E10**
C17	**20.96**	21.15	21.15	21.16	21.17	21.16	21.11
C18	177.80	152.40	146.90	113.60	147.60	118.90	**94.86**
C19	2.03E3	1.78E3	1.73E3	1.22E3	1.76E3	1.34E3	**927.80**
C20	61.73	42.06	42.84	28.58	42.77	23.70	**15.56**
C21	2.37E5	1.60E5	1.55E5	9.25E4	1.63E5	8.95E4	**5.32E4**
Total	1	0	0	3	0	0	17

6 Discussion and Conclusions

After the studying the behavior of monarch butterflies in North America, in 2015, Wang *et al.* designed a kind of swarm intelligence algorithm namely monarch butterfly optimization (MBO) for global unstrained optimization problems. In MBO, the butterfly adjusting rate (*BAR*) is fixed and unchangeable during the whole optimization process when implementing butterfly adjusting operator. In this paper, a self-adaptive strategy is introduced to adjust the butterfly adjusting rate, which is changeable all the time. Also, as most evolutionary algorithms, crossover operator is further used to improve the utilization of information in butterfly population in order to enhance the quality of the solutions. Crossover rate can be self-adaptively adjusted as the optimization goes. At last, 21 constrained benchmark functions are used to verify the effectiveness of the proposed SaMBO algorithm, and the experimental results indicate that self-adaptive strategy and crossover operator can improve significantly the performance of the basic MBO algorithm when addressing constrained functions.

Except the merits of SaMBO approach mentioned above, the following points should be further clarified and focused. Firstly, though butterfly adjusting rate is changed as MBO goes, its value is only related with the current generation and maximum generation. More intelligent butterfly adjusting rate should be redesigned. Secondly, migration operator is not updated in the current work, so in the future research, migration operator should be redesigned in order to further improve the performance of MBO algorithm. Thirdly, in the current work, only 21 standard constrained benchmark functions are solved by the proposed algorithms; in the future research, more real world problems from engineering applications should be solved by the proposed SaMBO algorithm. We believe, these researches will surely further improve the effectiveness and efficiency of the proposed SaMBO algorithm.

Acknowledgements. This work was supported by the Natural Science Foundation of Jiangsu Province (No. BK20150239) and National Natural Science Foundation of China (No. 61503165).

References

1. Wang, G.-G., Tan, Y.: Improving metaheuristic algorithms with information feedback models. IEEE Trans. Cybern. (2017). https://doi.org/10.1109/TCYB.2017.2780274. http://ieeexplore.ieee.org/document/8237198/
2. Wang, G.-G., Cai, X., Cui, Z., Min, G., Chen, J.: High performance computing for cyber physical social systems by using evolutionary multi-objective optimization algorithm. IEEE Trans. Emerg. Top. Comput. (2017). https://doi.org/10.1109/TETC.2017.2703784. https://ieeexplore.ieee.org/document/7927724/
3. Yi, J.-H., Wang, J., Wang, G.-G.: Improved probabilistic neural networks with self-adaptive strategies for transformer fault diagnosis problem. Adv. Mech. Eng. **8**, 1–13 (2016)
4. Duan, H., Luo, Q.: New progresses in swarm intelligence-based computation. Int. J. Bio-Inspired Comput. **7**, 26–35 (2015)
5. Kennedy, J., Eberhart, R.: Particle swarm optimization. In: Proceeding of the IEEE International Conference on Neural Networks, pp. 1942–1948. IEEE (1995)
6. Wang, G.-G., Gandomi, A.H., Alavi, A.H., Deb, S.: A hybrid method based on krill herd and quantum-behaved particle swarm optimization. Neural Comput. Appl. **27**, 989–1006 (2016)
7. Wang, G.-G., Gandomi, A.H., Yang, X.-S., Alavi, A.H.: A novel improved accelerated particle swarm optimization algorithm for global numerical optimization. Eng. Comput. **31**, 1198–1220 (2014)
8. Sun, Y., Jiao, L., Deng, X., Wang, R.: Dynamic network structured immune particle swarm optimisation with small-world topology. Int. J. Bio-Inspired Comput. **9**, 93–105 (2017)
9. Mirjalili, S., Wang, G.-G., Coelho, L.d.S.: Binary optimization using hybrid particle swarm optimization and gravitational search algorithm. Neural Comput. Appl. **25**, 1423–1435 (2014)
10. Geem, Z.W., Kim, J.H., Loganathan, G.V.: A new heuristic optimization algorithm: harmony search. Simulation **76**, 60–68 (2001)
11. Wang, G., Guo, L., Wang, H., Duan, H., Liu, L., Li, J.: Incorporating mutation scheme into krill herd algorithm for global numerical optimization. Neural Comput. Appl. **24**, 853–871 (2014)
12. Wang, H., Yi, J.-H.: An improved optimization method based on krill herd and artificial bee colony with information exchange. Memetic Comput. **10**(2), 177–198 (2018). https://doi.org/10.1007/s12293-017-0241-6
13. Sulaiman, N., Mohamad-Saleh, J., Abro, A.G.: Robust variant of artificial bee colony (JA-ABC4b) algorithm. Int. J. Bio-Inspired Comput. **10**, 99–108 (2017)
14. Wang, G.-G., Deb, S., Gandomi, A.H., Zhang, Z., Alavi, A.H.: Chaotic cuckoo search. Soft. Comput. **20**, 3349–3362 (2016)
15. Wang, G.-G., Gandomi, A.H., Zhao, X., Chu, H.E.: Hybridizing harmony search algorithm with cuckoo search for global numerical optimization. Soft. Comput. **20**, 273–285 (2016)

16. Wang, G.-G., Gandomi, A.H., Yang, X.-S., Alavi, A.H.: A new hybrid method based on krill herd and cuckoo search for global optimization tasks. Int. J. Bio-Inspired Comput. **8**, 286–299 (2016)
17. Yang, X.S., Deb, S.: Engineering optimisation by cuckoo search. Int. J. Math. Model. Numer. Optim. **1**, 330–343 (2010)
18. Cui, Z., Sun, B., Wang, G.-G., Xue, Y., Chen, J.: A novel oriented cuckoo search algorithm to improve DV-Hop performance for cyber-physical systems. J. Parallel Distr. Comput. **103**, 42–52 (2017)
19. Kumaresan, T., Palanisamy, C.: E-mail spam classification using S-cuckoo search and support vector machine. Int. J. Bio-Inspired Comput. **9**, 142–156 (2017)
20. Tan, Y.: Fireworks Algorithm-A Novel Swarm Intelligence Optimization Method. Springer, Heidelberg (2015). https://doi.org/10.1007/978-3-662-46353-6
21. Yang, X.-S.: Nature-Inspired Metaheuristic Algorithms. Luniver Press, Frome (2010)
22. Zhang, J.-W., Wang, G.-G.: Image matching using a bat algorithm with mutation. Appl. Mech. Mater. **203**, 88–93 (2012)
23. Xue, F., Cai, Y., Cao, Y., Cui, Z., Li, F.: Optimal parameter settings for bat algorithm. Int. J. Bio-Inspired Comput. **7**, 125–128 (2015)
24. Wang, G.-G., Chu, H.E., Mirjalili, S.: Three-dimensional path planning for UCAV using an improved bat algorithm. Aerosp. Sci. Technol. **49**, 231–238 (2016)
25. Wang, G.-G., Deb, S., Coelho, L.d.S.: Earthworm optimization algorithm: a bio-inspired metaheuristic algorithm for global optimization problems. Int. J. Bio-Inspired Comput. (2015). https://doi.org/10.1504/IJBIC.2015.10004283. http://www.inderscience.com/info/ingeneral/forthcoming.php?jcode=ijbic
26. Wang, G.-G., Deb, S., Gao, X.-Z., Coelho, L.d.S.: A new metaheuristic optimization algorithm motivated by elephant herding behavior. Int. J. Bio-Inspired Comput. **8**, 394–409 (2016)
27. Meena, N.K., Parashar, S., Swarnkar, A., Gupta, N., Niazi, K.R.: Improved elephant herding optimization for multiobjective DER accommodation in distribution systems. IEEE Trans. Ind. Inform. (2017). https://doi.org/10.1109/TII.2017.2748220. https://ieeexplore.ieee.org/document/8024030/
28. Wang, G.-G., Deb, S., Coelho, L.d.S.: Elephant herding optimization. In: 2015 3rd International Symposium on Computational and Business Intelligence (ISCBI 2015), pp. 1–5. IEEE (2015)
29. Wang, G.-G.: Moth search algorithm: a bio-inspired metaheuristic algorithm for global optimization problems. Memet. Comput. **10**(2), 151–164 (2018). https://doi.org/10.1007/s12293-016-0212-3
30. Feng, Y., Wang, G.-G.: Binary moth search algorithm for discounted 0-1 knapsack problem. IEEE Access **6**, 10708–10719 (2018)
31. Simon, D.: Biogeography-based optimization. IEEE Trans. Evol. Comput. **12**, 702–713 (2008)
32. Wang, G., Guo, L., Duan, H., Wang, H., Liu, L., Shao, M.: Hybridizing harmony search with biogeography based optimization for global numerical optimization. J. Comput. Theor. Nanosci. **10**, 2318–2328 (2013)
33. Wang, G.-G., Gandomi, A.H., Alavi, A.H.: An effective krill herd algorithm with migration operator in biogeography-based optimization. Appl. Math. Model. **38**, 2454–2462 (2014)
34. Yang, X.S.: Firefly algorithm, stochastic test functions and design optimisation. Int. J. Bio-Inspired Comput. **2**, 78–84 (2010)
35. Wang, G.-G., Guo, L., Duan, H., Wang, H.: A new improved firefly algorithm for global numerical optimization. J. Comput. Theor. Nanosci. **11**, 477–485 (2014)

36. Feng, Y., Wang, G.-G., Wang, L.: Solving randomized time-varying knapsack problems by a novel global firefly algorithm. Eng. Comput-Germany (2017). https://doi.org/10.1007/s00366-017-0562-6

37. Gandomi, A.H., Alavi, A.H.: Krill herd: a new bio-inspired optimization algorithm. Commun. Nonlinear Sci. Numer. Simul. **17**, 4831–4845 (2012)

38. Wang, G.-G., Gandomi, A.H., Alavi, A.H.: A chaotic particle-swarm krill herd algorithm for global numerical optimization. Kybernetes **42**, 962–978 (2013)

39. Wang, G.-G., Gandomi, A.H., Alavi, A.H., Hao, G.-S.: Hybrid krill herd algorithm with differential evolution for global numerical optimization. Neural Comput. Appl. **25**, 297–308 (2014)

40. Wang, G.-G., Guo, L., Gandomi, A.H., Hao, G.-S., Wang, H.: Chaotic krill herd algorithm. Inf. Sci. **274**, 17–34 (2014)

41. Wang, G.-G., Gandomi, A.H., Alavi, A.H., Deb, S.: A multi-stage krill herd algorithm for global numerical optimization. Int. J. Artif. Intell. Tools **25**, 1550030 (2016)

42. Guo, L., Wang, G.-G., Gandomi, A.H., Alavi, A.H., Duan, H.: A new improved krill herd algorithm for global numerical optimization. Neurocomputing **138**, 392–402 (2014)

43. Wang, G.-G., Deb, S., Cui, Z.: Monarch butterfly optimization. Neural Comput. Appl. (2015). https://doi.org/10.1007/s00521-015-1923-y

44. Zou, D.-X., Wang, G.-G., Pan, G., Qi, H.: A modified simulated annealing algorithm and an excessive area model for the floorplanning with fixed-outline constraints. Front. Inf. Technol. Electron. Eng. **17**, 1228–1244 (2016)

45. Zou, D.-X., Wang, G.-G., Sangaiah, A.K., Kong, X.: A memory-based simulated annealing algorithm and a new auxiliary function for the fixed-outline floorplanning with soft blocks. J. Ambient Intell. Humaniz. Comput. (2017). https://doi.org/10.1007/s12652-017-0661-7

46. Chen, S., Chen, R., Wang, G.-G., Gao, J., Sangaiah, A.K.: An adaptive large neighborhood search heuristic for dynamic vehicle routing problems. Comput. Electr. Eng. (2018). https://doi.org/10.1016/j.compeleceng.2018.02.049

47. Li, Z.-Y., Yi, J.-H., Wang, G.-G.: A new swarm intelligence approach for clustering based on krill herd with elitism strategy. Algorithms **8**, 951–964 (2015)

48. Nan, X., Bao, L., Zhao, X., Zhao, X., Sangaiah, A.K., Wang, G.-G., Ma, Z.: EPuL: an enhanced positive-unlabeled learning algorithm for the prediction of pupylation sites. Molecules **22**, 1463 (2017)

49. Wang, G., Guo, L., Duan, H.: Wavelet neural network using multiple wavelet functions in target threat assessment. Sci. World J. **2013**, 1–7 (2013)

50. Wang, G.-G., Guo, L., Duan, H., Liu, L., Wang, H.: The model and algorithm for the target threat assessment based on Elman_AdaBoost strong predictor. Acta Electronica Sinica **40**, 901–906 (2012)

51. Feng, Y., Wang, G.-G., Gao, X.-Z.: A novel hybrid cuckoo search algorithm with global harmony search for 0-1 Knapsack problems. Int. J. Comput. Intell. Syst. **9**, 1174–1190 (2016)

52. Liu, K., Gong, D., Meng, F., Chen, H., Wang, G.-G.: Gesture segmentation based on a two-phase estimation of distribution algorithm. Inf. Sci. **394–395**, 88–105 (2017)

53. Duan, H., Zhao, W., Wang, G., Feng, X.: Test-sheet composition using analytic hierarchy process and hybrid metaheuristic algorithm TS/BBO. Math. Probl. Eng. **2012**, 1–22 (2012)

54. Rizk-Allah, R.M., El-Sehiemy, R.A., Wang, G.-G.: A novel parallel hurricane optimization algorithm for secure emission/economic load dispatch solution. Appl. Soft Comput. **63**, 206–222 (2018)

55. Zou, D., Li, S., Wang, G.-G., Li, Z., Ouyang, H.: An improved differential evolution algorithm for the economic load dispatch problems with or without valve-point effects. Appl. Energy **181**, 375–390 (2016)

56. Srikanth, K., Panwar, L.K., Panigrahi, B.K., Herrera-Viedma, E., Sangaiah, A.K., Wang, G.-G.: Meta-heuristic framework: quantum inspired binary grey wolf optimizer for unit commitment problem. Comput. Electr. Eng. (2017). https://doi.org/10.1016/j.compeleceng.2017.07.023. https://www.sciencedirect.com/science/article/pii/S0045790617302057

57. Zou, D.-X., Deb, S., Wang, G.-G.: Solving IIR system identification by a variant of particle swarm optimization. Neural Comput. Appl. (2016). https://doi.org/10.1007/s00521-016-2338-0

58. Rizk-Allah, R.M., El-Sehiemy, R.A., Deb, S., Wang, G.-G.: A novel fruit fly framework for multi-objective shape design of tubular linear synchronous motor. J. Supercomput. **73**, 1235–1256 (2017)

59. Wang, G., Guo, L., Duan, H., Liu, L., Wang, H., Shao, M.: Path planning for uninhabited combat aerial vehicle using hybrid meta-heuristic DE/BBO algorithm. Adv. Sci. Eng. Med. **4**, 550–564 (2012)

60. Yi, J.-H., Lu, M., Zhao, X.-J.: Quantum inspired monarch butterfly optimization for UCAV path planning navigation problem. Int. J. Bio-Inspired Comput. (2017). http://www.inderscience.com/info/ingeneral/forthcoming.php?jcode=ijbic

61. Feng, Y., Wang, G.-G., Deb, S., Lu, M., Zhao, X.: Solving 0-1 knapsack problem by a novel binary monarch butterfly optimization. Neural Comput. Appl. **28**, 1619–1634 (2017)

62. Wang, G.-G., Deb, S., Zhao, X., Cui, Z.: A new monarch butterfly optimization with an improved crossover operator. Oper. Res. Int. J. (2016). https://doi.org/10.1007/s12351-016-0251-z

63. Feng, Y., Yang, J., Wu, C., Lu, M., Zhao, X.-J.: Solving 0-1 knapsack problems by chaotic monarch butterfly optimization algorithm. Memetic Comput. **10**(2), 135–150 (2016). https://doi.org/10.1007/s12293-016-0211-4

64. Ghanem, W.A.H.M., Jantan, A.: Hybridizing artificial bee colony with monarch butterfly optimization for numerical optimization problems. Neural Comput. Appl. (2016). https://doi.org/10.1007/s00521-016-2665-1

65. Feng, Y., Wang, G.-G., Li, W., Li, N.: Multi-strategy monarch butterfly optimization algorithm for discounted {0-1} knapsack problem. Neural Comput. Appl. (2017). https://doi.org/10.1007/s00521-017-2903-1

66. Feng, Y., Yang, J., He, Y., Wang, G.-G.: Monarch butterfly optimization algorithm with differential evolution for the discounted {0-1} knapsack problem. Acta Electronica Sinica **45** (2017)

67. Feng, Y., Wang, G.-G., Dong, J., Wang, L.: Opposition-based learning monarch butterfly optimization with Gaussian perturbation for large-scale 0-1 knapsack problem. Comput. Electr. Eng. **67**, 454–468 (2018). https://doi.org/10.1016/j.compeleceng.2017.12.014

68. Wang, G.-G., Deb, S., Gandomi, A.H., Alavi, A.H.: Opposition-based krill herd algorithm with Cauchy mutation and position clamping. Neurocomputing **177**, 147–157 (2016)

69. Chen, S., Chen, R., Gao, J.: A monarch butterfly optimization for the dynamic vehicle routing problem. Algorithms **10**, 107 (2017)

70. Faris, H., Aljarah, I., Mirjalili, S.: Improved monarch butterfly optimization for unconstrained global search and neural network training. Appl. Intell. **48**, 445–464 (2018)

71. Wu, G., Mallipeddi, R., Suganthan, P.N.: Problem definitions and evaluation criteria for the CEC 2017 competition on constrained real-parameter optimization (2017)

72. Wang, G.-G., Gandomi, A.H., Alavi, A.H.: Stud krill herd algorithm. Neurocomputing **128**, 363–370 (2014)

Collaborative Firefly Algorithm for Solving Dynamic Control Model of Chemical Reaction Process System

Yuanbin Mo$^{(\boxtimes)}$, Yanyue Lu, and Yanzhui Ma

Guangxi University for Nationalities, Nanning 530006, Guangxi, China
674148582@qq.com

Abstract. Chemical reaction system, dynamic operation can significantly increase the average rate of reaction, improve the time-average selectivity of complex reactions and enhance the molecular weight distribution of certain free-radical polymerization reactions, overcome the thermodynamic limitations of reversible reactions. It even can be used as integrated means of exothermic/endothermic reaction and catalytic reaction/catalyst regeneration, opens up new ways to strengthen and control the reaction process, reduce waste emissions, and increase economic and social benefits. Therefore, it has great significance to model, simulate and calculate the process of chemical reaction. In this paper, a cooperative firefly algorithm is proposed to solve the optimal dynamic model of chemical reaction. The characteristics of the proposed algorithm are analyzed in detailed and the simulation results of the algorithm are given. It provides a feasible solution to solve such problems and the simulation results also show the effectiveness of the proposed algorithm.

Keywords: Chemical reactor · Dynamic system optimal control
Firefly algorithm · Numerical solution

1 Introduction

The chemical reaction process is a dynamic process, and the optimal state of the system can be achieved under optimal steady state in the process of chemical reaction. Therefore, the task of process control is to suppress the influence of various disturbance factors to make the system as stable as possible in the optimal stationary state. However, further studies have shown that, for some reaction systems, artificially changing the operating conditions, the flow direction of the reaction mixture, or the position of the feed to allow the system to perform under non-steady conditions can significantly improve the time-averaged performance of the reaction. It can also improve the stability of the system and reduce the sensitivity of the parameters [1, 2]. For some chemical reaction systems, dynamic operation can significantly increase the average rate of reaction, improve the time-average selectivity of complex reactions, and improve certain free-radical polymerizations. The molecular weight distribution breaks through the thermodynamic limitations of reversible reactions and can even be used as an integrated method for the integration of exothermic/endothermic reactions, catalytic reactions/catalyst regeneration, and a new approach has been opened up for

© Springer International Publishing AG, part of Springer Nature 2018
Y. Tan et al. (Eds.): ICSI 2018, LNCS 10941, pp. 445–452, 2018.
https://doi.org/10.1007/978-3-319-93815-8_42

strengthening and control of reaction processes, reduction of waste emissions, improvement of economic and social benefits. Therefore, it has great significance to model, simulate and calculate the process of chemical reaction and have received extensive attention.

2   2-Chlorophenol Supercritical Water Oxidation Kinetic Equation

The chemical reaction process is a dynamic process. A dynamic process is usually a differential system in mathematics; instead, the temperature, pressure, concentration, feed rate, etc. can be controlled during the reaction to better achieve the desired reaction. The purpose, in mathematics, is expressed as a control u(t), and the goal can mathematically represent J. Therefore, a mathematical simulation of a chemical reaction process can be expressed as:

$$max(min)\, J(u) = \Phi\left[x(t_f), t_f\right] + \int_{t_0}^{t_f} \Psi(x(t), u(t))dt$$
$$s.t. \qquad \frac{dx}{dt} = f(x(t), u(t)), x(t_0) = x_0 \tag{1}$$

In the formula, X is a control variable which is related substance involved in a chemical reaction, u is the temperature, pressure, and flow rate, which are called control variables (or manipulated variables).

This is a dynamic optimal control problem. At present, domestic and foreign researches on the solution to the optimization of chemical process dynamics can be divided into two categories: the solution of the analytical solution and the solution of the numerical solution. The analytical method is further divided into a vibrational method and a dynamic programming method based on the Bellman best principle [3, 4]. Compared with the analytical method, the numerical solution method is more favored by the engineering community. The numerical solution approximates the control quantity function by n piecewise functions and is a constant function on each segment. In this way, the problem of solving the control quantity function is transformed into solving the n-dimensional optimization problem. Numerical solutions can be directly applied to process operation control from the perspective of computer control. Xiao and Zhou [5] used numerical solution to control the beer fermentation process and achieved good results; Xu and Luo [6] and others used numerical solutions to study the regenerator margin analysis and control design of the catalytic cracking unit. The final design results can meet the technical requirements. And it can achieve good automatic control; these are fully explain the superiority of the numerical solution.

The Firefly Algorithm (FA) was a heuristic intelligent optimization method proposed by the British Cambridge scholar Yang in 2008 [7, 8]. The basic idea of the method is derived from the social behaviors of fireflies such as searching food, attract mates and so on which based on the fact that the firefly adults use the biological properties of luminescence. After the algorithm was put forward, it has received attention and research from many scholars at home and abroad, and it has been successfully applied in combinatorial optimization [9], path planning [10], image processing [11], and economic dispatch [12]. Similar to other optimization algorithms, the basic FA algorithm has a large randomness, and there is a problem that the convergence speed is slow and the solution accuracy is not high. In order to solve these problems, this paper integrated some strategies to the basic firefly algorithm in order to enhance its performance. The improved algorithm is used to solve the classical dynamic optimization problems and apply to the dynamic model of chemical reactors, the simulation results indicates that the proposed algorithms obtain ideal results

2.1 Basic Firefly Algorithm (FA)

In the natural world, there are about more than 2,000 kinds of fireflies, most species emit their unique fluorescence. The actual purpose of the firefly is currently unknown. It is generally believed that fireflies use flash signals to attract the opposite sex or to attract potential prey and achieve courtship or foraging purposes. The firefly algorithm is a stochastic optimization algorithm designed to simulate the social behavior of this luminescent biological property. There are two key elements in the Firefly algorithm: its own brightness and attractiveness. Self-illumination reflects the position of the firefly. The firefly with low brightness is attracted by the brightness and moves toward the bright firefly. The attraction affects the distance the firefly needs to move, and the brightness of each individual is determined by the movement of the firefly. And the degree of attraction has been continuously updated to achieve the goal of goal optimization [8].

In the Firefly algorithm [7], the degree of attraction of the firefly is proportional to the magnitude of the brightness, and the brightness is determined by the objective function. A firefly is located at the coordinate X. Its brightness I can be taken as I (X) = f(X). The better the position of X, the greater its brightness, and the attractiveness of other individuals along with them. As the distance increases, it becomes smaller, and in the process of fluorescence transmission, it is absorbed by the propagation medium. Therefore, the degree of attraction is also related to the medium absorption factor. Therefore, the intensity I of a firefly pair from its r can be expressed as relative brightness

$$I(r) = I_0 e^{-\gamma r_{ij}} \tag{2}$$

where I_0 is the fluorescence intensity at a distance from the firefly pair $r = 0$, γ is the medium absorption factor, and r_{ij} is the Euclidean distance from firefly i to firefly j. The degree of attraction of fireflies' β is defined as:

$$\beta = \beta_{min} + (\beta_0 - \beta_{min})e^{-\gamma r^2} \tag{3}$$

where β_0 is the attraction of the firefly to the distance, and β_{min} is the smallest attraction, $\beta_{min} = 2$. The mobile formula that the firefly i is attracted by the firefly j is:

$$x_i = x_i + \beta(x_j - x_i) + \alpha\left(rand - \frac{1}{2}\right) \tag{4}$$

where x_i, x_j represents the location of firefly i and j, α is the step factor, and *rand* is the random factor that obeys the uniform distribution in the interval [0, 1].

2.2 Collaborative Search Strategy

In the firefly algorithm, each firefly individual is a D-dimensional vector whose goal is to produce the best solution. For a D-dimensional vector, one of its dimensions may find the optimal value in an iteration, but the individual's fitness value is calculated by the D-dimensional vector, so it is very likely that the individual is not the optimal result. The optimal value of the dimension found by this individual will also be discarded. We hope to find the optimal value of each element in the vector through the cooperation of each individual, and then obtain a better solution. In this paper, the cooperative search strategy is applied to FA and a Cooperative Firefly Algorithm(CFA) is proposed. All the individuals in the population find the optimal solution through the exchange and cooperation of their own information. In CFA, the optimal position is gbest and f(x) is the objective function. Respectively use the j (1, ..., D) dimension of each firefly individual instead of the corresponding element in gbest to become new-gbest and substitute the target function to calculate the fitness value. If f(newgbest) is better than f(gbest), then Replace gbest with newgbest to find the optimal value for the j dimension.

2.3 Collaborative Firefly Algorithm for Solving Dynamic Optimization Problems

The control period [t1, t2] is divided into m segments. Within each segment, all control variables and state variables remain unchanged. The value of the control variables in each segment composes the sequence u_0, u_1, ..., u_{n-1}, then the dynamic control problem is transformed into the m-dimensional optimization problem. In this regard, the steps to apply various intelligent algorithms are:

Step1: A group of individuals is initialized to form an initial population of a certain size. Each individual is a randomly generated sequence of control variables u_0, u_1, ..., u_{m-1}.

Step2: Apply the sequence of control variables of each individual to the controlled object, obtain the corresponding state trajectory, and then calculate the performance indicators of each group in the population according to the objective function, including the numerical solution of differential equations.

Step3: Determine if the termination condition is satisfied. If it is satisfied, terminate the calculation and output the optimal result; otherwise, proceed to the next step.

Step4: Calculate the next-generation group by each step of the firefly algorithm, then perform a collaborative search for each individual, return to Step2, and continue to run.

2.4   Performance Test of Algorithm

The Cooperative Firefly Algorithm was tested using the example of [3], as shown in Eq. (5). The literature [5] uses the principle of minima to obtain the theoretical solution of the optimal control variable. The corresponding target optimal value is 19.2910.

$$\min J(u) = 1/2 \int_0^1 (x^2 + u^2)dt$$
$$s.t. \quad \frac{dx}{dt} = -x + u, x(0) = 10, -6 \leq u \leq 2 \tag{5}$$

Apply FA and CFA respectively to solve, its parameters: Step length factor $\alpha_0 = 0.9$, maximum attraction, minimum attraction, medium absorption factor, The step size a adopts an adaptive change that gradually decreases with the number of iterations. The step size factor is $\alpha_0 = 0.9$, the maximum attraction degree is $\beta_0 = 0.1$, the minimum attraction degree is $\beta_{min} = 0.1$, the medium absorption factor $\gamma = 1$, the step length α is adaptive, and it decreases with the increase of iteration times. Its update formula is:

$$\alpha = \alpha(10^*(-4)/\alpha_0) * (1/NGen) \tag{6}$$

where α_0 is 0.9, $NGen$ is the maximum number of iterations. Feasible range of u from $[-6, 2]$. to 10 portions of the feasible region, approximate step curve, state variables are obtained by Runge-Kutta method. The calculation of the value of the objective function with the trapezoidal method, two algorithms are run 10 times, the number of iterations is 100, and the population is 50, the optimal income value of the objective function respectively. 20.6512 and 19.4528, the control curve as shown in Figs. 1, 2. From the last best value, we can see that CFA is better than FA, but we must see that the solution to the system is numerically solved. Therefore, there will be errors in the solution process, and the error will also be diffused. But because the numerical method is consistent and only depends on the effect of optimization, CFA is indeed better than FA.

2.5   Solution of Dynamic Model of Chemical Reaction Process in Tubular Reactor

The performance of the algorithm is further analyzed by the application of the model of tubular reactor in reference [13]. The mathematical model is as follows:

$$\max J(z_f) = 1 - x_A(z_f) - x_B(z_f)$$

$$s.t. \begin{cases} \dfrac{dx_A}{dz} = u(z)[10x_B(z) - x_A(z)] \\[2mm] \dfrac{dx_B}{dz} = -u(z)[10x_B(z) - x_A(z)] \\[2mm] \qquad\qquad -[1 - u(z)]x_B(z) \\[2mm] \qquad 0 \leq u(z) \leq 1 \\[2mm] x_A(0) = 1, x_B(0) = 0, z_f = 12 \end{cases} \tag{7}$$

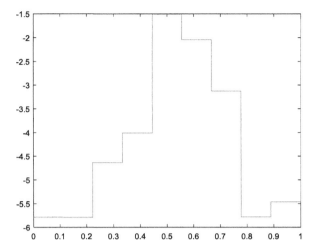

Fig. 1. The control curve obtained by the firefly algorithm.

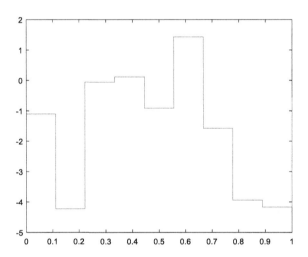

Fig. 2. Control curve obtained by cooperative firefly algorithm.

In the reactor, reaction of A occurs under the action of two kinds of catalysts. z is the length of the tubular reactor. $u(z)$ indicates the content of the first catalyst at the midpoint of the tube Z. The optimization purpose is to the catalyst. The optimal distribution is taken so that the concentration of the target product C is maximized at the end of the reaction. The results obtained are compared with the relevant literature, as shown in the following Table 1.

Table 1. Calculation results.

Method or Ref.	Discrete (N)	Performance (index)
Ref. [13]		0.476946
ACA [14]	4	0.47615
IGA [15]	100	0.4768
GA [16]	100	0.47668
IKBCA [17]	20	0.4753
	100	0.47768–0.47770
IKEA [16]	10	0.475
	20	0.4757
	100	0.47761–0.47768
CFA	10	0.473582 (NGen = 500)
	20	0.475933 (NGen = 700)
	100	0.4777903–0.47862 (NGen = 5000)

2.6   Analysis of Result

It is not easy to solve the dynamic optimization problem. From the results of the algorithm, this paper proposes that the CFA algorithm is effective, and with the increase of the sub-point, the result is better, which has a great relationship with the algorithm's collaborative local search. Some points of the method are not optimal, but one of the components is already the optimal component. In other searches, this component may be overlooked, and the collaborative search method is how to tap such components and make full use of it in the search process. In the lead role, and because it is an improvement on the single-dimensional progressive search. Therefore, this search method is also more suitable for solving high-dimensional optimization problems, so when the sub-point reaches 100, the result is ideal. In general, the performance of the algorithm is similar to that of other algorithms. However, considering that the system gives the solution to the state differential equations using numerical methods to solve the problem, the results of the algorithm have certain errors. But the results from the algorithm and other algorithms comparing the results, the results are still relatively satisfactory, which provides a feasible method for solving the problem.

3   Summary

The dynamic optimization of the chemical reaction process is a common problem in chemical process optimization. However, it is difficult to solve the problem numerically. The solving includes solving dynamic system which is differential equations and the integral calculation of the objective function, and has to control u(t) to achieve the goal of optimization, however, the relationship between u(t) and the goal cannot be obtained in general cases. Numerical simulation is a way of studying this kind of problem. This paper presents an alternative method to solve the dynamic optimization problem of chemical reactors, and the test results are good, but the research on this issue is far from over, but it is constantly exploring and advancing.

Acknowledgments. This work is supported by the Project supported by the National Natural Science Foundation of China (Grant No. 21466008, 21566007).

References

1. Matros, Y.S.: Unsteady-state Processes in Catalytic Reactor. Li Chengyue, Yan Zequn, trans. Science Press, Beijing, October 1994
2. Huang, Z., Wu, G.: Catalytic reaction processes and mechanism under forced oscillation. Chem. Eng. Prog. (5), 10–15 (1987)
3. Gong, X.: Computation Method for Optimal Control Problem. Science Press, Beijing (1979)
4. Zhong, H.: Mathematical Method of Optimal Control and Its Application. Jiangsu Science and Technology Press, Nanjing (1982)
5. Xiao, J., Zhou, Z.: Application of Ant colony optimization in beer fermentation control. Inf. Control **33**(4), 508–512 (2004)
6. Xu, F., Luo, X.: Mathematical description of dynamic analysis and control design of catalytic cracker regenerator based on dynamic optimization (I) dynamic optimization. J. Chem, Ind. Eng. **60**(3), 675–682 (2009)
7. Yang, X.S.: Nature-inspired Metaheuristic Algorithms. Luniver Press (2008)
8. Yang, X.-S.: Firefly algorithms for multimodal optimization. In: Watanabe, O., Zeugmann, T. (eds.) SAGA 2009. LNCS, vol. 5792, pp. 169–178. Springer, Heidelberg (2009). https://doi.org/10.1007/978-3-642-04944-6_14
9. Sayadi, M.K., Ramezanian, R., Ghaffari-Nasab, N.: A discrete firefly meta-heuristic with local search for make span minimization in permutation flow shop scheduling problems. Int. J. Ind. Eng. Comput. **1**(1), 1–10 (2010)
10. Srivatsava, P.R., et al.: Optimal test sequence generation using firefly algorithm. Swarm Evol. Comput. **8**, 44–45 (2013)
11. Horng, M.-H., Liou, R.-J.: Multilevel minimum cross entropy threshold selection based on the firefly algorithm. Expert Syst. Appl. **38**, 14805–14811 (2011)
12. Guo, L., Li, X., Gu, W.: Improved firefly algorithm to solve blocking pipeline scheduling problem. J. Intell. Syst. **8**(1), 33–38 (2013)
13. Roy, J.: Optimization of chemical reactors with respect to flow configuration. J. Optim. Theory Appl. **2**(4), 240–259 (1968)
14. Rajesh, J., Gupta, K., Kusumaker, H.S., Jayaraman, V.K., Kulkarni, B.D.: Dynamic optimization of chemical processes using ant colony framework. Comput. Chem. **25**(6), 583–595 (2001)
15. Zhang, B., Chen, D.: Iterative genetic algorithm and its application in feeding optimization of bioreactors. CIESC J. **56**(1), 100–104 (2005)
16. Peng, X., Geng, R., Du, W., Qian, F.: An improved knowledge evolution algorithm and its application in chemical industry dynamic optimization. J. Chem. Ind. Eng. **63**(3), 841–850 (2012)
17. Liu, Z., Du, W., Pei, R., Qian, F.: Culture algorithm based on knowledge improvement and its application in chemical industry dynamic optimization. CIESC J. **61**(11), 2889–2895 (2010)

Predator-Prey Behavior Firefly Algorithm for Solving 2-Chlorophenol Reaction Kinetics Equation

Yuanbin Mo[✉], Yanyue Lu, and Fuyong Liu

Guangxi University for Nationalities, Nanning 530006, Guangxi, China
674148582@qq.com

Abstract. 2-Chlorophenol is a kind of representative organic waste water. With the environmental pollution becoming increasingly serious, and the large amount of waste discharged and the increasing difficulty of treatment, the research on the kinetics of the oxidation of supercritical water of 2-chlorophenol has important significant. Aiming at the phenomenon that the Glowworm Swarm Optimization (GSO) algorithm has slow convergence, low precision and easy to get trapped into local optimum, this paper presents an improved version of the GSO based on the behavior of predator-prey and biological predator, and we call it dual population Glowworm Swarm Optimization (GSOPP). The algorithm accelerates the convergence speed by introducing strategies such as chase and escape and variation among populations, and can obtain a more accurate solution. Tested by three standard test functions, the results showed that the improved GSOPP algorithm had better performance than the basic GSO algorithm. Finally, the algorithm was applied to estimate the parameter estimation of the supercritical water oxidation kinetics of 2-chlorophenol, and satisfactory results were obtained.

Keywords: 2-chlorophenol · Reaction kinetics equation
Firefly algorithm (GSO) · Predator-prey behavior · Mutation strategy
Parameter estimation

1 Introduction

With the development of industrial and agricultural production, environmental pollution has become increasingly serious. The waste of the three wastes is large and the processing difficulty is increasing day by day. Among them, organic wastewater is the most difficult to handle. For most organic waste liquids, waste water and organic sludge, the supercritical water oxidation method has a fast reaction rate, complete oxidation, and a removal rate of 99.9% or more in a short residence time. Therefore, supercritical water oxidation is a promising technology for the treatment of organic pollution. The application of supercritical water oxidation technology to organic wastewater treatment, removal rate is the most important indicator, it is affected by the reaction temperature, reaction pressure, residence time, the amount of oxidant and the presence or absence of catalysts and other factors. Accurately estimating the reaction kinetic parameters can then accurately calculate the influence of the removal rate of

© Springer International Publishing AG, part of Springer Nature 2018
Y. Tan et al. (Eds.): ICSI 2018, LNCS 10941, pp. 453–462, 2018.
https://doi.org/10.1007/978-3-319-93815-8_43

each factor, thus laying the foundation for the design and optimization of industrial devices. The artificial firefly swarm optimization algorithm is a new swarm intelligence optimization algorithm. The algorithm is easy to fall into local extremum during the optimization performance process. Therefore, aiming at the problem of parameter estimation in this paper, it is proposed to use the predator-prey behavior to improve the algorithm and improve the performance of the algorithm. It can also be used to estimate the kinetic parameters of the supercritical water oxidation reaction of 2-chlorophenol.

2   2-Chlorophenol Supercritical Water Oxidation Kinetic Equation

The application of supercritical water oxidation technology to organic wastewater treatment is the most important indicator. The 2-chlorophenol is a representative organic wastewater, and its global reaction kinetics equation [1] is:

$$r_A = A \, exp\left(-\frac{E_a}{RT}\right)[2CP]^a[O_2]^b[H_2O]^c \tag{1}$$

In the formula, A, E_a, a, b and c are the kinetic parameters to be determined. A is the pre-factor, r_A is the reaction speed of 2-chlorophenol, E_a is the activation energy, R is the gas constant, T is the reaction temperature (°C), and $[2CP]$ is the reaction rate of 2-chlorophenol in the reactor, $[O_2]$ is the oxygen concentration in the reactor, $[H_2O]$ is the water concentration in the reactor, a is the 2-chlorophenol reaction order, and b is the reaction order of oxygen, c is the reaction order of water. The dependent variable is the 2-chlorophenol removal rate. Let the sample size be M and the measured value of the 2-chlorophenol removal rate of the is ample be r_i, the estimated value is r_i^*. The principle of parameter estimation is to minimize the value of EQS in Eq. (2), which is the objective function.

$$EQS = \sum_{i=1}^{M}\left(r_i - r_i^*\right)^2 \tag{2}$$

3   Firefly Algorithm (GSO)

Glowworm Swarm Optimization (GSO) is a new swarm intelligence optimization algorithm proposed by two Indian scholars Krishnanad and Ghose in 2005 [1, 2]. This algorithm is a group intelligent behavior that simulates the use of fluorescein information by fireflies. It has been successfully applied to sensor noise testing [3], simulation robot [4], numerical integration [5] and knapsack problem [6]. This algorithm is similar to other swarm intelligence algorithms. It has the advantages such as it doesn't require gradient information of the objective function, it is easy to implement and has strong robustness. However, it still has disadvantage with regard to slow convergence, low precision and easy to fall into local optima.

In the basic firefly algorithm, each fireflies carries Lucifer in with the same initial value and has its own decision domain. Each iteration consists of two phases, the Lucifer in update phase and the firefly motion phase.

Lucifer in renewal phase: During this phase, each fireflies updates Lucifer in according to the formula (3). The intensity of fluorescein is related to the corresponding fitness value at the position of the firefly. With the higher of luciferin, the location of the glowworm is better which means the fitness value is better.

$$l_i(t) = (1 - \rho)l_i(t - 1) + \gamma J(x_i(t)) \tag{3}$$

In the formula, $l_i(t)$ is the value of Lucifer for the i glowworm in t iteration, $\rho \in (0, 1)$ is the parameter for controlling the Lucifer in value, γ is the parameter for evaluating the function value, $x_i(t)$ is the position of the firefly i after the t iteration, and $J(x)$ is Fitness evaluation function.

Firefly movement phase: During this phase, fireflies i select neighbors with a certain probability (fireflies j need to be neighbors of fireflies i, fireflies must satisfy j within the decision domain of i and j have higher fluorochrome values than i). The firefly j moves toward it, and the probability selection formula is shown in Eq. (4). The position of firefly i is updated by Eq. (3), and the decision area is updated at the end of the exercise phase according to Eq. (4). Through the constant movement of the fireflies, more fireflies eventually gather around fireflies with higher fitness values. Path probability selection formula:

$$p_{ij}(t) = \frac{l_j(t) - l_i(t)}{\sum_{k \in N_i(t)} l_k(t) - l_i(t)} \tag{4}$$

Location update formula:

$$x_i(t + 1) = x_i(t) + s^* \left(\frac{x_j(t) - x_i(t)}{||x_j(t) - x_i(t)||} \right) \tag{5}$$

In the formula, $x_i(t) \in R^m$ denotes the position of Firefly i in the real space of m-dimension, $||\blacksquare||$ denotes the standard Euclidean distance operator, and $s > 0$ denotes the moving step. Decision domain update formula:

$$r_d^i(t + 1) = \min\{r_s, \max\{0, r_d^i(t) + \beta(n_t - |N_i(t)|)\}\} \tag{6}$$

In the formula, r_s is the perceived radius of the firefly, β is a proportionality constant, n_t is a parameter that controls the number of neighboring fireflies in the neighborhood, and $|N_i(t)|$ is the number of neighboring fireflies in the neighborhood of the fireflies.

4   GSO Algorithm Based on Predator-Prey Behavior

4.1   Biological Predator-Prey Behavior

The predator-prey behavior of biological populations is a common behavior in ecosystems. Predation is a phenomenon in which a species captures another species and consumes all or part of another species' body to obtain nutrition directly to maintain its own life. The former is called the predator, the latter is called the eater, also known as bait. In the long-term predation process, organisms form a predation strategy for hunting food, such as the exchange of pheromone among groups, the choice of easy-to-prey species [7–9], sneak attack, chase, and collective predation [10]. However, the prey species usually adopt three kinds of anti-hunting strategies such as concealment, avoidance and self-defense [11].

4.2   GSOPP Algorithm Model

Group intelligence algorithm is an algorithm designed to simulate biological behavior. Fully mining the characteristics of the creature and embedding it in the algorithm will help to improve the optimization performance of the algorithm and improve the ability of the algorithm to jump out of the local extremism. Predator's collective predation strategy and prey escaping strategy are embedded into the GSO algorithm. Fireflies are divided into two groups: predator and prey. A moving "nest" is set for each population. The center of the optimal 10 fireflies is centered, with the radius of the algorithm's initial search range being the radius. The predator population approaches the firefly of the prey population at a certain number of iterations. At this time, the prey population of fireflies' escapes from the individual of its closest predator group, thus being dispersed in a larger range, which is beneficial to the global search of the algorithm, called the GSOPP algorithm. In the algorithm, it is assumed that the better the fitness value of the prey population, the worse the physical quality, i.e., the poor ability to escape, can be easily captured.

In the GSOPP algorithm, predator predation strategies are simulated in the following three aspects: First, set a search range for the predator group fireflies (take 5% of the length of the search area). Second, the individuals of the predator group search for prey fireflies whose pre-existing values are better than their own value as prey, and select the prey object that has the best fitness value as the prey. Third, the predator's move to the prey is set to five times, if the predator finds a better position in the movement and stops moving, the predator thinks that the predation was successful. Otherwise, the predator fails. The formula for moving is shown in Eq. (7). If the predator does not search for prey or prey fails, the predator moves one step to the "nest" of the predator group. The length of the search range is moved to jump out of the area. The equation for moving is shown in Eq. (8). Since each predator attacks the prey with the best fitness value in the range, the prey can be the predation target of multiple predators, which reflects the collective predation behavior of the organism.

$$x_i^{k+1} = x_i^k + s^* \left(\frac{py_j - x_i^k}{||py_j - x_i^k||} \right) \tag{7}$$

$$x_i(t+1) = x_i(t) + d \frac{X}{|X|} \tag{8}$$

In the above formula, k is an integer from 0 to 4, x_i^{k+1} is the position of the predator i in the $k + 1$ th quarry, x_i^0 is the position of the predator i before moving to the prey, s is the step length, and py_j is the predator Prey position, $j(x)$ is the fitness function, d is the length of the predator search range, and X is the predator group nest.

The evasion strategy of the prey is manifested in the GSOPP: when the predator attacks the prey, the prey will issue a warning to inform the prey of the firefly to leave the predator's search range; the prey's fireflies are trying to avoid being preyed and try to be closest to themselves. The predator fireflies escaped and each fireflies set to their neighbors were approached once, in order from the highest fluorescein neighbor to the lowest neighbor, the equation is shown in (9). If the prey finds a better position in the process of flight, stops fleeing and thinks that it has escaped successfully, otherwise it flees and fails, and the prey is killed by the predator and is eliminated. In order to maintain the scale of the prey population, a new firefly is produced at the center of the eliminated fireflies' neighbors. If the fireflies are eliminated without neighbors, a new firefly is randomly generated within the prey population 'nest'.

$$x_i^{h+1} = x_i^h - s^* \left[\frac{dx_j - x_i^h}{||dx_j - x_i^h||} + \frac{x_i^{h+1} - x_i^h}{||x_i^{h+1} - x_i^h||} \right] J\left(x_j^h\right) \leq J\left(x_j^0\right) \tag{9}$$

Among them, x_i^{h+1} is the position of the firefly j in the prey population after the $h + 1$th neighbor to the neighbor, x_j^0 is the position of the prey firefly j before the predator, s is the step length, and dx_j is the firefly of the predator closest to the firefly j in the current distance from the prey population. In the position, x^h is the Lucifer in h firefly position in the neighborhood of Firefly j, and $J(x)$ is the fitness value function.

In order to improve the accuracy of the algorithm, this paper adopts a variable step size. If the predatory behavior occurs, the optimal position of the two groups does not change, and the step length is updated according to formula (10).

$$s = 0.9^w * s_0 + s_{min} \tag{10}$$

In the above equations, s is the current step size, s_0 is the initial step size, s_{min} is the lower limit of the step size, and w is the number of predation times where the optimal position of the two groups does not change after the predation behavior occurs.

When the firefly in the prey population is in a stagnant state, the predator firefly closest to it has no obvious effect of repelling it, and it cannot make it out of the local optimum, which will affect the performance of the algorithm. In this paper, the position variation method is used to increase the rejection effect. That is, if there is no change in the optimal positions of the 20 consecutive generations of prey populations during the iteration process, a firefly of prey is selected at random, and the position of the dimension in the dimension is selected randomly according to the formula (11). Variation occurs. Since the positional variation of a firefly that randomly selects prey does not disrupt the structure of the population, statistically speaking, each position of each firefly of prey mutates at the same probability.

$$x_{ik_j}(t) = 2r * x_{ik_j}(t) \tag{11}$$

In the above formula, $0 < k_j \leq m, x_{ik_j}(t)$ is the position of firefly i in k_j dimensions on the t iteration, which is a random number distributed uniformly between [0, 1].

4.3 The Flow of GSOPP Algorithm

The flow of the GSOPP algorithm can be briefly described as:

Step1 : Initialization. Initialize each parameter, randomly initialize the positions of the individuals of predator and prey within the target function search area;

Step2 : Calculate the optimal position of the population of two populations, update the fluorescein value according to formula (1);

Step3 : Determine whether the two populations meet the condition of rejection, i.e. if mod(t, K) = 0, execute Step4, and otherwise go to Step6;

Step4 : Calculate the position of the two nests, update the position of the predator population according to formula (7) or (8), update the position of the prey population according to formula (9), and generate a new firefly in the neighbor's center position or nest to replace the eliminated individual, Update the decision radius of each firefly in the two populations and move to the next step;

Step5 : Calculate the optimal position of the two groups. If there is no change, update the step according to formula (10); otherwise, go to Step7;

Step6 : Update the firefly information of two populations according to the basic GSO algorithm;

Step7 : Determine if the end condition is satisfied. If satisfied, the algorithm terminates and outputs the optimal solution; otherwise, go to Step2.

4.4 The Performance Test of the GSOPP Algorithm

4.4.1 Basic Test Functions

Select three basic test functions to test the performance of the GSOPP algorithm.

$$f_1 = \sum_{i=1}^{10} x_i^2 \tag{12}$$

$$f_2 = \sum_{i=1}^{10} \left[x_i^2 - 10\cos(2\pi x_i) + 10 \right] \tag{13}$$

$$f_3 = \frac{1}{4000} \sum_{i=1}^{10} x_i^2 - \prod_{i=1}^{10} \cos\left(\frac{x_i}{\sqrt{i}}\right) + 1 \qquad (14)$$

4.4.2   Algorithm Parameter Settings

In the GSO algorithm, the parameters use the common settings of the basic firefly algorithm (see Table 1). The number of populations is 60, and the step size is 3. In the GSOPP algorithm, the number of two populations is taken as 30, K is taken as 50, and the remaining parameters are set the same as the basic GSO.

Table 1. Parameter settings.

ρ	γ	β	n_t	l_0
0.4	0.6	0.08	5	5

4.4.3   Test Results

Both GSOPP and GSO run independently 20 times. The results obtained are shown in Table 2. Table 2 shows the best, worst, and average values of the two algorithms for solving each function. Figures 1, 2 and 3 depicts the average optimal value of the two algorithms in the process of solving each function.

Table 2. Comparison of the results of 20 tests of two algorithm.

Function	Algorithm	Worst	Average value	The optimal value
f_1	GSO	0.12356829	0.08951171	0.04300191
	GSOPP	5.029459e−07	1.251858e−07	3.748987e−10
f_1	GSO	21.62967483	11.56450137	5.24693823
	GSOPP	5.453582e−07	1.549574e−07	1.882350e−09
f_3	GSO	1.79858405	0.89537797	0.20542943
	GSOPP	1.589373e−06	1.173826e−07	6.725298e−11

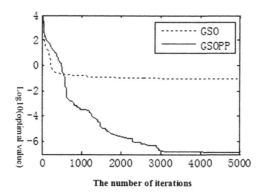

Fig. 1. The average optimal value change curve for Solution f_1.

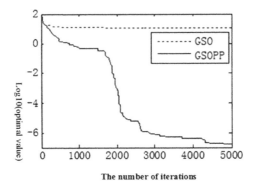

Fig. 2. The average optimal value change curve for Solution f_2.

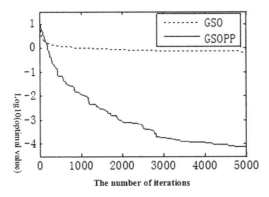

Fig. 3. The average optimal value change curve for Solution f_3.

From Table 2, it can be seen that the accuracy of the three basic test functions of the GSOPP algorithm is far better than that of the GSO.

5   GSOPP Estimation of Kinetic Parameters for the Supercritical Water Oxidation Reaction of 2-Chlorophenol

GSOPP was used to estimate the kinetic parameters of Eq. (1). The experimental data were taken from the literature [1]. The samples consisted of 62 groups including temperature, pressure, residence time, $[2CP]$, $[O_2]$, $[H_2O]$ and 2-chlorophenol. Removal rate, GSOPP parameter settings are shown in Sect. 4.4.2. The optimal value of GSOPP operation is EQS = 25.8875. The chaos genetic algorithm (CGA) is used in the literature [13], and the classical non-classification is used in [1]. Linear regression (NLR), literature [12] uses a hybrid genetic algorithm for parameter estimation. The results are shown in Table 3.

Table 3. Kinetic parameters estimation of 2 chlorophyll oxidation in supercritical water.

Method	A	E_a	a	b	c	EQS
GSOPP	95.12	44327	0.8083	0.4123	0.4314	**25.8875**
HACS [12]	63.5	45625.9	0.8081	0.4444	0.3239	**25.8921**
CGA [13]	70.4	45153.2	0.8181	0.4750	0.3267	**25.8920**
NLR [1]	**100.0**	**46200.0**	**0.8800**	**0.4100**	**0.3400**	**25.8920**

It can be seen from the table that the function value of the objective function is insensitive to the variable. In the case of large variation of the independent variable, the value of the function still changes very small, which is very difficult to find the optimal value. The results of the three algorithms also illustrate this problem. The results of the three algorithms are almost identical. The algorithm proposed in this paper has a greater improvement than the previous three results in terms of optimal results.

The estimation of chemical kinetic parameters is a common optimization problem. The form seems simple, its error response surface is often quite complex and has many local extreme. The conventional optimization algorithm is easily trapped in the local extreme region. The supercritical water oxidation kinetic parameters are estimated. The results indicate that GSOPP has a strong global search capability and has its place in parameter estimation.

6 Summary

The predator-prey behavior of organisms is embedded into the artificial firefly algorithm, and the population of the algorithm is divided into two populations. When searching, the number of iterations occur at intervals predatory behavior. At this point, the firefly of the Predator group continuously chases the best prey in its search range. Prey's fireflies continue to flee their nearest Predator fireflies while approaching their neighbors. This mechanism prey with better anti-predator behavior as a guide mechanism for the search, the algorithm has strong global search capability. And the algorithm obtained more satisfactory results in estimating 2-chlorophenol supercritical water oxidation reactor kinetic parameters.

Acknowledgments. This work is supported by the Project supported by the National Natural Science Foundation of China (Grant No. 21466008, 21566007).

References

1. Li, R., Savage, P.E., Szmukler, D.: 2-Chlorophenol oxidation in supercritical water: global kinetics and reaction products. AIChE J. **39**, 178–187 (1993)
2. Krishnanand, K.N., Ghose, D.: Glowworm swarm optimization: a new method for optimizing multi-modal functions. Int. J. Comput. Intell. Stud. **1**(1), 93–119 (2009)

3. Krishnanand, K.N.: Glowworm swarm optimization: a multimodal function optimization paradigm with applications to multiple signal source localization tasks. Indian Institute of Science [S. l.] (2007)
4. Krishnanand, K.N., Ghose, D.A.: Glowworm swarm optimization based multi-robot system for signal source localization. Berlin, Germany [s.n.] (2009)
5. Krishnanand, K.N., Ghose, D.: Chasing multiple mobile signal sources: a glowworm swarm optimization approach. In: Proceedings of the 3rd Indian International Conference on Artificial Intelligence [S. l.]. IEEE Press (2007)
6. Yang, Y., Zhou, Y.: Glowworm swarm optimization algorithm for solving numerical integral. Commun. Comput. Inf. Sci. **13**(4), 389–394 (2011)
7. Gong, Q., Zhou, Y., Yang, Y.: Artificial glowworm swarm optimization algorithm for solving 0-1 knapsack problem. Adv. Mater. Res. **144**(143), 166–171 (2011)
8. Shang, Y.: Predatory behaviour in animals. Bull. Biol. **36**(2), 13–14 (2001)
9. Ward, Z.: The importance of certain assemblages of iers as "information-center" for food finding. Ibis **115**, 517–531 (1973)
10. Roberts, D.: Imitation and suggestion in animals. Bull. Animal Behav. **1**, 11–19 (1941)
11. Yuan, M.: Animal predation strategy and anti-predator strategy. Educ. Sci. **6**(15), 87 (2009)
12. He, Y., Chen, D., Wu, X.: Estimation of kinetic parameters using hybrid ant colony system. J. Chem. Ind. Eng. (China) **56**(3), 487–491 (2005)
13. Yan, X., Chen, D., Hu, S., Ding, J.: Estimation of kinetic parameters using chaos genetic algorithms. J. Chem. Ind. Eng. (China) **53**(8), 810–814 (2002)

Hybrid Optimization Algorithms

A Hybrid Evolutionary Algorithm for Combined Road-Rail Emergency Transportation Planning

Zhong-Yu Rong, Min-Xia Zhang, Yi-Chen Du, and Yu-Jun Zheng[✉]

College of Computer Science and Technology,
Zhejiang University of Technology, Hangzhou 310023, China
`yujun.zheng@computer.org`

Abstract. As one of the most critical components in disaster relief operations, emergency transportation planning often involves huge amount of relief goods, complex hybrid transportation networks, and complex constraints. In this paper, we present a new emergency transportation planning model which combines rail and road transportation and supports transfer between the two modes. For solving the problem, we propose a novel hybrid algorithm that integrates two meta-heuristics, water wave optimization (WWO) and particle swarm optimization (PSO), whose operators are elaborately adapted to effectively balance the exploration and exploitation of the search space. Experimental results show that the performance of our method is better than a number of well-known heuristic algorithms on test instances.

Keywords: Emergency transportation planning
Water wave optimization (WWO) · Particle swarm optimization (PSO)
Hybrid algorithm

1 Introduction

Nowadays we are facing an increasing number of disasters, including floods, earthquakes, communicable diseases, terrorist attacks, etc., which can cause huge damages to people. Emergency transportation of disaster relief goods to the affected areas plays a crucial role in controlling and mitigating the damages after disasters. But unlike commercial transportation operations, emergency transportation operation planning has some special characteristics:

- There can be a huge amount of relief goods which are required to be delivered with restricted transport capacities and within a very limited time.
- The cost of transportation is not considered as a primary factor.
- Emergency transportation plans often have much higher priority than commercial ones.
- The environment can be dynamic, stochastic and hard to forecast.

© Springer International Publishing AG, part of Springer Nature 2018
Y. Tan et al. (Eds.): ICSI 2018, LNCS 10941, pp. 465–476, 2018.
https://doi.org/10.1007/978-3-319-93815-8_44

Emergency transportation planning problems are a special class of the general transportation problems, most of which are known to be NP-hard [3]. Thus, it is difficult for conventional mathematical optimization methods to solve medium- and large-size problem instances. To overcome this difficulty, many studies have been conducted on the use of evolutionary algorithms (EAs) to effectively solve the problems. Ding [6] modeled an emergency logistics distribution routing optimization problem to seek the shortest delivery time. They developed an improved ant colony algorithm that adds swarming behavior of artificial fish swarm algorithm (AFSA) [11] into ant colony optimization (ACO) [7] for path selection. Berkoune et al. [1] formulated an emergency transportation problem for minimizing the total transportation duration, and solved the problem using a genetic algorithm (GA) [9] that uses much less computational time than the exact CPLEX solver. Bozorgi et al. [2] introduced a new robust mixed-integer nonlinear programming (MINLP) model for disaster relief logistics problems. They developed a modified particle swarm optimization (PSO) [10] that uses discrete-continuous encoding method, and reinitializes several particles after running predetermined iterations to keep the diversity. In [20] Zheng et al. proposed a multi-objective fuzzy optimization problem of emergency transportation planning, where the uncertainty is tackled by three correlated fuzzy ranking criteria. They developed a cooperative evolutionary algorithm that divides the integrated problem into a set of subcomponents, evolves the sub-solutions concurrently, and brings together the sub-solutions to construct complete solutions. In [23] Zhou et al. presented another multi-objective optimization problem for multi-period dynamic emergency resource scheduling, and proposed a multi-objective evolutionary algorithm (MOEA) based on decomposition that uses simulated binary crossover (SBX) [4] operator and real mutation operator to optimize two objectives. However, most of the researches consider only one transportation mode (typically, road transportation). Interested readers can refer to [18] for a survey of meta-heuristic algorithms for emergency transportation problems.

In this paper, we consider a novel emergency transportation planning problem, where relief goods can be delivered not only via either road or rail, but also via a path that transfers between the two transportation modes. We then propose a hybrid optimization method that integrates two swarm intelligence algorithms, water wave optimization (WWO) [19] and PSO, to efficiently solve the problem. Experiments show that the hybrid algorithm outperforms a set of well-known heuristic algorithms on the test set.

In the rest of the paper, Sect. 2 formulates the problem, Sect. 3 proposes our algorithm, Sect. 4 gives the experimental results, and Sect. 5 concludes.

2   Problem Description

Our emergency transportation planning problem considers that there are a road transportation network $G = \langle N, E \rangle$ and a rail transportation network $G' = \langle N', E' \rangle$, where N and N' are nodes and E and E' are edges of the networks. We assume that $N' \subseteq N$, i.e., each rail node (station) is connected into the road network. For any two nodes i and j, we use d_{ij} and d'_{ij} to denote the road distance and rail distance between i and j, respectively.

We have a set I of supply sources and a set J of receiving targets ($I, J \subseteq N$). The quantity of relief goods required by each target j is r_j, and the quantity of relief goods that source i can provide is a_i. We also identify a set of $K \subset N'$ of intermediate rail stations, and thus consider the following four possible transportation modes from each $i \in I$ to each $j \in J$:

- Transportation from i to j directly by road.
- Transportation from i to j directly by rail, where $i \in N'$ and $j \in N'$.
- Transportation from i to an intermediate $k \in K$ by road and then from k to j by rail, where $i \in N \backslash N'$ and $j \in N'$.
- Transportation from i to an intermediate $k \in K$ by rail and then from k to j by road, where $i \in N'$ and $j \in N \backslash N'$.

For each $i \in I$ or $k \in K$, we use C_i or C_k to denote the maximum amount of goods that can be sent from i or k by road; for each $i \in I \cap N'$ or $k \in K \cap N'$, we use C'_i or C'_k to denote the maximum amount of goods that can be sent from i or k by rail.

The problem needs to determine the following decision variables:

- x_{ij}, the quantity of goods to be delivered from source i to destination j by road directly.
- x'_{ij}, the quantity of goods to be delivered from source i to destination j by rail directly.
- x_{ijk}, the quantity of goods to be delivered from source i through intermediate station k to destination j, first by road and then by rail.
- x'_{ijk}, the quantity of goods to be delivered from source i through intermediate station k to destination j, first by rail and then by road.

Time is the most critical factor in our emergency problem. The road and rail transportation time between two nodes i and j are empirically estimated as:

$$t_{ij} = (x_{ij})^\alpha d_{ij} \tag{1}$$
$$t'_{ij} = (x'_{ij})^{\alpha'} d'_{ij} \tag{2}$$

where α and α' are two positive constants less than 1. And the time for the transition from road mode to rail mode and that from rail to road are respectively estimated as:

$$\Delta t_{ijk} = (x_{ijk})^{\beta_k} \tag{3}$$
$$\Delta t'_{ijk} = (x'_{ijk})^{\beta'_k} \tag{4}$$

where β_k and β'_k are two positive constants less than 1 representing the loading/unloading capability of station k. Thus, the road-rail tand rail-road transportation time are respectively calculated as:

$$t_{ijk} = t_{ik} + \Delta t_{ijk} + t'_{kj} \tag{5}$$
$$t'_{ijk} = t'_{ik} + \Delta t'_{ijk} + t_{kj} \tag{6}$$

The objective of the problem is to minimize the quantity weighted arrival time of all relief goods, and the problem is formulated as follows:

$$\min\ f = \sum_{i \in I} \sum_{j \in J} \left(x_{ij} t_{ij} + x'_{ij} t'_{ij} + \sum_{k \in K} (x_{ijk} t_{ijk} + x'_{ijk} t'_{ijk}) \right) \tag{7}$$

s.t. Eqs. (1)–(6)

$$\sum_{i \in I} \left(x_{ij} + x'_{ij} + \sum_{k \in K} (x_{ijk} + x'_{ijk}) \right) \geq r_j, \quad j \in J \tag{8}$$

$$\sum_{j \in J} \left(x_{ij} + x'_{ij} + \sum_{k \in K} (x_{ijk} + x'_{ijk}) \right) \leq a_i, \quad i \in I \tag{9}$$

$$\sum_{j \in J} \left(x_{ij} + \sum_{k \in K} x_{ijk} \right) \leq C_i, \quad i \in I \tag{10}$$

$$\sum_{j \in J} \left(x'_{ij} + \sum_{k \in K} x'_{ijk} \right) \leq C'_i, \quad i \in I \cap N' \tag{11}$$

$$\sum_{i \in I} \sum_{j \in J} x_{ijk} \leq C'_k, \quad k \in K \tag{12}$$

$$\sum_{i \in I} \sum_{j \in J} x'_{ijk} \leq C_k, \quad k \in K \tag{13}$$

$$x_{ij}, x'_{ij}, x_{ijk}, x'_{ijk} \in \mathbb{Z}^+, \quad i \in I, j \in J, k \in K \tag{14}$$

To handle constraints (8)–(13), we define the following penalty functions:

$$P_1(j) = \begin{cases} 0, & \text{if } \sum_{i \in I} \left(x_{ij} + x'_{ij} + \sum_{k \in K} (x_{ijk} + x'_{ijk}) \right) \geq r_j \\ r_j - \sum_{i \in I} \left(x_{ij} + x'_{ij} + \sum_{k \in K} (x_{ijk} + x'_{ijk}) \right), & \text{else} \end{cases} \tag{15}$$

$$P_2(i) = \begin{cases} 0, & \text{if } \sum_{j \in J} \left(x_{ij} + x'_{ij} + \sum_{k \in K} (x_{ijk} + x'_{ijk}) \right) \leq a_i, \\ \sum_{i \in I} \left(x_{ij} + x'_{ij} + \sum_{k \in K} (x_{ijk} + x'_{ijk}) \right) - a_i, & \text{else} \end{cases} \tag{16}$$

$$P_3(i) = \begin{cases} 0, & \text{if } \sum_{j \in J} \left(x_{ij} - \sum_{k \in K} x_{ijk} \right) \leq C_i \\ \sum_{j \in J} \left(x_{ij} - \sum_{k \in K} x_{ijk} \right) - C_i, & \text{else} \end{cases} \tag{17}$$

$$P_4(i) = \begin{cases} 0, & \text{if } \sum_{j \in J} \left(x'_{ij} - \sum_{k \in K} x'_{ijk} \right) \leq C'_i \\ \sum_{j \in J} \left(x'_{ij} - \sum_{k \in K} x'_{ijk} \right) - C'_i, & \text{else} \end{cases} \tag{18}$$

$$P_5(k) = \begin{cases} \sum\limits_{i \in I} \sum\limits_{j \in J} x_{ijk} - C'_k, & \text{if } \sum\limits_{i \in I} \sum\limits_{j \in J} x_{ijk} > C'_k \\ 0, & \text{else} \end{cases} \tag{19}$$

$$P_6(k) = \begin{cases} \sum\limits_{i \in I} \sum\limits_{j \in J} x'_{ijk} - C_k, & \text{if } \sum\limits_{i \in I} \sum\limits_{j \in J} x_{ijk} > C_k \\ 0, & \text{else} \end{cases} \tag{20}$$

And thus the objective function is transformed to the following form (where M is large positive constant):

$$\begin{aligned} \min \; f = & \sum_{i \in I} \sum_{j \in J} \left(x_{ij} t_{ij} + x'_{ij} t'_{ij} + \sum_{k \in K} (x_{ijk} t_{ijk} + x'_{ijk} t'_{ijk}) \right) \\ & + M \Big(\sum_{j \in J} P_1(j) + \sum_{i \in I} (P_2(i) + P_3(i)) + \sum_{i \in I \cap N'} P_4(i) + \sum_{k \in K} (P_5(k) + P_6(k)) \Big). \tag{21} \end{aligned}$$

3   A Hybrid Evolutionary Algorithm for the Problem

We propose a hybrid EA combing WWO and PSO, denoted as CPS-WWO, to efficiently explore in the solution space of the problem. WWO [19] is a relatively new meta-heuristic, where each solution $\mathbf{x}$ is analogous to a wave, and its wavelength $\lambda_{\mathbf{x}}$ is set inversely proportional to its fitness. At each generation, WWO propagates each solution to a new position within the range proportional to $\lambda_{\mathbf{x}}$, such that better solutions can exploit smaller areas around them while worse solutions explore wider areas in the search space. WWO also has a refraction operator for improving the diversity and a breaking operator for performing intensive local search.

As most population-based EAs, our algorithm first randomly initializes a set of solutions, each being encoded as a $\big(|I||J| + |I \cap N'||J \cap N'| + |I||K||J \cap N'| + |I \cap N'||K||J|\big)$-dimensional vector like:

$$\underbrace{\{x_{1,1}, ..., x_{ij}, ...;}_{|I||J|} \underbrace{x'_{1,1}, ..., x'_{ij}, ...;}_{|I \cap N'||J \cap N'|} \underbrace{x_{1,1,1}, ..., x_{ijk}, ...;}_{|I||K||J \cap N'|} \underbrace{x'_{1,1,1}, ..., x'_{ijk}, ...\}}_{|I \cap N'||K||J|}$$

where each x_{ij}, x'_{ij}, x_{ijk} and x'_{ijk} are set as random values in $[0, \min(a_i, C_i)]$, $[0, \min(a_i, C'_i)]$, $[0, \min(a_i, C'_k)]$ and $[0, \min(a_i, C_k)]$, respectively.

For this problem, in order to increase the convergence speed, we adapt the WWO propagation operator by incorporating the PSO movement operator to evolve each solution $\mathbf{x}$ as follows:

$$v_{\mathbf{x}}(d) = w \cdot v_{\mathbf{x}}(d) + r_1 \cdot c \cdot \big(pbest_{f_d(\mathbf{x})}(d) - x(d) \big) \tag{22}$$

$$x'(d) = x(d) + v_{\mathbf{x}}(d) + r_2 \cdot \lambda_{\mathbf{x}} \cdot L(d) \tag{23}$$

where c is the PSO learning coefficient (set as 1.4944 as in [12]), r_1 and r_2 are two random numbers in $[0, 1]$, $pbest_x$ is the history personal best of $\mathbf{x}$, $L(d)$ is the length of the dth dimension of the search range, and the inertial weight w linearly decreases from an upper limit w_{max} to a lower limit w_{min} with generation [14]. Here, in (22) we use the comprehensive learning strategy of PSO [12], where at each dimension d $\mathbf{x}$ learns from a different exemplar solution $f_d(\mathbf{x})$ (determined as the winner of two randomly chosen solutions), which can avoid local optima more effectively than learning from $pbest_x$ and $gbest$ in the classical PSO [22].

After each generation, the wavelength of each $\mathbf{x}$ is updated as:

$$\lambda_{\mathbf{x}} = \lambda_{\mathbf{x}} \cdot \xi^{-(f(worst)-f(\mathbf{x})+\epsilon)/(f(worst)-f(gbest)+\epsilon)} \tag{24}$$

where ξ is a constant 1.0026 [19] and ϵ is a small value to avoid divide-by-zero.

During evolution, if a solution $\mathbf{x}$ does not improve its fitness over h_{max} (typically set to 12) consecutive generations, the refraction operator resets it to a new random solution to increase population diversity. When a new global best is found by propagation, the breaking operator conducts a local search around it by generating k_{max} (typically set to 12) neighboring solutions $\mathbf{x}'$ as:

$$x'(d) = x(d) + N(0,1) \cdot \gamma \cdot L(d) \tag{25}$$

where γ is the breaking coefficient, and $N(0,1)$ denotes a Gaussian random number with mean 0 and standard deviation 1. When producing a new solution, any float value will be rounded to the nearest integer, and any value situates outside the search range will be set to the nearest boundary value.

We also let the algorithm's population size n linearly decreases from an upper limit n_{max} to a lower limit n_{min} to better balance the exploration and exploitation [17]. Algorithm 1 shows the framework of the hybrid algorithm.

4   Computational Experiment

We test the performance of our CPS-WWO algorithm on a set of nine problem instances summarized in Table 1 (where D denotes the dimension of the problem, and the penalty constant M is set to 10000 for all the instances). Instances #1–#3 are derived from the 2010 Zhouqu mudslides, #4–#6 are from the 2008 Wenchuan earthquake, and the others are randomly generated.

The control parameters of CPS-WWO are tuned as $\gamma = 0.25$, $n_{max} = 50$, $n_{min} = 6$, $w_{max} = 0.5$ and $w_{min} = 0.1$. For comparison, we also implement the following seven algorithms (whose parameters are also fine-tuned):

- The PSO for integer programming [15]. The learning coefficients $c_1 = c_2 = 2$, $w_{max} = 0.9$ and $w_{min} = 0.4$.
- The basic WWO [19] (adapted for integer programming by rounding floats to the nearest integers), where $\gamma = 0.25$, $k_{max} = 12$, $h_{max} = 12$, and $n = 50$.
- The blended biogeography-based optimization (B-BBO) algorithm [13,16], whose maximum emigration rate and emigration rate are both set to 1.

Algorithm 1. The CPS-WWO algorithm for the considered problem.

---

1 Randomly initialize a population of n solutions;
2 **while** *stop criterion is not satisfied* **do**
3   **for** *each solution* $\mathbf{x}$ *in the population* **do**
4   Produce a new solution $\mathbf{x}'$ according to Eqs. (22) and (23);
5   **if** $f(\mathbf{x}') < f(\mathbf{x})$ **then**
6   **if** $f(\mathbf{x}') < f(gbest)$ **then**
7   Break $\mathbf{x}'$ into $k_{\max}$ neighboring solutions according to Eq. (25);
8   Update *gbest* with the best among $\mathbf{x}'$ and the neighboring solutions;
9   Replace $\mathbf{x}$ with $\mathbf{x}'$;
10   **else**
11   **if** $\mathbf{x}$ *has not been improved for* $h_{\max}$ *consecutive generations* **then**
12   Replace $\mathbf{x}$ with a new randomly generated solution;
13   Update $\lambda_{\mathbf{x}}$ according to Eq. (24);
14   Update w and n;
15 **return** the best solution found so far.

- The integer encoding differential evolution (IEDE) [5], whose scaling factor is 0.5 and crossover rate is 0.9.
- An improved integer coded genetic algorithm (ICGA) [8], whose crossover rate is 0.8 and mutation rate is 0.2.
- The ecogeography-based optimization (EBO) algorithm [21], whose maximum emigration rate and emigration rate are both set to 1, and the initial immaturity index is set to 0.8.
- The comprehensive learning PSO (CLPSO) [12], where $c = 1.49445$, $w_{\max} = 0.9$ and $w_{\min} = 0.4$.

The experiments are conducted on a computer of Intel Core i7-4510U processor and 8 GB memory. Each algorithm is run 50 times with different random seeds on each test instance, using the same termination condition that NFEs reaches $50D$ to ensure a fair comparison.

Table 2 presents the experimental results obtained by the eight algorithms on the instances, where "mean" denotes the average fitness value over the 50 runs, "std" is standard deviation, and "max" and "min" are the maximum and minimum fitness values of each algorithm among the 50 runs. The values in boldface indicate the best mean value and minimum value among the eight algorithms on each instance. We also perform nonparametric Wilcoxon rank sum tests between the results of CPS-WWO and each of the other algorithms on each instance, where h value of 1^+ indicates that the result of CPS-WWO significantly better than the corresponding algorithm with 95% confidence, 0 implies no difference and 1^- demonstrates worse.

On the smallest size instance #1, CPS-WWO, IEDE, CLPSO, and EBO obtain the same best mean value and minimum value; on the second smallest

Table 1. A summary of problem instances

Instance	$|I|$	$|J|$	$|K|$	D
#1	3	3	1	25
#2	4	3	3	58
#3	6	5	5	146
#4	8	6	7	396
#5	10	7	7	550
#6	12	7	9	840
#7	15	8	10	1325
#8	18	9	12	2106
#9	20	11	14	3300

instance #2, CPS-WWO obtains the best minimum value while EBO obtains the best mean value. On the remaining instances, CPS-WWO always uniquely obtains both the best mean value and best minimum values, which demonstrates that the proposed algorithm is the best among the eight comparative algorithms. Among the other seven algorithms, EBO exhibits the second best performance; IEDE exhibits the third best performance on instances #3–#6, but it is outperformed by most of the others on instances #7–#9, showing that IEDE is not suitable for large-size instances. In terms of statistical tests, the performance of CPS-WWO is significantly better than ICGA, B-BBO, PSO, and WWO on all the nine instances, better than EBO on eight instances, and better than IEDE and CLPSO on seven instances. Comparatively speaking, the performance gap between our CPS-WWO and the second best algorithm becomes more significant with the increase of instance size, which indicates that CPS-WWO has not only high efficiency but also good scalability for this problem.

The performance advantage of CLPSO over PSO is also significant, which is the reason why we use the comprehensive learning strategy in CPS-WWO. In general, the performance of WWO and CLPSO is not so superior to the other comparative algorithms, but their combination outperforms not only the two individual ones but also the others, which validates the effectiveness of the evolutionary operators of CPS-WWO we designed for the problem.

Figure 1 presents the convergence curves of the algorithms on the nine instances, where y-axis denotes the mean value and x-axis denotes the generations. As we can see, the convergence speed of CPS-WWO is not always the fastest. In fact, CPS-WWO converges very slow in the very early phase (approximately the first 10% or less of the whole running time, while B-BBO, PSO and ICGA converge fast in this stage), but its speed soon becomes very fast and overtakes all the others. The reason is that both the WWO propagation and CLPSO learning operators are not very effective in locating optima or near-optima very fast (as we can see that WWO and CLPSO also converge slow in the very early phase); but with the progress of evolution, more and more better

Table 2. The experimental results on the test instances

ID	Metric	ICGA	IEDE	PSO	B-BBO	WWO	CLPSO	EBO	CPS-WWO
#1	mean	2.70E+03	**2.20E+03**	2.23E+03	2.72E+03	2.29E+03	**2.20E+03**	**2.20E+03**	2.20E+03
	std	2.11E+02	0.00E+00	2.21E+03	6.26E+02	9.52E+01	0.00E+00	0.00E+00	0.00E+00
	max	3.06E+03	2.20E+03	2.27E+03	4.43E+03	2.45E+03	2.20E+03	2.20E+03	2.20E+03
	min	2.42E+03	**2.20E+03**	2.32E+03	2.27E+03	2.21E+03	**2.20E+03**	**2.20E+03**	2.20E+03
	h	1+	0	1+	1+	1+	0	0	
#2	mean	9.65E+03	4.65E+03	6.15E+03	6.85E+03	1.05E+04	4.46E+03	**4.10E+03**	4.16E+03
	std	2.95E+03	1.20E+02	4.81E+02	9.93E+02	2.98E+03	1.21E+02	7.48E+01	1.09E+02
	max	1.49E+04	4.77E+03	7.24E+03	9.32E+03	1.56E+04	4.67E+03	4.26E+03	4.38E+03
	min	6.25E+03	4.43E+03	5.58E+03	5.88E+03	7.31E+03	4.31E+03	4.03E+03	**4.01E+03**
	h	1+	0	1+	1+	1+	0	1−	
#3	mean	2.87E+04	7.40E+03	1.06E+04	1.26E+04	4.02E+04	7.30E+03	6.93E+03	**6.39E+03**
	std	1.16E+04	2.73E+02	5.36E+02	3.74E+03	1.22E+04	1.61E+02	2.21E+02	2.37E+02
	max	5.26E+04	8.00E+03	1.14E+04	2.21E+04	6.41E+04	7.54E+03	7.25E+03	6.77E+03
	min	1.09E+04	7.02E+03	9.77E+03	9.30E+03	2.74E+04	6.97E+03	6.69E+03	**5.96E+03**
	h	1+	1+	1+	1+	1+	1+	1+	
#4	mean	4.41E+04	7.05E+03	8.08E+03	1.46E+04	5.20E+04	7.41E+03	6.35E+03	**5.32E+03**
	std	2.34E+04	3.34E+02	3.27E+02	4.80E+03	8.77E+03	6.84E+02	1.41E+02	2.36E+02
	max	8.33E+04	7.70E+03	8.41E+03	2.29E+04	6.33E+04	8.44E+03	6.57E+03	5.71E+03
	min	2.38E+04	6.59E+03	7.53E+03	1.10E+04	3.63E+04	6.60E+03	6.13E+03	**4.94E+03**
	h	1+	1+	1+	1+	1+	1+	1+	
#5	mean	8.56E+04	1.14E+04	1.83E+04	4.01E+04	1.17E+05	1.68E+04	1.13E+04	**9.22E+03**
	std	1.79E+04	6.21E+02	2.06E+03	2.41E+04	3.75E+04	4.14E+03	4.30E+02	3.80E+02
	max	1.08E+05	1.23E+04	2.14E+04	8.97E+04	1.82E+05	2.27E+04	1.20E+04	9.52E+03
	min	5.40E+04	1.06E+04	1.49E+04	1.61E+04	7.68E+04	1.19E+04	1.08E+04	**8.30E+03**
	h	1+	1+	1+	1+	1+	1+	1+	
#6	mean	8.14E+04	1.96E+04	8.13E+03	3.46E+04	1.24E+05	7.16E+03	6.24E+03	**6.06E+03**
	std	1.97E+04	1.01E+04	6.09E+02	1.52E+04	3.28E+04	3.38E+02	1.14E+02	1.90E+02
	max	1.10E+05	4.26E+04	9.14E+03	6.70E+04	1.78E+05	7.54E+03	6.49E+03	6.39E+03
	min	4.86E+04	8.47E+03	7.35E+03	1.79E+04	7.77E+04	6.74E+03	6.11E+03	**5.75E+03**
	h	1+	1+	1+	1+	1+	1+	1+	
#7	mean	7.86E+05	6.90E+05	2.23E+05	4.92E+05	1.07E+06	2.92E+04	1.88E+04	**1.76E+04**
	std	1.71E+05	7.84E+05	1.53E+05	6.53E+04	2.17E+05	1.98E+03	8.19E+02	6.09E+02
	max	1.15E+06	2.20E+06	5.89E+05	6.12E+05	1.41E+06	3.19E+04	2.05E+04	1.89E+04
	min	6.04E+05	1.08E+05	3.85E+04	4.17E+05	7.83E+05	2.65E+04	1.77E+04	**1.66E+04**
	h	1+	1+	1+	1+	1+	1+	1+	
#8	mean	5.84E+05	1.04E+06	1.44E+05	5.89E+05	6.51E+05	5.56E+04	6.02E+04	**3.42E+04**
	std	1.23E+05	9.06E+04	1.68E+05	9.68E+04	9.73E+04	4.70E+04	3.49E+03	5.86E+03
	max	7.44E+05	1.15E+06	4.53E+05	7.75E+05	8.01E+05	1.88E+05	6.68E+04	4.93E+04
	min	3.47E+05	8.53E+05	3.42E+04	4.46E+05	5.10E+05	3.52E+04	5.49E+04	**2.95E+04**
	h	1+	1+	1+	1+	1+	1+	1+	
#9	mean	2.29E+06	4.18E+06	7.70E+05	7.93E+05	3.01E+06	1.08E+05	5.28E+04	**1.83E+04**
	std	3.19E+05	1.24E+05	6.17E+04	7.47E+04	3.76E+05	6.97E+04	5.86E+04	1.16E+03
	max	2.84E+06	4.29E+06	9.04E+05	9.50E+05	3.45E+06	1.96E+05	1.66E+05	2.02E+04
	min	1.81E+06	3.92E+06	6.93E+05	6.82E+05	2.35E+06	4.65E+04	2.24E+04	**1.72E+04**
	h	1+	1+	1+	1+	1+	1+	1+	

solutions are found, and the combined propagation-movement operator together with the breaking operator show good performance in not only producing more promising solutions but also avoiding being trapped in local optima. In general, the overall convergence speed of CPS-WWO is fast enough and is suitable for most emergency conditions.

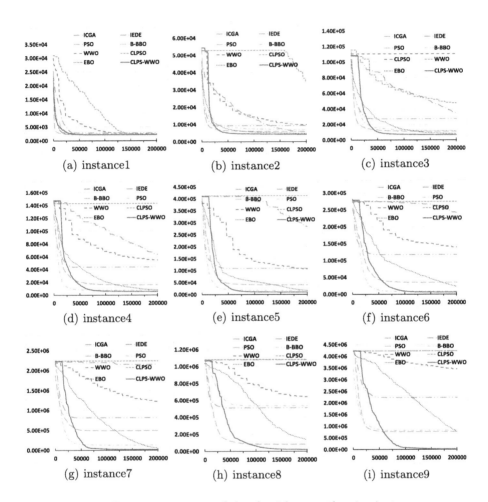

Fig. 1. Convergence curves of the algorithms on the nine instances.

5   Conclusion

The paper presents a new emergency transportation planning problem combining rail and road transportation, and proposes a hybrid algorithm integrating

WWO with CLPSO to efficiently solve the problem. Experimental results demonstrate the performance advantage of our hybrid algorithm over not only the two individual ones but also the other popular meta-heuristics.

Air transportation is another important mode in relief delivery, and it is often combined with road transportation but rarely combined with rail transportation. Ongoing work will studies an extended problem integrating the three modes and rail-road and air-road transfers. The algorithm is expected to be further improved for the extended problem.

Acknowledgments. This work is supported by National Natural Science Foundation (Grant No. 61473263) of China.

References

1. Berkoune, D., Renaud, J., Rekik, M., Ruiz, A.: Transportation in disaster response operations. Socio-Eco. Plan. Sci. **46**(1), 23–32 (2012)
2. Bozorgi, A.A., Jabalameli, M.S., Alinaghian, M., Heydari, M.: A modified particle swarm optimization for disaster relief logistics under uncertain environment. Int. J. Adv. Manuf. Technol. **60**(1), 357–371 (2012)
3. Bruno, J., Coffman, E.G., Sethi, R.: Scheduling independent tasks to reduce mean finishing time. Commun. ACM. **17**(7), 382–387 (1974)
4. Deb, K., Agrawal, R.B.: Simulated binary crossover for continuous search space. Comput. Syst. **9**(2), 115–148 (1995)
5. Deng, C., Yang, Y.: Integer encoding differential evolution algorithm for integer programming. In: International Conference Information Engineering and Computer Science, pp. 1–4 (2010)
6. Ding, H.: Research of emergency logistics distribution routing optimization based on improved ant colony algorithm. In: International Conference on Artificial Intelligence and Computational Intelligence, pp. 430–437 (2011)
7. Dorigo, M., Birattari, M., Stutzle, T.: Ant colony optimization. IEEE Comput. Intell. Mag. **1**(4), 28–39 (2006)
8. Golestani, S., Raoofat, M., Farjah, E.: An improved integer coded genetic algorithm for security constrained unit commitment problem. In: IEEE International Power Energy Conference, pp. 1251–1255 (2008)
9. Holland, J.H.: Adaptation in Natural and Artificial Systems: An Introductory Analysis with Applications to Biology, Control and Artificial Intelligence. MIT Press, Cambridge (1975)
10. Kennedy, J., Eberhart, R.: Particle swarm optimization. In: IEEE International Conference on Neural Networks, vol. 4, pp. 1942–1948 (1995)
11. Li, L.X., Shao, Z.J., Qian, J.X.: An optimizing method based on atonomous animats: fish-swarm algorithm. Syst. Eng. Theor. Pract. **22**(11), 32–38 (2002)
12. Liang, J.J., Qin, A.K., Suganthan, P., Baskar, S.: Comprehensive learning particle swarm optimizer for global optimization of multimodal functions. IEEE Trans. Evol. Comput. **10**(3), 281–295 (2006)
13. Ma, H., Simon, D.: Blended biogeography-based optimization for constrained optimization. Eng. Appl. Artif. Intell. **24**(3), 517–525 (2011)
14. Shi, Y., Eberhart, R.: A modified particle swarm optimizer. In: Proceedings of the IEEE World Congress on Computational Intelligence, pp. 69–73 (1998)

15. Tan, Y., Gao, H.M., Zeng, J.C.: Particle swarm optimization for integer programming. Syst. Eng. Theory. Pract. **24**(5), 126–129 (2004)
16. Wang, Z.C., Wu, X.B.: Hybrid biogeography-based optimization for integer programming. Sci. World J. **2014**(5), 672–983 (2014)
17. Zhang, B., Zhang, M.-X., Zhang, J.-F., Zheng, Y.-J.: A water wave optimization algorithm with variable population size and comprehensive learning. In: Huang, D.-S., Bevilacqua, V., Prashan, P. (eds.) ICIC 2015. LNCS, vol. 9225, pp. 124–136. Springer, Cham (2015). https://doi.org/10.1007/978-3-319-22180-9_13
18. Zhang, M.X., Zhang, B., Zheng, Y.-J.: Bio-inspired meta-heuristics for emergency transportation problems. Algorithms **7**(1), 15–31 (2014)
19. Zheng, Y.J.: Water wave optimization: a new nature-inspired metaheuristic. Comput. Oper. Res. **55**, 1–11 (2015)
20. Zheng, Y., Ling, H.: Emergency transportation planning in disaster relief supply chain management: a cooperative fuzzy optimization approach. Soft. Comput. **17**(7), 1301–1314 (2013)
21. Zheng, Y.J., Ling, H.F., Xue, J.Y.: Ecogeography-based optimization: enhancing biogeography-based optimization with ecogeographic barriers and differentiations. Comput. Oper. Res. **50**(10), 115–127 (2014)
22. Zheng, Y., Ling, H., Xue, J., Chen, S.: Population classification in fire evacuation: a multiobjective particle swarm optimization approach. IEEE Trans. Evol. Comput. **18**(1), 70–81 (2014)
23. Zhou, Y.W., Liu, J., Zhang, Y.T., Gan, X.H: A multi-objective evolutionary algorithm for multi-period dynamic emergency resource scheduling problems. Transp. Res. Part E. **99**, 77–95 (2017)

A Fast Hybrid Meta-Heuristic Algorithm for Economic/Environment Unit Commitment with Renewables and Plug-In Electric Vehicles

Zhile Yang[1], Qun Niu[2], Yuanjun Guo[1(✉)], Haiping Ma[3], and Boyang Qu[4]

[1] Shenzhen Institute of Advanced Technology,
Chinese Academy of Sciences, Shenzhen, China
`yj.guo@siat.ac.cn`
[2] School of Mechatronics and Automation, Shanghai University, Shanghai, China
[3] College of Mathematics, Physics and Information,
Shaoxing University, Shaoxing, China
[4] School of Electrical and Information Engineering,
Zhongyuan University of Technology, Zhengzhou, China

Abstract. To tackle with the urgent scenario of significant green house gas and air pollution emissions, it is pressing for modern power system operators to consider environmental issues in conventional economic based power system scheduling. Likewise, renewable generations and plug-in electric vehicles are both leading contributors in reducing the emission cost, however their integrations into the power grid remain to be a remarkable challenging issue. In this paper, a dual-objective economic/emission unit commitment problem is modelled considering the renewable generations and plug-in electric vehicles. A novel fast hybrid meta-heuristic algorithm is proposed combing a binary teaching-learning based optimization and the self-adaptive differential evolution for solving the proposed mix-integer problem. Numerical studies illustrate the competitive performance of the proposed method, and the economic and environmental cost have both been remarkably reduced.

1 Introduction

Paris climate conference have set an ambitious goal for human beings: to limit no more than 2 °C rise of temperature increase by the year 2050. The only way to realise this goal is to significantly reduce the fossil fuel consumption and green house gas emission. In this regard, power generation and transportation are both the foremost contributors. A holistic approach is to intelligently integrate significant renewable energy resources and plug-in electric vehicles into the thermal power generations [16]. Unit commitment (UC) is to minimize the economic cost by determining the 24-h power plant generation agenda, while maintaining several system constraints [1]. Current state-of-the-art methods for UC including conventional mathematical approaches involving dynamic programming [5],

© Springer International Publishing AG, part of Springer Nature 2018
Y. Tan et al. (Eds.): ICSI 2018, LNCS 10941, pp. 477–486, 2018.
https://doi.org/10.1007/978-3-319-93815-8_45

Lagrangian relaxation [3] and priority list [4], as well as the meta-heuristic methods such as genetic algorithm [1], particle swarm optimization (PSO) [11] etc. In addition to the real-valued optimization, binary optimization has also been utilized such as binary PSO [10] and binary GSA [19] etc. Multi-objective problems considering economic and emission have also been studied [2,13]. Though numerous of methodologies have been proposed, the inadequate results in stability and accuracy call for more powerful computational tools [15]. In addition, the significant integrations of new participants such as the renewable energy generations (REGs) and plug-in electric vehicles (PEVs) propose remarkable challenges for the operators.

The wind and solar power generations and the partly/fully coordinated plug-in electric vehicles provide opportunities for both reducing the thermal plant fuel costs and environmental emissions. However, the strong intermittent behaviours of renewable generations and unpredicted charging behaviours may lead to significant fluctuations, which call for a more intelligent and flexible scheduling method. Some researchers have integrated REGs and PEVs into the unit commitment to proposed intelligent method to analyse the economic factor [17] and emission factor [7,11]. The results remain conservative and the convergence speed is relatively slow. In this paper, an economic/environmental unit commitment problem considering substantial REGs and PEVs is proposed namely EEUCRP. A fast hybrid meta-heuristic algorithm (FHMA) is proposed, combining a binary teaching-learning based optimization, a self-adaptive differential evolution (SaDE) [6] and a lambda iteration method, for solving the novel EEUCRP problem. The algorithm performance in regarding both economic and emission sectors are evaluated and analyzed.

The rest of this paper is presented as follow: Sect. 2 formulates the EEUCRP problem, followed by the FHMA method proposed in Sect. 3. Section 4 presents the numerical study and analysis. Section 5 concludes the paper.

2   Problem Formulation

In this section, an EEUCRP problem is formulated considering two objectives including economic and emission costs and several system constraints such as power generation and power demand limits. The details of the EEUCRP problem is illustrated as following parts.

2.1   Objective Function

The objectives considered in this paper include the economic and emission sector respectively.

Fuel cost. Fuel cost occurs due to the burning of coal, gas and other fossil fuels in heating up the water. The detailed equation of fuel cost is shown as follow:

$$F_{j,t}^{fuel}(P_{j,t}) = a_j + b_j P_{j,t} + c_j P_{j,t}^2 \tag{1}$$

where $F_{j,t}^{fuel}$ and $P_{j,t}$ denote the cost of fuel and power output of the jth unit in the t time interval. a_j, b_j and c_j denote the cost coefficients.

Start-Up cost. Due to the complex psychical process of thermal plants, the start-up operation of a unit sees two piece-wise cost $SU_{j,t}$, denoted as cold start cost $SU_{C,j}$ and hot start cost $SU_{H,j}$. The hour of off-line duration $TOFF_{j,t}$ once exceeds the cold hour $T_{cold,j}$, an extra cost should be accounted for specific unit as shown below,

$$SU_{j,t} = \begin{cases} SU_{H,j}, \ if \ MDT_j \leq TOFF_{j,t} \leq MDT_j + T_{cold,j} \\ SU_{C,j}, \ if \ TOFF_{j,t} > MDT_j + T_{cold,j} \end{cases} \tag{2}$$

MDT_j and MUT_j are minimum down and up time. To accumulate the total economic cost, the totally T time (normally 24 h in day ahead schedule) is taken in to account as denoted below,

$$C_{eco} = \sum_{t=1}^{T} \sum_{j=1}^{n} [F_{j,t}^{fuel}(P_{j,t})u_{j,t} + SU_{j,t}(1 - u_{j,t-1})u_{j,t}] \tag{3}$$

where C_{eco} denotes the total economic cost. $u_{j,t}$ is the the binary decision variable of given units. Therefore, the decision variables are the real valued power output $P_{j,t}$ and binary $u_{j,t}$, both requires the proposed algorithm to be determine.

Emission cost. The emission cost is also modelled in a quadratic formulation denoted as below,

$$F_{j,t}^{emi}(P_{j,t}) = \alpha_j + \beta_j P_{j,t} + \gamma_j P_{j,t}^2 \tag{4}$$

where $F_{j,t}^{emi}$ is the emission cost while α_j β_j and γ_j denote the emission cost coefficients. The total emission cost C_{emi} is presented as below,

$$C_{emi} = \sum_{t=1}^{T} \sum_{j=1}^{n} [F_{j,t}^{emi}(P_{j,t})u_{j,t}] \tag{5}$$

Total cost. In a result, a total cost C_{total} consists of the economic and emission cost and is show below,

$$min \ C_{total} = C_{eco} + \omega C_{emi} \tag{6}$$

In the total cost equation, a weighting factor ω is defined to normalize the number scale of the proposed two objectives. Note that the units of the dual objectives are completely different, similar converted method have been used in the economic/emission load dispatch problem [7] to transfer the dual goals into a single one.

2.2   Constraints

Generation limit. Due to the power capacity of generators, the generation limited is modelled as follow,

$$u_{j,t}P_{j,min} \leq P_{j,t} \leq u_{j,t}P_{j,max} \tag{7}$$

where $P_{j,min}$ and $P_{j,max}$ are the minimum and maximum power output of jth.

Power demand limit. The demand limit equation is defined as follows,

$$\sum_{j=1}^{n} P_{j,t}u_{j,t} + P_{wind,t} + P_{solar,t} = P_{D,t} + P_{PEV,t} \tag{8}$$

$P_{D,t}$ is the predicted power demand at time t and $P_{PEV,t}$ denotes the power contribution of PEVs aggregator. $P_{wind,t}$ and $P_{solar,t}$ are wind and solar renewable power contributions respectively.

Spinning reserve limit. The $P_{D,t}$ is a predicted power and may witness some unexpected rise in the real application. In this regard, a spinning reserve limit is in need to provide sufficient reserve for real-time power balance, which is shown below,

$$\sum_{j=1}^{n} P_{j,max}u_{j,t} + P_{wind,t} + P_{solar,t} \geq P_{D,t} + SR_t + P_{PEV,t}. \tag{9}$$

where SR_t is the spinning reserve at t time slot. The inequality illustrates that the accumulated generations should exceed the proposed reserve capacity, ensuring the adequate power to meet up the unpredicted load.

Minimum up/down time limit. Coal based thermal units require relatively longer period to warm up and cool down when dispatched and therefore suffer minimum off-line and on-line time constraints denoted as below,

$$u_{j,t} = \begin{cases} 1, & if\ 1 \leq TON_{j,t-1} < MUT_j \\ 0, & if\ 1 \leq TOFF_{j,t-1} < MDT_j \\ 0\ or\ 1, & otherwise \end{cases} \tag{10}$$

where MUT_j and MDT_j denote the minimum up and down time. The binary decision variable is forcedly adjusted when the given limit is violated.

PEVs power limit. The PEVs interaction with the power system is practically aggregated acting as a flexible generator or controllable load. The PEVs power $P_{PEV,t}$ is another important decision variable in the problem formulation. In the PEVs power limit, the aggregator is deemed to provide sufficient power for PEVs users in daily use and the constraint is modelled as follow,

$$\sum_{t=1}^{T} P_{PEV,t} = P_{EV,total} \tag{11}$$

where the $P_{EV,total}$ is the total power that needs to be provided from the power grid. In the proposed EEUCRP problem, the maximum charging and discharging power boundary of PEVs aggregator is limited as follows:

$$P_{EVD,t,max} \geq P_{PEV,t} \geq P_{EVC,t,max} \tag{12}$$

In (12), the $P_{EVD,t,max}$ and $P_{EVC,t,max}$ denote the maximum charging and discharging power from/to the power system.

3   Proposed Fast Hybrid Meta-Heuristic Algorithm

In this paper, we propose a fast hybrid meta-heuristic algorithm (MA) combing a binary teaching-learning based optimization, a self adaptive differential evolution and a lambda iteration method for solving the EEUCRP complex problem.

3.1   Binary Teaching-Learning Based Optimization

Teaching learning based optimization is a recent proposed popular MA and has shown competitive performance in solving numerous engineering optimization problem [8,18]. A binary TLBO method is proposed in [14] and adopted in this research. Similar to the original TLBO, two phases are considered namely binary teacher phase and binary learner phase respectively.

Binary teacher phase utilize a best performance binary solution T_{bi} to act as a teacher to share his/her knowledge to the students as shown below,

$$V_{ij}^{new} = rand_1 \times (T_{bi} - L_F M_{bi}) \tag{13}$$

where the M_{bi} denotes the mean value of all the binary particles and V_{ij}^{new} denotes the new generated velocity. L_F is a integer learning factor selected as either 1 or 2. The novel velocity V_{ij}^{new} is then used in a binary transfer function to generate a new population of binary particles.

In addition to the binary teacher phase, a binary learner phase is presented to enable the interactions among students and shown as follow,

$$V_{ij}^{new} = rand_2 \times (V_{ik} - V_{ij}) \tag{14}$$

In the Eq. (14), V_{ij} and V_{ik} denote the current and another particles in the velocity population. The new generated V_{ij}^{new} from both phase will be used to generate binary particles by transferring the probability in selecting the binary variables Pr are defined in the transfer function shown as below,

$$Pr(V_{ij}^{new}) = |tanh(V_{ij}^{new})|; \tag{15}$$

Utilizing the proposed probability, the binary variable x_{ij} is denoted as below,

$$x_{ij} = \begin{cases} 1 - x_{ij}, & if \ rand_3 < Pr(V_{ij}^{new}) \\ x_{ij}, & otherwise \end{cases} \tag{16}$$

The binary TLBO aims to fast determine the binary on/off status of power units and provide fundamental binary solutions to the EEUCRP problem. Besides the binary optimization, the PEVs power generation also remains to be optimized, where we apply the popular self-adaptive differential evolution [6] for solving the problem, which is not detailed in this paper.

3.2   Proposed Fast Hybrid Meta-Heuristic Algorithm for EEUCRP Problem

The proposed EEUCRP problem is a mix-integer non-convex optimization problem bearing two types of real-valued variables and one type of binary variables. The proposed FHMA is illustrated as the following procedures:

1. Initialization:
   (a) Import power system data such as economic and environment coefficients of the units generation capacity, minimum up/down time, as well as power demand etc.;
   (b) Import wind and solar generation data, PEVs data and relevant constraints;
   (c) Initialize the number of particles Np, the maximum iteration number $Iter_{max}$ and the crossover and probability parameters of FHMA;
   (d) Generate a new population of particles for both Binary TLBO and SaDE, determine the binary statues according to the initial velocity;
   (e) Check the power system constraints (7)–(10) and PEVs constraints (11)–(12), update u_{ij} and $P_{PEV,t}$ to comply with the constraints;
2. FHMA process:
   (a) Calculate the objective function C_{total}, select the teacher for BTLBO;
   (b) Generate the V_{ij}^{new} according to the binary teaching phase (13);
   (c) Generate $P_{PEV,t}$ according to SaDE process;
   (d) Calculate the probability of each binary status Pr based on the Eq. (15);
   (e) Generate a new population u_{ij} according to the (16);
   (f) Check the power system constraints (7)–(10), PEVs constraints (11)–(12) and update the population to prevent violating the constraints;
   (g) Calculate the objective function C_{total}, and reserve the better particles;
   (h) If the iteration is less than $iter_{max}$, go back to 2-a, otherwise, go to the end.

The detailed constraints handling method are referred to [17], where the lambda iteration method is integrated for solving the economic load dispatch for online units.

4   Numerical Results and Analysis

The proposed FHMA method is designed for solving the EEUCRP problem, which considers multiple power system participants and is therefore intractable to be solved. We analyse two cases in the paper: the economic only case and the economic and environmental case. The well adopted 10 unit benchmark system [9] is employed to analyse the economic and environmental factor.

4.1   Case 1: Economic only UC

In this case, we only consider the economic factor in the EEUCRP analysis. The number of particles Np of FHMA method is set as 20 and the maximum iteration number $iter_{max}$ is as 100 due to the double function evaluations of TLBO. To eliminate the randomness, 10 different trails are adopted in the test. The mutation factor F and crossover rate CR for SaDE is set as 0.8 and 0.3 respectively. In regarding the plug-in electric vehicles, 50000 PEVs are supposed to be online and joining in the coordinated charging and discharging aggregator service. To demonstrate the significant optimization ability, we adopt the Case 1-1 to compare with the results in [12], where all the PEVs are supposed to be the grid support one with 0 MW power required from the grid and no renewable generations are integrated. Suppose 20% of PEVs users are willing to provide the service and each PEV is equipped with a 15 kWh battery. An average of 50% state of charge are available for the PEVs to discharge. Also it should be noted that the power electronics devices may suffer a 15% power cost and 85% charging and discharging efficiency is assumed. In this case maximum charging and discharging capacity of PEVs are +63.75 MW and −63.75 MW respectively.

On the other hand in Case 1–2, in order to compare the algorithm performance, we adopt the data from [10], where the wind generation varies from 0 to 25.50 MW and the maximum solar generation is 38.06 MW along 24 h. The results of the both cases have been presented in Table 1, where the best, worst and average results are shown. The both sub-cases are tested in an Intel Core i7-6700 CPU with 2.4 GHz and 8 GB RAM system.

Table 1. Case 1: Numerical results for EEUCRP problem with economic only factor

Scenario ($/day)	GA-LR [12]			FHMA		
	Cost ($/day)			Cost ($/day)		
	Best	Worst	Mean	Best	Worst	Mean
Case 1–1: No REG	561821	566281	564050	561527	566206	563750
Scenario ($/day)	BPSO-IPSO [10]			FHMA		
	Cost ($/day)			Cost ($/day)		
	Best	Worst	Mean	Best	Worst	Mean
Case 1–2: With REG	553172	-	-	541501	545590	543678

It could be observed from the Table 1 that the proposed FHMA out performs the GA-LR [12] method in PEVs integration Case 1–1 test on all the best, worst and average results. In addition, a more significant result improvement could be found in Case 1–2 compared with BPSO-IPSO [10] method. In the both tests, the proposed FHMA method has a 294 \$/day saving in Case 1–1 and 11671 \$/day cost reduction in Case 1–2. The result distributions of 10 trials achieve by FHMA is shown in Fig. 1. In Fig. 1, the results of two sub-cases distributes evenly within the range of a few thousands, which is lower than 2% in regarding the deviations, showing strong stability of the proposed methods. The computational time is averagely 9.03 s, which is significantly faster than the previous UC tests.

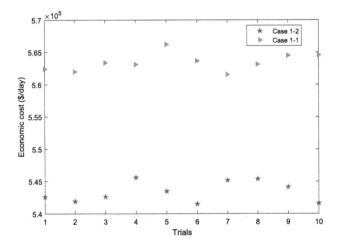

Fig. 1. Result distributions of 10 trials in Case 1 by FHMA method

4.2   Case 2: Economic and Emission UC

In Case 2, the proposed FHMA method is eventually applied for solving the EEUCRP problem. The power system data including the emission coefficients could be found in [2]. The renewable settings and PEVs relevant parameters are the same with the Case 1. However, we assume that the PEVs, besides providing power buffer service, request power to support the everyday use. The average travelling distance is 32.88 miles [16], equivalent to 8.22 kWh power necessity per day for a single PEV. Therefore, a total 411 MW power is required to support the daily commute of PEVs. To investigate the impact of different selections of weighting factor ω on the economic and emission performance, we choose the weighting factor ω as 0.1, 0.2, 0.5, 1, 2, 5 and 10, and each test with 10 independent trials. The optimal results of economic, emission and total costs are illustrated in Table 2.

It could be observed in Table 2 that the results are various under different selections of weighting factor ω. The optimal economic cost among all the scenarios are 550313 \$/day in $\omega = 5$, while the minimum emission achieved is

Table 2. Case 2: Result of different selection ω for EEUCRP problem

ω	C_{eco} ($/day)		C_{emi} (lb/day)		C_{total}	
	Best	Worst	Best	Worst	Best	Worst
0.1	550818	554245	72310	73360	558154	561476
0.2	551418	555809	71910	73146	565985	570235
0.5	550912	554341	72248	73118	587270	590575
1	550533	554367	72390	73381	623739	626852
2	552605	555752	72271	72862	697968	700578
5	550313	554259	72456	73066	915191	918945
10	551059	554574	72300	72972	1277303	1283231

71910 lb/day. Comparing with the results in Case 1, the results not only achieve an optimal cost for both economic and emission, but also provide sufficient power for PEVs daily use. This have shown the effectiveness of the proposed FHMA method, which provides a useful tool for solving the complex power system scheduling problem.

5   Conclusion

In this paper, a novel fast hybrid meta-heuristic method is proposed for solving the economic/emission unit commitment problem considering the renewable energy generations and plug-in electric vehicles. The novel FHMA algorithm combining a binary teaching-learning based optimization method, a self adaptive differential evolution method to solve the sub-problem of economic load dispatch. Numerical study have shown the competitive performance of the problem comparing with the state-of-the-art method for solving integrated UC problem. The both economic and emission cost are reduced by integrating the renewable generations and flexible charging and discharging of plug-in electric vehicles.

Acknowledgment. This paper is financially supported by National Science Foundation of China (No. 51607177, 61773252, 61673404).

References

1. Kazarlis, S.A., Bakirtzis, A., Petridis, V.: A genetic algorithm solution to the unit commitment problem. IEEE Trans. Power Syst. **11**(1), 83–92 (1996)
2. Li, Y.F., Pedroni, N., Zio, E.: A memetic evolutionary multi-objective optimization method for environmental power unit commitment. IEEE Trans. Power Syst. **28**(3), 2660–2669 (2013)
3. Ongsakul, W., Petcharaks, N.: Unit commitment by enhanced adaptive lagrangian relaxation. IEEE Trans. Power Syst. **19**(1), 620–628 (2004)

4. Osório, G., Lujano-Rojas, J., Matias, J., Catalão, J.: A new scenario generation-based method to solve the unit commitment problem with high penetration of renewable energies. Int. J. Electr. Power Energy Syst. **64**, 1063–1072 (2015)
5. Padhy, N.: Unit commitment using hybrid models: a comparative study for dynamic programming, expert system, fuzzy system and genetic algorithms. Int. J. Electr. Power Energy Syst. **23**(8), 827–836 (2001)
6. Qin, A., Huang, V., Suganthan, P.: Differential evolution algorithm with strategy adaptation for global numerical optimization. IEEE Trans. Evol. Comput. **13**(2), 398–417 (2009)
7. Qu, B., Zhu, Y., Jiao, Y., Wu, M., Suganthan, P., Liang, J.: A survey on multi-objective evolutionary algorithms for the solution of the environmental/economic dispatch problems. Swarm Evol. Comput. **38**, 1–11 (2018)
8. Rao, R., Savsani, V., Vakharia, D.: Teaching-learning-based optimization: a novel method for constrained mechanical design optimization problems. Comput.-Aided Des. **43**(3), 303–315 (2011)
9. Saber, A.Y., Venayagamoorthy, G.K.: Intelligent unit commitment with vehicle-to-grid—a cost-emission optimization. J. Power Sources **195**(3), 898–911 (2010)
10. Saber, A.Y., Venayagamoorthy, G.K.: Plug-in vehicles and renewable energy sources for cost and emission reductions. IEEE Trans. Industr. Electron. **58**(4), 1229–1238 (2011)
11. Saber, A.Y., Venayagamoorthy, G.K.: Resource scheduling under uncertainty in a smart grid with renewables and plug-in vehicles. IEEE Syst. J. **6**(1), 103–109 (2012)
12. Talebizadeh, E., Rashidinejad, M., Abdollahi, A.: Evaluation of plug-in electric vehicles impact on cost-based unit commitment. J. Power Sources **248**, 545–552 (2014)
13. Trivedi, A., Srinivasan, D., Pal, K., Saha, C., Reindl, T.: Enhanced multiobjective evolutionary algorithm based on decomposition for solving the unit commitment problem. IEEE Trans. Industr. Inform. **11**(6), 1346–1357 (2015)
14. Yang, Z., Li, K., Zhang, L.: Binary teaching-learning based optimization for power system unit commitment. In: 2016 UKACC 11th International Conference on Control (CONTROL), pp. 1–6, August 2016
15. Yang, Z., Li, K., Foley, A.: Computational scheduling methods for integrating plug-in electric vehicles with power systems: a review. Renew. Sustain. Energy Rev. **51**, 396–416 (2015)
16. Yang, Z., Li, K., Niu, Q., Xue, Y.: A comprehensive study of economic unit commitment of power systems integrating various renewable generations and plug-in electric vehicles. Energy Convers. Manage. **132**, 460–481 (2017)
17. Yang, Z., Li, K., Niu, Q., Xue, Y.: A novel parallel-series hybrid meta-heuristic method for solving a hybrid unit commitment problem. Knowl.-Based Syst. **134**, 13–30 (2017)
18. Yang, Z., Li, K., Niu, Q., Xue, Y., Foley, A.: A self-learning TLBO based dynamic economic/environmental dispatch considering multiple plug-in electric vehicle loads. J. Mod. Power Syst. Clean Energy **2**(4), 1–10 (2014)
19. Yuan, X., Ji, B., Zhang, S., Tian, H., Hou, Y.: A new approach for unit commitment problem via binary gravitational search algorithm. Appl. Soft Comput. **22**, 249–260 (2014)

A Hybrid Differential Evolution Algorithm and Particle Swarm Optimization with Alternative Replication Strategy

Lulu Zuo[1], Lei Liu[1], Hong Wang[1(✉)], and Lijing Tan[2(✉)]

[1] College of Management, Shenzhen University, Shenzhen 518060, China
ms.hongwang@gmail.com
[2] College of Management, Shenzhen Institute of Information Technology,
Shenzhen 518172, China
mstlj@163.com

Abstract. A new hybrid algorithm, combining Particle Swarm Optimization (PSO) and Differential Evolution (DE), is presented in this paper. In the proposed algorithm, an alternative replication strategy is introduced to avoid the individuals falling into the suboptimal. There are two groups at the initial process. One is generated by the position updating method of PSO, and the other is produced by the mutation strategy of DE. Based on the alternative replication strategy, those two groups are updated. The poorer half of the population is selected and replaced by the better half. A new group is composed and conducted throughout the optimization process of DE to improve the population diversity. Additionally, the scaling factor is used to enhance the search ability. Numerous simulations on eight benchmark functions show the superior performance of the proposed algorithm.

Keywords: Particle Swarm Optimization · Differential evolution algorithm
Alternative replication strategy

1 Introduction

Particle Swarm Optimization (PSO), proposed by Kennedy and Eberhart [1], is a well-known global intelligence optimization algorithm. On the basis of individual perception and social perception, the particles of PSO are replaced to enhance the speed of convergence and search accuracy in every iteration. Since then, many modifications have been developed. A recent version of modification was to update the particle positions by using two selected functions and combining individual experiences to avoid getting into the local optimum [2]. A fitness function was defined in [3] to identify the parameters of nonlinear dynamic hysteresis model. To a certain extent, the algorithm improves the convergence of the progress. However, a common problem occurring in the simulation experiments is still the premature clustering in the early part of iteration procedure.

Differential Evolution (DE) [4] is a population-based method of function optimization like Genetic algorithm (GA), including mutation, crossover, and selection. In DE, new individuals are generated from the information of multiple previous

© Springer International Publishing AG, part of Springer Nature 2018
Y. Tan et al. (Eds.): ICSI 2018, LNCS 10941, pp. 487–497, 2018.
https://doi.org/10.1007/978-3-319-93815-8_46

individuals to get out of stagnation. Hence, some improved DE algorithms are proposed for getting better consequents. An improvement of DE with Taguchi method of sliding levers had the powerful ability of global search and obtained a better solution [5]. The fuzzy selection operation was used in an improved DE to reduce the complexity of multiple attribute decisions and enhance population diversity [6]. Though the DE has some advantages in global optimization, there is a dependency on controlling parameters which are not easy to decide when confronting high-dimensional complex problems.

In view of the advantages and disadvantages of PSO and DE, many hybrid algorithms of PSO and DE are described to combine the advantages of both and better solve various practical problems. The hybrid PSO and DE with population size reduction (HPSODEPSR) [7] can achieve optimal or near optimal solution faster than other comparison algorithms. The Bacterial Foraging Optimization (BFO) hybridized [8] with PSO and DE was introduced to effectively handle the dynamic economic dispatch problem. In order to improve the diversity and make each subgroup achieve a different optimal solution in the range of fitness values, Zuo and Xiao [9] used a hybrid operator and multi-population strategy performing the PSO and DE operation in turn. A novel hybrid algorithm PSO-DE [10] jumped out of stagnation, increased the speed of convergence and improved the algorithm's performance. A modified algorithm hybridizing PSO and DE with an aging leader and challengers was advanced to find the optimal parameters of PID controller quickly [11]. Though those hybrid algorithms improve the performance of the original algorithms (i.e. PSO and DE), premature stagnation is still a major problem.

This paper presents a novel hybrid algorithm of PSO and DE (DEPSO) with alternative replication strategy to overcome the above-mentioned problems. In the proposed algorithm, population is separated into two groups which are generated by two different methods, i.e. velocity updating strategy of PSO and mutative strategy of DE. A novel population are produced according to alternative replication strategy. The poor half of the population is eliminated while the other half is reproduced for the new evolution. In order to enhance the diversity of the population, the scaling factor of DEPSO is adjusted according to the linear decreasing rule.

The remaining paper is organized as follows. A brief introduction of PSO algorithm and DE algorithm is provided in Sect. 2. In Sect. 3, the hybrid algorithm of PSO and DE with alternative and replication strategy is described in detail. Section 4 gives experimental results of the Simulations on benchmark functions. Finally, the conclusion is presented in Sect. 5.

2   Description of Algorithms

2.1   Particle Swarm Optimization

In standard PSO algorithm, a group of particles flies in the search space to find the optimal location. The particles are given random positions x and velocities v in the initiate progress. In each iteration, the best position of each particle $pbest_{id}$ and the best position of global $gbest_{id}$ are learnt, which leads the particle to the new position. Equations (1)–(2) are the updated rule [1]:

$$v_{id}^{G+1} = \omega v_{id}^G + c_1 rand(0,1)(pbest_{id}^G - x_{id}^G) + c_2 rand(0,1)(gbest_{id}^G - x_{id}^G) \quad (1)$$

$$x_{id}^{G+1} = x_{id}^G + v_{id}^{G+1}, i = 1,..,N, d = 1,...,D \quad (2)$$

$$\omega = \omega_{max} - (\omega_{max} - \omega_{min}) * G/G_{max} \quad (3)$$

where x_{id} and v_{id} are the position and velocity of the ith particle, respectively, N is the number of particles, and D is the dimensions of search space, c_1 and c_2 are acceleration factors. Finally, ω is the inertia weight adjusted by Eq. (3) in [12], ω_{max} and ω_{min} are the maximum and the minimum value of inertia weight, respectively. G and G_{max} are the current number of iteration and the maximum number of iteration, separately.

2.2   Differential Evolution Algorithm

DE, proposed by Storn and Price [4], has the significant effect on solving application problems. The outline of DE can be described as follows:

Step 1: initialize individuals according to the upper and lower bounds of search space, and evaluate the fitness of each individual.
Step 2: compare the fitness of every individual and record the best individual.
Step 3: generate new vectors through mutation process. The mutation rule is as follows Eq. (4):

$$v_i = x_{r1} + F(x_{r2} - x_{r3}), i = 1,..,N \quad (4)$$

where N is the number of individuals, x_i is the ith individual and v_i is the updated i^{th} vector through mutating. F is the scaling factor, r_1, r_2 and r_3 not equal to each other are randomly selected from $[1, N]$.

Step 4: cross populations and mutant vectors to get a trial vector. Equation (5) is the crossover formula:

$$u_{ij} = \begin{cases} v_{ij} & if\,(rand_j(0,1) \le CR)\,or\,j = j_{rand} \\ x_{ij} & otherwise \end{cases}, j = 1...D \quad (5)$$

where D is the number of parameters, while u_{ij} represents the ith individual at the jth search space after crossing operation. CR is the crossover probability, and j_{rand} is a randomly selected index in the range of $[0, D]$.

Step 5: The greedy algorithm (i.e. Eq. (6)) is used to select individuals for the next iteration process.

$$x_i = \begin{cases} u_i & \text{if } f(u_i) \leq f(x_i) \\ x_i & \text{otherwise} \end{cases} \tag{6}$$

3 DEPSO Algorithm with Alternative Replication Strategy

Due to rapid information search, the suboptimal solutions might be more frequently obtained by PSO. Different from the PSO, population of DE tends to be more diversity as the number of iterations increases but consumes more computational complexity. To take advantages of those two algorithms, in this paper, a new hybrid DEPSO method is proposed to improve the search capability of particles with smaller computational time.

For the purpose of preventing individuals from sinking into suboptimal solution, we use the following alternative replication strategy to optimize the initial particles of each iteration.

At the beginning of each iteration, a new group P_1 is generated by PSO algorithm (i.e. Eqs. (1)–(2)). Considering the optimal value of every individual x_{pbest}, another group P_2 is renewed by the mutation process of DE algorithm (i.e. Eq. (7)). Based on the fitness value, we compare the updated groups (i.e. P_1 and P_2) with the initial group P_0 and preserve the better individuals to form new P_1 and P_2.

$$x_i = F(x_{pbest} - x_i) + F(x_{r4} - x_{r5}), \ i = 1 \dots N \tag{7}$$

where N is individuals' number, x_i is the i individuals, F is the scaling factor, and r_4 and r_5 are indexes selected from $[1, N]$.

Sort the individuals of new groups (i.e. P_1 and P_2) according to the fitness values, and the sorted groups are also compared to retain the superior individuals constituting a group P_3. The new group P_3 eliminates half of the individuals with poor fitness values, and the rest of the individuals are reproduced to keep the number of individuals.

In order to overcome the shortcoming of population reduction, the mutation factor decreases linearly with the number of iterations increasing in the mutation procedure. The scaling factor is controlled in Eq. (8).

$$F = F_{\max} - (F_{\max} - F_{\min}) * G/G_{\max} \tag{8}$$

where F_{max}, F_{min}, G, and G_{max} are the maximum mutation factor, minimum mutation factor, the current number of iteration and the maximum number of iteration, respectively.

Finally, DE algorithm is re-simulated based on the group which is obtained using the alternative replication strategy. The scheme of DEPSO is described as follows in detail:

Step 1:   initialize the position and velocity of every individual, and generate initial group P_0.

Step 2:   calculate the fitness of each individual, and evaluate the best solution of each individual *pbest* and the best solution of all individuals *gbest*.

Step 3:   update the position and velocity of individuals using Eqs. (1)–(2), and generate new group P_1.

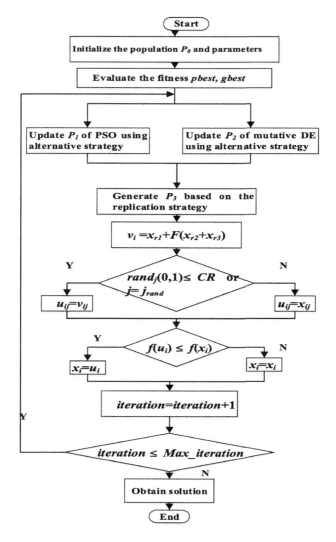

Fig. 1. Flowchart of DEPSO

Step 4:   mutate the initial individuals (i.e. Eq. (7)) and introduce a new group P_2.
Step 5:   calculate the fitness of two groups (i.e. P_1 and P_2), and compare the fitness with the initial group P_0 to update the groups P_1 and P_2, respectively.
Step 6: P_1 and P_2 are sorted based on the fitness. A new group P_3 is constituted of the superb individuals in the comparison of the sorted groups. The group P_3 is updated by alternative replication strategy.
Step 7:   new vectors are formed by the group P_3 in the light of mutation process (i.e. Eq. (4)).
Step 8:   Equation (5) is applied to get trial vectors through the crossover of individuals and mutant vectors in DE algorithm.
Step 9:   select the best individuals using Eq. (6) and new offspring P_0 are introduced to execute the iterative procedure. Figure 1 presents the flowchart of DEPSO.

4   Experiments and Analysis

4.1   Benchmark Functions and Algorithms

To verify the performance of the proposed DEPSO algorithm, eight benchmark functions [13] (i.e. Sphere f_1, SumPowers f_2, Rosenbrock f_3, Quartic f_4, Rastrigin f_5, Griewank f_6, Ackley f_7, Schwefel2.22 f_8) are applied to test the improved algorithm. One important reason for choosing these eight functions is that they contain unimodal functions (i.e. f_1, f_2, f_3, and f_4) and multimodal functions (i.e. f_5, f_6, f_7, and f_8). Additionally, these functions are minimum problems and the minimum value is known to be zero. The performance of DEPSO is demonstrated through eight benchmark functions and compared with some classic algorithms, i.e. PSO, DE, Genetic algorithm (GA) [14], Artificial Bee Colony algorithm (ABC) [15, 16], and Bacterial Foraging Optimization (BFO) [17]. All functions are tested on these optimization algorithms through MATLAB R2014a software.

4.2   Experimental Parameters

The similar parameters of six optimization algorithms are set as follows: the size of the population is 50, the maximum iterative number is set to 5000. Each function is run 30 times with the search space dimension 30, 50, and 80. The parameters of GA, ABC and BFO are from [18] except the reproduction's number of BFO is 25. More parameters setting of PSO, DE and DEPSO are shown as follows: In PSO, $c_1 = c_2 = 2$, $\omega_{max} = 0.9$, and $\omega_{min} = 0.4$; In DE, $CR = 0.5$, and F ranges from 0.4 to 0.9; In DEPSO, c_1, c_2, ω_{max} and ω_{min} are the same as PSO. CR and F are the same as DE. The values are the results of multiple simulations.

Table 1. Experiment results on benchmark functions

Funs.	D	Ret.	PSO	DE	GA	ABC	BFO	DEPSO
f_1	30	mean	4.73E−33	1.86E−40	2.76E−06	1.47E−17	3.98E−01	**0.00E+00**
		std	1.43E−32	1.86E−40	2.07E−06	2.62E−17	8.93E−02	**0.00E+00**
	50	mean	4.75E−14	2.03E−16	6.49E−04	2.02E−02	4.36E−01	**0.00E+00**
		std	6.19E−14	6.72E−17	8.40E−06	2.49E−03	6.02E−01	**0.00E+00**
	80	mean	5.83E−05	3.26E−05	4.12E−02	6.91E+03	1.01E+00	**0.00E+00**
		std	6.91E−05	4.26E−07	1.01E−02	5.58E+02	1.42E+00	**0.00E+00**
f_2	30	mean	3.34E−58	1.90E−81	3.43E−07	3.89E−01	1.54E−04	**0.00E+00**
		std	4.39E−58	2.66E−81	2.37E−07	4.81E−01	2.17E−04	**0.00E+00**
	50	mean	1.53E−12	4.18E−26	5.25E−07	5.31E+09	2.06E−04	**0.00E+00**
		std	1.99E−12	5.86E−26	2.64E−09	5.03E+09	2.91E−04	**0.00E+00**
	80	mean	1.92E+09	2.42E+00	4.25E−07	1.55E+28	1.08E−03	**0.00E+00**
		std	2.64E+09	1.02E+00	3.64E−08	1.04E+28	1.52E−03	**0.00E+00**
f_3	30	mean	6.15E+01	**2.11E+01**	7.79E+01	5.56E+01	4.92E+01	2.63E+01
		std	4.87E+01	**2.53E−01**	7.07E+01	4.29E+01	2.78E+01	1.80E+00
	50	mean	1.24E+02	4.60E+01	9.47E+01	5.28E+07	1.02E+02	**4.53E+01**
		std	1.11E+02	3.62E−01	3.22E+01	1.08E+07	7.46E+01	**1.79E−01**
	80	mean	3.36E+02	1.57E+02	2.37E+02	3.46E+09	1.84E+02	**7.69E+01**
		std	4.59E+01	5.97E+00	1.07E+02	6.57E+08	1.48E+02	**9.56E−01**
f_4	30	mean	4.79E−48	3.79E−61	7.06E−17	2.69E−17	1.25E−01	**0.00E+00**
		std	6.20E−48	4.01E−61	1.43E−17	2.91E−17	1.77E−01	**0.00E+00**
	50	mean	5.84E−20	1.07E−24	7.39E−12	3.46E−01	9.02E−01	**0.00E+00**
		std	8.03E−20	9.60E−25	4.91E−13	2.38E−01	1.28E+00	**0.00E+00**
	80	mean	1.63E−08	1.99E−09	7.48E−09	1.83E+01	3.34E+00	**0.00E+00**
		std	1.69E−08	9.76E−10	2.52E−09	2.18E+00	4.73E+00	**0.00E+00**
f_5	30	mean	4.90E+01	1.31E+03	1.76E+01	1.94E+03	3.66E+02	**0.00E+00**
		std	2.59E+01	1.29E+02	6.53E−01	3.11E+01	5.17E+02	**0.00E+00**
	50	mean	1.50E+02	3.76E+03	2.31E+02	5.41E+03	5.78E+02	**0.00E+00**
		std	4.27E+01	4.86E+02	1.98E+02	3.31E+02	8.17E+02	**0.00E+00**
	80	mean	4.02E+02	8.44E+03	1.72E+03	1.07E+04	1.39E+03	**0.00E+00**
		std	3.02E+01	3.43E+02	4.60E+02	3.05E+02	1.96E+03	**0.00E+00**
f_6	30	mean	**0.00E+00**	**0.00E+00**	7.75E−03	1.74E−11	1.04E−02	**0.00E+00**
		std	**0.00E+00**	**0.00E+00**	1.07E−02	2.46E−11	1.41E−02	**0.00E+00**
	50	mean	9.86E−03	**0.00E+00**	1.20E−02	1.73E−01	2.19E−02	**0.00E+00**
		std	5.66E−14	**0.00E+00**	1.95E−03	1.03E−01	3.05E−02	**0.00E+00**
	80	mean	9.77E−02	2.86E−05	1.68E−01	6.18E+01	2.55E−02	**0.00E+00**
		std	1.24E−01	1.15E−05	2.54E−02	1.84E+00	3.57E−02	**0.00E+00**

(*continued*)

Table 1. (*continued*)

Funs.	D	Ret.	PSO	DE	GA	ABC	BFO	DEPSO
f_7	30	mean	1.15E−14	4.44E−15	3.46E+00	3.74E−09	6.76E−01	**8.88E−16**
		std	5.02E−15	0.00E+00	6.07E−01	2.38E−09	8.28E−01	**0.00E+00**
	50	mean	5.77E−07	3.39E−09	5.58E+00	2.74E−01	7.49E−01	**8.88E−16**
		std	7.10E−07	2.87E−10	7.20E−01	1.72E−01	9.64E−01	**0.00E+00**
	80	mean	1.98E−02	1.13E−03	4.15E+00	1.14E+01	8.33E−01	**4.44E−15**
		std	1.37E−02	1.75E−04	1.44E+00	8.78E−02	1.11E+00	**0.00E+00**
f_8	30	mean	1.26E−21	3.59E−24	2.22E+00	3.42E−15	1.85E+00	**0.00E+00**
		std	1.76E−21	1.92E−24	2.06E−01	1.25E−15	2.01E+00	**0.00E+00**
	50	mean	8.29E−11	3.03E−10	2.10E+00	1.77E−04	3.59E+00	**0.00E+00**
		std	3.55E−11	2.39E−11	2.47E−01	3.58E−06	4.27E+00	**0.00E+00**
	80	mean	1.08E−04	1.09E−03	2.88E+00	9.71E+00	5.93E+00	**0.00E+00**
		std	1.03E−04	4.51E−05	9.88E−01	9.38E−01	7.34E+00	**0.00E+00**

4.3   Experiment Results and Discussion

To get experiment results, all benchmark functions are executed by coding these search methods. The mean fitness value and the standard deviation obtained by six optimization algorithms are displayed in Table 1. The bold type is used to underline the best of all the numerical results attained by comparing six optimization algorithms. Figure 2 lists the convergence curves of different test functions gotten by all the algorithms with the dimension 50. In Fig. 2, in order to make the curves clear, the results are the logarithm with base 10.

As shown in Table 1, DEPSO algorithm almost gets the optimal mean and standard deviation among all the algorithms for the eight benchmark functions. It means that the hybrid DEPSO algorithm is better than other algorithms in terms of search accuracy. Additionally, the proposed algorithm obtains the minimum values (i.e. zero) on functions of Sphere, SumPowers, Quartic, Rastrigin, Griewank, and Schwefel2.22. It means that the convergence precision of the DEPSO algorithm is high in the selected functions.

In terms of dimensionality, the DEPSO can perform better than other algorithms when the dimension is increasing. From Fig. 2, we can conclude the convergent speed of DEPSO algorithm is significantly faster than other algorithms and the convergent results are closer to optimal values. Altogether, the performance of DEPSO algorithm performs better whether in unimodal functions or in multimodal functions.

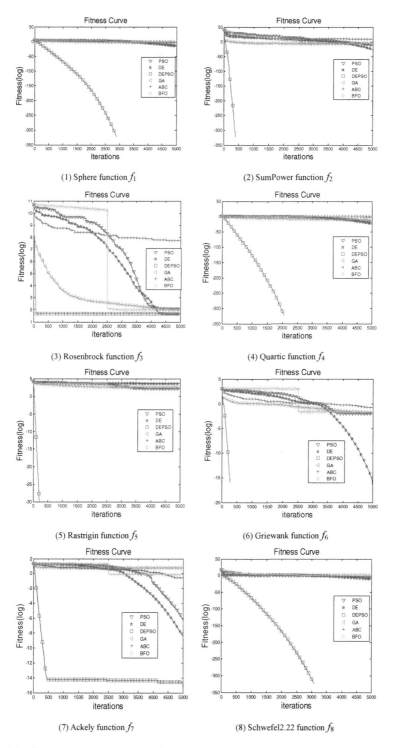

(1) Sphere function f_1

(2) SumPower function f_2

(3) Rosenbrock function f_3

(4) Quartic function f_4

(5) Rastrigin function f_5

(6) Griewank function f_6

(7) Ackely function f_7

(8) Schwefel2.22 function f_8

Fig. 2. The iteration process of the algorithms when the dimensionality is 50

5   Conclusion

A hybrid algorithm integrating the advantages of PSO and DE is proposed in this paper. The results show that the DEPSO algorithm outperforms other algorithms in terms of mean and standard deviation. Though DE with nonlinearly decreasing mechanism of scaling factor can obtain the similar solutions on some benchmark functions (e.g., Rosenbrock and Rastrigin), the convergence speed is not good than the proposed DEPSO method. Thus, the proposed alternative replication strategy can enhance the performance of the hybrid algorithm. Our future study will focus on the application of the proposed algorithm to solve the real-world problems and more hybrid methods will be developed to obtain better solutions.

Acknowledgment. This work is partially supported by The National Natural Science Foundation of China (Grants No. 61472257), Natural Science Foundation of Guangdong Province (2016A030310074), Guangdong Provincial Science and Technology Plan Project (No. 2013B040403005), and Research Foundation of Shenzhen University (85303/00000155).

References

1. Kennedy, J., Eberhart, R.C.: Particle swarm optimization. In: IEEE International Conference on Neural Networks, Piscataway, pp. 1942–1948 (1995)
2. Guedria, N.B.: Improved accelerated PSO algorithm for mechanical engineering optimization problems. Appl. Soft Comput. **40**(40), 455–467 (2016)
3. Zhang, J., Xia, P.: An improved PSO algorithm for parameter identification of nonlinear dynamic hysteretic models. J. Sound Vib. **389** (2016)
4. Storn, R., Price, K.: Differential evolution – a simple and efficient heuristic for global optimization over continuous spaces. J. Global Optim. **11**(4), 341–359 (1997)
5. Tsai, J.T.: Improved differential evolution algorithm for nonlinear programming and engineering design problems. Neurocomputing **148**, 628–640 (2015)
6. Pandit, M., Srivastava, L., Sharma, M.: Environmental economic dispatch in multi-area power system employing improved differential evolution with fuzzy selection. Appl. Soft Comput. **28**, 498–510 (2015)
7. Ali, A.F., Tawhid, M.A.: A hybrid PSO and DE algorithm for solving engineering optimization problems. Appl. Math. Inf. Sci. **10**(2), 431–449 (2016)
8. Vaisakh, K., Praveena, P., Rao, S.R.M.: A bacterial foraging PSO — DE algorithm for solving reserve constrained dynamic economic dispatch problem. In: 2011 IEEE International Conference on Fuzzy Systems, pp. 153–159 (2011)
9. Zuo, X., Xiao, L.: A DE and PSO based hybrid algorithm for dynamic optimization problems. Soft. Comput. **18**(7), 1405–1424 (2014)
10. Liu, H., Cai, Z., Wang, Y.: Hybridizing particle swarm optimization with differential evolution for constrained numerical and engineering optimization. Appl. Soft Comput. **10**(2010), 629–640 (2010)
11. Moharam, A., El-Hosseini, M.A., Ali, H.A.: Design of optimal PID controller using hybrid differential evolution and particle swarm optimization with an aging leader and challengers. Appl. Soft Comput. **38**, 727–737 (2016)
12. Shi, Y., Eberhart, R.: A modified particle swarm optimizer. In: Proceedings of IEEE International Conference Evolutionary Computation, Anchorage, pp. 69–73 (1998)

13. Niu, B., Liu, J., Zhang, F., Yi, W.: A cooperative structure-redesigned-based bacterial foraging optimization with guided and stochastic movements. In: Huang, D.-S., Jo, K.-H. (eds.) ICIC 2016. LNCS, vol. 9772, pp. 918–927. Springer, Cham (2016). https://doi.org/10. 1007/978-3-319-42294-7_82

14. Holand, J.H.: Adaption in natural and artificial systems. Control Artif. Intell. **6**(2), 126–137 (1975)

15. Karaboga, D.: An idea based on honey bee swarm for numerical optimization. Engineering Faculty, Computer Engineering Department, Erciyes University, Technical report - TR06 (2005)

16. Karaboga, D., Basturk, B.: A powerful and efficient algorithm for numerical function optimization: Artificial Bee Colony (ABC) algorithm. J. Global Optim. **39**(3), 459–471 (2007)

17. Passino, K.M.: Biomimicry of bacterial foraging for distributed optimization and control. IEEE Control Syst. **22**(3), 52–67 (2002)

18. Wang, H., Zuo, L., Liu, J., Yang, C., Li, Ya., Baek, J.: A comparison of heuristic algorithms for bus dispatch. In: Tan, Y., Takagi, H., Shi, Y., Niu, B. (eds.) ICSI 2017. LNCS, vol. 10386, pp. 511–518. Springer, Cham (2017). https://doi.org/10.1007/978-3-319-61833-3_54

A Hybrid GA-PSO Adaptive Neuro-Fuzzy Inference System for Short-Term Wind Power Prediction

Rendani Mbuvha[1,3]([✉]), Ilyes Boulkaibet[1], Tshilidzi Marwala[1],
and Fernando Buarque de Lima Neto[2]

[1] School of Electrical and Electronic Engineering,
University of Johannesburg, Johannesburg, South Africa
rendani.mbuvha@wits.ac.za, {ilyesb,tmarwala}@uj.ac.za
[2] School of Engineering, University of Pernambuco, Recife, Brazil
fbln@ecomp.poli.br
[3] School of Statistics and Actuarial Science,
University of Witwatersrand, Johannesburg, South Africa

Abstract. The intermittency of wind remains the greatest challenge to its large scale adoption and sustainability of wind farms. Accurate wind power predictions therefore play a critical role for grid efficiency where wind energy is integrated. In this paper, we investigate two hybrid approaches based on the genetic algorithm (GA) and particle swarm optimisation (PSO). We use these techniques to optimise an Adaptive Neuro-Fuzzy Inference system (ANFIS) in order to perform one-hour ahead wind power prediction. The results show that the proposed techniques display statistically significant out-performance relative to the traditional backpropagation least-squares method. Furthermore, the hybrid techniques also display statistically significant out-performance when compared to the standard genetic algorithm.

Keywords: ANFIS · GA · PSO · Hybrid GA-PSO · Wind power Prediction

1 Introduction

The main reservation around large scale adoption of wind energy is its intermittency as energy production is directly dependent on uncertain future atmospheric conditions [3]. Forecasting of short term wind energy production has thus become critical to operations management and planning for electricity suppliers [11]. Such forecasts can then be used for proactive reserve management and energy market trading to ensure that electricity load demands are optimally met [11,13].

Generally, statistical and machine learning methods have become increasingly prominent in wind power forecasting. These are mainly based on using historical wind power output to refine Numerical Weather Predictions (NWP)

© Springer International Publishing AG, part of Springer Nature 2018
Y. Tan et al. (Eds.): ICSI 2018, LNCS 10941, pp. 498–506, 2018.
https://doi.org/10.1007/978-3-319-93815-8_47

into localised predictions for the wind farms in question. Adaptive Neuro-Fuzzy Inference Systems (ANFIS) have also been prominent in wind power prediction literature. The authors in [4] propose a two stage ANFIS with the first stage refining the NWP winds speeds and while the second uses the refined wind speed estimate for wind power prediction. The authors in [9] compare ANFIS and ANNs in power predictions. Other techniques have included Bayesian Neural Networks [11], Classification and Regression Trees, Support Vector Regression and Random Forests [5]. A comprehensive review of the current state-of-the-art methods in wind power forecasting is given in [17].

There has also been work in creating hybrids between the genetic algorithm (GA) and particle swarm optimisation (PSO). A hybrid algorithm is proposed in [6], where randomly selected particles from the PSO are evolved using GA and returned to the PSO for further optimisation. The authors in [19] propose randomly partitioning the particle population into sections where PSO and GA are applied independently, and the results are then combined then re-partitioned after every iteration.

The objective of this paper is to investigate two hybrid GA-PSO algorithms, we then apply these two algorithms for training an ANFIS model for one-hour ahead wind power prediction. The rest of the paper is arranged as follows: Sect. 2 introduces our proposed hybrid GA-PSO algorithm and sets-out the ANFIS optimisation problem. Section 3 gives the experiment setup. Section 4 provides and discusses the results of the experiments. Section 5 gives the conclusions and possible future work.

2   Methods

In this paper, two hybrid methods based on GA and PSO are investigated in predicting one-hour ahead wind power production based on an ANFIS model.

2.1   Genetic Algorithm

The GA is inspired by the biological process of natural selection. In GA candidate solutions are individuals within the population. Each individual's fitness is evaluated on the basis of a cost function. At each iteration, three evolutionary procedures, selection, crossover and mutation, are executed in order to obtain a global minimum. First, certain individuals are sampled from the population (the selection step) for a crossover where parts of the selected individuals are randomly exchanged. Next, another set of randomly selected individuals are also mutated. In this paper, a continuous GA is used to optimise the parameters of the ANFIS model where the mutation is performed by adding a Gaussian noise to randomly selected parts of the vector of the unknown parameters. The process continues until the algorithm converge or a specified maximum number of iterations is executed.

2.2   Particle Swarm Optimisation

The PSO is one of the most recognised meta-heuristic optimisation algorithms which inspired by the natural process of flocking of birds in search for food. In the PSO algorithm, each particle in a swarm is considered as a candidate solution of the optimisation problem. In this algorithm, the position of each particle is updated in each iteration using the following equation:

$$P_{i+1} = P_i + V_{i+1} \tag{1}$$

Here V_{i+1} the particle's velocity which is updated by:

$$V_{i+1} = w_0 V_i + c_1 r_1 (P_{best} - P_i) + c_2 r_2 (G_{best} - P_i) \tag{2}$$

where w_0 is the inertia weight which maintains the previous velocity. c_1 is the particle's acceleration constant towards its personal best solution P_{Best}, while c_2 is the acceleration of the particle towards the best known position amongst all particles. r_1 and r_2 are randomly selected from a uniform distribution $U(0,1)$ to add randomness to the search space exploration. These updates continue until the algorithm converges or a specified maximum number of iterations is executed.

2.3   Proposed Approach

Generally, the main issue in GA is the lack of memory since the information contained by the candidate solution that has not been selected for crossover (or mutation) may be lost to future generations [6]. In this paper, two hybrid methods between GA and PSO are proposed such that the GA can be further improved by the memory and social learning elements of the PSO.

1. **GA with PSO Crossover (GA-PSO)** Here we adapt the GA crossover by probabilistically alternating between the standard GA crossover and the PSO velocity updates. A random number $R(i)$ is drawn from a $U(0,1)$ distribution. If $R(i)$ exceeds a threshold T PSO updates are performed instead of the GA crossover. This algorithm is shown in Fig. 1.
2. **GA with PSO initialisation (GAPSO-I)** Here we run the PSO algorithm for a limited number of iterations while the best particle obtained by the PSO is used as one of the individuals that initialise the GA population. This most similar to the algorithm proposed by [18]. However, we use only one particle from the PSO rather than a all the M best particles in the GA initialisation. We believe that using just best particle from the PSO with other random population members increases the search space of the GA. While using M particles could possibly localise the search.

2.4   Adaptive Neuro-Fuzzy Inference Systems

ANFIS are class of the fuzzy Inference Systems (FIS) that adaptively adjust membership functions and consequent parameters based on training data.

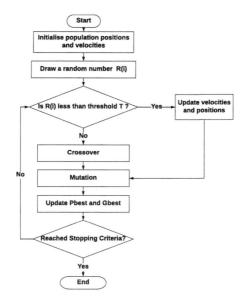

Fig. 1. Flowchart showing the GAPSO algorithm.

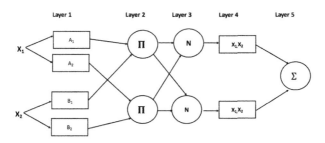

Fig. 2. Simple ANFIS architecture with two inputs and two rules.

Figure 2 shows an ANFIS architecture as proposed by [8]. ANFIS consists of five consecutive layers that sequentially process the information from inputs towards outputs. These five layers operate as follows:

Layer 1 is a fuzzification layer, where crisp inputs are converted into fuzzy set membership values. This is done using membership functions (MFs) which are bounded in range the $[0, 1]$. The output of the jth node in this layer will be of the form:

$$O_j^1 = \mu_{A_j}(x) \quad j=1, 2 \tag{3}$$

where $\mu_{A_j}(x)$ is the MF. In this paper, a Gaussian MF, as described in Eq. 4, are selected for the modelling process.

$$\mu_{A_j}(x) = \exp\left(-\frac{(x - p_j)}{\alpha_j}\right) \tag{4}$$

Layer 2 combines the incoming signals from the fuzzy sets in the previous layer using a T-norm operator. The result of this operation is the combined firing strength of each rule. If the chosen T-norm operator is multiplication then the output of the jth node in this layer is:

$$O_j^2 = w_j = \mu_{A_j}(x) \times \mu_{A_j}(x) \quad j=1,\ 2 \tag{5}$$

Layer 3 is a normalisation node where the relative firing strength of each rule is calculated as ratio of its firing strength w_j to the sum of the firing strengths of all rules. The normalised firing strength of the jth in this layer will be:

$$O_j^3 = \bar{w}_j = \frac{w_j}{w_1 + w_2} \quad j=1,\ 2 \tag{6}$$

Layer 4 calculates the consequent part of a Tagaki-Sugeno type FIS. The result is a linear combination of the inputs for each rule weighted by its respective normalised firing strength $\bar{w}_j$. This weighted linear combination is of the form:

$$O_j^4 = \bar{w}_j f_j = \bar{w}_j(a_j x_1 + b_j x_2 + c_j) \tag{7}$$

where a_j, b_j, c_j are unknown consequent parameters

Layer 5 performs an aggregation of the consequent values evaluated in the previous layer as an weighted average. The final output is therefore:

$$O_j^5 = \bar{w}_j = \sum_i \bar{w}_j f_i \tag{8}$$

The unknown parameters of the MFs in layer 1 and the linear coefficients in layer 4 need to be estimated from training data. Multiple optimisation techniques have been used for tuning these parameters [15]. A two-step process is suggested in [8] where the linear consequent parameters are optimised using Least Squares Estimation(LSE) in the forward pass, while the MF parameters are optimised using gradient decent in the backward pass. The authors in [14] use PSO for the MF parameters and LSE for consequent parameters. PSO is used for both the MF and consequent parameters in [16], while the genetic algorithm is used for both sets of parameters in [2]. In this paper, two algorithms based on the combination of GA and PSO are proposed for estimating these parameters.

3   Experiments

In this section, the relative performance of the proposed hybrid methods is investigated when training an ANFIS for predicting one-hour ahead wind power production on the Norwegian wind farm dataset.

3.1 Dataset

The Norwegian wind farm dataset consists of 7384 records covering the period from January 2014 to December 2016 [11]. The dataset features include the windfarm online capacity, one and two hour lagged historical power production values as well as NWP estimates of humidity, temperature and wind speed.

We randomly split the data into 70% for training and 30% for testing. The model performance is evaluated on the basis of Root Mean Square Error (RMSE) as defined in Eq. 9 for observation series T and corresponding model prediction series Y.

$$RMSE = \sqrt{\frac{1}{N} \sum_{i=1}^{N} (T_i - Y_i)^2} \qquad (9)$$

3.2 Model Setup

An ANFIS with 3 Gaussian MFs for each input was trained using the following methods:

1. Hybrid backpropagation least squares (BP-LS) method of [8]
2. The normal GA [2]
3. The proposed GAPSO
4. The GAPSO-I

Table 1. List of additional parameters

	Parameter	Value
GAPSO/GAPSO-I	Inertia weight	1
	Personal learning coefficient	1.6
	Global learning coefficient	2
	GAPSO random number Threshold (T)	0.75

In-order to allow for the stochastic effects of random initialisation we repeat the training of each algorithm 30 times. This also allows us to perform statistical significance tests on the results using a non-parametric Kruskal-Wallis(KW) [12] and post-hoc bonferorni [7] test for pairwise comparisons. In all cases, the ANFIS is first initialised using Fuzzy C-Means clustering [1]. Training iterations for each of the algorithms is capped at a maximum of 1500 iterations. A population size of 40 is used of the GA, GAPSO and GAPSO-I. Table 1 shows a list of the additional parameters settings.

4 Results and Discussions

Figures 3 and 4 shows the results of the experiments described in Sect. 3.

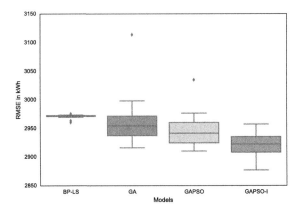

Fig. 3. Boxplot showing the distribution of testing RMSE from the 30 trials of each method

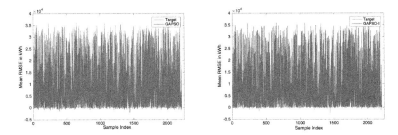

Fig. 4. Left, Graph showing the mean predictions from the GAPSO and true targets for each of the samples in testing set. Right, Graph showing the mean predictions from the GAPSO-I and true targets for each of the samples in testing set.

The boxplot in Fig. 3 shows the distribution of testing RMSE from the different models. It can be seen from the plot that evolutionary techniques show lower testing mean RMSE with the GAPSO-I showing the lowest mean RMSE of 2919.60 kWh.

The results also show that the RMSE for the evolutionary techniques have greater variation than the BP-LS as there are more stochastic elements in the algorithms rather than just in the initialisation of the backpropagation in the BP-LS.

We also see from Table 2 that while the BP-LS displays the lowest training RMSE of 2955.34 kWh it displays the highest the testing mean RMSE of 2971.57 kWh. This indicates the common problem of over-fitting to the training data displayed by gradient based methods [10].

A KW statistical test performed on the testing RMSE gives a p-value of $1.07e-12$, indicating that the differences in model performance are statistically significant. A further Bonferroni test for pair-wise differences shows that the difference between the testing RMSE from the evolutionary techniques and the

Table 2. Results showing the mean RMSE from 30 trails of ANFIS trained by the various optimisation algorithms for one-hour ahead wind power prediction.

Model	Mean training RMSE (kWh)	Mean testing RMSE (kWh)
BP-LS	2955.34	2971.57
GA	3012.07	2959.54
GAPSO	2998.24	2941.02
GAPSO-I	2989.17	2919.60

BP-LS is statistically significant in all cases at an acceptance level of $\alpha = 0.05$. The Bonferroni test also showed that the GAPSO-I had a statistically significant lower RMSE than all the other methods.

5   Conclusions and Future Work

In this paper, two hybrid GA-PSO techniques were proposed for optimising ANFIS parameters. We applied these techniques in predicting one-hour ahead wind power production on the Norwegian wind farm dataset. The results showed that both hybrid methods produce statistically significant lower RMSE than the traditional BP-LS. Furthermore, the GAPSO-I displayed statistically significant out-performance when compared to the normal GA and the GAPSO.

Future improvements to this work could explore longer horizons in wind power prediction such as 24 h [11]. An ANFIS version of the two stage modelling wind power framework such as that in [20] could also be adopted. The effect of different types of membership functions on the predictive performance can also be explored.

References

1. Bezdek, J.C., Ehrlich, R., Full, W.: FCM: the fuzzy c-means clustering algorithm. Comput. Geosci. **10**(2–3), 191–203 (1984)
2. Cárdenas, J.J., Garcia, A., Romeral, J., Kampouropoulos, K.: Evolutive ANFIS training for energy load profile forecast for an IEMS in an automated factory. In: IEEE 16th Conference on Emerging Technologies & Factory Automation (ETFA), 2011, pp. 1–8. IEEE (2011)
3. Ernst, B., Oakleaf, B., Ahlstrom, M.L., Lange, M., Moehrlen, C., Lange, B., Focken, U., Rohrig, K.: Predicting the wind. IEEE Power Energy Mag. **5**(6), 78–89 (2007)
4. Eseye, A.T., Zhang, J., Zheng, D., Ma, H., Jingfu, G.: A double-stage hierarchical ANFIS model for short-term wind power prediction. In: 2017 IEEE 2nd International Conference on Big Data Analysis (ICBDA), pp. 546–551, March 2017
5. Fischer, A., Montuelle, L., Mougeot, M., Picard, D.: Statistical learning for wind power: a modeling and stability study towards forecasting. Wind Energy **20**(12), 2037–2047 (2017). we.2139

6. Garg, H.: A hybrid PSO-GA algorithm for constrained optimization problems. Appl. Math. Comput. **274**, 292–305 (2016)
7. Hochberg, Y., Tamhane, A.C.: Distribution-Free and Robust Procedures, pp. 234–273. Wiley, New York (2008)
8. Jang, J.S.R.: ANFIS: adaptive-network-based fuzzy inference system. IEEE Trans. Syst. Man Cybern. **23**(3), 665–685 (1993)
9. Kassa, Y., Zhang, J.H., Zheng, D.H., Wei, D.: Short term wind power prediction using ANFIS. In: 2016 IEEE International Conference on Power and Renewable Energy (ICPRE), pp. 388–393, October 2016
10. MacKay, D.J.: Bayesian model comparison and backprop nets. In: Advances in Neural Information Processing Systems, pp. 839–846 (1992)
11. Mbuvha, R.: Bayesian Neural Networks for Short Term Wind Power Forecasting. Master's thesis, KTH, School of Computer Science and Communication (CSC) (2017)
12. McKight, P.E., Najab, J.: Kruskal-wallis test. Corsini Encyclopedia of Psychology (2010)
13. Potter, C.W., Negnevitsky, M.: Very short-term wind forecasting for tasmanian power generation. IEEE Trans. Power Syst. **21**(2), 965–972 (2006)
14. Pousinho, H., Mendes, V., Catalão, J.: A hybrid PSO-ANFIS approach for short-term wind power prediction in Portugal. Energy Convers. Manag. **52**(1), 397–402 (2011)
15. Salleh, M.N.M., Hussain, K.: A review of training methods of ANFIS for applications in business and economics. Int. J. u- e-Serv. Sci. Technol. **9**(7), 165–172 (2016)
16. Sargolzaei, A., Faez, K., Sargolzaei, S.: A new method for foetal electrocardiogram extraction using adaptive nero-fuzzy interference system trained with PSO algorithm. In: IEEE International Conference on Electro/Information Technology (EIT), 2011, pp. 1–5. IEEE (2011)
17. Wang, X., Guo, P., Huang, X.: A review of wind power forecasting models. Energy Procedia **12**, 770–778 (2011). the Proceedings of International Conference on Smart Grid and Clean Energy Technologies (ICSGCE 2011)
18. Yu, S., Wei, Y.M., Wang, K.: A PSO-GA optimal model to estimate primary energy demand of China. Energy Policy **42**, 329–340 (2012)
19. Zhang, Q., Ogren, R.M., Kong, S.C.: A comparative study of biodiesel engine performance optimization using enhanced hybrid PSO-GA and basic GA. Appl. Energy **165**, 676–684 (2016)
20. Zhang, Y., Wang, J., Wang, X.: Review on probabilistic forecasting of wind power generation. Renew. Sustain. Energy Rev. **32**, 255–270 (2014)

Multi-Objective Optimization

A Decomposition-Based Multiobjective Evolutionary Algorithm for Sparse Reconstruction

Jiang Zhu[1,2], Muyao Cai[1], Shujuan Tian[1(✉)], Yanbing Xu[1], and Tingrui Pei[1]

[1] College of Information Engineering, Xiangtan University, Xiangtan 411105, China
sjtianwork@xtu.edu.cn

[2] National Engineering Laboratory for Robot Visual Perception and Control Technology, Hunan University, Changsha 410082, China

Abstract. Sparse reconstruction is an important method aiming at obtaining an approximation to an original signal from observed data. It can be deemed as a multiobjective optimization problem for the sparsity and the observational error terms, which are considered as two conflicting objectives in evolutionary algorithm. In this paper, a novel decomposition based multiobjective evolutionary algorithm is proposed to optimize the two objectives and reconstruct the original signal more exactly. In our algorithm, a sparse constraint specific differential evolution is designed to guarantee that the solution remains sparse in the next generation. In addition, a neighborhood-based local search approach is proposed to obtain better solutions and improve the speed of convergence. Therefore, a set of solutions is obtained efficiently and is able to closely approximate the original signal.

Keywords: Sparse reconstruction · Multiobjective optimization
Evolutionary algorithm · Decomposition · Differential evolution

1 Introduction

Compressive sensing (CS) is a novel theoretical framework for information acquisition and processing, proposed by Candes et al. [1,2,6,12]. It breaks through this limit and dramatically reduces, under certain conditions, the amount of data we need to sample. Therefore, it can be widely applied to mass data acquisition and processing. As an essential step in compressive sensing, the performance of sparse reconstruction directly affects whether the CS framework is practical.

According to CS theory, the high-dimensional original signal is projected to obtain a set of measurement data with smaller dimensionality. Theoretically, sparse reconstruction can recover the original signal from the measurement data based on the prior knowledge that the signal could be transformed into a sparse one. As a matter of fact, it is hard to completely eliminate the additive noise in a true signal observation process, thus the ground-truth signal x_{tr} is approximated

© Springer International Publishing AG, part of Springer Nature 2018
Y. Tan et al. (Eds.): ICSI 2018, LNCS 10941, pp. 509–519, 2018.
https://doi.org/10.1007/978-3-319-93815-8_48

by the solution in the problem with noise $\boldsymbol{n}$. This problem could be formulated as the following problem:

$$\min_{\boldsymbol{x}} \|\boldsymbol{x}\|_0 \quad s.t. \quad \|\boldsymbol{y} - A\boldsymbol{x}\|_2^2 \leq \sigma, \tag{1}$$

where $\boldsymbol{x} = (x_1, ..., x_m)^T$ is a signal vector; $\boldsymbol{y} = (y_1, ..., y_d)^T$ is a measurement vector; $A = (a_{ij})^{d \times m}$ is a sensing matrix with $d < m$ that is full-rank and overcomplete; σ is a nonnegative parameter to estimate the degree of noisiness of the data under the observation process and $\|\boldsymbol{x}\|_0$ denotes the number of nonzero elements in the vector $\boldsymbol{x}$, which represents the sparsity of the signal.

Most of traditional algorithms consider the constrained formula as a single objective function by introducing a Lagrange multiplier [9,16]. In order to find an optimal solution, specific problems need specific multipliers, that always depend on the weights of the two terms of the sparse reconstruction (the sparsity and the measurement error). However, it is hard to choose the proper weights in many practical situations. Usually it needs some experiments for finding best value for correspond situation without any additional knowledge, which is time-comsuming. For the purpose of avoiding this difficulties and finding interesting solutions more easily, a more universal and robust algorithm is necessary for sparse reconstruction. The population-based methods like multi-objective evolutionary algorithms [4,7] are considered as a better alternative for this problem.

This paper proposes a decomposition-based multiobjective evolutionary algorithm for sparse reconstruction (MOSR/D), which applies the multiobjective evolutionary algorithm based on decomposition (MOEA/D) [11,17] to solve the sparse reconstruction problem. The proposed algorithm decomposes sparse reconstruction into several scalar subproblems, and then addresses them with a differential evolution operator considering sparse constraint. Besides this, a neighborhood-based local search approach is employed to improve the speed of convergence and the performance of the solutions. Finally a group of Pareto solutions, which are tradeoffs between the two terms of the SR, can be obtained in a single run. The Pareto front (PF), i.e., the sets of objective victors of these solutions, can be readily visualized in the objective space [10]. It is extremely useful for decision makers to find the solution they want. It has been proved that the best approximation to the original signal is always located in PF.

This paper is organized as follows. Section 2 describes the proposed algorithm in detail. In Sect. 3, the MOSR/D is compared with other conventional algorithms and the experimental results are shown. Section 4 concludes this paper.

2   Methodology

In this section the proposed decomposition-based multiobjective evolutionary algorithm for sparse reconstruction is described. First, a multiobjective SR model is given, and then the MOSR/D is described in detail. In this algorithm, a differential evolution operator based on sparse constraint is designed and a neighborhood-based local search is applied to obtain better solutions efficiently.

2.1 Decomposition-Based Multiobjective Evolutionary Algorithm for Sparse Reconstruction

In order to obtain a close approximation for sparse reconstruction, its sparsity and observational error should be as small as possible. Traditional sparse reconstruction algorithms transform the objective function into a single term using weighting parameters, but this is sensitive to the specific datasets and result in fluctuations in the reconstruction performance. To overcome this drawback, sparse reconstruction can be expressed as a bi-objective optimization model while minimizing the two terms

$$\min_{\boldsymbol{x}} F(\boldsymbol{x}) = \min_{\boldsymbol{x}}(\|\boldsymbol{x}\|_0, \|\boldsymbol{y} - A\boldsymbol{x}\|_2^2)$$
$$subject\ to\quad \boldsymbol{x} \in \Omega, \tag{2}$$

where Ω is the variable space. This model is more robust than the conventional ones, and its solutions can meet the various requirements of a decision maker in that a group of different solutions are produced at the same time.

For the purpose of resolving the multi-objective sparse reconstruction model, a multiobjective evolutionary algorithm MOSR/D based on MOEA/D is proposed in this paper. This algorithm decomposes the sparse reconstruction problem into a certain number of scalar optimization problems, called subproblems, by a weighted aggregation of the objectives. Then the subproblems are solved by evolving a population of solutions. The current population consists of the best solutions obtained so far for each subproblem. For each subproblem, a neighborhood relationship is defined based on the distance between the corresponding weight vectors. According to [17], the optimal solutions of the neighboring subproblems should be very similar and only the information from these neighboring subproblems is used to optimize each solution.

The approach of decomposition makes a difference to the performance of the algorithm. Tchebycheff approach is one of the most popular methods [13]. It converts the problem of approximating the PF into a certain number of subproblems, and could be used in our algorithm. In the sparse reconstruction problem there are two objectives (the observational error and the sparsity) to be solved. Suppose $\boldsymbol{\lambda} = (\lambda_1, \lambda_2)^T$ is a weight vector, where $\lambda_1 \geq 0$, $\lambda_2 \geq 0$ and $\lambda_1 + \lambda_2 = 1$. Then the corresponding Pareto optimal solutions can be obtained from the subobjective functions as follows:

$$\min_{\boldsymbol{x}}\ g^{te}(\boldsymbol{x}|\boldsymbol{\lambda}, \boldsymbol{z}^*) = \max\{\lambda_1|f_1(\boldsymbol{x}) - z_1^*|, \lambda_2|f_2(\boldsymbol{x}) - z_2^*|\}$$
$$subject\ to\quad \boldsymbol{x} \in \Omega, \tag{3}$$

where $\boldsymbol{z}^* = (z_1^*, z_2^*)^T$ denotes the ideal point, i.e., $z_1^* = \min\{f_1(\boldsymbol{x})|\boldsymbol{x} \in \Omega\}$ and $z_2^* = \min\{f_2(\boldsymbol{x})|\boldsymbol{x} \in \Omega\}$. Each subproblem is related to others. After the decomposition steps, each subproblem will be optimized by a collaborative method employing the information from other subproblems.

Combining all the Pareto optimal vectors in the objective space, an approximation to the Pareto front can be obtained. With the evolution of the population of solutions, the set of Pareto optimal vectors should be closer to the real Pareto front. The procedure of our algorithm is given in Algorithm 1. It contains both the initialization and a loop.

Algorithm 1. MOSR/D

Input:
The objectives of MOSR/D $f_1(\boldsymbol{x})$, $f_2(\boldsymbol{x})$;
The number of weight vectors in the neighborhood of each weight vector T;
The number of subproblems decomposed N;
A termination criterion.
Output:
The ultimate population $P = \{\boldsymbol{x^1}, ..., \boldsymbol{x^N}\}$;
The set of Pareto objective vectors PF $= \{FV^1, ..., FV^N\}$.
1: **Step 1) Initialization:**
2: Generate a set of weight vectors $\boldsymbol{\lambda^1}, ..., \boldsymbol{\lambda^N}$ by a problem-specific method;
3: Calculate the Euclidean distances between each two weight vectors and pick the T closest weight vectors to each weight vector out; For each $i = 1, ..., N$, set $D(i) = \{i_1, ..., i_T\}$, where $\boldsymbol{\lambda^{i1}}, ..., \boldsymbol{\lambda^{iT}}$ are the T closest weight vectors to $\boldsymbol{\lambda^i}$;
4: Randomly initialize a population P including the points $\boldsymbol{x^1}, \boldsymbol{x^2}, ..., \boldsymbol{x^N}$ in the variable space; Set $FV^i = F(\boldsymbol{x^i})$;
5: Generate $\boldsymbol{z} = \{z_1, z_2\}^T$ by a problem-specific method.
6: **Step 2) Cycling:**
7: **repeat**
8:    **for** $i = 1$ to N **do**
9:       A sparse constraint specific differential evolution operator is used on solution $\boldsymbol{x^i}$ to obtain $\boldsymbol{v}$;
10:       Apply a neighborhood-based local search approach on solution $\boldsymbol{v}$ to produce $\boldsymbol{v'}$;
11:       Update of Neighboring Solutions:
12:       **for** each index $j \in D(i)$ **do**
13:          **while** $g^{te}(\boldsymbol{v'}|\lambda, z) \leq g^{te}(\boldsymbol{x^j}|\lambda, z)$ **do**
14:             $\boldsymbol{x^j} \leftarrow \boldsymbol{v'}$, $FV^j \leftarrow F(\boldsymbol{v'})$
15:          **end while**
16:       **end for**
17:    **end for**
18: **until** Termination condition is satisfied
19: **return** P and PF.

In the initialization, firstly we should set the weight vectors with an uniform distribution in the objective space, i.e., ensure the same angle between each two weight vectors. Then P, an initial population of the solutions to the subproblems, is generated randomly in the specific domain. To ensure our search strategy is useful for solutions with different sparsities, different sparsities from 1 to m are assigned to the solutions in this initial population. The Euclidean distance between the corresponding weight vectors of each subproblem is found, and then be used to estimate the neighboring relationship among the subproblems. Based on this we can select the T closest ones as the neighborhood of each subproblem.

In the evolution step, a new genetic operator, called the sparse constraint specific differential evolution (SpaDE) operator, and a neighborhood-based local search method are employed on the current solution to search for a better one. These two methods are described in the following subsections. The termination condition could be set as a certain number of generations. When it is satisfied, then the evolution is stopped and the ultimate population and PF are obtained.

2.2   A Sparse Constraint Specific Differential Evolution Operator

In MOSR/D, after decomposition of the SR problem, a sparse constraint specific differential evolution operator is applied to the current generation population in this algorithm, due to several advantages, e.g., it is an efficient scheme for global optimization and it is simple to implement.

The procedure of SpaDE is described in Algorithm 2 in detail. It contains the following four steps: mutation, crossover, sparse constraint, and selection. Mutation and crossover operations are used to search for a new solution around the current one, and selection chooses the better one from two solutions. Due to the decomposition of the whole MOP into scalar subproblems, the conventional selection operator for scalar optimization can be directly used in our algorithm. So we can compare the solutions after differential evolution with the original solutions and pick the better one directly based on the values of the subobjective function in (3). These operators lead the solutions to converge to the Pareto front straightforwardly and rapidly.

Even though the DE operator has shown great performance on the SR problem, its use also gives rise to another difficulty. After a mutation using the DE operator, the sparsity of the solutions has already increased to approximately three times what it was before. In order to obtain a close approximation to the ground-truth signal, it is necessary to execute a specific operator that will enforce a sparsity of solution similar to that of the ground-truth one. Therefore, we propose a method, referred to as sparse constraint, to maintain the sparsity of the solutions. The process of sparse constraint is illustrated by an example in Fig. 1, where C is a vector which include m elements and represent the solution after a crossover operation, x^i is the target solution vector, and S is the new vector produced. Based on the elements of x^i, we decide whether to pass the nonzero elements of C to S. When the corresponding coefficients of x^i and C include a zero value and a non-zero one, the corresponding coefficients of S will be assigned a zero with probability p.

Note that the setting of the probability p plays a significant role in this approach. Some investigation has been done, as follows. Supposing k is the sparsity of the original signal and m is its dimension, and ignoring the situation where the value of the elements in the same index of the vectors x^v and vector x^l are equal (a remote possibility), the sparsity of the difference between x^v and x^l can be written as

$$k_s = k + (m - k) \times \frac{k}{m} = 2k - \frac{k^2}{m}. \tag{8}$$

Algorithm 2. Sparse Constraint Specific Differential Evolution Operator

---

Input:

The target solution $\boldsymbol{x}^i = (x_1, ..., x_k, ..., x_m)^T$;

The solutions to neighboring subproblems $\boldsymbol{x}^{i1}, ..., \boldsymbol{x}^{iT}$;

The scale parameter F;   The crossover parameter CR;

The weight vector $\boldsymbol{\lambda}^i$;   The reference point $\boldsymbol{z}$.

Output:

A new solution to the target subproblem $\boldsymbol{v} = \{v_1, ..., v_m\}$.

1: **Mutation**

Randomly select three neighboring solution vectors $\boldsymbol{x}^u, \boldsymbol{x}^v$ and $\boldsymbol{x}^l$ from the neighborhood of the target solution.

Generate a individual $\boldsymbol{B} = (b_1, ..., b_k, ..., b_m)^T$ from

$$B = x^u + F \cdot (x^v - x^l), \tag{4}$$

2: **Crossover**

Generate a trial vector $\boldsymbol{C} = \{c_1, ..., c_j, ...c_m\}$ through a binomial crossover as

$$c_j = \begin{cases} b_j \text{ if rand}(0,1) < \text{CR or } j = j_{rand}, \\ x_j^i \text{ otherwise.} \end{cases} \tag{5}$$

3: **Sparse Constraint**

Generate a new vector $\boldsymbol{S} = \{s_1, ..., s_j, ...s_m\}$ by comparing $\boldsymbol{C}$ and the target solution $\boldsymbol{x}^i$:

$$s_j = \begin{cases} 0 \quad c_j = x_j^i = 0 \text{ or rand}(0,1) < p, \\ c_j \text{ otherwise.} \end{cases} \tag{6}$$

4: **Selection**

Apply the objective of the corresponding target subproblem to estimate the vectors:

$$v = \begin{cases} S \quad g^{te}(S|\lambda^i, z) < g^{te}(x^i|\lambda^i, z), \\ x^i \text{ otherwise.} \end{cases} \tag{7}$$

5: **return** v.

Then this difference is multiplied by a weight F and the product is added to the vector $\boldsymbol{X}^u$, so the sparsity of newpoint after mutation becomes

$$k_m = k_s + (m - k_s) \times \frac{k}{m} = 3k + \frac{3k^2}{m} + \frac{k^3}{m^2}. \tag{9}$$

Note that the sparsity of the solution after mutation k_m increases to about three times what it was before, when $m \gg k$. In our approach of sparse constraint, we should restore the sparsity of solutions to k by finding a reasonable probability p. According to (8) and the situations above, the nonzero elements come from three parts:

$$\begin{cases} k_1 = 0; \\ k_2 = k_m \times \frac{m-k}{m} + (m - k_m) \times \frac{k}{m}; \\ k_3 = k_m \times \frac{k}{m}. \end{cases} \tag{10}$$

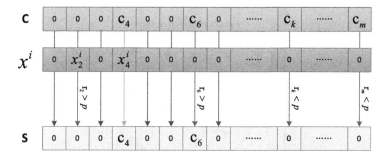

Fig. 1. The sparse constraint process

In the hope of obtaining a solution with sparsity k, the following equation can be derived.

$$k_1 + k_2 \times (1 - p) + k_3 = p \tag{11}$$

Finally, the optimal probability p is set to

$$p = \frac{3m^3 - 6km^2 + 4k^2m - k^3}{4m^3 - 9km^2 + 7k^2m - 2k^3}. \tag{12}$$

Based on the condition that $n \gg k$, the optimal p is approximately 0.75. Therefore, the probability p is set to 0.75 in the sparse constraint approach to improve the performance of our algorithm.

2.3   Neighborhood-Based Local Search

In order to improve the performance of the algorithm and the speed of convergence, a neighborhood-based local search approach proposed in this paper is applied to the solutions after the genetic operator. For each solution v from SpaDE, we obtain a new solution v' through searching with the information of the target solution and other solutions in its neighboring subproblems. As seen in Fig. 2, the arrows represent different weight vectors, black points are the current optimal solutions we have found so far, the area under shadow is neighborhood of the current weight vector, i.e., the red one. Our method use only the solutions in the neighborhood of current subproblem to search its actual optimal solution.

Suppose that $f(\boldsymbol{x}) = \frac{1}{2}\|A\boldsymbol{x} - \boldsymbol{y}\|_2^2$ and $c(\boldsymbol{x}) = \|\boldsymbol{x}\|_1$. Obviously the $c(\boldsymbol{x})$ is separable. Then, an updated solution $\boldsymbol{x}^{k+1}$ can be calculated by minimizing the linearized function of the previous solution $\boldsymbol{x}^k$ with IST [3,8] in the SR problem

$$\boldsymbol{x}^{k+1} = \min_x f(\boldsymbol{x}^k) + (\boldsymbol{x} - \boldsymbol{x}^k)^T \nabla f(\boldsymbol{x}^k) + \frac{1}{2}(\boldsymbol{x} - \boldsymbol{x}^k)^T H(\boldsymbol{x}^k)(\boldsymbol{x} - \boldsymbol{x}^k) + \tau c(\boldsymbol{x})$$

$$\approx \min_x (\boldsymbol{x} - \boldsymbol{x}^k)^T \nabla f(\boldsymbol{x}^k) + \frac{\alpha^k}{2}\|A\boldsymbol{x} - \boldsymbol{y}\|_2^2 + \tau\|\boldsymbol{x}\|_1$$

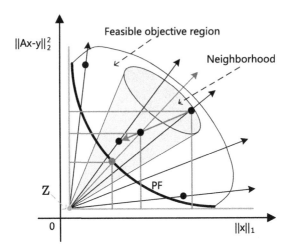

Fig. 2. Neighborhood-based local search

$$= \frac{1}{2}\|\boldsymbol{x} - \boldsymbol{u}^k\|_2^2 + \frac{\tau}{\alpha^k}\|\boldsymbol{x}\|_1$$
$$= soft(\boldsymbol{u}^k, \frac{\tau}{\alpha^k}) \tag{13}$$

where $soft(b, \frac{\tau}{2})$ is the soft-thresholding function [5]. The parameter α^k is set by a Barzilai–Borwein (Spectral) Method in [14]. The diagonal matrix $\alpha^k \boldsymbol{E}$ denotes an estimate of the Hessian matrix $H(\boldsymbol{x}^k) = \nabla^2 f(\boldsymbol{x}^k)$ and

$$\boldsymbol{u}^k = \boldsymbol{x}^k - \frac{1}{\alpha^k} \nabla f(\boldsymbol{x}^k). \tag{14}$$

In order to incorporate the soft-threshold function into our algorithm, it is important to choose appropriate values for $\boldsymbol{x}^k$ and $\boldsymbol{x}^{k-1}$. After several generations of our algorithm, the current solutions of the population should be close to the optimal solutions. Due to the similarity between the optimal solutions to two neighboring subproblems, it is considered a feasible method to select two of the present solutions to the neighboring subproblems as $\boldsymbol{x}^k$ and $\boldsymbol{x}^{k-1}$. After these steps, we can find better solutions that are close to the Pareto front, and then get a close approximation to the original signal.

3   Experimental Study

In this section we describe an simulation experiment to demonstrate the superiority of the MOSR/D by comparing this algorithm against another six popular traditional approaches for sparse reconstruction. These six approaches are OMP, basis pursuit (BP), homotopy methods, sparse reconstruction by separable approximation (SpaRSA), the fast iterative shrinkage thresholding algorithm (FISTA), and the alternating direction method (ADM). Toolboxes for these methods can be found in [15].

Algorithm 3. Neighborhood-based local search

Input:

The population after SpaDE operator $v^1, ..., v^N$;

The number of subproblems N;   The weight vectors $\lambda^1, ..., \lambda^N$;

The number of neighboring subproblems T;   The reference point z.

Output:

The new solutions v'.

1: **for** $i = 1$ to N **do**

2:    set $D(i) = i_1, ..., i_T$, where $\lambda^{i1}, ..., \lambda^{iT}$ are the T closest weight vectors to λ^i;

3:    select two indices i_a, i_b from $D(i)$;

4:    **if** $g^{te}(v^{i_a}|\lambda^i, z) \leq g^{te}(v^{i_b}|\lambda^i, z)$ **then**

5:        $x^k \leftarrow v^{i_a}, x^{k-1} \leftarrow v^{i_b}$;

6:    **else**

7:        $x^k \leftarrow v^{i_b}, x^{k-1} \leftarrow v^{i_a}$;

8:    **end if**

9:    Compute x^{k+1} by x^k and x^{k-1};

10:    $v' \leftarrow x^{k+1}$.

11: **end for**

In this experiment, the setting of the simulation experiment is set as follows. The dimension of the ground-truth signal m is 2000. The observation vector y is polluted by an additive white noise, in which the coefficients are distributed with mean 0 and standard deviation $\delta = 0.01$. The value of the tolerance σ is set to 0.3 and λ is fixed at 0.02 for the compared algorithms.

Table 1. Average reconstruction error of the MOEA/D and other algorithms with different projection dimensions

Projection dimension	OMP	BP	Homotopy	SpaRSA	FISTA	ADM	MOSR/D
800	1.026	0.631	0.640	0.650	0.657	0.657	0.510
1000	0.793	0.603	0.565	0.568	0.564	0.558	0.437
1200	0.831	0.618	0.508	0.498	0.515	0.520	0.394
1400	0.978	0.721	0.485	0.473	0.475	0.472	0.382
1600	1.024	0.902	0.461	0.460	0.456	0.471	0.387
1800	1.316	1.329	0.446	0.439	0.440	0.441	0.371

In Table 1, the sparsity ratio k/m is set to 0.15, and the projection dimension d of the observation matrix d varies from 800 to 1800, in intervals of 200. From this table we can see how the reconstruction error changes with d in different algorithms. Obviously MOEA/D has the lowest average reconstruction error, meaning it outperforms the other algorithms.

In Table 2, the projection dimension is fixed at $d = 1200$ while the sparsity ratio is varied over the range $k/m = 0.1$–0.4. As can be seen in this table, the

Table 2. Average reconstruction error of the MOEA/D and other algorithms with different sparsity ratios

Sparsity ratio	OMP	BP	Homotopy	SpaRSA	FISTA	ADM	MOSR/D
0.10	0.296	0.561	0.394	0.397	0.392	0.407	0.364
0.15	0.801	0.631	0.524	0.526	0.524	0.522	0.397
0.20	0.948	0.686	0.611	0.619	0.603	0.613	0.447
0.25	1.081	0.715	0.688	0.681	0.672	0.689	0.495
0.30	1.209	0.760	0.740	0.727	0.730	0.735	0.530
0.35	1.296	0.802	0.767	0.771	0.766	0.773	0.554
0.40	1.339	0.831	0.795	0.796	0.792	0.792	0.589

MOEA/D has a better performance than the other algorithms for sparse reconstruction, except for OMP with $k/m = 0.1$. However, considering that the OMP method works worse when the sparsity varies from 0.15 to 0.4, MOSR/D is a better choice for sparse reconstruction on the whole.

4   Conclusion

This paper has proposed a multi-objective model for sparse reconstruction, in which the observational error and an enforced sparsity are employed as the two objectives and minimized simultaneously. A novel algorithm named MOSR/D has been designed to solve this model and obtain a set of tradeoffs between the two objectives. These tradeoffs are useful for a decision maker to reconstruct the original sparse signal exactly. In particular, a sparse constraint specific differential evolution operator is incorporated to obtain a closer approximation to the original signal, and a neighborhood-based local search approach is used to speed up the convergence of our algorithm. Results of simulation experiments have demonstrated that our algorithm outperforms other conventional algorithms for sparse reconstruction. Future work is going to focus on incorporating MOSR/D into significant applications and designing effective methods for finding the best tradeoff along the Pareto front.

Acknowledgements. This work is supported by the National Natural Science Foundation of China (61602397, 61672447, 61602398, 61711540306) and the Postgraduate Research and Innovation Project of Hunan Province of China (CX2017B338) and CERNET Innovation Project (NGII20160310) and Natural Science Foundation of Hunan Province of China (2017JJ3316) and the Research Foundation of Hunan Provincial Educational Department of China (16C1547).

References

1. Candès, E.J., Romberg, J., Tao, T.: Robust uncertainty principles: exact signal reconstruction from highly incomplete frequency information. IEEE Trans. Inf. Theor. **52**(2), 489–509 (2006)
2. Candès, E.J., Wakin, M.B.: An introduction to compressive sampling. IEEE Sig. Process. Mag. **25**(2), 21–30 (2008)
3. Daubechies, I., Defrise, M., De Mol, C.: An iterative thresholding algorithm for linear inverse problems with a sparsity constraint. Commun. Pure Appl. Math. **57**(11), 1413–1457 (2004)
4. Deb, K.: Multi-objective evolutionary algorithms. In: Kacprzyk, J., Pedrycz, W. (eds.) Springer Handbook of Computational Intelligence, pp. 995–1015. Springer, Heidelberg (2015). https://doi.org/10.1007/978-3-662-43505-2_49
5. Donoho, D.L.: De-noising by soft-thresholding. IEEE Trans. Inf. Theor. **41**(3), 613–627 (1995)
6. Donoho, D.L.: Compressed sensing. IEEE Trans. Inf. Theor. **52**(4), 1289–1306 (2006)
7. Gong, M., Li, H., Luo, E., Liu, J., Liu, J.: A multiobjective cooperative coevolutionary algorithm for hyperspectral sparse unmixing. IEEE Trans. Evol. Comput. **21**(2), 234–248 (2017)
8. Herrity, K.K., Gilbert, A.C., Tropp, J.A.: Sparse approximation via iterative thresholding. In: Proceedings of the 31st International Conference on Acoustics, Speech and Signal Processing, vol. 3, p. III (2006)
9. Mallat, S.G., Zhang, Z.: Matching pursuits with time-frequency dictionaries. IEEE Trans. Sig. Process. **41**(12), 3397–3415 (1993)
10. Miettinen, K.: Nonlinear Multiobjective Optimization, vol. 12. Springer, New York (2012). https://doi.org/10.1007/978-1-4615-5563-6
11. Trivedi, A., Srinivasan, D., Sanyal, K., Ghosh, A.: A survey of multiobjective evolutionary algorithms based on decomposition. IEEE Trans. Evol. Comput. **21**(3), 440–462 (2017)
12. Tsaig, Y., Donoho, D.L.: Extensions of compressed sensing. Sig. Proces. **86**(3), 549–571 (2006)
13. Wang, L., Zhang, Q., Zhou, A., Gong, M., Jiao, L.: Constrained subproblems in a decomposition-based multiobjective evolutionary algorithm. IEEE Trans. Evol. Comput. **20**(3), 475–480 (2016)
14. Wright, S.J., Nowak, R.D., Figueiredo, M.A.: Sparse reconstruction by separable approximation. IEEE Trans. Sig. Process. **57**(7), 2479–2493 (2009)
15. Yang, A.Y.: l-1 benchmark package. http://people.eecs.berkeley.edu/~yang/software/l1benchmark/l1benchmark.zip
16. Yang, A.Y., Sastry, S.S., Ganesh, A., Ma, Y.: Fast L1-minimization algorithms and an application in robust face recognition: a review. In: Proceedings of 17th IEEE International Conference on Image Processing, pp. 1849–1852. IEEE (2010)
17. Zhang, Q., Li, H.: MOEA/D: a multiobjective evolutionary algorithm based on decomposition. IEEE Trans. Evol. Comput. **11**(6), 712–731 (2007)

A Novel Many-Objective Bacterial Foraging Optimizer Based on Multi-engine Cooperation Framework

Shengminjie Chen[1], Rui Wang[2], Lianbo Ma[2(✉)], Zhao Gu[2],
Xiaofan Du[2], and Yichuan Shao[3]

[1] Faculty of Science, Kunming University of Science and Technology,
Kunming, China
[2] College of Software, Northeastern University, Shenyang, China
malb@swc.neu.edu.cn
[3] Shenyang University, Shenyang 110044, China

Abstract. In order to efficiently manage the diversity and convergence in many-objective optimization, this paper proposes a novel multi-engine cooperation bacterial foraging algorithm (MCBFA) to enhance the selection pressure towards Pareto front. The main framework of MCBFA is to handle the convergence and diversity separately by evolving several search engines with different rules. In this algorithm, three engines are respectively endowed with three different evolution principles (i.e., Pareto-based, decomposition-based and indicator-based), and their archives are evolved according to comprehensive learning. In the foraging operations, each bacterium is evolved by reinforcement learning (RL). Specifically, each bacterium adaptively varies its own run-length unit and exchange information to dynamically balance exploration and exploitation during the search process. Empirical studies on DTLZ benchmarks show MCBFA exhibits promising performance on complex many-objective problems.

Keywords: Multi-engine · Reinforcement learning
Bacterial forging algorithm · Many-objective optimization

1 Introduction

Many real-world problems can be formulated mathematically as a many-objective optimization problem (MaOP) [1], usually with more than three conflicting objectives. Intuitively, the aim of an algorithm for MaOPs is to find a set of optimal trade-off solutions between a numbers of objectives, which are also called the Pareto-optimal solutions (PS). Obviously, these high-dimensional MaOPs are more difficult than those with two or three objectives, because with the increasing number of objectives, the percentage of nondominated solutions for MaOPs increases rapidly, which inevitably causes the difficulty of estimating the solutions' similarity. Evolutionary algorithms (EAs) have been deeply investigated and treated in the literature [2]. Pareto optimality is the popular paradigm, such as NSGA-II [3] and SPEA2 [4]. However, these algorithms encounter severe degradation in performance on MaOPs, because they would

© Springer International Publishing AG, part of Springer Nature 2018
Y. Tan et al. (Eds.): ICSI 2018, LNCS 10941, pp. 520–529, 2018.
https://doi.org/10.1007/978-3-319-93815-8_49

lose the diminishing selection pressure over non-dominated solutions with the number of objectives increasing.

In order to resolve this issue, a large number of approaches have been proposed recently, such as decomposition-based approach [5], quality indicator-based approach [6], and augmenting selection pressure approach [7]. Among those, several novel paradigms exhibit large potential with excellent experimental results, such as NSGAIII [8] and two-archive MOEA [9]. NSGAIII uses a set of reference points to guide the selection process over nondominated solutions in the high-dimensional objective space. The two-archive MOEA is to respectively assign Pareto-based and indicator-based metrics to the two archives, in order to handle the convergence and diversity separately [10]. Note that recently many bacterial swarm based algorithms are proposed to take advantage of the success of bacterial intelligence. The main strength of bacterial foraging optimization (BFO) algorithms lies in its excellent exploitation ability, which compares favorably with other EAs [11, 12]. However, compare to the in-depth investigation of other algorithms on MaOPs, few affords are paid to use BFO and its variants to resolve the MaOPs.

Inspired by above works, we proposed a new multi-engine cooperation bacterial foraging algorithm (MCBFA). Specifically, in the colony-level interaction, the decomposition-based engine (DE), the Pareto-based engine (PE) and the indicator-based engine (IE) are concurrently evolved to maintain diversity and convergence. In the individual-level searching, the bacterial foraging operations are selected as the basic search rule. Then the Q-learning method is used to dynamically balance exploration and exploitation during the search process. By integrating these mechanisms, the single-population BFO has been extended to a multi-population multi-level cooperation model for many-objective optimization.

The remainder of the paper is given as follows. Section 2 describes the main framework of multi-engine Cooperation bacterial foraging paradigm. In Sect. 3, the proposed algorithm is presented in detail. Section 4 presents a series of experiments on a set of benchmarks to evaluate effectiveness of the proposed algorithm. Section 5 outlines the conclusions.

2 Proposed Framework

2.1 Basic Idea

The multi-engine cooperation framework is developed as shown in Fig. 1. In the framework, three types of search engines are evolved independently with different dominance relations, so as to tackle convergence and diversity separately. Each engine is composed of a set of solutions with the same evolution strategy. Specifically, the Pareto-based engine (PE) is to enhance the diversity of population, the indicator-based engine (IE) attempts to guide the population to converge to the true PF quickly, and the decomposition-based engine (DE) is responsible to further make up the loss of selection pressure. In this approach, the DE, PE and IE work cooperatively with different archive-updating rules and fitness-evaluation approaches. As shown in Fig. 1, the general framework of MCFBA consists of multi-archive management mechanism,

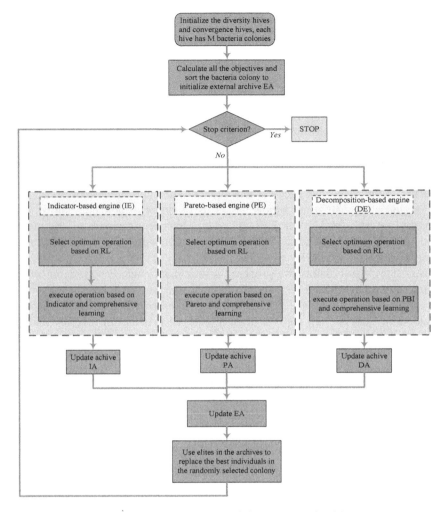

Fig. 1. The basic flowchart of the proposed algorithm

comprehensive learning, reinforcement learning, and basic foraging operators, which is composed of chemotaxis, reproduction, elimination-dispersal and crossover. The details are given below.

2.2 Multi-archive Maintenance

Figure 2 shows the hybrid multi-archive management mechanism, where three heterogeneous archives are updated independently based on different dominance relations, and then they are merged in the global archive EA by a specific selection scheme. For the sake of simplification, we employ only one colony in each engine.

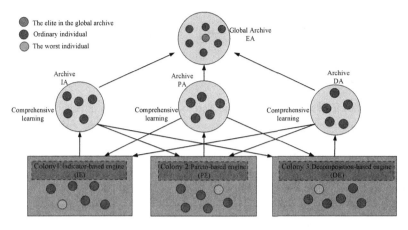

Fig. 2. The schematic diagram of comprehensive learning and archive management in MCBFA

Archive for Decomposition-Based Engine. In DE, the penalty-based boundary interception (PBI) is employed as fitness assignment, since its effectiveness has been verified in [8]. Here an ideal point Z^* is used as a reference point, and the diversity function is defined as

$$\text{PBI}(P, \lambda) = d_1 + \theta d_2 \tag{1}$$

where d_1 is the distance between the Z^* and a point P, and d_2 is the distance between the point P and the weight vector λ. Essentially, d_1 is used to measure the closeness to PF, while d_2 is used to maintain the diversity of population. Then θ is to combine d_1 and d_2 into a single value. Then, d_1 and d_2 are calculated as:

$$d_1 = \frac{\left\| (P - Z^*)^T \lambda \right\|}{\|\lambda\|} \tag{2}$$

$$d_2 = \left\| P - \left(Z^* + d_1 \frac{\lambda}{\|\lambda\|} \right) \right\| \tag{3}$$

Archive for Indicator-Based Engine. The quality indicator $I\varepsilon+$ is used in IE and its archive IA to improve the convergence. Suppose there are two solution sets A and B, then $I\varepsilon+$ is defined as [13]:

$$I_{\varepsilon+}(A, B) = \min\{\forall y \in B \, \exists x \in A : f_i(x) - \varepsilon \leq f_i(y) \, for \, i \in \{1, \ldots, m\}\} \tag{4}$$

where x and y are solution vectors, m is the number of objectives. Intuitively, it represents the minimum shift weight of each dimension of the objectives. Then it is used to assign fitness to individuals in IE as

$$Fit_{I\varepsilon+}(x) = \sum_{y\in P\backslash\{x\}} -e^{-I_{\varepsilon+}(y,x)/0.05} \qquad (5)$$

where P is the population. Essentially, $Fit_{I\varepsilon+}(x)$ can be directly employed as the dominance relation.

Archive for Pareto-Based Engine. The Pareto-based PE aims at diversity promotion over a set of non-dominated solutions by using its archive PA. Accordingly, only non-dominated solutions in the population can be selected into PA. Although the proportion of non-dominant solutions is increasing with the growth of generations, it is still very effective in the initial phase. The redundant individual is deleted based on the crowding distance when PA is overflowed.

Algorithm 1. Manage archive *EA*

Input: *size_EA*   /*the fixed size of *EA**/.

1. $A = DA \cup IA \cup PA$

2. For all $x \in A$ do

3. $Fit_{I\varepsilon+}(x) = Fit_{I\varepsilon+}(x) + \sum_{x\in A\backslash\{x^*\}} -e^{-I_{\varepsilon+}(x^*,x)/0.05}$

4. End for.

5. Sort all x according to $Fit_{I\varepsilon+}(x)$.

6. While ($|A|$ > *size_EA*)

7. $x_{min} = \{x\,|\,\min(Fit_{I\varepsilon+}(x)), x \in A\}$

8. $A = A \backslash x_{min}$

9.   For all $x \in A$ do

10. $Fit_{I\varepsilon+}(x) = Fit_{I\varepsilon+}(x) + \sum_{x\in A\backslash\{x^*\}} -e^{-I_{\varepsilon+}(x^*,x)/0.05}$

11.   End for.

12. End While

13. $EA = A$.

17. Return *EA*.

Global Archive. As shown in Fig. 2, the newly solutions in DA, IA and PA are merged together into EA in each generation. EA is maintained as Algorithm1. Due to good performance and low complexity, the indicator $I\varepsilon+$ is used. In principle, the EA has the combinable merits of DA, PA and IA in the environmental selection. Furthermore, the information exchange between individuals and populations can be enhanced via comprehensive learning in parallel at each individual updating step. That is, the bacterium x_i in an engine uses one randomly selected neighbor x_j in another engine to generate a new one. Obviously, this can improve the efficiency of information exchange among archives.

3 The MCBFA Algorithm

Based on the above framework, MCBFA contains four operations, namely chemotaxis, swimming & tumbling, reproduction, and elimination-dispersal are adopted as basic search rules. In order to select appropriate operation at each step, the Q-learning is used in the algorithm [16]. Specifically, Q-learning selects an optimal action by observing the current state and then enters next state, as shown in Fig. 3.

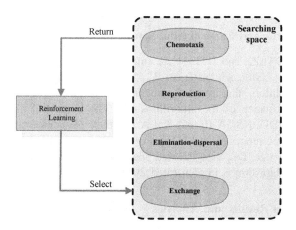

Fig. 3. The proposed MCBFO structure

First, the operation space of bacterial foraging colony is designed as a 4×4 matrix called Q-table, as illustrated in Table 1. Then, each individual implements it. Suppose the state of the individual is Elimination-dispersal, the optimal operation is performed as chemotaxis based on potential reward-maximization. Finally, the individual receives a feedback based on the performance variation of population. The data item (Elimination-dispersal, Chemotaxis) of Q-table is updated as

$$Q(s_r, o_r) = Q(s_r, o_r) + \partial[l_{r+1} + \gamma \max_a Q(s_{t+1}, a) - Q(s_t, a_t)] \qquad (6)$$

$$\partial(t) = 1 - (0.9 * \frac{iter}{\max Cycle}) \qquad (7)$$

Table 1. A specific example of the Q-table

State	Operation			
	Chemotaxis	Reproduction	Elimination-dispersal	Crossover
Chemotaxis	−0.3	0	0	−0.03
Reproduction	0	0	0	0
Elimination-dispersal	0.9	0	0	0
Crossover	1	0	0	0

where γ represents a discount factor range of 0 to 1, l_{r+1} is the immediate reward in its current state s_r by executing a operation o_r, ∂ is the coefficient of learning in [0, 1].

In the operation-level process, the proposed algorithm is similar to the classical algorithm.

4 Benchmark Test

4.1 Test Functions and Experimental Setup

DTLZ1, DTLZ2, DTLZ3 and DTLZ4 are employed to verify the performance of the proposed algorithm. For each instance, *3, 5, 8,* and *10* objectives are respectively considered. In addition, the inverted generational distance (IGD) is employed to evaluate the performance of the algorithms [3]. The compared algorithms include MOEA/D, MOEA/DD, NSGA-III and KnEA and their parameters are set to the same with their original references [5, 8, 14, 15]. For MCBFA, the population size of DE, PE and IE is *N/3*, the size_DE, size_PE and size_IE are equal to *N/3*, size_AE = *N/2*. In addition, each algorithm is implemented 20 times independently on each problem.

4.2 Computation Results and Analysis

The mean and standard deviation values of IGD are given in Table 1 where the best items are highlighted in bold. From the table, it can be found that MCBFA performs more powerfully than other peer algorithms, mainly due to its adopted multi-engine cooperation and comprehensive learning strategies.

Specifically, MCBFA does best on 5-objective DTLZ1 instance, and ranks second on 8-objective instance. Similar observations are obtained on DTLZ2, MOCBFA performs best on 5-objective DTLZ2 instance, while MOEA/DD also obtains powerful performance on 10-objective instance. MCBFA performs best on the DTLZ3 instances, ranking first or second on most of the test instances. Note that the performance of NSGA-III is approximately equivalent to those of MCBFA on DTLZ test instances. On DTLZ4. MCBFA also obtains remarkable performance, while NSGAIII performs more competitively than MCBFA on 8-objective instances. MCBFA are slightly better than MOEA/D on 5-objective instances. Generally, MCBFA performs better than other algorithms on most of test instances. For DTLZ2 and DTLZ4, MCBFA and MOEA/DD performs very closely. Intuitively, MCBFA and MOEA/DD are better than

Table 2. Mean and standard deviation results of IGD obtained by the algorithms

Problem	M	MCBFA	MOEA/D	MOEA/DD	KnEA	NSGAIII
DTLZ1	3	2.504e−02(5.645e−06)	2.431e−02(7.657e−06)	**1.651e−02(7.652e−09)**	5.051e−02(2.346e−02)	2.475e−02(2.251e−07)
	5	**5.254e−02(5.961e−06)**	5.350e−02(9.150e−06)	5.561e−02(1.912e−06)	2.353e−01(7.021e−02)	5.425e−02(8.578e−06)
	8	9.521e−02 (6.832e−05)	**9.520e−02(7.769e−06)**	9.758e−02(9.758e−06)	2.732e−01(1.021e−01)	9.543e−02(4.324e−05)
	10	1.246e−01(9.759e−04)	1.342e−01(9.695e−06)	1.243e−01(8.795e−06)	1.235e + 01(1.221e + 01)	**1.195e−01(6.594e−05)**
DTLZ2	3	4.543e−02(9.761e−07)	4.163e−02(5.634e−08)	4.031e−02(9.760e−08)	**4.027e−02(9.437e−04)**	4.038e−02(1.002e−06)
	5	**2.010e−01(4.022e−06)**	2.016e−01(1.579e−07)	2.021e−01(2.341e−07)	2.013e−01(3.483e−03)	2.014e−01(1.471e−07)
	8	2.504e−01(7.257e−06)	**3.094e−01(9.753e−07)**	3.113e−01(7.114e−06)	1.818e + 01(3.559e−03)	4.261e−01(2.425e−05)
	10	4.482e−01(3.421e−06)	4.568e−01(3.272e−05)	**4.362e−01(6.439e−04)**	6.745e−01(3.032e−04)	6.410e−01(6.825e−06)
DTLZ3	3	5.621e−02(3.015e−07)	3.867e−02(1.025e−05)	**3.756e−02(8.216e−07)**	6.827e−02(6.134e−03)	4.046e−02(4.217e−06)
	5	3.261e−01(8.420e−08)	5.211e−01(3.320e−06)	5.249e−01(4.218e−05)	5.429e−01(6.726e−02)	**2.449e−01(8.152e−06)**
	8	**4.212e−01(5.263e−02)**	4.240e−01(3.252e−04)	4.219e−01(6.060e−05)	4.564e + 00(1.084e + 01)	5.353e−01(9.213e−02)
	10	**5.018e−01(2.120e−04)**	5.727e−01(3.487e−05)	5.361e−01(6.217e−04)	3.732e + 01(9.656e + 01)	6.421e−01(1.025e−01)
DTLZ4	3	4.543e−02(3.180e−06)	4.781e−02(3.111e−07)	**3.368e−02(1.143e−06)**	5.316e−02(8.131e−04)	4.040e−02(1.983e−06)
	5	2.021e−01(2.541e−07)	2.025e−01(6.244e−03)	2.201e−01(1.204e−07)	**1.912e−01(7.124e−04)**	2.012e−01(1.458e−04)
	8	3.514e−01(2.535e−07)	4.001e−01(6.413e−03)	3.678e−01(4.563e−06)	3.952e−01(4.010e−04)	**3.512e−01(6.032e−02)**
	10	**4.710e−01(5.262e−06)**	5.011e−01(8.105e−03)	4.827e−01(5.219e−03)	5.214e−01(5.373e−04)	6.2063e−01(8.924e−03)

other algorithms. For DTLZ1 and DTLZ3, smaller IGD values are found by MCBFA, which indicates the effeteness of MCBFA (Table 2).

4.3 Computation Complexity Analysis

Within one generation, the computation complexity of MCBFA mainly performs the following operations: (1) the decomposition-based engine, (2) the Pareto-based engine, (3) the indicator-based engine. For a population size N, an optimization problem of M objectives, the computational complexity of the decomposition-based engine is O (MNT), where T is the number of the reference vectors. The runtime of the Pareto-based engine is $O(MN^2)$. And the indicators-based needs a runtime of $O(MN^2)$. To sum up, the computation complexity of MCBFA is $O(MN^2)$.

5 Conclusions

This paper presents a new framework based on bacterial foraging paradigm called MCBFA to solve MaOPs. MCBFA approximates an outstanding converged and properly distributed PF by evolving three cooperative bacteria populations with different evolution regulation. Specifically, in the colony-to-colony interaction, the decomposition-based engine, the Pareto-based engine and the indicator-based engine communicate with each other based on the comprehensive learning mechanism, which essentially enhance the population diversity. In the inter-colony evolution, the Q-learning is incorporated into the framework to expedite its local search ability. Experiments have been conducted on a set of many-objective benchmarks. Experimental results show that MCBFA is significant superior or at least comparable to its competitors in terms of IGD. For future research, it is interesting to investigate the performance of MCBFA on more instances and further improve performance on large-scale problems.

Acknowledgements. This work is supported by National Natural Science Foundation of China under Grant No. 6177021519 and No. 61503373 and supported by Fundamental Research Funds for the Central University (N161705001), Liaoning PhD startup fund:optimization model and algorithm of power scheduling for microgrid, Postdoctoral fund in China under Grant No. 2016M601332.

References

1. Gong, Y.J., Li, J.J., Zhou, Y., Li, Y., Chung, S.H., Shi, Y.H., et al.: Genetic learning particle swarm optimization. IEEE Trans. Cybern. **46**(10), 2277 (2016)
2. Lopez, E.M., Coello, C.A.C.: Improving the integration of the IGD+ indicator into the selection mechanism of a Multi-objective Evolutionary Algorithm. In: Evolutionary Computation. IEEE (2017)
3. Deb, K., Pratap, A., Agarwal, S., Meyarivan, T.: A fast and elitist multiobjective genetic algorithm: NSGA-II. IEEE Trans. Evol. Comput. **6**(2), 182–197 (2002)

4. Zitzler, E., Laumanns, M., Thiele, L.: SPEA2: improving the strength pareto evolutionary algorithm (2001)
5. Zhang, Q., Li, H.: MOEA/D: a multionbjective evolutionary algorithm based on decomposition. IEEE Trans. Evol. Comput. **11**(6), 712–731 (2007)
6. Trautmann, H., Wagner, T., Brockhoff, D.: R2-EMOA: focused multiobjective search using R2-indicator-based selection. In: Nicosia, G., Pardalos, P. (eds.) LION 2013. LNCS, vol. 7997, pp. 70–74. Springer, Heidelberg (2013). https://doi.org/10.1007/978-3-642-44973-4_8
7. Köppen, M., Yoshida, K.: Substitute distance assignments in NSGA-II for handling many-objective optimization problems. In: Obayashi, S., Deb, K., Poloni, C., Hiroyasu, T., Murata, T. (eds.) EMO 2007. LNCS, vol. 4403, pp. 727–741. Springer, Heidelberg (2007). https://doi.org/10.1007/978-3-540-70928-2_55
8. Deb, K., Jain, H.: An evolutionary many-objective optimization algorithm using reference-point-based nondominated sorting approach, Part I: solving problems with box constraints. IEEE Trans. Evol. Comput. **18**(4), 577–601 (2014)
9. Ma, L., Cheng, S., Wang, X., Huang, M., Shen, H., He, X., et al.: Cooperative two-engine multi-objective bee foraging algorithm with reinforcement learning. Knowl. Based Syst. **133**, 278–293 (2017)
10. Ma, L., Zhu, Y., Zhang, D.: Niu, B: A hybrid approach to artificial bee colony algorithm. Neural Comput. Appl. **27**(2), 387–409 (2016)
11. Chen, H., Niu, B., Ma, L., et al.: Bacterial colony foraging optimizationl. Neurocomputing **137**(2), 268–284 (2014)
12. Ma, L., Wang, X., Huang, M., Lin, Z., Tian, L., Chen, H.: Two-level master-slave RFID networks planning via hybrid multiobjective artificial bee colony optimizer. IEEE Trans. Syst. Man Cybern. Syst. **PP**(99), 1–20 (2017)
13. Zitzler, E., Künzli, S.: Indicator-based selection in multiobjective search. In: Yao, X., et al. (eds.) PPSN 2004. LNCS, vol. 3242, pp. 832–842. Springer, Heidelberg (2004). https://doi.org/10.1007/978-3-540-30217-9_84
14. Li, K., Deb, K., Zhang, Q., Kwong, S.: An evolutionary many-objective optimization algorithm based on dominance and decomposition. IEEE Trans. Evol. Comput. **19**(5), 694–716 (2015)
15. Zhang, X., Tian, Y., Jin, Y.: A knee point-driven evolutionary algorithm for many-objective optimization. IEEE Trans. Evol. Comput. **19**(6), 761–776 (2015)
16. Watkins, C.J.C.H., Dayan, P.: Technical note: Q-learning. Mach. Learn. **8**(3–4), 279–292 (1992)

Multi-indicator Bacterial Foraging Algorithm with Kriging Model for Many-Objective Optimization

Rui Wang[1], Shengminjie Chen[2], Lianbo Ma[1(✉)], Shi Cheng[3], and Yuhui Shi[4]

[1] College of Software, Northeastern University, Shenyang, China
malb@swc.neu.edu.cn
[2] Faculty of Science, Kunming University of Science and Technology, Kunming, China
[3] School of Computer Science, Shaanxi Normal University, Xi'an, China
[4] Department of Computer Science and Engineering, Southern University of Science and Technology, Shenzhen, China

Abstract. In order to efficiently reduce computational expense as well as manage the diversity and convergence in many-objective optimization, this paper proposes a novel multi-indicator bacterial foraging algorithm with Kriging model (K-MBFA) to guide the search process toward the Pareto front. In the proposed algorithm, a set of preferential individuals for the improved Kriging model are appropriately selected according to the different indicators. Specifically, the stochastic ranking technique is adopted to avoid the search biases of different indicators, which would lead the population to converge to local region of the Pareto front. With several test instances from DTLZ sets with 3, 5, 8 and 10 objectives, K-MBFA is verified to be significantly superior to other compared algorithms in terms of inverted generational distance (IGD).

Keywords: Multi-indicator · Bacterial forging algorithm
Many-objective optimization · Kriging model

1 Introduction

Many-objective optimization refers to optimization problems that involve a set of conflicting objectives, often more than three objectives [1]. Intuitively, the main goal of an optimization algorithm for MaOPs is to obtain a set of optimal compromises between these objectives, which are also termed as Pareto-optimal solutions (PS). As the number of objectives increases, these MaOPs become more difficult to be tackled due to the inability of the nondominance or Pareto-based paradigms to approximate Pareto front (PF). Due to their heuristic features and population-based paradigm, evolutionary algorithms (EAs) exhibit strong search ability on multi-objective optimization problems (MOPs). Among these, Pareto-based EAs are the commonly used scheme, such as NSGA-II [2] and SPEA2 [3].

Compared with low-dimensional MOPs, the curse of dimensionality in MaOPs has caused severe performance deterioration for MOEAs, because (1) The increasing

© Springer International Publishing AG, part of Springer Nature 2018
Y. Tan et al. (Eds.): ICSI 2018, LNCS 10941, pp. 530–539, 2018.
https://doi.org/10.1007/978-3-319-93815-8_50

number of objectives result in the loss of algorithmic selection pressure during the search process and (2) the high-dimensional search space largely weakens the efficiency of the algorithmic operator. Especially, the large search space makes the algorithm more computationally expensive, even nearly stagnant during the evolutionary process.

In order to address the first issue, a considerable number of methods have been developed, such as aggregation-based algorithms [4], preference-based algorithms [5], and relaxed dominance-based algorithms [6]. Among those, the indicator-based approaches are rather simple because the final solutions are evaluated by using the indicators [7]. However, a single indicator would mislead the population evolution towards some local regions of PF [8, 9]. For examples, the $I\varepsilon+$ in IBEA prefers the convergence to the diversity [10], and another indicator I_{SDE} will prefer the diversity instead [11]. Accordingly, multiple indicators with different biases, can work cooperatively for environmental selection, which is conductive to maintain the diversity and convergence in the search process. As for the second issue, surrogate models are usually beneficial to reduce the computation cost of algorithms. The Kriging model [12] is especially utilized for the adaptive approximation of complex problems and it further evaluates errors of the approximation by using the Gaussian function. This approach is helpful for decision makers to locate additional sample points so as to improve accuracy.

It is stressed that recently a number of bacterial foraging algorithms (BFAs) have been developed based on intelligent bacterial behaviors to evolve towards optimal regions. Compared with other EAs, the main merit of the BFA algorithm lies in its more powerful exploitation ability in complex environments [13]. Motivated by the above, a multi-indicator bacterial foraging algorithm with Kriging model called K-MBFA is proposed. Specifically, a set of preferential points for the improved Kriging model are selected according to multiple indicators. Furthermore, the stochastic ranking technique is designed to manage the implementation sequence of the inconsistent indicators. By incorporating these strategies, the BFA has been extended to an effective optimizer for many-objective optimization.

The rest of the paper is given as follows. Section 2 describes the enhanced optimization framework based on Kriging model. In Sect. 3, the proposed K-MBFA algorithm is presented in detail. Section 4 presents comprehensive experiments on a set of test instances to evaluate effectiveness of the proposed algorithm. Section 5 outlines the conclusions.

2 Enhanced Global Optimization Based on Kriging Model

In the proposed model, a number of uniformly-distributed individuals are initialized by the Latin hypercube sampling (LHS) method [14]. The Kriging model for each objective function is constructed by interpolating these initial individuals. A set of indicators including $I\varepsilon+$, I_{SDE} and PBI are used to select the preferred solution from the Kriging model by using the estimated objective functions, as shown in Fig. 1. The binary addictive indicator $I\varepsilon+$ is maximized by the algorithm and then the candidates for additional solutions are identified. Afterwards, the Kriging models are reconstructed

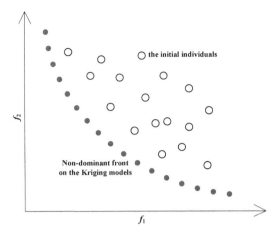

Fig. 1. Reference point definition using an ideal point of solutions on the Kriging models

by the initial and additional individuals. The procedures of K-MBFA are shown in Fig. 2. A classic BFA is adopted by K-MABC to explore preferred solutions based on indicators what is are properly selected.

The ordinary Kriging Model represents the unknown function $f(x)$, which is formulated as

$$f(x) = a(x) + b(x) \tag{1}$$

where x is an m-dimensional decision vector, $a(x)$ is a global model, and $b(x)$ is a Gaussian process with $N(0, \sigma^2)$, which represents a local error with the global model. The correlation between $b(x_i)$ and $b(x_j)$ is strongly correlated to the distance between x_i and x_j. Here, we use the Gaussian function with a weighted distance to define the correlation as

$$Corr(b(x_i), b(x_j)) = \exp(-\sum_{k=1}^{m} \omega^k (x_i^k - x_j^k)^2) \tag{2}$$

where $\omega^k (0 \leq \omega^k < \infty)$ is the weight factor of the kth element of an m-dimensional weight vector ω. These weights maintain the anisotropy of the Kriging model and improve its accuracy. The predictor and uncertainty of the Kriging are expressed as

$$\tilde{f}(x) = \tilde{b}(x) + r(x)^T R^{-1} (f - \tilde{b}) \tag{3}$$

$$v^2(x) = \tilde{\sigma}^2 (1 - r(x)^T R^{-1} r(x) + \frac{(1 - 1^T R^{-1} r(x))^2}{1^T R^{-1} 1}) \tag{4}$$

where $\tilde{b}(x)$ is the approximated value of $b(x)$, R express the $n \times n$ matrix whose (i, j) element is $Corr(b(xi), b(xj))$, $r(x)$ is an n-dimensional vector whose ith element is $Corr(b(xi), b(xj))$, and then f and $\tilde{b}$ are formulized as follows when there are n solutions

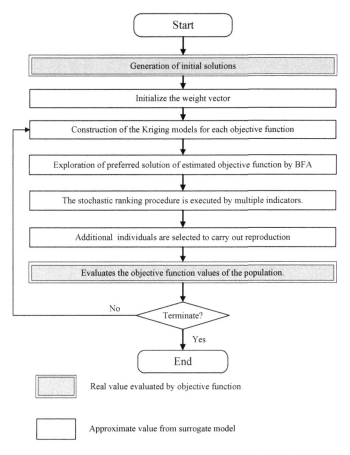

Fig. 2. Flowchart of the K-MBFA.

$$f = (f(x^1) \ldots f(x^n))^T \tag{5}$$

$$\tilde{b} = (\tilde{b}(x^1) \ldots \tilde{b}(x^n))^T \tag{6}$$

ω, $\tilde{b}(x)$ and $\tilde{\sigma}^2$ (approximated σ^2) are the unknown parameters in the Kriging model. By maximizing the likelihood function, the unknown parameters are obtained [15].

Based on the Kriging model, the EI value, which is the expected objective function improvement from the current non-domination solution, is calculated according to the improvement value $I(x)$, expressed as

$$I(x) = \max(f_{ref} - f, 0) \tag{7}$$

$$EI(x) = \int_{-\infty}^{f_{ref}} (f_{ref} - f)\lambda(f)df \tag{8}$$

where λ is the probability of f, the density function is denoted by $N(\tilde{f}(x), v^2(x))$, f_{ref} is the reference value of f, namely the minimum value of $f(x)$. Accordingly, EI(x) can be treated as the approximate value of the objective function.

3   The K-MBFA Algorithm

In K-MBFA, a stochastic ranking is used to select preferred solution based on multiple indicators. Assuming that that the population contains N individuals, while $N/2$ individuals need to be selected, the algorithm is to rank individuals for $N/2$ times. All pairs of adjacent individuals are compared by the values of a randomly chosen indicator during each sweep. The termination condition for the sweep is that there is no change in the rank ordering. The parameter $P(p_1, p_2)$ is the tradeoff between multiple indicators. The first $N/2$ individuals are selected as additional solutions when the ranking procedure terminates. The flowchart of the stochastic ranking is shown in Algorithm 1.

Algorithm 1: The stochastic ranking procedure

Input : $P_t = \{p_1, ..., p_N\}$ (The population)

Output: P_{t+1} (Sorted population that will be reproduced)

1.   **for** Counter=1 to $|P_t|/2$ **do**

2.   **for** i=1 to $|P_t|-1$ **do**

3.   I=random(I_1, I_2, I_3)

4.   **if** $I(u_i)$ is worse than $I(u_{i+1})$ **then**

5.   Swap(u_i, u_{i+1})

6.   **end**

7.   **end**

8.   **if** no swap done **then**

9.   Break

10.   **end**

11. **end**

12. $P_{t+1} = \{u_1, ..., u_{N/2}\}$

Accordingly, any suitable indicator can be applied in algorithm. Considering convergence and diversity, the indicators PBI, Iε+ [10] and I$_{SDE}$ [11] are chosen for

K-MBFA. These three indicators have been proved to be effective in terms of convergence or diversity and are low computational expenditure.

The aggregation function $I_1(x)$ by the penalty-based boundary interception (PBI) approach is defined as follows:

$$PBI(P,a) = d_1 + \delta d_2 \tag{9}$$

$$I_1(x) = \min(PBI(P,\alpha)) \tag{10}$$

where d_1 is the distance between the origin and the certain point P, and d_2 is the perpendicular distance from the weight vector α. The main idea of PBI is shown in Fig. 3 in a two-dimensional objective space. And then δ is a preset parameter that combines d_1 and d_2 into a single value that maintain the diversity and convergence of individuals. The formula to measure d_1 and d_2 are given as:

$$d_1 = \frac{p^T w}{\|w\|} \tag{11}$$

$$d_2 = \left\| P - d_1 \left(\frac{w}{\|w\|} \right) \right\| \tag{12}$$

The binary addictive ε-indicator and the corresponding $I_2(x)$ can be defined as:

$$I_{\varepsilon+}(x,y) = \min_\varepsilon(f_i(x) - \varepsilon \leq f_i(y), i \in \{1, \ldots, m\}) \tag{13}$$

$$I_2(x) = \sum_{y \in A, y \neq x} -e^{-I_{\varepsilon+}(x,y)/0.05} \tag{14}$$

where A is the population of all individuals. This indicator is employed to analysis dominance relation in the multi-objective optimization. In addition, I_2 is also used as the fitness assignment for each bacterium.

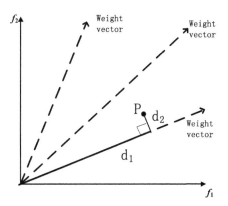

Fig. 3. Illustration of the PBI function

The I_{SDE} and the corresponding $I_3(x)$ for measuring solutions are defined as:

$$I_{SDE}(x,y) = \sqrt{\sum\nolimits_{1 \leq i \leq m} sd(f_i(x),f_i(y))^2} \tag{15}$$

$$I_3(x) = min_{(y \in A, y \neq x)}\{I_{SDE}(x,y)\} \tag{16}$$

where

$$sd(f_i(x),f_i(y)) = \begin{cases} f_i(y) - f_i(x) & if\ f_i(x) < f_i(y) \\ 0 & otherwise \end{cases} \tag{17}$$

4 Experiment Results

4.1 Test Functions and Experimental Setup

A suit of benchmark functions are employed namely DTLZ1–DTLZ4 with 3, 5, 8, and 10 objectives to evaluate the performance of the proposed algorithm. The Inverse Generational Distance (IGD) metric is used to measure the performance of the involved algorithms. The proposed algorithm is compared with four state-of-the-art algorithms, namely MOEA/D, MOEA/DD, NSGA-III and KnEA. The compared algorithms are adjusted to be the same as their original references. For the proposed K-MBFA, The number of initial solutions generated by LHS is set to $(11m - 1)$ suggested in [15] and additional individuals are added until the total number of initial and additional individuals reaches 200. Other parameters for BFA are listed as: Step size C = 0.05, P_{ed} = 0.25, the swimming & tumbling maximum step size Ns = 1, the number of reproduction N_{re} = 50 and number of elimination-dispersal N_{ed} = 20. The number of fitness evaluation is set to 10000 and the independent run times are set to 30.

4.2 Computation Results and Analysis

The mean and standard deviation values of IGD by the five algorithms over 20 independent runs are reported in Table 1 where the best items are highlighted in bold. From the table, it is clearly observed that K-MBFA performs more powerfully than other peer algorithms, mainly due to its adopted Kriging model and multi-indicator cooperation strategies.

To be specific, K-MBFA obtains the first ranks on 5- and 10-objective DTLZ2 instances, and achieves the first ranks on 10-objective DTLZ3 instance, while KnEA also obtains competent performance on 8-objective DTLZ4 instance. On DTL1, K-MBFA performs a little worse than NSGAIII, still better than MOEA/D, MOEA/DD and KnEA. Especially, for the more complex DTLZ4 instances where the distribution of the points on PF is strongly nonuniform, K-MBFA obtains a significantly better approximation than that of NSGAIII and MOEA/DD. Generally, K-MBFA obtains better performance than that of other algorithms on most test instances. For DTLZ3 and

Table 1. Mean and standard deviation results of IGD obtained by K-MBFA

Problem	M	K-MBFA	MOEA/D	MOEA/DD	KnEA	NSGAIII
DTLZ1	3	1.726e−02(5.378e−03)	5.954e−02(5.437e−02)	1.380e−02(5.717e−08)	1.470e−02(7.320e−08)	**1.370e−02(2.702e−07)**
	5	1.175e−01(1.648e−02)	2.101e−01(7.398e−02)	6.333e−02(8.219e−06)	6.333e−02(7.422e−07)	**6.332e−02(8.386e−07)**
	8	1.860e−01(9.864e−03)	3.336e−01(1.183e−01)	**9.722e−02(5.737e−05)**	9.725e−02(1.893e−05)	9.727e−02(8.699e−07)
	10	**1.012e−01(1.408e−02)**	2.164e+01(1.453e+01)	1.133e−01(1.119e−04)	1.133e−01(2.404e−06)	1.134e−01(8.846e−05)
DTLZ2	3	3.802e−02(4.658e−04)	4.290e−02(8.608e−05)	3.638e−02(3.377e−08)	**3.635e−02(4.167e−08)**	3.638e−02(4.588e−09)
	5	**1.711e−01(8.337e−04)**	1.847e−01(1.896e−03)	1.949e−01(1.108e−07)	1.949e−01(9.604e−08)	1.949e−01(1.006e−07)
	8	3.481e−01(1.795e−03)	3.627e−01(6.662e−04)	**3.149e−01(1.077e−06)**	3.159e−01(5.022e−06)	3.152e−01(1.236e−04)
	10	**4.352e−01(4.922e−04)**	4.572e−01(2.418e−03)	4.376e−01(6.486e−06)	4.376e−01(7.273e−06)	5.147e−01(1.098e−01)
DTLZ3	3	3.883e−02(1.712e−03)	5.445e−02(5.590e−03)	3.640e−02(1.442e−05)	3.639e−02(7.940e−07)	**3.638e−02(3.993e−06)**
	5	2.702e−01(3.672e−02)	6.605e−01(3.067e−01)	1.949e−01(3.620e−05)	1.949e−01(1.022e−06)	**1.923e−01(9.715e−07)**
	8	5.531e−01(2.855e−02)	**2.491e−01(1.355e−01)**	3.149e−01(2.617e−05)	3.149e−01(5.811e−06)	6.113e−01(3.375e−03)
	10	**1.156e−01(6.443e−01)**	4.908e+01(1.792e−02)	4.378e−01(5.253e−04)	4.376e−01(2.171e−05)	5.424e−01(1.489e−01)
DTLZ4	3	3.874e−02(5.384e−04)	4.313e−02(5.714e−04)	3.638e−02(3.451e−08)	**3.630e−02(5.483e−08)**	3.640e−02(3.948e−06)
	5	**1.720e−01(8.266e−04)**	1.807e−01(2.905e−03)	4.207e−01(6.419e−08)	1.949e−01(1.406e−08)	1.949e−01(3.171e−05)
	8	**3.479e−01(7.946e−04)**	3.542e−01(6.150e−03)	4.276e−01(5.224e−06)	3.549e−01(3.782e−06)	3.780e−01(8.925e−02)
	10	**4.205e−01(1.907e−03)**	5.0436e−01(6.972e−04)	4.346e−01(1.820e−05)	4.976e−01(1.321e−05)	6.181e−01(9.449e−03)

DTLZ4, the performance of K-MBFA is relatively close to that of MOEA/DD. Generally, K-MBFA and MOEA/DD perform more powerfully than other algorithms, which indicates K-MBFA has great potential to handle complex multi-objective problems.

4.3 Computation Complexity Analysis

Given an MaOP with m objectives and a population size of N, the computation complexity of each generation of K-MBFA is given as: first, constructing Kriging models for each objective requires $O(mN)$. Second, determining preferred solution by using estimated objective function needs $O(mN^2)$. Third, the computation complexity of the stochastic ranking process is $O(mN^2)$. In summary, the computational complexity of K-MBFA is $O(mN^2)$ better than MOEA/DD, at the same level of NSGA-III, MOEA/D and KnEA. Due to fitness evaluation by Kriging model, the former is less time-consuming than the latter in practice.

5   Conclusions

This paper presents a new evolutionary optimization algorithm based on bacterial foraging paradigm called K-MBFA to solve MaOPs. K-MBFA uses the Kriging model to reduce computational expense during the search process, and adopts the stochastic ranking technique to manage the implementation of multiple indicators. These mechanisms can guide the search process of the algorithm toward the Pareto front quickly.

To be specific, in K-MBFA, a set of preferential individuals for the improved Kriging model are determined based on the specific indicators. Meanwhile, the stochastic ranking technique is designed deliberately to balance the search of different indicators. Extensive experiments have been conducted on a set of well-known test functions. Computation results verify that K-MBFA is significant superior or at least comparable to its competitors in terms of IGD. In the future, it is worthwhile to further investigate the performance of K-MBFA in more problems by accurate statistical tests.

Acknowledgements. This work is supported by National Natural Science Foundation of China under Grant No. 6177021519 and No. 61503373 and supported by Fundamental Research Funds for the Central University (N161705001), Shenzhen Science and Technology Innovation Committee (ZDSYS201703031748284).

References

1. Gong, Y.-J., Chen, W.-N., Zhang, J., Li, Y., Zhang, Q., et al.: Distributed evolutionary algorithms and their models. Appl. Soft Comput. **34**(C), 286–300 (2015)
2. Deb, K., Pratap, A., Agarwal, S., Meyarivan, T.: A fast and elitist multiobjective genetic algorithm: NSGA-II. IEEE Trans. Evol. Comput. **6**(2), 182–197 (2002)
3. Zitzler, E., Laumanns, M., Thiele, L.: SPEA2: improving the strength pareto evolutionary algorithm (2001)

4. Zhang, Q., Li, H.: MOEA/D: a multiobjective evolutionary algorithm based on decomposition. IEEE Trans. Evol. Comput. **11**(6), 712–731 (2007)
5. Deb, K., Jain, H.: An evolutionary many-objective optimization algorithm using reference-point-based nondominated sorting approach, part i: solving problems with box constraints. IEEE Trans. Evol. Comput. **18**(4), 577–601 (2014)
6. Köppen, M., Yoshida, K.: Substitute distance assignments in NSGA-II for handling many-objective optimization problems. In: Obayashi, S., Deb, K., Poloni, C., Hiroyasu, T., Murata, T. (eds.) EMO 2007. LNCS, vol. 4403, pp. 727–741. Springer, Heidelberg (2007). https://doi.org/10.1007/978-3-540-70928-2_55
7. Chen, H., Niu, B., Ma, L., Su, W.: Bacterial colony foraging optimization. Neurocomputing **137**(2), 268–284 (2014)
8. Ma, L., Cheng, S., Wang, X., Huang, M., Hai, H., He, X.: Cooperative two-engine multi-objective bee foraging algorithm with reinforcement learning. Knowledge-Based Systems (2017)
9. Ma, L., Zhu, Y., Zhang, D., Niu, B.: A hybrid approach to artificial bee colony algorithm. Neural Comput. Appl. **27**(2), 387–409 (2016)
10. Zitzler, E., Künzli, S.: Indicator-based selection in multiobjective search. In: Yao, X., et al. (eds.) Parallel Problem Solving from Nature - PPSN VIII, PPSN 2004. LNCS, vol. 3242, pp. 832–842. Springer, Heidelberg (2004). https://doi.org/10.1007/978-3-540-30217-9_84
11. Li, M., Yang, S., Liu, X.: Shift-based density estimation for pareto-based algorithms in many-objective optimization. IEEE Trans. Evol. Comput. **18**(3), 348–365 (2014)
12. Matheron, G.: Principles of geostatistics. Econ. Geol. **58**(8), 1246–1266 (1963)
13. Rani, R.R., Ramyachitra, D.: Multiple sequence alignment using multi-objective based bacterial foraging optimization algorithm. Biosystems **150**, 177 (2016)
14. Mckay, M.D., Beckman, R.J., Conover, W.J.: A comparison of three methods for selecting values of input variables in the analysis of output from a computer code. Technometrics **21**(2), 239–245 (2000)
15. Jeong, S., Minemura, Y., Obayashi, S.: Optimization of combustion chamber for diesel engine using Kriging model. JFST **1**, 138–146 (2006)
16. Jones, D.R., Schonlau, M., Welch, W.J.: Efficient global optimization of expensive black-box functions. J. Global Optim. **13**(4), 455–492 (1998)

An Improved Bacteria Foraging Optimization Algorithm for High Dimensional Multi-objective Optimization Problems

Yueliang Lu[1] and Qingjian Ni[2(✉)]

[1] College of Software Engineering, Southeast University, Suzhou, China
[2] School of Computer Science and Engineering, Southeast University, Nanjing, China
nqj@seu.edu.cn

Abstract. In this paper, an improved bacterial foraging optimization algorithm (BFO), which is inspired by the foraging and chemotactic phenomenon of bacteria, named high dimensional multi-objective bacterial foraging optimization (HMBFO) is introduced for solving high dimensional multi-objective optimization (MO) problems. The high-dimension update strategy is presented in this paper to solve the problem that the global Pareto solutions can be hardly obtained by traditional MBFO in high-dimension MO problems. According to this strategy, the position of bacteria not only can be rapidly updated to the optimal solution, but also can enhance the searching precision and reduce chemotaxis dependency remarkably. Moreover, the penalty mechanism is considered for solving the inequality constraints MO problems, and three different performance metrics (Hypervolume, Convergence metric, Spacing metric) are introduced to evaluate the performances of algorithms. Compared with the other four evolutionary MO algorithms (MBFO, MOCLPSO, MOPSO, PESA2), the simulation result shows that in most cases, the proposed algorithm carries out better than the other existing algorithms, it has high efficiency, rapid speed of convergence and strong search capability of global Pareto solutions.

1 Introduction

Many real-world optimization problems have two or more objectives [1], and these objectives in multi-objective optimization (MO) problems are mutual contradiction and competition. Without the objectives evaluating information, those optimization problems will be solved by a set of optimal solutions (Pareto-optimal solutions). Thus how to obtain the global Pareto-optimal solutions is the hottest spot of recent research.

In the past few decades, there are some novel ways to solve the MO problems. Many algorithms are classics and landmark which include vector evaluated genetic algorithm (VEGA), nondominated sorting genetic algorithm II (NSGA-II) [2], the Pareto envelope-based selection algorithm (PESA), PESA-II [3], the

© Springer International Publishing AG, part of Springer Nature 2018
Y. Tan et al. (Eds.): ICSI 2018, LNCS 10941, pp. 540–549, 2018.
https://doi.org/10.1007/978-3-319-93815-8_51

Pareto evolutionary algorithm (SPEA), SPEA-2 [4]. Many algorithms are innovative computing and popular in recent years which include multi-objective particle swarm optimization (MOPSO) [5], multi-objective comprehensive learning particle swarm optimization (MOCLPSO) [6], the nondominated neighbor immune algorithm (NNIA) [7], model-based multi-objective estimation of distribution algorithm (RM-MEDA) [8], bee optimization algorithm (BOA) [9]. Different algorithms have its own unique features as well as using different ways to solve the MO problems.

There are many popular swarm intelligence algorithms especially the Bacteria Foraging Optimization (BFO) [10]. In recent years, BFO has been used in many important areas [11,12]. With the research fervorization of MO problems, BFO algorithm has been introduced to solve those problems [13], and then it was applied rapidly [14,15].

With the complexity of MO problems, the dimension of those problems are getting higher and higher. In the paper [13], it is clear and detailed explanation that the performance of MBFO is hardly to obtain the Pareto solution in the high-dimension MO problems, therefore, this paper proposes a BFO Algorithm to improve the performance based on those problems. In the High-dimension multi-objective bacteria foraging optimization (HMBFO), we create a high-dimension update strategy for improving the performance of BFO in high-dimension MO problems.

This paper is organized as follows. Section 2 introduces the basic concept of MO problems. In Sect. 3, there are some brief introduction about BFO algorithm and the extend of MBFO algorithm. The high-dimension update strategy and its theoretical proof are showed in Sect. 4. The simulation is given in Sect. 5. Finally, in Sect. 6, we conclude this paper.

2   MO Problems and Three Evaluation Indices

Unlike the single objective optimization problems, in MO problems, the improvement of one objective is at the cost of deteriorating the others, and it must obtain a solution set for compromising all of the objectives [14]. A set of decision vectors are considered in this study which represent global Pareto-optimal sets. All vectors in the true Pareto-optimal sets are non-dominated by any vectors in the breathing spaces.

There are three usual evaluation indices, Hypervolume, Convergence metric and Spacing metric [16].

Hypervolume: Hypervolume is used to calculate the covered volume in the global Pareto-optimal sets. As the minimize multi-objective problem, the dash area, which is created by Pareto points and reference point, is the hypervolume. And the smaller value of objectives or the larger the number of Pareto points, the bigger the hypervolume. The hypervolume can be calculated as follow

$$V_H((x_0, ..., x_m)) = \sum_{i=1}^{m} (x_{i+1} - x_i)(f(x_0) - f(x_i)) \tag{1}$$

Thus, the function of hypervolume is extended as follow

$$V_H = volume(\bigcup_{i=1}^{|Q|} v_i) \tag{2}$$

Convergence Metric: Convergence metric which also named Generational distance (GD) is used to describe the distance between searched non-dominated solutions and the actual Pareto-optimal front.

The $Sg = \{Sg^1, Sg^2, ..., Sg^M\}$ denote the global Pareto-optimal solutions, and the current Pareto-optimal solutions $Sp = \{Sp^1, Sp^2, ..., Sp^M\}$ are calculated by the proposed algorithm, and the function of convergence metric as follow

$$Cm(Sp) = \frac{\sum_{i=1}^{|Sp|} d_i}{|Sp|} \tag{3}$$

where

$$d_i = \min_{j=1}^{|Sg|} \sqrt{\sum_{k=1}^{D} \left(\frac{f_k(Sp^i) - f_k(Sg^j)}{f_k^{max} - f_k^{min}} \right)} \tag{4}$$

f_k^{min} and f_k^{max} denote the minimum and maximum values of the in the kth objective respectively.

Spacing Metric: The current Pareto-optimal solutions are also used in calculating,

$$S = \sqrt{\frac{1}{|A| - 1} \sum_{i=1}^{|A|} (\bar{L} - L_i)^2} \tag{5}$$

where

$$L_i = \min_j \left\{ \sum_{k=1}^{D} |f_k(Sp_i) - f_k(Sp_j)| \right\}, \quad i, j = 1, 2, ..., |Sp| \tag{6}$$

$\bar{L}$ is the average value for all L_i. It is denoted that the distribute of Pareto solutions are equidistant, if $S = 0$. It is clearly described that these three indices evaluate the performance of different aspects of the algorithm in [16]. Hypervolume considers the Convergence and diversity, Convergence metric calculates the convergence, and Spacing metric concentrate on the distribution of the solutions.

3   Bacteria Foraging Optimization Algorithm

In BFO [10], firstly, the positions of all bacteria are initialized. The chemotaxis operation is performed through tumbling and swimming. But before each the bacteria tumbling, the group behavior of *E.coli* is executed, which intricate and stable spatio-temporal patterns are formed in semisolid nutrient medium. Through the cell-to-cell signaling released, the current bacterium is influenced by attractant signal and repellent signal produced by the others bacteria which helps current bacteria to aggregate into groups as well as move to concentric patterns of swarms with high bacterial density.

$$G(S^l, S_{\varepsilon,\kappa,o}) = \sum_{\imath}^{D} G(S^l, S^{\imath}_{\varepsilon,\kappa,o})$$

$$= \sum_{\imath=1}^{D} \left[-d_{att} \cdot exp \left(-w_{att} \cdot \sum_{i=1}^{N}(s^{\imath.i} - s^{l,i})^2 \right) \right] \quad (7)$$

$$+ \sum_{\imath=1}^{D} \left[-h_{rep} \cdot exp \left(-w_{rep} \cdot \sum_{i=1}^{N}(s^{\imath.i} - s^{l,i})^2 \right) \right]$$

where $G(S^l, S_{\varepsilon,\kappa,o})$ is the cost function which denote the information cost from changed the population distribution, when the cost value of $G(S^l)$ is dominated by the cost value $G(S^l, S_{\varepsilon,\kappa,o})$, the lth bacterium will move to the concentric of the population, d_{att} and w_{att} are the depth and width of the released attractant signal, h_{rep} and w_{rep} are the height and width of repellant signal respectively; $S^{\imath}_{\varepsilon,\kappa,o}$ represent the position of $\imath$th bacterium at εth chemotactic step, κth reproductive step and oth elimination/dispersal steps. The tumbling operation which generated a random direction vector is executed after executing group behavior.

$$\varphi(l) = \frac{\Delta(l)}{\sqrt{\Delta^T(l) \cdot \Delta(l)}} \quad (8)$$

Where $\varphi(l)$ is the random direction; $\Delta(l)$ represents a D-dimension vector whose all elements lie in of lth bacterium. In this tumbling direction, if the current bacterium is not dominated by the next bacterium, it tumbles again. If it is dominated, the swim behavior is executed, and the way can be described as follow

$$S^l_{\varepsilon+1,\kappa,o} = S^l_{\varepsilon,\kappa,o} + C(l) \cdot \varphi(l) \quad (9)$$

Where $C(l)$ denotes the certain step. When times of swimming steps equal N_s, the chemotaxis operation will be terminated. According the natural law of survival of the fittest, the reproduction behavior is introduced. The less healthy bacteria die, and the other healthier bacteria division, which are placed in the same location.

The elimination/dispersal step is the way to help the population jumping out the local optimum. In this step, some bacteria will be initialized, and the initialization probability is Pb.

4   High-Dimension Update Strategy

The strengths and weaknesses of the MBFO can be thoroughly studied by test problems with different characteristics. MBFO performs well either in diversity or general distance in test problems, which have lower dimensional variables. But comparatively high values of converge and diversity metric were showed in test problems which have higher dimensional variables [13]. Therefore, in this paper, a high-dimension update strategy is introduced to improve the performance of MBFO.

As the progress of optimizing, it is supposed that obtaining the best solution can spend n times optimization in one dimension, however, in thirty dimensions, it will be spend n^{30} times. Thus the performance of simple exploration and optimization unable to meet the needs for dimension growth, it is imperative to increase information interaction. It is simple but important theory that each two or more vectors which are not parallel with each other can donate every vectors, and using specific strategy can obtain the specific connection between new created vectors with basic vectors. The Pareto solutions are nondominated with each other, thus the probability of parallel each other in Pareto solutions almost are zero. The new solutions which are created by algorithm based on Pareto solutions must be in the feasible region, therefore the optimal space area must be the simply connected space [14].

M donates the number of basic Pareto solution, D represents the dimension number of the solution's space area. Firstly, the probability which decision the distribution of new solution randomly in specific area.

$$P_i = \frac{\rho}{M} \cdot rand[-1,1] \quad i = 1, 2, ..., M \tag{10}$$

where ρ is the constant quantity which control the range of specific area.

$$\gamma_j^k = \sum_{\substack{i=1 \\ i \neq j}}^{M} P_i \cdot Sp_i^k + (1 - \sum_{\substack{i=1 \\ i \neq j}}^{M} P_i) \cdot Sp_j^k \quad j = 1, 2, ..., M \quad k = 1, 2, ..., D \tag{11}$$

where γ_j^k denote the kth dimension of the jth new solution and Sp is the solution in Pareto solutions. After updating strategy, the jth new bacteria can be describe as follow

$$S_j = \{\gamma_j^1, ..., \gamma_j^k, ..., \gamma_j^D\} \tag{12}$$

This updating strategy can be simplified as follow

$$\gamma_j^k = \sum_{i=1}^{M} P_i \cdot (Sp_i^k - Sp_j^k) + Sp_j^k \tag{13}$$

Thus in (14), we can see the new bacteria S_j is generated around Sp_j according to the others Sp_i.

Range Limited: According to (12) (13), in S_j, there are D formulas, and combined the polynomial, we can obtain the function

$$\sum_{k=1}^{D} \gamma_j^k = \sum_{i=1}^{M} P_i \cdot (\sum_{k=1}^{D} Sp_i^k - \sum_{k=1}^{D} Sp_j^k) + \sum_{k=1}^{D} Sp_j^k \tag{14}$$

In (14), the value of Sp are known in the Pareto solutions, therefore the range of new bacterial S_j is a space area which is surrounded by many hyperplanes and decided by the probability P. And the max and min hyperplanes respectively are

$$\sum_{k=1}^{D} \gamma_j^k = \sum_{i=1}^{M} \left| \frac{\rho}{M} \cdot \left(\sum_{k=1}^{D} Sp_i^k - \sum_{k=1}^{D} Sp_j^k \right) \right| + \sum_{k=1}^{D} Sp_j^k \tag{15}$$

$$\sum_{k=1}^{D} \gamma_j^k = -\sum_{i=1}^{M} \left| \frac{\rho}{M} \cdot \left(\sum_{k=1}^{D} Sp_i^k - \sum_{k=1}^{D} Sp_j^k \right) \right| + \sum_{k=1}^{D} Sp_j^k \tag{16}$$

Thus ρ is the key variable for controlling the range of specific area.

5 Simulation

In this paper, MBFO, MOCLPSO, MOPSO, PESA2 are introduced to compare the performance of the HMBFO algorithm. And the number of populations is 30, and the iterate number is 50. In HMBFO, $Nc = 50$, $Ns = 10$, $Nre = 4$, $Ned = 2$, $C = 0.1$, $M = 4$, $\rho = 0.5$.

In this study, Zitzler-Deb-Thiele's function N.1 (ZDT1), ZDT2, ZDT3, ZDT4, ZDT6 [17], Osyczka and Kundu function (OAK) [18], those function are two objectives; Deb-L Thiele-M Laumanns-E Zitzler function N.1 (DTLZ1), DTLZ2, DTLZ3, DTLZ4, DTLZ5, DTLZ7 [19], those function are three objectives. Those all benchmark problems are used to evaluate the performance of the algorithms.

In ZDT1-ZDT3 and DTLZ1-DTLZ5, they are set that $D = 30$, and in ZDT4,OAK and ZDT6, $D = 6$. In those classical MO problems, the constraints of OAK and DTLZ7 are the inequality constraints. In the process of solving the equality constraints problems, the variable equality constraints can be substituted into objective equations, but inequality constraints can not. Thus it is the best way that those inequality constraints functions are transformed to the approach of penalty functions [20].

$$f_j^*(\bar{x}) = f_j(\bar{x}) + \tau \cdot \sum_{i=1}^{m} (e^{max(g_i(\bar{x}),0)} - 1)^2 \quad j = 1, 2, ..., M \tag{17}$$

where τ is the penalty factor, $max\{\}$ denotes outputting the maximum value.

The Hypervolume considers the convergence and diversity, thus it is the best choice to evaluate the performance of algorithms, but, the calculated amount shows exponential growth as the number of objections grows. Thus, in this paper, for two objective problems, the Hypervolume index is used to evaluate the convergence and diversity of algorithm. And for three objective problems, it will use the Convergence metric calculates the convergence, and Spacing metric concentrate on the distribution of the solution.

Thus, the hypervolume simulation results of five algorithms for 30 times based on ZDT1, ZDT2, ZDT3, ZDT4, ZDT6, OAK are showed form Fig. 1.

Firstly, in OAK, 51% of PESA2 are the penalty value, thus PESA2 is not participated in comparison in this MO problem. In Fig. 1, the hypervolume of

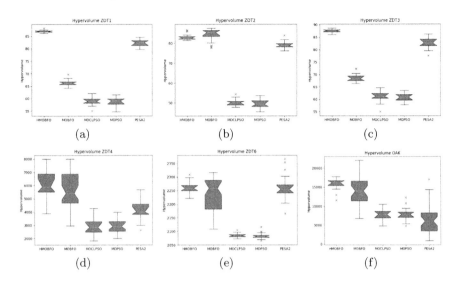

Fig. 1. Hypervolume

HMBFO in ZDT1, ZDT3, OAK are superior to the MBFO's, and we can see that HMBFO obtain the best value in five problems.

In ZDT2, ZDT4 and ZDT6, the performance of two algorithm are difficult to distinguish. Therefore, the hypervolume value in every iteration are showed in the Fig. 2.

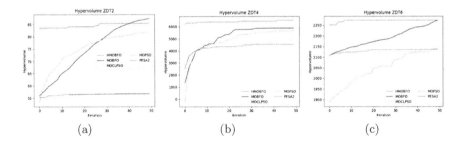

Fig. 2. Iterative curve of hypervolume

In Fig. 2, it is clear that the convergence rates of HMBFO are faster than MBFO's. And the robust of HMBFO is the best. Thus, it is proved that this improvement is effective for introducing the high-dimension update strategy.

In DTLZ7, 95% values of PESA2 are the penalty values, thus in this problem, its also not participated in comparison.

In Fig. 3, it is showed that the Convergence metric five algorithms in DTLZ1, DTLZ2, DTLZ3, DTLZ4, DTLZ5 and DTLZ7, where in DTLZ1,

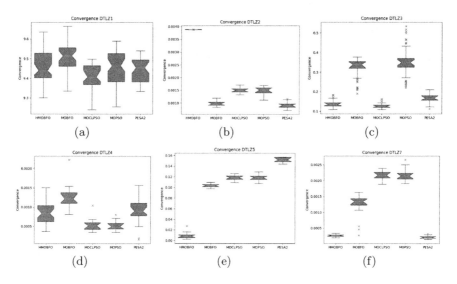

Fig. 3. Convergence metric

DTLZ3, DTLZ4, DTLZ5 and DTLZ7, the convergence of HMBFO is better than MBFO's. In DTLZ2, DTLZ3, DTLZ4 and DTLZ7, those are regarded as getting to the Pareto optimization surface because the convergence value is less than 10^{-1}.

Then, the distribution of the algorithms are showed in Fig. 4.

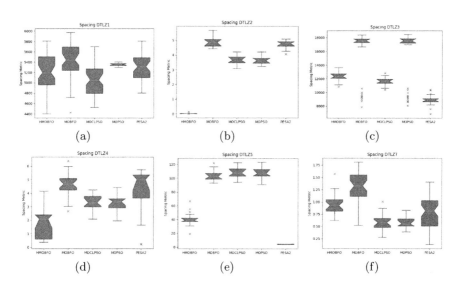

Fig. 4. Spacing metric

In Fig. 4, all the spacing of HMBFO are superior to the MBFO's, thus it is also proved that this improvement is effective for introducing the high-dimension update strategy.

6   Conclusion

In this paper, High Dimensional Multi-objective Bacterial Foraging Optimization (HMBFO) based on Multi-objective Bacterial Foraging Optimization (MBFO) is proposed. The theory of high-dimension update strategy is introduced in HMBFO, which can veritably accelerate the convergence promptly and have strong capability of global Pareto solutions searching and robust. Penalty function is also a better choice for solving the inequality constraints MO problems. Three performance metrics: Hypervolume, Convergence metric, Spacing metric are used to evaluate and compare the performance of the algorithms in this paper. The simulation results have testified the ability of HMBFO in finding Pareto-optimal solutions. Through comparing with four other multi-objective optimization evolutionary algorithms in Figs. 1, 2, 3 and 4, HMBFO distinctly outperforms MBFO, MOCLPSO and MOPSO, and in most cases transcend the PESA2. In the future, the strengths and weaknesses of the proposed algorithm can be showed in the in-depth study. For instance in Fig. 2, it is clearly showed that if the number of iteration is increased, the hypervolume of MBFO will better than HMBFO, Thus, although the high-dimension update strategy improved the convergence, the ability of deep exploration is limited. Therefore, more powerful and complicated HMBFO variants are possible to appear in the future, if we enhance the ability of high-dimension update strategy in the earlier iteration, and weaken or omit it in the later.

References

1. Deb, K.: Multi-Objective Optimization Using Evolutionary Algorithms, vol. 16. Wiley, Hoboken (2001)
2. Niu, X., Liu, K., Zhang, Y., Xiao, G., Gong, Y.: Multiobjective optimization of multistage synchronous induction coilgun based on NSGA-II. IEEE Trans. Plasma Sci. **45**(7), 1622–1628 (2017)
3. Prata, B.d.A.: A multiobjective metaheuristic approach for the integrated vehicle and crew scheduling. J. Transp. Lit. **10**(2), 10–14 (2016)
4. He, F., Shen, K., Guan, L., Jiang, M.: Research on energy-saving scheduling of a forging stock charging furnace based on an improved SPEA2 algorithm. Sustainability **9**(11), 2154 (2017)
5. Azaza, M., Wallin, F.: Multi objective particle swarm optimization of hybrid microgrid system: a case study in Sweden. Energy **123**, 108–118 (2017)
6. Zhang, G., Li, Y.: A memetic algorithm for global optimization of multimodal nonseparable problems. IEEE Trans. Cybern. **46**(6), 1375–1387 (2016)
7. Liu, R., Wang, R., He, M., Wang, X.: Improved artificial weed colonization based multi-objective optimization algorithm. In: Yue, D., Peng, C., Du, D., Zhang, T., Zheng, M., Han, Q. (eds.) LSMS/ICSEE -2017. CCIS, vol. 762, pp. 181–190. Springer, Singapore (2017). https://doi.org/10.1007/978-981-10-6373-2_19

8. Mohagheghi, E., Akbarzadeh-T, M.R.: Multi-objective estimation of distribution algorithm based on voronoi and local search. In: 6th International Conference on Computer and Knowledge Engineering (ICCKE) 2016, pp. 54–59. IEEE (2016)

9. Ma, L., Cheng, S., Wang, X., Huang, M., Shen, H., He, X., Shi, Y.: Cooperative two-engine multi-objective bee foraging algorithm with reinforcement learning. Knowl. Based Syst. **133**, 278–293 (2017)

10. Passino, K.M.: Biomimicry of bacterial foraging for distributed optimization and control. IEEE Control Syst. **22**(3), 52–67 (2002)

11. Verma, O.P., Parihar, A.S.: An optimal fuzzy system for edge detection in color images using bacterial foraging algorithm. IEEE Trans. Fuzzy Syst. **25**(1), 114–127 (2017)

12. Keshari, A., Mishra, N., Shukla, N., McGuire, S., Khorana, S.: Multiple order-up-to policy for mitigating bullwhip effect in supply chain network. Ann. Oper. Res., 1–26 (2017)

13. Niu, B., Wang, H., Wang, J., Tan, L.: Multi-objective bacterial foraging optimization. Neurocomputing **116**, 336–345 (2013)

14. Yi, J., Huang, D., Fu, S., He, H., Li, T.: Multi-objective bacterial foraging optimization algorithm based on parallel cell entropy for aluminum electrolysis production process. IEEE Trans. Ind. Electron. **63**(4), 2488–2500 (2016)

15. Rani, R.R., Ramyachitra, D.: Multiple sequence alignment using multi-objective based bacterial foraging optimization algorithm. Biosystems **150**, 177–189 (2016)

16. Durillo, J.J., Nebro, A.J., Alba, E.: The jMetal framework for multi-objective optimization: design and architecture. In: IEEE Congress on Evolutionary Computation (CEC) 2010, pp. 1–8. IEEE (2010)

17. Zitzler, E., Deb, K., Thiele, L.: Comparison of multiobjective evolutionary algorithms: empirical results. Evol. Comput. **8**(2), 173–195 (2000)

18. Maimos, M., Konfe, B.O., Koussoube, S., Some, B.: Alienor method for nonlinear multi-objective optimization. Appl. Math. **2**(02), 217 (2011)

19. Deb, K., Thiele, L., Laumanns, M., Zitzler, E.: Scalable multi-objective optimization test problems. In: Proceedings of the 2002 Congress on Evolutionary Computation 2002, CEC 2002, vol. 1, pp. 825–830. IEEE (2002)

20. Bayram, İ., Bulek, S.: A penalty function promoting sparsity within and across groups. IEEE Trans. Sign. Proces. **65**(16), 4238–4251 (2017)

A Self-organizing Multi-objective Particle Swarm Optimization Algorithm for Multimodal Multi-objective Problems

Jing Liang[1], Qianqian Guo[1], Caitong Yue[1], Boyang Qu[2(✉)], and Kunjie Yu[1]

[1] School of Electrical Engineering, Zhengzhou University,
Zhengzhou 450001, China
{liangjing,yukunjie}@zzu.edu.cn, 18137780112@163.com,
zzuyuecaitong@163.com
[2] School of Electric and Information Engineering,
Zhongyuan University of Technology, Zhengzhou 450007, China
qby1984@hotmail.com

Abstract. To solve the multimodal multi-objective optimization problems which may have two or more Pareto-optimal solutions with the same fitness value, a new multi-objective particle swarm optimizer with a self-organizing mechanism (SMPSO-MM) is proposed in this paper. First, the self-organizing map network is used to find the distribution structure of the population and build the neighborhood in the decision space. Second, the leaders are selected from the corresponding neighborhood. Meanwhile, the elite learning strategy is adopted to avoid premature convergence. Third, a non-dominated-sort method with special crowding distance is adopted to update the external archive. With the help of self-organizing mechanism, the solutions which are similar to each other can be mapped into the same neighborhood. In addition, the special crowding distance enables the algorithm to maintain multiple solutions in the decision space which may be very close in the objective space. SMPSO-MM is compared with other four multi-objective optimization algorithms. The experimental results show that the proposed algorithm is superior to the other four algorithms.

Keywords: Self-organizing · Multimodal multi-objective problems
Multi-objective particle swarm optimizer · Elite learning strategy

1 Introduction

In real world, many problems have two or more conflicting objectives to be optimized. For these problems, an improvement of one objective may lead to degradation in others. Multi-objective optimization algorithms provide a best tradeoff solution set instead of a single solution. The solution set is known as the Pareto solution set (PS) in the search space and the set of all the vectors in the objective space corresponding to the PS is called Pareto front (PF).

© Springer International Publishing AG, part of Springer Nature 2018
Y. Tan et al. (Eds.): ICSI 2018, LNCS 10941, pp. 550–560, 2018.
https://doi.org/10.1007/978-3-319-93815-8_52

There are some problems which have more than one solution corresponding to the same point in the objective space. The literature [1] identified the existence of problems with multiple PSs. Liang referred to this class of problems as multimodal multi-objective problems [2]. Niching methods are applied to locate the multiple optimal solutions and keep them from being deleted. However, classic niching methods such as fitness sharing, crowding, and speciation are sensitive to the value of niching parameters [3]. Yue adopted an index-based ring topology [4] to form stable niches without any niching parameters and proposed non-dominated-sort method with special crowding distance (Non-dominated-scd-sort) to maintain multiple solutions [5].

For most multi-objective problems, under mild conditions, both the PS and the PF are $(m-1)$ dimensional piecewise continuous manifolds [6]. Based on the regularity, many multi-objective evolutionary algorithms have been proposed. MOEA/D decomposed a multi-objective problem into a set of subproblems by a set of predefined weight vectors [7]. RM-MEDA clustered the PS by using the local principal component analysis and sampled new solutions from the built model [8]. Zhou used self-organizing map (SOM) to establish the neighborhood relationship and to generate offspring with the neighboring solutions [9].

Particle swarm optimization algorithm is a simple and robust algorithm [10]. The fast convergence of particle swarm optimization leads to the loss of diversity to some extent. Some mechanisms have been proposed to address this issue. Decomposition strategy maintains diversity by ensuring each sub-region has a solution in the objective space [11–13]. Mutation operator helps the algorithm to jump out of local optimal location [14, 15]. Different neighbor relationships of particles have been introduced to select neighbor best and sharing information [16, 17].

When solving multimodal multi-objective problems, the neighbor leaders play an important role in local search. Inspired by the characteristics of multi-objective optimization problems and the neighbor property of SOM, a self-organizing multi-objective particle swarm optimization algorithm for solving multimodal multi-objective problems (SMPSO-MM) is proposed in this paper. Self-organizing map network is used to gather good and similar solutions together in hidden layers in MOPSO and to build neighboring relationship in decision space.

The rest of this paper is organized as follows: Sect. 2 briefly describes the multi-objective problems and multi-objective particle swarm optimization algorithm. Section 3 presents the self-organizing multi-objective particle swarm algorithm in detail. Experimental results and analysis are shown in Sect. 4. Finally, conclusions are drawn in Sect. 5.

2   Related Works

2.1   Multi-objective Problems (MOPs)

A continuous multi-objective optimization problem can be formulated as follows:

$$\text{Min } F(x) = (f_1(x), f_2(x), \ldots, f_m(x)) \text{ s.t. } x = (x_1, x_2, \ldots, x_n) \in \Omega \quad (1)$$

where $\Omega = [a_i, b_i]^n$ is feasible region of the search space; x is a n-dimensional decision vector bounded in Ω; m is the number of objective functions. $F: \Omega \rightarrow R^m$ consists of m objective functions to be optimized and R^m denotes the objective space. In the following texts, some important definitions for multi-objective problems are given.

Definition 1 (Pareto Dominance). A decision vector x is said to dominate decision vector y (denoted as $x \prec y$). If and only if

$$(\forall i \in \{1, 2, \ldots, m\} : f_i(x) \leq f_i(y)) \wedge (\exists j \in \{1, 2, \ldots, m\} : f_i(x) < f_i(y)) \quad (2)$$

Definition 2 (Pareto Optimal Solution). A decision vector x is said to be Pareto optimal solution with respect to Ω if

$$\neg \exists y \in \Omega : y \prec x \quad (3)$$

Definition 3 (Pareto Optimal Set, PS). is defined as:

$$\mathbf{PS} = \{x \in \Omega | \neg \exists y \in \Omega : y \prec x\} \quad (4)$$

Definition 4 (Pareto Front, PF). is defined as:

$$\mathbf{PF} = \{F(x) | x \in \mathbf{PS}\} \quad (5)$$

2.2   Multi-objective Particle Swarm Optimization Algorithm (MOPSO)

In MOPSO, each particle represents a potential solution. Assuming there are N particles in the swarm and the searching space is n-dimensional hyperspace. The position and velocity of particle i are represented as $x_i = (x_{i1}, x_{i2}, \ldots, x_{in})$ and $v_i = (v_{i1}, v_{i2}, \ldots, v_{in})$ respectively. They are updated according to the following equations:

$$v_i(t+1) = w * v_i(t) + c_1 r_1 (x_{pbest_i} - x_i(t)) + c_2 r_2 (x_{nbest_i} - x_i(t)) \quad (6)$$

$$x_i(t+1) = x_i(t) + v_i(t+1) \quad (7)$$

where t is the iteration; w is inertia factor; c_1 and c_2 are two constants which affect acceleration; r_1 and r_2 are two random variables in the range (0,1); *pbest* and *nbest* represent personal best and neighbor best position of the ith particle, respectively.

3 The Details of SMPSO-MM

3.1 Leaders Selection in Neighborhood

The proposed SMPSO-MM algorithm uses SOM to find the distribution of current population (**POP**) and external archive (**EXA**). Newly generated non-dominated solutions are training sets (**TS**) for updating SOM model. SOM clusters similar solutions into same neighborhood. Non-dominated-scd-sort method [5] is used to selected *nbest* from neighborhood. **Algorithm 1** presents the details of selecting *nbest*.

The process of composing *nbest* pool is illustrated in Fig. 1. The solutions assigned to neighboring neurons of winning neuron u compose the *nbest* pool. The advantages of this selection method are presented as: (1) the weights are constantly updated by new non-dominated solutions, so SOM can reflect the distribution of PS more accurately; (2) the *nbest* is close to particle in the decision space; (3) different leaders can promote the diversity and locate more multimodal solutions.

Algorithm 1: The procedure of selecting *nbest*

1. **Find the index of neighboring neurons**

   Calculate the geographical distance $\left\|z^u - z^{u'}\right\|_2$, I_k^u is the index of the kth nearest neuron to neuron u in the representation layer.

2. **Update SOM model**

   2.1. Update learning rate $\eta = \eta_0 * (1 - \dfrac{t}{maxT})$, learning radius $\sigma = \sigma_0 * (1 - \dfrac{t}{maxT})$ / t is the current iteration, $maxT$ is maximum iteration.

   2.2. Find the winning neuron of $x \in$ **TS** : $u' = \arg \min_{1 \le u \le N} \left\|x - w^u\right\|_2$

   2.3. Locate the neighborhood neurons to be updated: $U = \{1 \le u \le N \wedge \left\|z^u - z^{u'}\right\|_2 < \sigma\}$

   2.4. Update the weights in U. $w_{t+1}^u = w_t^u + \eta(t) * \exp(\left\|z^u - z^{u'}\right\|_2)(x - w_t^u)$

3. **POP and EXA partition**

   3.1. Map $x_i \in$ **POP** to SOM and find the winning neuron u. Each unit is assigned to one particle;

   3.2. Map $x_i \in$ **EXA** to SOM and *unit2nbest* records the index of particles assigned to each neuron. The number of particles assigned to each unit is unlimited.

4. **Select *nbest* for particles**

   4.1. nPool= unit2nbest{ I_k^u };/ nPool records the *nbest* pool of particle i;

   4.2. Select the first one as *nbest* according to Non-dominated-scd-sort method.

3.2 The Elite Learning Strategy

The elite learning strategy is applied to offspring generation. Operating mutation on the best location can enhance global search ability and help the algorithm to jump out of local optimal location.

Fig. 1. The process of composing *nbest* pool

$$x_j = nbest_j + Gauss(0, pr^2) \times (b_j - a_j) \quad \text{if } rand < pr \qquad (8)$$

where a_j and b_j are the upper and lower bounds of jth dimension. The $Gauss(0, pr^2)$ is a random number of a Gaussian distribution with a zero mean and a stand deviation pr. The pr decreases linearly with the iteration increases. According to the Gaussian distribution, the greater value of pr can make the position have a larger variation range, which is beneficial for global search in the early stage. In the later stage of evolution, variation range is small which is beneficial for local search.

3.3   Procedure of SMPSO-MM

The procedure of SMPSO-MM is described in **Algorithm 2**. The weights of SOM are initialized as **POP**. The *nbest* selected from the neighborhood leads the particles flying to promising locations. The elite learning strategy is applied in generating offspring operator to increase the diversity of population. And Non-dominated-scd-sort method [5] is adopted to update **EXA** and keep diversity both in decision and objective space. The Non-dominated-scd-sort method firstly sorts the particles according to dominance relationship. Then the crowding distance in decision space and objective space are calculated. The particles with larger crowding distance are preferred. Details of the method can be referred to the literature [5].

Algorithm 2: The procedure of SMPSO-MM
---
1. **Initialize population and self-organizing map**
1.1   Initialize **POP** $= \{x^1, x^2, ..., x^N\}$, $\mathbf{v} = \{v^1, v^2, ..., v^N\}$; **EXA=POP**; **Pbest=POP**.
1.2   Initialize SOM model: $\{w^1, w^2, ..., w^N\}$=**POP** ; **TS=POP**; learning rate η_0, learning radius σ_0.

2. **Optimization loop**
2.1.   Select *nbest* according to **Algorithm 1**.
2.2.   Generate offspring according to equation (6-7) and elite learning strategy.
2.3.   Update the **EXA** and **TS**
       tmpEXA $= $ **EXA**$(t) \cup $ **POP**$(t+1)$; /t is the current iteration
       EXA$(t+1)$=non-dominated particles in **tmpEXA**;
       TS=EXA$(t+1)\backslash$ **EXA**(t);
3. **Stop if a stop criterion is satisfied, otherwise repeat the Optimization loop.**
---

4   Experimental Results

The multimodal multi-objective test functions used in this paper include MMF1–MMF8 [5] and three other functions named SYM-PART simple [18], SYM-PART rotated [18] and Omni-test function [19] with $n = 3$.

The Pareto set proximity (*PSP*) [5] and inverted generational distance in the objective space (*IGDf*) are adopted as metrics to evaluate the performance of the algorithms. The big value of *PSP* means the convergence and diversity of obtained solutions in decision space are good. The small value of *IGDf* means the obtained solutions in objective space are well distributed.

SMPSO-MM is compared with other four algorithms including MOPSO/D [11], Omni-optimizer [19], DN-NSGAII [2] and MO-Ring-PSO-SCD [5]. The parameters of algorithms are the same to the corresponding literature.

For SMPSO-MM, the parameters of PSO are same as literature [5]: $c_1 = c_2 = 2.05$, $w = 0.7298$; the parameters of SOM are same as literature [9]: topological structure 1×100, $\eta_0 = 0.7$, $\sigma_0 = \mathrm{sqrt}(1^2 + 100^2)/2$; the value of *pr* in elite learning decreases linearly from 0.2 to 0.05 with the iteration increases, the value of *pr* is set according to the experimental results. For all algorithms, the population size N is 100; the EXA size is 800; Maximum evaluation number is 60000. All experiments are carried out 25 times independently.

4.1   The Rationality of Neighborhood Built by SOM

To verify the rationality of the neighborhood relationship, the distribution of *nbest* candidates in the evolutionary process for MMF2 are shown in Fig. 2. The figure shows that the *nbest* candidates selected based on the neighboring relationship are close

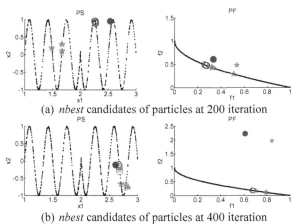

(a) *nbest* candidates of particles at 200 iteration

(b) *nbest* candidates of particles at 400 iteration

...is solution in **EXA**; ★ is particle *i*, ☆ is *nbest* candidate of particle *i*;
● is particle *j*, ○ is *nbest* candidate of particle *j*;

Fig. 2. *nbest* candidates of particles in the process of evolution

to particle both in the decision space and objective space. It verifies the rationality of the neighborhood relationship as the particle can fly to the near position by learning from neighboring leader to promote local search.

4.2   Results of Compared Algorithms

In Fig. 3, MOPSO/D, Omni-optimizer, DN-NSGAII, MO-Ring-PSO-SCD and SMPSO-MM are numbered 1, 2, 3, 4 and 5 respectively. The results show that mean *PSP* values of SMPSO-MM are the highest for all test functions. MO-Ring-PSO-SCD ranks second. The *IGDf* and *rank* shown in Table 1 reveal that SMPSO-MM is the second best and Omni-optimizer obtains the best distribution in decision space. The *rank* value is the mean rank on all test functions. In fact, the performances of compared algorithms are close to each other except MOPSO/D. The reason is that the four algorithms all consider the distribution in the objective space.

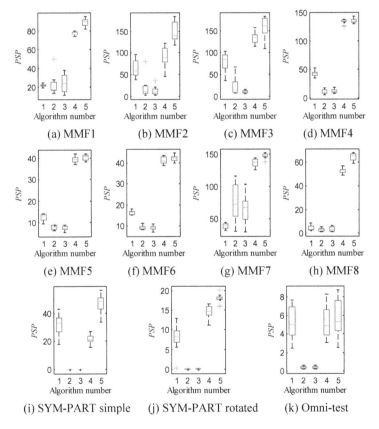

Fig. 3. The box-plots of *PSP* values of different algorithms. The numbers on the horizontal axis of each plot indicate the following algorithms: 1 = MOPSO/D, 2 = Omni-optimizer, 3 = DN-NSGAII, 4 = MO-Ring-PSO-SCD, 5 = SMPSO-MM.

Table 1. The *IGDf* values of different algorithms

Functions	MOPSO/D	Omni-optimizer	DN-NSGAII	MO-Ring-PSO-SCD	SMPSO-MM
MMF1	2.30E–03 [5]	6.69E–04 [2]	8.46E–04 [4]	7.95E–04 [3]	**6.61E–04** [1]
	(2.77E–04)	(3.08E–05)	(5.73E–05)	(4.25E–05)	(2.98E–05)
MMF2	3.62E–03 [4]	2.86E–03 [2]	**1.84E–03** [1]	5.22E–03 [5]	2.89E–03 [3]
	(4.87E–04)	(7.37E–03)	(3.87E–03)	(6.45E–04)	(2.04E–04)
MMF3	3.38E–03 [4]	**6.29E–04** [1]	1.04E–03 [2]	4.04E–03 [5]	2.33E–03 [3]
	(2.05E–04)	(2.00E–05)	(8.43E–04)	(5.10E–04)	(1.19E–04)
MMF4	1.65E–03 [5]	6.40E–04 [2]	7.79E–04 [4]	6.62E–04 [3]	**6.29E–04** [1]
	(1.21E–04)	(4.72E–05)	(6.04E–05)	(7.09E–05)	(4.15E–05)
MMF5	2.34E–03 [5]	6.51E–04 [2]	8.03E–04 [4]	7.36E–04 [3]	**6.50E–04** [1]
	(2.58E–04)	(1.43E–05)	(3.93E–05)	(1.63E–05)	(2.64E–05)
MMF6	2.00E–03 [5]	6.44E–04 [2]	7.84E–04 [4]	6.81E–04 [3]	**6.27E–04** [1]
	(1.22E–04)	(2.24E–05)	(3.58E–05)	(2.04E–05)	(2.88E–05)
MMF7	2.06E–03 [5]	6.69E–04 [2]	9.19E–04 [4]	6.71E–04 [3]	**6.44E–04** [1]
	(2.52E–04)	(2.01E–05)	(4.19E–05)	(2.46E–05)	(2.14E–05)
MMF8	1.46E–03 [4]	**7.23E–04** [1]	8.47E–04 [3]	1.16E–03 [5]	8.42E–04 [2]
	(1.07E–04)	(2.28E–05)	(3.18E–05)	(6.36E–05)	(1.91E–05)
SYM-PART simple	7.55E–03 [4]	**2.89E–03** [1]	2.94E–03 [2]	9.15E–03 [5]	3.96E–03 [3]
	(1.76E–03)	(2.93E–04)	(3.22E–04)	(1.40E–03)	(5.85E–04)
SYM-PART rotated	1.67E–02 [5]	**3.12E–03** [1]	3.67E–03 [2]	1.39E–02 [4]	1.15E–02 [3]
	(3.52E–03)	(3.88E–04)	(3.12E–04)	(2.60E–03)	(1.56E–03)
Omni-test	9.98E–01 [5]	9.97E–01 [3]	9.97E–01 [4]	**9.79E–01** [1]	9.82E–01 [2]
	(2.28E–04)	(2.32E–04)	(3.40E–04)	(1.81E–03)	(1.69E–03)
Rank	4.64	1.73	3.09	3.63	1.91

4.3 The Effect of the Size of External Archive

Different external archive (EXA) sizes affect the performance of the algorithm especially for multimodal multi-objective problems. Figure 4 shows the result of *PSP* values with different external sizes. The test functions are MMF1, MMF4, MMF8 and SYM-PART simple. *PSP* values increase as the EXA size grows for most test functions. The large size of EXA allows more non-dominated solutions to locate more solutions. And the small size increases the challenge to maintain solutions uniformly.

In order to study how the performances of the algorithm are affected by the EXA size, different EXA sizes of all algorithms are applied on MMF3, MMF8, SYM-PART simple and SYM-PART rotated test functions. The results reported in Fig. 5 confirm

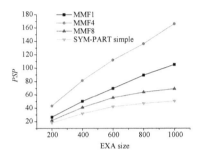

Fig. 4. The *PSP* values with different external sizes of SMPSO-MM

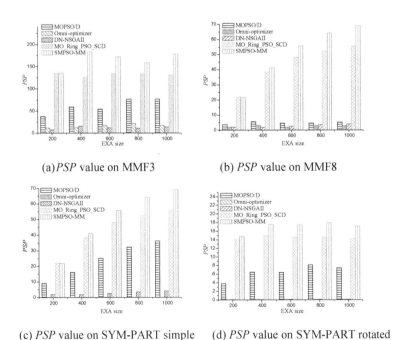

(a)*PSP* value on MMF3   (b) *PSP* value on MMF8

(c) *PSP* value on SYM-PART simple   (d) *PSP* value on SYM-PART rotated

Fig. 5. The *PSP* values with different external size of different algorithms.

that the performances of the algorithms are affected by varying EXA sizes. SMPSO-MM is superior to other algorithms for most sizes of EXA.

5 Conclusion

In this paper, we proposed a new multi-objective particle swarm algorithm with self-organizing mechanism to solve multimodal multi-objective problems. A new strategy to build the neighborhood and select neighborhood leaders is applied in MOPSO. The SOM network can reflect the distributions of current particles and non-dominated solutions in the decision space. The elite learning strategy promotes the diversity and avoids the premature of algorithm. Experimental results show that the proposed algorithm can locate the multiple solutions in the decision space and have a good distribution on Pareto front in the objective space for multimodal multi-objective problems.

Acknowledgments. The work is supported by National Natural Science Foundation of China (61473266 and 61673404), Project supported by the Research Award Fund for Outstanding Young Teachers in Henan Provincial Institutions of Higher Education of China (2014GGJS-004) and Program for Science & Technology Innovation Talents in Universities of Henan Province in China (16HASTIT041 and 16HASTIT033), Scientific and Technological Project of Henan Province (152102210153).

References

1. Preuss, M., Kausch, C., Bouvy, C., Henrich, F.: Decision space diversity can be essential for solving multiobjective real-world problems. In: Ehrgott, M., Naujoks, B., Stewart, T., Wallenius, J. (eds.) Multiple Criteria Decision Making for Sustainable Energy and Transportation Systems. Lecture Notes in Economics and Mathematical Systems, vol. 634. Springer, Heidelberg (2010). https://doi.org/10.1007/978-3-642-04045-0_31
2. Liang, J.J., Yue, C.T., Qu, B.Y.: Multimodal multi-objective optimization: a preliminary study. In: IEEE Congress on Evolutionary Computation, pp. 2451–2461 (2016)
3. Li, X., Epitropakis, M.G., Deb, K., Engelbrecht, A.: Seeking multiple solutions: an updated survey on niching methods and their applications. IEEE Trans. Evol. Comput. **21**(4), 518–538 (2017)
4. Li, X.: Niching without niching parameters: particle swarm optimization using a ring topology. IEEE Trans. Evol. Comput. **14**(1), 150–169 (2010)
5. Yue, C.T., Liang, J.J., Qu, B.Y.: A multi-objective particle swarm optimizer using ring topology for solving multimodal multi-objective problems. IEEE Trans. Evol. Comput. (2017). (https://doi.org/10.1109/tevc.2017.2754271)
6. Li, H., Zhang, Q.F.: Multiobjective optimization problems with complicated pareto sets, MOEA/D and NSGA-II. IEEE Trans. Evol. Comput. **13**(2), 284–302 (2009)
7. Wang, L.P., Zhang, Q.F., Zhou, A.M., Gong, M.G., Jiao, L.C.: Constrained subproblems in decomposition based multiobjective evolutionary algorithm. IEEE Trans. Evol. Comput. **20**(3), 475–480 (2016)
8. Zhang, Q.F., Zhou, A.M., Jin, Y.C.: RM-MEDA: a regularity model-based multiobjective estimation of distribution algorithm. IEEE Trans. Evol. Comput. **12**(1), 41–63 (2008)

9. Zhang, H., Zhou, A.M., Song, S.M., Zhang, Q.F., Gao, X.Z., Zhang, J.: A self-organizing multiobjective evolutionary algorithm. IEEE Trans. Evol. Comput. **20**(5), 792–806 (2016)
10. Kennedy, J., Eberhart, R.: Particle swarm optimization. In: IEEE International Conference on Neural Networks, vol. 4, pp. 1942–1948 (1995)
11. Dai, C., Wang, Y.P., Ye, M.: A new multi-objective particle swarm optimization algorithm based on decomposition. Inf. Sci. **325**, 541–557 (2015)
12. Fei, L.I., Liu, J.C., Shi, H.T., Zi-ying, F.U.: Multi-objective particle swarm optimization algorithm based on decomposition and differential evolution. Control Decis. **32**(3), 403–410 (2017)
13. Wei, L.X., Fan, R., Li, X.: A novel multi-objective decomposition particle swarm optimization based on comprehensive learning strategy. In: 36th Chinese Control Conference, pp. 2761–2766 (2017)
14. Dong, W.Y., Kang, L.L., Zhang, W.S.: Opposition-based particle swarm optimization with adaptive mutation strategy. Soft. Comput. **21**(17), 5081–5090 (2017)
15. Chen, C.C.: Optimization of zero-order TSK-type fuzzy system using enhanced particle swarm optimizer with dynamic mutation and special initialization. Int. J. Fuzzy Syst. (2018). (https://doi.org/10.1007/s40815-018-0453-z)
16. Liang, J.J., Suganthan, P.N.: Dynamic multi-swarm particle swarm optimizer with local search. In: IEEE Congress on Evolutionary Computation, vol. 1, pp. 522–528 (2005)
17. Zhao, S.Z., Suganthan, P.N.: Two-lbests based multi-objective particle swarm optimizer. Eng. Optim. **43**(1), 1–17 (2011)
18. Rudolph, G., Naujoks, B., Preuss, M.: Capabilities of EMOA to detect and preserve equivalent pareto subsets. In: Obayashi, S., Deb, K., Poloni, C., Hiroyasu, T., Murata, T. (eds.) EMO 2007. LNCS, vol. 4403, pp. 36–50. Springer, Heidelberg (2007). https://doi.org/10.1007/978-3-540-70928-2_7
19. Deb, K., Tiwari, S.: Omni-optimizer: a procedure for single and multi-objective optimization. In: Coello Coello, C.A., Hernández Aguirre, A., Zitzler, E. (eds.) EMO 2005. LNCS, vol. 3410, pp. 47–61. Springer, Heidelberg (2005). https://doi.org/10.1007/978-3-540-31880-4_4

A Decomposition Based Evolutionary Algorithm with Angle Penalty Selection Strategy for Many-Objective Optimization

Zhiyong Li[1(✉)], Ke Lin[1], Mourad Nouioua[1], and Shilong Jiang[2]

[1] Key Laboratory for Embedded and Network Computing of Hunan Province, College of Computer Science and Electronic Engineering, Hunan University, Changsha, China
{zhiyong.li,kelin_0808}@hnu.edu.cn, mouradnouioua@gmail.com
[2] PKU-HKUST Shenzhen-HongKong Institution, Shenzhen, China
jiangshilong03@126.com

Abstract. Evolutionary algorithms (EAs) based on decomposition have shown to be promising in solving many-objective optimization problems (MaOPs). First, the population (or objective space) is divided into K subpopulations (or subregions) by a group of uniform distribution reference vectors. Later, subpopulations are optimized simultaneously. In this paper, we propose a new decomposition based evolutionary algorithm with angle penalty selection strategy for MaOPs (MOEA-APS). In the environmental selection process, in order to prevent the solutions located around the boundary of the subregion from being simultaneously selected into the next generation which will affect negatively on the performance of the algorithm, a new angle similarity measure (AS) is calculated and used to punish the dense solutions. More precisely, after selecting a good solution x for a sub population, the solutions whose angle similarity with x exceeding η or pareto dominated by x will be directly punished. Moreover, The threshold η is not fixed, but decided by the distribution of the solutions around x. This mechanism allows to improve diversity of population. The experimental results on DTLZ benchmark test problems show that the results of the proposed algorithm are very competitive comparing with four other state-of-the-art EAs for MaOPs.

Keywords: Many-objective optimization · Decomposition Evolutionary algorithm

1 Introduction

The multi-objective optimization problems (MOPs) are defined as the problems that involve more than one conflicting objective to be optimized simultaneously, MOPs can be formulated as follows:

© Springer International Publishing AG, part of Springer Nature 2018
Y. Tan et al. (Eds.): ICSI 2018, LNCS 10941, pp. 561–571, 2018.
https://doi.org/10.1007/978-3-319-93815-8_53

$$\min F(x) = (f_1(x), f_1(x), ..., f_m(x))$$
$$subject\ to\ x \in \prod_{i=1}^{D} [a_i, b_i], \tag{1}$$

where $\prod_{i=1}^{D} [a_i, b_i]$ is the decision space with $x = \{x | x = (x_1, x_2, ..., x_D)\}$, $a_j < x_j < b_j, j = 1, 2, ..., D$, being the decision vector, D is the dimension, a_j and b_j are constants, and m is the number of objectives. For any two decision vectors, $x, y \in \prod_{i=1}^{D} [a_i, b_i]$, we say x is pareto dominate $y(x \prec y)$, if

$$\forall i \in \{1, 2, ..., m\} : f_i(x) \leq f_i(y)$$
$$\exists i \in \{1, 2, ..., m\} : f_i(x) < f_i(y). \tag{2}$$

When no solution $x \in \prod_{i=1}^{D} [a_i, b_i]$ exists such that $F(x)$ dominates $F(x^*)$, x^* is called a pareto optimal solution.

Although the multi-objective evolutionary algorithms (MOEAs) have been successfully applied for MOPs, they unfortunately encounter severe difficulties on solving the optimization problems that have more than three objectives, which are often called the many-objective optimization problems (MaOPs)[1]. The major reason behind these difficulties is the exponentially increase of the number of nondominant solutions when the number of objectives increases. Moreover, the traditional MOEAs lack the selection pressure toward pareto front (PF).

Over the last decades, many-objective optimization has become a really hot issue because of its wide applications and great importance. Accordingly, a number of MOEAs have been especially designed for MaOPs. Globally, the proposed MOEAs can be classified on four categories:

- *Convergence enhancement based approaches.* These methods modify the domination relationship to increase the selection pressure on the PF, such as grid-dominance [2], Ranking-Dominance [3] and Fuzzy-Based Pareto Optimality [4]. However, one or more parameters have a significant effect on the performances of these methods.
- *Performance indicator based approaches.* In these approaches, such as fast HV-based EA (HypE) [5], the ε-metric based EAs [6], and stochastic ranking EA [7], the notion of pareto dominance is not used and the selection pressure is enhanced, but high computational complexity is needed.
- *Objective reduction based approaches.* These algorithms are based on the application of certain dimensionality reduction techniques to deal with the hardness of the MaOPs, such as principal component analysis (PCA) [8] and unsupervised feature selection [9].
- *The decomposition-based approaches.* Generally, these approaches include two techniques, namely weight aggregation-based techniques [10] and reference vector-based techniques [11–13]. Besides, Penalty Boundary Intersection (PBI) [14], weight sum [15] and Tchebycheff [15] are the most commonly used decomposition methods.

Among the above methods, decomposition based MOEAs are very promising for many-objective optimization. In fact, decomposition based selection can not only overcome the disadvantage of indistinguishable solutions in high-dimensional objective space, but also, maintain population diversity on coarse granularity. Additionally, decomposition based approaches has an acceptable computational effort comparing with other methods. However, most of the current reference vector-based MOEAs only consider the convergence or diversity of solutions in each subregion while ignore the diversity of the solutions between subregions. Therefore, in this paper we propose a decomposition based evolutionary algorithm with angle penalty selection strategy for MaOPs (MOEA-APS). Besides, The population (or objective space) is divided into K subpopulations (or subregions) by a group of uniform distribution reference vectors which are optimized simultaneously. Moreover, in order to obtain pareto solution set with better convergence and distribution, The angle similarity AS between any two solutions is calculated and used to punish the dense solutions which are located near the boundary of the subspace. The main contributions of this paper are summarized as follows:

(1) AS is defined by calculating the acute angle of any two solutions objective vector, which is very suitable to represent the similarity of two solutions. The more consistent their direction is, the more similar the two solutions are. Notice that, in the positive real spaces, the angle range of any two solutions is in $[0, \pi/2]$ which is convenient to calculate.

(2) In our proposed angle penalty selection strategy (APS), after selecting a good solution x for a sub population, the solutions whose angle similarity with x exceeding η or pareto dominated by x will be punished. This mechanism allows to effectively prevent the dense solutions from entering the next generation of population.

(3) The threshold η is not fixed. Whether the solution is punished or not is decided by the distribution of solutions around x.

The rest of the paper is organized as follows: Sect. 2 is devoted to the description of the proposed algorithm MOEA-APS. In Sect. 3 we present and discuss the experimental results. Finally, Sects. 4 concludes the paper.

2   Proposed Algorithm

MOEA-APS algorithm belongs to the reference vector-based MOEAs. Besides, the population of MaOPs is divided into several subpopulations by a set of uniformly distributed reference vectors and each subpopulation evolves independently in parallel with others. In the environmental selection, a fixed number of solutions is chosen for each subregion. As shown in Fig. 1(a), solution B is slightly better than C in terms of PBI value. Thus, solutions A and B will be selected for subregions 2 and 3 respectively. However, we can remark that it is better to choose the solution A and C and ignore B because this solution is very close to A in its neighborhood subregion 2. Instead of taking on consideration

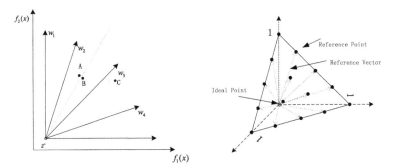

(a) Distribution of solutions in a popula- (b) Set of reference points in a normal-
tion after decomposition   ized hyper-plan when $m = 3$ and $H = 4$

Fig. 1. Distribution of solutions and reference points generation

the quality of the solution only in the subregion itself to the detriment of the
density of solutions in the adjacent subregions, which will affect negatively on
the diversity of the whole population. The APS strategy is proposed which allows
us to overcome the above mentioned problem. The pseudocode of MOEA-APS
is presented in Algorithm 1.

Algorithm 1. Framework of MOEA-APS

Input:
  1) the maximal number of generation $t_{\max}$;
  2) a set of uniformly distributed unit reference vectors $V = \{v_1, ...v_K\}$;
Output:
  $P_{t_{\max}}$
1: $P_0 = Initialization(P)$
2: Compute the acute angle between any two reference vectors and then work out the closest
   m reference vectors to each reference vector. For each $i = 1, ..., K$ set $B(i) = \{i_1, ...i_m\}$, where
   $v_{i_1}, ..., v_{i_m}$ are the closest m reference vectors to v_i
3: **while** $t < t_{\max}$ **do**
4:     $P_t' = offspring - creation(P_t)$;
5:     $Q_t = P_t' \cup P_t$;
6:     $P_{t+1} = Angle\_Penalty\_Selection\_Strategy(Q_t, V_t, B)$;
7:     $t = t+1$;
8: **end while**
9: **return** $P_{t_{\max}}$

2.1   Reference Vectors Generation

In MOEA-APS algorithm, the Das and Dennisos systematic method [16] is used
to generate a set of uniformly distributed reference vectors $v_i = (v_i^1, ..., v_i^m), i = \{1, ..., K\}$, the generated reference vectors allows to decompose the objective
space into K subregions. More precisely, K points are generated on the hyper-
plane with a uniform spacing of $\delta = 1/H$, where $H(H > 0)$ is the number of
divisions in each objective coordinate. The size of reference points (K) is given
by $K = C_{H+m-1}^{m-1}$, where m is the number of objectives. When $m > 8$, the reference points are generated via a two-layer sampling scheme [12] with two values of
H. Figure 1(b) shows a simple example of the generated reference vectors when
$m = 3$ and $H = 4$.

2.2   Angle Similarity Calculation and Population Decomposition

The angle similarity AS between a solution x_i and other solution x_j is given as by Eq. 3:

$$AS_j(x_i) = \arccos(\theta_{i,j}), j = 1, .., |Q|$$
$$\cos(\theta_{i,j}) = \frac{\sum_{k=1}^{m} f_k'(x_i) \times f_k'(x_j)}{\sqrt{\sum_{k=1}^{m} f_k'(x_i)^2} \times \sqrt{\sum_{k=1}^{m} f_k'(x_j)^2}}, \tag{3}$$

where m is the number of objectives, $f'(x) = f(x) - Z^*, Z^* = (f_1^{\min}, ..., f_m^{\min})$. AS is very suitable for the representation of the similarity between the two vectors. The smaller the acute angle between solutions x_i and x_j, the greater the similarity is. If $AS_j(x_i) < \eta, j = 1, ...|Q|$ and η is the angle similarity penalty threshold, we say that x_i and x_j are similar solutions.

Reference vectors can explicitly divide the objective space into K subregions $\{\Omega^1, \Omega^2, ..., \Omega^K\}$:

$$\Omega^i = \{f'(x) \in R_+^m | \arg \min_{v_i \in V} \{AS_{v_i}(x)\}, \tag{4}$$

where $f(x)$ is in Ω^i if and only if v^i has the smallest acute angle to $f(x)$ among all the K reference vectors. Population decomposition is described in lines 3 to 9 of Algorithm 2.

Algorithm 2. *Angle_Penalty_Selection_Strategy*(Q_t, V_t, B)

Input:
    1) generation index t;
    2) population Q_t;
    3) reference vectors $V = \{v_1, ...v_K\}$;
    4) B : the index of closest M reference vectors to each reference vector.
Output:
    the next generation population P_{t+1}
1: Compute $AS_j(x_i), i = 1, ... |Q_t|, j = 1, ... |Q_t|$, the acute angle similarity between any two objective vectors
2: % objective space decomposition %
3: **for** $x \in Q_t$ **do**
4:    **for** $v \in V_t$ **do**
5:       calculate the acute angle: $AS_v(x) = \arccos(x, v)$
6:    **end for**
7:    $index(x) = v : \arg \min_{v \in V}\{AS_v(x)\}$
8: **end for**
9: According to index, Q_t is divided to K Sub populations, $subP = \{p_1, ...p_K\}$
10: % Angle penalty strategy %
11: **for** $k = 1 : K$ **do**
12:    **if** all solutions in p_k are punished **then**
13:       select solution $x_i = \arg \min_{x_i \in p_k} PBI(x_i)$
14:    **else**
15:       select solution $x_i = (\arg \min_{x_i \in p_k} PBI(x_i)) \wedge (x_i \notin \psi_{punished})$
16:    **end if**
17:    $punishing\_individuals(x, Q_t, B(i), \psi_{punished}, AS, subP)$;
18: **end for**
19: **return** P_{t+1}

2.3   Angle Penalty Selection Strategy

As shown in Fig. 1(a), the solutions that are located around the boundary of subregions (namely subregion boundary solutions) are more likely to be very close. These solutions are very similar and dense in objective space. Therefore, when updating any subregion, the subregion boundary solutions should be punished. More precisely, once a good solution in a subregion is selected, the similar solutions will not be considered temporarily when updating its subregions which allows us to avoid the similar solutions to be selected simultaneously. If all the solutions in a subregion are punished, the solution x with minimum PBI value will be directly selected as the next generation solution. Otherwise, the x with the minimum PBI value is selected from the solutions that are not punished (see line 12 to 16 of Algorithm 2).

2.4   Punishing Individuals Process

After the selection of a solution x, the solutions that have a large angle similarity with x or the solutions that are dominated by x will be directly punished. Given a solution $x_i \in subx$, the angle similarity penalty threshold η of x_i is defined by:

$$\eta = \min_{j \in subn} \ AS_j \ (x_b)$$
$$x_b = \arg\min_{b \in subn} \ AS_b \ (x_i), \tag{5}$$

where $subn$ is one of the neighborhood subregions of $subx$, x_b represents the solution that has the greatest angle similarity with x_i in $subn$. In other words, x_b is the subregion boundary solution in $subn$. η represents the minimum acute angle between x_b and the other solutions located in $subn$. If the angle similarity $AS_p(x_i)$ between the solutions in $subn$ and x_i satisfies $AS_p(x_i) < \eta$, then the solution x_p will be punished and added to the punished solutions set $\psi_{punished}$:

$$\psi_{punished} = \{x_p | AS_p(x_i) < \eta\}, p = 1, ... |subn| \tag{6}$$

It is worth mentioning that the proposed threshold η not only considers the density between the selected solution x and the other solutions in its neighborhood subregions, but it also takes into consideration the density of all solutions in the neighborhood subregions. By this way, the diversity of the whole population will be further improved. Algorithm 3 describes the punishment process individuals. Besides, lines 1 to 3 show that each solution pareto dominated by the solution x_i will be punished.

3   Experimental Results

In order to asses the performance of the proposed algorithm MOEA-APS, empirical experiments are conducted on the widely used benchmark test suites named DTLZ [17] and MOEA-APS is compared with four other state-of-the-art MOEAs for MaOPs, namely NSGAIII [12], MOEA/D-PBI [10], GrEA [2], and RVEA [13].

Algorithm 3. $punishing\_individuals(x_i, Q_t, indexB, \psi_{punished}, AS, subP)$

Input:
    1) the selected solution x_i;
    2) the merged population Q_t;
    3) $indexB$: the index of the closest m reference vectors to the vector which x associates to;
    4) AS : the acute angle similarity between any two objective vectors;
    5) $subP = \{p_1, ... p_K\}$: K Sub populations
Output:
    the punished solutions $\psi_{punished}$
1: **for** all $x_i : x \prec x_i, x_i \in Q_t$ **do**
2:    $\psi_{punished} = \psi_{punished} \cup \{x_i\}$
3: **end for**
4: **for** $i = 1 : length(indexB)$ **do**
5:    $subn = p_{indexB(i)}$
6:    **if** $(\sim isempty(subn))$ **then**
7:       %find the closest solution x_b to x_i from $subn$%
8:       $x_b = \arg\min\limits_{b \in subn} AS_b (x_i)$
9:       $\eta = \min\limits_{j \in subn} AS_j (x_b)$
10:    **end if**
11:    **for** all $x_j : AS_j(x_i) < \eta, x_j \in subn$ **do**
12:       $\psi_{punished} = \psi_{punished} \cup \{x_j\}$
13:    **end for**
14: **end for**
15: **return** $\psi_{punished}$

The widely used IGD [18] metric and HV metric [19] are both used as a performance indicators during the comparisons. IGD measures the average distance from a set of reference points P^* in the PF to the approximation set P that can measure the convergence of the obtained solutions. On the other hand, HV metric [19] can simultaneously measure the convergence and diversity of the obtained solutions. Notice that, The lower the IGD value is (or the larger the HV value is), the better the obtained solution set P quality is.

3.1 General Parameter Settings

The general parameters settings of MOEA-APS as well as the other state-of-the-art MOEAs are summarized as follows:

(1) Population size N and divisions H for generating reference vectors are shown in Table 1. (2) The settings of div in GrEA are the same as in RVEA. (3) The SBX crossover is $p_c = 1$ and its distribution index is $\eta_c = 30$. Polynomial mutation $p_m = 1/n$ and its distribution index is $\eta_m = 20$. Neighborhood size T in MOEA/D is 20, the probability of selecting in the neighborhood is 0.9. (4) Penalty parameter θ in PBI is 5. (5) The reference points P^* is composed by uniformly sampling 10000 points over the true PF. Setting of reference points for HV computation for DTLZ1 and DTLZ2-4 are $(1.0, ..., 1.0)^T$ and $(2.0, ..., 2.0)^T$ respectively. (6) The number of decision variables is set as $D = m + k - 1$, and $k = 5$ for DTLZ1, $k = 10$ for DTLZ2-4. During experiments, for each problem, we independently run each algorithm 10 times.

Table 1. The general settings of divisions, reference points and population sizes

No. of objectives (m)	Divisions (H)	Reference vectors	Popsize
3	$H = 12$	91	91
5	$H = 6$	210	210
8	$H_1 = 3, H_2 = 2$	156	156
10	$H_1 = 3, H_2 = 2$	275	275
15	$H_1 = 2, H_2 = 1$	135	135

3.2   Simulation Results and Analysis

As mentioned above, we compare the performance of the proposed MOEA-APS with four state-of-the-art MOEAs. Table 2 shows the IGD metric values of the four compared algorithms for each DTLZ test instance with 3, 5, 8, 10 and 15-objective in 10 independent runs. The best values for each test instance are highlighted in bold. Similarly, Table 3 shows the statistical results of the HV metric. Although the results presented in Table 2 show that the proposed MOEA-APS performs slightly better or similarly comparing to other algorithms in term of convergence. The experimental results in Table 3 confirm the effectiveness of the proposed APS strategy. Indeed, the devoted APS strategy allows improving further the diversity of the population under the premise of ensuring the convergence. In short, the proposed MOEA-APS algorithm is competitive in comparison with four state-of-the-art MOEAs.

In addition to the previous results and in order to visually observe the performance of the compared algorithms, the parallel coordinates of the non dominated front obtained by the five algorithms on DTLZ1 with 15-objective are depicted in Fig. 2. We can remark that MOEA-APS, NSGAIII, MOEAD-PBI and RVEA can obtain a solution set with good convergence and wide distribution. The proposed MOEA-APS has a slightly better performance comparing with the three other algorithms, whereas GrEA completely fails to reach the true PF of this instance. The distributions of the nondominated solutions obtained by the five compared algorithms on DTLZ4 with 3 objectives are depicted in Fig. 3. We can see that, MOEA-APS, NSGAIII and RVEA algorithms are able to generate evenly distributed solutions with an advantage to our proposed MOEA-APS comparing to NSGAIII and RVEA, additionally, unlike the three precedent algorithms, it is clear that MOEAD-PBI fails to generate evenly distributed solutions.

Table 2. Statistical results (mean and standard deviation) of the IGD values obtained by the five algorithms on DTLZ1-4. The best results are in bold type.

Problem	m	FEs	MOEA-APS	NSGAIII	MOEAD-PBI	GrEA	RVEA
	3	36400	**6.2150e-4 (1.04e-4)**	7.2039e-4 (3.55e-4)	1.5666e-3 (1.36e-3)	1.0310e-1 (8.45e-2)	1.3553e-3 (5.45e-4)
	5	126000	**4.1284e-4 (9.15e-5)**	4.3546e-4 (8.76e-5)	6.4928e-4 (3.42e-4)	2.1603e-1 (4.12e-2)	5.2237e-4 (3.22e-5)
DTLZ1	8	117000	**1.8787e-3 (4.29e-4)**	4.4107e-2 (6.46e-2)	5.4237e-3 (3.76e-4)	3.5028e-1 (1.08e-1)	2.9376e-3 (2.77e-4)
	10	275000	**1.9228e-3 (2.15e-4)**	5.2499e-3 (2.56e-3)	2.3955e-3 (3.29e-4)	3.4937e-1 (1.47e-1)	3.1337e-3 (1.38e-4)
	15	202500	**2.5236e-3 (7.20e-4)**	8.5352e-2 (1.43e-1)	2.3630e-2 (7.45e-4)	4.4555e-1 (3.34e-2)	2.8436e-3 (1.84e-4)
	3	22750	9.1960e-4 (1.19e-4)	1.0753e-3 (5.35e-5)	**5.4442e-4 (8.74e-5)**	7.3594e-2 (8.88e-4)	8.1682e-4 (1.91e-4)
	5	73500	1.8030e-3 (1.65e-4)	2.6807e-3 (3.94e-4)	**8.6769e-4 (1.09e-4)**	1.4512e-1 (2.09e-3)	1.5616e-3 (9.41e-5)
DTLZ2	8	78000	5.8219e-3 (4.13e-4)	1.9876e-1 (3.29e-1)	**2.3041e-3 (1.59e-4)**	3.0421e-1 (1.99e-3)	5.6278e-3 (3.62e-4)
	10	206250	5.0041e-3 (1.52e-4)	3.2408e-1 (2.75e-1)	**2.0810e-3 (5.05e-5)**	3.4515e-1 (9.59e-4)	5.4928e-3 (1.35e-4)
	15	135000	**6.0961e-3 (1.19e-3)**	6.9244e-1 (6.97e-2)	1.0783e-2 (5.95e-3)	4.7746e-1 (3.33e-3)	9.2489e-3 (1.16e-3)
	3	91000	2.3041e-3 (2.41e-3)	4.3101e-3 (2.52e-3)	5.3214e-3 (1.07e-3)	1.5781e-1 (1.44e-1)	**1.4041e-3 (8.09e-4)**
	5	210000	**1.1162e-3 (2.43e-4)**	3.4290e-3 (7.68e-4)	5.1683e-3 (1.98e-3)	6.0240e-1 (3.88e-1)	1.4306e-3 (4.08e-4)
DTLZ3	8	156000	1.0520e-2 (2.43e-3)	1.1390e+0 (1.03e+0)	1.0826e-2 (6.08e-3)	1.3460e+0 (5.33e-1)	**8.9336e-3 (3.97e-3)**
	10	412500	3.4853e-2 (2.68e-4)	6.6158e-1 (6.72e-1)	4.0694e-1 (5.57e-1)	1.2649e+0 (4.90e-4)	**4.8921e-3 (4.52e-4)**
	15	270000	9.0106e-3 (1.14e-3)	2.0973e+1 (1.32e+1)	8.4953e-1 (6.86e-1)	2.6922e+2 (2.82e+1)	**8.7292e-3 (1.86e-3)**
	3	54600	**1.8935e-4 (1.51e-5)**	5.4067e-4 (1.96e-5)	3.5375e-1 (3.06e-1)	7.2661e-2 (1.22e-3)	2.0120e-4 (2.27e-5)
	5	210000	**2.5140e-4 (3.62e-5)**	1.3790e-3 (3.02e-4)	1.1450e-1 (1.98e-1)	1.4696e-1 (7.47e-3)	3.3253e-4 (6.58e-5)
DTLZ4	8	195000	7.5698e-2 (1.26e-1)	1.7674e-1 (2.99e-1)	2.7210e-1 (2.35e-1)	3.0645e-1 (1.75e-3)	**7.3847e-3 (8.46e-3)**
	10	550000	3.5794e-3 (1.37e-4)	4.1622e-3 (7.34e-4)	2.3126e-1 (8.90e-2)	3.4374e-1 (1.16e-1)	**3.3423e-3 (2.28e-4)**
	15	405000	6.1523e-3 (2.67e-4)	4.2515e-1 (3.67e-1)	2.7229e-1 (1.49e-1)	4.6349e-1 (3.15e-3)	**5.2482e-3 (3.84e-4)**

Table 3. Statistical results (mean and standard deviation) of the HV values obtained by the five algorithms on DTLZ1-4. The best results are in bold type.

Problem	m	FEs	MOEA-APS	NSGAIII	MOEAD-PBI	GrEA	RVEA
	3	36400	1.3979e-1 (1.17e-4)	1.3958e-1 (4.54e-4)	1.3965e-1 (3.24e-4)	9.7840e-2 (1.60e-2)	**1.3990e-1 (4.99e-5)**
	5	126000	**4.9318e-2 (7.24e-6)**	4.9297e-2 (4.62e-6)	4.9310e-2 (9.48e-6)	3.6608e-2 (8.87e-3)	4.9308e-2 (2.10e-6)
DTLZ1	8	117000	**8.3537e-3 (5.06e-7)**	8.3457e-3 (1.47e-5)	8.3504e-3 (5.84e-7)	3.6013e-3 (8.41e-4)	8.3532e-3 (3.98e-7)
	10	275000	**2.5322e-3 (2.17e-8)**	2.5320e-3 (3.44e-7)	2.5320e-3 (6.45e-8)	1.0633e-3 (5.80e-4)	2.5322e-3 (6.61e-8)
	15	202500	**1.2749e-4 (1.66e-9)**	1.2380e-4 (3.52e-6)	1.2743e-4 (1.37e-8)	6.2752e-5 (2.82e-5)	1.2747e-4 (1.83e-9)
	3	22750	7.4399e-1 (3.41e-4)	**7.4442e-1 (9.00e-5)**	7.4430e-1 (8.08e-5)	7.2483e-1 (6.66e-4)	7.4414e-1 (2.11e-4)
	5	73500	1.3077e+0 (6.00e-4)	1.3074e+0 (6.65e-4)	1.3079e+0 (5.97e-4)	1.3075e+0 (1.07e-3)	**1.3080e+0 (9.46e-4)**
DTLZ2	8	78000	1.9824e+0 (5.25e-4)	1.9784e+0 (4.68e-4)	1.9800e+0 (7.55e-4)	**1.9868e+0 (1.55e-3)**	1.9803e+0 (2.47e-4)
	10	206250	**2.5167e+0 (4.66e-4)**	2.4430e+0 (9.75e-2)	2.5154e+0 (3.97e-4)	2.4994e+0 (3.94e-3)	2.5154e+0 (3.55e-4)
	15	135000	**4.1388e+0 (2.67e-4)**	3.5157e+0 (4.94e-1)	4.1379e+0 (5.18e-4)	4.0510e+0 (6.02e-3)	4.1356e+0 (5.00e-3)
	3	91000	**7.4220e-1 (1.15e-3)**	7.3797e-1 (4.20e-3)	7.3895e-1 (3.73e-3)	6.1769e-1 (1.46e-1)	7.4057e-1 (1.59e-3)
	5	210000	**1.3085e+0 (1.18e-3)**	1.3062e+0 (1.47e-3)	1.3040e+0 (2.52e-3)	2.9860e-1 (2.68e-1)	1.3073e+0 (1.01e-3)
DTLZ3	8	156000	1.9368e+0 (5.97e-2)	1.5172e+0 (8.57e-1)	1.6265e+0 (7.75e-1)	1.1763e+0 (1.08e-1)	**1.9763e+0 (2.77e-3)**
	10	412500	2.3453e+0 (3.49e-2)	2.5139e+0 (8.98e-4)	2.5137e+0 (5.04e-4)	2.9299e+0 (8.12e-2)	**2.5152e+0 (3.95e-4)**
	15	270000	**4.1380e+0 (6.19e-4)**	0.0000e+0 (0.00e+0)	4.1249e+0 (2.88e-2)	0.0000e+0 (0.00e+0)	4.1379e+0 (6.01e-4)
	3	54600	**7.4483e-1 (1.61e-5)**	7.4464e-1 (1.17e-4)	4.3718e-1 (3.12e-1)	6.0312e-1 (2.70e-1)	7.4481e-1 (2.99e-5)
	5	210000	**1.3088e+0 (4.89e-4)**	1.3080e+0 (9.37e-4)	1.2453e+0 (8.67e-2)	1.3081e+0 (2.07e-3)	1.3087e+0 (8.81e-4)
DTLZ4	8	195000	1.9830e+0 (8.56e-4)	1.9231e+0 (1.25e-1)	1.8512e+0 (1.27e-1)	**1.9877e+0 (2.34e-3)**	1.9806e+0 (4.08e-4)
	10	550000	**2.5168e+0 (3.30e-4)**	2.4347e+0 (1.11e-1)	2.4130e+0 (4.22e-2)	2.5047e+0 (2.52e-3)	2.5154e+0 (6.17e-4)
	15	405000	**4.1400e+0 (4.10e-4)**	3.6055e+0 (2.72e-1)	4.0930e+0 (3.74e-2)	4.0616e+0 (5.19e-3)	4.1345e+0 (8.56e-3)

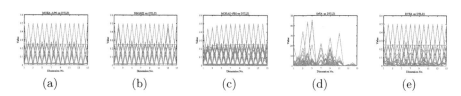

(a)   (b)   (c)   (d)   (e)

Fig. 2. Parallel coordinates of the nondominated front obtained by each algorithm on 15-objective DTLZ1 for the run associated with the median HV value. (a) MOEA-APS. (b) NSGAIII. (c) MOEAD-PBI. (d) GrEA. (e) RVEA

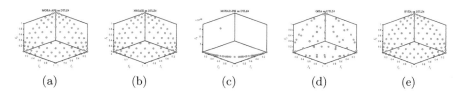

(a)   (b)   (c)   (d)   (e)

Fig. 3. Nondominated solutions obtained by each algorithm on 3-objective DTLZ4 in the run associated with the median HV value. (a) MOEA-APS. (b) NSGAIII. (c) MOEAD-PBI. (d) GrEA. (e) RVEA.

4   Conclusion

In this paper, a new evolutionary algorithm called MOEA-APS is developed for MaOPs. Besides, a new proposed APS is used as the main selection criterion, the proposed APS allows to effectively prevent the dense solutions being selected simultaneously as well as it allows to greatly improve the diversity of the population. Moreover, a non fixed penalty threshold η varies according to the density of the solution is used.

The performance of MOEA-APS is validated through a series comparative experiments with four other well-known MOEAs. The results obtained by our proposed MOEA-APS are very competitive.

Acknowledgment. This work was partially supported by the National Natural Science Foundation of China (No.61672215, U1613209).

References

1. Ishibuchi, H., Tsukamoto, N., Nojima, Y.: Behavior of evolutionary many-objective optimization. In: Tenth International Conference on Computer Modeling and Simulation, pp. 266–271 (2008)
2. Yang, S., Li, M., Liu, X., Zheng, J.: A grid-based evolutionary algorithm for many-objective optimization. IEEE Trans. Evol. Comput. **17**(5), 721–736 (2013)
3. Kukkonen, S., Lampinen, J.: Ranking-dominance and many-objective optimization. In: IEEE Congress on Evolutionary Computation, CEC 2007, pp. 3983–3990 (2007)
4. He, Z., Yen, G.G., Zhang, J.: Fuzzy-based pareto optimality for many-objective evolutionary algorithms. IEEE Trans. Evol. Comput. **18**(2), 269–285 (2014)
5. Bader, J., Zitzler, E.: Hype: an algorithm for fast hypervolume-based many-objective optimization. Evol. Comput. **19**(19), 45–76 (2011)
6. Basseur, M., Zitzler, E.: A preliminary study on handling uncertainty in indicator-based multiobjective optimization. In: Rothlauf, F., et al. (eds.) EvoWorkshops 2006. LNCS, vol. 3907, pp. 727–739. Springer, Heidelberg (2006). https://doi.org/10.1007/11732242_71
7. Li, B., Tang, K., Li, J., Yao, X.: Stochastic ranking algorithm for many-objective optimization based on multiple indicators. IEEE Trans. Evol. Comput. **20**(6), 924–938 (2016). https://doi.org/10.1109/TEVC.2016.2549267. ISSN 1089-778X
8. Saxena, D.K., Duro, J.A., Tiwari, A., Deb, K.: Objective reduction in many-objective optimization: linear and nonlinear algorithms. IEEE Trans. Evol. Comput. **17**(1), 77–99 (2013)
9. Pez Jaimes, A., Coello Coello, C.A., Chakraborty, D.: Objective reduction using a feature selection technique. In: Proceedings of Genetic and Evolutionary Computation Conference, GECCO 2008, Atlanta, GA, USA, pp. 673–680, July 2008
10. Zhang, Q., Li, H.: MOEA/D: a multiobjective evolutionary algorithm based on decomposition. IEEE Trans. Evol. Comput. **11**(6), 712–731 (2007)
11. Liu, H.L., Gu, F., Zhang, Q.: Decomposition of a multiobjective optimization problem into a number of simple multiobjective subproblems. IEEE Trans. Evol. Comput. **18**(3), 450–455 (2014)

12. Deb, K., Jain, H.: An evolutionary many-objective optimization algorithm using reference-point-based nondominated sorting approach, part i: Solving problems with box constraints. IEEE Trans. Evol. Comput. **18**(4), 577–601 (2014)
13. Cheng, R., Jin, Y., Olhofer, M., Sendhoff, B.: A reference vector guided evolutionary algorithm for many-objective optimization. IEEE Trans. Evol. Comput. **20**(5), 773–791 (2016)
14. Das, I., Dennis, J.E.: Normal-boundary intersection: a new method for generating the pareto surface in nonlinear multicriteria optimization problems. SIAM J. Optim. **8**(3), 631–657 (1998)
15. Hillermeier, C.: Nonlinear Multiobjective Optimization. Birkhaser Verlag, Basel (2001)
16. Das, I., Dennis, J.E.: Normal-boundary intersection: a new method for generating the pareto surface in nonlinear multicriteria optimization problems. SIAM J. Optim. **8**(3), 631–657 (2000)
17. Deb, K., Thiele, L., Laumanns, M., Zitzler, E.: Scalable test problems for evolutionary multiobjective optimization. In: Abraham, A., Jain, L., Goldberg, R. (eds.) Evolutionary Multiobjective Optimization. Springer, London (2005). https://doi.org/10.1007/1-84628-137-7_6
18. Bosman, P.A.N., Thierens, D.: The balance between proximity and diversity in multiobjective evolutionary algorithms. IEEE Trans. Evol. Comput. **7**(2), 174–188 (2003)
19. Zitzler, E., Thiele, L.: Multiobjective evolutionary algorithms: a comparative case study and the strength pareto approach. IEEE Trans. Evol. Comput. **3**(4), 257–271 (1999)

A Personalized Recommendation Algorithm Based on MOEA-ProbS

Xiaoyan Shi, Wei Fang$^{(\boxtimes)}$, and Guizhu Zhang

School of IoT Engineering, Jiangnan University, Wuxi, Jiangsu, China
fangwei@jiangnan.edu.cn

Abstract. As a technology based on statistics and knowledge discovery, recommendation system can automatically provide appropriate recommendations to users, which is considered as a very effective tool for reducing information load. The accuracy and diversity of recommendation are important objectives of evaluating an algorithm. In order to improve the diversity of recommendation, a personalized recommendation algorithm Multi-Objective Evolutionary Algorithm with Probabilistic-spreading and Genetic Mutation Adaptation (MOEA-PGMA) based on Personalized Recommendation based on Multi-Objective Evolutionary Optimization (MOEA-ProbS) is proposed in this paper. Low-grade and unpurchased items are preprocessed before predicting the scores to avoid recommending low-grade items to users and improve recommendation accuracy. By introducing adaptive mutation, the better individuals will survive in the evolution with a smaller mutation rate, and worse individuals will eliminate. The experimental results show that MOEA-PMGA has a higher population search ability compared to MOEA-ProbS, and has improved the accuracy and diversity on the optimal solution set.

1 Introduction

Faced with a huge amount of data, it becomes very difficult for users to find the goods or information they are interested in [1]. As a technology based on statistics and knowledge discovery, recommendation system takes advantage of e-commerce sites to provide commodity information and advice, helping users decide what products to buy and complete the purchase process like the sales staff [2].

With the rapid development of the times, the types of data have become more and more abundant and only considering recommendation accuracy is not enough. In order to meet the personalized needs of users, introducing some other performance indexes such as diversity and novelty is necessary. Since diversity and high accuracy are contradictory of a recommendation system, recommending a variety of products to users may reduce the recommendation accuracy [3]. Therefore, a challenge the recommendation system faces is how to develop a recommendation technology that can achieve high accuracy and diversity at the same time.

© Springer International Publishing AG, part of Springer Nature 2018
Y. Tan et al. (Eds.): ICSI 2018, LNCS 10941, pp. 572–579, 2018.
https://doi.org/10.1007/978-3-319-93815-8_54

Personalized algorithms based on multi-objective evolution continue to emerge. Zang and Hurley [4] proposed a recommendation technique. The technique considered the balance of accuracy and diversity into a quadratic programming problem and developed multiple strategies to solve the optimization problem. Zhou [5] introduced the hybrid algorithm combining HeatS with probability distribution algorithm. Heats algorithm is used to increase diversity, while ProbS algorithm is used to improve the accuracy. The basis of this hybrid algorithm is a basic method of weighted linear set. Therefore, the weights should be appropriately adjusted to make accurate and diverse recommendations. Adomavicius and Kwon [6] proposed a series of commodity ranking technologies that can achieve relatively accurate recommendation and diversity. Zuo et al. [7] proposed a multi-objective recommendation algorithm combining MOEA and ProbS to improve the diversity with high accuracy. However, with the number of population iterations increasing, the crowding degree between the optimal solution set is getting higher and higher, and the population shows premature convergence.

In this paper, the MOEA-ProbS algorithm is analyzed, and it is modified in the application of recommendation problem to improve the accuracy and diversity of the optimal solution set. In the module of predicting grade, because the MOEA-ProbS algorithm does not distinguish between items that users have purchased with low scores and those that are not purchased, the algorithm may repeatedly recommend low grade products to users. MOEA-PGMA makes improvements according to this. The grade will be set to -1 if the items are not purchased. The grade will be set to 0 if the items get low evaluating scores. The grade is 1 if the items get high evaluating scores. In the process of evolution, with the increase of the iteration number, the premature convergence of the population leads to the decrease of diversity. MOEA-PGMA uses adaptive mutation rate so that the better individuals will participate in the evolution with a smaller mutation rate, and the worse individuals are the opposite. The experimental results show that the improved algorithm can have more reliable searching ability with the same population size, and the optimal solution can be improved greatly in diversity and accuracy.

2   Background

2.1   Definition of Recommendation Problem

In general, the recommendation problem is defined as follows. Suppose the C set contains all the users in the system, and the S set contains all the recommended items in the system. The matrix R contains users' rating data for products, so R is used to indicate the users' degree of preference for the items. For example, i is an element of the C set, and the commodity α is an element of the S set. The user's rating level for the product is 0–5. It defines that if the user's rating level is equal to or greater than 3, it means that they like the item. For example, $R(i, \alpha)$ which represents the degree of user i's preference for item α is equal to 4, then user i likes the item α. In general, the number of products evaluated by one user is small, so the first step of product recommendation is to predict the user's preference for unknown products through a certain recommendation method. Usually, items with high ratings will be recommended to users [9], as Eq. (1).

$$\forall i \in C, \alpha = argmaxR\,(i, \alpha)\,\alpha \in S \tag{1}$$

2.2   Multi-objective Optimization

Multi-objective optimization is designed to optimize the function as Eq. (2), where $x = [x_1, x_1..., x_d] \in \Omega$. x is the decision vector and Ω is the decision space of D dimensions.

$$minF\,(x) = (f_1\,(x)\,, f_2\,(x)\,, ..., f_m\,(x))^T \tag{2}$$

Since the maximum problem can be converted into a minimum problem, we consider the minimum problem as shown in Eq. (2). X_A and X_B the decision vector sets are given. If $f(X_A) \leq f(X_B)$ for all $f(X_A)$ and $f(X_B)$, then $X_A > X_B$, namely X_A dominates X_B. If there isn't another group of vector X^*, where $X^* > X$, then vector X is the optimal solution. The set of all the optimal solutions is the optimal set (3).

$$PS = \{x \in \Omega | \neg x^* \in \Omega, x^* > x\} \tag{3}$$

The image of pareto set in the target function space becomes the pareto front, which is defined as (4). The goal of MOEA is to figure out how to approximate the real pareto front.

$$PF = \{F(x) | x \in PS\} \tag{4}$$

2.3   MOEA-ProbS

In order to ensure that the recommended set has a high diversity with high accuracy, Zuo et al. [7] proposes the MOEA-ProbS algorithm. The algorithm starts with the users commodity evaluation record, and the users with similar preference are divided into the same group. The Probs algorithm is used to predict the evaluation score of unpurchased products in the group. A group of recommendation for each user in the group is built in the predictive scoring system to initialize the population chromosome. The optimal solution set is produced and recommended to the user through the operation of evolution.

3   MOEA-PGMA

3.1   Improved ProbS Algorithm

ProbS is suitable for the recommendation system without definite rating, and $R(i, \alpha)$ is 0 or 1 in the evaluation matrix R, where 0 means that the user does not collect the commodity α, and 1 indicates that the user has collected the commodity α. In MOEA-ProbS, commodities with a score of 3 and above are set to 1, and commodities with a score lower than 3 or not collected are set to 0. Then, when recommending commodities with higher score to users, it is possible to recommend the products with lower evaluation score to users since the algorithm does not distinguish between the commodities with low evaluation score and the uncollected commodities.

In general, users are less likely to buy low-scoring commodities twice. Therefore, in the improved ProbS algorithm, uncollected commodities rating will be set to -1, and low-scoring commodities rating will be set to 0 and high-scoring commodities rating will be set to 1. The commodities with high score will be recommended according to the rating list of the commodities that the user has not purchased.

3.2   Adaptive Mutation Rate for Multi-objective

The mutation operator is designed to maintain a certain diversity of population, so that the genetic algorithm has the ability to jump out of local optimum before convergence. In general genetic algorithms, the population uses a fixed global mutation rate. When the mutation rate is very small, the mutation will hardly affect the population, which is not conducive to the introduction of new genes. When the mutation rate is too high, it is possible to destroy the good genes of the population, which is not conducive to the convergence of the algorithm.

Therefore, different mutation rates can be applied to different individuals in the population. The better individuals in the population have a smaller mutation rate, which can get better retention and the accumulation of good models through cross-recombination, while worse individuals in the population can enhance their ability to explore with a larger mutation rate.

In order to adjust the individual mutation rate in the population smoothly, Xiong [8] proposes the Sigmoid function as (5), where p_m^i is the mutation rate of the ith individual in the descending order of moderate value of the population.

$$p_m^i = \begin{cases} \frac{0.5}{1+e^{-\alpha_1(i-N_S)}}, i \le N_s \\ \frac{0.5}{1+e^{-\alpha_2(i-N_S)}}, i \ge N_s \end{cases} \tag{5}$$

The curve shape of p_m^i is controlled by two parameters. α_i is the shape factor and N_S is the demarcation point of the population. N_S is used to control the division of fine and poor individuals. Figure 1 shows the curve after normalization of the population, where the parameters α_1, α_2 and N_S are set to 0.2, 0.1, 0.5.

Since the adaptive mutation rate proposed by Xiong is only applicable to single-objective genetic algorithm, this method is improved to apply to multi-objective genetic application. Before adjusting mutation rate dynamically, the dominance hierarchy and crowding degree of individual population are calculated. Sort the individuals according to the individual dominance hierarchy and crowding degree. The individual mutation rate is adjusted dynamically according to the sorting result. The principle is that with different dominance hierarchies, individuals with lower dominance hierarchies have smaller mutation rates.

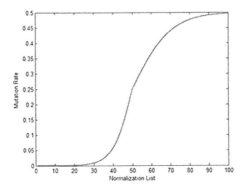

Fig. 1. Adjustment of mutation rate

With the same dominance hierarchy, individuals with higher crowding degree have a smaller mutation rate.

3.3   The Proposed Algorithm

The steps of the proposed algorithm combining improved Probs and adaptive mutation rate are as follows.

(1) Predicting the evaluation score with Probs according to the score record.
(2) Initializing population T, the number of individuals is N_0.
(3) Generating EPOP by selecting operator and crossover operator.
(4) Calculating the individual accuracy and diversity of EPOP, performing the mutation operation on the same individual with different mutation rate according to the P_m curve, generating the next generation population.
(5) Juding whether or not to meet the stop condition, yes to step 6 or to step 3 to continue.
(6) Outputing the current optimal solution as the results.

4   Experiment

4.1   Parameters Settings

In order to test the improvement effect of the adaptive mutation rate, the same experiment parameters as the MOEA-Probs are used in this paper except mutation rate. The mutation rate used by MOEA-Probs is 0.8, and this article uses the mutation rate as Eq. (5). The parameters are set as shown in Table 1.

4.2   Results and Analysis

To test the performance of the improved algorithm, this paper takes the same data set Movielens [9] as MOEA-Probs. The data set contains 943 users and

Table 1. Parameters setting

Parameters	Setting
Length of recommendation list	10
Population size	100
Number of iteration	3000
Crossover probability	0.8
Mutation probability	$p_m^i = \begin{cases} \frac{0.5}{1+e^{-\alpha_1(i-N_S)}}, i \leq N_s \\ \frac{0.5}{1+e^{-\alpha_2(i-N_S)}}, i \geq N_s \end{cases}$

1,682 films. By using the k-means clustering method, the data set is divided into four groups. Since the Probs algorithm is applicable to the 0–1 rating system, an item grade will be rated as 1 if its score is equal or greater than 3. An items grade will be set to 0 if their scores are less than 3 or the item isn't collected. At the same time, 80% of the data is randomly selected as training set, and the remaining data is used as test set.

Hypervolume is one of the most important indexes in the field of multi-objective optimization. It can simultaneously measure the convergence and diversity of the algorithm. The larger the hypervolume value is, the better the solution is. Therefore, in order to test the performance of MOEA-PMGA, the hypervolume is used as the performance index. MOEA-PMGA and MOEA-ProbS are compared using the same data set. The experimental results are as Fig. 2 and Table 2.

Table 2. Compare the hypervolume value of the two algorithms

Algorithm	Movielens1	Movielens2	Movielens3	Movielens4
MOEA-ProbS	0.0802	0.1394	0.0941	0.1636
MOEA-PMGA	0.1073	0.1568	0.1110	0.2274

The experimental results show that the MOEA-PGMA improves a lot in diversity and accuracy than MOEA-Probs. MOEA-PGMA has a higher accuracy than MOEA-Probs since it avoids recommending low-scoring movies. In addition, the improved algorithm adopts adaptive mutation rate after pareto ranking, top-ranking chromosome participating in mutation with a relatively lower probability, low-ranking chromosome participating in mutation with a relatively higher probability. Therefore, taking the method of adaptive mutation rate has achieved both elite retention and recommendation diversity improvement. The hypervolume value of MOEA-PGMA is higher than MOEA-Probs, which indicates that MOEA-PMGA has better convergence and higher diversity than MOEA-Probs.

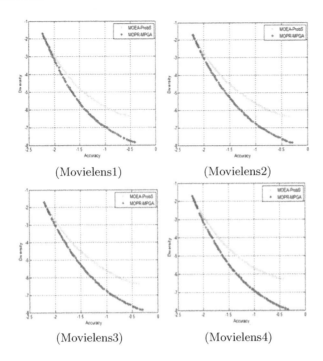

(Movielens1)   (Movielens2)

(Movielens3)   (Movielens4)

Fig. 2. Results comparison of MOEA-ProbS and MOEA-PGMA

5   Conclusions

In this paper, a general improved multi-objective recommendation algorithm is proposed to optimize the recommendation accuracy and diversity. The improved ProbS algorithm is used to improve the accuracy and the diversity is improved with adaptive mutation rate. The experimental results show that the improved MOEA-ProbS algorithm can make multiple recommendations to the same user more efficiently.

Acknowledgement. This work was partially supported by the National Natural Science Foundation of China (Grant Nos. 61673194, 61105128), Key Research and Development Program of Jiangsu Province, China (Grant No. BE2017630), the Postdoctoral Science Foundation of China (Grant No. 2014M560390), Six Talent Peaks Project of Jiangsu Province (Grant No. DZXX-025).

References

1. Du, H.: Research on recommendation algorithm based on network structure, pp. 1–57. Beijing University of Posts and Telecommunications, Beijing (2012)
2. Hou, Z.: Personalized recommendation study of e-commerce websites in user behavior mode. Comput. Inf. Technol. (4), 4–7 (2011)

3. Zuo, Y.: An evolutionary multi-objective algorithm based on global optimization and local learning, pp. 1–135. Xidian University, Xian (2016)
4. Zhang, M., Hurley, N.: Avoiding monotony: improving the diversity of recommendation lists. In: Proceedings of the ACM Conference on Recommender Systems, New York, pp. 123–130 (2008)
5. Zhou, T., Kuscsik, Z., Liu, J.G., Medo, M., Wakeling, J.R., Zhang, Y.C.: Solving the apparent diversity-accuracy dilemma of recommender systems. Proc. Natl. Acad. Sci. **107**(10), 4511–4515 (2010)
6. Adomavicius, G., Kwon, Y.: Improving aggregate recommendation diversity using ranking-based techniques. IEEE Trans. Knowl. Data Eng. **24**(5), 896–911 (2012)
7. Zuo, Y., Gong, M., Zeng, J., Ma, L., Jiao, L.: Personalized recommendation based on evolutionary multiobjective optimization. IEEE Comput. Intell. Soc. **10**(1), 52–62 (2015)
8. Xiong, J.: Mutation rate and adaptive population number genetic algorithm. J. Southeast Univ. (Natural Science Version) (4), 553–556 (2004)
9. Adomavicius, G., Tuzhilin, A.: Toward the next generation of recommender systems: a survey of the state-of-the-art and possible extensions. IEEE Trans. Knowl. Data Eng. **17**(6), 734–749 (2005)

Large-Scale Global Optimization

Adaptive Variable-Size Random Grouping for Evolutionary Large-Scale Global Optimization

Evgenii Sopov[✉]

Reshetnev Siberian State University of Science and Technology,
Krasnoyarsk, Russia
evgenysopov@gmail.com

Abstract. In recent years many real-world optimization problems have had to deal with growing dimensionality. Optimization problems with many hundreds or thousands of variables are called large-scale global optimization (LSGO) problems. Many well-known real-world LSGO problems are not separable and are complex for detailed analysis, thus they are viewed as the black-box optimization problems. The most advanced algorithms for LSGO are based on cooperative coevolution with problem decomposition using grouping methods, which form low-dimensional non-overlapping subcomponents of a high-dimensional objective vector. The standard random grouping can be applied to the wide range of separable and non-separable LSGO problems, but it does not use any feedback from the search process for creating more efficient variables combinations. Many learning-based dynamic grouping methods are able to identify interacting variables and to group them into the same subcomponent. At the same time, the majority of the proposed learning-based methods demonstrate greedy search and perform well only with separable problems. In this study, we proposed a new adaptive random grouping approach that create and adaptively change a probability distribution for assigning variables to subcomponents. The approach is able to form subcomponents of different size or can be used with predefined fix-sized subcomponents. The results of numerical experiments for benchmark problems are presented and discussed. The experiments show that the proposed approach outperforms the standard random grouping method.

Keywords: Cooperative co-evolution · Random grouping
Large-scale global optimization

1 Introduction

Optimization problems with many hundreds or thousands of objective variables are called large-scale global optimization (LSGO) problems. LSGO is still a challenging problem for mathematical and evolutionary optimization techniques. Moreover, many real-world LSGO problems are usually complex and not well-studied, so they are viewed as black-box optimization problems even the objective has analytical representation (using mathematical formula). Evolutionary algorithms (EAs) have proved their efficiency at solving many complex real-world optimization problems. However,

© Springer International Publishing AG, part of Springer Nature 2018
Y. Tan et al. (Eds.): ICSI 2018, LNCS 10941, pp. 583–592, 2018.
https://doi.org/10.1007/978-3-319-93815-8_55

their performance usually decreases when the dimensionality of the search space increases. Black-box LSGO problems have become a great challenge even for EAs as we have no information about the search space to include it into a certain algorithm. Another challenge is nonseparability that excludes a straightforward variable-based decomposition. Nevertheless, some assumptions about the continuous search space can be done, and there exist many efficient LSGO techniques.

The most advanced algorithms for LSGO are based on cooperative coevolution (CC) with problem decomposition using grouping methods. The decomposition methods are based on divide-and-conquer strategy, which decomposes LSGO problems into multiple low-dimensional non-overlapping subcomponents. The standard random grouping can be applied to the wide range of separable and non-separable LSGO problems, but it does not use any feedback from the search process for creating more efficient variables combinations. There is a lack of efficient learning-based approaches for dynamic grouping, which are able to identify interacting variables and to group them into the same subcomponent. The majority of the proposed learning-based methods perform well only with separable LSGO problems and fail in solving non-separable problems and problems with overlapping variables. Many dynamic grouping techniques use greedy approaches for identifying interacting variables (for example, weighted and differential grouping [1, 2]). As known, EAs realize a combination of exploration and exploitation strategies on different stages of the search process. And, it is obvious that different stages may need different problem decomposition for better performance.

In this study, we proposed a new adaptive random grouping approach. The idea behind the approach is based on the Population-Level Dynamic Probabilities (PDP) adaptation strategy that applies EA's operations using probabilities based the success rates of the operations [3]. The proposed approach create and adaptively change a probability distribution for assigning variables to subcomponents. The approach is able to form subcomponents of different size or can be used with predefined fix-sized subcomponents. The CMA-ES algorithm [4] is used as the core EA in the CC scheme.

The rest of the paper is organized as follows. Section 2 describes related work. Section 3 describes the proposed approach. In Sect. 4 the results of numerical experiments are discussed. In the Conclusion the results and further research are discussed.

2 Related Work

There exist a great variety of different LSGO techniques that can be combined in two main groups: non-decomposition methods and cooperative coevolution (CC) algorithms. The first group of methods are mostly based on improving standard evolutionary and genetic operations. But the best results and the majority of approaches are presented by the second group. The CC methods decompose LSGO problems into low dimensional sub-problems by grouping the problem subcomponents. CC consists of three general steps: problem decomposition, subcomponent optimization and subcomponent coadaptation (merging solutions of all subcomponents to construct the complete solution). The problem decomposition is a critical step. There are many subcomponent grouping methods, including: static grouping [5], random dynamic grouping [2] and learning dynamic grouping [1, 6].

The learning dynamic grouping seems to be the most perspective approach as it collects and uses feedback information for improving the decomposition stage. There were proposed a CC Algorithm based on the correlation matrix [7], a CC with Variable Interaction Learning (CCVIL) [8], an automated decomposition approach (DECC-DG) with differential grouping [1] and many others. A good survey on LSGO and methods is proposed in [9].

The majority of the learning dynamic grouping techniques demonstrates too greedy adaptation, thus performs well only with separable LSGO problems. For example, DECC-DG is based on the mathematic definition of separability and uses this information for the grouping. At the same time, there exist many approaches in the field of EAs for solving self-adaption and self-configuration problems that use a stochastic adaptation strategy. One of the most popular and efficient techniques is called Population-Level Dynamic Probabilities (or PDP) [3]. The PDP implements EAs' actions using some distribution of probabilities. The probabilities are adapted based on the success rates of the previously applied actions. In this study we will combine ideas of the random grouping and the PDP.

3 Proposed Approach

The following optimization problem is considered:

$$f(X) \rightarrow \min_{X \in R^n}, \tag{1}$$

where $X = (x_1, \ldots, x_i, \ldots, x_n)$ and $x_i \in \left[x_i^{min}, x_i^{max} \right]$, $i = \overline{1, n}$.

We will use the following notations:

- *cycle* is a period than the optimization problem is being solved using the certain decomposition, t denotes a cycle number ($t = 0$ is used for the initialization step);
- *numCycles* is the maximum number of cycles;
- *maxFEs* is a maximum number of function evaluations for the optimization problem;
- s_j is a low-dimensional subcomponent of a candidate-solution X;
- EA_{s_j} is the EA that optimizes the *i*-th subcomponent;
- *popSize* is a size of population for EAs;
- *fitness*(X) is a fitness function for a candidate-solution X, which is based on an objective function for the given optimization problem, the fitness function is maximized;
- *bestFound* is the fitness value of the best-found solution and *bestFound*$_j(t)$ is the fitness value of the best-found solution obtained by the EA_{s_j} within the *t*-th cycle;
- *popAverageFitness*$_j(t)$ denotes average performance of the EA_{s_j}, and it is mean value of the average fitness in the EA_{s_j}'s populations over generations within the *t*-th cycle.

The general scheme for the proposed adaptive variable-size random grouping algorithm (AVS-RG CC) contains the following steps:

1. Initialization.
2. Set $t = 1$ to start a new *cycle*.
3. Perform the adaptive random grouping and decompose the n-dimensional problem into k subcomponents. The sizes of the groups are $\{s_1, \ldots, s_j, \ldots, s_k\}$ and $\sum_{j=1}^{k} s_j = n$.

   Set $j = 1$.
4. Optimize the j-th subcomponent with a certain EA (EA_{s_j}) for a predefined number of Fitness Evaluations (*FE*). If T is a predefined number of generations within a cycle for EAs with a fixed size of population then $FE = T * popSize$.
5. If $j < k$ then set $j = j + 1$ and go to Step 4 else go to Step 6.
6. If $t < numCycles$ then set $t = t + 1$ and go to Step 3 for the next *cycle* else Stop.

We will discuss some steps of the AVS-RG CC in details.

At the grouping stage (step 3), we need to combine all components of the X into k groups. The sizes of the groups are: $s_1, \ldots, s_i, \ldots, s_k$ and $\sum_{j=1}^{k} s_j = n$.

In many well-studied techniques, the sizes are equal, $s_1 = \ldots = s_i = \ldots = s_k = s$ and $s \cdot k = n$. In the random grouping method, the sizes are also equal and the groups are filled with variables at random without repetition. This means that we do not use any feedback information about the success of the grouping.

We will introduce a probability distribution $P(t)$ that defines a chance for each variable to be assigned to a specific group:

$$P(t) = (p_1(t), \ldots, p_i(t), \ldots, p_n(t)). \tag{2}$$

Here each component of $P(t)$ is a vector that represent a distribution:

$$p_i(t) = \left(p_i^1(t), p_i^2(t), \ldots, p_i^k(t)\right), \; p_i^j(t) = P\left(x_i \in s_j\right) \text{ and } \sum_{j=1}^{k} p_i^j(t) = 1 \tag{3}$$

On the initialization step, if any a priori information about component grouping is absent, random uniform distribution is used. The groups are filled without repetition using the probability: $p_i^j(t = 0) = \frac{1}{k}$. The grouping based on the random uniform distribution will be equivalent to the random grouping method.

In this study, we propose a novel approach that introduces the feedback based on the performance of a search algorithm on the previous cycles, which was obtained with the given grouping. The approach adaptively changes the probability distribution $P(t)$

and defines the chance to each component of candidate-solutions to be assigned to a specific group.

There exist at least three strategies of applying the probability distribution for the component grouping:

1. Let $s_1 = \ldots = s_i = \ldots = s_k = s = const.$

   At the grouping stage, we start from x_1, calculate the corresponding probability and assign the component to a chosen group until the group is filled up. Then we go to x_2, x_3 and so on.

2. Let $s_i \in [s_{min}, s_{max}]$, $\forall i$ and $\sum_{j=1}^{k} s_j = n.$

   In this case, sizes of groups can be different in the given range, but the number of groups is still equal to k.

3. Let $s_i \in [0, n]$, $\forall i$ and $\sum_{j=1}^{k} s_j = n.$

   In this case, sizes of groups can be different and the number of the groups may vary between 1 and k.

It is obvious that the third case is more flexible and universal, and we will use it in this study.

After each cycle, we need to estimate the performance for the search algorithm for adapting the distribution P in order to increase probabilities for successful variable-subcomponent links. The performance metric can be used as a feedback for estimating the current component grouping. As we use the PDP-like adaption, we will divide of subcomponents' EAs into two subsets: EAs with successful grouping (denoted as bEA) and all the rest EAs (wEA). Variable-subcomponent links that correspond to sub-components of the bEA set will increase their probabilities in the distribution P by decreasing probabilities of links corresponding to the wEA set.

We will include in the bEA set all EAs that have improved the best-found solution obtained within the previous cycle. If a new best-found solution was not found, we will estimate the average performance of EAs over the last cycle and will rank EAs. A predefined percentage of EAs with high ranks (denoted as α) will be included into the bEA set, the rest - into the wEA set.

Finally, we can use the following algorithm for adapting the probability distribution based on the feedback information:

Algorithm 1: Adapting the probability distribution

$t = \overline{1, numCycle}$
$sumP = 0$
if $\left(\exists EA_j: bestFound_j(t) > bestFound(t-1)\right)$
$\quad \forall j = \overline{1, k}$
$\quad$ if $\left(bestFound_j(t) > bestFound(t-1)\right)$
$\quad\quad \forall i = \overline{1, n}$
$\quad\quad$ if $\left(\left(i \notin S_j\right) \wedge \left(\left(p_i^j(t) - \Delta p\right) \geq \theta\right)\right)$
$\quad\quad\quad sumP += \Delta p$
$\quad\quad\quad p_i^j(t) -= \Delta p$
$\quad \forall j = \overline{1, k}$
$\quad \forall i = \overline{1, n}$
$\quad$ if $\left(i \in S_j\right)$
$\quad\quad p_i^j(t) += \dfrac{sumP}{\left|\{EA_j, j=\overline{1,k}: \left(bestFound_j(t) > bestFound(t-1)\right)\}\right|}$
else
$\quad \{bEA, wEA\} = rank(\alpha\%, popAverageFitness_j(t))$
$\quad \forall j = \overline{1, k}$
$\quad$ if $\left(EA_j \in wEA\right)$
$\quad\quad \forall i = \overline{1, n}$
$\quad\quad$ if $\left(\left(p_i^j(t) - \Delta p\right) \geq \theta\right)$
$\quad\quad\quad sumP += \Delta p$
$\quad\quad\quad p_i^j(t) -= \Delta p$
$\quad \forall j = \overline{1, k}$
$\quad$ if $\left(EA_j \in bEA\right)$
$\quad\quad \forall i = \overline{1, n}$
$\quad\quad p_i^j(t) += \dfrac{sumP}{|wEA|}$

Here Δp defines amount of changes in probabilities and θ is a threshold that guarantees some non-zero probability for each variable-subcomponent link. We can define these two parameters using the predefined number of cycles (*numCycle*):

$$\Delta p = \gamma * \frac{1}{numCycle}, \gamma > 0, \quad (4)$$

$$\theta = \frac{1}{numCycle}, \quad (5)$$

where γ is a learning rate, and values higher than 1 will lead to greedy adaptation. If the given optimization problem is fully separable problem and $\gamma = 1$, then we will need exactly *numCycle* cycles to redistribute all linkage probabilities.

4   Experimental Settings and Results

To estimate the proposed approach performance, we have used benchmark problems from the CEC 2013 Special Session and Competition on Large-Scale Global Optimization [10]. These problems represent a wider range of real-world large-scale optimization problems and provide convenience and flexibility for comparing various evolutionary algorithms specifically designed for large-scale global optimization. The benchmark contains LSGO problems of 4 types: fully-separable problems, partially separable problems, problems with overlapping subcomponents and non-separable problems. As known, collecting and analyzing statistics on LSGO problem solving need essential computational costs. In this study, we have chosen only one problem of each type for estimating performance of the AVS-RG CC algorithm. These problems are f2 - Shifted Rastrigin's Function (fully-separable), f6 - Shifted and Rotated Ackley's Function (partially separable, contains 7-nonseparable and 1-separable subcomponents), f12 - Shifted Rosenbrock's Function (overlapping subcomponents) and f15 - Shifted Schwefel's Function (fully non-separable).

The experimental results are compared with some state-of-the-art decomposition methods. We have chosen the differential evolution based cooperative coevolution with random dynamic grouping (DECC-G) [1] and Covariance Matrix Adaptation Evolution Strategy using Cooperative Coevolution (CC-CMA-ES) [6], because these algorithms represent the general CC decomposition ideas and are in Top-4 of CEC'13 and CEC'15 Competitions on Large-Scale Global Optimization. We have also included the Cooperative Co-evolution with Differential Grouping algorithm (DECC-DG) [1], because it implements an automatic decomposition approach.

All experimental settings are as proposed in [10]. The settings are:

- Dimensions for all problem are D = 1000;
- For each problem the best, worst, median, mean, and standard deviation of the 25 independent runs are evaluated;
- Maximum number of fitness evaluations is *MaxFE* = 3.0e+6.

The AVS-RG CC algorithm settings are:

- Number of cycles is *numCycles* = 50;
- Maximum number of subcomponents k = 5, 10 and 20;
- CMA-ES algorithm is used for optimizing each subcomponents;
- Population sizes and number of generations for each CMA-ES are *popSize* = 200, T = 60 for k = 5, *popSize* = 100, T = 60 for k = 10 and *popSize* = 50, T = 60 for k = 20;
- $\gamma = 1$;
- $\alpha = 20\%$.

The experimental results are presented in Tables 1, 2, 3 and 4.

Table 1. Experimental results on the f2 problem from CEC 2013 LSGO competition.

	CC-CMA-ES	DECC-G	DECC-DG	AVS-RG (k = 5)	AVS-RG (k = 10)	AVS-RG (k = 20)
Best	1.09e+03	9.90e+02	1.24e+04	5.65e+03	5.21e+03	3.17e+03
Median	1.33e+03	1.03e+03	1.42e+04	5.87e+03	5.59e+03	4.15e+03
Worst	1.56e+03	1.07e+03	1.66e+04	6.27e+03	5.98e+03	5.11e+03
Mean	1.33e+03	1.03e+03	1.44e+04	5.93e+03	5.60e+03	4.15e+03
StDev	1.11e+02	2.26e+01	1.36e+04	1.29e+02	1.08e+03	4.45e+02

Table 2. Experimental results on the f6 problem from CEC 2013 LSGO competition.

	CC-CMA-ES	DECC-G	DECC-DG	AVS-RG (k = 5)	AVS-RG (k = 10)	AVS-RG (k = 20)
Best	5.61e+03	6.96e−08	7.51e+04	6.72e+03	5.87e+03	2.03e+03
Median	9.93e+05	6.08e+04	1.27e+05	5.82e+05	3.73e+05	4.44e+05
Worst	1.01e+06	1.10e+05	1.81e+05	1.19e+06	7.42e+05	8.65e+05
Mean	5.83e+05	4.85e+04	1.23e+05	5.98e+05	3.73e+05	4.44e+05
StDev	4.79e+05	3.98e+04	3.29e+04	2.73e+05	1.69e+05	1.96e+05

Table 3. Experimental results on the f12 problem from CEC 2013 LSGO competition.

	CC-CMA-ES	DECC-G	DECC-DG	AVS-RG (k = 5)	AVS-RG (k = 10)	AVS-RG (k = 20)
Best	9.77e+02	9.80e+02	1.01e+11	9.80e+02	1.15e+03	1.90e+03
Median	9.85e+02	1.03e+03	1.42e+11	2.20e+03	3.15e+03	8.30e+03
Worst	2.43e+03	1.20e+03	1.78e+11	3.59e+03	5.15e+03	1.47e+04
Mean	1.27e+03	1.04e+03	1.43e+11	2.28e+03	3.16e+03	8.30e+03
StDev	4.26e+02	5.76e+01	1.89e+10	6.01e+02	9.30e+02	2.96e+03

Table 4. Experimental results on the f15 problem from CEC 2013 LSGO competition.

	CC-CMA-ES	DECC-G	DECC-DG	AVS-RG (k = 5)	AVS-RG (k = 10)	AVS-RG (k = 20)
Best	2.31e+07	4.63e+07	3.19e+06	5.91e+07	4.88e+07	1.03e+08
Median	2.85e+07	6.01e+07	5.01e+06	8.47e+07	6.09e+07	2.52e+08
Worst	4.89e+07	7.15e+07	7.94e+06	1.12e+08	7.92e+07	4.33e+08
Mean	3.03e+07	6.05e+07	5.19e+06	8.55e+07	6.40e+07	2.68e+08
StDev	6.08e+06	6.45e+06	1.13e+06	1.22e+7	7.03e+06	7.64e+07

As we can see from Tables, the proposed approach has demonstrated the performance comparable with the state-of-art techniques. The AVS-RG CC outperforms the DECC-DG algorithm on the f2, f6 and f12 problems, but yields to it on the f15 problem. At the same time, the performance of the AVS-RG CC algorithm is stable over all types of LSGO problems.

The experimental results shows that the efficient maximum number of subcomponents k depends on the type of the given LSGO problem. Smaller values of k are preferable for non-separable problems and problems with overlapping subcomponents, bigger values are preferable for separable problems.

5   Conclusions

In this paper a novel technique for LSGO based on the adaptive random grouping approach that create and adaptively change a probability distribution for assigning variables to subcomponents. The AVS-RG CC algorithm uses feedback information on the performance of the search process with the certain grouping and increases probabilities for successful variable-subcomponent links. One of the advantages on the approach is the possibility of generating subcomponents of different size. The experimental results has demonstrated that the performance of the AVR-RG algorithm is comparable with the state-of art techniques.

In further work, we will implement the proposed approach the CUDA parallel computation framework for carrying out more experiments. We will estimate the performance of the approach with all remained benchmark problems from the CEC'13 and will provide more detailed analysis of the algorithm' parameters.

Acknowledgements. This research is supported by the Ministry of Education and Science of Russian Federation within State Assignment № 2.1676.2017/ПЧ.

References

1. Omidvar, N.B., Li, X., Mei, Y., Yao, X.: Cooperative co-evolution with differential grouping for large scale optimization. IEEE Trans. Evol. Comput. **18**(3), 378–393 (2014)
2. Yang, Z., Tang, K., Yao, X.: Large scale evolutionary optimization using cooperative coevolution. Inform. Sci. **178**(15), 2985–2999 (2008)
3. Niehaus, J., Banzhaf, W.: Adaption of operator probabilities in genetic programming. In: Miller, J., Tomassini, M., Lanzi, P.L., Ryan, C., Tettamanzi, A.G.B., Langdon, W.B. (eds.) EuroGP 2001. LNCS, vol. 2038, pp. 325–336. Springer, Heidelberg (2001). https://doi.org/10.1007/3-540-45355-5_26
4. Omidvar, M.N., Li, X.: A comparative study of CMA-ES on large scale global optimisation. In: Li, J. (ed.) AI 2010. LNCS (LNAI), vol. 6464, pp. 303–312. Springer, Heidelberg (2010). https://doi.org/10.1007/978-3-642-17432-2_31
5. Potter, M., De Jong, K.A.: Cooperative coevolution: an architecture for evolving coadapted subcomponents. Evol. Comput. **8**(1), 1–29 (2000)
6. Liu, J., Tang, K.: Scaling up covariance matrix adaptation evolution strategy using cooperative coevolution. In: Intelligent Data Engineering and Automated Learning – IDEAL 2013, pp. 350–357 (2013)
7. Ray, T., Yao, X.: A cooperative coevolutionary algorithm with correlation based adaptive variable partitioning. In: IEEE Congress on Evolutionary Computation, (CEC 2009), pp. 983–989 (2009)

8. Chen, W., Weise, T., Yang, Zh., Tang, K.: Large-scale global optimization using cooperative coevolution with variable interaction learning. In: Schaefer, R., Cotta, C., Kołodziej, J., Rudolph, G. (eds.) PPSN 2010. LNCS, vol. 6239, pp. 300–309. Springer, Heidelberg (2010). https://doi.org/10.1007/978-3-642-15871-1_31
9. Mahdavi, S., Shiri, M.E., Rahnamayan, S.: Metaheuristics in large-scale global continues optimization: a survey. Inf. Sci. **295**, 407–428 (2015)
10. Li, X., Tang, K., Omidvar, M.N., Yang, Zh., Qin, K.: Benchmark functions for the CEC 2013 special session and competition on large-scale global optimization. Technical report, Evolutionary Computation and Machine Learning Group, RMIT University, Australia (2013)

A Dynamic Global Differential Grouping for Large-Scale Black-Box Optimization

Shuai Wu[1], Zhitao Zou[2], and Wei Fang[1(✉)]

[1] School of IoT Engineering, Jiangnan University, Wuxi, China
fangwei@jiangnan.edu.cn
[2] School of Science, Jiangnan University, Wuxi, China

Abstract. Cooperative Co-evolution (CC) framework is an important method to tackle Large Scale Black-Box Optimization (LSBO) problem. One of the main step in CC is grouping for the decision variables, which affects the optimization performance. An ideal grouping result is that the relationship of decision variables in intra-group is stronger as possible and those in inter-groups is weaker as possible. Global Differential Grouping (GDG) is an efficient grouping method based on the idea of partial derivatives of multivariate functions, and it can automatically resolve the problem by maintaining the global information among variables. However, once the grouping result by GDG is determined, it will no longer be updated and will not be automatically adjusted with the evolution of the algorithm, which may affect the optimization performance of the algorithm. Therefore, based on GDG, a Dynamic Global Differential Grouping (DGDG) strategy is proposed for grouping the decision variables in this paper, which can update the grouping results with the evolution processing. DGDG works with Particle Swarm Optimization (PSO) algorithm in this paper, which is termed as CC-DGDG-PSO. The experimental results based on the LSBO benchmark functions from CEC'2010 show that DGDG algorithm can improve the performance of GDG.

Keywords: Large-Scale Black-Box Optimization
Cooperative Co-evolution · Dynamic · Differential Grouping

1 Introduction

Large Scale Global Optimization (LSGO) problems refer to the problems with a large number of decision variables to be optimized, usually thousands or even more [1]. In LSGO problems, there is a case where the objective function does not have an explicit analytical formula [3], which is usually called Large Scale Black-Box Optimization (LSBO) problem [4]. LSBO problems are often encountered in research and industrial fields [5]. For instance, in the optimization problem of fluid-based airplane wing shapes, there are more than 2500 variables need to be optimized [6,7]. The optimization of LSBO problems is encountered two main issues: (1) the characteristics of black-boxes and the problem often have

© Springer International Publishing AG, part of Springer Nature 2018
Y. Tan et al. (Eds.): ICSI 2018, LNCS 10941, pp. 593–603, 2018.
https://doi.org/10.1007/978-3-319-93815-8_56

complex features such as nonlinear, non-convex and non-differentiable; (2) large-scale decision variables.

Cooperative Co-evolution (CC) [8], which is based on the idea of divide-and-conquer, is an algorithmic framework for solving LSBO problems by decomposing the problem into some sub-problems. Since the CC framework can decompose the LSBO problem into some sub-problems that the optimization algorithm can process, it has become an important method to solve the LSBO problem in recent years [1,2]. But one of the key issues is how to divide the problem effectively with high accuracy [2,9].

The research on the grouping strategy can divide into three categories: fixed grouping, stochastic grouping and grouping based on learning mechanism. Dividing the problem into some sub-problems with the pre-fixed groups is called fixed grouping strategy, i.e., the problem with n variables can divide into m sub-problems with s variables ($n = m \cdot s, 1 \leq s \leq \frac{n}{2}$) [10]. The fixed grouping strategy performed better on separable problems. However, the size of sub-problems and the composition of variables are all pre-determined, and the correlation between variables is not considered. Therefore, it usually shows weak optimization ability in nonseparable problems. In order to study the correlation between variables and place the associated variables as much as possible in the same sub-problem, the researchers proposed a stochastic grouping method in which variables in sub-problems are assigned in a random way and variables change with the evolution process. In [11,12], Yang et al., designed a decomposition strategy that randomly assigned variables to a fixed number of groups to increase the probability of the associated variables entering the same group. However, when the number of associated variables exceeds 5 in a group, the effect of this strategy becomes weak [13]. Later, Yang et al. proposed a multi-level co-evolutionary approach (MLCC) to solve the problem that the optimal number of groups in [12] is determined difficultly [14,15], but the size of each group is still equal. Grouping based on learning mechanism, that is, before or during the implementation of the optimization algorithm, through the analysis of certain features to learn the relationship between variables so that grouping the variables clearly. Ray and Yao proposed a method of grouping variables according to the best fitness of the first 50% of individuals [16]. Later, Singh and Ray improved this method [17]. In order to improve the variable grouping method of MLCC [14,18] proposed a new method of adaptively obtaining the size of variable groupings. Liu and Tang have implemented problem decomposition based on the features of evolutionary algorithms [19,20]. In [21], a grouping method based on the idea of partial derivative of multivariate functions is proposed to realize the automatic decomposition of the problem. This method obtains very accurate grouping results in most of the test functions of CEC'2010 [22]. However, to some extent, it depends on the pre-defined threshold, and the accuracy of problem decomposition will decrease with the increasing of the complexity of the problem (unevenness of sub-problems, large difference contribution of sub-problems, and the increase of the correlation between variables) [23]. In [5], Mei proposed a GDG approach to reduce the dependency of the pre-defined threshold and addressed the missing relationship among variables [21]. However, there are some drawbacks in the decomposition of complex optimization problems and the judgment of the complexity of correlation between variables. And once the results of variable grouping are determined, they are no longer updated, which can not reflected the influence of evolution process on the correlation between variables.

In this paper, we propose a new GDG method named Dynamic GDG (D-GDG) to address the lack of GDG method, which can dynamically adjust the grouping of variables with process.

The rest of the paper is organised as follows: The definition of LSBO problem and CC framework are introduced in Sect. 2. Then, the introduction of GDG method and the proposed algorithm, named Dynamic GDG (D-GDG), is described in Sect. 3. The experimental studies are presented in Sect. 4. Finally, conclusions is described in Sect. 5.

2   The Definition of LSBO Problem and CC Framework

2.1   The Definition of LSBO Problem

Without loss of generality, a LSBO problem can be stated as follows:

$$min \ f(\mathbf{x}) \tag{1}$$

where $\mathbf{x} = (x_1, x_2, \ldots, x_D)$ is a D-dimensional *decision vector*, and each $x_i(i = 1, \ldots, D)$ is called a *decision variable*. D, the number of decision variables, is the dimension of search space. The real value of D is generally relatively large, usually in the hundreds to thousands. $f(\mathbf{x})$ is the *objective function* to be minimized.

2.2   CC Framework

The main step of CC framework can be stated as follows:

***Step 1* variables grouping**: Divide the original problem into multiple sub-problems. The method of dividing is more important. The bad dividing method will lead to strong coupling between groups and affect the optimization performance of the whole algorithm. Therefore, the design of the divide and conquer strategy is the most crucial step to improve the algorithm's performance.

***Step 2* the optimization of sub-problems**: To solve each sub-problem independently, this step should select the optimizer with significant performance. It can optimize the sub-problems in a round-robin fashion or independently optimize with the parallel program.

***Step 3* the merge of sub-problems**: Use the solution of the current sub-problem and the best solution of other sub-problems to synthesize a complete solution vector and evaluate the fitness of this solution vector.

The pseudocode of CC framework is stated as follows:

Algorithm 1. CC(f,lb,ub,D)

1: /* *(Phase 1): Decomposition* */
2: groups ← grouping(f,lb,ub,D);
3: /* *(Phase 2): Optimization* */
4: /* *Initialization* */
5: pop ← rand(popsize, D);
6: (best,bestval) ← *min f(pop)* ;
7: **for** i ← 1 **to** Cycle **do**
8:     **for** j ← 1 **to** $size(groups)$ **do**
9:         indices ← groups[j];
10:        subpop ← pop[:,indices];
11:        /* *Use sub-optimizer*/
12:        subpop ← $optimizer(best, subpop, FE)$;
13:        pop[:, indicies]← subpop;
14:        (best, bestval) ← min(f(pop));
15:    **end for**
16: **end for**

---

3 Dynamic Global Differential Grouping

No matter what kind of decomposition method is adopted, the main goal of variable decomposition is to place the interrelated variables in the same group and separate the unrelated variables. Therefore, the core idea of variable decomposition is to find the correlation between variables. There are some related features such as *completely separable, completely nonseparable, partially separable, overlapping* between variables in LSBO problem. In a black-box environment, the information related to the problem what we have only know is the number of variables and its domain with the output of the objective function corresponding to different inputs. The relationship between the variables are completely unknown. Therefore, analyse the relationship between variables by evaluating the fitness of objective function is a viable option.

3.1 Global Differential Grouping

The GDG method is extended from the Differential Grouping (DG) method. Assume that there are optimization problems as follows:

$$F(x_1, x_2, x_3, x_4) = x_1^2 + x_2 x_3^{-3} + x_3 x_4 + x_4^2 \qquad (2)$$

First, when the DG method detects the codependency of x_2 and x_3, the two variables are grouped together and the variables x_2 and x_3 are eliminated from the variable pool. Next, it is detected that x_3 and x_4 are interdependent and put in another group. So the interdependence between x_2 and x_4 can not be detected. Therefore, there are some drawback like this, missing some correlation variables which should have divided into a same group in some optimization problem. Mei proposed a GDG method based on DG method. Instead of the step of variable elimination in DG method, Mei calculated all the difference of objective function fitness in the algorithm and obtained a complete difference matrix. Then every element of difference matrix compared with a sufficiently small threshold ϵ to get a correlation matrix containing only 0 and 1. Finally, the decomposition of the variables can be modelled as the computation of the connected components of the graph with the node adjacency matrix, which can be easily solved using *breadth-first search* or *depth-first search* [5]. The GDG method greatly improve the accuracy of grouping.

3.2 Dynamic GDG (D-GDG)

The GDG method is the same as the DG method in that all of them determine the variable grouping before algorithm is ran and the grouping result runs through the whole optimization process. Both methods do not consider the appropriate adjustment of the grouping of variables as the optimization process advances, which may not adapt to the current distribution of solutions. In this paper, based on the basic idea of GDG method, the original data matrix that reflects the connection between two variables is derived from the general idea of partial derivation of multivariate functions. Through the standardization of the original data matrix and the establishment of the fuzzy relation matrix, the fuzzy clustering method is used to realize the dynamic clustering of variables. And through limiting the size of each variable group by setting the upper and lower bounds of the variable grouping scale, according to the state of the algorithm during operation, the grouping of variables is adaptively adjusted to promote the optimization of the problem.

The pseudocode of DGDG is described in Algorithm 2. An example of DGDG is given blow to explain DGDG algorithm. Firstly, the original difference matrix Λ obtained by DGDG algorithm using the method to compute the original difference matrix described in GDG algorithm. Assumed we have got the *Lambda* matrix shown in Eq. (3). Then, the Candidate threshold vector $\epsilon\_vec = (0, 1, 2, 4, 5)$ are obtained by sorting and de-duplicating each element in the Λ matrix. DGDG introduces a hyperparameter, α, which represents the number of fuzzy clustering, i.e., the times of variables grouping in whole algorithm ran process. Assumed α is equal to 2 in our example. So the distance between two adjacent selected thresholds, *step* is equal to 2, the floor of the size of ϵ_vec divided by α. And all selected thresholds is vector $(5, 2, 0)$. Finally, the GDG method is used for each threshold one by one. For instance, assumed the threshold currently to be processed is 2. Then, a matrix Θ is obtained from Λ and $\epsilon(\epsilon \in \epsilon\_vec)$. The entry Θ_{ij} takes 1 if $\Lambda_{ij} > \epsilon$, and 0 otherwise. The Θ matrix is shown in Eq. (4). Considering Θ matrix as the adjacency matrix of a graph, we got two groups, $\{x_1, x_5\}$ and $\{x_2, x_3, x_4\}$.

$$\varLambda = \begin{pmatrix} 0\ 1\ 2\ 1\ 4 \\ 1\ 0\ 4\ 5\ 2 \\ 2\ 4\ 0\ 2\ 2 \\ 1\ 5\ 2\ 0\ 2 \\ 4\ 2\ 2\ 2\ 0 \end{pmatrix} \tag{3}$$

$$\varTheta = \begin{pmatrix} 0\ 0\ 0\ 0\ 1 \\ 0\ 0\ 1\ 1\ 0 \\ 0\ 1\ 0\ 0\ 0 \\ 0\ 1\ 0\ 0\ 0 \\ 1\ 0\ 0\ 0\ 0 \end{pmatrix} \tag{4}$$

Algorithm 2. DGDG(f,lb,ub,D,α)

1: $\varLambda \leftarrow calcDiffMat(f, D, lb, ub)$ //computing the original difference matrix using the method described in paper [5]
2: $\epsilon\_vec \leftarrow unique(sort(diff(:)))$ //obtaining the candidate threshold vector
3: idx $\leftarrow size(\epsilon\_vec)$
4: step $\leftarrow floor(size(\epsilon\_vec)/\alpha)$
5: *Initialize the best solution, bestx, bestval*
6: **while** idx > 0 **do**
7:     $\epsilon \leftarrow \epsilon\_vec(idx)$
8:     $\varTheta \leftarrow \varLambda > \epsilon$
9:     groups $\leftarrow grouping(\varTheta)$
10:    (bestx,bestval) $\leftarrow sub\_optimizer(f, lb, ub, D, groups, bestx, bestval)$ //using sub-optimizer to find the best solution according to the current solution and current groups
11:    idx $\leftarrow$ idx - step
12: **end while**

---

4   Experimental Results and Discussions

4.1   Experimental Settings

In order to show the effect of the proposed DGDG method for solving the LSBO problem, the proposed DGDG algorithm is evaluated on the CEC'2010 LSGO benchmark functions and use PSO optimal algorithm as sub-optimizer. The final results obtained by CC-DGDG-PSO are compared with CC-GDG-PSO proposed by Mei et al. The stop criterion $maxFEs = 3 \times 10^6$ is a commonly-used setting. Besides this parameter, there is only one parameter related to DGDG (Algorithm (2))- α. Three different values $(3, 6, 9)$ for α are took to experiment on DGDG algorithm. All the compared algorithms were run 25 times independently to reduce the randomness of experiment.

The CEC'2010 LSGO benchmark functions which consist of 20 1000 − *dimensional* benchmark function (f_1 to f_{20}) can be divided into three categories, fully separable ($f_1 - f_3$), partially separable ($f_4 - f_{18}$), fully non-separable ($f_{19} - f_{20}$).

4.2   Results and Discussions

Tables 1, 2, 3 respectively shows the minimal, median, mean and standard deviation of fitness values obtained by the 25 independent runs of the compared algorithms on fully separable functions ($f_1 - f_3$), partially separable functions ($f_4 - f_{18}$), fully non-separable functions ($f_{19} - f_{20}$) of the CEC'2010 LSGO benchmark functions. CC-GDG-PSO indicates the GDG grouping method is adopted. CC-DGDG-PSO3, CC-DGDG-PSO6, CC-DGDG-PSO9, respectively indicate the DGDG grouping method with different α value $(3, 6, 9)$ is adopted.

Overall, it is seen that CC-DGDG-PSO6 performs much better than CC-DGDG-PSO3 and CC-DGDG-PSO9 over 20 benchmark functions from all tables. The three algorithm obtained the same magnitude global optimal solution over most of functions respectively, while CC-DGDG-PSO6 has a rather small global optimal solution over the three functions f_7, f_8, and f_{12} belonged to partially separable functions, which is orders of magnitude lower than CC-DGDG-PSO3 and CC-DGDG-PSO9.

From Tables 1 and 3, which respectively consist of fully separable functions and fully non-separable functions, it is obviously that CC-DGDG-PSO performs much better than CC-GDG-PSO algorithm. CC-GDG-PSO performs better than CC-DGDG-PSO only on functions $f_5, f_6, f_{10}, f_{11}, f_{15}, f_{16}$ and f_{18}, from Table 2. But the global optimal solutions they obtained are the same in magnitude. However, CC-DGDG-PSO performs much better than CC-GDG-PSO in most of this

Table 1. Minimal, median, mean standard deviation of the fitness values obtained by the 25 independent runs of the compared algorithms on fully separable functions of the CEC'2010 benchmark functions ($f_1 - f_3$)

Function		CC-fGDG-PSO	CC-DGDG-PSO3	CC-DGDG-PSO6	CC-DGDG-PSO9
f_1	Min	4.27E−01	8.00E−02	**5.30E−02**	1.30E−01
	Median	1.36E+03	1.74E+00	1.82E−01	4.65E−01
	Mean	1.06E+05	4.93E+00	2.43E−01	5.51E−01
	Std	4.72E+05	8.05E+00	2.18E−01	3.66E−01
f_2	Min	7.36E+03	7.44E+03	7.27E+03	**7.12E+03**
	Median	7.85E+03	7.74E+03	7.66E+03	7.54E+03
	Mean	7.86E+03	7.74E+03	7.62E+03	7.56E+03
	Std	2.30E+02	1.52E+02	1.85E+02	2.15E+02
f_3	Min	1.20E+01	6.01E+00	4.35E+00	**3.63E+00**
	Median	1.30E+01	6.60E+00	5.10E+00	4.14E+00
	Mean	1.30E+01	6.75E+00	5.11E+00	4.09E+00
	Std	8.00E−01	4.50E−01	4.17E−01	2.59E−01

Table 2. Minimal, median, mean standard deviation of the fitness values obtained by the 25 independent runs of the compared algorithms on partially separable functions of the CEC'2010 benchmark functions ($f_4 - f_{18}$)

Function		CC-fGDG-PSO	CC-DGDG-PSO3	CC-DGDG-PSO6	CC-DGDG-PSO9
f_4	Min	4.69E+11	**1.72E+11**	2.84E+11	2.53E+11
	Median	1.06E+12	3.44E+11	5.19E+11	6.23E+11
	Mean	1.14E+12	3.78E+11	5.61E+11	6.54E+11
	Std	4.56E+11	1.23E+11	1.94E+11	2.02E+11
f_5	Min	**2.71E+08**	2.85E+08	3.62E+08	3.13E+08
	Median	3.47E+08	5.32E+08	4.56E+08	4.80E+08
	Mean	3.46E+08	5.09E+08	4.71E+08	4.91E+08
	Std	3.57E+07	1.12E+08	7.13E+07	1.13E+08
f_6	Min	**2.43E+06**	3.54E+06	2.73E+06	2.20E+06
	Median	3.47E+06	4.98E+06	4.05E+06	4.35E+06
	Mean	3.58E+06	8.78E+06	5.95E+06	8.04E+06
	Std	1.00E+06	6.66E+06	5.17E+06	6.42E+06
f_7	Min	5.73E+03	4.40E−01	**9.01E−04**	3.80E−03
	Median	5.95E+05	3.26E+00	2.92E−02	1.02E−01
	Mean	1.21E+05	5.60E+00	8.48E−02	2.11E−01
	Std	1.61E+05	6.79E+00	1.96E−01	2.58E−01
f_8	Min	1.63E+02	1.04E+02	**5.26E−04**	3.01E+02
	Median	3.43E+07	1.15E+07	1.10E−02	2.08E+06
	Mean	4.63E+07	1.53E+07	9.50E+03	1.77E+07
	Std	4.02E+07	2.04E+07	4.70E+04	3.36E+07
f_9	Min	4.97E+06	5.61E+06	4.70E+06	**4.33E+06**
	Median	7.84E+06	7.52E+06	6.11E+06	5.78E+06
	Mean	7.86E+06	7.37E+06	6.23E+06	5.89E+06
	Std	1.31E+06	9.96E+05	7.79E+05	8.96E+05
f_{10}	Min	**7.44E+03**	8.95E+03	8.31E+03	8.50E+03
	Median	7.81E+03	9.73E+03	9.40E+03	9.43E+03
	Mean	7.81E+03	9.82E+03	9.50E+03	9.44E+03
	Std	1.94E+02	5.05E+02	4.93E+02	4.50E+02
f_{11}	Min	**7.70E+01**	1.11E+02	1.02E+02	1.07E+02
	Median	8.60E+01	1.32E+02	1.20E+02	1.24E+02
	Mean	8.60E+01	1.34E+02	1.21E+02	1.25E+02
	Std	4.62E+00	1.70E+01	8.61E+00	8.45E+00
f_{12}	Min	4.60E+01	1.00E+01	9.80E−01	**4.43E−01**
	Median	4.57E+02	1.80E+01	1.83E+00	9.36E−01
	Mean	9.22E+02	2.10E+01	2.00E+00	9.15E−01
	Std	1.47E+03	1.20E+01	7.70E−01	2.41E−01

(Continued)

Table 2. *(Continued)*

Function		CC-fGDG-PSO	CC-DGDG-PSO3	CC-DGDG-PSO6	CC-DGDG-PSO9
f_{13}	Min	5.04E+02	3.96E+02	**1.15E+02**	1.50E+03
	Median	9.61E+02	1.06E+03	1.91E+03	2.86E+03
	Mean	1.01E+03	1.22E+03	2.05E+03	3.03E+03
	Std	3.99E+02	5.25E+02	8.25E+02	1.38E+03
f_{14}	Min	1.55E+07	1.61E+07	1.59E+07	**1.30E+07**
	Median	1.81E+07	2.08E+07	1.82E+07	1.70E+07
	Mean	1.83E+07	2.12E+07	1.89E+07	1.66E+07
	Std	1.78E+06	2.48E+06	2.26E+06	1.67E+06
f_{15}	Min	**7.30E+03**	1.03E+04	9.92E+03	9.96E+03
	Median	7.80E+03	1.09E+04	1.08E+04	1.11E+04
	Mean	7.76E+03	1.10E+04	1.09E+04	1.10E+04
	Std	2.67E+02	4.92E+02	6.00E+02	5.10E+02
f_{16}	Min	**1.34E+02**	2.44E+02	2.17E+02	2.18E+02
	Median	1.44E+02	2.57E+02	2.42E+02	2.31E+02
	Mean	1.45E+02	2.60E+02	2.42E+02	2.33E+02
	Std	5.78E+00	1.10E+01	1.00E+01	1.40E+01
f_{17}	Min	1.18E+03	3.18E+02	**2.10E+02**	2.85E+02
	Median	2.51E+03	4.36E+02	3.23E+02	4.19E+02
	Mean	2.73E+03	4.52E+02	3.27E+02	4.22E+02
	Std	1.26E+03	1.04E+02	7.30E+01	7.70E+01
f_{18}	Min	**1.32E+03**	1.71E+03	4.70E+03	3.00E+03
	Median	2.23E+03	3.76E+03	1.05E+04	7.42E+03
	Mean	2.47E+03	4.84E+03	1.12E+04	9.42E+03
	Std	9.17E+02	2.51E+03	4.83E+03	6.32E+03

Table 3. Minimal, median, mean standard deviation of the fitness values obtained by the 25 independent runs of the compared algorithms on fully non separable functions of the CEC'2010 benchmark functions ($f_{19} - f_{20}$)

Function		CC-fGDG-PSO	CC-DGDG-PSO3	CC-DGDG-PSO6	CC-DGDG-PSO9
f_{19}	Min	3.28E+05	8.31E+04	**7.63E+04**	8.31E+04
	Median	4.95E+05	1.14E+05	1.14E+05	1.08E+05
	Mean	4.85E+05	1.20E+05	1.13E+05	1.11E+05
	Std	8.61E+04	2.18E+04	2.15E+04	2.13E+04
f_{20}	Min	5.09E+07	2.02E+03	2.13E+03	**1.89E+03**
	Median	2.63E+08	2.43E+03	2.30E+03	2.22E+03
	Mean	3.19E+08	2.43E+03	2.35E+03	2.22E+03
	Std	2.01E+08	1.83E+02	1.68E+02	2.56E+02

functions. This may be caused by the fact that the CC-GDG-PSO is grouped before the algorithm runs and the algorithm reaches convergence early on some functions e.g. f_7, f_8. However, the CC-DGDG-PSO will be regrouped during the operation of the algorithm so that the originally converged state diverge again to get better results.

5   Conclusions

This paper proposed a Dynamic-GDG method for variable decomposition, which addresses the issue that the GDG method can not be dynamically adjusted with the evolution of the algorithm in the variable decomposition of LSBO problems. By solving 20 test functions of CEC'2010 LSGO benchmark functions, it is known that the optimization result of the algorithm can be improved by the DGDG method. Next, we will continue to study the strategy of dynamic variable decomposition to further improve the optimal effect of LSBO problems.

Acknowledgement. This work was partially supported by the National Natural Science foundation of China (Grant Nos. 61673194, 61105128), Key Research and Development Program of Jiangsu Province, China (Grant No. BE2017630), the Postdoctoral Science Foundation of China (Grant No. 2014M560390), Six Talent Peaks Project of Jiangsu Province (Grant No. DZXX-025). National Key R&D Program of China, Project (Grant No. 2017YFC1601800).

References

1. Mahdavi, S., Shiri, M.E., Rahnamayan, S.: Metaheuristics in large-scale global continues optimization: a survey. Inf. Sci. **295**, 407–428 (2015)
2. Zhou, Z.-H., Chawla, N.V., Jin, Y., Williams, G.J.: Big data opportunities and challenges: discussions from data analytics perspectives [discussion forum]. IEEE Comput. Intell. Mag. **9**(4), 62–74 (2014)
3. Scheerlinck, K., Vernieuwe, H., Baets, B.D.: Zadeh's extension principle for continuous functions of non-interactive variables: a parallel optimization approach. IEEE Trans. Fuzzy Syst. **20**(1), 96–108 (2012)
4. Schaul, T.: Studies in continuous black-box optimization. Universität München (2011)
5. Mei, Y., Omidvar, M.N., Li, X., Yao, X.: A competitive divide-and-conquer algorithm for unconstrained large-scale black-box optimization. ACM Trans. Math. Softw. **42**(2), 13 (2016)
6. Mucherino, A., Fuchs, M., Vasseur, X., Gratton, S.: Variable neighborhood search for robust optimization and applications to aerodynamics. In: Lirkov, I., Margenov, S., Waśniewski, J. (eds.) LSSC 2011. LNCS, vol. 7116, pp. 230–237. Springer, Heidelberg (2012). https://doi.org/10.1007/978-3-642-29843-1_26
7. Vanderplaats, G.N.: Very large scale optimization. National Aeronautics and Space Administration, Langley Research Center (2002)
8. Potter, M.A., De Jong, K.A.: A cooperative coevolutionary approach to function optimization. In: Davidor, Y., Schwefel, H.-P., Männer, R. (eds.) PPSN 1994. LNCS, vol. 866, pp. 249–257. Springer, Heidelberg (1994). https://doi.org/10.1007/3-540-58484-6_269

9. Potter, M.A., De Jong, K.A.: Cooperative coevolution: an architecture for evolving coadapted subcomponents. Evol. Comput. **8**(1), 1–29 (2000)
10. van den Bergh, F., Engelbrecht, A.P.: A cooperative approach to particle swarm optimization. IEEE Trans. Evol. Comput. **8**(3), 225–239 (2004)
11. Yang, Z., Tang, K., Yao, X.: Differential evolution for high-dimensional function optimization. In: IEEE Congress on Evolutionary Computation, pp. 3523–3530. IEEE (2007)
12. Yang, Z., Tang, K., Yao, X.: Large scale evolutionary optimization using cooperative coevolution. Inf. Sci. **178**(15), 2985–2999 (2008)
13. Omidvar, M.N., Li, X., Yang, Z., Yao, X.: Cooperative co-evolution for large scale optimization through more frequent random grouping. In: IEEE Congress on Evolutionary Computation, pp. 1–8. IEEE (2010)
14. Yang, Z., Tang, K., Yao, X.: Multilevel cooperative coevolution for large scale optimization. In: IEEE Congress on Evolutionary Computation, pp. 1663–1670. IEEE (2008)
15. Yang, Z.: Nature inspired real-valued optimization and applications. University of Science and Technology of China (2010)
16. Ray, T., Yao, X.: A cooperative coevolutionary algorithm with Correlation based Adaptive Variable Partitioning. In: IEEE Congress on Evolutionary Computation, pp. 983–989 (2009)
17. Singh, H.K., Ray, T.: Divide and conquer in coevolution: a difficult balancing act. In: Sarker, R.A., Ray, T. (eds.) Agent-Based Evolutionary Search. ALO, vol. 5, pp. 117–138. Springer, Heidelberg (2010). https://doi.org/10.1007/978-3-642-13425-8_6
18. Omidvar, M.N., Mei, Y., Li, X.: Effective decomposition of large-scale separable continuous functions for cooperative co-evolutionary algorithms. In: IEEE Congress on Evolutionary Computation, pp. 1305–1312 (2014)
19. Liu, J., Tang, K.: Scaling up covariance matrix adaptation evolution strategy using cooperative coevolution. In: Yin, H., Tang, K., Gao, Y., Klawonn, F., Lee, M., Weise, T., Li, B., Yao, X. (eds.) IDEAL 2013. LNCS, vol. 8206, pp. 350–357. Springer, Heidelberg (2013). https://doi.org/10.1007/978-3-642-41278-3_43
20. Liu, J.: CMA-ES and decomposition strategy for large scale continuous optimization problem. University of Science and Technology of China (2014)
21. Omidvar, M.N., Li, X., Mei, Y., Yao, X.: Cooperative co-evolution with differential grouping for large scale optimization. IEEE Trans. Evol. Comput. **18**(3), 378–392 (2014)
22. Tang, K., Li, X., Suganthan, P.N., Yang, Z., Weise, T.: Benchmark functions for the CEC2010 special session and competition on large-scale global optimization (2010)
23. Omidvar, M.N., Li, X., Tang, K.: Designing benchmark problems for large-scale continuous optimization. Inf. Sci. **316**, 419–436 (2015)

A Method to Accelerate Convergence and Avoid Repeated Search for Dynamic Optimization Problem

Weiwei Zhang$^{(\boxtimes)}$, Guoqing Li, Weizheng Zhang, and Menghua Zhang

School of Computer and Communication Engineering,
Zhengzhou University of Light Industry, Zhengzhou 450000, Henan, China
weizheng008@126.com

Abstract. Most of the optimization problems are dynamic in real world. When dealing with the dynamic optimization problems, the evolutionary algorithms always suffer from low accuracy and diversity loss. One of the main reasons of low accuracy is that the population cannot convergent to the optima in limit computational cost. And one of the main reasons of diversity loss is that some areas are searched repeatedly while leave the others unsearched deal to the unbalanced attraction from local optima. To cope with the deficiency, two strategies are proposed in this paper. One is called Searching Gbest, which searches for a better solution along each dimension of the best one in the population to accelerate the convergence, and the other is predicting convergence, which deletes the population if it has the trend of converge to the searched area to avoid the repeatedly search. The proposed methods are tested on PSO with multiple populations. The experiments on the Moving Peaks Benchmark show that the methods can improve optima tracking ability, avoid repeatedly search and save the computing resources effectively.

Keywords: Dynamic optimization · Particle swarm optimization algorithm
Predictive mechanism · Moving Peaks Benchmark

1 Introduction

Dynamic Optimization Problems (DOPs) exists extensively in real life. To solve these problems, swarm intelligence algorithms, such as ant colony optimization (ACO), particle swarm optimization (PSO), and so on are widely employed [1]. Generally, a dynamic optimization problem can be summarized as follows.

$$Optimize f\,(X,\,t)\ =\ f\left(x_1, x_2, x_3, \ldots x_n, t\right) \tag{1}$$

Where $X = (x_1,\ x_2,\ x_3, \ldots x_n)$ is the decision vector in the range of R and each dimension of the search space is defined between $x_j^{lb} < x_j < x_j^{ub}$ for j = 1, 2.... n. x_j^{lb} and x_j^{ub} are the lower boundary and the upper boundary for each dimension. f is the objective function to be optimized, which will change over the time, t [2].

© Springer International Publishing AG, part of Springer Nature 2018
Y. Tan et al. (Eds.): ICSI 2018, LNCS 10941, pp. 604–611, 2018.
https://doi.org/10.1007/978-3-319-93815-8_57

In the past years, some researchers have done a lot of research on dynamic optimization by using swarm intelligence. Many strategies aim for handling the dynamics [3, 4] are proposed. For example, the methods of increasing diversity after a change, determining the moment to react to change, the methods of searching and tracking the optimal solution [3]. To effectively maintain the balance of population diversity and convergence and track the optimal solution after the environmental changed, some algorithms divide the population into multiple sub-populations and search for each independent sub-areas simultaneously [5, 7, 8]. In this situation, the convergence ability of the subpopulation has big influence to the precision of the final results. To improve the searching precision, a strategy call searching Gbest is proposed. Moreover, repeat search to the same area could lead to the computational resource wastes. To avoid repeated search, predicting convergence is presented.

2   Related Work

Evolutionary algorithms always suffer from diversity loss when dealing with optimization in dynamic environment. The converged population in the process of searching optima is hard to redistribute after environmental change and lead to the poor performance. To maintain the diversity of population, many methods have been proposed [3, 4]. Among them, multi-population method is mostly adopted. In addition, the memory based method and prediction method are also widely used as assistance.

2.1   Multi-population Methods

Multi-populations method divides a population into many subpopulations in a certain way. Each subpopulation simultaneously searches for an optimal solution in an independent sub-region [3, 5]. Li and Yang proposed an algorithm called CPSO, which the number of populations is dynamic. If the overlap range of two subpopulations is greater than a certain threshold, the two subpopulations merge into one and it will have more opportunities to search for the best solution [5]. Shams and Salwani proposed an algorithm called Multi-pop-ABC, which divides the population into multiple subpopulations to exploit and explore the search process, and it used artificial bee colony algorithm and obtained a good result compared to others algorithms in MPB [8].

2.2   Memory-Based Methods

When fitness landscape shows up repeatedly or has some kind of relations. The reuse of the acquired historical information could be benefit for the performance. Historical information can guide us to search for a better solution with purpose [3, 7]. Halder and Das proposed a method called external archive (Ar) based on memory [7]. If a cluster or a subpopulation is converge, the cluster will be delete and its best solution is preserved in Ar. B Nasiri proposed a new method, which uses a BSP tree to store important information in the iteration process [9, 10].

2.3   Prediction and Optima Tracking

Prediction and optima tracking are the other useful methods when the fitness landscape has some kind of relations between environmental changes. Prediction mechanism can save a lot of computing resources and improve the performance of the algorithm. Yazdani and Nasiri proposed an algorithm called FTMPSO [6], in order to explore a better solution, it searches for a better solution near the current optimal solution at the end of each iteration. Wang and Xiong proposed a method to predicted the location of the new solution, where is based on the idea that it create the prediction areas before the changes occur [11].

To accelerate the convergence and save computational resource, this paper proposes two methods named searching Gbest and predicting convergence for moving peaks problem.

3   The Methods

The proposed method is based on the basic particle swarm optimization, it uses clustering to divides the population into multiple subpopulations and each subpopulation search for an optimal solution in an independent sub-area simultaneously, and the *Gbest* is the best one in the whole population.

3.1   Searching Gbest

In order to search a better solution, the best solution of the population noted as Gbest is selected. Then a better solution within the range of radius R of Gbest along each dimension is searched. It is worth noticed that this approach is used at the beginning of each generation. It is equivalent to searching for a better solution around Gbest throughout the iteration rather than search a better solution around the Gbest when subpopulations have converged. The pseudocode of Searching Gbest is presented in Algorithm 1.

Algorithm 1.   Searching Gbest

---

1   *if i<=SearchNum do*

2   *Temp_gbest=gbest*

3   *for* each dimension d of *gbest* do

4   *Temp_gbest[d]=gbest[d]+rand(-R,R);*

5   *if f(Temp_gbest)>f(gbest) do*

6   *gbest[d]=Temp_gbest[d];*

7   *end*

8   *End*

9   *End*

Note that *rand(-R, R)* means generate a random number within the range of −R to R. *gbest* stands for the best solution at present and *Temp_gbest* is temporary variable.

3.2   Predicting Convergence

Two subpopulations may converge to the same peak in the process of optima searching. To save computational resource, one subpopulation should be deleted to ensure that a peak can only be tracked by a single population [6, 7]. It is very important to determine whether the population converges in multi-population methods. In this paper, we proposed a new method called predicting convergence and have adopted a predictable way to avoid two peaks in one peak and reduce the waste of computing resources. The proposed method is shown in Algorithm 2 as follows.

Algorithm 2. Predicting Convergence

---

1 *for* each subpopulation *sub(i) do*

2   *for* each convergence subpopulation *csub(j) do*

3   *Num=0;*

4   *for* each dimension *n do*

5   *if* |*sub(i,n)-csub(j,n)*|<*m do*

6   *Num=Num+1;*

7   *end*

8   *end*

9   *end*

10   *if Num= Dimension do*

11   subpopulation *sub(i)* and convergence subpopulation *csub(j)*is considered in the same peak;

12   Delete subpopulation *sub(i)*;

13   *end*

14 *end*

In Algorithm 2, *sub(i, n)* represents the *n-th* dimension of the individual with highest fitness in *i-th* subpopulation at present and *csub(j, n)* represents the *n-th* dimension of the individual with highest fitness in the *j-th* convergence subpopulation. If each dimension of the *i-th* subpopulation is in the radius m of each dimension of the *j-th* convergent subpopulation, it considers the *i-th* subpopulation is moving toward the *j-th* convergent subpopulation and two subpopulations may converge to the same peak in the next evolutionary process. In this case, one of them will be deleted.

4   Experiment and Discussion

4.1   Moving Peaks Benchmark

Moving Peaks Benchmark (MPB) is a classic benchmark for dynamic optimization problems and it is widely used in DOPs. Individuals track the highest peaks which height, width and location change in new environment [1, 5]. For the D dimensional landscape, the problem is defined as follows.

$$F(x,t) = \max_{i=1\ldots p} \frac{H(i)_t}{1 + W(i)_t \sum_{j=1}^{D}(x(j)_t - X(i,j)_t)^2} \tag{2}$$

where $H(i)_t$ and $W(i)_t$ are the height and width of the *i-th* peak at time t respectively. $X(i,j)_t$ is *j-th* dimension of the location of the *i-th* peak at time t. p represents the number of peaks and calculating the maximum value by the max function [2, 5]. The position of each peak is shifted in a random direction. The parameter shift length s controls the severity of the problem dynamics. For more details about MPB, please refer to the paper [1]. Note that standard setting is adopted in the paper and the default settings and definition of MPB is presented at Table 1.

Table 1. Default settings for the MPB

Parameter	Value	Parameter	Value
Number of peaks, p	5, 10, 20, 50, 100	Shift length, s	1.0
Change frequency	5000	Number of dimension, D	5
Height severity	7.0	Correlation coefficient	0
Width severity	1.0	Height range	[30, 70]
Peak shape	Cone	Width range	[1.0, 12.0]
Basic function	No	Initial height	50

Each experiment runs 30 times independently.

4.2   SearchGbest Effect

Searching Gbest works for accelerate convergence. To show the effect of the proposed method, the *Searching Gbest* is added to PSO with multiple population. We also hired two other methods to compare with it. One is *No SearchGbest*, in which nothing is added. The other is *Ndim SearchGbest*, in which a set of five individuals within a radius of R is generated around *Gbest*. The experimental results are shown in Fig. 1.

From Fig. 1 we can observe that the proposed method called *Searching Gbest* could improve the searching precision. The method accelerates population convergence and has more opportunities to search for a better solution. It's equivalent to enhance a local search around the current solution. Note that it only searches once for each dimension within the radius R range in each generation.

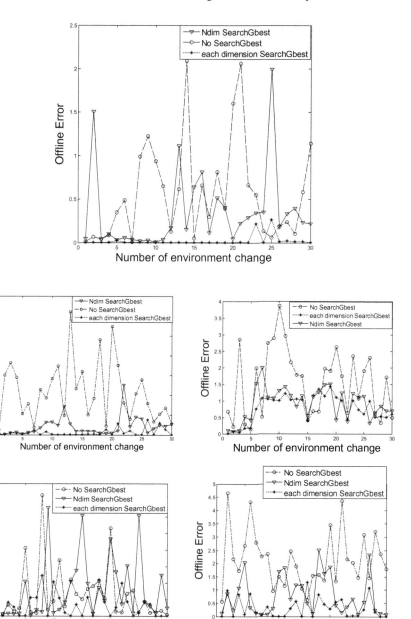

Fig. 1. Comparison of searching Gbest, No SearchGbest and Ndim SearchGbest on MPB with 5, 10, 20, 50, 100 peaks, respectively. X-axis represents the number of environmental changed with p peaks and Y-axis represents the offline error

4.3 The Effect of Predicting Convergence

We test the Predicting Convergence on MPB with 20 peaks. The distribution of the population in 2D of before and after environmental changed, and with and without Predicting Convergence are shown in Fig. 2.

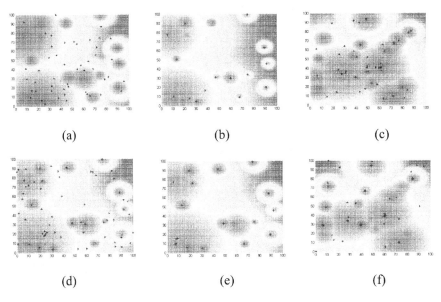

(a)   (b)   (c)

(d)   (e)   (f)

Fig. 2. Population distribution on MPB with 20 peaks: (a) the initial population (b) population distribution before environmental change with Predicting Convergence (c) population distribution before environmental change without Predicting Convergence (d) population distribution after environmental change, random individuals are introduced (e) the converged population with Predicting Convergence (f) the converged population distribution without Predicting Convergence

Figure 2(a) shows the initial random population distribution. After the population evolves for a certain time, the population will converge to some of the certain optimal area. Figure 2(b) and (c) show the population distribution of converged population with and without proposed Predicting Convergence respectively before change happens. We can observe that the proposed method can effectively avoid more than one subpopulations converge to one peak. In order to maintain population diversity, some random particles are introduced after environmental changed which is shown in Fig. 2(d). Figure 2(e) and (f) presents the population distribution with and without prediction convergence method before and after the environmental changed, respectively. Due to the preserved individuals from last environment, the populations can quickly converge. The prediction convergence method maintains the good distribution of the population through comparing Fig. 2(e) and (f). It can be observed that the method is effective for avoiding subpopulations repeatedly searching for a certain area.

5 Conclusions and Future Work

In the paper, searching Gbest is proposed to enhance local search ability and accelerate convergence of the population. Moreover, Predicting Convergence is proposed to avoid repeatedly search and save computing resources. Experiments on MPB show that the proposed methods could improve the performance of the algorithm.

Acknowledgment. The work is supported by the Natural Science Foundation of China (No. 61403349, 61402422, 61501405), Funding program for key scientific research projects of universities in Henan province (No. 18A210025), Science and technology research key project of basic research projects in education department of Henan province (No. 15A520033, No. 14B520066) and Postgraduate Technology Innovation Project in Zhengzhou University of Light Industry (No. 2017032).

References

1. Branke, J.: Memory enhanced evolutionary algorithms for changing optimization problems. In: IEEE Congress on Evolutionary Computation, pp. 1875–1882. IEEE, Washington, DC (1999)
2. Zhang, W.W., Yen, G., Wang, X.: An immune inspired framework for optimization in dynamic environment. In: 2016 IEEE Congress on Evolutionary Computation (CEC), pp. 1800–1807. IEEE, Vancouver, BC (2016)
3. Li, C.H., Nguyen, T.T., Yang, M., Yang, S.X.: Multi-population methods in unconstrained continuous dynamic environments: the challenges. Inf. Sci. **296**(1), 95–118 (2015)
4. Mavrovouniotis, M., Li, C.H., Yang, S.X.: A survey of swarm intelligence for dynamic optimization: algorithms and applications. Swarm Evol. Comput. **33**, 1–17 (2017)
5. Yang, S.X., Li, C.H.: A clustering particle swarm optimizer for locating and tracking multiple optima in dynamic environments. IEEE Trans. Evol. Comput. **14**(6), 959–974 (2010)
6. Yazdani, D., Nasiri, B.: A novel multi-swarm algorithm for optimization in dynamic environments based on particle swarm optimization. Appl. Soft Comput. **13**(4), 2144–2158 (2013)
7. Halder, U., Das, S., Maity, D.: A cluster-based differential evolution algorithm with external archive for optimization in dynamic environments. IEEE Trans. Cybern. **43**(3), 881–897 (2013)
8. Nseef, S.K., Abdullah, S., Turky, A., Kendall, G.: An adaptive multi-population artificial bee colony algorithm for dynamic optimisation problems. Knowl.-Based Syst. **104**(1), 14–23 (2016)
9. Nasiri, B., Meybodi, M.R.: History-driven firefly algorithm for optimisation in dynamic and uncertain environments. Int. J. Bio-Inspired Comput. **8**(5), 326–339 (2016)
10. Nasiri, B., Meybodi, M.R., Ebadzadeh, M.M.: History-driven particle swarm optimization in dynamic and uncertain environments. Neurocomputing **172**(8), 356–370 (2016)
11. Wan, S.Z., Xiong, S.W., Liu, Y.: Prediction based multi-strategy differential evolution algorithm for dynamic environments. In: 2012 IEEE Congress on Evolutionary Computation, Brisbane, pp. 1–8. IEEE, QLD (2012)
12. Zhang, W.W., Lin, J.J., Jing, H.L., Zhang, Q.W.: A novel hybrid clonal selection algorithm with combinatorial recombination and modified hypermutation operators for global optimization. Comput. Intell. Neurosci. **2016**(1), 1–16 (2016)

Optimization of Steering Linkage Including the Effect of McPherson Strut Front Suspension

Suwin Sleesongsom[1(✉)] and Sujin Bureerat[2]

[1] Department of Aeronautical Engineering and Commercial Pilot,
International Academy of Aviation Industry,
King Mongkut's Institute of Technology Ladkrabang, Bangkok 10520, Thailand
suwin.se@kmitl.ac.th
[2] Sustainable and Infrastructure Development Center,
Department of Mechanical Engineering, Faculty of Engineering,
KhonKaen University, KhonKaen City 40002, Thailand

Abstract. This paper proposes to optimise the steering linkage including an effect of McPherson strut front suspension. Usually, the suspension is exerted with an impact force due to uneven road, which dynamically changes to performance of a steering linkage. The present work proposes to study an effect of suspension to performance of steering mechanism with comparative study of steering mechanism with and without suspension system, which is included in optimization problem. The performance is minimised in both turning radius and steering error, that is called multi-objective optimisation problems. The model of McPherson strut front suspension is simplified model but it is sufficient accuracy. The results show that the suspension is an important effect on the optimisation design and the optimisation results show that the design concept leads to effective design of rack and pinion steering linkages satisfying both steering error and turning radius criteria.

Keywords: Rack-and-pinion steering linkage · Steering error
Turning radius · Multi-objective optimization
Population-based incremental learning: McPherson strut

1 Introduction

Steering linkages can categorise in two groups for passenger car or personal car, sometime it is group as four-bar and six-bar linkages. The former is widely used for the old passenger car, which used rigid axle. The last group is presently popular for personal car or modern cars. Both group still in used at the present due to two reasons that are eases of construction and operation [1]. The optimum synthesis of the planar four-bar linkage fulfilling the Ackermann principle has been proposed by many researcher [1–14] by using gradient based [1, 4, 14] and non-gradient based [2, 3, 5, 13] optimizer with an objective function perform in single objective or multi-objective optimization. At the present we know that the six-bar linkage can design to accord with the Ackerman principal than the old one, so it makes the mechanism is popular in

© Springer International Publishing AG, part of Springer Nature 2018
Y. Tan et al. (Eds.): ICSI 2018, LNCS 10941, pp. 612–623, 2018.
https://doi.org/10.1007/978-3-319-93815-8_58

studying the performance enhancement. Very recent work by Sleesongsom and Bureerat [15] proposed minimise steering error and turning radius to find the steering linkage layout with can compromise in both objectives. Steering error ($\delta\theta_O$) is the different angle between the outer front wheel axle made by the actual steering linkage (θ_O) and Ackermann principle (θ_{OA}) as shown in Fig. 1.

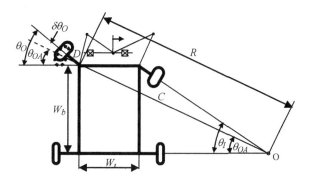

Fig. 1. Steering error [15].

To protect the wheel from wear and skidding, the steering linkages should keep minimum steering error. The steering error equation is shown in the following equation

$$\delta\theta_O(\theta_I) = |\theta_O(\theta_I) - \theta_{OA}(\theta_I)| \tag{1}$$

where θ_O is the actual angle made by the outer front wheel during turning and θ_{OA} is the correct angle for the same wheel based on the Ackermann principle. The formulation of the actual angle and the correct angle can see in reference [15]. For the turning radius, it makes the car more nimble driving in the narrow way and traffic jam. The smallest turning radius R_{min} at the full turn is shown as

$$R_{min} = D + C = D + W_b / \sin\theta_{O,max} \tag{2}$$

where D is a kingpin length, C is the distance from the instantaneous centre of turning to the kingpin, and $\theta_{O,max}$ is the actual maximum angle made by the outer front wheel during full turning [15].

From our review of literature, it is found a few research did about dimensional design of steering linkage including the McPherson strut suspension effect except the work by Felzien and Cronin [11], they considered combining the McPherson suspension and steering linkage models in the minimization of steering error. Later, Zhou et al. [13] proposed the optimization of the steering error included the effect of toe-in angle changing due to wheel jumping. Furthermore, this combination of steering linkage and McPherson suspension has been used to study the steering kickback performance [16]. In this study proposed a simplified planar model of steering system is used to minimize the vibration of the steering wheel. The most of the past researches focus on modeling accuracy of the McPherson strut suspension in both two and three dimensions rather than considering the effect on steering system [17–21].

The purpose of this research is to optimise the dimension of a six-bar steering mechanism that including the effect of McPherson strut suspension when exerting with the impulse load. The optimizers are used in this study is the best scheme from our previous work [15], which is an adaptation of the hybrid multi-objective real-code population-based incremental learning and differential evolution (RPBIL-DE). The previous result is used to comparative performance with the present work to study the effect of the McPherson strut suspension in designing the steering linkage. The model of the McPherson strut front suspension is composed of lump mass of wheel and its support and strut suspension. The system has sixth degree of freedom exert with impulse load due to uneven road. The design problem is set to minimize the steering error and turning radius that are conflicting objectives. The optimization problems are assigned as minimization of the maximum steering error and the turning radius.

The rest of this paper is organised as follows. Simplified model of steering linkage and McPherson strut front suspension are presented in Sect. 2. The optimisation problem and RPBIL-DE are detailed in Sect. 3. The design results are given in Sect. 4, while the conclusions of this study are drawn in Sect. 5.

2 Simplified Model of the System

To include the effect of suspension system into dimensional synthesis problem of the steering linkage, the model of McPherson suspension system should be sufficient accuracy to simulate the change of toe in angle cause by uneven road. This angle knows as changing due to uneven road act with the suspension [13]. The system is showed in Fig. 2 is composed of the suspension system and steering system. The wheel and supporting equipment is modelled with six degrees of freedom as shown in Fig. 2(b). The whole wheel is modelled as a single object with appropriate inertial properties. This model is adapted from [16]. Flexible lower arm is modelled by spring line in the x-direction, while the flexible tie rod is modelled by a spring line in x-y plane has an angle θ_3 respect to a steering rack axis as shown in Fig. 3. Usually tie rod is built as part of supporting kingpin as a result it can neglect to consider the flexible of this member.

The equation of motion for this model can be derived by considering the centre of mass C displaces from its original position due to a car moves pass an uneven road. The wheel with supporting is idealized as a rigid body of mass m attached to lower arm, tie rod and McPherson strut that model with three degree of linear spring, except the strut is modelled with stiffness and damping constant. These elements are independence in each direction. Considering impulse forces due to uneven road exert on wheel at the centre of mass. The origin G of the fixed global coordinate system $G\,\bar{X}\bar{Y}\bar{Z}$ is located at the centre of mass C at static equilibrium. Under working condition the displacement of the centre of mass C will be measured by $x_c, y_c, z_c, \theta_x, \theta_y, \theta_z$.

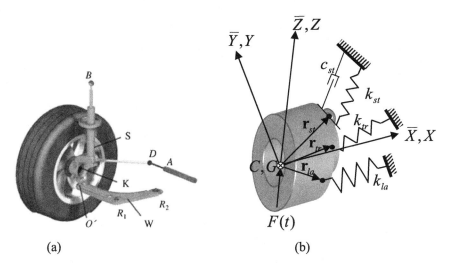

Fig. 2. (a) Model of the steering system [17] (b) simplified model of the suspension system

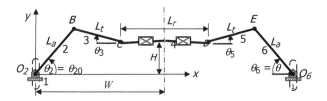

Fig. 3. Six-bar planar rack-and-pinion steering linkage configuration [15].

Linear spring behaviour is expressed with the following relation:

$$\mathbf{F} = k(\mathbf{r} - \mathbf{r}_0) = k\delta\mathbf{r} \tag{3}$$

where k is spring stiffness, r_0 is the position of the un-stretched spring, $\mathbf{r}$ is the position vector of the spring under the force $\mathbf{F}$, and $\delta\mathbf{r}$ is a spring translational vector.

A rigid body of the whole wheel attached with a linear equivalent springs due to a strut suspension, lower arm and tie rod is given in Fig. 4. From the figure, the position vector of the i-th spring can be expressed with respect to the centroid position as

$$\mathbf{r}_i = \mathbf{r}_c + \mathbf{r}_{ci} \tag{4}$$

where r_i is the position vector of spring i, r_c is the position vector of the mass centre, r_{ci} is the potion vector of spring i with respect to the mass centre.

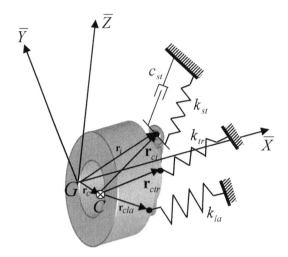

Fig. 4. Vector position of spring position relative with center of mass.

When the body is in motion due to uneven road supplied force to wheel, the derivation of the vectors in Eq. (4) can be written as

$$\delta \mathbf{r}_i = \delta \mathbf{r}_c + \delta \mathbf{r}_{ci} \tag{5}$$

As the centroid and the i-th point are at the same body, we can have

$$\delta \mathbf{r}_i = \delta \mathbf{r}_c + \delta \boldsymbol{\theta} \times \mathbf{r}_{ci} \tag{6}$$

where $\delta \boldsymbol{\theta}$ is the vector of rotation displacements of the body. The translation and rotation vectors can be defined as

$$\delta \mathbf{r}_c = \begin{bmatrix} u_x \\ u_y \\ u_z \end{bmatrix}, \qquad \delta \boldsymbol{\theta} = \begin{bmatrix} \theta_x \\ \theta_y \\ \theta_z \end{bmatrix} \tag{7}$$

where u_i is the translation in i-th direction and θ_i is the angular displacement in the i-th axis. The rigid body has 6 degrees of freedom. By substituting (7) into (6), we have

$$\delta \mathbf{r}_i = \begin{bmatrix} u_x + \theta_y r_{ci,z} - \theta_z r_{ci,y} \\ u_y + \theta_z r_{ci,x} - \theta_x r_{ci,z} \\ u_z + \theta_x r_{ci,y} - \theta_y r_{ci,x} \end{bmatrix} = \begin{bmatrix} 1 & 0 & 0 & 0 & r_{ci,z} & -r_{ci,y} \\ 0 & 1 & 0 & -r_{ci,z} & 0 & r_{ci,x} \\ 0 & 0 & 1 & r_{ci,y} & -r_{ci,x} & 0 \end{bmatrix} \begin{bmatrix} u_x \\ u_y \\ u_z \\ \theta_x \\ \theta_y \\ \theta_z \end{bmatrix} = \mathbf{T}_i \mathbf{d} \tag{8}$$

where $\mathbf{T}_i$ is called a transformation matrix for the i-th spring and $\mathbf{d}$ is the displacement vector of the body. As a result, elastic potential energy of the i-th spring is

$$U_i = \frac{1}{2}k_i\delta\mathbf{r}_i^T\delta\mathbf{r} = \frac{1}{2}\mathbf{d}^T(k_i\mathbf{T}_i^T\mathbf{T}_i)\mathbf{d} = \frac{1}{2}\mathbf{d}^T\mathbf{K}_i\mathbf{d} \tag{9}$$

If the spring-mass system has n linear springs, the total elastic potential energy can be computed as:

$$U = \frac{1}{2}\mathbf{d}^T\left(\sum_{i=1}^{n}\mathbf{K}_i\right)\mathbf{d} = \frac{1}{2}\mathbf{d}^T\mathbf{K}\mathbf{d} \tag{10}$$

where $\mathbf{K}$ is the stiffness matrix of the system. The kinetic energy or the work due to inertial forces can be computed as

$$T = \frac{1}{2}\mathbf{m}\delta\dot{\mathbf{r}}_c^T\delta\dot{\mathbf{r}}_c + \frac{1}{2}\delta\dot{\boldsymbol{\theta}}^T\mathbf{I}\delta\dot{\boldsymbol{\theta}} = \frac{1}{2}\dot{\mathbf{d}}^T\mathbf{M}\dot{\mathbf{d}} \tag{11}$$

where

$$\mathbf{M} = \begin{bmatrix} \mathbf{m} & \mathbf{0} \\ \mathbf{0} & \mathbf{I} \end{bmatrix} = \begin{bmatrix} m & 0 & 0 & 0 & 0 & 0 \\ 0 & m & 0 & 0 & 0 & 0 \\ 0 & 0 & m & 0 & 0 & 0 \\ 0 & 0 & 0 & I_{xx} & -I_{xy} & -I_{xz} \\ 0 & 0 & 0 & -I_{yx} & I_{yy} & -I_{yz} \\ 0 & 0 & 0 & -I_{zx} & -I_{zy} & I_{zz} \end{bmatrix} \tag{12}$$

m is body mass, and $\mathbf{I}$ is the matrix of moments of inertia. Due to axis symmetrical of wheel mass moment $\mathbf{I}$ is a diagonal matrix.

Viscous damping due to McPherson strut, which is used to dissipate kinetic energy is a nonconservative force that may considered by using the Rayleigh dissipation function. This function assumes that the damping forces are proportional to the velocities, which can adapt from (11) as shown as follow.

$$\mathbf{F} = \frac{1}{2}\dot{\mathbf{d}}^T\mathbf{C}\dot{\mathbf{d}} \tag{13}$$

Equation of motion can be derive by performing Lagrange's equation as result as follow

$$\mathbf{M}\ddot{\mathbf{d}} + \mathbf{C}\dot{\mathbf{d}} + \mathbf{K}\mathbf{d} = \mathbf{F}(t) \tag{14}$$

$\mathbf{F}(t)$ is impulse force due to uneven road can directly add to Eq. (14) in form of initial conditions are $x_0 = 0$ and $v_0 = \hat{F}/m$. In this work, numerical solutions of the system of differential equations in (14) can be carried out by using the Newmarks integration technique. Vibration due to uneven road can cause changing of toe angle α [13] it can approximate $\alpha = \theta_z$. The change of toe angle is

$$\delta\alpha = |\alpha_0 - \alpha_i| = |\theta_{z0} - \theta_{zi}| \tag{15}$$

The computation of the steering error and turning radius of the six-bar linkage as shown in Eqs. (1–2) is detailed in our previous work [15]. The model of the six-bar linkage is shown in Fig. 3. The interference of steering linkage and McPherson suspension pass the design variables are L_a, L_t, and H can affect to steering error, so the steering error in Eq. (2) can be derive to:

$$\delta\theta_O = |\theta_O + \delta\alpha - \theta_{OA}| \tag{16}$$

where $\delta\alpha$ can increasing or decreasing the steering error. The purpose of this research is to minimise the steering error that effect by changing of toe angle, such that the measuring this angle signal should be measure in maximum in a time interval T.

3 Optimisation Problem and RPBIL-dE

3.1 Optimisation Problem

The multi-objective optimization problem is assigned to minimize the steering error and turning radius, is shown as:

$$
\begin{aligned}
\text{Minimize} \quad & \left\{ \begin{aligned} f_1(\mathbf{x}) &= \max|\delta\theta_O(\theta_I)| \ ; \theta_I \in [0^\circ, 40^\circ] \\ f_2(\mathbf{x}) &= R_{\min} \end{aligned} \right\} \\
\text{Subject to} \quad & \theta_{6,\max} - \theta_{60} \geq 40^\circ \\
& f_1 \leq 0.75^\circ \\
& f_1 \leq 5\,\text{m} \\
& \{0.1, 0, 0\}^T \leq \mathbf{x} \leq \{0.3, 0.3, 0.3\}^T\,\text{m}
\end{aligned} \tag{17}
$$

where $\mathbf{x} = \{L_a, L_t, H\}^T$, $\delta\theta_O = |\theta_O + \delta\alpha - \theta_{OA}|$, and $\delta\alpha = \theta_z$, and $\mathbf{x} = \{L_a, L_t, H\}^T$

3.2 RPBIL-dE

From our previous studies [15, 22–25], MHs are the most popular optimisers for solving dimensional design problems. Population based incremental learning (PBIL) is one optimizer in group of an estimation distribution algorithm (EDA), which is still popular due to its easy to apply for a single- and multi-objective optimization problem [15, 24, 25]. Furthermore, this technique is hybrid with the most en efficient technique that is called Differential Evolutionary (DE), so it is undisputed the performance of this hybridization as showed in the previous studied [15, 26]. The hybridization of real-code population-based incremental learning and differential evolution (RPBIL-DE) for multi-objective optimization has been proposed by Pholdee and Bureerat [24, 26] to solve a truss structure problem. It is found is one of the top performers for constrained truss optimization and later it has an adaptation for solving several practical multiob-jective optimization problem [15]. The later study found the best optimizer is RPBIL-DE using DE/best/2/bin operators and the constraint relaxation scheme 3, where the second best is RPBIL-DE using an opposition-based DE/best/2/bin mutation operator and the constraint relaxation scheme 3. The present work we propose to use this technique in this study. For the detail of these optimisers can see in [15].

4   Design Results

The first objective of this research is to find the optimal dimensions of a rack-and-pinion steering linkage while minimizing the steering error and the minimum turning radius, which is considered the effect of vibration of suspension system exerted with impulse force duet to an uneven road. All important dimensions of the car are from [1] and other parameters of suspension system are given in Table 1. Some of them are collected from the experiment in our laboratory i.e. the mass moment of inertia, whole mass, length of member etc.

The PBIL-DE that chooses for this study is applied to solve the problem with the population size of 50 and the number of iterations being 80. The external Pareto archive size is set to be 100. Other parameters are assigned as $n_I = 40$ where each probability tray produces five design solutions. The crossover rate and the probability of choosing an element from an offspring in the binary DE crossover are set as $p_c = 0.7$ and $CR = 0.5$ respectively. Two variant of RPBIL-DE is used to examine in this study can be detailed as:

RPBIL-DE2: using DE/best/2/bin mutation operator and the mutated offspring c can be calculated as

$$c = p + F(q_1 - r_1) + F(q_2 - r_2) \tag{18}$$

Table 1. Dimensions of a small car and other parameters

	Initial dimension (mm)
Wheel base, W_b	2175
Wheel track, W_t	1215
Rack length, L_r	678
Kingpin length, D	300
Whole wheel mass	17.15 kg
I_{XX}, I_{YY}, I_{ZZ}	11.57, 11.78, 11.78 kg/m^2
Modulus of rigidity of spring	80 GPa
Diameter of coil spring	0.01203 m
Number of round spring	6
Outside diameter of spring	0.14
Diameter of tie rod and lower arm	0.0129 m
Young's modulus of tie rod	207 GPa
Diameter of lower arm	0.0285 m
Lower arm length	0.36 m

where F is a uniform random number sampling a new in the interval [0.25, 0.75]. q_1, r_1, q_2, and r_2 are chosen from the current real code population at random. From the previous studied this technique is the best technique.

RPBIL-DE3: using the opposition-based DE/best/2/bin mutation operator where the mutated offspring c can be calculated using (18) with F being in the interval [−0.75, 0.75]. Both of variant of the optimiser still use with relaxation scheme [15]. The constraints in (17) are handled by using the non-dominated sorting for MOEAs can see more in [15].

The comparative results of two optimisers of the multiobjective design problem with 30 runs for each algorithm, the obtained results are reported in Table 2. The values in the table is the hypervolume (HV) of a Pareto front explored by the algorithms where is the reference point used for computing the hypervolume indicator is same with the previous study [15] at $\{f_1, f_2\} = \{1°, 5.0$ m$\}$. The higher hypervolume means the better result. Other descriptive statistics are showed in the same table that use to descript the results. For the present design result, the best optimizer is RPBIL-DE23 using DE/best/2/bin operators and the constraint relaxation 3 outperforms the second one as show with highlight colour in Table 2. It means that the technique has been proposed in the previous study is undisputed in the performance enhancement to the optimizers. The performance enhancement technique is composed of both the variant of mutation and the constraint handling scheme. From the same table the best standard deviation or minimum standard deviation is the RPBIL-DE23 that means this technique also more consistency than other technique.

Table 2. Comparative results for Case-1–4 with a new technique

	With Suspension		Without Suspension	
	RPBIL- DE23	RPBIL-DE33	RPBIL- DE23	RPBIL-DE33
mean	0.26148	0.256908	0.3585	0.3532
min	0.078219	0.082133	0.2968	0.3120
max	0.365626	0.367476	0.3651	0.3650
Std	0.111091	0.113763	0.0143	0.0148

Furthermore, the comparative result of the optimization problem with and without consider the effect of suspension system exert with force due to an uneven road as shown in Table 2. The last two columns are the optimum data from our previous work in [15], which is design without consideration of the effect of suspension system. The results show the best hypervolume of the design result with considering the suspension system is lower than the design result without considering the suspension system. It means that the effect of suspension system is degraded the optimum design result of the design problem without considered the suspension system.

Some configuration of the design solutions are selected from Fig. 5 where the corresponding linkages are displayed in Fig. 6(a). A method used to select some design

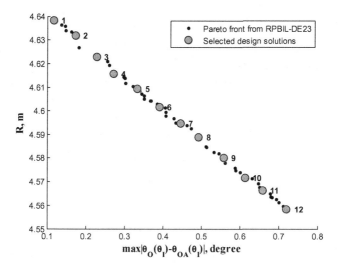

Fig. 5. Best Pareto front from RPBIL-DE23 with suspension.

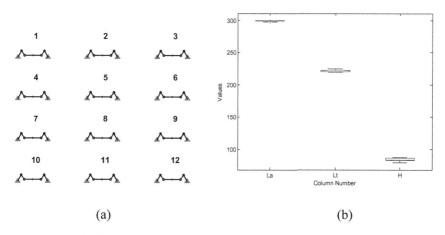

(a)   (b)

Fig. 6. (a) some selection linkage (b) distribution of link dimensions.

solution set is an even Pareto filter technique [27]. The distribution of the design variable of Fig. 5 displays in box-plots as shown in Fig. 6(b). The figure shows those solutions have slightly different dimensions than the previous study especially the design variable H is increased in distribution, while the other parameter are decreased. The changing is caused by the effect of suspension system, which is occurred to sustain the effect of toe angle.

5 Conclusions

This paper presents technique to find the optimum parameters of steering linkage included an effect of McPherson strut front suspension. The simplified model of McPherson strut suspension system is proposed in this study. The effect of interference mechanism is a cause of undesired effect on optimum design result. This is a reason why the suspension is included in optimisation design, which guarantees that the proposed design concept leads to effective design of rack and pinion steering linkages that can use the linkage in practicability.

For future study, the reliability design approach will develop to handle uncertainties that take place due to an interference mechanism.

Acknowledgement. The authors are grateful for the financial support provided by *King Mongkut's Institute of Technology Ladkrabang*, the Thailand Research Fund, and the Post-doctoral Program from Research Affairs, Graduate School, Khon Kaen University (58225).

References

1. Hanzaki, A.R., Rao, P.V.M., Saha, S.K.: Kinematic and sensitivity analysis and optimization of planar rack-and-pinion steering linkages. Mech. Mach. Theory **44**, 42–56 (2009)
2. Simionescu, P.A., Beale, D.: Optimum synthesis of the four-bar function generator in its symmetric embodiment: the Ackermann steering linkage. Mech. Mach. Theory **37**, 1487–1504 (2002)
3. Ettefagh, M.M., Javash, M.S.: Optimal synthesis of four-bar steering mechanism using AIS and genetic algorithms. J. Mech. Sci. Technol. **28**, 2351–2362 (2014)
4. Zhao, J.S., Liu, X., Feng, Z.J., Dai, J.S.: Design of an Ackermann-type steering mechanism. J. Mech. Eng. Sci. **227**, 2549–2562 (2013)
5. Peñuñuri, F., Peón-Escalante, R., Villanueva, C., Pech-Oy, D.: Synthesis of mechanisms for single and hybrid tasks using differential evolution. Mech. Mach. Theory **46**(10), 1335–1349 (2011)
6. Simionescu, P.A., Smith, M.R., Tempea, I.: Synthesis and analysis of the two loop translational input steering mechanism. Mech. Mach. Theory **35**(7), 927–943 (2000)
7. Carcaterra, A., D'Ambrogio, W.: A function generating differential mechanism for an exact solution of the steering problem. Mech. Mach. Theory **33**(5), 535–549 (1998)
8. Simionescu, P.A., Smith, M.R.: Applications of Watt II function generator cognates. Mech. Mach. Theory **35**, 1535–1549 (2000)
9. Simionescu, P.A., Smith, M.R.: Four- and six-bar function cognates and over constrained mechanism. Mech. Mach. Theory **36**, 913–924 (2001)
10. Zarak, C.E., Townsend, M.A.: Optimal design of rack-and-pinion steering linkages. J. Mech. Des. **105**, 220–226 (1983)
11. Felzien, M.L., Cronin, D.L.: Steering error optimization of the McPherson strut automotive front suspension. Mech. Mach. Theory **20**, 17–26 (1985)
12. Simionescu, P.A., Smith, M.R.: Initial estimates in the design of rack-and-pinion steering linkages. J. Mech. Des. **122**, 194–200 (2000)
13. Zhou, B., Li, D., Yang, F.: Optimization design of steering linkage in independent suspension based on genetic algorithm. In: Proceedings of Computer-Aided Industrial Design and Conceptual Design, Wenzhou, China, pp. 45–48 (2009)

14. Kim, S.I., Kim, Y.Y.: Topology optimization of planar linkage mechanisms. Int. J. Numer. Methods Eng. **98**, 265–286 (2014)
15. Sleesongsom, S., Bureerat, S.: Multiobjective optimization of a steering linkage. J. Mech. Sci. Technol. **30**(8), 3681–3691 (2016)
16. Szczotka, M.: Simulation and optimisation of the steering kickback performance. J. Theor. Appl. Mech. **49**(1), 187–208 (2011)
17. Mantaras, D.A., Luque, P., Vera, C.: Development and validation of a three-dimensional kinematic model for the McPherson steering and suspension, mechanisms. Mech. Mach. Theory **39**(6), 603–619 (2004)
18. Habibi, K.H., Shirazi, K.H., Shishesaz, M.: Roll steer minimization of McPherson-Strut suspension system using genetic algorithm method. Mech. Mach. Theory **43**, 57–67 (2008)
19. Lee, H.G., Won, C.J., Kim, J.W.: Design sensitivity analysis and optimization of Mcpherson suspension system. In: Proceedings of the World Congress on Engineering, London, UK (2009)
20. Qin, D., Yang, J., Zhu, Q., Du, P.: Simulation and optimization of MPV Suspension System Based on ADAMS. In: Proceedings of the World Congress on Structural and Multidisciplinary Optimization, Sydney, Australia (2015)
21. Knapczyk, J., Kucybaa, P.: Simplified planar model of a car steering system with rack and pinion and McPherson suspension. IOP Conf. Ser. Mater. Sci. **148**, 012011 (2016)
22. Phukaokaew, W., Sleesongsom, S., Bureerat, S.: Four-bar linkage path synthesis using meta-heuristics-algorithm comparison. Paper Presented in 7th TSME – ICOME, Chiang Mai, Thailand (2016)
23. Sleesongsom, S., Bureerat, S.: Four-bar linkage path generation through self-adaptive population size teaching-learning based optimization. Knowl. Based Syst. **135**, 180–191 (2017)
24. Sleesongsom, S., Bureerat, S.: Alternative constraint handling technique for four-bar linkage path generation. IOP Conf. Ser. Mater. Sci. Eng. **324**, 012012 (2018)
25. Sleesongsom, S., Bureerat, S.: Topology optimisation using MPBILs and multi-grid ground element. Appl. Sci. **8**, 271 (2018)
26. Pholdee, N., Bureerat, S.: Hybridisation of real-code population-based incremental learning and differential evolution for multiobjective design of trusses. Inf. Sci. **223**, 136–152 (2013)
27. Sleesongsom, S.: Multiobjective optimization with even Pareto filter. Paper Presented in 4th International Conference on Natural Computation, Jinan, China (2008)

Multi-scale Quantum Harmonic Oscillator Algorithm with Individual Stabilization Strategy

Peng Wang[1]([✉]), Bo Li[2,3], Jin Jin[2,3], Lei Mu[1], Gang Xin[2,3], Yan Huang[4], and XingGui Ye[2,3,5]

[1] College of Computer Science and Technology,
Southwest Minzu University, Chengdu 610225, China
wp002005@163.com
[2] Chengdu Institution of Computer Application of China Academy of Science,
Chengdu 610041, China
[3] University of Chinese Academy of Sciences, Beijing 100049, China
[4] Huaiyin Normal University, Huaiyin 223300, China
[5] Cloud Computing and Big Data Center,
China Unicom Fujian Branch, Fuzhou 350007, China

Abstract. Multi-scale quantum harmonic oscillator algorithm (MQH-OA) is a novel global optimization algorithm inspired by wave function of quantum mechanics. In this paper, a MQHOA with individual stabilization strategy (IS-MQHOA) is proposed utilizing the individual steady criterion instead of the group statistics. The proposed strategy is more rigorous for the particles in the energy level stabilization process. A more efficient search takes place in the search space made by the particles and improves the exploration ability and the robustness of the algorithm. To verify its performance, numerical experiments are conducted to compare the proposed algorithm with the state-of-the-art SPSO2011 and QPSO. The experimental results show the superiority of the proposed approach on benchmark functions.

Keywords: Multi-scale quantum harmonic oscillator algorithm
Optimization algorithm · Individual stabilization · Wave function

1 Introduction

Optimal problems always encountered in scientific, engineering or management fields. It takes too much time to solve real world problems with traditional optimization methods, and they cannot be solved effectively. In the past decades, researchers have developed hundreds of optimization techniques to tackle these problems inspired from biological evolution or physical world, such as Simulated annealing (SA) [1], Genetic algorithm (GA) [2], Ant colony optimization (ACO) [3], Particle swarm optimization (PSO) [4], Fireworks algorithm (FWA) [5,6]

© Springer International Publishing AG, part of Springer Nature 2018
Y. Tan et al. (Eds.): ICSI 2018, LNCS 10941, pp. 624–633, 2018.
https://doi.org/10.1007/978-3-319-93815-8_59

and Brain storm optimization algorithm (BSO) [7]. These algorithms are proved to be effective and efficient in real-life optimization problems.

In recent years, inspired from quantum mechanics, many new quantum optimization algorithms have emerged. In [8], Deutsch-Jozsa quantum algorithm (DQA) is successfully applied in a quantum computer to solve a purely mathematical problem with fewer steps than classical computer. Quantum annealing algorithm (QAA) [9] uses the tunnel effect of quantum transition mechanism to minimize multidimensional functions. In [10], a quantum-inspired evolutionary algorithm (QEA) is proposed which is based on the concept and principles of quantum computing, such as quantum bit and superposition of states. In [11], a quantum genetic algorithm (QGA) is proposed which takes advantage of quantum computing quantum parallelism, quantum entanglement properties. [12] uses a Q-bit string as a representation, and proposes the quantum-inspired differential evolution algorithm (QDE). Quantum particle swarm optimization (QPSO) [13] employs delta potential well to solve the objective function. The ground states wave function of the quantum system bounded by delta potential well are employed as a sampling function to explore the global minimum. QPSO outperforms the original PSO in search ability and has fewer parameters to control. But as many other PSOs, it is easy to fall into local optimum in solving high-dimensional complex optimization problems.

Motivated by probability interpretation of quantum wave function, a novel quantum meta-heuristic methodology named multi-scale quantum harmonic oscillator algorithm (MQHOA) is proposed [14], which is used to solve optimal problems such as integer programming, k-means clustering, multi-project scheduling and so on. [15] uses limited Markov chain theoretics to analyze the convergence characteristics of MQHOA. [16] proposes a partition algorithm based on MQHOA for multimodal optimization. [17] demonstrates the uncertainty relationship between global searching accuracy and local searching accuracy for the first time. [18] presents an optimized K-means clustering algorithm based on the MQHOA. In [19], an application of MQHOA is applied in assignment problem for multiple nodes with multiple targets. [20] improves the MQHOA with energy level stabilizing process analogizing to quantum harmonic oscillator's wave function. All of the following work is based on [20].

The energy level stabilization process plays an important role in MQHOA. This process determines whether the swarm have located the optimal solution space. The group statistical properties reflect the global distribution of the particles and used to determine this process. This mechanism has a disadvantage of only focus on the statistical properties of the swarm, ignoring individual characteristics. If the particle gets trapped in a local optimum and then causes the premature of the algorithm. A MQHOA with individual stabilization strategy (IS-MQHOA) is proposed which focus more on individual stabilization. The individual strategy is more critical to the particles and enables the algorithm to execute sampling multiple times in solution space. It enhances the global exploration ability of the algorithm.

This paper is organized as follows. After the introduction, Sect. 2 reviews the related work and discussed the theoretical of IS-MQHOA in details. Experiment results and analysis are presented in Sect. 3. Finally, conclusion and further discussion are given in Sect. 4.

2 Theoretical Analysis of IS-MQHOA

2.1 Theoretical Background

In quantum mechanical theory, every non-relativistic particle in an electric field moves randomly in the space where there are different energy levels between high potential energy states and the ground state. Particles move randomly in the space where the higher the energy level of $E_i (i = 1, 2..., n)$, the more active and unstable. The Zero Energy State E_0 is the most stable state, in which particles just stay still to keep balance. The gradual transition of particles from high energy to low energy levels can be seen as a gradual convergence process.

In the real world, the optimization problem $f(x)$ is usually to find the optimal solution from the solution space. The mathematical model established is generally abstract, complex and difficult to solve. According to quantum theory and quantum annealing method, the optimization problem can be transformed into the problem of finding ground state under a potential well $V(x)$. Meanwhile, the wave function reflects the probability of the optimal solution at each energy level. The appearance probability of particles in the quantum space can be demonstrated by time-independent Schrödinger equation. The time-independent Schrödinger equation is written as:

$$E\psi(x) = \left(-\frac{\hbar^2}{2m}\frac{d^2}{dx^2} + V(x)\right)\psi(x) \tag{1}$$

In linear algebra terminology, (1) is an eigenvalue equation, where E represents the system energy of stationary state, $\psi(x)$ represents the probability amplitude, $|\psi|^2$ represents the probability distribution of the particles in the electric field, $\hbar = h/2\pi$ (h represents the Planck constant), $V(x)$ indicates the potential energy and bound condition which is too complicated to express analytically.

It is assumed in [21] that the objective function $f(x)$ could be regarded as the potential energy $V(x)$ in Schrödinger equation. It is difficult to solve the $f(x)$ and $V(x)$ in the real world. The transition of particles from high energy levels to the ground state could be regarded as a convergence process in function evaluation. According to this model, an objective function $f(x)$ of an optimization problem can be seen as the potential well of bound states $V(x)$ in quantum system. Accordingly, (1) can be rewritten as the following form:

$$E\psi(x) = \left(-\frac{\hbar^2}{2m}\frac{d^2}{dx^2} + f(x)\right)\psi(x) \tag{2}$$

where the $V(x)$ in (1) is replaced by $f(x)$ in (2). According to Taylor's theorem, a function can be approximated by using a finite number of terms of its Taylor series. The function $f(x)$ in (2) is expanded by Taylor second-order as the following equation:

$$f(x) = f(x_0) + f'(x_0)(x - x_0) + \frac{f''(x_0)}{2!}(x - x_0)^2 + \dots \tag{3}$$

where x_0 is an optimal solution. $f(x_0)$ is a constant. The derivative of the constant term is zero, and the first derivative is zero at the optimal solution in (3). Then, the function $f(x)$ is transformed into the following equation:

$$f(x) \approx \frac{f''(x_0)}{2}(x - x_0)^2 \tag{4}$$

where $f''(x_0)$ can be seen as a spring constant k in a harmonic motion.

$$f(x) = \frac{1}{2}kx^2 \tag{5}$$

where $f(x)$ is defined as the potential energy of a quantum harmonic oscillator, k is the resilience coefficient. In quantum theory, the quadratic of wave function probability amplitude $\psi(x)$ in (2) reflects the probability distribution of particles. Equation (5) is substituted into (2) to get the wave function $\psi(x)$ as the following formula:

$$\psi(x) = \sum_{i=1}^{n} \psi_i(x) = \sum_{i=1}^{n} \frac{1}{\sqrt{2\pi}\sigma} exp(-\frac{(x - \mu_i)^2}{2\sigma^2}) \tag{6}$$

where μ represents the mean value of the optimal solutions, σ denotes the standard deviation of the current optimal solutions. The smaller the σ, the narrower the search space. It can be observed in (6) from high energy levels to the ground state corresponding to process of the wave function of quantum harmonic oscillator changes from an intertwined of n Gaussian functions to an overlapped Gaussian function.

2.2   Framework of MQHOA

Inspired from laws of quantum motion, MQHOA's basic idea is to map the objective function to quantum harmonic oscillator constraint state through Taylor second-order approximation, so as to the optimization problems can be converted to solve the ground state wave function quantum harmonic oscillator problem under different scales.

MQHOA is characterized by three principle components tightly connected with each other: energy level stabilization phase, energy level transition phase and scale decrease phase. In the energy level stable phase, particles explore the adjacent space in order to locate a better optimal solution. When all of the particles finish the exploration and exploitation for better solutions, the group statistics (GS) is used to evaluate the status of the swarm. The difference of variance is calculated before and after sampling. If the difference is less than the current scale, the swarm is considered to be in stable status in current scale. In the energy level transition phase, the main task is to eliminate the particle with the worst fitness in the swarm. The strategy is to use the mean value of the swarm's position to replace the particle with the worst fitness. This strategy ensures the diversity of the swarm with generating a new particle every iteration. In the third phase, the scale decrease phase adopts the strategy of reducing the scale by half, so the algorithm repeats the energy level from high to low in a smaller scale. The changing process from large scale to small scale corresponding to the gradual transition from global search to local search algorithm.

2.3   Stabilization Strategy in Energy Level Stabilization

Two different strategies are depicted in Fig. 1. Figure 1(a) represents the group stabilization strategy(GS). Figure 1(b) represents the individual stabilization strategy(IS). X, X' are two vectors that consists of particles. X is consist of $x_1, x_2, ..., x_i (i = 1, 2, 3, ..., k)$. X' is consist of $x'_1, x'_2, ..., x'_i (i = 1, 2, 3, ..., k)$. Where x_i represents the potential optimal solution, x'_i is the corresponding particle generated by Gaussian distribution with center x_i and variance σ. The two expressions represent the stabilization condition.

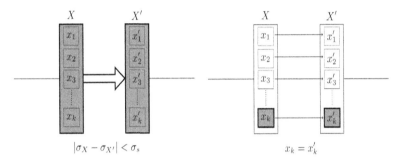

(a) Group Stabilization strategy   (b) Individual Stabilization strategy

Fig. 1. Different strategies in energy level stable phase

The process of GS is that algorithm generates a new sampling positions x'_i for all sampling particles $x_i (i = 1, 2, 3, ..., k)$ in a normal distributions $N(x_i, \sigma^2)$. If the new position corresponds to a smaller function value: $f(x'_i) < f(x_i)$, the x_i is replaced by x'_i until the $|\sigma_X - \sigma_{X'}| < \sigma_s$. Figure 1(b) demonstrates the principle of IS-MQHOA. IS-MQHOA concerns the stability of the individual particle. By continuously sampling, particles move for the better optimal solution in the solution space. The optimal position of particle updates if the particle makes progress. The individual stabilization strategy makes each particle resampled until current particle's position is no longer replaced. The σ_{min} determines the location accuracy of the algorithm results. When the current scale is less than the preset accuracy, the algorithm stops and outputs the optimal results.

The IS determines the stability of the swarm through the stability of the individual. It is more critical with the energy stabilization than the GS. Strict constraints strategy makes the algorithm execute energy level stabilization several times. It enhances the global exploration of the particle in the solution space. Exploration is defined as searching for the new regions in the search space, while exploitation is defined as visiting the regions within the neighborhood of previously visited individuals. The exploration task is accomplished mainly in the energy level stabilization phase. And the exploitation task mainly achieved by the energy level decreased phase. The judgement strategy of the energy stable phase determined how to keep a proper trade-off between exploration and exploitation of optimal solutions. IS enables the algorithm to perform multiple searches in the solution space, enhance the global optimization ability of the algorithm.

2.4   IS-MQHOA Process

The pseudo code of IS-MQHOA is described as follows:

Algorithm 1. IS-MQHOA Pseudo code

---
initialize k, σ_{min}, LB, UB, $\sigma_s = UB - LB$.
randomly generate x_i, $(i = 1, ..., k)$ in $[LB, UB]$.
calculate the standard deviation σ_k for all x_i.
while $(\sigma_s > \sigma_{min})$ **do**
$\quad$ **while** $(\sigma_k > \sigma_s)$ **do**
$\quad\quad$ set $Flag_{stable} = 0$.
$\quad\quad$ **while** $(Flag_{stable} == 0)$ **do**
$\quad\quad\quad$ $Flag_{stable} = 1$.
$\quad\quad\quad$ $\forall\, x_i$, generate $x'_i \sim N(x_i, \sigma_s^2)$.
$\quad\quad\quad$ $\forall\, x_i$ and x'_i, if $f(x'_i) < f(x_i)$ then $x_i = x'_i$, $Flag_{stable} = 0$.
$\quad\quad$ **end**
$\quad\quad$ calculate the standard deviation σ_k for all x_i.
$\quad\quad$ update the worst solution: $x^{worst} = x^{mean}$.
$\quad$ **end**
$\quad$ $\sigma_s = \sigma_s/2$.
end
output $x^{best}, f(x^{best})$.

The initial search range is $[LB, UB]$. The number of particles is k. The σ_{min} is the accuracy of the optimal solution. $\sigma_s = UB - LB$. The x^{mean} is the mean value of x_i: $f(x^{mean}) = mean(f(x_i))$. The x^{worst} is the worst solution of x_i: $f(x^{worst}) = argmax(f(x_i))$

3   Experimental Results and Discussions

In this section, there are 6 benchmark functions used in the following experiments. The benchmark functions, search ranges and optimums are listed in

Table 1. The benchmark functions are divided into two categories: unimodal function and multimodal function. Usually, unimodal function is used to test the ability of local search algorithm, and multimodal function is used to test the ability of the global search. Function f_1–f_3 are multimodal functions. Function f_4–f_6 are unimodal functions. Two experiments are conducted. One is to compare the performance of IS-MQHOA with MQHOA. The other one is to compare the performance of IS-MQHOA with SPSO2011 and QPSO.

Table 1. Benchmark functions

Function name	Benchmark function	Range	Optimum
Ackley	$f_1 = -20exp(-0.2\sqrt{\frac{1}{n}\sum_{i=1}^{n}x_i^2})$ $-exp(\frac{1}{n}\sum_{i=1}^{n}cos(2\pi x_i))[+20+e]$	$[-32,32]$	0
Dixon-Price	$f_2 = (x_1-1)^2 + \sum_{i=2}^{n}i(2x_i^2-x_{i-1})^2$	$[-10,10]$	0
Griewank	$f_3 = \frac{1}{4000}\sum_{i=1}^{n}x_i^2 - \prod_{i=1}^{n}cos\left(\frac{x_i}{\sqrt{i}}\right)+1$	$[-100,100]$	0
Sphere	$f_4 = \sum_{i=1}^{n}x_i^2$	$[-100,100]$	0
SumSqure	$f_5 = \sum_{i=0}^{n-1}ix_i^2$	$[-10,10]$	0
Zakharov	$f_6 = \sum_{i=1}^{n}x_i^2 + (\sum_{i=1}^{n}0.5ix_i)^2 + (\sum_{i=1}^{n}0.5ix_i)^4$	$[-5,10]$	0

The experiments are conducted in MATLAB 2014b (Windows7, Intel Core i5-2600, 2.6 GHZ, 8G RAM). In the simulations, SPSO2011 is tested using the population size of 20 and maximum iterations number of 1e5. The scope of inertia weight is set as $[0.4, 0.9]$. As for QPSO, the simulation parameters are: $w = 1/(2ln2)$, $c1 = 1/2 + ln(2)$, $c2 = 1/2 + ln(2)$, maximum iterations number of 2000, the number of population is 20. For IS-MQHOA, the number of particles $k = 20$, σ_{min}=1e−6. Each algorithm runs 50 independent trials on every benchmark function.

To validate the performance of studied algorithm, the following evaluation criterions are calculated: the optimal solutions, mean values, standard deviations(Std), and SR(success rate). The optimal solution indicates the exploitation ability of the algorithm, the mean value indicates the solution quality of the algorithm, and the standard deviation represents the stability of the algorithm. The SR represents the robust of the algorithm and it's value equals to the number of finding the optimal solutions divided by the number of runs. When the accuracy of the optimal solution is less than $1e-5$, it is considered that the optimal solution is located.

3.1 Compared with the MQHOA

In the first experiment, IS-MQHOA is compared with MQHOA in dimension 20. The average results are obtained after 50 independent runs of the algorithm. Table 2 shows the experimental results.

Table 2. Comparison of results for IS-MQHOA, MQHOA in dimension 20

		f_1	f_2	f_3	f_4	f_5	f_6
IS-MQHOA	Best	3.27E−06	6.67E−01	1.70E−11	7.42E−12	2.48E−10	1.45E−10
	Mean	5.01E−06	6.67E−01	1.53E−10	1.96E−11	1.38E−09	3.42E−10
	Std	1.07E−06	3.61E−09	4.04E−11	7.90E−12	1.08E−09	1.23E−10
	SR	100%	0%	100%	100%	100%	100%
MQHOA	Best	6.66E−06	6.67E−01	3.93E−12	2.08E−11	5.91E−10	2.99E−10
	Mean	2.94E−01	6.67E−01	5.47E−03	5.04E−11	2.38E−09	6.80E−10
	Std	6.16E−01	7.75E−09	9.04E−03	1.47E−11	1.15E−09	2.95E−10
	SR	78%	0%	62%	100%	100%	100%

From Table 2, it can be observed that IS-MQHOA successfully finds the global optimal solution with 100% success rate on all of the test functions except for $f_2(0\%)$ for multimodal function. MQHOA fails to find the global optimal solution. The success rates are $f_1(78\%)$, $f_2(0\%)$, $f_3(62\%)$. IS-MQHOA enables the particles of the swarm take a close search of the solution space and improves the robust ability of the algorithm. IS-MQHOA and MQHOA get stuck in the local minima and fails to locate the optimal solution on f_2 in 50 runs. The Dixon-Price(f_2) is shaped like a valley and the global minimum is inside a long, narrow, parabolic shaped flat valley. To converge to the global minimum is difficult. For the unimodal functions f_4–f_6, IS-MQHOA and MQHOA can find the best optimal solution in 50 runs. But IS-MQHOA can get a higher accuracy of optimal solutions. From the mean value and standard deviation criterions, the results are on an order of magnitude, but the IS-MQHOA gets smaller values. Through the analysis of experimental results, the performance of the proposed algorithm has been improved in both global search ability and local search ability due to the more sufficient energy level stabilization process.

3.2 Compared with SPSO2011, QPSO

In this experiment, the performance of the IS-MQHOA is compared with the recently developed SPSO2011 and QPSO in dimension 50. The average results are obtained after 50 independent runs of the algorithm. Table 3 shows the experimental results.

For the multimodal functions, none of the compared algorithms find the optimal solution with probability 1 in 50 runs and trapped into local optimum with a larger probability. The success rates of SPSO, QPSO for f_1, f_2 equal to 0 in all 50 runs. Ackley(f_1) function is characterized by a nearly flat outer region, and a large hole at the centre. The results of the compared algorithm on f_3 are relatively good. The success rates are over 50%. For the unimodal functions, IS-MQHOA finds the optimal solution with a 100% success rate on f_4–f_6. It verifies that IS shows excellent global search capability and the ability to locate the optimal solution. SPSO2011 can find the optimal solution with a 100% success rate except $f_5(4\%)$, $f_6(0\%)$. QPSO is trapped in local optimum on

Table 3. Comparison of results for IS-MQHOA, SPSO2011,QPSO in dimension 50

		f_1	f_2	f_3	f_4	f_5	f_6
IS-MQHOA	Best	8.67E−06	6.67E−01	2.03E−11	1.16E−10	5.20E−08	3.77E−09
	Mean	1.12E+00	6.67E−01	2.02E−03	2.27E−10	8.86E−08	8.26E−09
	Std	9.50E−01	9.62E−08	4.84E−03	9.71E−11	2.07E−08	3.10E−09
	SR	10%	0%	82%	100%	100%	100%
SPSO2011	Best	1.65E+00	6.67E−01	9.28E−07	8.63E−07	1.22E−06	1.02E−02
	Mean	2.36E+00	8.16E−01	4.14E−03	9.53E−07	6.78E−03	9.24E−02
	Std	3.95E−01	3.31E−01	5.48E−03	3.30E−08	1.00E−02	7.71E−02
	SR	0%	0%	60%	100%	4%	0%
QPSO	Best	4.38E−04	6.67E−01	4.09E−07	9.77E −06	1.21E−06	5.19E+01
	Mean	9.86E−03	3.07E+00	3.30E−03	3.76E−04	6.34E−05	1.16E+02
	Std	2.93E−02	2.27E+00	6.40E−03	6.53E−04	9.15E−05	3.92E+01
	SR	0%	0%	56.7%	33%	20%	0%

the unimodal function. The success rates are $f_4(33\%)$, $f_5(20\%)$, $f_6(0\%)$. QPSO employs a quantum delta potential well model, which is relatively flat at both end and a sharp convergence process in the center position. This makes the algorithm premature. The experimental results also prove the theory. From the mean value, standard deviation respective, the results of IS-MQHOA are better than SPSO2011 and QPSO. The optimal solutions of IS-MQHOA are more accurate less than 1e−8.

4 Conclusion

In this paper, a novel multi-scale quantum harmonic oscillator algorithm with individual stabilization strategy (IS-MQHOA) is proposed. The proposed strategy improves the exploration performance of MQHOA while maintaining its exploitation performance. IS strategy enables the algorithm to execute energy level stabilization process several times which increases the exploration capability of the particle in the solution space. The experimental results show that IS-MQHOA improves the performance of the original MQHOA and outperforms SPSO2011 and QPSO on 6 benchmark functions in a statistically meaningful way. As a future work, it is important for quickly solving practical applications that we can gain more knowledge on how to improve our algorithm.

Acknowledgment. This work is supported by Fundamental Research Funds for the Central Universities of China (2017NZYQN27), Science and Technology Planning Project of Guangdong Province, China (2016B090918062), National Natural Science Foundation of China (60702075,71673032).

References

1. Kirkpatrick, S.: Optimization by simulated annealing: quantitative studies. J. Stat. Phys. **34**(5–6), 975–986 (1984)
2. Holland, J.H.: Erratum: genetic algorithms and the optimal allocation of trials. SIAM. J. Sci. Comput. **2**(2), 88–105 (1973)
3. Dorigo, M., Maniezzo, V., Colorni, A.: Ant system: optimization by a colony of cooperating agents. IEEE Trans. Syst. Man. Cybern. A. **26**(1), 29–41 (1995)
4. Kennedy, J., Eberhart, R.: Particle swarm optimization. In: IEEE ICNS 1995, vol. 4, pp. 1942–1948 (2002)
5. Li, J., Tan, Y.: Loser-out tournament based fireworks algorithm for multi-modal function optimization. IEEE Trans. Evol. Comput. **PP**(99), 1 (2017)
6. Tan, Y., Zhu, Y.: Fireworks algorithm for optimization. In: ICSI, pp. 355–364 (2010)
7. Shi, Y.: Brain storm optimization algorithm. In: ICSI, pp. 303–309 (2011)
8. Chuang, I.L., Vandersypen, L.M., Zhou, X., et al.: Experimental realization of a quantum algorithm. Nature **393**(6681), 143–146 (1998)
9. Finnila, A.B., Gomez, M.A., Sebenik, C., Stenson, C., Doll, J.D.: Quantum annealing: a new method for minimizing multidimensional functions. Chem. Phys. Lett. **219**(5–6), 343–348 (1994)
10. Han, K.H.: Quantum-inspired evolutionary algorithm for a class of combinatorial optimization. IEEE Trans. Evol. Comput. **6**(7), 580–593 (2002)
11. Rylander, B., Soule, T., Foster, J.A., et al.: Quantum genetic algorithms. In: GECCO, p. 373 (2000)
12. Draa, A., Batouche, M., Talbi, H.: A quantum-inspired differential evolution algorithm for rigid image registration. In: ICCI 2004, pp. 408–411 (2004)
13. Sun, J., Xu, W., Feng, B.: A global search strategy of quantum-behaved particle swarm optimization. In: IEEE CIS, vol. 1, pp. 111–116 (2004)
14. Wang, P., Huang, Y., Ren, C., et al.: Multi-scale quantum harmonic oscillator for high-dimensional function global optimization algorithm. Chin. J. Electron. **41**(12), 2468–2473 (2013)
15. Wang, P.C., Wang, P.C., Qian, X.: Simulated harmonic oscillator algorithm and its global convergence analysis. Comput. Eng. **39**(3), 209–212 (2013)
16. Zj, L., Jx, A., Wang, P.: Partition-based MQHOA for multimodal optimization. Acta Automatica Sinica **42**(2), 235–245 (2015)
17. Wang, P., Huang, Y.: Physical model of multi-scale quantum harmonic oscillator optimization algorithm. J. Front. Comput. Sci. Chi. 1271–1280 (2015)
18. Haitao, Y., Wang, P., Zi, L.: Optimized k-means clustering algorithm based on simulated harmonic oscillator. Comput. Eng. Appl. **48**(30), 122–127 (2012)
19. Mu, L., Qu, X., Wang, P.: Application of multi-scale quantum harmonic oscillator algorithm for multifactor task allocation problem in WSANs. In: ICIVC, pp. 1004–1009 (2017)
20. Wang, P., Huang, Y.: MQHOA algorithm with energy level stabilizing process. J. Commun. **37**(7), 79–86 (2016)
21. Lorenzo, S., Giuseppe, E.S., Erio, T.: Optimization by quantum annealing: lessons from simple cases. Phys. Rev. B. **72**(1), 014303 (2005)

Author Index

Aggarwal, Garvit II-513
Aggarwal, Swati II-513
Aguila, Alexander II-174
Aguilera-Hernández, Doris II-471
Akhmedova, Shakhnaz I-68
An, Xinqi II-225
Antonov, M. A. I-3
Arbulú, Mario I-304

Bacanin, Nebojsa I-283
Balaguera, Manuel-Ignacio I-51, II-452
Bariviera, Aurelio F. II-153
Bing, Liu II-295
Bogomolov, Alexey I-361
Boulkaibet, Ilyes I-498
Brester, Christina I-210
Bureerat, Sujin I-612

Cai, Li I-273
Cai, Muyao I-509
Chao, Yen Tzu II-305
Chen, Chao II-329, II-413
Chen, Di II-132
Chen, Guang I-421
Chen, Jianjun I-191
Chen, JianQing I-125
Chen, JingJing II-361
Chen, Jinlong II-461, II-483, II-493, II-500
Chen, Jinsong I-295
Chen, Jou Yu II-249
Chen, Li I-317
Chen, Mingsong II-552
Chen, Pei Chi II-432
Chen, Shengminjie I-520, I-530
Chen, Xianjun II-461, II-483, II-493, II-500
Chen, Xiaohong II-267, II-275, II-351
Chen, Xu I-166
Chen, Zhihong I-201
Cheng, Jian II-361
Cheng, Ming Shien II-249, II-305, II-423,
    II-432
Cheng, Shi I-530
Cui, Ning II-361
Cui, Zhihua I-432

de Lima Neto, Fernando Buarque I-498
DeLei, Mao II-295
Deng, Zhenqiang II-132
Deras, Ivan II-164
Dong, Shi II-552
Dorta, Rafael Gómez II-164
Du, Xiaofan I-520
Du, Yi-Chen I-465

Ebel, Henrik II-89
Eberhard, Peter II-89, II-102

Fan, Long II-225
Fan, Qinqin I-243
Fang, Wei I-572, I-593
Fei, Rong II-563
Frantsuzova, Yulia I-22
Fu, Changhong II-102

Gaitán-Angulo, Mercedes I-51, II-471
Gan, Xiaobing I-410
Gao, Chao I-191
Gao, Shangce I-384, I-397
Garg, Ayush II-513
Geng, Shineng II-25
Geng, Shuang I-410, II-275
Gong, Lulu I-201
Gong, Xiaoju II-212
Graven, Olaf Hallan II-74
Gu, Feng II-36
Gu, Zhao I-520
Guan, Zengda II-286
Guo, Fangfei I-201
Guo, Ling I-101
Guo, Qianqian I-550
Guo, Ruiqin II-132
Guo, Weian I-42
Guo, Yi-nan II-361
Guo, Yinan II-399
Guo, Yuanjun I-477
Guo, Zhen II-493

Hai, Huang II-122
Han, Song II-399

Hao, Guo-Sheng   I-432
Hao, Zhiyong   II-267
Hao, Zhou   II-122
He, Haiyan   I-201
He, Jun   II-413
He, Weixiong   II-112
He, Yuqing   II-36
Henao, Linda Carolina   II-471
Henry, Maury-Ardila   II-174
Hernández-Fernández, Lissette   II-164
Hernández-Palma, Hugo   II-189, II-440
Hong, Liu   II-15
Hsu, Ping Yu   II-249, II-305, II-423, II-432
Hsu, Tun-Chieh   I-78
Hu, Xi   I-58
Hu, Rongjing   II-258
Huang, Chen Wan   II-249, II-305, II-423, II-432
Huang, Hai   II-132
Huang, Kaishan   I-223
Huang, Min   I-113
Huang, Shih Hsiang   II-249, II-305, II-423, II-432
Huang, Yan   I-624

Inga, Esteban   II-174
Ivutin, Alexey   I-22, II-43
Izquierdo, Noel Varela   II-164

Ji, Junkai   I-384, I-397
Jia, Songmin   I-421
Jia, Yongjun   II-483
Jianbin, Huang   II-15
Jiang, Entao   I-410
Jiang, Shilong   I-153, I-561
Jiang, Si-ping   I-317
Jiao, Licheng   I-327
Jiménez-Delgado, Genett   II-189, II-440
Jin, Jin   I-624
Jin, Ye   I-374

Kang, Rongjie   II-25
Kao, Yen Hao   II-423
Karaseva, M. V.   I-91
Ko, Yen-Huei   II-249, II-305, II-423
Kolehmainen, Mikko   I-210

Kotov, Vladislav   I-361
Kovalev, D. I.   I-91
Kovalev, I. V.   I-91
Kustudic, Mijat   I-410

Lanzarini, Laura   II-153
Larkin, E. V.   I-3
Larkin, Eugene   I-22, I-361, II-43
Lei, Hong Tsuen   II-249, II-305, II-423
Lei, Xiujuan   I-101
Lezama, Omar Bonerge Pineda   II-164
Li, Baiwei   II-339
Li, Bin   II-542
Li, Bo   I-624
Li, Decai   II-36
Li, Geng-Shi   I-145
Li, Guoqing   I-604
Li, Hao   I-273
Li, Lei   I-201
Li, Peidao   I-327
Li, Sheng   I-397
Li, Wei   II-339
Li, Xiaomei   II-522
Li, Xuan   I-179
Li, Yangyang   I-327
Li, Yinghao   II-132
Li, Zhiyong   I-153, I-561
Li, Zili   II-314
Liang, Jing   I-101, I-550
Liang, Jinye   I-201
Liao, Qing   I-243
Lima, Liliana   II-174
Lin, Ke   I-561
Ling, Haifeng   II-112
Lis-Gutiérrez, Jenny-Paola   I-51, II-452, II-471
Liu, Chen   II-530
Liu, Feng-Zeng   I-273
Liu, Fuyong   I-453
Liu, Ganjun   I-179
Liu, Guangyuan   I-327
Liu, Henzhu   II-142
Liu, Huan   I-350
Liu, Lei   I-487, II-267, II-275, II-351
Liu, Qun   II-370
Liu, Tingting   II-267, II-275, II-351
Liu, Xi   II-53

Liu, Yuxin I-191
Losev, V. V. I-91
Lu, Hui II-202
Lu, Yanyue I-445, I-453
Lu, Yueliang I-540
Luo, Wei II-102
Luqian, Yu II-380
Lv, Jianhui I-113
Lv, Lingyan I-191

Ma, Haiping I-477
Ma, Jun II-258
Ma, Lianbo I-520, I-530
Ma, Yanzhui I-445
Malagón, Luz Elena II-452
Mao, Meixin II-314
Martínez, Fredy I-304, II-66
Marwala, Tshilidzi I-498
Mbuvha, Rendani I-498
Meng, Hongying II-370
Miyashita, Tomoyuki I-251
Mo, Yuanbin I-445, I-453, II-389
Mu, Lei I-624
Mu, Yong II-258

Nand, Parma II-3
Naryani, Deepika II-513
Neira-Rodado, Dionicio II-189, II-440
Ni, Qingjian I-540
Niu, Ben I-223, I-341, I-350
Niu, Qun I-477
Nouioua, Mourad I-153, I-561
Novikov, Alexander I-22, II-43

Ortíz-Barrios, Miguel II-189, II-440

Pacheco, Luis II-66
Pan, Hang II-461, II-483, II-493, II-500
Parque, Victor I-251
Pei, Tingrui I-509
Penagos, Cristian II-66
Peng, Yingying I-410
Perez, Ramón II-174
Phoa, Frederick Kin Hing I-78
Portillo-Medina, Rafael I-51, II-471
Prassida, Grandys Frieska II-305
Privalov, Aleksandr I-361

Qiao, Chen II-542
Qiu, Xinchen I-201
Qu, Boyang I-477, I-550

Raghuwaiya, Krishna II-3
Ren, Jiadong II-235
Ren, Ke II-329, II-413
Rendón, Angelica I-304
Retchkiman Konigsberg, Zvi I-14
Rong, Chen II-380
Rong, Zhong-Yu I-465
Ryzhikov, Ivan I-210

Santana, Patricia Jimbo II-153
Saramud, M. V. I-91
Saveca, John I-233
Semenkin, Eugene I-68, I-210
Shao, Yichuan I-520
Sharma, Bibhya II-3
Shen, Jianqiang I-42
Shi, Jinhua II-202
Shi, Lihui II-483
Shi, Xiaoyan I-572
Shi, Yubin II-370
Shi, Yuhui I-530
Si, Chengyong I-42
Sleesongsom, Suwin I-612
Song, Bo II-522
Sopov, Evgenii I-583
Sørli, Jon-Vegard II-74
Stanovov, Vladimir I-68
Strumberger, Ivana I-283
Sun, Jiandang II-235
Sun, Ke-Feng II-542
Sun, Manhui II-142
Sun, Yanxia I-233
Sun, Yuehong I-374

Tai, Xiaolu I-201
Takagi, Hideyuki I-263
Tan, Fei I-132
Tan, Lijing I-295, I-487
Tan, Ying I-101, I-263
Tang, Qirong II-102, II-132
Tang, Renjun II-500
Tang, Zhiwei II-399
Tian, Shujuan I-509

Todo, Yuki   I-384, I-397
Troncoso-Palacio, Alexander   II-440
Troshina, Anna   I-22, II-43
Tuba, Eva   I-283
Tuba, Milan   I-283

Vanualailai, Jito   II-3
Vargas, María-Cristina   II-452
Vasechkina, Elena   I-32
Vásquez, Carmen   II-174
Viloria, Amelec   I-51, II-164, II-174, II-452, II-471

Wang, Chen   I-317
Wang, ChunHui   I-125
Wang, Cong   II-25
Wang, Dan   I-374
Wang, Feishuang   II-329
Wang, Gai-Ge   I-432
Wang, Hong   I-223, I-487
Wang, Huan   I-295
Wang, Jingyuan   II-329
Wang, Lei   I-42
Wang, Na   II-563
Wang, Peng   I-624
Wang, Qingchuan   II-339
Wang, Rui   I-520, I-530
Wang, Wei   II-530
Wang, Weiguang   II-552
Wang, Xiaolin   II-399
Wang, Xiaoru   II-339
Wang, Xingwei   I-113
Wang, Yanzhen   II-53
Wang, Yong   II-413
Wang, Youyu   II-25
Wang, Zenghui   I-233
Wang, Zirui   II-399
Weng, Sung-Shun   I-223, II-351
Wu, Guohua   II-563
Wu, Miao   II-399
Wu, Shuai   I-593
Wu, Tao   I-58

Xia, Bin   I-132
Xiao, Bing   I-273
Xiao, Lu   I-295
Xin, Gang   I-624
Xiu, Jiapeng   II-530
Xu, Bin   I-166

Xu, Qingzheng   II-563
Xu, Xiaofei   II-329, II-413
Xu, Yanbing   I-509
Xu, Ying   I-201
Xu, Zhe   I-384
Xuan, Shibin   II-389
Xun, Weiwei   II-53

Yachi, Hanaki   I-384
Yan, Tang   II-295
Yan, Xiaohui   I-341, I-350
Yang, Chen   II-267, II-275, II-351
Yang, Heng   II-563
Yang, Hongling   II-389
Yang, Jianjian   II-399
Yang, Liying   II-36
Yang, Shaowu   II-142
Yang, Xuesen   I-223
Yang, Zhengqiu   II-530
Yang, Zhile   I-477
Yao, Jindong   I-201
Ye, XingGui   I-624
Yi, Wei   II-53
Yi, Xiaodong   II-53
Yin, Peng-Yeng   I-145
Yu, Jun   I-263
Yu, Kunjie   I-550
Yu, Yang   I-384, I-397
Yuan, Fenggang   I-397
Yue, Caitong   I-550

Zeng, Li   II-314
Zeng, Qinghao   II-461
Zeng, Qingshuang   II-235
Zexing, Zhou   II-122
Zhang, Chao   I-201
Zhang, Gangqiang   II-370
Zhang, Guizhu   I-572
Zhang, Hongda   II-36
Zhang, JunQi   I-125
Zhang, Menghua   I-604
Zhang, Min-Xia   I-465
Zhang, Pei   II-361
Zhang, Qingyi   I-113
Zhang, Rui   II-461, II-483
Zhang, Ruisheng   II-258
Zhang, Tao   I-179, II-225
Zhang, Weiwei   I-604
Zhang, Weizhen   I-604

Zhang, Xiangyin   I-421
Zhang, Xiaotong   II-235
Zhang, Zhanliang   II-112
Zhang, Zili   I-191
Zhao, Ruowei   I-201
Zhao, Xin   II-225
Zhao, Zhao   II-314
Zheng, Yu-Jun   I-465
Zheng, Ziran   II-212
Zhi, Li   II-15

Zhou, Rongrong   II-202
Zhou, Xinling   II-552
Zhu, Jiang   I-509
Zhu, Ming   I-201
Zhu, Tao   II-112
Zhu, XiXun   I-125
Zhuo, Yue   II-522
Zou, Sheng-rong   I-317
Zou, Zhitao   I-593
Zuo, Lulu   I-295, I-487